# Good University Guide 2026

# THE TIMES
# THE SUNDAY TIMES

# Good University Guide 2026

## WHERE TO GO AND WHAT TO STUDY

ZOE THOMAS

Published in 2025 by Times Books

An imprint of HarperCollins Publishers
Robroyston Gate
Glasgow G33 1JN
www.harpercollins.co.uk

HarperCollins Publishers
Macken House, 39/40 Mayor Street Upper,
Dublin 1, D01 C9W8, Ireland

First published in 1993. Thirty-first edition 2025.

© Times Media Ltd 2025

The Times® and The Sunday Times® are registered trademarks of Times Media Ltd

ISBN 978-0-00-873213-4

Main league table and individual subject tables compiled by UoE Consulting Limited.

Please see Chapters 1 and 10 for a full explanation of the sources of data used in the ranking tables.
The data providers do not necessarily agree with the data aggregations or manipulations appearing
in this book and are also not responsible for any inference or conclusions thereby derived.

Text: Zoe Thomas
Data and editorial consultant: Nick Rodrigues
Project editor: Peter Dennis
Design and layout: Davidson Publishing Solutions

# Contents

# About the Author

Zoe Thomas is a journalist and education writer. She has worked on *The Times and Sunday Times Good University Guide* since 2005 and is a former staff journalist for the Sunday newspaper.

For the past 14 years, she has written extensively for the *Guide*, both its UK and Irish editions, and its sister publication *The Sunday Times Schools Guide, Parent Power*, the annual review of Britain's leading primary and secondary schools. She has a degree in media studies from the University of Sussex.

## Acknowledgments

We would like to thank the many individuals who have helped with this edition of *The Times and Sunday Times Good University Guide*, particularly Helen Davies, editor of T*he Sunday Times Good University Guide*, and John O'Leary, journalist, education consultant and the former author of this *Guide*. Thanks also go to Nick Rodrigues at *The Sunday Times*, Peter Dennis, Harley Griffiths, Samuel Fitzgerald and Warren Shore at HarperCollins Publishers and to Sophie Bradford, Andy Farquhar, Fiona Kugele and Nicki Horseman (consultant) at UoE Consulting Limited, which has compiled the main university league table and the individual subject tables for this *Guide* on behalf of *The Times, The Sunday Times* and HarperCollins Publishers. For his work devising our social inclusion ranking, thanks go to Alastair McCall, data journalist and deputy director of the Centre for Education and Employment Research at the University of Buckingham.

Thank you to the members of *The Times and Sunday Times Good University Guide* Advisory Group for their time and expertise: Christine Couper, director of CouperJones higher education consultants; James Galbraith, senior strategic planner, University of Edinburgh; Josh Gulrajani, former head of data and insights at Bath Spa and current director of quality and planning at Aston University; Daniel Monnery, chief strategy officer, Northumbria University; Gary Russell, head of strategic planning and performance, Northumbria University; Jackie Njoroge, director of strategy, University of Salford; Helen Eustace, head of planning, Aberystwyth University; David Totten, head of planning, Queen's University, Belfast; Jenny Walker, Senior Planning Officer, Loughborough University; Em Bailey, deputy director strategic planning and performance, Heriot-Watt University; and Jack Ruane, university league managers at People & Planet. Thanks also go to Emily Raven, Kathryn Heywood and Samantha Ayling of Jisc for their technical advice; and to Shannon Corbishley, Gareth Powell, Adam Finlayson, and Hannah White at the Office for Students. We also wish to thank all the university staff who assisted in providing information for this edition

# Timeline to a University Place

This book will help you find a university place in September 2026. Though it may seem a long way off, the journey from sixth form to Freshers' Week involves a busy schedule of activities and deadlines that applicants need to tick off in good time. Being prepared for each step as it comes will give you greater flexibility and more options later down the line.

Those applying for degrees in medicine, veterinary medicine and dentistry have an earlier application deadline (October 15, 2025) than the majority of applicants. This is the same date that Cambridge and Oxford universities also require applications to have been submitted.

Relevant work experience is required for some degrees including medicine, as are aptitude and pre-assessment tests (detailed further in Chapter 2).

Use the dates below to find the key stages to a university place.

## Key dates

### February to July 2025
This is the time for chewing things over. What subject are you interested in studying? Where would you like to study it? The chapters of this book will help you whittle down your options with regards to choosing a subject and a university.

### March 2025 onwards
Go to university Open Days. They are the best way of getting a feel for a university, its location, and what studying in a particular department or faculty would be like. Applicants need to prebook places and should go to as many Open Days as they can, within reason. Plan carefully and make each one count. Virtual Open Days and events are also offered; they cut down the schlepping on trains and motorways and can fill the gaps where making another trip is not an option. For Open Day dates, consult each university's website – as detailed in Chapter 12.

### July 2025
Registration starts for UCAS Apply, the online application system through which you will apply to universities. You will have a maximum of five choices when you complete your form.

### September 2025
UCAS will begin to accept completed applications.

### October 15, 2025
Deadline for applications to Oxford or Cambridge (you can only apply to one of them), and for applications to any university to study medicine, dentistry or veterinary medicine. Some courses require you to have completed a pre-application assessment test by this date.

### January 15, 2026
Deadline for applications for all other universities and subjects (excluding a few art and design courses with a March 2026 deadline). This is the last date you can apply by, but it is better to get your application in beforehand; aim for the end of November 2025.

### End of March 2026

Universities should have given you decisions on your applications by now if you submitted them by January 15, 2026.

### April 2026 onwards

Apply for student loans to cover tuition fees and living costs.

### Early May 2026

By this time, you should have responded to all university decisions. You must select a first choice, and if your first offer is conditional, a second choice, and reject all other offers.

Once you have accepted an offer, apply for university accommodation if you are going to need it. Universities have their own housing application deadlines – getting in early will often guarantee a space and may allow you first dibs on your choice of room.

### First week of August 2026

Scottish examination results. If your results meet the offer from your first choice (or, failing that, your second choice), your place at university will be confirmed. If not, you can enter Clearing for Scottish universities to find a place on another course.

### Second week of August 2026

A-level results announced. If your results meet the offer from your first choice (or, failing that, your second choice), your place at university will be confirmed. If not, you can enter Clearing. If you did better than expected and want to "trade up" you can use the "decline my place" button in your application and enter Clearing.

### Mid to late September 2026

Arrive at university for Freshers' Week.

# How This Book Can Help You

What and where to study are the fundamental decisions in making a successful university application.

### How do I choose a course?

Most degrees last three or sometimes four years, some even longer, so you will need enthusiasm for, and some aptitude in, the subject. Also consider whether studying full-time or part-time will be best for you.

» The first half of Chapter 2 provides advice on choosing a subject area and selecting relevant courses within that subject.

» Chapter 10 provides details for 70 different subject areas. For each subject there is specific advice and a league table that provides our ranking of universities offering courses.

### How will my choice of subject affect my employment prospects?

The course you choose will influence your job prospects after you graduate, so your initial subject decision will have an impact on your life long after you have finished your degree.

» The employment prospects and average starting salaries for the main subject groups are given in Chapter 3.

» The subject tables in Chapter 10 give the employment prospects for each university offering a course.

» Universities are working to increase the employability of their graduates. Examples are given in Chapter 3 and in the profiles in Chapter 12.

### How do I choose a university?

While choosing your subject comes first, the place where you study also plays a major role. You will need to decide what type of university you wish to go to: campus, city or smaller town? How well does the university perform in league tables? How far is the university from home? Is it large or small? Is it specialist or general?

» Central to our *Guide* is the main *Times and Sunday Times* league table in Chapter 1. This ranks the universities by assessing their performance not just according to teaching quality and the student experience but also through seven other factors, including research quality, UCAS entry points, and graduate employment prospects.

» The second half of Chapter 2 provides advice on the factors to consider when choosing a university.

» Chapter 12, the largest chapter in the book, contains a page on each university, giving a general overview of the institution as well as data on student numbers, contact details, accommodation provision, and the latest fees available. Note that fees and student support for 2026–27 will not be confirmed until August 2025, and you must check these before applying.

» For those considering Oxford or Cambridge, details of admission processes and profiles of all the undergraduate colleges can be found in Chapter 11.

» Chapter 8 gives advice about student life; focusing on alcohol, drugs, mental health and staying safe on campus.

» Specific advice for international students coming to study in the UK is given in Chapter 9.

## How do I apply?

» Chapter 5 outlines the application procedure for university entry. It starts by advising you on how to complete the UCAS application, and then takes you through the process that we hope will lead to your university place for autumn 2026.

## Can I afford it?

Note that most figures in Chapter 4 refer to 2024 and there will be changes for 2026, which you will need to check.

» Chapter 4 describes how the system of tuition fees and finance works. It looks at what you are likely to be charged, depending upon where in the UK you plan to study, and how much you can borrow. It also looks at other forms of financial support (including university scholarships and bursaries), and how to plan your budget.

» Chapter 7 provides advice on finding somewhere to live while you are at university. Sample accommodation charges for each university are given in Chapter 10.

## How do I find out more?

*The Times and Sunday Times Good University Guide* website at **www.thetimes.co.uk/uk-university-rankings** will keep you up to date with developments throughout the year and contains further information and online tables (subscription required).

The UCAS website **www.ucas.com** offers a wealth of helpful advice and information, as do individual university websites. Statistical information can be found on the Discover Uni website **discoveruni.gov.uk**.

# Introduction

On the face of it an extra £285 a year for a university education is not much. In the grand scheme of student finance, it is a relatively trivial sum when added to the student loans accrued by undergraduates, who already know they are in for a hefty bill (around £43,800, at the last count). But the increase in tuition fees to £9,535 per year in 2025–26 marks a profound shift in higher education policy, coming as it does after an eight-year fees moratorium. The incoming Labour government introduced the hike four months after winning the election in July 2024. It had little choice. The long-term fees freeze plus a period of high inflation had caused the real terms value of £9,250 teaching income to shrink to £6,000. The paucity of tuition income has caused widespread financial instability in the sector. Recruitment from overseas has been challenging too, at a time when UK universities were particularly in need of shoring up their finances with the much higher tuition fees paid by international students. In the spring of 2024 the Office for Students, the regulator of higher education in England, forecast that 40% of English universities would run budget deficits in 2024 and warned of closures and mergers. Many have had to make difficult decisions to cut budgets, lose jobs and close courses.

Announcing the increase, Bridget Phillipson, Secretary of State for Education, referenced the need "to put our world-leading higher education sector on a secure footing: in order to face the challenges of the next decade, and to ensure that all students have confidence that they will receive the world-class higher education experience they deserve." Higher education is inextricably linked with the political picture; universities drive economic growth and have civic roles in communities. They are one of the country's best exports with "a key role to play in enhancing the UK's reputation across the globe," the education secretary affirmed. Whether local institutions or global centres, UK universities power industry with skilled workforces and innovation. And they stimulate social mobility.

For university applicants and current students, though, the affordability of day-to-day life tends to be the more pressing concern. In this matter the government's reforms were even handed: while raising the cap on tuition in line with retail price inflation of 3.1% it made the same uplift to maintenance loans. This funding for living costs has become notorious for falling short of most students' actual financial needs, like tuition fees suffering an erosion to its value amid inflation and higher prices. In many cases it does not even cover the rent. Parents and carers make up the difference, as much as they can afford to, and students with part-time jobs are increasing their hours – not an easy juggle with degree-level academia.

Making ends meet on a student budget during a cost of living crisis is not for the faint of heart, but undergraduates are proving resourceful. Find out more about all things student finance in Chapter 4.

As the fiscal lens through which deciding what and where to study gets more focused, applicants need to strike a sensible balance between following their dreams and getting into debt unwisely when choosing what and where to study. Investigate the findings of the new Graduate Outcomes survey in Chapter 3, which shows what graduates are doing 15 months after finishing their degrees. Ideally, in the subjects you want to apply to study, you will see high proportions in high-skilled jobs and/or postgraduate study, and far fewer in jobs deemed low-skilled, or unemployed. We also include salary data within the subject summaries in Chapter 10, though this has never been an ingredient of our rankings.

University is still a positive, life-changing experience for most who choose it. Government figures in 2023 showed 87.7% of working-age graduates in employment compared to 69.7% of non-graduates and earning £40,000 median salaries, compared with £29,500 among those without a degree. And while the lofty aspirations of studying solely for the passion of learning have given way to an emphasis on securing a good graduate career, the potential for intellectual inspiration remains among the attractions of university.

In 2023 there were 757,000 applications for full-time undergraduate places through UCAS, down by almost 10,000 on the record level from 2022 and slowing "the journey to a million" applications that UCAS has predicted by the end of the decade. Within the overall decline however was undimmed demand for high-tariff universities by 18-year-old applicants – in step with the age group's population surge that is working its way up secondary schools.

There are modifications to the admissions process which new applicants will experience. On its website UCAS now shows the actual entry grades achieved by previous students before they started university degree courses, rather than just grades institutions request. This gives some idea of how flexible they are likely to be if the candidate misses a grade or two. It has also tweaked the application form, introducing three structured questions to the personal statement instead one long free-text essay. The introductions are aimed at widening participation, as is the waiving of the £28.50 application fee for applicants who receive free school meals.

Fairness of admissions is discussed in greater depth in Chapter 6, The Diversity Index, which is also the home of the seventh edition of our dedicated social inclusion league table. Topped once again by Wrexham University in north Wales, the table ranks universities according to nine measures of social inclusion. It reveals how successful (or not) UK universities are at delivering on their social role to attract and retain students with academic potential from all backgrounds. Today's applicants want to know about the composition of the student body they will be joining, and this table helps them in that quest.

In Chapter 8, Staying Safe and Seeking Help on Campus, we look at how students' mental health is being impacted by the multiple pressures on them, and the provision of support available at university. Drinking, drug-taking and personal safety on campuses are also front and centre in the chapter, which aims to set a realistic tone. For parents, it offers helpful advice on how it is possible to give your child their autonomy while also checking in with them.

Most graduates do not regret going to university and carry fond memories of their undergraduate years with them through life – along with career advantages and intellectual enrichment. The right university cannot be pinpointed simply by a league table, but this *Guide* should provide all the information needed to draw up a shortlist for further investigation, which will help you make the right choice in the end.

## Evolving higher education

In the 31 years that this book has been published, higher education has experienced numerous changes. Graduates used to have 30 years after leaving university to pay off their student debt before the government wrote it off completely, regardless of how much had been repaid. Since 2023–24 however, the deadline for repaying student loans increased to 40 years and the earnings threshold for repayment dropped to £25,000. More graduates than ever will need to repay their student loan in full to the government, plus interest. The previous government's rhetoric about "rip-off degree courses" and free speech on campus has been overtaken by the Labour administration's focus on five priorities for reform of the higher education system: play a stronger role in expanding access and improving outcomes; make a stronger contribution to economic growth; play a greater civic role; raise the bar further on teaching standards, maintaining and improving our world-class reputation; and underpinning all other priorities with a sustained efficiency and reform programme.

Covid's intervening years make Brexit feel like a lifetime ago, but it was only on January 31, 2020 that Britain's withdrawal from the European Union completed. The move brought significant change for students from EU countries, Iceland, Liechtenstein, Norway (EEA) and Switzerland, who lost eligibility to UK "home" fees and funding. Instead, since the 2021–22 academic year, they have qualified for the higher rate of "international" tuition rates payable by those from the rest of the world. The UK also left the Erasmus foreign exchange programme, an EU operation, and replaced it with the Turing Scheme – a national version that had funding confirmed until 2024–25 and dwindling rates of engagement from UK universities.

The pattern of applications and enrolments has changed since the original introduction of higher fees in 2012. Students are opting in larger numbers for subjects that they think will lead to well-paid jobs. While there has been a recovery in some arts and social science subjects, the trend towards the sciences and some vocational degrees is unmistakeable. Application numbers within computer science, business-related subjects, medicine, law and engineering were strong in the 2023 cycle. Nursing and teaching courses experienced downturns in applications, and the decline in languages at degree level is ongoing. Most students take a degree at least partly to improve their career prospects, so some second-guessing of the employment market is inevitable. But most graduate jobs are not subject-specific, and even the keenest future forecasters are hard-pressed to predict employment hotspots four or five years ahead – which is when today's applicants will be looking for jobs.

The latest Teaching Excellence Framework (TEF) exercise, carried out by the Office for Students (OfS), published its results in December 2023. Ratings of gold, silver, bronze and "requires improvement" were awarded by a TEF panel of independent academic experts and student representatives. As well as their overall ratings, each higher education provider has a rating for the two 'aspects' of the TEF: the student experience (encompassing the National Student Survey metrics plus evidence from submissions) and student outcomes (continuation, completion, progression, plus evidence from the submissions). You can find out which ratings were achieved where in Chapter 12 University Profiles. The TEF looks at 109 of the 134 universities profiled in the *Guide*. The other 25 institutions fall outside the survey's area (no Scottish, Welsh or Northern Irish universities were included). Of the 109 surveyed, 34 were given an overall "Gold" rating (with 15 of these also achieving gold in the Student Experience and Student Outcome measures); 68 achieved "silver" and 7 were rated "bronze" overall. Only one institution (Goldsmith's) dipped below "bronze" in the student experience category to "requires improvement".

## Using this *Guide*

The merger of *The Times and Sunday Times* university guides 11 years ago began a new chapter in the ranking of higher education institutions in the UK. The two guides had 35 editions between them and, in their new form, provide the most comprehensive and authoritative assessments of undergraduate education at UK universities. Now in its fourth year in our main ranking, Hartpury University is the most recent addition to our league table and ministers are keen for new institutions to shake up the higher education system. Even those with university titles – the first criterion for inclusion in our table – take time to build up the body of data required to make meaningful comparisons.

Some famous names in UK higher education have never been ranked because they do not fit the parameters of a system that is intended mainly to guide full-time undergraduates. The Open University, for example, operates entirely through distance learning, while the London and Manchester Business Schools have no undergraduates. Birkbeck, University of London, which operates a broadly part-time course model, has dropped out of the table, though we still publish a profile of it in Chapter 12.

There are now 70 subject tables, and others will be added in due course because there is growing demand for information at this level. Successive surveys have found that students are more influenced by subject rankings than those for whole institutions.

A handful of changes to the basic methodology have been introduced, to best reflect the evolving higher education landscape. There is no longer a measure of service and facilities spend – this was removed due to questions over the relevance of such data, and our concerns over the influence of quite small changes year on year on an institution's overall ranking. Meanwhile, for the second year we have included the People & Planet indicator – based on an assessment of universities against 14 ethical and environmental criteria that measure an institution's sustainability. It is also the second year that the graduate outcomes measure is weighted 1.5 (up from 1) to reflect the importance of employability to applicants evaluating their options. Further detail on the metrics included in our league table follows in Chapter 1.

The methodology for the new edition remains stable. The *Guide* has always put a premium on consistency in the way that it uses the statistics published by universities and presents the results. The overriding aim is to inform potential students and their parents and advisers, not to make judgements on the performance of universities. As such, it differs from the government's Teaching Excellence Framework (TEF), which uses some of the same statistics but makes allowance for the prior qualifications of students and uses an expert and student panel to place the results in context.

Our tables use the raw data produced by universities to reflect the undergraduate experience, whatever advantages or disadvantages those institutions might face. We also rank 131 universities, while the TEF uses only three bands, leaving almost half of the institutions in our table on the same middle tier.

## This year's tables

Ranked No 1 in the main academic league table is the London School of Economics and Political Science (LSE). It has beaten last year's winner and this year's runner-up St Andrew's, as well as both Oxford and Cambridge. It is the first time Britain's social sciences powerhouse LSE has topped the table in our 31-year history. Improving rates of student satisfaction, expressed in successive National Student Surveys (NSS), have been key to LSE's rise through the ranks. Only five years ago it was 112th for satisfaction with the wider undergraduate experience; it now places =40th based on our NSS analysis. In the heart of London, equidistant from parliament and the City, the university has long had a stellar record at getting students into high-paying careers. This year it is No 2 (up from fifth last year) in our analysis of graduate prospects, with 92.5% of leavers in highly skilled jobs or returning to study 15 months after finishing their degree. Chances to take part in networking with employers, become an intern or otherwise engage with the world of work are built into most courses. Refurbishments made to LSE's campus include the Norman Foster-designed LSE Library – one of the largest in the world devoted to the economic and social sciences and containing unique historical collections. The Marshall Building opened in 2022, adding a sports centre and café, academic departments, music practice rooms and study spaces on one of London's oldest squares – the 17th-century Lincoln's Inn Fields. The developments have been achieved without compromising on sustainability and LSE is ranked 25th by People & Planet for 2023–24. Free speech is championed: "If you come here expect to encounter ideas you hate, that bite, that go to your identity", said Larry Kramer, president and vice-chancellor of LSE. All first-year undergraduates take a compulsory interdisciplinary module called LSE100, which teaches them how to debate controversial issues. Its many accomplishments have earned LSE our University of the Year title, on top of its No 1 ranking.

Meanwhile, Northumbria University's climb six places up the league table has helped it to take the Modern University of the Year. The Newcastle university was recently awarded more than £9 million to create the UK Research and Innovation AI Centre for Doctoral Training in Citizen-Centred AI. The University of Reading has been named Sustainable University of the Year – having reduced its carbon emissions by more than 60% since 2009 and cut waste by 35% against baselines. Reading is also one of the leading universities for the study of climate change.

It may have slipped to fourth place in our institutional ranking, but Cambridge is again the most successful university among our subject rankings. It tops 19 of the 70 tables – one of them (History) jointly with St Andrews, which is No 1 in seven tables; Oxford (in third place overall and with former prime minister William Hague as its 160th chancellor) heads six; Loughborough leads five subject tables; the LSE, Imperial, UCL and Glasgow each come top in four rankings; Queen's Belfast takes the top spot in three tables while Durham, Glasgow Caledonian, Strathclyde and Warwick are first in two tables each. Seven other universities top one table each.

St Andrews is our Scottish University of the Year, and also takes the University of the Year for Student Experience award. It was the first university to break the Oxbridge duopoly at the top of our academic league table three years ago, and has maintained the lead over its rivals, while topping the Scottish institutions. In our analysis of the National Student Survey St Andrews ranks top for the broad experience and second for teaching quality. Queen's Belfast remains Northern Ireland's top university by a clear margin. Swansea is our Welsh University of the Year – up four places to rank 37th it has two campuses at either end of the city's waterfront and offers career support as well as sea views: many of its degrees are offered as four-year courses with a year spent in industry or abroad. University of the Arts London (UAL) wins Specialist University of the Year. Up two places to rank =40th UAL is comprised of six distinct colleges and its superb facilities dot the capital. Innovation across the creative fields is long established and UAL is second for art and design in the QS World University Rankings 2024 for the sixth year running (behind only Royal College of Art, a postgraduate institution).

Impressive risers in our table include Birmingham Newman, which has gained 35 places to =90th, where it ties with Gloucestershire – which has a new vice chancellor in former UCAS chief executive Dame Clare Marchant – and experienced the second-biggest uplift of 22 places. Salford is our third-largest riser (up 19 places to 72nd). Going in the opposite direction, Buckingham has fallen 58 places to 114th and Queen Margaret in Edinburgh is down 42 places to =105th.

Ranked sixth in our main league table, Imperial College London is our University of the Year for Graduate Employment for the fourth time in four years. The UK's only university to specialise in science, engineering, technology, medicine and business has a stellar teaching record. It tops our graduate prospects index, based on 95.9% who had moved on to highly skilled jobs or further study within 15 months of completing their course. In 10th place overall, our Sports University of the Year is Loughborough. Athletes who have studied and trained at Britain's leading sporting university won an astonishing 35 medals at 2024's Olympics and Paralympics in Paris. The campus hosts superb facilities and is the base for governing bodies of England Netball, England and Wales Cricket, British Weightlifting, British Swimming, British Triathlon, and British Athletics. Loughborough teams topped the British Universities and Colleges Sport (BUCS) league in 2023–24 for the 43rd consecutive time.

## Making the right choices

This *Guide* is intended as a starting point to finding the right course, a tool to help navigate the statistical minefield that applicants face as universities present their performance in the best possible light. There is advice on fees and financial questions, as well as all-important employment issues, along with the usual ranking of universities and 70 subject tables.

While some of the leading universities have expanded considerably in recent years, most will remain selective, particularly in popular subjects. Although the offer rate is still promising for now, that does not mean that all students secure the university or course of their dreams. The demand for places is far from uniform, and even within the same university the level of competition will vary between subjects. The entry scores quoted in the subject tables in Chapter 10 offer a reliable guide to the relative levels of selectivity, but the figures are for entrants' actual qualifications. The standard offers made by departments will invariably be lower, and the grades those departments are prepared to accept are often lower still.

Making the right choice requires a mixture of realism and ambition. Most sixth-formers and college students have a fair idea of the grades they are capable of attaining, within a certain margin for error. Even with five course choices, there is no point in applying for a degree where the standard offer is so far from your predicted grades that rejection is virtually certain. If your results do turn out to be much better than predicted, there will be an opportunity through Clearing to trade up to an alternative university.

Since the relaxation of recruitment restrictions, universities that once took pride in their absence from Clearing have continued to recruit after A-level results day. As a result, the use of insurance choices – the inclusion of at least one university with lower entrance standards than your main targets – has been declining. It is still a dangerous strategy, but there is now more chance of picking up a place at a leading university if you aimed too high with all your first-round choices. Some may even come to you if you sign up to the system that allows universities to approach unplaced candidates on Results Day if their grades are similar to those of other entrants.

**The long view**

School-leavers who will enter higher education in 2026 were not born when our first league table was published and most will never have heard of polytechnics, even if they attend a university that once carried that title. But it was the award of university status to the 34 polytechnics, over a quarter of a century ago, that was the inspiration for the first edition of *The Times Good University Guide*. The original poly, the Polytechnic of Central London, had become the University of Westminster. Bristol Polytechnic became the University of the West of England, and Leicester Polytechnic morphed into De Montfort University. The new *Guide* charted the lineage of the new universities and offered the first-ever comparison of institutional performance in UK higher education.

The university establishment did not welcome the initiative. The vice-chancellors described the table as "wrong in principle, flawed in execution and constructed upon data which are not uniform, are ill-defined and in places demonstrably false". The league table has changed considerably since then, and its results are taken rather more seriously.

While consistency has been a priority for the *Guide* throughout its 31 years, only five of the original 14 measures have survived. Some of the current components – notably the National Student Survey – did not exist in 1992, while others have been modified or dropped at the behest of the expert group of planning officers from different types of universities that meets annually to review the methodology and make recommendations for the future. The newest addition is the sustainability metric from People & Planet, now in its second year of inclusion in our league table metrics and weighted 0.5, keeping up with the contemporary concerns of climate change. We have increased the weighting of graduate prospects within the methodology to 1.5, again reflecting current priorities for students.

While ranking is hardly popular with academics, the relationship with universities has changed radically, and this *Guide* is quoted on numerous university websites. As Sir David Eastwood, when he was vice-chancellor of the University of Birmingham, said in launching an official report on university league tables that he commissioned as chief executive of the Higher Education Funding Council for England: "We deplore league tables one day and deploy them the next."

Most universities have had their ups and downs over the years, with the notable exceptions of Oxford (in third place this year) and Cambridge (ranked fourth). Both benefit from top research grades and also have famously high entry standards, the largest proportions of first and upper-second class degrees, and consistently good scores on every other measure. Even so, these are the lowest positions the country's two most famous universities have held in the 31-year history of the rankings, and it is the first time Cambridge has failed to place in the top three. Topping the league table this year is the London School of Economics and Political Science (LSE), which has beaten runner-up St Andrews and its Oxbridge rivals to No 1 for the first time. An increased focus on career prospects in a tough graduate jobs market and improved feedback from students have helped LSE to climb from fourth place to first this year, and take our University of the Year title. In our National Student Survey analysis it ranks top for the broad experience and 2nd for teaching quality. Consistently in the top 10, Durham has powered up two places to fifth this year, while Imperial has slipped one spot to rank sixth. Bath and Warwick have retained their customary positions within the top 10, where they are joined by Loughborough – another regular at the top end of the table.

There have been spectacular rises. As Thames Valley University in 2001, West London was bottom of our rankings. It is =57th this year. Lincoln is another former incumbent of the bottom spot (in 1999) when it was the University of Lincolnshire and Humberside. It is 56th this year.

Since this book was first published, the number of universities has increased by a third and the full-time student population has rocketed. Individual institutions are almost unrecognisable from their 1993 forms. Nottingham, for example, had fewer than 10,000 students then, compared with more than 35,000 now. Manchester Metropolitan, the largest of the former polys, has experienced similar growth. Yet there are universities now which would have been too small and too specialist to qualify for the title in 1992. The diversity of UK higher education is celebrated as one of its greatest strengths, and the modern universities are neither encouraged nor anxious to compete with the older foundations on some of the measures in our table.

If Labour makes good on its intentions the coming years will bring more transformation in higher education. This year's school leavers have the advantage of coming after the lockdown years and they have a head start on the 18-year-old population boom that has yet to explode competition for places.

# 1 The University League Table

## What makes a top university?

*The Times and Sunday Times University Guide* weighs up university performance measures and combines them in a straightforward way that has armed generations of students with the knowledge and insights to make informed choices. The table in this chapter focuses on the fundamentals of undergraduate education and makes meaningful comparisons. Every element of the table has been chosen for the light it shines on the experience undergraduates encounter during their degrees, and their future prospects.

When tuition fees were first introduced in 1998, higher education became accountable for the investment it represented to students, their families and to taxpayers more widely. Information and statistics about universities and students came thick and fast as universities and the government adopted a commendably transparent approach to sharing information. Prior to this sharing of educational facts and figures, the somewhat nebulous notion of "reputation" was what largely counted as the means of judging a university's quality. The disclosure of data about higher education helps applicants to make informed decisions about what and where to study but navigating this abundance of publicly available information can be a complicated and at times confusing process. This is where our *Guide* can help.

The information contained within our league table gives readers the chance to look under the bonnet of universities' performance. To get the most out of its content, it is worth reading through this introduction to our league table in order to gain an understanding of the measures used. There is no panel of "experts" involved in creating our league table: statistics do the talking instead. Critics may have reasons to discount any of the measures we use, but the package has struck a chord with readers. Our ranking has built a reputation as the most authoritative arbiter of changing fortunes in higher education.

Over 31 years of publication, our *Guide* has maintained consistency in its evaluations, confident that the measures used are the best currently available for the task. Some changes have been forced upon us though, naturally enough during the course of nearly three decades, and others we have introduced in step with the evolving higher education and broader landscapes. In our new edition we have once again included a sustainability metric from

People & Planet, and we have boosted the weighting of graduate outcomes to keep up with the contemporary concerns of climate change and career prospects. We will consider the introduction of further data sources in the future.

When universities stopped assessing teaching quality by subject, our table lost its most heavily weighted measure. However, we now have the benefit of the National Student Survey (NSS), which allows us to reflect the student experience. More than two-thirds of final-year undergraduates give their views on the quality of their courses, a remarkable response rate that makes the results impossible to dismiss.

The student satisfaction measure is split in two: "teaching quality" and "student experience" – explained in more detail further down this chapter. Teaching quality is favoured over student experience in our table and accounts for 67% of the overall student satisfaction score, with student experience making up the remaining 33%.

The basic information that applicants need in order to judge universities and their courses does not change, however. A university's entry standards, staffing levels, completion rates, degree classifications and graduate employment rates are all vital pieces of intelligence for anyone deciding where to study. Research grades, while not directly involving undergraduates, bring with them considerable funds and enable a university to attract top academics.

The measures used are kept under review by a steering group of university administrators and statisticians, which meets annually and confers on an ad hoc basis more often than that. The raw data that go into the table in this chapter and the 70 subject tables in Chapter 10 are all in the public domain and are sent to universities for checking before any scores are calculated.

The various official bodies concerned with higher education do not publish league tables, and the Higher Education Statistics Agency (HESA), which supplies most of the figures used in our tables, does not endorse the way in which they are aggregated. But there are now numerous exercises, from the Teaching Excellence Framework to the annual "performance indicators" published by HESA on everything from completion rates to research output at each university, that invite comparisons.

Scrutiny of institutional league table positions is best carried out in conjunction with an examination of the relevant subject table – it is the course, after all, that will dominate your undergraduate years and influence your subsequent career.

## How *The Times and Sunday Times* league table works

The table is presented in a format that displays the raw data, wherever possible. In building the university league table, scores for student satisfaction (covering satisfaction with teaching quality and with the wider student experience), research quality and graduate prospects were weighted by 1.5; People & Planet scores were weighted by 0.5; and all other indicators were weighted by 1.

For entry standards, student-staff ratios, first-class and 2.1 degrees and graduate prospects, the score was adjusted for subject mix. For example, it is accepted that engineering, law and medicine graduates will tend to have better graduate prospects than their peers from English, psychology and sociology courses. Comparing results in the main subject groupings helps to iron out differences attributable simply to the range of degrees on offer. This subject-mix adjustment means that it is not possible to replicate the scores in the table from the published indicators because the calculation requires access to the entire dataset.

The indicators were combined using a common statistical technique known as z-scores, to ensure that no indicator has a disproportionate effect on the overall total for each university, and the totals were transformed to a scale with 1,000 for the top score. The z-score technique makes it impossible to compare universities' total scores from one year to the next, although their relative positions in the table are comparable. Individual scores are dependent on the top performer: a university might drop from 60% of the top score to 58% but still have improved, depending on the relative performance of other universities.

Only where data are not available from HESA are figures sourced directly from universities. Where this is not possible, scores are generated according to a university's average performance on other indicators, apart from the measures for research quality and student/staff ratio, where no score is created.

The organisations providing the raw data for the tables are not involved in the process of aggregation, so are not responsible for any inferences or conclusions we have made. Every care has been taken to ensure the accuracy of the tables and accompanying information, but no responsibility can be taken for errors or omissions.

*The Times* and *The Sunday Times* league table uses nine important indicators of university activity, based on the most recent data available at the time of compilation:

» Teaching quality
» Student experience
» Research quality
» Entry standards
» Student/staff ratio

» Continuation rate
» Good honours
» Graduate prospects
» People & Planet

### Teaching quality and student experience

The student satisfaction measure is divided into two components which give final-year undergraduates' views of the quality of their courses. The National Student Survey (NSS) published in 2022, inclusive of overall satisfaction for all UK universities, was the source of the data. After a consultation with the steering group, *The Times and The Sunday Times Good University Guide 2026* used an average from the relaunched National Student Survey (NSS) 2023 and 2024 data. The National Student Survey covers seven aspects of a course, which are grouped into themes.

» The teaching quality indicator reflects the average scores of the teaching, learning opportunities, assessment and feedback, and academic support themes. Students answer on a scale from 1 (top) to 4 (bottom), and the score in the table is based on the percentage of positive responses (options 1 and 2).
» The student experience indicator is drawn from the average NSS scores in the organisation and management, learning resources, and student voice themes. Students answer on a scale from 1 (top) to 4 (bottom) and the score in the table is based on the percentage of positive responses (options 1 and 2).
» Teaching quality accounts for 67% of the overall score covering student satisfaction, with student experience making up the remaining 33%.
» The survey is based on the opinion of final-year undergraduates rather than directly assessing teaching quality. Most undergraduates have no experience of other universities, or different courses, to inform their judgements. Although all the questions relate to courses, rather than other aspects of the student experience, some types of university – notably medium-sized campus universities – tend to do better than others, while those in London, in particular, tend to do worse.

### Research quality

This is a measure of the quality of the research undertaken in each university. The information was sourced from the 2021 Research Excellence Framework (REF), a peer-review exercise used to evaluate the quality of research in UK higher education institutions undertaken by the UK Higher Education funding bodies.

The overall quality of research is based on the 2021 REF. The output of the REF gave each institution a profile in the following categories: 4\* world-leading; 3\* internationally excellent; 2\* internationally recognised; 1\* nationally recognised and unclassified. The funding bodies have directed more funds to the very best research by applying weightings.

For the current edition of the *Guide*, we used the weightings adopted by UK Research and Innovation (UKRI) and Research England, published in 2020. A 4\* output was weighted by a factor of 4, and 3\* was weighted by a factor of 1. Outputs of 2\* and 1\* carry zero weight. The score was weighted to account for the number of staff in each unit of assessment. The score is presented as a percentage of the maximum possible score of 3. To achieve the maximum score, all staff would need to be at 4\* world-leading level. There are no scores in this category for Buckingham (as a private university it fell outside of REF 2021).

### Entry standards

This is the average score, using the UCAS tariff (see page 33), of new students under the age of 21 who took A and AS-Levels, Scottish Highers and Advanced Highers and other equivalent qualifications (e.g. International Baccalaureate). It measures what new students achieved rather than the entry requirements suggested by the universities. Two years of data were used to partially offset the inflation in tariffs caused by pandemic disruption. The first pandemic year 2019–20 was double-weighted to balance the teacher-assessed grades given for university entry in 2021–22. The original sources of data for this measure are data returns made by the universities to HESA.

» Using the UCAS tariff, each student's examination results were converted to a numerical score. HESA then calculated an average for all students at the university. The results have then been adjusted to take account of the subject mix at the university.

» A score of 144 represents three As at A-level. Although the vast majority of the top 40 universities in the table have average entry standards of at least 144, it does not mean that everyone achieved such results – let alone that this was the standard offer. Courses will not demand more than three subjects at A-level, and offers are pitched accordingly. You will need to reach the entry requirements set by the university, rather than these scores.

### Graduate prospects

This measure is the percentage of full-time, UK-resident graduates working in a high-skilled job and/or undertaking further study 15 months after graduation. The high-skilled employment marker is derived from the new Graduate Outcomes survey, based on 2021–22 graduates and published in 2024. The results have been adjusted for subject mix.

### Good honours

This measure is the percentage of graduates achieving a first or upper-second class degree. The results have been adjusted to take account of the subject mix at the university. The data comes from HESA for 2021–22. The original sources of data for this measure are data returns made by the universities to HESA.

» Four-year first degrees, such as MChem, are treated as equivalent to a first or upper-second.
» Scottish Ordinary degrees (awarded after three years of study) are excluded.
» Universities control degree classification, with some oversight from external examiners.

There have been suggestions that, since universities have increased the numbers of good honours degrees they award, this measure may not be as objective as it should be. However, it remains a key measure of a student's success and employability.

## Continuation rates

This is the percentage of UK-domiciled full-time undergraduate students still in higher education after one year who either continue at the same provider, or transfer to another UK institution as recorded in the year after entry. Two years' of data were used in the calculation this year to balance out the change in continuation rates due to pandemic disruption. The pre-pandemic year (2018–19) was double weighted to account for 2020–21 scores.*

## Student-staff ratio

This is a measure of the average number of full-time equivalent students to each member of the academic staff, apart from those purely engaged in research. In this measure, a low value is better than a high value. The data comes from HESA for 2021–22. The original sources of data for this measure are data returns made by the universities themselves to HESA.

» The figures, as calculated by HESA, allow for variation in employment patterns at different universities. A low value means that there are a small number of students for each academic member of staff, but this does not, of course, ensure good teaching quality or contact time with academics.

» Student/staff ratios vary by subject; for example, the ratio is usually low for medicine. In building the table, the score is adjusted for the subject mix taught by each university.

» Adjustments are also made for students who are on industrial placements, either for a full year or for part of a year.

## People & Planet

Universities are assessed against 14 ethical and environmental criteria that measure an institution's sustainability. Approximately 45% of marks come from universities' performance on environmental indicators, such as carbon reduction, waste and recycling, water reduction, and use of renewable energy, which are taken from the HESA 2021–22 Estates Management Record covering the period from August 1, 2022, to July 31, 2023. The remaining marks, 55%, are based on analysis of institutional policies on sustainable issues that affect all campus stakeholders, made public by universities online, including the food that is served on campus, a university's investments, its curricula, its careers and recruitment activities, workers' rights, and many others.

*Falmouth University has no score due to missing 2020–21 data.

| Rank | 2023 rank | | Teaching quality (%) | Student experience (%) | Research quality (%) | Entry standards (UCAS pts) | Graduate prospects (%) | Good honours (%) | Continuation rate (%) | Student-staff ratio | Total | Page |
|---|---|---|---|---|---|---|---|---|---|---|---|---|
| 1 | 4 | London School of Economics | 81.6 | 79.6 | 68 | 182 | 92.5 | 93.9 | 98 | 12.8 | 63.4 | 383 |
| 2 | 1 | St Andrews | 88.9 | 86.4 | 53.8 | 208 | 87.6 | 94.8 | 97.5 | 11.9 | 45.2 | 409 |
| 3 | 2 | Oxford | 85 | 71.1 | 67 | 200 | 90.4 | 94.1 | 98.5 | 10.3 | 59.4 | 396 |
| 4 | 3 | Cambridge | 84.2 | 73.3 | 69.7 | 206 | 90.4 | 92.8 | 99.2 | 11.6 | 46.7 | 332 |
| 5 | 7 | Durham | 82.7 | 76.1 | 55.9 | 183 | 88.8 | 91.9 | 97.3 | 13.5 | 62.9 | 346 |
| 6 | 5 | Imperial College London | 81.6 | 79.9 | 73.9 | 200 | 95.9 | 92.8 | 96.8 | 11.9 | 40.4 | 367 |
| 7 | 6 | University College London | 79.1 | 78.3 | 66.8 | 179 | 87.5 | 92.4 | 96.6 | 10.9 | 71.4 | 429 |
| 8 | 8 | Bath | 84 | 83.8 | 53 | 172 | 88.7 | 90.9 | 97.8 | 15.3 | 46.6 | 316 |
| 9 | 9 | Warwick | 84 | 82.2 | 60.9 | 172 | 86.4 | 85.8 | 96.4 | 13.9 | 48.6 | 431 |
| 10 | 10 | Loughborough | 84.1 | 84.7 | 52.5 | 155 | 86.3 | 88.3 | 97.2 | 14.1 | 47.6 | 385 |
| 11 | 16 | Bristol | 79.3 | 75.9 | 66.2 | 167 | 83.7 | 89.4 | 97.6 | 13.9 | 70.3 | 328 |
| 12 | 14 | Lancaster | 84.2 | 81.9 | 57.4 | 148 | 82.1 | 86.1 | 96.4 | 14 | 47.1 | 372 |
| 13 | 11 | Exeter | 81.1 | 79.6 | 57.5 | 158 | 81.9 | 89.5 | 97.2 | 16.1 | 64.5 | 353 |
| 14 | 18 | Sheffield | 84.4 | 83.1 | 59.1 | 153 | 82.9 | 86.5 | 96.5 | 14.4 | 45.1 | 413 |
| 15 | 19 | Aberdeen | 85.2 | 83.3 | 38.7 | 185 | 82.2 | 89.1 | 94.9 | 15.1 | 43 | 308 |
| 16 | 12 | Glasgow | 78.9 | 73.8 | 61.2 | 206 | 82.3 | 88.2 | 95.6 | 14.4 | 34.5 | 355 |
| =17 | 13 | Edinburgh | 75.4 | 72.5 | 61.5 | 191 | 81.3 | 91.9 | 96.8 | 12.3 | 39.4 | 350 |
| =17 | 15 | York | 80.7 | 77.9 | 62.8 | 152 | 82.7 | 83.1 | 96.5 | 14.2 | 45.6 | 440 |
| 19 | 17 | Southampton | 80.4 | 76.8 | 60.1 | 153 | 84.3 | 86.6 | 97 | 14 | 42.9 | 418 |
| 20 | 20 | Strathclyde | 83.9 | 80.2 | 53.1 | 203 | 83 | 81.2 | 93.5 | 18.8 | 40.9 | 421 |
| 21 | 21 | Surrey | 85.9 | 84.7 | 53.3 | 138 | 83.7 | 78.5 | 94.5 | 14.4 | 38.4 | 424 |
| 22 | 22 | Birmingham | 79.3 | 76.3 | 61.9 | 154 | 84.2 | 86.6 | 96.9 | 14.6 | 43.1 | 320 |
| 23 | =29 | Liverpool | 81.6 | 80.7 | 55.6 | 143 | 82 | 85.6 | 96 | 13.6 | 55.1 | 379 |
| =24 | 27 | King's College London | 77.3 | 73.3 | 64.2 | 166 | 85.1 | 88.8 | 94.4 | 14 | 75.4 | 370 |
| =24 | =34 | Reading | 83.3 | 81.6 | 51.1 | 125 | 80.4 | 82 | 93.9 | 15.8 | 81.8 | 404 |

| Rank | 2023 rank | | Teaching quality (%) | Student experience (%) | Research quality (%) | Entry standards (UCAS pts) | Graduate prospects (%) | Good honours (%) | Continuation rate (%) | Student-staff ratio | Total | Page |
|---|---|---|---|---|---|---|---|---|---|---|---|---|
| 26 | 31 | Queen's Belfast | 81.5 | 79.4 | 52 | 151 | 87.1 | 80.9 | 95.2 | 15.4 | 52 | 403 |
| =27 | =34 | Leicester | 82.7 | 82.7 | 53.6 | 130 | 81 | 83 | 95.7 | 14.4 | 46.7 | 377 |
| =27 | 23 | Manchester | 77.1 | 72.9 | 64.4 | 164 | 80.8 | 86.8 | 96.2 | 13.9 | 58.5 | 386 |
| 29 | 24 | Leeds | 76.6 | 75.6 | 57 | 161 | 81 | 88.8 | 96.3 | 14.4 | 58.2 | 373 |
| =30 | 37 | Newcastle | 79.2 | 77.3 | 53.6 | 146 | 82.4 | 83.6 | 96.3 | 14.3 | 59.6 | 389 |
| =30 | 32 | Nottingham | 80.9 | 77.2 | 56.1 | 149 | 83.3 | 85.5 | 96.1 | 15.7 | 48.6 | 393 |
| 32 | 25 | Cardiff | 78.8 | 76.1 | 56.7 | 148 | 85.1 | 81 | 96 | 13.9 | 52.7 | 334 |
| 33 | 26 | East Anglia | 81 | 77.6 | 58 | 135 | 81 | 85.4 | 93.9 | 13.4 | 41.2 | 347 |
| 34 | =29 | Royal Holloway, London | 80.8 | 78.9 | 53.6 | 133 | 78.7 | 83 | 94.7 | 15.9 | 33.9 | 408 |
| 35 | 38 | Aston | 81.6 | 81.5 | 40.9 | 129 | 82.6 | 82.9 | 96.2 | 17 | 57.1 | 314 |
| 36 | 33 | Dundee | 82.2 | 74.7 | 51.1 | 179 | 83 | 83 | 94.4 | 15.4 | 30.6 | 345 |
| 37 | 41 | Swansea | 81.5 | 77.9 | 47.5 | 134 | 81 | 82.5 | 94.2 | 15.9 | 73 | 426 |
| 38 | 48 | Sussex | 82.1 | 80.9 | 52.9 | 136 | 73 | 80.9 | 96.1 | 16.9 | 48.7 | 425 |
| 39 | 46 | Queen Mary, London | 78.2 | 76 | 58.7 | 147 | 78.6 | 88 | 95 | 15.6 | 60.3 | 402 |
| =40 | 42 | Arts London | 79.8 | 73.7 | 46 | 145 | 60.5 | 80.3 | 93 | 11.5 | 75.6 | 313 |
| =40 | 52 | Kent | 81 | 77.2 | 52.9 | 126 | 72.1 | 84.8 | 94.2 | 16.5 | 60.2 | 369 |
| 42 | 43 | Nottingham Trent | 84.8 | 81.2 | 41.9 | 123 | 71.5 | 72.1 | 94.6 | 15.1 | 71.1 | 394 |
| 43 | 49 | Northumbria | 81.7 | 78.5 | 40.6 | 141 | 78.4 | 79.8 | 90.7 | 15.5 | 63.8 | 391 |
| 44 | 50 | Glasgow Caledonian | 81.8 | 78.6 | 38.5 | 169 | 81.2 | 86.4 | 92.1 | 22.6 | 57.1 | 356 |
| 45 | 40 | Ulster | 84.8 | 81.1 | 47.8 | 129 | 77.8 | 82.8 | 91.9 | 18.3 | 37 | 428 |
| =46 | =56 | Essex | 83 | 80.9 | 50 | 118 | 72.1 | 82 | 90.8 | 14.6 | 50.7 | 352 |
| =46 | 59 | Manchester Metropolitan | 84 | 80.8 | 43.7 | 130 | 71.6 | 78.2 | 92.1 | 18 | 77.6 | 387 |
| 48 | 39 | Aberystwyth | 87.3 | 85 | 38.7 | 123 | 72.4 | 70.5 | 94.4 | 14.9 | 30.6 | 310 |
| 49 | 66 | City, London | 79.9 | 79.7 | 51.5 | 134 | 78.9 | 82.6 | 92.4 | 18.2 | 54.6 | 339 |
| 50 | 61 | Oxford Brookes | 82.6 | 77.6 | 32.8 | 116 | 77.8 | 73.6 | 93.8 | 13 | 52.6 | 397 |

| Rank | 2023 rank | | Teaching quality (%) | Student experience (%) | Research quality (%) | Entry standards (UCAS pts) | Graduate prospects (%) | Good honours (%) | Continuation rate (%) | Student-staff ratio | Total | Page |
|---|---|---|---|---|---|---|---|---|---|---|---|---|
| 51 | 64 | Heriot-Watt | 77.5 | 75.7 | 48.7 | 172 | 82.8 | 81.1 | 91.7 | 18.4 | 20.2 | 362 |
| 52 | 45 | St Mary's, Twickenham | 86.7 | 81.5 | 29.4 | 110 | 79.8 | 75.3 | 89 | 16.4 | 38.7 | 411 |
| 53 | 36 | Harper Adams | 85.4 | 75.3 | 19.5 | 126 | 74 | 75.2 | 95.6 | 13.8 | 26.5 | 360 |
| 54 | 58 | Coventry | 84 | 80.1 | 33.8 | 116 | 74.4 | 78.3 | 88.5 | 13 | 63.9 | 340 |
| 55 | 65 | Portsmouth | 84.3 | 81 | 39.1 | 115 | 75.1 | 76.3 | 92.7 | 15.8 | 48.5 | 400 |
| 56 | 55 | Lincoln | 83.4 | 78.6 | 38.4 | 120 | 72.9 | 74.6 | 94.1 | 15.1 | 45.4 | 378 |
| =57 | 68 | Keele | 80.6 | 77.3 | 42 | 124 | 78.6 | 80 | 94.5 | 15.1 | 50 | 368 |
| =57 | 47 | West London | 86.3 | 82.4 | 28.7 | 119 | 69.4 | 78.4 | 88.2 | 12.9 | 71.2 | 433 |
| 59 | 60 | Edinburgh Napier | 82.8 | 78.9 | 32.9 | 153 | 80 | 83.5 | 89.6 | 21.4 | 51.7 | 351 |
| 60 | 67 | Hull | 84.5 | 79.9 | 42.4 | 126 | 75.8 | 75.7 | 90.7 | 16.5 | 60.1 | 366 |
| 61 | 62 | Robert Gordon | 86.2 | 79.8 | 20.8 | 156 | 81.6 | 73.3 | 91.7 | 19.2 | 52.7 | 405 |
| 62 | =53 | Chichester | 84.3 | 74.5 | 20.1 | 126 | 74.8 | 75.1 | 92.6 | 15.2 | 43.5 | 338 |
| 63 | =53 | Stirling | 79.9 | 75.6 | 43.8 | 171 | 75.3 | 73.3 | 92.1 | 19.2 | 35.1 | 420 |
| 64 | 44 | Bangor | 80.4 | 74.9 | 51.3 | 125 | 71.6 | 76.5 | 91.9 | 15.7 | 67.2 | 315 |
| 65 | 28 | SOAS, London | 73.9 | 65.6 | 51.9 | 144 | 75.4 | 86.3 | 91.8 | 15 | 13.9 | 415 |
| =66 | =70 | Liverpool John Moores | 83.2 | 81 | 32.8 | 139 | 73.7 | 75.3 | 91.6 | 18.1 | 51.3 | 381 |
| =66 | 78 | Cardiff Metropolitan | 83 | 78.9 | 32 | 127 | 74.4 | 76.7 | 89.7 | 18.9 | 75.3 | 335 |
| 68 | 72 | West of England | 80.5 | 75.9 | 35.7 | 126 | 76.2 | 75.3 | 92.2 | 16.8 | 71.7 | 432 |
| 69 | 79 | St George's, London | 78.6 | 69 | 48.8 | 146 | 91.6 | 84.2 | 95 | 14.2 | 25.8 | 410 |
| 70 | =70 | Plymouth | 80.4 | 74.9 | 38.6 | 129 | 79.7 | 73.8 | 92.5 | 16.7 | 66.8 | 398 |
| 71 | 87 | Brighton | 81 | 73.9 | 41.4 | 114 | 73.3 | 80.1 | 91.2 | 16 | 56.2 | 327 |
| 72 | 91 | Salford | 81 | 76.2 | 37.8 | 127 | 76.6 | 76.4 | 90.9 | 18.1 | 70.9 | 412 |
| 73 | 51 | Falmouth | 82.3 | 75.6 | 48.8 | 127 | 58.1 | 78 | n/a | 14.3 | 35.1 | 354 |
| 74 | 84 | Abertay | 86.5 | 82.8 | 24.6 | 150 | 70.9 | 83 | 86.6 | 22.8 | 28.1 | 309 |
| 75 | 83 | Plymouth Marjon | 88.3 | 81.3 | 17.4 | 120 | 75.7 | 76.5 | 86.5 | 16.9 | 37 | 399 |

| Rank | 2023 rank | | Teaching quality (%) | Student experience (%) | Research quality (%) | Entry standards (UCAS pts) | Graduate prospects (%) | Good honours (%) | Continuation rate (%) | Student-staff ratio | Total | Page |
|---|---|---|---|---|---|---|---|---|---|---|---|---|
| 76 | 74 | Bath Spa | 81.8 | 74 | 29.3 | 111 | 64.8 | 87.5 | 92.8 | 19.6 | 68.9 | 317 |
| 77 | 82 | Derby | 84.5 | 79.5 | 21 | 119 | 73.4 | 71.3 | 88.4 | 14.9 | 62.1 | 344 |
| =78 | 76 | Huddersfield | 81.6 | 77.6 | 31.1 | 124 | 75 | 74.5 | 89.6 | 14.6 | 49.3 | 365 |
| =78 | 80 | Arts Bournemouth | 81 | 74.8 | 23 | 145 | 58.3 | 73.3 | 94.6 | 14.4 | 53.1 | 312 |
| 80 | 96 | Goldsmiths, London | 77.2 | 69.3 | 45.5 | 128 | 67.1 | 87.2 | 88.4 | 13.4 | 26.1 | 358 |
| 81 | 75 | Norwich Arts | 82.7 | 76.6 | 38.8 | 130 | 61.9 | 77.5 | 90.7 | 15.3 | 30.1 | 392 |
| 82 | 81 | Bournemouth | 79.1 | 74.9 | 30.7 | 113 | 75.9 | 76.9 | 91.5 | 18.3 | 71.9 | 325 |
| 83 | 95 | Hertfordshire | 83.6 | 80.1 | 39.2 | 107 | 73.1 | 75.8 | 91.1 | 17.6 | 46.8 | 363 |
| =84 | 69 | Edge Hill | 78.7 | 74.7 | 26.3 | 131 | 77.6 | 77.1 | 92 | 15.1 | 20.9 | 349 |
| =84 | =85 | Sheffield Hallam | 79.6 | 73.8 | 36 | 117 | 75.5 | 74.4 | 92 | 17.1 | 57.1 | 414 |
| 86 | =89 | Bishop Grosseteste | 89.5 | 83.3 | 11.3 | 110 | 76.6 | 64.2 | 90.1 | 17.6 | 39 | 323 |
| 87 | 73 | Creative Arts | 80.3 | 70.8 | 41.2 | 135 | 56.8 | 73.8 | 91.1 | 12.6 | 41 | 341 |
| 88 | 101 | Leeds Beckett | 83.2 | 79.7 | 26.7 | 110 | 70.8 | 73.5 | 90.4 | 17.5 | 47.6 | 375 |
| 89 | 100 | Chester | 81.3 | 74.8 | 21.1 | 122 | 76.3 | 76.8 | 91 | 15.1 | 33.8 | 337 |
| =90 | =112 | Gloucestershire | 80.9 | 73.5 | 21 | 118 | 76.4 | 59 | 91.3 | 15.4 | 64.5 | 357 |
| =90 | 125 | Birmingham Newman | 87.7 | 83.9 | 13.3 | 107 | 73.9 | 71.2 | 87.2 | 16.7 | 22.4 | 322 |
| 92 | =89 | Leeds Arts | 83.5 | 78.5 | 6 | 149 | 59.4 | 75.4 | 96.6 | 16.5 | 20.1 | 374 |
| 93 | 77 | York St John | 84.7 | 79.5 | 19.6 | 112 | 69.1 | 73.5 | 91.5 | 17.7 | 29.6 | 441 |
| =94 | 88 | Liverpool Hope | 85.1 | 79.5 | 22.3 | 117 | 65.2 | 72.7 | 90.1 | 14.9 | 28.2 | 380 |
| =94 | 97 | South Wales | 83.6 | 74.9 | 27.5 | 119 | 71.1 | 71.6 | 90.2 | 16.6 | 44 | 417 |
| 96 | 111 | Central Lancashire | 83 | 77.8 | 30.4 | 126 | 74.3 | 67.4 | 86.8 | 15.6 | 57.4 | 336 |
| 97 | 98 | Kingston | 82.4 | 78.5 | 34.6 | 121 | 66.1 | 70.8 | 91.8 | 18.1 | 49.8 | 371 |
| 98 | 109 | Solent, Southampton | 84.4 | 78.6 | 12.6 | 113 | 66 | 72.3 | 90.4 | 15.3 | 42.1 | 416 |
| 99 | 103 | Worcester | 80.9 | 76.8 | 15.3 | 118 | 78.6 | 65.1 | 90.5 | 17.2 | 72.6 | 438 |
| 100 | 116 | London South Bank | 81.6 | 75.8 | 28.8 | 110 | 75.4 | 77.9 | 88.2 | 17.1 | 41.8 | 384 |

| Rank | 2023 rank | | Teaching quality (%) | Student experience (%) | Research quality (%) | Entry standards (UCAS pts) | Graduate prospects (%) | Good honours (%) | Continuation rate (%) | Student-staff ratio | Total | Page |
|---|---|---|---|---|---|---|---|---|---|---|---|---|
| 101 | =93 | Staffordshire | 79.1 | 71.4 | 30 | 120 | 73.7 | 75.6 | 89.5 | 17.4 | 52.2 | 419 |
| 102 | 105 | Greenwich | 81.7 | 78.2 | 32.9 | 118 | 70.6 | 70.8 | 90.7 | 20.9 | 67.2 | 359 |
| 103 | =85 | Winchester | 81 | 74.8 | 22 | 113 | 69 | 72.8 | 92.9 | 18.1 | 44.8 | 436 |
| 104 | 102 | Teesside | 82.5 | 75.7 | 28 | 118 | 79.2 | 75.3 | 86.6 | 17.2 | 39.4 | 427 |
| =105 | 63 | Queen Margaret, Edinburgh | 80.2 | 72.9 | 27.3 | 164 | 67 | 81.5 | 91.1 | 20.6 | 21 | 401 |
| =105 | =93 | Sunderland | 83.9 | 78 | 30.5 | 121 | 64.7 | 73.2 | 86.3 | 13.9 | 34.2 | 423 |
| =107 | 110 | Birmingham City | 81 | 76.6 | 29 | 123 | 70.4 | 63.3 | 90.6 | 17.1 | 62.7 | 321 |
| =107 | =119 | Brunel London | 79.3 | 78 | 34 | 120 | 69.4 | 68 | 92.5 | 18.2 | 54.8 | 329 |
| 109 | 114 | Canterbury Christ Church | 81.4 | 73.9 | 26.1 | 102 | 75.1 | 70.2 | 87.6 | 16.2 | 57.4 | 333 |
| 110 | 117 | Wales Trinity St David | 87.1 | 81.2 | 23.8 | 138 | 59.6 | 70.6 | 88.1 | 20.3 | 61.1 | 430 |
| 111 | 108 | Bradford | 77.1 | 73 | 29.9 | 126 | 77.9 | 80.1 | 91.2 | 20.1 | 41.4 | 326 |
| 112 | 92 | Leeds Trinity | 81 | 74.3 | 15.1 | 108 | 73 | 71.3 | 89.3 | 18.1 | 33.5 | 376 |
| 113 | =119 | De Montfort | 79.7 | 76.2 | 27.4 | 108 | 69.3 | 70.6 | 89.8 | 18.3 | 74.5 | 343 |
| 114 | =56 | Buckingham | 79.5 | 69.2 | n/a | 121 | 76.4 | 80.9 | 92.6 | n/a | n/a | 330 |
| 115 | 122 | Wrexham | 87.8 | 81.4 | 13.3 | 118 | 74.7 | 69 | 83.7 | 22.4 | 62.2 | 439 |
| 116 | =112 | Hartpury | 87.6 | 78.6 | 15.8 | 124 | 60 | 66.1 | 88.9 | 16.7 | n/a | 361 |
| 117 | 121 | Middlesex | 84 | 80.6 | 30.4 | 108 | 64.7 | 68.5 | 86.1 | 15.8 | 22.3 | 388 |
| 118 | 99 | Roehampton | 83.5 | 78.4 | 45.9 | 102 | 58.1 | 72.2 | 89.4 | 17.9 | 23.1 | 406 |
| 119 | =106 | Bolton | 83.9 | 78 | 10.6 | 117 | 74.8 | 69.7 | 86.5 | 15.1 | 14 | 324 |
| 120 | 123 | Westminster | 79.6 | 79.1 | 39.7 | 118 | 61.2 | 71.2 | 89.7 | 19.6 | 48.4 | 435 |
| 121 | 126 | West of Scotland | 83.2 | 74.7 | 19.2 | 139 | 73.5 | 74.6 | 84.9 | 22.4 | 34.9 | 434 |
| 122 | 127 | Buckinghamshire New | 86.6 | 79.1 | 17.6 | 109 | 69.3 | 57.6 | 84.7 | 16.7 | 43.3 | 331 |
| 123 | 118 | Wolverhampton | 82.7 | 75.9 | 21.6 | 109 | 73.4 | 71.1 | 86 | 15.6 | 13.2 | 437 |
| 124 | =106 | Suffolk | 82.2 | 75.1 | 21.8 | 114 | 72 | 71.7 | 79.7 | 13.1 | 43.2 | 422 |
| 125 | 128 | Northampton | 81.1 | 76 | 13.8 | 109 | 69.7 | 66.5 | 88.5 | 17.4 | 46.6 | 390 |

| Rank | 2023 rank | | Teaching quality (%) | Student experience (%) | Research quality (%) | Entry standards (UCAS pts) | Graduate prospects (%) | Good honours (%) | Continuation rate (%) | Student-staff ratio | Total | Page |
|------|-----------|---|------|------|------|------|------|------|------|------|------|------|
| **126** | 131 | East London | 86.4 | 80.1 | 22.8 | 105 | 63.6 | 74.2 | 87.5 | 25 | 29.5 | 348 |
| **127** | 124 | London Metropolitan | 84.5 | 79.8 | 29.2 | 102 | 63.4 | 74.3 | 79.1 | 19.3 | 42.4 | 382 |
| **128** | 129 | Cumbria | 75.7 | 69.7 | 13.6 | 122 | 74.8 | 67.4 | 88.4 | 18.1 | 39.3 | 342 |
| **129** | 130 | Bedfordshire | 82.4 | 76.4 | 30 | 108 | 66.7 | 64.5 | 77.3 | 24.5 | 77.2 | 318 |
| **130** | 115 | Anglia Ruskin | 80.1 | 73 | 30.2 | 113 | 69 | 72.2 | 88 | 18.4 | 57.8 | 311 |
| **131** | 104 | Royal Agricultural | 63.9 | 62.8 | 24.2 | 115 | 68.7 | 68 | 93.2 | 21.3 | 18.3 | 407 |

# 2 Choosing What and Where to Study

Making informed but also aspirational decisions about a degree course is key to ensuring a wise choice that is likely to stand the test of time. There are around 35,000 undergraduate courses in Britain, as totted up by UCAS for 2024–25 entry. This *Guide* features 135 universities, and there are many colleges that applicants of certain specialisms will also be considering. Such breadth of choice may seem overwhelming, but by this point applicants will be used to the choice that runs through education. Those from the UK will already have selected GCSEs and A-levels, or Higher and Advanced Higher subjects, from a vast array of options.

Figuring out what to study and where to study it is the next decision. It is a big one; this is a milestone that will impact the rest of your life, to one extent or another, on many levels – from the intellectual and professional to the social and personal. Careers, scholarship and friendships are shaped during the undergraduate years. Mind-boggling though it will seem to sixth-formers filling out their UCAS applications, the university they go to could be the place they meet the person they end up marrying.

Widespread research has found that students decide on their degree subject before thinking about the institution at which they will study it. Enjoying their subject is a guiding principle for those making selections, but employability prospects are also increasingly taken into consideration – a trend that has gathered steam since the pandemic. A UCAS survey of around 20,000 undergraduate applicants in the 2022 admissions cycle found that more than nine out of ten students said it was "extremely important" or "important" that their course was "good value". Just under half of those surveyed said that either career pathway or prospects were the motivation behind their degree. But, thinking forward, skills and a meaningful job came out as more important than earnings, while student wellbeing and happiness was seen as the best measure of "value". The research results showed notable differences in responses depending on what subject applicants had chosen, with those applying to maths putting far higher importance on graduate earnings data relative to those applying to education courses. Similarly, more than half of those choosing communications courses, such as journalism and publishing, cited information about networking opportunities as critical to their decision-making.

Naturally, all considerations are under the microscope of affordability, with the government forecasting that the average debt among students who started their course in 2023–24 will be £42,900. Finance is in even sharper focus within decision making, given the rising cost of living and the new "Plan 5" student loan repayment scheme, which will result in a greater proportion of graduates repaying their debt than did under the previous system. This is covered in more detail in Chapter 4, The Bottom Line.

But the charms of university remain increasingly attractive; not even a global health pandemic stalled the upward trajectory of applications and enrolments to UK higher education institutions. The popularity of going to university has been projected to be undented by the rising cost of living, although the financial pinch is likely to impact the quality of students' experiences in one way or another.

Some subjects and some universities carry more prestige than others. Such judgements are worth bearing in mind, as your future CV will be assessed according to them. This kind of thinking may not sit easily with everyone, but employers treat universities and subjects as yardsticks, not just the results gained on courses. Certain universities, however, may not occupy our upper rankings, but they might have particularly strong departments for individual subjects. Make the most of out of this *Guide*, and cross reference the subject-by-subject information in Chapter 10 with the university profiles and rankings in Chapter 12. The options are not endless, but they are many.

The new Graduate Outcomes survey shows what graduates of the subjects you are interested in are doing 15 months after finishing their degrees. Ideally, you will see high proportions in high-skilled jobs and/or postgraduate study, and far fewer in jobs deemed low-skilled, or unemployed. It is a useful tool for new applicants

Be realistic in your choices. The course you apply to should be within your capabilities, although it will also need to keep you interested for three years-plus. A degree should broaden your options later in life, so be sensible about choosing one that can do that for you while keeping an eye on the career horizon. The technological advancements of the fourth industrial revolution are continually reshaping the world of work, and you want to be abreast of developments. Narrowing your focus at degree stage could limit what is open to you in five to 10 years' time. This *Guide* can inform you of what is possible, and what will make a wise choice.

### Is higher education for you?
Being carried along with the flow is too easy. Maybe all your friends are going to university, or your parents expect it. If you apply for a course in your strongest A-level subject, things should work out OK and your career will look after itself, right? Or perhaps your driving motivation is to leave home in search of the UK's best live music or clubbing scenes, or simply to put a sizeable portion of motorway between you and your parents. Such considerations are natural and will not necessarily lead to disaster. But now is the time to question whether university is the best way of fulfilling your ambitions. There are degree apprenticeships or training schemes at big firms which could equally help you achieve what you want, minus the need to take out a student loan. If studying for A-levels or equivalent qualifications has felt like torture, now may not be the time for you to go to university. Perhaps a job would be better, and possibly a return to education later in life would suit you more. Love of a subject is an excellent reason for taking a degree; it will help you focus your course search on those that reflect your passion. But if a degree is a means to a career for you, look carefully at employment rates for any courses you consider.

## Setting your priorities

The majority of graduate jobs are not subject-specific; employers value the transferable skills that higher education confers. Rightly or wrongly, however, most employers are influenced by which university you went to, as mentioned above, so the choice of institution remains important.

Consider boosting your CV while studying by choosing a university that offers some sort of employment-related scheme. It could be work experience built into your degree, or a particularly active careers service.

## Narrowing down your options

Although competition for places is going to get fiercer as the 18-year-old population surges in the decade ahead, for now a scramble for places affects a relatively small proportion of courses that attract intense competition, and there are plenty of places at good universities for candidates with sufficient qualifications. For older applicants returning to education, relevant work experience and demonstrable interest in a subject may be enough to win a place.

Too much choice is more of an issue. Start filtering your options by:

» Choosing a subject – or subject area – first, rather than a university. This can reduce the field considerably as not all universities offer all subjects.
» Then factor in personal preferences such as location and type of university – campus or city? – and, by this point, you may already have the beginnings of a manageable list.
» Next up is course content and what life is really like for students. Today's budding undergraduates are at an advantage in this regard. As well as having access to the informative and accurate contents of university prospectuses and websites, they can connect with current students online and do some digging. Most universities have an "Ask a Student" function, or similar, on their website, which provides them with a link to a student ambassador for a live chat or call back.

Another helpful source of information is **www.thestudentroom.com**, the country's largest online student community. You may already have used it while studying for your A-levels. The peer-to-peer platform offers forums for students to discuss their options, ask for advice and build relationships. Current students on the courses and at the universities you are interested in may be happy to share their appraisals – although bear in mind that what they tell you may be biased in some direction or another. Cross-reference anything you have been told with factual sources of information such as ours, or the UCAS website.

The National Student Survey is an objective source of information which is available online, with a range of additional data about the main courses at each institution, at **www.officeforstudents.org.uk/advice-and-guidance/student-information-and-data**.

Visiting the university will give a truer picture yet; better still go to the department where you would be studying.

## What to study?

As well as an interest that is sustainable for three-plus years in the subject you pick, you need to ensure you have the right qualifications to meet its entry requirements. Many economics degrees require mathematics A-level, for example, while most medical schools demand chemistry or biology. The UCAS website is a good starting point; it contains subject profiles and entrance requirements (**www.ucas.com**), while universities' own sites offer more detailed information.

The Russell Group of 24 leading universities' Informed Choices website is another go-to source of information regarding required subjects (**informedchoices.ac.uk**).

## UCAS tariff scores for main qualifications:

| A-levels | | AS-levels | |
|---|---|---|---|
| Grade | Points | Grade | Points |
| A* | 56 | A | 20 |
| A | 48 | B | 16 |
| B | 40 | C | 12 |
| C | 32 | D | 10 |
| D | 24 | E | 6 |
| E | 16 | | |

| Scottish Advanced higher | | Scottish higher | |
|---|---|---|---|
| Grade | Points | Grade | Points |
| A | 56 | A | 33 |
| B | 48 | B | 27 |
| C | 40 | C | 21 |
| D | 32 | D | 15 |

| BTec Level 3 | | | |
|---|---|---|---|
| National Diploma (post-2016) | | Extended Certificate | |
| Grade | Points | Grade | Points |
| D* | 28 | D* | 56 |
| D | 24 | D | 48 |
| M | 16 | M | 32 |
| P | 8 | P | 16 |

| International Baccalaureate* | | | |
|---|---|---|---|
| Higher level | | Standard level | |
| H7 | 56 | S7 | 28 |
| H6 | 48 | S6 | 24 |
| H5 | 32 | S5 | 16 |
| H4 | 24 | S4 | 12 |
| H3 | 12 | S3 | 6 |

*The Extended Essay and Theory of Knowledge course are awarded A12, B10, C8, D6, E4
For Foundation Diploma, Extended Diploma and other BTec levels see UCAS website
For other qualifications see: ucas.com/ucas/ucas-tariff-points

## Your school subjects and the UCAS tariff

The official measure by which your results will be judged is the UCAS tariff, which gives a score for each grade of most UK qualifications considered relevant to university entrance, as well as for the International Baccalaureate (IB). The points system is shown in the table above. Two-thirds of offers are made in grades, rather than tariff points. This means universities may stipulate the grades they require in specific subjects, and determine which vocational qualifications are relevant to different degrees. In certain universities, some departments, but not others, will use the tariff to set offers. Course profiles on the UCAS website and/or universities' own sites should show whether offers are framed in terms of grades or tariff points. It is important to find out which, especially if you are relying on points from qualifications other than A-level or Scottish Highers.

Entry qualifications listed in the *Guide* relate not to the offers made by universities, but to the actual grades achieved by successful candidates who are under 21 on entry. For ease of comparison, a tariff score is included even where universities make their offers in grades.

### 'Soft' subjects

These are another big factor in what and where you study. The Russell Group scrapped its controversial list of preferred A-levels in 2019, after criticism that it contributed to a devaluation of creative and arts subjects. Previously however the group's Informed Choices website had a list of "facilitating subjects" comprising: maths and further maths, English, physics, biology, chemistry, geography, languages (classical and modern) and history, which are required by many degrees and welcomed by Russell Group universities generally.

The website advised sixth-formers to pick the majority of their A-levels from this list and to include at most one "soft" subject. Although these "soft subjects" were not listed specifically, a previous Informed Choices report named media studies, art and design, photography and business studies among the subjects that would normally be given this label. The current Informed Choices website offers more personalised guidance on A-level choices.

The facilitating subjects list may be gone, but its legacy is entrenched – which applicants to these universities should be very aware of when selecting their A-levels. It is better to keep more doors open than close any off at sixth form.

For most courses at most universities, there are no such restrictions, as long as your main subjects or qualifications are relevant to the degree you hope to take. Even so, the Russell Group lists are an indication of the subjects that admissions tutors may take more or less seriously, especially if you plan to apply to at least one leading university. Although only the London School of Economics has published a list of "non-preferred" subjects (see page 35), others may take a less formal approach but still apply similar weightings.

General studies is a separate matter, and some universities still do not regard it as a full A-level for entry purposes, while others – including some leading institutions – do.

### Vocational qualifications

The Education Department downgraded many vocational qualifications in school league tables from 2014. This has added to the confusion surrounding the value placed on diplomas and other qualifications by universities. The engineering diploma has won near-universal approval from universities (for admission to engineering courses, and possibly some science degrees), but some of the other diplomas are in fields that are not on the curriculum of the most selective universities. Regardless of the points awarded under the tariff, it is essential to contact universities directly to ensure that a diploma or another vocational qualification will be an acceptable qualification for your chosen degree.

### Admission tests

The growing numbers of applicants with high grades at A-level have encouraged the introduction of separate admission tests for some of the most oversubscribed courses. There are national tests in medicine and law that are used by some of the leading universities, while Oxford and Cambridge have their own tests in a growing number of subjects. The details are listed on page 36. In all cases, the tests are used as an extra selection tool, not as a replacement for A-level or other general qualifications.

### Making a choice

Your A-levels or Scottish Highers may have been straightforward to choose, but the range of subjects at university is vast. Even subjects you have studied at school may be quite different at degree level – some academic economists prefer their undergraduates not to have taken A-level economics because they approach the subject so differently. Other students are disappointed because they appear to be going over old ground when they continue with a subject that they enjoyed at school. Universities now publish quite detailed syllabuses, and applicants are advised to go through the fine print.

The greater difficulty comes in judging your suitability for the many subjects that are not on the school or college curriculum. Philosophy and psychology sound fascinating (and are), but you may have no idea what degrees in either subject entail – for example, the level of statistics that may be required. Forensic science may look exciting on television – more glamorous than plain chemistry – but it opens fewer doors, as the type of work portrayed in *Silent Witness* is very hard to find.

## Academic or vocational?

There is frequent and often misleading debate about the differences between academic and vocational higher education. It is usually about the relative value of taking a degree, as opposed to a directly work-related qualification. But it also extends to higher education itself, with jibes about so-called "Mickey Mouse" degrees in areas that were not part of the higher education curriculum when most of the critics were students.

Such attitudes ignore the fact that medicine and law are both vocational subjects, as are architecture, engineering and education. They are not seen as any less academic than geography or sociology, but for some reason social work or nursing, let alone media studies and sports science, are often looked down upon. The test of a degree should be whether it is challenging and a good preparation for working life. Both general academic and vocational degrees can do this.

---

### "Traditional academic" and "non-preferred" subjects

The London School of Economics expects applicants to offer at least two of the traditional subjects listed below, while any of the non-preferred subjects listed should only be offered together with two traditional subjects.

**Traditional subjects**

» Ancient history
» Biology
» Classical civilisation
» Chemistry
» Computing
» Economics
» Electronics
» English (English language, English literature and English language and literature)
» Further mathematics
» Geography
» Government and politics
» History
» Languages: modern foreign, classic and community
» Law
» Mathematics
» Music
» Philosophy
» Physics
» Psychology
» Religious studies
» Sociology

**Non-preferred subjects**

» Any applied A-level
» Accounting*
» Art and design
» Business studies
» Citizenship studies
» Communication and culture
» Creative writing
» Design and technology
» Drama/theatre studies
» Film studies
» Health and social care
» Home economics
» Information and communication technology
» Leisure studies
» Media studies
» Music technology
» Physical education/sports studies
» Travel and tourism

*The LSE Department of Accounting considers accounting equally with other generally preferred subjects. Therefore, it will consider accounting alongside one other subject from the non-preferred list. However, the majority of departments continue to regard accounting as a non-preferred subject.
Critical thinking, general studies, global perspectives and research, knowledge and enquiry, project work and thinking skill are normally excluded subjects and will only be considered as a fourth A-level. They will not be accepted as part of a contextual offer.
**Source:** LSE

## Admissions tests

Some of the most competitive courses now have additional entrance tests. The most significant tests are listed below. Note that registration for many of the tests is before 15th October and you will need to register for them as early as possible. All the tests have their own websites. Institutions requiring specific tests vary from year to year and you must check course website details carefully for test requirements. In addition, over 50 universities also administer their own tests for certain courses. Details are given at: **www.ucas.com/undergraduate/applying-university/admissions-tests**

### Law

**Law National Admissions Test (LNAT):** for entry to law courses at Bristol, Cambridge, Durham, Glasgow, King's College London, London School of Economics, Oxford, SOAS, University College London. Register from August; tests held from September to July (but some universties will not accept LNAT results taken as late as July). .

### Science, technology, engineering, and mathematics

**Sixth Term Examination Papers (STEP):** for entry to mathematics and mathematics with physics at Cambridge, and mathematics at Warwick and Imperial College London. Registration opens at the beginning of March for testing in June. For more information visit **ocr.org.uk/students/step-mathematics**

**The Test of Mathematics for University Admission (TMUA):** for entry to mathematics, economics and computer science courses. Used for courses at Cambridge, Durham, Imperial College London, London School of Economics and Political Science, and Warwick. Visit **esat-tmua.ac.uk** for registration and test dates.

**Mathematics Admissions Test (MAT):** for entry to computer science; computer science and philosophy; mathematics/ mathematics and statistics; mathematics and computer science; and mathematics and philosophy at Oxford. For registration and dates visit **ox.ac.uk/admissions/undergraduate/applying-to-oxford/guide/admissions-tests/mat**

**Engineering and Science Admissions test (ESAT):** used by Imperial College London and Cambridge. Register from the beginning of August for testing in October and January.

### Medical subjects

**University Clinical Aptitude Test (UCAT):** for entry to medical and dental schools at Aberdeen, Anglia Ruskin, Aston, Bangor, Birmingham, Brighton and Sussex Medical School, Bristol, Brunel, Cambridge, Cardiff, Central Lancashire, Chester, Dundee, East Anglia, Edge Hill, Edinburgh, Exeter, Glasgow, Hull York Medical School, Imperial College London, Keele, Kent and Medway Medical School, King's College London, Lancaster, Leeds, Leicester, Liverpool, Manchester, Newcastle, Nottingham, Oxford, Plymouth, Queen Mary University of London, Queen's University Belfast, Sheffield, Southampton, St Andrews, St George's, University of London, Sunderland, Surrey, Swansea, Warwick and Worcester. Check **ucat.ac.uk** for registration and test dates.

**Graduate Medical School Admissions Test (GAMSAT):** for graduate entry to medicine at Brunel, Chester, Exeter, Imperial College London, Keele, Liverpool, Nottingham, Plymouth (and for dentistry), St Andrews, St George's Medical School, Sunderland, Surrey, Swansea, Ulster, and Worcester. The GAMSAT test is offered in March and September (**gamsat.acer.org**)

**Health Professions Admissions Test (HPAT-Ulster):** for certain health profession courses at Ulster. The HPAT–Ireland test window is typically in the latter half of February, check **hpat-ireland.acer.org**.

### Cambridge University

Pre-interview or at-interview assessments take place for most subjects. Full details given on the Cambridge admissions website. See also LNAT, ESAT, STEP, TMUA and UCAT above.

### Oxford University

Pre-interview tests take place in many subjects and candidates are required to register by early October. Full details given on the Oxford admissions website. Tests usually at candidate's educational institution. See also LNAT, MAT and BMAT above.

It is clear that the prospect of much higher graduate debt is encouraging more students into job-related subjects. This is understandable and, if you are sure of your future career path, possibly also sensible. But much depends on what that career is – and whether you are ready to make such a long-term commitment. Some of the programmes that have attracted public ridicule, such as surf science or golf management, may narrow graduates' options to a worrying extent, but often boast strong employment records.

As you would expect, many vocational courses are tailored to particular professions. If you choose one of these, make sure that the degree is recognised by the relevant professional body (such as the Engineering Council or one of the institutes) or you may not be able to use the skills that you acquire. Most universities are only too keen to make such recognition clear in their prospectus; if no such guarantee is published, contact the university department running the course and seek assurances. In education, for example, by no means do all degrees qualify you to teach.

Even where a course has professional recognition, a further qualification may be required to practise. Both law and medicine, for example, demand additional training to become a fully qualified solicitor, barrister or doctor. Neither degree is an automatic passport to a job: only about half of all law graduates go into the profession. Both law and medicine also offer a postgraduate route into the profession for those who have taken other subjects as a first degree.

Law conversion courses, though not cheap, are increasingly popular, and there are a growing number of graduate-entry medical degrees.

One way to ensure that a degree is job-related is to take a "sandwich" course, which involves up to a year in business or industry. Students often end up working for the organisation which provided the placement, while others gain valuable insights into a field of employment – even if only to discount it. The drawback with such courses is that, like the year abroad that is part of most language degrees, the period away from university inevitably disrupts living arrangements and friendship groups. But most of those who take this route find that the career benefits make this a worthwhile sacrifice. Growing numbers of traditional degrees now offer shorter periods of work experience.

Employers' organisations calculate that more than half of all graduate jobs are open to applicants from any subject, and recruiters for the most competitive graduate training schemes often prefer traditional academic subjects to apparently relevant vocational degrees.

| Most popular subject areas by applications 2023 | |
|---|---|
| 1 Law | 163,325 |
| 2 Computer science | 128,125 |
| 3 Psychology (non-specific) | 122,965 |
| 4 Economics | 104,065 |
| 5 Design studies | 95,615 |
| 6 Medicine (non-specific) | 88,705 |
| 7 Sport and exercise sciences | 79,040 |
| 8 Sociology | 76,055 |
| 9 Management studies | 73,665 |
| 10 Business studies | 70,680 |

Source: UCAS End of Cycle report 2024

| Most popular subject areas by acceptances 2023 | |
|---|---|
| 1 Law | 29,830 |
| 2 Psychology (non-specific) | 26,025 |
| 3 Business studies | 22,505 |
| 4 Business and management (non-specific) | 21,885 |
| 5 Computer science | 21,080 |
| 6 Design studies | 18,545 |
| 7 Sport and exercise sciences | 16,040 |
| 8 Language and Area studies | 15,785 |
| 9 Adult nursing | 14,795 |
| 10 Economics | 14,485 |

Source: UCAS End of Cycle report 2024

## Subject areas covered in this *Guide*

The list below gives each of the 70 subject areas that are covered in detail later in the book (in Chapter 10). For each subject area in that chapter, there is specific advice, a summary of employment prospects and a league table of universities that offered courses in 2020–21, ranked on the basis of an overall score calculated from research quality, entry standards, teaching quality, student experience and graduate employment prospects.

Accounting and Finance
Aeronautical and Manufacturing
   Engineering
Agriculture and Forestry
American Studies
Anatomy and Physiology
Animal Science
Anthropology
Archaeology and Forensic Science
Architecture
Art and Design
Bioengineering and Biomedical
   Engineering
Biological Sciences
Building
Business
Celtic Studies
Chemical Engineering
Chemistry
Civil Engineering
Classics
Communication and Media Studies
Computer Science
Creative Writing
Criminology
Dentistry
Drama, Dance and Cinematics
East and South Asian Studies
Economics
Education
Electrical and Electronic Engineering
English
Food Science
French
General Engineering
Geography and Environmental Sciences
Geology

German
History
History of Art
Hospitality, Leisure, Recreation and
   Tourism
Iberian Languages
Information Systems and Management
Italian
Land and Property Management
Law
Liberal Arts
Linguistics
Materials Technology
Mathematics
Mechanical Engineering
Medicine
Middle Eastern and African Studies
Music
Natural Sciences
Nursing
Pharmacology and Pharmacy
Philosophy
Physics and Astronomy
Physiotherapy
Politics
Psychology
Radiography
Russian
Social Policy
Social Work
Sociology
Sport Science
Subjects Allied to Medicine
Theology and Religious Studies
Town and Country Planning and
   Landscape
Veterinary Medicine

Newspapers, for example, may prefer a history graduate to one with a media studies degree, while many classics graduates end up in the business world.

A good degree classification and the right work experience are more important than the subject for most non-technical jobs. But it is hard to achieve a good result on a course that you do not enjoy, so scour prospectuses, and email or phone university departments, to ensure that you know what you are letting yourself in for.

## Studying more than one subject

If more than one subject appeals, you could consider Joint Honours – degrees that combine two subjects – or even Combined Honours, which will cover several related subjects. Such courses obviously allow you to extend the scope of your studies, but they should be approached with caution. Even if the number of credits suggests a similar workload to Single Honours, covering more than one subject inevitably involves extra reading and often more essays or project work.

Applicants should also be sure to discuss their even-handed interest in both subjects in the personal statement of their UCAS form.

Many students choose a "dual" to add a vocational element to make themselves more employable – business studies with languages or engineering, for example, or media studies with English. Others want to take their studies in a particular direction, perhaps by combining history with politics, or statistics with maths. Some simply want to add a completely unrelated interest to their main subject, such as conservation biology and music production (offered at Liverpool Hope).

At most universities, however, it is not necessary to take a degree in more than one subject in order to broaden your studies. The spread of modular programmes ensures that you can take courses in related subjects without changing the basic structure of your degree. The number and scope of the combinations offered at many of the larger universities is extraordinary. Indeed, it has been criticised by academics who believe that "mix-and-match" degrees can leave a graduate without a rounded view of a subject. But if you are looking for breadth and variety, scrutinise university websites and prospectuses closely as part of the selection process.

## What type of course?

Once you have a subject, you must decide on the level and type of course. Most readers of this *Guide* will be looking for full-time degree courses, but higher education is much broader than that. You may have neither the time or the money needed for a full-time commitment of three or four years at this point in life.

## Part-time courses

Tens of thousands of people each year opt for a part-time course – usually while holding down a job – to continue learning and to improve their career prospects. The numbers studying this way have dropped considerably, but loans are available for students whose courses occupy between a quarter and three-quarters of the time expected on a full-time course. Repayments are on the same conditions as those for full-time courses, except that you will begin repaying the April four years after the start of your course, or the April after you finish or leave your course, whichever comes first, even if the course has not been completed by then. The downside is that universities have increased their fees in the knowledge that part-time students will be able to take out student loans to cover fees, and employers are now less inclined to fund their employees on such courses.

At Birkbeck, University of London, a compromise has been found with full-time courses taught in the evening. For courses classified as part-time, students pay fees in proportion to the number of credits they take. Part-time study can be exhausting unless your employer gives you time off, but if you have the stamina for a course that will usually take twice as long as the full-time equivalent, this route should still make a degree more affordable. Part-time students tend to be highly committed to their subject, and many claim that the quality of the social life associated with their course makes up for the quantity of leisure time enjoyed by full-timers.

## Distance learning

The pandemic showed that undergraduate teaching and learning is more possible to achieve remotely than many might have thought pre-Covid. If you are confident that you can manage without regular face-to-face contact with teachers and fellow students, distance learning is an option. Courses are delivered mainly or entirely online or through correspondence, although some programmes offer a certain amount of local tuition. The process might sound daunting and impersonal, but students of the Open University (OU), all of whom are educated in this way, are frequently among the most satisfied in the country, according to the results of the annual National Student Survey. Attending lectures or oversized seminars at a conventional university can be less personal than regular contact with your tutor at a distance – factors that mainstream universities have cottoned on to since being forced to pivot to remote teaching and learning in the pandemic.

This mode of study gives students ultimate flexibility to determine when and where they study. Distance learning is becoming increasingly popular for the delivery of professional courses, which are often needed to supplement degrees. The OU takes students of all ages, including school-leavers, not just mature students.

In addition, Massive Open Online Courses (MOOCs) are provided by many of the leading UK and American universities, usually free of charge. As yet, most such courses are the equivalent of a module in a degree course, rather than the entire qualification. Some are assessed formally but none is likely to be seen by employers as the equal of a conventional degree, no matter how prestigious the university offering the course. For those who are uncertain about committing to a degree, or who simply want to learn more about a subject without needing a high-status qualification, they are ideal. MOOCs are also used by sixth-formers to extend their subject knowledge and demonstrate their enthusiasm and capability to admissions tutors. They are certainly worth considering for inclusion in a personal statement and/or to spark discussion at an interview.

A number of UK universities offer MOOCs through the Futurelearn platform, run by the Open University (**www.futurelearn.com**). But the beauty of MOOCs is that they can come from all over the world. Perhaps the best-known providers are Coursera (**www.coursera.org**), which originated at Stanford University, in California, and now involves a large number of American and international universities including Edinburgh, and edX (**www.edx.org**), which numbers Harvard among its members.

## Foundation degrees

Even if you are set on a full-time course, you might not want to commit yourself for three or more years. Two-year vocational Foundation degrees have become a popular route into higher education in recent years. Many other students take longer-established two-year courses, such as Higher National Diplomas or other diplomas tailored to the needs of industry or parts of the health service. Those who do well on such courses usually have the option of converting their qualification into a full degree with further study, although many are satisfied without immediately staying on for the further two or more years that will be required to complete a BA or BSc.

## Foundation courses
A growing number of short courses, usually lasting a year, are designed for students who do not have the necessary qualifications to start a degree in their chosen subject. Foundation courses in art and design have been common for many years and are the chosen preparation for a degree at leading departments, even for many students whose A-levels would win them a degree place elsewhere. Access courses perform the same function in a wider range of subjects for students without A-levels, or for those whose grades are either too low or in the wrong subjects to gain admission to a particular course. Entry requirements are modest, but students have to reach the same standard as regular entrants to progress to a degree.

## Other short courses
A number of universities are experimenting with two-year degrees, encouraged by the government, squeezing more work into an extended academic year. The so-called "third semester" makes use of the summer vacation for extra teaching, so that mature students, in particular, can reduce the length of their career break. But only at the University of Buckingham, the UK's longest-established private university, is this the dominant pattern for degree courses. Other private institutions are following suit.

## Earn while you learn
Degree apprenticeships are a serious alternative to university. They give students the best of both worlds by combining study at degree level with extended work experience at a named industrial or business partner. The government wants more degree apprenticeships and universities are expanding their offerings, which include accountancy, cybersecurity, law, finance, economic and social research, computing, nursing, healthcare sciences, data science, management and some branches of engineering. The average salary while learning is £18,000 but for some it is as high as £26,000. The hours are usually longer than for undergraduates and they have less holiday but degree apprentices graduate debt-free.

The UCAS website has begun giving degree apprenticeships a bigger showing, so that every applicant who logs into the UCAS Hub now sees the most relevant apprenticeship opportunities for them alongside degree courses. Its Career Finder service helps students find jobs and apprenticeships. Applications for an apprenticeship are made directly to employers and, if successful, a student is then linked to a university to study part-time for the associated degree.

UCAS Chief Executive (Interim), Sander Kristel, said: "As we journey towards one million undergraduate applicants by the end of the decade, we can expect to see more applications to higher education and a more competitive landscape emerge. By enabling the visibility of both pathways, students will be able to explore all their options to make the best decision for their future career aspirations. Likewise, employers will be able to tap into a new future talent pipeline to meet their business needs and fill critical skills shortages."

Results of a survey by UCAS, published in October 2023, showed the number of its users searching for apprenticeships soared by 62.4% in 2023 compared to the same point in 2022 (81,023 in 2023 versus 49,881 in 2022), while views of apprenticeship roles increased by 85% (108,978 in 2023 versus 58,666 in 2022).

## Multiverse

Applicants can also make a direct application to the company. Weigh up the options on the government's "Find an Apprenticeship" page (**www.gov.uk/apply-apprenticeship**). Once you register, you can set up email and text alerts to inform you about new apprenticeship roles. You can also find a range of vacancies at **www.ratemyapprenticeship.co.uk**, which carries thousands of reviews.

Such apprenticeships take up to six years to complete and leave the graduate with a Bachelor's or even a Master's degree. Employers including Deloitte, PwC, BMW, Microsoft and the BBC are offering higher-level apprenticeships, although naturally not all are with household names such as these.

## Yet more choice

No single guide can allow for personal preferences in choosing a course. You may want one of the many degrees that incorporate a year at a partner university abroad, or to try an exchange via the government's Turing Scheme, which has replaced Erasmus post-Brexit. Either might prove a valuable experience and add to your employability. Or you might prefer a January or February start to the traditional autumn start – there are plenty of opportunities for this, and not only at post-1992 universities.

In some subjects – particularly engineering and the sciences – the leading degrees may be Masters courses, taking four years rather than three (in England). In Scotland, most degree courses take four years and some at the older universities will confer a Masters qualification.

Those who come with A-levels may apply to go straight into the second year. Relatively few students take this option, but it is easy to imagine more doing so in future at universities that charge students from other parts of the UK the full £9,250 for all years of the course.

## Where to study

Several factors might influence your choice of university or college. Obviously, you need to have a reasonable chance of getting in, you may want reassurance about the university's reputation, and its location will probably be important to you as well. On top of that, most applicants have views about the type of institution they are looking for – big or small, old or new, urban or rural, specialist or comprehensive.

Campus universities tend to produce the highest levels of student satisfaction, but big city universities continue to attract sixth-formers in the largest numbers. You may surprise yourself by choosing somewhere that does not conform to your initial criteria but working through your preferences is another way of narrowing down your options.

## Entry standards

Unless you are a mature student or have taken a gap year, your passport to your chosen university will probably be a conditional offer based on your predicted grades, previous exam performance, personal statement, and school or college reference.

Supply and demand dictate whether you will receive an offer, conditional or otherwise (see Chapter 5). Beyond the national picture, your chances will be affected both by the university and the subject you choose. A few universities (but not many) at the top of the league tables are heavily oversubscribed in every subject; others will have areas in which they excel but may make relatively modest demands for entry to other courses. Even in many of the leading universities, the number of applicants for each place in languages or engineering is still not high. Conversely, three As at A-level will not guarantee a place on one of the top English or law

## Universities with highest and lowest offer rates

| Highest | | Lowest | |
|---|---|---|---|
| University for the Creative Arts | 94.5% | University of Oxford | 19.2% |
| Bishop Grosseteste University | 93% | University of Cambridge | 21.8% |
| Aberystwyth University | 92.6% | University of St Andrews | 24.7% |
| University of Sussex | 92.2% | London School of Economics and Political Science | 26.1% |
| St Mary's University, Twickenham | 91.5% | University College London | 29.5% |
| SOAS University of London | 90% | University of Edinburgh | 29.7% |
| University of Kent | 89.8% | Imperial College London | 30.1% |
| Northumbria University | 89.3% | King's College London | 39.3% |
| Nottingham Trent University | 88.5% | St George's, University of London | 40% |
| Canterbury Christ Church University | 88% | University of the Arts, London | 43.2% |

UCAS: Applications 2022

degrees, but there are enough universities running courses to ensure that three Cs will give you a chance somewhere.

University websites and prospectuses and the UCAS website will give you the "standard offer" for each course, but in some cases, this is pitched deliberately low in order to leave admissions staff extra flexibility. The standard A-level offer for medicine, for example, may not demand A*s, but nearly all successful applicants will have one or more.

In Scotland, and increasingly elsewhere in the UK, universities have started to publish two sets of standard offers: their normal range and another with lower grades for applicants from disadvantaged backgrounds.

Contextual offers are a similar practice elsewhere in the UK and are increasingly widespread, using contextualised information about applicants' backgrounds to reduce the entry grades.

As already noted, the average entry scores in our tables give the actual points obtained by successful applicants – many of which are far above the offer made by the university, but which give an indication of the pecking order at entry. The subject tables (in Chapter 10) are, naturally, a better guide than the main table (in Chapter 1), where average entry scores are influenced by the range of subjects available at each university.

### Best paid graduates

(Median salary 15 months after graduating)

| | | |
|---|---|---|
| 1 | Imperial College London | £36,000 |
| 2 | London School of Economics | £35,000 |
| 3 | Cambridge | £33,750 |
| =4 | University College London | £32,000 |
| =4 | Oxford | £32,000 |
| 6 | Warwick | £31,000 |
| 7 | King's College | £30,786 |
| 8 | Bath | £30,600 |
| =9 | Durham | £30,000 |
| =9 | Queen Mary London | £30,000 |

HESA 2020–21 graduates

### Location

The most obvious starting point is the country you study in. Most degrees in Scotland take four years, rather than the UK norm of three, which makes them more expensive for students who come from outside Scotland, especially given the loss of the year's salary you might have been earning after graduation. Chapter 4 goes into the details of the system, but suffice to say that students from Scotland pay no fees, while those from the rest of the UK do. Nevertheless, Edinburgh and St Andrews remain particularly popular with English students, despite charging them £9,250 a year for the full four years of a degree starting in 2024.

The number of English students going to Scottish universities has increased almost every year since the fees went up, even though there would be no savings, perhaps because the institutions have tried harder to attract them. Fees – or the lack of them – are by no means the only influence on cross-border mobility: the number of

**Most popular universities by main scheme applications 2022**

| | | |
|---|---|---|
| 1 | University of Manchester | 93,450 |
| 2 | UCL (University College London) | 77,615 |
| 3 | Edinburgh University | 71,135 |
| 4 | King's College, London | 69,300 |
| 5 | University of Leeds | 69,085 |
| 6 | Manchester Metropolitan Universityl | 62,025 |
| 7 | University of Bristol | 61,490 |
| 8 | University of Nottingham | 56,890 |
| 9 | University of Birmingham | 56,645 |
| 10 | University of Warwick | 47,130 |

Source: UCAS End of Cycle report 2022

Scots going to English universities rose sharply, despite the cost, probably because the number of places is capped in Scotland, but not any longer in England.

## Close to home

Far from crossing national boundaries, however, students also choose to study near home, whether or not they continue to live with their family. This is understandable for Scots, who will save themselves tens of thousands of pounds by studying at their own fees-free universities.

But there is also a gradual increase in the numbers choosing to study close to home either to cut living costs or for personal reasons, such as family circumstances, a girlfriend or boyfriend, continuing employment or religion. Some simply want to stick with what they know.

A recent survey of sixth-formers by University College London found that one in three students starting university in 2023 may opt to live at home, due to rising costs and family needs affecting the "Covid generation" of school-leavers. Before the pandemic about 20% of first year undergraduates in England lived at home while studying, including mature students. The UCL report found that as many as 34% of 18-year-old school-leavers was considering staying at home if accepted by their first-choice university when exam results were published. The survey found that students from disadvantaged families were more likely to be affected by the financial challenges of studying away from home.

The trend for full-time students who do go away to study, is to choose a university within about two hours' travelling time. The assumption is that this is far enough to discourage parents from springing unannounced visits, but close enough to make the occasional trip home to get the washing done, have a decent meal and see friends. The leading universities recruit from all over the world, but most still have a regional core.

## City universities

The most popular universities, in terms of total applications, are nearly all in big cities with other major centres of population within the two-hour travelling window. Students are drawn by the best nightclubs, top sporting events, high-quality shopping, cultural diversity and access to leading galleries, museums and theatres. Especially for those who live in cities already, city universities are a magnet. The big universities also, by definition, offer the widest range of subjects, although that does not mean that they necessarily have the specific course that is right for you. You might not actually go clubbing a lot or hit the shops that much, in spite of the inspiring marketing material that suggests you will, either because you cannot afford to, or because student life is more focused on the university than the city, or even because you are too busy studying.

## Campus universities

City universities are the right choice for many young people, but it is worth bearing in mind that the National Student Survey shows that the highest satisfaction levels tend to be at smaller universities, often those with their own self-contained campuses. It seems that students identify more closely with institutions where there is a close-knit community and the social life is based around the students' union rather than the local nightclubs – at least in the first-year when more students tend to live in campus accommodation. There may also be a better prospect of regular contact with tutors and lecturers, who are likely to live on or near the campus.

Few UK universities are in genuinely rural locations, but some – particularly among the more recently promoted – are in relatively small towns. Several longer-established institutions in Scotland and Wales also share this type of setting, where the university dominates the town.

## Importance of Open Days

By far the best way to be confident that any university is for you is to visit. The pattern of Open Days varies and many offer virtual as well as physical events.

Our profiles in Chapter 12 give each university's website for the latest information. Schools often restrict the number of open days that sixth-formers can attend in term-time, but some universities offer a weekend alternative. A full calendar of events is available at **www.opendays.com**.

Bear in mind, if you only attend one or two, that the event has to be badly mismanaged for a university not to seem an exciting place to someone who spends their days at school, or even college. Try to get a flavour of several institutions before you make your choice.

## How many universities to pick?

When that time comes, of course, you will not be making one choice but five; four if you are applying for medicine, dentistry or veterinary science. (Full details of the application process are given in Chapter 5.) Tens of thousands of students each year eventually go to a university that did not start out as their first choice, either because they did not get the right offer or because they changed their mind along the way.

UCAS rules are such that applicants do not list universities in order of preference anyway – indeed, universities are not allowed to know where else you have applied. So do not pin all your hopes on one course; take just as much care choosing the other universities on your list.

## The value of an 'insurance' choice

Until recently, nearly all applicants included at least one "insurance" choice on that list – a university or college where entry grades were significantly lower than at their preferred institutions. This practice has been in decline, presumably because candidates expecting high grades think they can pick up a lower offer either in Clearing or through UCAS Extra, the service that allows applicants rejected by their original choices to apply to courses that still have vacancies after the first round of offers. However, it is easy to miscalculate and leave yourself without a place that you want. You may not like the look of the options in Clearing, leaving yourself with an unwelcome and potentially expensive year off.

The lifting of recruitment restrictions in 2015 has increased competition between universities and seen more of the leading institutions taking part in Clearing. For those with good grades, this makes it less of a risk to apply only to highly selective universities. However, if you are at all uncertain about your grades, including an insurance choice remains a sensible course of action.

Even if you are sure that you will match the standard offers of your chosen universities, there is no guarantee that they will make you an offer. Particularly for degrees demanding three As or more at A-level, there may simply be too many highly qualified applicants to offer places to all of them.

The main proviso for insurance choices, as with all others, is that you must be prepared to take up that place. If not, you might as well go for broke with courses with higher standard offers and take your chances in Clearing, or even retake exams if you drop grades. Thousands of applicants each year end up rejecting their only offer when they could have had a second, insurance, choice.

**Reputation**

The reputation of a university is something intangible, usually built up over a long period and sometimes outlasting reality. Before universities were subject to external assessment and the publication of copious statistics, reputation was rooted in the past. League tables are partly responsible for changing that, although employers are often still influenced by what they remember as the university pecking order when they were students.

The fragmentation of the British university system into groups of institutions is another factor: the Russell Group (**www.russellgroup.ac.uk**) represents 24 research-intensive universities, nearly all with medical schools; the million+ group (**www.millionplus.ac.uk**) contains many of the former polytechnics and newer universities; the University Alliance (**www.unialliance.ac.uk**) provides a home for 16 universities, both old and new, that identify themselves as professional and technical institutions; while GuildHE (**www.guildhe.ac.uk**) represents specialist colleges and the newest universities.

The Cathedrals Group (**www.cathedralsgroup.ac.uk**) is an affiliation of 15 church-based universities and colleges, some of which are also members of other groups.

| **Top 10 Universities for Quality of Teaching, feedback and support 2022 by % of students satisfied** | | **Top 10 Universities for Overall Student Experience 2022 by % of students satisfied** | |
| --- | --- | --- | --- |
| 1 Bishop Grosseteste | 89.5% | 1 St Andrews | 86.4% |
| 2 St Andrews | 88.9% | 2 Aberystwyth | 85% |
| 3 Plymouth Marjon | 88.3% | =3 Surrey | 84.7% |
| 4 Wrexham | 87.8% | =3 Loughborough | 84.7% |
| 5 Birmingham Newman | 87.7% | 5 Birmingham Newman | 83.9% |
| 6 Hartpury | 87.6% | 6 Bath | 83.8% |
| 7 Aberystwyth | 87.3% | =7 Bishop Grosseteste | 83.3% |
| 8 Wales Trinity St David | 87.1% | =7 Aberdeen | 83.3% |
| 9 St Mary's, Twickenham | 86.7% | 9 Sheffield | 83.1% |
| 10 Buckinghamshire New | 86.6% | 10 Abertay | 82.8% |

**Source:** National Student Survey 2022     **Source:** National Student Survey 2022

Many of today's applicants will barely have heard of a polytechnic, let alone be able to identify which of today's universities had that heritage, but most will know which of two universities in the same city has the higher status. While that should matter far less than the quality of a course, it would be naïve to ignore institutional reputation entirely if that is going to carry weight with a future employer. Some big firms restrict their recruitment efforts to a small group of universities (see Chapter 3), and, however shortsighted that might be, it is something to bear in mind if a career in the City or a big law firm is your ambition.

## Facilities

The quality of campus facilities is an important factor in choosing a university for most students. Only the course and the university's location tend to have a higher priority. Accommodation is the main selling point for those living away from home, but sports facilities, libraries (24-hour, ideally) and computing equipment also play an important part. Even upgraded campus nightclubs have become part of the facilities race that has followed the introduction of higher fees.

Many universities guarantee first-year students accommodation in halls of residence or university-owned flats. It is a good idea to know what happens after that. Are there enough places for second or third-year students who want them, and if not, what is the private market like? Rents for student houses vary quite widely across the country and there have been tensions because of a shortage of student accommodation in places, and sometimes with local residents in some cities. All universities offer specialist accommodation for disabled students – and are better at providing other facilities than most public institutions.

Special-interest clubs and recreational facilities, as well as political activity, tend to be based in the students' union – sometimes known as the guild of students. In some universities, the union is the focal point of social activity, while in others the attractions of the city seem to overshadow the union to the point where facilities are underused. Students' union websites are included with the information found in the university profiles (Chapter 12).

## University or college?

This *Guide* is primarily concerned with universities, the destination of choice for the vast majority of higher education students. But there are other options – and not just for those searching for lower fees. A number of specialist higher education colleges offer a similar, or sometimes superior, quality of course in their particular fields. The subject tables in Chapter 10 chart the successes of various colleges in art, agriculture, music and teacher training in particular.

Some colleges of higher education are not so different from the newer universities and may acquire that status themselves in future years.

## Further education colleges

The second group of colleges offering degrees are further education (FE) colleges. These are often large institutions with a wide range of courses, from A-levels to vocational subjects at different levels, up to degrees in some cases. Although their numbers of higher education students have been falling in recent years, the current fee structure presents them with an opportunity because they tend not to bear all the costs of a university campus. For that reason, too, they may not offer a broad student experience of the type that universities pride themselves on, but the best colleges respond well to the local labour market and offer small teaching groups and effective personal support.

FE colleges are a local resource and tend to attract mature students who cannot or do not want to travel to university. Many of their higher education students apply nowhere else. But, as competition for university places has increased, they also have become more of an option for school-leavers to continue their studies, as they always have been in Scotland.

Statistical comparisons of FE colleges, with their predominantly local, mature student populations, against universities, where undergraduates make up the main numbers, are not reliable. But it should be noted that the proportion of college graduates unemployed six months after graduation tends to be higher than at universities, and average graduate salaries lower.

Both further and higher education colleges are audited by the Quality Assurance Agency and appear in the National Student Survey, as well as the Teaching Excellence Framework. In all three, their results usually show wide variation. Some demonstrate higher levels of satisfaction among their students than most universities, for example, while others are at the bottom of the scale.

### Private universities and colleges

Courses are mainly in business and law, and also in some other specialist fields (see pages 442–3). These were relatively insignificant in terms of size until recently, but the current fee regime may cause numbers at private universities and colleges to grow.

By far the longest established – and the only one to meet the criteria for inclusion in our main table – is the University of Buckingham, which is profiled on page 330. The best-known "newcomer" currently is BPP University, which became a full university in 2013 and offers degrees, as well as shorter courses, in both law and business subjects. Like Buckingham, BPP offers two-year degrees with short vacations to maximise teaching time.

Northeastern University London, formerly New College of the Humanities, graduated its first students in 2015, and offers a liberal-arts-inspired curriculum. Having started out with fees of nearly £18,000 a year for all undergraduates, the college is now matching the "public sector" at £9,250 a year.

Two other private institutions have been awarded full university status. Regent's University, attractively positioned in London's Regent's Park, caters particularly for the international market with courses in business, arts and social science subjects priced at £20,500–£25,000 a year for 2023–24. However, about half of the students at the not-for-profit university, which offers British and American degrees, are from the UK or other parts of Europe.

The University of Law, as its name suggests, is more specialised. It has been operating as a college in London for more than 100 years and claims to be the world's leading professional law school. It offers law degrees, as well as professional courses, with fees for three-year degrees set at £9,250 per year in 2024–25 for UK students and £11,100 per year for the two-year version. The university has 17 UK campuses, in locations including London (where it has two), Nottingham, Birmingham, Bristol, Chester, Guildford, Manchester and Leeds, as well as at Exeter, East Anglia, Reading, and Liverpool universities.

There are also growing numbers of specialist colleges offering degrees, especially in the business sector. The London Institute of Banking & Finance (formerly ifs School of Finance), also dates back more than 100 years and now has university college status for its courses in finance and banking.

The Dyson Institute of Engineering and Technology, based at Malmesbury, in Wiltshire, welcomed its first 33 undergraduates in 2017 and began awarding its own degrees three years later. Funded entirely by Sir James Dyson, there are no fees, and students work at the nearby

## Checklist

Choosing a subject and a place to study is a major decision. Make sure you can answer these questions:

### Choosing a course

» Will my course enable my career and income goals?
» Do I want to study something I know from school, or something new?
» Are my qualifications right for the course?
» Will I enjoy my studies and stick with them?
» Will there be work experience opportunities?
» Will I cope with the demands made on myself?
» Is there good academic and wellbeing support?

### Choosing a university

» Does my dream university offer the right course?
» Do I prefer a campus, city or smaller town setting?
» Is the student population predominantly male or female? Does it matter to me?
» Should I stay close to home to save money?
» How much will accommodation and study extras cost?
» What do students already there think of the university?
» I come from a state school, will I fit in?

---

Dyson headquarters for 47 weeks a year. The New Model in Technology and Engineering, in Hereford, has received more than £20million in government funding and promises to give students a "head start on becoming a work-ready, world-conscious engineer".

The London Interdisciplinary School was founded in 2017. Based in Whitechapel, east London it had its own degree awarding powers from inception and offers a unique degree in interdisciplinary problems and methods. It takes time to build a track record, but there should be a market in the area it offers.

## Sources of information

With more than 130 universities to choose from, the Discover Uni and UCAS websites, as well as guides such as this one, are the obvious places to start your search for the right course.

Discover Uni includes figures for average salaries at course level, as well as student satisfaction ratings and some information on contact hours, although this does not distinguish between lectures and seminars. The site does not make multiple comparisons easy to carry out, but it does contain a wealth of information for those who persevere. Once you have narrowed down the list of candidates, you will want to go through undergraduate prospectuses. All are available online and many universities still print hard copies, should you want a hefty book that includes details of every course to arrive in the post. Beware of generalised claims about the standing of the university, the quality of courses, friendly atmosphere and legendary social life. Stick to the factual information.

While the material that the universities publish about their own qualities is less than objective, much of what you will find on the internet may be completely unreliable, for different reasons. A simple search on the name of a university will turn up spurious comparisons of everything from the standard of lecturing to the attractiveness of the students.

These can be seriously misleading and are usually based on anecdotal evidence, at best. Make sure that any information you consider comes from a reputable source and, if it conflicts with your impression, try to cross-check it with this *Guide* and the institution's own material.

**Useful websites**

The best starting point is the UCAS website (**www.ucas.com**), there is extensive information on courses, universities and the whole process of applying to university. UCAS has an official presence on Facebook (**www.facebook.com/ucasonline**) and X (**@UCAS_online**) and now also has a series of video guides (**www.youtube.com/user/ucasonline**) on the process of applying, UCAS resources and comments from other students.

For statistical information which allows limited comparison between universities (and for full details of the National Student Survey), visit: **www.discoveruni.gov.uk**

On appropriate A-level subject choice, visit **www.informedchoices.ac.uk**

Narrowing down course choices: **www.ukcoursefinder.com**

For a full calendar of university and college open days: **www.opendays.com**

Students with disabilities: Disability Rights UK: **www.disabilityrightsuk.org/guidance-resources**

# 3 Assessing Graduate Job Prospects

Some people have always known what they want to be when they grow up. Others have a standout talent leading them down certain pathways when it comes to university. Many would-be undergraduates, though, are unclear what their job might turn out to be at the point of filling out their UCAS applications. University is not the only, or even a guaranteed, route into a rewarding profession. But those opting for higher education do so with the hope for a future career that offers fulfilment, social standing, and at least above-average pay. Degree selection for some can be a heart-or-head situation: should you follow your heart and study a subject you love, regardless of where it might lead? Or should you choose a degree with a more secure career route?

Trends in application numbers depict a generation conscious of securing well-paid careers after graduating. And why wouldn't they? The jobs market has never been so competitive, even for graduates armed with a good 2.1 or a first. "In 2023 one in three students had a definite job offer by the end of February," reports Martin Birchall, the editor of The Times Top 100 Graduate Employers, whereas in 2024 not only had the number of job offers dropped, "but there are fewer graduate vacancies for the year ahead. Employers in the top 100 get 40–50 applications per vacancy," he explains. With the rising cost of a degree and of living more generally, along with the hopes and fears of parents on their shoulders there is a lot to play for. The 2023 admissions cycle showed buoyant student enrolments in business and management, medicine and dentistry, law, and STEM subjects as well as a sharp uplift in computing-related degrees. Meanwhile there were fewer enrolments on courses in design and creative and performing arts, nursing, education and teaching, and modern languages.

The trends tally with graduate salary analysis by *The Sunday Times* in September 2024 which showed the best-paid university leavers in Britain to be computer science graduates from Imperial College London, earning an average salary of £65,000 within 15 months of finishing their degrees. At the other end of the scale were graduates of drama, dance and cinematics courses at the University of Bristol, taking home an average of £21,000. Although graduate salaries are perhaps the most obvious way of evaluating whether a degree represents a good bet, they have never been used as a performance measure by *The Times* and *The Sunday*

*Times Good University Guide* league table rankings. Few would argue that trainee nurses and teachers, for example, should be put off going to university because the professions they are studying towards do not promise megabucks. The social value of some professions may outweigh their financial gains but there is still job security to be found, as well as the rewarding elements of the work. Salaries are also liable to variations including whether a university is located in an area of high or low employment, with high or low wages. We list average salaries for each of the 70 subject groups in this chapter's second table, without including them in our league table calculations.

From the government's perspective, a degree should provide value for money to the taxpayer as well as to the student, partly because so many student loans will not be fully paid back – even under the new terms: if graduates either never earn above or slip below earning £25,000 for students in England who enrolled from 2023 onwards (or £27,295 for those who began their studies before 2023) they do not need to make student loan repayments.

For those who study for a degree, it still pays to go to university – by a clear margin. Figures published in June 2024 by the government showed 87.7% of working-age graduates were employed in 2023, compared with 69.7% of non-graduates, while 67% of working-age graduates were in high-skilled employment compared with 23.7% of those who did not go to university. The average salary was £40,000 for graduates, compared with £29,500 for non-graduates, and this gap has remained at about £10,000 since 2007. However, the gap for young graduates – those aged 21 to 30 – has shrunk proportionally from 35% in 2007, when they earned £23,000 compared with a £17,000 salary for non-graduates, to 21% in 2023, when young graduates' average earnings were £31,500, compared with £26,000 for non-graduates. But there

## Median earnings by degree subject five years after graduation (2015–16 graduates)

| | | | |
|---|---|---|---|
| Medicine and dentistry | £47,200 | Biosciences | £24,900 |
| Economics | £37,700 | Law | £24,900 |
| Engineering | £34,000 | Materials and technology | £24,900 |
| Pharmacology, toxicology and pharmacy | £33,300 | Allied health | £24,800 |
| Mathematical sciences | £32,900 | Celtic studies | £24,500 |
| Veterinary sciences | £31,800 | Education and teaching | £23,800 |
| Physics and astronomy | £31,500 | Sport and exercise sciences | £23,800 |
| Architecture, building and planning | £31,000 | Combined and general studies | £23,400 |
| Medical sciences | £30,700 | English studies | £23,400 |
| Chemistry | £28,500 | Health and social care | £23,100 |
| Nursing and midwifery | £28,200 | General, applied and forensic sciences | £22,700 |
| Politics | £28,100 | Media, journalism and communications | £22,700 |
| Computing | £27,400 | Psychology | £22,300 |
| Languages and area studies | £27,400 | Sociology, social policy and anthropology | £22,300 |
| Business and management | £26,700 | Agriculture, food and related studies | £20,500 |
| Geography, earth and environmental studies | £26,700 | Creative arts and design | £20,100 |
| History and archaeology | £25,600 | Performing arts | £19,800 |
| Philosophy and religious studies | £25,600 | | |

**Source:** Department for Education, Graduate Outcomes, November 2024

is some encouraging news: Stephen Isherwood, chief executive of the Institute of Student Employers, says graduate pay is on the increase. "We saw it for the first time last year, when the average graduate salary went up from £31,000 to £32,000," he says. "This year we expect our salary survey to show graduate salaries going up above inflation for a second year running."

Keeping an eye on the future is wise. At the same time, experts advise that other than needing a certain degree for a specific field of work, you should go for a subject that is likely to provide an enjoyable and fulfilling experience – which you will likely do best in. Applying to a degree you have no interest in just because it promises a high salary could cause frustration and failing to complete the course – a costly and confidence-crushing experience. Figuring out what your values are and the kind of individual you want to be as you grow older is another way of narrowing the field; a sustainable way of life may trump money.

Nick Hillman, the director of the Higher Education Policy Institute, said: "It is still very much worth going to university. You earn more and you pretty much have insurance against unemployment when there's a recession or downturn. Also, it's very difficult to enter most professions nowadays if you don't have a degree. That is just the labour market considerations." The UK Labour Force Survey, run by the Office for National Statistics (ONS), showed that graduates remained at a career advantage over those without degrees during the Covid-19 outbreak: while unemployment increased during coronavirus, graduates suffered less acutely than those without degrees. Graduates are among the highest-skilled workers and play an important role in the economy, they promote innovation and growth. Graduates are also more occupationally and geographically mobile, which helps explain their employment in times of crisis. As well as specific capabilities related to their subject, graduates have more general transferable skills – such as writing, communication and critical thinking – that contribute to greater career resilience when the world is in extremis.

Over a working lifetime the Institute for Fiscal Studies (IFS) calculated in 2020 that male graduates can expect to be about £130,000 better off than if they had not gone to university, after student loan repayments and extra taxes. For women, this figure is £100,000. Once enrolled, working hard to get a high degree classification also helps, and of course some professions are bigger earners than others. Use our *Guide* to assess graduate prospects by subject area and by university, and to get an idea of the sort of salaries to expect soon after finishing a degree.

## Graduate prospects in *Good University Guide* rankings

The measure we use to assess graduate prospects takes account of the rates of employment for graduates in the 70 subject areas in our *Guide* and distinguishes between types of work.

The Graduate Outcomes (GO) survey is now in its fifth year, having replaced the Destination of Leavers from Higher Education (DLHE) survey. Both measure the same thing: what graduates do next, but the previous system gathered information six months after graduation, whereas GO conducts its survey 15 months after graduates have finished their degrees.

The longer timeframe better reflects changes in work patterns, with many graduates doing internships, travelling or sampling the jobs market before plumping for a career path. We look at the proportion of graduates in high-skilled jobs and/or postgraduate study. This *Guide* uses a definition of a high-skilled job from the Higher Education Statistics Agency (HESA), which conducts the GO survey.

# What graduates are doing 15 months after leaving university by subject studied

| Subject | Employed in high-skilled job % | Employed in high-skilled job and studying % | Studying % | Employed in lower-skilled job % | Employed in lower-skilled job and studying % | Unemployed % | Total with positive outcome % |
|---|---|---|---|---|---|---|---|
| Veterinary Medicine | 92 | 2 | 1 | 1 | 0 | 2 | 95 |
| Medicine | 81 | 8 | 5 | 0 | 0 | 0 | 94 |
| Nursing | 89 | 4 | 1 | 2 | 0 | 1 | 94 |
| Radiography | 88 | 3 | 2 | 3 | 0 | 2 | 93 |
| Physiotherapy | 87 | 4 | 1 | 2 | 0 | 3 | 91 |
| Dentistry | 81 | 7 | 1 | 0 | 0 | 3 | 88 |
| General Engineering | 78 | 3 | 4 | 6 | 0 | 4 | 86 |
| Civil Engineering | 77 | 5 | 4 | 6 | 1 | 4 | 85 |
| Building | 75 | 8 | 0 | 8 | 0 | 4 | 83 |
| Subjects Allied to Medicine | 74 | 4 | 4 | 8 | 1 | 3 | 83 |
| Electrical & Electronic Engineering | 72 | 3 | 6 | 8 | 0 | 5 | 81 |
| Chemical Engineering | 68 | 4 | 8 | 8 | 0 | 6 | 80 |
| Land & Property Management | 68 | 9 | 2 | 10 | 0 | 4 | 80 |
| Natural Sciences | 50 | 6 | 22 | 7 | 0 | 6 | 78 |
| Mechanical Engineering | 68 | 4 | 5 | 10 | 0 | 7 | 77 |
| Materials Technology | 53 | 3 | 21 | 10 | 1 | 5 | 77 |
| Bioengineering & biomedical engineering | 58 | 4 | 15 | 10 | 0 | 5 | 77 |
| Town & Country Planning & Landscape | 66 | 4 | 6 | 12 | 1 | 4 | 77 |
| Architecture | 67 | 5 | 5 | 9 | 0 | 8 | 76 |
| Aeronautical & Manufacturing Engineering | 65 | 2 | 8 | 13 | 0 | 5 | 76 |
| Physics & Astronomy | 52 | 4 | 20 | 10 | 0 | 7 | 75 |
| Pharmacology & Pharmacy | 59 | 7 | 9 | 7 | 1 | 6 | 75 |
| Chemistry | 51 | 4 | 19 | 11 | 0 | 6 | 74 |
| Mathematics | 56 | 7 | 11 | 11 | 1 | 7 | 74 |
| Computer Science | 65 | 4 | 4 | 11 | 1 | 9 | 73 |
| Economics | 58 | 9 | 6 | 13 | 1 | 5 | 73 |
| Geology | 53 | 3 | 18 | 13 | 0 | 5 | 73 |
| Education | 64 | 4 | 5 | 17 | 1 | 4 | 72 |
| Food Science | 60 | 2 | 9 | 18 | 1 | 3 | 71 |
| Social Work | 61 | 4 | 4 | 19 | 1 | 4 | 70 |
| Information Systems & Management | 62 | 4 | 2 | 17 | 0 | 8 | 69 |
| German | 56 | 2 | 10 | 18 | 1 | 5 | 68 |
| Geography & Environmental Sciences | 52 | 4 | 11 | 19 | 1 | 5 | 67 |
| Anatomy & Physiology | 42 | 5 | 19 | 16 | 2 | 5 | 66 |
| Celtic Studies | 35 | 13 | 17 | 17 | 5 | 0 | 65 |
| Middle Eastern & African Studies | 49 | 5 | 10 | 17 | 1 | 10 | 64 |
| Liberal Arts | 49 | 5 | 10 | 22 | 1 | 4 | 64 |
| Theology & Religious Studies | 49 | 5 | 10 | 21 | 2 | 4 | 63 |
| Italian | 46 | 5 | 12 | 22 | 1 | 6 | 63 |

| | | | | | | |
|---|---|---|---|---|---|---|
| French | 50 | 2 | 11 | 21 | 1 | 6 | **63** |
| Agriculture & Forestry | 53 | 5 | 5 | 32 | 0 | 3 | **63** |
| Iberian Languages | 49 | 4 | 9 | 22 | 0 | 8 | **62** |
| Law | 45 | 6 | 10 | 20 | 2 | 5 | **62** |
| Biological Sciences | 39 | 3 | 19 | 20 | 1 | 6 | **61** |
| Politics | 46 | 5 | 10 | 22 | 1 | 7 | **61** |
| Sport Science | 46 | 5 | 9 | 24 | 1 | 3 | **61** |
| Anthropology | 43 | 5 | 12 | 24 | 1 | 6 | **60** |
| Business, Management & Marketing | 53 | 4 | 3 | 26 | 1 | 7 | **60** |
| Music | 49 | 4 | 6 | 26 | 1 | 6 | **59** |
| Communication & Media Studies | 54 | 2 | 3 | 26 | 1 | 8 | **59** |
| Philosophy | 42 | 5 | 11 | 22 | 1 | 6 | **59** |
| English | 43 | 4 | 12 | 23 | 1 | 6 | **58** |
| Russian | 42 | 8 | 9 | 29 | 2 | 3 | **58** |
| Accounting & Finance | 44 | 10 | 3 | 26 | 3 | 6 | **56** |
| Classics & Ancient History | 36 | 4 | 15 | 23 | 1 | 6 | **55** |
| History | 37 | 4 | 14 | 26 | 2 | 5 | **55** |
| Linguistics | 38 | 3 | 15 | 28 | 1 | 6 | **55** |
| Art & Design | 51 | 2 | 3 | 30 | 1 | 8 | **55** |
| Archaeology & Forensic Science | 40 | 5 | 10 | 27 | 2 | 6 | **54** |
| American Studies | 38 | 2 | 12 | 31 | 1 | 6 | **52** |
| Hospitality, Leisure, Recreation & Tourism | 45 | 2 | 4 | 37 | 1 | 6 | **51** |
| Social Policy | 40 | 4 | 7 | 34 | 1 | 6 | **51** |
| Drama, Dance & Cinematics | 45 | 2 | 3 | 33 | 1 | 8 | **51** |
| East & South Asian Studies | 36 | 3 | 12 | 29 | 2 | 9 | **51** |
| History of Art, Architecture & Design | 41 | 1 | 7 | 32 | 3 | 6 | **50** |
| Sociology | 36 | 4 | 9 | 32 | 2 | 7 | **49** |
| Animal Science | 35 | 3 | 11 | 36 | 2 | 5 | **48** |
| Psychology | 34 | 5 | 9 | 32 | 2 | 5 | **48** |
| Criminology | 37 | 4 | 6 | 36 | 2 | 5 | **48** |
| Creative Writing | 36 | 3 | 6 | 30 | 2 | 10 | **46** |

**Note:** This table is ranked on the proportion of graduates in high-skilled jobs after further study, and those combining low-skilled jobs with further study.
**Source:** HESA (Higher Education Statistics Agency) 2022–23

# What graduates are earning 15 months after graduation by subject studied

| | Subject | High-skilled work (median) £ | Low- and medium-skilled work (median) £ |
|---|---|---|---|
| 1 | Dentistry | 42,000 | – |
| 2 | Medicine | 35,000 | – |
| =3 | Pharmacology & Pharmacy | 33,000 | 21,050 |
| =3 | Veterinary Medicine | 33,000 | – |
| 5 | Economics | 31,000 | 23,750 |
| 6 | Natural Sciences | 30,700 | 10,500 |
| 7 | Social Work | 30,007 | 21,419 |
| =8 | Aeronautical and Manufacturing Engineering | 30,000 | 23,500 |
| =8 | Chemical Engineering | 30,000 | 23,500 |
| =8 | Computer Science | 30,000 | 21,000 |
| =8 | Electrical and Electronic Engineering | 30,000 | 23,250 |
| =8 | General Engineering | 30,000 | 24,500 |
| =8 | Materials Technology | 30,000 | 12,000 |
| =8 | Mathematics | 30,000 | 21,500 |
| =8 | Mechanical Engineering | 30,000 | 24,500 |
| =8 | Middle Eastern and African Studies | 30,000 | – |
| =8 | Physics & Astronomy | 30,000 | 21,250 |
| 18 | Building | 29,000 | 25,225 |
| 19 | Civil Engineering | 28,800 | 23,000 |
| =20 | Bioengineering and biomedical engineering | 28,000 | 21,000 |
| =20 | Philosophy | 28,000 | 21,100 |
| =22 | East and South Asian Studies | 27,500 | 20,750 |
| =22 | Liberal Arts | 27,500 | 12,000 |
| =22 | Politics | 27,500 | 21,676 |
| =25 | Anatomy & Physiology | 27,000 | 20,850 |
| =25 | Business, Management & Marketing | 27,000 | 22,400 |
| =25 | Celtic Studies | 27,000 | – |
| =25 | Chemistry | 27,000 | 21,500 |
| =25 | Classics & Ancient History | 27,000 | 21,000 |
| =25 | German | 27,000 | 11,476 |
| =25 | Information Systems and Management | 27,000 | 25,000 |
| =25 | Town and Country Planning and Landscape | 27,000 | 23,250 |
| 33 | Iberian Languages | 26,900 | 22,500 |
| 34 | Anthropology | 26,775 | 20,500 |
| 35 | Accounting & Finance | 26,750 | 21,500 |
| =36 | Agriculture and Forestry | 26,500 | 24,000 |
| =36 | Land & Property Management | 26,500 | 21,392 |
| =36 | Russian | 26,500 | 12,000 |
| 39 | Radiography | 26,404 | – |
| 40 | Food Science | 26,325 | 21,000 |
| =41 | Biological Sciences | 26,000 | 21,000 |
| =41 | Education | 26,000 | 19,000 |

| | | | |
|---|---|---:|---:|
| =41 | French | 26,000 | 22,700 |
| =41 | Geography & Environmental Sciences | 26,000 | 21,390 |
| =41 | Geology | 26,000 | 19,500 |
| =41 | History | 26,000 | 20,750 |
| =41 | Italian | 26,000 | 12,300 |
| =41 | Physiotherapy | 26,000 | – |
| =41 | Subjects Allied to Medicine | 26,000 | 20,750 |
| 50 | Nursing | 25,675 | 11,000 |
| =51 | Sociology | 25,500 | 21,250 |
| =51 | Theology & Religious Studies | 25,500 | 20,350 |
| =53 | American Studies | 25,000 | 19,800 |
| =53 | English | 25,000 | 20,302 |
| =53 | History of Art, Architecture and Design | 25,000 | 22,500 |
| =53 | Hospitality, Leisure, Recreation & Tourism | 25,000 | 21,650 |
| =53 | Linguistics | 25,000 | 20,500 |
| =53 | Music | 25,000 | 20,250 |
| =53 | Social Policy | 25,000 | 21,000 |
| =53 | Sport Science | 25,000 | 20,750 |
| 61 | Psychology | 24,800 | 20,200 |
| 62 | Criminology | 24,700 | 20,750 |
| 63 | Law | 24,500 | 21,000 |
| =64 | Art & Design | 24,000 | 20,500 |
| =64 | Creative Writing | 24,000 | 19,500 |
| =64 | Drama, Dance and Cinematics | 24,000 | 20,750 |
| 67 | Archaeology and Forensic Science | 23,500 | 20,000 |
| 68 | Animal Science | 23,400 | 20,000 |
| =69 | Architecture | 23,000 | 21,500 |
| =69 | Communication and Media Studies | 23,000 | 20,650 |

**Note:** This table is ranked by the median salary of those in highly-skilled employment in each subject area. Where high-skilled salaries are equal, medium-skilled salaries are used as a separator.

**Source:** HESA (Higher Education Statistics Agency), Graduate Outcomes Survey, published July 2024
Covers graduates in employment and self-employment/freelance work, first degree UK-domiciled students only

## Future-proof degrees?

The average Briton changes careers or jobs five to seven times during their lifetime. So, your first job after university doesn't have to be for ever, and experience is transferable. Everyone knows that there have been changes to the world of work in the last few decades, however reminding young people that the jobs they will do have not been invented yet can be unhelpful, dispiriting and confusing. Advances in robotics and artificial intelligence mean some jobs are on the way out, but roles needed to develop new technologies and new solutions are expanding. Automation is changing professions, not wiping them out entirely. The stuff that makes us different from machines, such as emotional intelligence, analytical skills and caring, will be vital in the future jobs market, as will creativity and resilience. A rounded university education with experience both in and out of the classroom or laboratory will help to hone such "soft" skills. As for resilience, Gen Z students have survived a pandemic and they run the gauntlet of social media's distorted realities every day. They may be better at gatekeeping their wellbeing than their parents' generation, but this does not mean they lack resilience.

Parents' well-meant career advice is often 20 or 30 years out of date. Careers experts recommend finding something you care about, and something you are good at, and linking the two to find a job that will be rewarding. Some suggest looking at the United Nations' Sustainable Development Goals (SDGs) and aligning careers to them: improving health and education, reducing inequality, spurring economic growth and conserving the environment – these are problems whose solutions are long-term, and their higher purpose chimes with the interests of the current generation of students. By keeping your eye on the horizon to see what trends and changes are coming, you stand a chance of picking a future-proof field of work.

## Graduate employment and underemployment

Competition for graduate jobs, with their salary premium over a working lifetime, remains stiff. The Annual Population Survey carried out by the Office of National Statistics (ONS) estimates that there were over 15 million people with degree or equivalent qualifications working in the UK at the end of 2020, and that 43% of the UK working-age population (aged 16–64) had a degree or equivalent.

The high proportion of graduates in the overall population means that they may now take longer than their predecessors to find the right career opening. Employers' ideas of which jobs require a degree, and of the roles for which they prefer graduates change over time. Nurses have not always been required to take a degree, but the job now needs skills that were not part of the profession 25 years ago. The same is true of many occupations. Even in jobs where it may be possible to do the work involved without a degree, having taken one makes it easier to get hired in the first place. The Department of Education estimates that by 2035 48% of jobs in the UK will require at least an undergraduate degree, up from 36% in 2020.

Surveys have found that a sizeable proportion of graduates consider themselves working in a job that does not require a degree – an experience known as being underemployed. Scoping out a job via internships rather than going for whatever is immediately available for the highest salary can be a wise move.

## The graduate labour market

The contents of this *Guide* – particularly in the subject tables – should help to create a nuanced picture. A close examination of individual universities' employment rates in your subject – possibly supplemented by the salary figures on the Discover Uni website – will tell you whether national trends apply to your chosen course (**discoveruni.gov.uk**).

Even without the cost of living crisis, health pandemic and Brexit, for the boom years of graduate employment to return, there will have to be stronger recruitment by small and medium-sized companies, as well as the big battalions. The number of self-employed graduates will increase, in line with universities reporting growing demand for their business start-up and incubator services. If you are considering the graduate entrepreneur route, explore what your chosen university offers, because business hub services vary considerably in scale and sophistication.

## Subject choice and career opportunities

For those thinking of embarking on higher education in 2026, the signs are still positive. But in any year, some universities and some subjects produce better returns than others. The tables on the pages that follow give a more detailed picture of the differences between subjects at a national level, while the rankings in Chapters 1 and 10 include figures for each university and subject area.

In the employment table, subjects are ranked according to the proportion employed in jobs categorised by HESA as high-skilled, and include those undertaking further study, whether or not combined with a high-skilled job. As mentioned earlier, some similar tables do not make a distinction between different sorts of work, which can mislead applicants into thinking all universities and subjects offer positive career outcomes.

The definitions of both a high-skilled and a graduate job are controversial. But HESA relies on the Standard Occupational Classification, a complex series of definitions drawn up by the ONS. New universities, in particular, often claim that the whole concept of a graduate job immediately after graduation fails to reflect reality for their alumni. In any case, a degree is about enhancing your whole career, not just your first job out of college.

That said, the tables in this chapter will help you assess whether your course is likely to pay off in career terms, at least to start with. They show both the amount you might expect to earn with a degree in a specific subject, and the odds of being in work. They reflect the experience 15 months after graduation of those who completed their degrees in 2022, so the picture may have improved by the time you leave university. The pattern of success rates for specific subjects and institutions, however, are unlikely to have changed radically.

It is worth considering that at age 25 the average male graduate earns 5% more per year than the average female graduate, even though women are more likely to get first-class or upper second degrees. By the age of 30 – before most graduates start having children – the gender pay gap in annual earnings has extended to 25%. Without maternity leave to explain such a pay gulf, analysts have suggested it may be down to women choosing degrees that are less likely to translate into as high-paying careers as their male counterparts.

The table of employment statistics from the new GO survey reveals some unexpected results. For example, only 60.8% of business, management and marketing graduates are working in high-skilled jobs or doing further study, though this is slightly more than the 59.4% of accounting and finance graduates who achieved similar positive outcomes. The Celtic studies graduates, town and country planners, economists and food scientists fare a lot better. All seven branches of engineering are in the top 21 subjects for starting salaries, and all are in the top 20 for graduate outcomes.

The employment table also shows that graduates in some subjects – especially sciences such as physics and astronomy, biological sciences, chemistry and geology – are more likely to undertake further study than in others, such as those in art and design or hospitality.

A range of professions now regard a Masters degree as a basic entry-level qualification. Those going into subjects such as art and design appreciate that these, too, have their own career peculiarities. Periods of freelance or casual work are common at the start of a career and may become an enduring choice. Less surprisingly, doctors, vets and nurses are virtually guaranteed a job, but dentists (often in the top three) have been overtaken by radiographers and physiotherapists in the latest survey.

The second table, on pages 56–57, gives average earnings of those who graduated in 2022, recorded 15 months after leaving university. It contains interesting, and in some cases surprising, information about early career pay levels. Few would have placed social work in the top 15 for graduate pay. Nursing has dropped to 41st, having been in the top 30 in data from the year before.

It is important, of course, to consider the differences between starting salaries and the long-term prospects of different jobs. Over time, the accountants may well end up with bigger rewards, despite being £665 a year worse off than the nurses in our early-career snapshot.

In any case, it is important to realise that once you ignore the higher incomes available to medics and other elite professionals, early graduate incomes vary less than you might think from subject to subject.

Eight subjects (aeronautical and manufacturing engineering; chemical engineering; economics; electrical and electronic engineering; general engineering; materials technology; mechanical engineering; and natural sciences) tie at £30,000 in our salary ranking. Another eight subjects (agriculture and forestry; business, management and marketing; food science; geology; Iberian languages; physiotherapy; politics; and Russian) tie at £26,000. A further seven tie at £24,000 (American studies; history of art, architecture and design; hospitality, leisure, recreation and tourism; linguistics; social policy; sociology; and sport science).

There is so little between them, in fact, that where high-skilled salaries are equal, medium-skilled salaries are used as a separator. That's why you should consider the lifetime earnings you might derive from these subjects, and your own interests and inclinations, at least as much as this snapshot.

### Enhancing your employability
Graduate employability has become the holy grail of degree education since higher fees were introduced in most of the UK. Virtually every university has an initiative to enhance their graduates' prospects. Many have incorporated specially designed employability modules into degree courses; some are certificating extracurricular activities to improve their graduates' CVs; and many more are stepping up their efforts to provide work experience to complement degrees. Opinion is divided on the value of such schemes.

Some of the biggest employers restrict their recruitment activities to a small number of universities, believing that these institutions attract the brightest minds and that trawling more widely is not cost-effective. The High Fliers survey reported that ten universities targeted by the largest number of leading graduate employers in 2023–2024 were Birmingham, Manchester, Nottingham, Leeds, Bristol, Warwick, University College London, Southampton, Durham and Exeter.

Some top law firms and others in the City of London have introduced institution-blind applications, but big employers' links with their favourite recruiting grounds are likely to continue. Widening the pool of universities from which they set out to recruit is costly, and can seem unnecessary if employers are getting the people they think they need. They will expect outstanding candidates who went to other universities to come to them, either on graduation or later in their careers. But most graduates do not work in the City, and most students do not go to universities at the top of the league tables.

### University schemes
To hit the ground running as a graduate, students are advised to connect with their university careers service in their first term, where they can access mock assessment centres and practice sessions for the online personality and aptitude tests used by many employers, and get help building their first LinkedIn profile. Increasingly, companies are working with universities to help to shape their curriculums. Today many more degrees than in the past include the chance to study in industry or work abroad – including courses at Russell Group universities. Modules designed to develop the skills needed to succeed in the workplace are embedded within degrees, or students are offered help to find and complete an internship. Make the most of your university's alumni network too.

## The value of work experience

The majority of graduate jobs are open to applicants from any discipline. For these general positions, employers tend to be more impressed by a good degree from what they consider a prestigious university than by an apparently relevant qualification. Here numeracy, literacy and communication – the skills needed to function effectively in any organisation – are vitally important.

Specialist jobs, for example in engineering or design, are a different matter however. Employers may be much more knowledgeable about the quality of individual courses, and less influenced by a university's overall position in league tables, when the job relies directly on knowledge and skills acquired as a student. That goes for medicine and architecture as well as computer games design or environmental management.

In almost all fields of employment, however, work experience has become increasingly valuable. Research by High Fliers shows that work experience schemes have become an integral part of recruiting new graduates. Students who apply for work experience in their first or second year at university go through similar selection processes to graduates, which works as a kind of pre-vetting for a job after graduation. The number of paid placements has risen sharply. Many firms offer paid internships lasting eight to ten weeks to students in their penultimate summer at university (for law it's "vacation schemes" lasting one to three weeks). If you can make it through the lengthy application process, these internships can be a gateway to securing a prized "return offer", where you are invited back after you graduate to join full-time. Charities and social enterprises such as the 93% Club, Bright Network and Zero Gravity provide support and access to a rapidly developing pipeline into graduate internships and careers at a range of firms including KPMG.

Week-long taster experiences for first-year students are also an option, offered by big graduate employers such as PwC. These are usually held over the Easter break and are sometimes called "spring weeks". Bagging one is competitive: the application process starts in September, as soon as students arrive at university.

Sandwich degrees, which include extended programmes of up to a year at work, have always boosted employment prospects. Graduates frequently end up working where they undertook their placement. And while a sandwich year will make your course take longer, it will not cost a full year's-worth of tuition fees. Many conventional degrees now include shorter placements that should offer some advantages in the labour market.

If you opt for a traditional degree without a work placement, consider arranging your own part-time or temporary employment. The majority of full-time students now take jobs during term time, as well as in vacations, to make ends meet. But such jobs can boost your CV as well as your bank balance. "When you get to that final recruitment round at the assessment centre and they ask, 'Can you tell me where you worked with a team to solve a problem?' you can say, 'I organised a ski trip for 250 students,'" says Martin Birchall, who also edits The Times High Fliers Research. "That description brings alive your abilities and achievements."

## Plan early for your career

Whatever type of course you choose, it is sensible to start thinking about your future career early in your time at university. Students are wise to dispel the growing tendency to convince themselves that there will be plenty of time to apply for jobs after graduation. In the current employment market, all but the most obviously brilliant graduates need to offer more than just a degree, whether it be work experience, leadership qualities demonstrated through clubs and societies, or commitment to voluntary activities. Many students finish a degree without knowing what they want to do, but a blank CV will not impress a prospective employer.

**Useful websites**

Prospects, the UK's official graduate careers website: **prospects.ac.uk**

For career advice, internships and student and graduate jobs: **milkround.com**

For graduate employment (and other) statistics: **discoveruni.gov.uk**

High Fliers research: **highfliers.co.uk**

# 4 The Bottom Line: Tuition Fees and Finance

University tuition fees are rarely far from the top of the political agenda. The Labour administration wasted no time in grasping the nettle when it came into power in 2024, implementing a dramatic sea change by ending the eight-year freeze on how much universities charge undergraduates for their degrees. From September 2025, tuition fees are rising in line with retail price inflation from £9,250 to £9,535. The plans cover a one-year increase, but fees are expected to rise in future years as well. The Institute for Fiscal Studies said that they could reach £10,680 by 2029–30. The move is intended to help secure the finances of universities, which have seen inflation erode the real-terms value of tuition fees to below £6,000, and has been welcomed by the vice chancellors organisation Universities UK.

The tuition fees hike is accompanied by a 3.1% uplift to means-tested maintenance loans, currently worth £10,227 for someone living away from home outside London or £13,348 for those in London. The increase will add a maximum of £414 extra. Also on the table was the reintroduction of maintenance grants, which were worth up to £3,500 until they were abolished in 2016 and did not have to be repaid, but these did not get the green light from the Treasury.

It's important to be aware that although undergraduates – current and new – will be charged £285 more a year for their university education from September 2025, these changes do not generate any upfront costs for them. The student loan repayment process remains the same, so the extra fees get added to the overall student loan debt, which only begins to be repaid once students have graduated and are earning over the repayment threshold.

From making ends meet on a shoestring to government reform of higher education finance, money matters are a constant for students. Most are likely to be more concerned with the affordability of their everyday living – which is reliant on access to sufficient maintenance loans – than the relatively modest changes to tuition fees. High inflation and the cost of the living crisis are playing out predictably for students, who report increasing their hours in part-time work and taking on multiple jobs to get by. Financial hardship is not confined to students from disadvantaged backgrounds, as financially stretched parents from middle-income households struggle to compensate the growing gap. Save the Student's National Money Survey 2024 found that maintenance loans fell short of living costs by £504 a month – more than double the shortfall of four years before. Parents need to cover the difference, "and some will actually want to pay maintenance costs in full up front, especially since most graduates will end up repaying any maintenance loans in full," notes Sarah Coles, head of personal finance at investment platform Hargreaves Lansdown.

The tuition fees move has been welcomed by vice chancellors but "An increase in tuition fees simply rubs salt into the wounds for students, and ignores the single biggest issue they currently face: huge real-terms cuts to maintenance funding," says Tom Allingham, student money expert from Save the Student. "Although extra cash was needed to address successive freezes to fees, we had hoped this would be met by increasing the government grant rather than adding to student debt. We're even more disappointed that they've decided to do this without taking any significant action on student maintenance funding … all we got was a 3.1% increase to the maintenance loan – in line with inflation, but nowhere near enough to start eroding the huge real-terms cuts we've seen to funding in recent years. With that in mind, we repeat our call that any action on maintenance loans and grants must involve increasing overall funding levels to catch up with inflation."

At the National Union of Students (NUS) Alex Stanley, the vice-president for higher education, said "Students are being asked to foot the bill to literally keep the lights and heating on in their uni buildings and prevent their courses from closing down. This is – and can only ever be – a sticking plaster. Universities cannot continue to be funded by an ever-increasing burden of debt on students."

The change to tuition fees follows the introduction of the "Plan 5" loan in 2023-24, which at the time represented the biggest shake-up to the sector's finance in more than a decade. Its terms mean more graduates than ever will repay their student loan in full to the government, plus interest. On the Plan 5 loan, which all new students now sign for, the repayment threshold has been lowered to £25,000 a year (from £27,295). The length of time over which graduates repay is 40 years (up from 30). So, those heading to university now will start paying back their loan sooner than those who went before them, and the changes mean many borrowers will still be paying off their student loan when they approach retirement. The loan interest rate has been cut, however, to the Retail Price Index (RPI) rate of inflation (having previously been RPI +3%).

The government forecasts that the average debt among students who started courses in 2023-24 will be £43,700 on Plan 5 (lower than the £45,600 forecasted for those who started in 2022-23). The boost for the Treasury is that 65% are predicted to repay the new style loan in full, more than double the proportion than repaid their full loans under the previous system (27%).

The changes effectively complete the transformation of student 'loans' into a sort of graduate tax, which is paid by those who went to university over their working lifetime in exchange for a degree. The new system will be fairer to the taxpayer, ministers say, by reducing the subsidy for university degrees. And for many who choose the university route, the value a degree will add to their earning potential down the road still makes the cost of student loan repayments worth it.

For new university applicants, the implications of the Plan 5 system make it worthwhile to calculate how much will be repaid depending on earning different salaries, to ensure that a degree is worth it financially. Repayments are 9% of everything earned above the £25,000 threshold. They should kick in during the early careers of the majority of graduates who have secured a high-skilled job; a glance at our salaries ranking (on pages 56–57) shows 51 of the 70 subjects tabled average median starting salaries that tip over the repayment trigger point of £25,000.

While university is increasingly expensive, the undergraduate experience is far more than a financial pact, and higher earnings later on in life will balance the copy book for most. The

Office for National Statistics released data in June 2024 which showed the average graduate earns £6,500 a year more than a non-graduate during their career. In today's prices, over a 45-year career, this could add up to as much as £292,500. Hargreaves Lansdown's Savings & Resilience Barometer found those with degrees were more likely to have enough savings and cash left at the end of the month, to own their own home and be on track for retirement than those without.

## Tuition fees history

Up until 1998, tuition at UK universities was free. The £1,000 annual fees introduced that year represented a seismic shift in higher education at the time, and in British society more widely. These fees were paid upfront by students at the start of the academic year. In 2006, fees were raised to £3,000 and a new system of variable deferred fees and tuition fees loans was introduced. From then on, fees rose gradually by inflation until 2012 when tuition fees were raised to £9,000 per year – a move met by protest marches, campus occupations and students voting with their feet as evidenced by a downturn in applications to university. Student finance reformed at the same time to include raising the repayment threshold to £21,000 and introducing a variable tiered rate of interest on student loans.

Fees up to £9,250 were first introduced in 2017–18 and stayed the same until 2025 when they are rising to £9,535. Application and enrolment numbers have regained the ground they lost in the immediate years after 2012, students appearing to have become resigned to the regime. There are some exceptions to these upper limits; private providers are not subject to fee caps, and the maximum fee for accelerated degree courses in England is £11,100 (rising to 11,440 in 2025–26). However, a fee loan will only be made available up to £9,535 and any shortfall must be met by the student.

Most students pay the maximum fees, but tuition costs vary more widely than the upper limits suggest, with bursaries and fee waivers bringing down the price for students from low-income households, while merit-based scholarships – which are sometimes, but not always linked to household incomes – are similarly valuable to those in receipt of them.

This *Guide* quotes the higher headline fees, but even these will vary according to whether you are from the UK or overseas, studying full-time or part-time, and whether you are taking a foundation degree or an honours programme. For 2024–25, international medical students at Imperial College London are paying £53,700 per year in tuition fees. Not far away at Kingston University, UK students on the early-years foundation course are being charged £7,000 per year in 2024–25 (a price likely to be cut to £5,197 from 2025–26 in line with changes to classroom-based foundation years). EU students who enrolled on courses in the UK before Brexit and who are completing their studies still qualify for "home fees" of £9,250–£9,535 per year. However, any who have joined since Britain left the EU are classed as international students – with higher fees to match. Here we focus on full-time honours degrees for UK undergraduates, and the EU students who escaped the higher international fees: these students make up the biggest group on any UK campus.

An important fact easy to overlook is that some universities guarantee fees will be fixed at the first-year rate for the whole of your course, while others make no such promise. Applicants are advised to check the fees pages of individual universities closely. It is also worth noting that during work placements or years abroad fees cannot exceed 20% of the full-year fee for work placements and up to 15% for a year abroad or Turing year. So, the costs incurred by extending an undergraduate degree to four years by adding a year abroad or in industry are mainly living-related.

## Fees and loans

Marginal fluctuations in fee levels and bursary provision between universities tend not to be the basis upon which applicants make their degree choices, however. Numbers from the poorest socio-economic groups are at record levels, although they remain severely underrepresented compared with more affluent groups. Most readers of *The Times and Sunday Times Good University Guide* will be choosing full-time undergraduate or foundation degree courses. The fees for 2025 entry are listed alongside each university's profile in Chapter 12 wherever available. Details of English universities' bursaries and scholarships are on the website of the Office for Students (OfS) in the pages on access and participation plans. Universities have their own fees and funding web pages as well, which are good places to source up-to-date information regarding financial help.

## Alternative options

Some further education colleges offer substantial savings on the cost of a degree, or offer foundation degrees, but they tend to have very local appeal and their subject range tends to be largely vocational. The private sector may grow in popularity, following the success of two-year degrees at the University of Buckingham and BPP University in particular. A two-year course gets you into the workforce faster and reduces spending on living costs. However, this approach also cuts out much chance of holiday earnings and of sandwich courses or placements, where students can often get paid and gain work experience. Tuition fees vary by course at BPP, with prices for international students from £8,000 for a Masters and from £9,000 for a Bachelors degree – massively lower than those charged to students from abroad by the mainstream UK universities. BPP received a "requires improvement" rating for the student experience in the government's Teaching Excellence Framework 2023 however, although it fared better for student outcomes with a silver.

## Degree apprenticeships

The option of studying for a degree with no fees at all, by taking a degree apprenticeship sponsored by an employer, is growing. Multiverse – the apprenticeship provider run by Euan Blair (son of Tony, the former Labour prime minister) – is the first apprenticeship provider granted a licence to award degrees on the job. Its subject focus is on data, technology, business, and software engineering. Many other degree apprenticeships are in professional areas, such as childcare, nursing, accounting, policing and social work, but there are others in the sciences, business subjects, some social sciences and IT. On the whole, students spend the majority of their time at work with their sponsoring employer – and receiving a wage, rather than having to access loans – with varying periods at university.

The degree versus degree apprenticeship debate is fairly even-handed. Financially, degree apprenticeships (called graduate apprenticeships in Scotland) are a no-brainer: you do not pay tuition fees, plus you get paid for a job that is building experience for your future career, rather than a typical part-time role just to boost your current account. Those who last the course of up to five years will be met with immediate employment, and many employers pay those who complete the qualification more than traditional graduates because they will have been with them for longer and be more valuable in the short term.

However, some feel that the apprenticeship route is too new for the long-term prospects to be certain, as is whether the qualification will have the same currency and be as portable as a traditional degree in mid-career. But barriers between vocational and academic education are being broken down, and the numbers enrolling on degree apprenticeships is rising: starts at Level 6 (Bachelors) and 7 (Masters) increased by 8.2% to 46,800 in 2022/23.

### Getting the best deal

Student support packages mean applicants can shop around, particularly if their family income is low. But the best deal, even in purely financial terms, is one that leads to a rewarding career. By all means compare the full packages offered by individual universities, but consider too whether marginal differences of a few hundred pounds in headline fees, repaid over 30 or 40 years, matter as much as the quality of the course and the likely advantages it will confer in the employment market. Scottish students can save themselves £28,605 by opting to study in their home country, based on a three-year degree starting in 2025. That is a very different matter to the much smaller saving that is available to students elsewhere in the UK.

### International students

For more information on international tuition fees, please refer to Chapter 9, Coming to the UK to Study.

### Financing your studies

Whatever changes in fees are dictated by government policies, the need for enough money to live on at university and the likelihood that this will involve incurring some debt is unerring. Most students take out both tuition fee and maintenance loans to cover the cost of studying and living. These are technically two types of funding, but the total amount borrowed is known as their Student Loan. It now costs almost £30,000 to pay for university tuition, and that is before rent, bills, food and some fun nights out. But try not to focus on the headline figures. Yes, there is going to be a debt and it is likely to be considerable, but student loan debts are not quite like other sorts of commercial borrowing – such as on credit cards or via a mortgage. As discussed earlier in this chapter, they increasingly work out more like a graduate tax.

Each UK country has its own student finance system. The following sections of this chapter relate to the loans and costs incurred by students from England, while the broader content relates to students aross the UK. The facts and figures for those from Northern Ireland, Wales and Scotland are detailed separately later in the chapter.

### Tuition fee loans

Full-time students can borrow up to the full amount of £9,535 needed to cover tuition fees wherever they study in the UK. Those studying an accelerated degree course could get up to £11,100. This loan is not dependent upon household income. New part-time students can apply for loans of up to £7,145 (the new rate from 2025–26) for tuition fees in an academic year. Students never get their hands on the tuition fee loans cash; the money is paid straight to the university. This way there is no risk of blowing the lot on something other than funding studies, or running late with payments.

### Maintenance loans

These are designed to help full-time home students pay for their living expenses – rent, food, travel, bills, going out, clothes, gym fees and so on. Maintenance loans are partly means-tested and the amount that can be borrowed depends on family income, whether the university is in London or elsewhere in the UK, and whether students live at home with their family or independently.

Maximum loan amounts in 2024–25:
» £8,610 for students living at their family home during term time.
» £10,227 for students living away from home, outside London.

» £13,348 for students living away from home, in London.

» £11,713 for students living and studying abroad for at least one term as part of their UK course.

## Maintenance loan entitlement, England 2024–25

| Household income | Living at home | Living away from home but not in London | Living away from home and studying in London |
|---|---|---|---|
| £25,000 or less | £8,610 | £10,227 | £13,348 |
| £30,000 | £7,887 | £9,497 | £12,606 |
| £35,000 | £7,163 | £8,766 | £11,863 |
| £40,000 | £6,440 | £8,035 | £11,120 |
| £42,875 | £6,024 | £7,614 | £10,692 |
| £45,000 | £5,716 | £7,304 | £10,377 |
| £50,000 | £4,993 | £6,573 | £9,634 |
| £55,000 | £4,269 | £5,842 | £8,891 |
| £58,307 | £3,790 | £5,359 | £8,400 |
| £60,000 | £3,790 | £5,111 | £8,148 |
| £62,347 | £3,790 | £4,767 | £7,799 |
| £65,000 | £3,790 | £4,767 | £7,405 |
| £70,000 | £3,790 | £4,767 | £6,662 |
| £70,098+ | £3,790 | £4,767 | £6,647 |

**Source:** Student Finance England

In general, students must be under 60 on the first day of the first academic year of their course. However, in England over-60s can access a lower means-tested loan for living costs, of up to £4,327.

Maintenance loans are paid straight into students' bank accounts in three instalments throughout the year. Budgeting to make each loan last until the next instalment is down to students. The final maintenance loan payment is a bit smaller than in the years before, because student life ends in June/July of that year, and with it the entitlement to a student loan.

For most 18-year-old freshers, the sight of their current account being hit with probably its biggest single cash injection ever may bring a rush of blood to the head. More sobering, however, may be the surprise that the interest clock starts ticking on the loan from the day of the initial payment, usually the first day of the first term. It keeps ticking until the April after students finish their course, which is when repayment may or may not begin – depending on the level of earnings. For part-time students earning over the threshold, repayment starts four years after starting to receive the loan, even if they are furthering their studies then rather than working.

Repayments are in line with those for tuition fee loans. But critics have said many low and middle-income students could be put off university by having to accrue more debt, and in 2020 the government reintroduced maintenance grants for nurses, as detailed below.

### NHS bursaries

Eligible full-time NHS students can apply for a bursary from the NHS, plus a £1,000 grant from the NHS and a reduced maintenance loan from Student Finance England. For those eligible for an NHS bursary, the NHS pays their standard tuition fees directly to their university.

All full-time nursing students qualify for £5,000 a year maintenance grant, paid pro-rata for part-time students – which is commonly known as the bursary. Those who plan on working in a branch of nursing suffering from severe shortages can also access a further £1,000. Beyond this, another £2,000 is accessible in childcare allowances. Only part of the bursary is means-tested, and some student nurses may be eligible to more bursary funding subject to the means-testing. Student nurses do not have to repay the maintenance grants, as they are not loans. And having the bursary doesn't impact student nurses' access to a full student loan through the Student Loans Company.

The NHS Business Services Authority has a Student Services Arm which runs the NHS Learning Support Fund, worth investigating by those planning to study health or social work.

### Interest rates

Student loan interest rates are based on the RPI, the rate at which prices rise. The interest rate changes every September, based on the RPI rate of inflation in the year to the previous March. Student loan interest rates are based on RPI and, as RPI can go up or down, interest rates can too. The RPI rate rocketed in recent years, due to high inflation, but was down to 3.4% in October 2024. As student loans are repaid over a long period, interest rate swings in either direction usually even themselves out. Student loans are fairly flexible; you do not pay if you are not earning enough, and you can overpay whenever you want. If students lose touch with the Student Loans Company, RPI plus 3% is automatically applied to their debt, and penalty charges kick in if anyone tries to avoid paying what they owe.

### The disappearing debt

After 40 years in England, or 30 under the old scheme (this varies a little elsewhere in the UK – please see further down this chapter), the debt is written off. Because the repayments seem modest for anyone with a qualifying income, and because of the 40- or 30-year rule, student debt is a lot more forgiving than a mortgage or a credit card, where the bills keep on coming even if you are out of work. The Student Loans Company is probably the only lender in Britain that hands out tens of thousands of pounds without a credit check.

### Repaying the student loan

Student loan debt works very differently from other types of borrowing. If you take a personal loan or a mortgage, for example, what you repay is based on how much is borrowed, the interest rate and the loan term. With student loan repayments what you repay is based solely on what you earn. The repayment threshold for the Plan 5 loan for all new students in England is currently £25,000 a year (£2,083 a month or £480 a week) before tax. The first Plan 5 repayments will be no earlier than the 2026/27 tax year. Once they hit the threshold, university-leavers then pay 9% of anything they earn above this level.

What you'll repay on a Plan 5 student loan

| Salary | What you'll repay each year |
| --- | --- |
| £24,000 | You don't pay |
| £26,000 | £90/year (9% of £1,000) |
| £35,000 | £900/year (9% of £10,000) |
| £50,000 | £2,250/year (9% of £25,000) |
| £100,000 | £6,750/year (9% of £75,000) |
| Source: moneysavingexpert.com | |

So, if you earn £30,000 you repay £243.45 a year. A graduate keeps repaying their loan until they have cleared it, or for 40 (or 30 for those on the outgoing loan) years from the April after they graduate. If they have not cleared it by then, the outstanding debt is written off. In other words, the interest added is not the interest paid. That depends on future earnings. Some graduates will not repay any interest and some will not earn enough to repay all of it. Unlike most debts, which are better to clear as early as possible, students should not start repaying student loans before the April after leaving university, as this can result in overpaying.

The Student Loans Company website has information to guide prospective students through these arrangements and also gives examples of levels of repayment (www. studentloanrepayment.co.uk).

### Living in one country, studying in another

As each of the countries of the UK develops its own distinctive system of student finance, the effects on students leaving home in one UK nation to go and study in another have become knottier. UK students who cross borders to study pay the tuition fees of their chosen university and are eligible for a fee loan, and maybe a partial grant, to cover them. They are also entitled to apply for the scholarships or bursaries on offer from that institution. Any maintenance loan or grant will still come from the awarding body of their home country. If you are in this position, you must check with the authorities in your home country about the funding you are eligible for. You should also contact your own government about support on offer if you are from the Channel Islands or the Isle of Man.

### Applying for support

English students should apply for grants and loans through Student Finance England, Welsh students through Student Finance Wales, Scottish students through the Student Awards Agency for Scotland, and those in Northern Ireland through Student Finance NI or their Education and Library Board. Applications should be made as soon as the offer of a place at university has been received. Don't expect things to happen automatically. For instance, students have to tell the Student Loans Company to pay the tuition fees they owe to the university. Following Britain's departure from the European Union, EU students are charged the same tuition fees as those paid by international students from further afield. International students may be considered for some scholarships and bursaries by individual institutions.

### How the fee system works

What follows is a summary of the position for British students in late 2024. Universities in England and Wales have committed to the same higher tuition fees from 2025. Scottish students studying in Scotland will continue to pay no tuition fees. Northern Ireland had yet to announce any changes to its fee structure.

While there are substantial differences between the four countries of the UK, there is one important piece of common ground. Upfront payment of fees is not compulsory, and students can take out a fee loan from the Student Loans Company to cover them. This is repayable in instalments after graduation when earnings reach £25,000 for new English students (£27,295 for those on the discontinued Plan 2 loan).

The most you can borrow to pay fees is £9,535, with lower sums for private colleges (up to £6,165) and part-time study, where the cap is £7,145 (from 2025–26) at public institutions and £4,625 at private ones. There are different levels of fees and support for UK students who are not from England.

New students enrolling at UK universities from all international countries, including those in the EU, will pay the same international rate, which is usually much higher than the home rate. EU students already registered on courses before December 31, 2020, qualify for the home rate of fees for the remainder of their course. The latest information on individual universities' fees at the time of going to press is listed alongside their profiles in Chapter 12. With changes, large or small, becoming almost an annual occurrence, it is essential to consult the websites of the relevant government agencies.

## Tuition fees by region for courses starting in 2024

| Student's home region | Studying in England | Studying in Scotland | Studying in Wales | Studying in Northern Ireland |
|---|---|---|---|---|
| England | Up to £9,250 | Up to £9,250 | Up to £9,250 | Up to £9,250 |
| Scotland | Up to £9,250 | No fee | Up to £9,250 | Up to £9,250 |
| Wales | Up to £9,250 | Up to £9,250 | Up to £9,250 | Up to £9,250 |
| Northern Ireland | Up to £9,250 | Up to £9,250 | Up to £9,250 | Up to £4,750 |
| EU and other international | Variable | Variable | Variable | Variable |

*This will not apply to Irish nationals living in the UK and Ireland whose right to study and to access benefits and services is preserved on a reciprocal basis for UK and Irish nationals under the Common Travel Area arrangement.

**Source:** UCAS/Scottish Government/Welsh Government

### Fees in England

In England, the maximum tuition fee for full-time undergraduates from the UK will be up to £9,535 a year in 2025–26 and up to £7,145 for part-time students. Most courses will demand the maximum rate or close to it. In many public universities, the lowest fees will be for foundation degrees and Higher National Diplomas (HND). Those for foundation degrees have been recently capped at £5,197, to align with the fees for HNDs. These two-year courses remain a cost-effective stepping stone to a full degree, or a qualification in their own right, at many universities and further education colleges. Those universities that offer extended work placements or a year abroad as part of a degree course, will charge much less than the normal fee for this "year out". The maximum cost for a placement year is 20% of the tuition fee, and for a full year abroad, 15%. If you spend only part of the year abroad, you will probably have to pay the whole £9,535.

### Fees and funding in Scotland

At Scottish universities and colleges, students from Scotland pay no fees directly. The universities' vice-chancellors and principals have appealed for charges to be introduced at some level to save their institutions from falling behind their English rivals in financial terms, but the Scottish government said in August 2024 it was committed to free education. Students whose home is in Scotland and who are studying at a Scottish university apply to the Student Awards Agency for Scotland (SAAS) to have their fees paid for them. Note, too, that three-year degrees are rare in Scotland, so most students can expect to pay four years of living costs.

Students from England, Wales and Northern Ireland studying in Scotland will pay fees at something like the scale that applies in England and will have access to finance at similar levels to those available for study in England. It is worth noting, however, that some courses offer considerable savings, such as Robert Gordon University in Aberdeen, for example, which has a fee of £6,860 per year (correct for 2024–25) for some four-year courses, including a BA in Accounting and Finance.

## Scottish maintenance bursaries and loans 2024–25

| Young student (under 25 at start of course) | | | | Independent student (25+) | | | |
|---|---|---|---|---|---|---|---|
| Income | Loan | Bursary | Total | Income | Loan | Bursary | Total |
| Up to £20,999 | £9,400 | £2,000 | £11,400 | Up to £20,999 | £10,400 | £1,000 | £11,400 |
| £21,000–£23,999 | £9,400 | £1,125 | £10,525 | £21,000–£23,999 | £10,400 | £0 | £10,400 |
| £24,000–£33,999 | £9,400 | £500 | £9,900 | £24,000–£33,999 | £9,900 | £0 | £9,900 |
| Over £34,000 | £8,400 | £0 | £8,400 | Over £34,000 | £8,400 | £0 | £8,400 |

Scottish paramedic, nursing and midwifery students studying in Scotland are eligible for bursaries of £10,000 for the first three years and £7,500 for the fourth year of a course, but only if they intend to stay and work in Scotland after qualifying. There is a separate dental bursary scheme.

**Source:** Students Awards Agency Scotland

The majority of Scottish universities offer a "free" fourth year for non-Scottish students to bring their total fees into line with English universities, but Edinburgh and St Andrews were charging £9,250 in all four years of their degree courses up to 2024–25. They had yet to confirm whether these would go up in line with the rest of the UK in 2025–26, at the time of writing.

### Student loans and grants for Scottish students
Scottish students pay no tuition fees at their own universities and can apply for up to £9,250 per year as a loan for fees elsewhere in the UK (presumably this will go up in line with the new fees, but Scotland's SAAS agency had not confirmed this at the time of writing). They must reapply for this loan each year.

Unlike the other UK countries, Scotland uses a band system to calculate the combination of bursary and loan, rather than precise household income. So, in 2024–25, students from a family with an income below £20,999 could get a £2,000 Young Students' Bursary (YSB) as well as a loan of £9,400 – making £11,400. For incomes from £21,000 to £23,999, the bursary is £1,125 and the loan remains the same – making £10,525, and for those earning £24,000 to £33,999, the bursary is £500 and the loan is still £9,400, making a total of £9,900. Above £34,000, no bursary is available and the maximum loan falls to £8,400.

These figures are the same regardless of whether students live at home or where they are studying in the UK. Higher loans but more limited bursaries are available for "independent" students – those who are married, mature (25 or over) or without family support. Maintenance support loans in Scotland are not available to students aged over 55, and students must be under 60 to enrol on the first day of their course.

Scotland's SAAS agency has the repayment threshold set at £31,395 for those on Plan 4. Interest is linked to the Retail Price Index, as in Northern Ireland. Repayments continue until the loan is paid off, with any outstanding amount being cancelled after 35 years. As elsewhere in the UK, there are special funds for people with disabilities and other special needs, and for those with children or adult dependants.

### Fees and funding in Wales
Welsh universities lifted the cap on tuition fees from £9,000 to £9,250 in 2024 and soon after committed to the same rise in tuition fees rise as England, to £9,535.

For 2024–25, the maximum maintenance award is £10,315 for students living at home,

£12,150 for those living away from home and outside London, and £15,170 for those studying in London. The Welsh government has said there will be a 1.6% rise to maintenance funding for 2025–26. These sums are mainly an outright grant to those from low-income households. So, if total household income is £18,370 or less, £8,100 of the total £12,150 maintenance award is a grant (and therefore does not need to be repaid) and only £4,050 a loan. But if income is over £59,200, then £11,150 is repayable and only £1,000 is a grant. The same logic applies to other levels of support, while part-time students can get a variable loan or grant that depends upon income and the intensity of their course. In addition, students in Wales are also able to apply for Welsh government support for parents of young children, for adult learners, for those with adult dependants and for those with disabilities. This support can cover carer costs as well as equipment and general expenditure.

Tuition fee loans are available to cover the whole £9,535 of tuition fees in Wales and for Welsh students in Scotland, England or Northern Ireland (£6,165 for a private provider). Those studying part-time in Wales (or at the Open University) can apply for a loan of up to £2,625. Elsewhere in the UK they can apply for up to £6,935, or for courses at private institutions, £4,625.

Wales has kept the Plan 2 repayment system, which means that new student borrowers will continue to use the £27,295 repayment threshold and 30-year repayment period. Interest repayments are at RPI up to RPI+3%.

## Student finance in Northern Ireland
The two universities of Northern Ireland are charging local students £4,750 a year for 2024–25. For students from elsewhere in the UK, the fee is £9,535 for Queen's Belfast in 2025–26 and £9,250 at Ulster in 2024–25 (though it is likely to follow suit with Queen's the following year).

Maintenance grants of up to £3,475 are available to students from households with incomes below £41,065 and these do not have to be repaid. There are maintenance loans of up to £5,250 for students living at home, up to £6,776 for those living away from home outside London, up to £9,492 for those studying in London away from home. The maximum loan is reduced by the size of any grant received. Loan repayments of 9% of salary start once income reaches £22,015 currently, a lower threshold than in England, Scotland or Wales, and interest is calculated on the Retail Price Index or 1% above base rate, whichever is lower. The loan will be cancelled after 25 years, quicker than elsewhere in the UK.

There are also special funds for people with disabilities and other special needs, and for those with children or adult dependants. Students studying in the Republic of Ireland can also borrow up to €3,000 a year to pay their Irish tuition contribution and may be able to get a bursary to study there. Tuition fee loans are available for the full amount of tuition fees, regardless of where you study in the UK.

## Affording to live and the cost of living crisis
No one has to pay tuition fees while they are a student, but you still have to find thousands of pounds in living costs to take a full-time degree. Stretching the student budget is an ever-present university challenge, and students have always proved resourceful. Analysis by numerous organisations including the NUS confirms what students already knew, that the maintenance loan does not provide enough money to cover the real cost of living – even before prices spiralled. University leaders say government forecasts of annual increases to maintenance loans have been inaccurate in each year since 2020–21. Without a mechanism in place to correct for inflation, it means a "significant real-terms cut" has been baked into the system – which the upcoming 3.1% increase is not sufficient to make up for.

Universities in the Russell Group collectively were spending seven-figure sums on direct financial aid and non-financial support measures in 2023–24. A third of Russell Group universities operated food banks for students, while many boosted their bursary and hardship funds to counteract rising living costs. They have also provided free and low-cost meals, free and subsidised travel, technology loans and money management advisors, as well as enhanced bursaries, grants and rent guarantor schemes for students from under-represented groups, who are at the most risk of dropping out of their studies because of financial challenges. A 2023 survey of Russell Group students revealed that 94% had concerns about living costs, while 1 in 4 were regularly going without food and other necessities due to financial hardship – a figure that rises to more than 3 in 10 for students from the most socioeconomically disadvantaged background.

Typically, the No 1 one source of topping up the coffers is parents, whose implied assistance is now more of an explicit one in the government's approach to student funding. Part-time jobs, savings and bursaries and scholarships also contribute to the student purse. The Student Money Survey 2024 from savethestudent.org found that average undergraduate spending was £1,104 per month (up from £1,078 per month in 2023 and £924 per month in 2022), with rent the biggest outlay at an average of £540 per month. The proportion of students receiving money from their parents dropped to 50% (from 53% in 2023 and from 59% in 2022) – suggesting that parents are also struggling with the rising cost of living. The amount they are contributing has soared, however, according to the annual NatWest Student Living Index for 2024, which found parent/family monetary support has increased by 57% year-on-year, up from £321.15 to £505.10 per month.

The Natwest index also found that students are spending more time than ever in part-time work, with an average of 46.39 hours per month – a 153% increase compared to 2023. Household bills were found to have jumped: In 2023, the biggest spend after rent was at the supermarket, in 2024 household bills overtook, with an average spend of £157.78, up from £34.48. Students were choosing nights without alcohol when it comes to socialising, which 61% did at least once a fortnight or more. Meanwhile average going out budgets of £46 per month were the lowest for three years, and only £3 a month higher than in pandemic-hit 2021.

### Budgeting

Help is at hand to avoid the financial abandon of splurging huge portions of a student loan in the first month. University websites, UCAS at **ucas.com/finance/managing-money/student-budgeting-tips** ; **savethestudent.org/save-money** and many others offer guidance on preparing a budget. List all likely income (loans, bursaries, part-time work, savings, parental support) and compare this with expected outgoings. It pays to be realistic, rather than too optimistic, about both sides of the equation.

Aldi, Lidl and other budget supermarkets are godsends when it comes to stretching the budget, even if shopping at one means needing to get a taxi home – share with a housemate and split the cost, there will still be significant savings on the prices at the nearby Tesco Express or Sainsbury's Local. No one is condoning binge drinking, but with "pre-drinks" before a night out popular, great savings can be made by stocking up on the budget versions of well-known drinks and snacks. Shopping online, while not offered by the budget supermarkets, can also be cost effective if you stick to own brand products, as the temptation of popping extra items into the trolley at will is removed and any delivery fee can be shared with housemates. Some parents like to send supermarket deliveries to their student.

Cookery how-tos on YouTube, TikTok, Instagram et al have brought meal prep guidelines to smartphones, bringing culinary skills to the tip of everyone's fingers. Sharing a meal with housemates is great for bonding, while leftovers in Tupperware are a weapon in the fight against blowing the budget on daily café lunches. The same goes for a carry-cup for hot drinks.

More than two-thirds of 18–24-year-olds reported they received no financial education at school, according to a report by the National Association of Student Money Advisors (NASMA). Keeping track of finances is not every student's idea of a good time but it is certain to provide greater freedom for enjoying university life. Most graduates will have to grapple with spreadsheets during their working life, and they make balancing the student budget simpler. Apps can help too, such as Snoop, which lets you connect all your bank accounts and credit cards on one dashboard, so you can keep track of spending. You can set yourself a budget for each spending category and it sends you summaries, showing where you could be overspending to help you cut costs.

Make full use of student travel cards and shopping discounts, and shop around for the best calls and data deals on mobile phones. Strength of will around social media advertising should also help with budgeting: Natwest's 2024 survey revealed that 73% of students had been influenced to make a purchase after seeing it on social media, with clothes/fashion the most popular purchase (50%), followed by skincare and makeup products (42%), and haircare products (27%).

---

## Funding timetable

It is vital that you sort out your funding arrangements before you start university. Each funding agency has its own arrangements, and it is very important that you find out the exact details from them. The timings below give general indications of key dates.

### March/April
» Online and paper application forms become available from funding agencies.
» You must contact the appropriate funding agency to make an application. This will be the funding agency for the region of the UK that you live in, even if you are planning to study elsewhere in the UK.
» Complete application form as soon as possible. At this stage, select the university offer that will be your first choice.
» Check details of bursaries and scholarships available from your selected universities.

### May/June
» Funding agencies will give you details of the financial support they can offer.
» Last date for making an application to ensure funding is ready for you at the start of term (exact date varies significantly between agencies).

### August
» Tell your funding agency if the university or course you have been accepted for is different from that originally given them.

### September
» Take letter confirming funding to your university for registration.
» After registration, the first part of funds will be released to you.

---

## Study costs

Some courses require much higher course spends than others, and extra financial support may be available for certain – but not all – things. Take out library text books or buy them second-hand from students who don't need them anymore to cut back on bills incurred by a long reading list. Lots of reference publications are available for free online too. The average student spent £18 per month on course materials, Save the Student's 2024 survey found.

## Overdrafts and credit cards

These are the more expensive forms of debt, and best avoided if at all possible. Many banks offer free overdraft facilities for students but going over the limit without prior arrangement can result in high charges. Credit cards can be useful if managed properly, ideally by setting up a direct debit to pay off the full balance every month, thus avoiding paying any interest. To pay only the minimum charge each month can end up costing a small fortune over a long period. Those inclined to spend impulsively without keeping track of spending are probably better off without a credit card and should stick with a debit card.

## Insurance

Most students arrive at university with laptops and other goodies such as games consoles, sports equipment, musical instruments, mobile phones and bikes that are tempting to thieves. It is estimated that around a third of students fall victim to crime at some point during university. A reasonable amount of cover for these items should be found by shopping around, without it costing you an arm and a leg. It may also be possible to add this cover cheaply to parents' domestic contents policy (probably at their expense).

## University scholarships and bursaries

Shop around for university bursaries, scholarships and sponsorship packages, and seek other forms of supplementary support. There may be fee reductions for groups including local students, which are usually detailed on university websites. There is funding for students with disabilities or family responsibilities; or for those taking subjects such as social work or medicine, with wide public benefit, as well as a range of charities with their own criteria. In some cases, bursaries may make the difference between being able to afford higher education and having to pass up a potentially life-changing opportunity. Some are worth up to £3,000 a year, although most are less generous than this, often because large numbers of students qualify for an award. Some scholarships are even more valuable, and are awarded for sporting and musical prowess, as well as academic achievement. Most scholarships are not means-tested, but a few are open only to students who are both high performers academically and from low-income families.

Some universities have substantial endowments to fund their bursaries and scholarships programmes, such as the prestigious London School of Economics and Political Science, which in recent years has awarded around £4million annually in scholarships and financial support to its undergraduates. Across the city at the University of West London about half of full-time students qualify for some form of financial assistance, which includes the UWL Aspire Bursary of £200 for student supplies and £1,000 a year undergraduate bursaries for those from low-income households.

The Scholarship Hub, a database of scholarships, suspects UK students could be missing out on funding worth over £150 million a year as organisations offering scholarships often struggle to get enough applications. The database is free, but it requires a subscription to access advice about how to apply and to use enhanced search tools. Most bursaries are means-tested, while scholarships are via open competition. Some universities offer eligible students the choice of accommodation discounts, fee waivers or cash.

Most also have hardship funds for those who find themselves in financial difficulties. Many charities for specific industries or professions have a remit to support education, and many have bursaries for anyone studying a related subject. The Directory of Grant-Making Trusts lists bodies that make one-off or regular awards to all kinds of causes, often including deserving students. Only available in hard copy, a library visit to see it for free could be worth the trip.

Take note of the application procedures for scholarships and bursaries. They vary between institutions, and even from course to course within institutions. Specific awards may have specific application deadlines. In some cases, the university will work out for you whether you are entitled to an award by referring to your funding agency's financial assessment. If your personal circumstances change part-way through a course, entitlement to a scholarship or bursary may be reviewed.

Advice on scholarships and bursaries is usually included in a university's website or prospectus and many institutions also maintain a helpline. Is the bursary or scholarship automatic or conditional? When will you find out whether your application has been successful? For some awards, this won't be until after exam results.

### Students with disabilities

Extra financial help is available to disabled students, whether studying full-time or part-time, through Disabled Students' Allowances, which are paid in addition to the standard student finance package. They are available for help with education-related conditions such as dyslexia, and for other physical and mental disabilities. They do not depend on income and do not have to be repaid. The cash is available for extra travel costs, equipment and to pay helpers. For 2024–25, the maximum amount available for eligible students in England for support – including a nonmedical helper, or specialist equipment – is £26,948 a year.

### Further sources of income

There are various types of support available for students in particular circumstances, other than the main loans, grants and bursaries. Support has broadened since the cost of living crisis started to impact students, and the NatWest Student Living Index 2024 shows that income from hardship loans/grants in term time jumped from just £5 a month in 2023 to £371 in 2024. Reliance on bank loans also climbed, from £31 a month in 2023 to £224 in 2024.

» Even without the rising cost of living, undergraduates in financial difficulties could apply for help from their university's student hardship fund. These provide support for anything from day-to-day study and living costs to unexpected or exceptional expenses. The university decides which students need help and how much to award them. These funds often target older or disadvantaged students, and finalists in danger of dropping out. The sums range up to a few thousand pounds, are not repayable and do not count against other income.

» Students with children can apply for a Childcare Grant. For 2024–25, this was up to £193.62 a week for a first child and up to £331.95 for two or more children. There was also a Parents' Learning Allowance of between £50 and £1,963 a year in 2024–25 for help with course-related costs.

» Students with a partner, or another adult family member who is financially dependent on them, can apply for an Adult Dependants' Grant of up to £ 3,438 a year for 2024–25.

**Part-time work**

A part-time term-time job is a fact of life for around half of students. The challenge is to not let the part-time job get in the way of studying. A survey by the NUS found that 59% of students who worked felt it had an impact on their studies, with 38% missing lectures and over a fifth failing to submit coursework because of their part-time jobs.

Student employment agencies, found on many university campuses, match employers with students seeking work, sometimes offering jobs within the university itself. They also ensure both minimum wages and the maximum number of hours worked in term time, typically 15 hours a week. Students sometimes make money from freelance work and student businesses, but most take casual work in shops, restaurants, bars and call centres. Most students get a job during the holidays, including those who don't have one in the term. Three in ten students reported having their own side hustle or business in Save the Student's 2024 survey, most with incomes of up to £500 a year but some reporting earnings in the thousands.

**Useful websites**

The "fees and funding" pages on university websites provide the most up-to-date information on costs of individual courses – especially for rates paid by international students, which vary.

Universities also publish details of the financial help available, and how to apply. It is essential to consult the latest information provided by government agencies. The following websites will outline any major developments.

England: **gov.uk/student-finance**
Wales: **studentfinancewales.co.uk**
Scotland: **saas.gov.uk**
Northern Ireland: **studentfinanceni.co.uk**
Office for Students: **officeforstudents.org.uk**

For the basics of fees, loans, grants and other allowances: **gov.uk/student-finance**

UCAS provides helpful advice: **ucas.com/money-and-student-life** as does student money website: **savethestudent.org**

All UK student loans are administered by the Student Loans Company: **gov.uk/government/organisations/student-loans-company**

HMRC information on the tax position of students: **gov.uk/student-jobs-paying-tax**

For finding out about availability of scholarships: **thescholarshiphub.org.uk** (requires subscription fee). Or go direct to university websites, where their scholarship and bursary provision will be detailed.

# 5 Making Your Application

The UK's predicted admissions system is unique among developed countries. It has been a long-running discussion in the higher education sector – with many arguing that applying to university without knowing your results lacks transparency and is hard for students to navigate. Detractors to the system also point to the unfairness of predicted grades, which can be unreliable as well as work against high achievers from disadvantaged backgrounds – whose grades are more likely to be under-predicted, evidence shows. But moving to a post-qualification model (PQA) is not hugely popular with exam boards, whose marking time would be squeezed, or universities – which may need to delay term start dates and reduce teaching time. In any case, plans to switch to a PQA model were officially shelved in 2022.

Moving on from the binary debate over pre- or post-qualification admissions the chief executive of UCAS, Dr Jo Saxton, believes a dynamic use of Clearing brings a third way into view. This is based on the growing numbers of applicants using UCAS' "decline my place" tool to switch to a different course, or applying direct to Clearing. Dr Saxton has said the practice reflects "students exercising the agency that they have in a marketised system", and that if harnessed correctly, it should mean more young people – particularly from disadvantaged backgrounds – securing the right courses for them.

Change is already underway with the admissions process, chiefly with the introduction of the new-style personal statement, which will be used by students applying for 2026 entry onwards. Instead of the 4,000-character essay, applicants must respond to three structured questions, detailed later in this chapter. It is hoped the shift will make the admissions process more fair. "The new approach with guided questions aims to give greater confidence to those students, as well as their teachers when advising on how to secure their dream course," Dr Saxton said.

All UK university admissions are handled through UCAS – the service formed in 1992 through the merger of UCCA and PCAS, the former university and polytechnic admissions systems. UCAS makes the process of applying to university as straightforward as possible. Everything happens online and applicants are provided with clear instructions, tips and suggestions of how best to navigate each section along the way.

The UCAS hub is your one-stop-shop for everything from details of more than 35,000 courses, open days and key dates, to top tips based on where you are in the application process, handy to-do lists and reminders to keep you on track. It also offers personalised careers information and advice and includes tools such as a personal statement builder, tariff calculator and apprenticeship finder.

Grades are the most important factor in winning a place at university, but what goes on the application form is more important than many students realise, and it pays to keep your eye on the ball at this stage on the journey to university. Applicants must decide on up to five choices months before they take their final exams, you do not have to use all five of them but doing so gives you the best chance of success.

## The application process

Almost all applications for full-time higher education courses go through UCAS, including those to the conservatoires, which come with separate guidance and processes on the UCAS website.

Applications for degree apprenticeships are exceptions to the rule, however, and should be made to employers rather than universities. Deadlines differ between employers. You can apply for as many apprenticeships as you want, on top of your university applications. Many recruit through the **www.gov.uk/apply-apprenticeship** website, which also has links to vacancy information, as does UCAS at **careerfinder.ucas.com**.

Some universities that have not filled all their places on conventional degrees, even during Clearing, will accept direct applications up to and sometimes after the start of the academic year, but UCAS is both the official route and the only way into the most popular courses.

## Registering with Apply

Applications kick off by registering with Apply. School and college students will be given a "buzzword" by their tutor or careers adviser – you need this in order to login to register. It links your application to the school or college so that the application can be sent electronically to your referee (usually one of your teachers) for your reference to be attached. If you are no longer at a school or college, you do not need a buzzword, but you will need details of your referee.

---

### The main screens to be completed in UCAS Apply

» Personal and contact details, and some additional non-educational details for UK applicants.
» Student finance arrangements (UK applicants only), and up to five course choices.
» Details of your education so far, including examination results and those still to be taken.
» Your employment history, listing any paid or voluntary work you have done.
» Your personal statement.
» A reference from one of your teachers.
» View all details to make sure they are correct and reflect your preferences.
» Pay for the application. For 2025–26 it costs £28.50 for up to five courses. This fee is waived for applicants in receipt of free school meals.

---

Apply is available 24 hours a day, and, when the time comes, information on the progress of your application may arrive at any time. More information is given on the UCAS website.

Clicking on "Apply" begins the process for providing your personal details and generating a username and password, as well as reminding you of basic points, such as amending your details in case of a change of address. You can register separate term-time and holiday addresses – a useful option for boarders, who could find offers and, particularly, the confirmation of a place, going to their school when they are miles away at home. Remember to keep a note of your username and password in a safe place.

Throughout the process, you will be in sole control of communications with UCAS and your chosen universities. Only if you nominate a representative and give them your unique nine-digit application number (sent automatically by UCAS when your application is submitted), can a parent or anyone else give or receive information on your behalf, perhaps because you are ill or out of the country.

Video guides on the application process are available on the UCAS website. Once you are registered, you can start to complete the Apply screens. The sections that follow cover the main screens.

## Personal details

This information is taken from your initial registration, and you will be asked for additional information, for example, on ethnic origin, to monitor equal opportunities in the application process. UK students will also be asked to complete a student finance section designed to speed up any loan application you might make. Applicants since 2024 entry have been able to select from "man | woman | I use another term | I prefer not to say" when asked for their gender identity.

UCAS also introduced seven new questions in 2023, as part of its commitment to widening participation. They allow students to self-declare important information about their circumstances, so they can be connected to the right support for their needs. The new questions cover:

- » Students estranged from their parents
- » Students with caring responsibilities
- » Students with parenting responsibilities
- » Refugees, asylum seekers and those with limited leave to remain in the UK
- » Students from UK Armed Forces families
- » UK Armed Forces veterans and Service leavers
- » A self-declared free school meals question

## Choices

In most subjects, you will be able to apply to a maximum of five universities and/or colleges. The exceptions are medicine, dentistry and veterinary science, where the maximum is four, but you can use your fifth choice as a back-up to apply for a different subject.

The other important restriction concerns Oxford or Cambridge, because you can only apply to one or the other; you cannot apply to both universities in the same year, nor can you apply for more than one course there. For both universities you may need to take a written test and submit examples of your work, depending on the course selected. In addition, for Cambridge, many subjects will demand a pre-interview assessment once the university has received your application from UCAS, while the rest will set written tests to be taken at interview.

The deadline for Oxbridge applications – and for all medicine, dentistry and veterinary science courses – is October 15. For all other applications the deadline is January 15 (or March 24 for some specified art and design courses). The other exceptions to this rule are the relatively small but growing number of courses that start in January or February. If you are considering one of these, contact the university concerned for application deadlines.

Most applicants use all five choices. But if you do choose fewer than five courses, you can still add another to your form up to June 30, as long as you have not accepted or declined any offers. Nor do you have to choose five different universities if more than one course at the same institution attracts you – if you are keen on one institution in particular, applying for one course with lower entrance requirements than the other is a good way of hedging your bets. Universities are not allowed to see where else you have applied, or whether you have chosen the same subject elsewhere. But they will be aware of multiple applications within their own institution. Remember that it is more difficult to write a convincing personal statement if it has to cover two subjects.

For each course you select, you will need to put the UCAS code on the form – and you should check carefully that you have the correct code and understand any special requirements that may be detailed on the UCAS description of the course. It does not matter in what order you enter your choices as all are treated equally. You will also need to indicate whether you are applying for a deferred entry (for example, if you are taking a gap year – see page 90).

**Education**

This is where you provide details of the schools and colleges you have attended, and the qualifications you have obtained or are preparing for. The UCAS website gives plenty of advice on the ways in which you should enter this information, to ensure that all your relevant qualifications are included with their grades. While UCAS does not need to see qualification certificates, it can double-check results with the examination boards to ensure that no one has exaggerated their results.

In the Employment section that follows, add details of any paid jobs you have had (unpaid or voluntary work should be mentioned in your personal statement).

**Personal statement**

Applicants for 2026 entry will be the first to submit the new-style personal statement. This has divided the format from one long piece of text into three separate questions, each with a minimum 350-character requirement. The overall 4,000-character limit (including spaces) is the same. The questions are:

**Question 1: Why do you want to study this course or subject?**
Showcase your motivations for studying the course or courses here, your knowledge of the subject area and interests, and your future plans and why this is a good fit for you.

**Question 2: How have your qualifications and studies helped you to prepare for this course or subject?**
Under this section, talk about how your studies or training relate to your chosen course, courses or subject area, the relevant skills you have that make you a great candidate, and any relevant educational achievements.

**Question 3: What else have you done to prepare outside of education, and why are these experiences useful?**
Use this section to highlight work experience, employment or volunteering, as well as personal life experiences or responsibilities. You can also bring in hobbies and extracurricular or outreach activities, achievements outside school or college, and for those no longer in full-time education, this is the place to mention what you've been doing since and how this has equipped you for your chosen course or courses.

By removing the daunting spectre of a personal statement blank page and providing these structured sub-headers, the process is intended to be easier for applicants to convey their very best talents and experiences. It is hoped that the new format will support the broadest range of applicants to succeed in their applications and remove the advantages that privileged applicants had with regards to coaching and support in writing personal statements.

"The 4,000 total character count remains the same, as does our advice to students," explains Courteney Sheppard, Head of Customer Contact at UCAS. "The personal statement is your opportunity to talk about you and why you want to enrol in a particular course, we encourage students to advocate for themselves, in their own words, and describe the ambitions, skills and experience that will make them suitable for the course."

This is the part of the application where you get to tell the universities why they should pick you. A part-time job, volunteering and other extracurricular activities can be useful ways of demonstrating that you have the skills and experience for university study. These could involve anything from learning survival skills during the Duke of Edinburgh's Award scheme to taking part in music or sports activities, or helping at a charity.

Don't just list your skills – be they communication and leadership or the ability to work in a team and manage time well – try to provide examples of when you have demonstrated them. Don't be tempted to make sentences complicated – keep them short and don't overuse the thesaurus. Avoid pretentious quotes, as well as clichés and phrases such as "from a young age", "as long as I can remember" and "I have always been interested in".

Admissions tutors want to see evidence of your interest, commitment and knowledge of your chosen subject. Avoid using the word "passion" – instead, let it jump off the page. If you enjoy reading, which many people do, say which authors or books inspire you, and why. Again, ensure your account is based on lived experiences, not what you think the UCAS admissions tutor would want you to say. Your UCAS form also has your teacher's reference and your statement should be in line with their summary of your abilities and interests.

While stopping short of exaggerating or out-and-out lying, this is an opportunity to promote yourself; if that makes you cringe and clam up, ask for help from your parents, friends and teachers. The personal statement is not the place to discuss exam grades – qualifications are covered elsewhere on your UCAS form. Academic staff in charge of admissions look for potential beyond the high grades that increasing numbers of candidates bring. To stand out, do your homework on your chosen degree, show an interest in the subject by listening to podcasts, following lecturers on X, and reading articles. Highlight the experiences you've gained that are related to the syllabus you are applying to – clubs you attend or run, lectures, visits, blogs you have written, work experience and wider reading around the subject.

Practical work experience or volunteering in medical or caring settings should be included by those applying to study medicine – but don't just list what you've done, reflect on what these experiences taught you about working as a doctor and how you are suited to the training and profession. The same approach goes for other vocational degrees; explain how you see yourself using the qualification. Work experience in any setting requires a similar approach; merely namechecking a prestigious company you have been lucky enough to get a placement at will not impress admissions tutors – tell them what you learnt from the organisation and how it relates to the degree you are applying to study.

Take advice from teachers and, if there is still time before you make your application, look for some subject-related activities that will help round out your statement. Mention the accomplishments that suggest you will turn out to be a productive member of the university and, eventually, a successful graduate. Leading activities outside your school or college are ideal, or other responsibilities you have taken on. Show the admissions tutors that you can take initiative and be self-disciplined, since higher education involves much more independent study than sixth-formers are used to.

Think hard about why you want to study your chosen subject – especially if it is one you have not taken at school or college – and align your interests and skills with the course.

---

## Timetable for applications for university admission in 2026

At the time of writing UCAS had not confirmed the exact dates for the application schedule. Please check the UCAS website for the most recent information.

### 2025

| | |
|---|---|
| January onwards | Find out about courses and universities. Check schedule of open days. |
| February onwards | Attend open days. |
| early July | Registration starts for UCAS Apply. |
| mid September | UCAS starts receiving applications. |
| October 2 | Final day for conservatoire music applications |
| October 15 | Final day for applications to Oxford and Cambridge, and for most courses in medicine, dentistry and veterinary science. |

### 2026

| | |
|---|---|
| January 29 | Final equal consideration date for applications for most other undergraduate courses |
| January 30–end June | New applications continue to be accepted by UCAS, but only considered by universities if the relevant courses have vacancies. |
| late February | Start of applications through UCAS Extra. |
| end March | Universities should have sent decisions on all applications received by January 29. |
| early May | Final time by which applicants have to decide on their choices if all decisions received by end March (exact date for each applicant will be confirmed by UCAS). **If you do not reply to UCAS, they will decline your offers.** UCAS must have received all decisions from universities if you applied by January 29. |
| early June | Final time by which applicants have to decide on their choices if all decisions received by early May. |
| start of July | Any new application received from this time held until Clearing starts. End of applications through UCAS Extra. |
| July 5 | International Baccalaureate results published (to be confirmed). Full Clearing opens. |
| early August | SQA results published. Scottish Clearing starts (to be confirmed). |
| mid August | A-level results published (to be confirmed). |
| end August | Last time for you to meet any offer conditions, after which a university might not accept you. |
| late October | End of period for adding Clearing choices and last point at which a university can accept you through Clearing. |

---

Showing commitment to the full course is important, so admissions officers are convinced you will get good results for its duration. Some applicants' five choices will cover more than one subject, and in this situation try to make more general comments about your academic strengths and enthusiasms and avoid focusing on just one of the courses.

If you are an international (EU and non-EU) student you should also include why you want to study in the UK, detail your English language skills, and any English courses or tests you've taken and why you want to be an international student, rather than study in your own country.

Mature students can talk about any alternative entry requirements you've used – such as an access course – that show skills and knowledge gained through previous experiences.

Take advantage of the help offered by your school or college. Your teachers see personal statements every year and will have a feel for ones that have gone down well for former students, despite the new format.

## International and EU students

Many universities will continue to accept applications from international students later in the year, until nearer the beginning of the course.

## References

Hand-in-hand with your personal statement goes the reference from your school, college or, in the case of mature students, someone who knows you well, but is not a friend or family member. Since 2014, even referees who are not your teachers have been encouraged to predict your grades, although they are allowed to opt out of this process. Whatever the source, the reference has to be independent – you are specifically forbidden to change any part of it if you send off your own application – but that does not mean you should not try to influence what it contains.

Most schools and colleges conduct informal interviews before compiling a reference, but it does no harm to draw up a list of the achievements that you would like to see included, and ensure your referee knows what subject you are applying for. Referees cannot know every detail of a candidate's interests and most welcome an aide-memoire.

The UCAS guidelines skirt around the candidate's right to see their reference, but it does exist. Schools' practices vary, but most now show the applicant the completed reference. Where this is not the case, the candidate can ask UCAS customer service to send a copy of their application as a subject access request, which includes the reference. Better, if you can, to see it before it goes off, in case there are factual inaccuracies that can be corrected.

## Timing

Applications are accepted from mid-September onwards, so the autumn half-term is a sensible target date for completing the process. Universities tend to start considering applications as soon as they arrive, so some early applicants will already be holding offers from universities. Other universities will not start making offers until after all applications are in, so offers will be sent out after January 15.

The general deadline for applications through UCAS is January 15, but even those received up to June 30 will be considered if the relevant courses still have vacancies. After that, you will be limited to Clearing, or an application for the following year. If your form arrives with the deadline looming, you may appear less organised than others; your application may therefore be one of a large batch that receives a more cursory first reading. Under UCAS rules, last-minute applicants should not be at a disadvantage, but why take the risk? The best advice is to get your application in early: before Christmas, or earlier if possible.

## Next steps

Once your application has been processed by UCAS, you will receive an email confirming that it has been sent to your chosen universities and summarising what will happen next. The email will also confirm your personal ID, which you can use to access "Track", the online system that allows you to follow the progress of your application. Check all the details carefully: you have 14 days to contact UCAS to correct any errors.

After that, it is just a matter of waiting for universities to make their decisions, which can take days, weeks or even months. Some obviously see an advantage in being the first to make an offer – it is a memorable moment to be reassured that at least one of your chosen institutions wants you. Others take much longer, perhaps because they have so many good applications to consider, or maybe because they are waiting to see which of their applicants withdraw when Oxford and Cambridge make their offers. Universities are asked to make all their decisions by the end of March, and most have done so long before that.

## Interviews

Unless you are applying for a professional training degree in health or education that brings you into direct contact with the public, the chances are you will not have a selection interview. For prospective medics, vets, dentists or teachers, a face-to-face (or video call) assessment of your suitability will be crucial to your chances of success. Likewise in the performing arts, the interview may be as important as your exam grades. Cambridge still interviews around 80% of applicants in all subjects and Oxford interviews about 40% to 45% of applicants, see Chapter 11, while a few of the other top universities also see a significant proportion. But the expansion of higher education has made it impractical to interview everyone, and many admissions experts are sceptical about interviews.

What has become more common, however, is the "sales" interview, where the university is really selling itself to the candidate. There may still be testing questions, but the admissions staff have already made their minds up and are actually trying to persuade you to accept an offer. Indeed, you will probably be given a clear indication at the end of the interview that an offer is on its way. The technique seems to work, perhaps because you have invested time and nervous energy in a sometimes lengthy trip, as well as acquiring a more detailed impression of both the department and the university.

The difficulty can come in spotting which type of interview is which. The "genuine" ones require extensive preparation, revisiting your personal statement and reading beyond the exam syllabus. Impressions count for a lot, so dress smartly – even if your interview is being held via video call – and make sure that you are on time. Have a question of your own ready, as well as being prepared to give answers.

While you would not want to appear ignorant at a sales interview, lengthy preparation might be a waste of valuable time during a period of revision. Naturally, you should err on the side of caution, but if your predicted grades are well above the standard offer and the subject is not one that normally requires an interview, it is likely that the invitation is a sales pitch. It is still worth going, unless you have changed your mind about the application.

## Offers

When your chosen universities respond to your application, there will be one of three answers:
» Unconditional Offer (U): This used to be a possibility only if you applied after satisfying the entrance requirements – usually if you were applying as a mature student, while on a gap year, after resitting exams or, in Scotland, after completing Highers. However, a number of universities competing for bright students now make unconditional offers to those who are

predicted high grades – just how high will depend on the university. If you are fortunate (and able) enough to receive one, do not assume that grades are no longer important because they may be taken into consideration when you apply for jobs as a graduate.

» Conditional Offer (C): The vast majority of students will still receive conditional offers, where each university offers a place subject to you achieving set grades or points on the UCAS tariff.

» Rejection (R): You do not have the right qualifications or have lost out to stronger competition.

English universities were banned from making "conditional unconditional" offers during the pandemic until September 2021. This type of offer – which only becomes unconditional once an applicant accepts it as their firm choice – was the focus of controversy pre-Covid, with more than 20 universities that were making the highest proportions of conditional unconditional offers named and shamed by the education secretary of the time, who argued that it was unethical to restrict such offers to those who made the university their first choice.

Universities UK (UUK), which represents the sector, published its code of fair admissions in 2022, setting out how processes must support "student choice". According to the code, universities should not make conditional unconditional offers, or offers with significantly lower grade requirements based on applicants making their institution a firm choice. Conditional unconditional offer-making has since fallen from a high of over 64,825 in 2019 to 4,860 in 2023.

Any remaining unconditional offers might tempt a candidate to lower their sights and accept a place that would not have been their first choice otherwise. As long as this is not the case, however, there is no reason to spurn such an offer if it comes, as long as you do not take your foot off the pedal in the run-up to exams.

If you have chosen wisely, you should have more than one offer to choose from, so you will be required to pick your favourite as your firm acceptance – known as UF if it was an unconditional offer and CF if it was conditional. Candidates with conditional offers can also accept a second offer, with lower grades, as an insurance choice (CI). You must then decline any other offers that you have.

You do not have to make an insurance choice – indeed, you may decline all your offers if you have changed your mind about your career path or regret your course decisions. But most people prefer the security of a back-up route into higher education if their grades fall short. Some 25,290 took up their insurance choice in 2023, representing 12% of UK 18-year-old applicants – more than did in the previous two admissions years but fewer than in 2019. You must be sure that your firm acceptance is definitely your first choice because you will be allocated a place automatically if you meet the university's conditions. You cannot change your mind at this stage because UCAS rules will not then allow a switch to your insurance choice.

The only way round those rules, unless your results are better than your highest offer (see Results Day, below), is through direct contact with the universities concerned. Your firm acceptance institution must be prepared to release you so that your new choice can award you a place in Clearing. Neither is under any obligation to do so but, in practice, it is rare for a university to insist that a student joins against their wishes.

## UCAS Extra

If things do go wrong and you receive five rejections, that need not be the end of your higher education ambitions. From late February until early July, you have another chance through

UCAS Extra, a listing of courses that still have vacancies after the initial round of offers. Extra is sometimes dismissed (wrongly) as a repository of second-rate courses. In fact, even in the boom years for applications, most Russell Group universities still have courses listed in a wide variety of subjects.

You will be notified if you are eligible for Extra and can then select courses marked as available on the UCAS website. You will be able to submit a new personal statement for Extra. Applications are made, one at a time, through UCAS Track. If you do not receive an offer, or you choose to decline one, you can continue applying for other courses. About half of those applying through Extra normally find a place and Extra remains a valuable route for those who need it. Why wait for the uncertainty of Clearing if there are places available on a course that you want?

### Results Day
Rule No 1 on results day is to be at home, or at least within easy communication – this is not the day to rely on intermittent wi-fi reception in a far-flung location. At 8am on the morning of A-level results day, Track informs those who have already won a place on their chosen course. However, it does not show your A-level results, these are obtained from your school or college.

If you get the grades stipulated in your conditional offer, the process should work smoothly, and you can begin celebrating. Track will let you know as soon as your place is confirmed, and the paperwork will arrive in a day or two. You can phone the university to double check, but it should not be necessary.

If the results are not what you hoped – and particularly if you just miss your grades – you need to be on the phone and taking advice from your school or college. In a year when results are better than expected, some universities will stick to the letter of their offers, perhaps refusing to accept your AAC grades when they had demanded ABB. When places are more liberally available, universities are more likely to forgive a dropped grade to take a candidate who is regarded as promising, rather than go into Clearing to recruit an unknown quantity. Admissions staff may be persuadable – particularly if there are extenuating personal circumstances. Try to get a teacher to support your case and be persistent. Showing commitment is a good thing.

If your results are lower than predicted, one option is to ask for papers to be re-marked, as growing numbers do each year. The school may ask for a whole batch to be re-marked, and you should ensure that your chosen universities know this. If your grades improve as a result, the university will review its decision, but, if by then it has filled all its places, you may have to wait until next year to start.

If you took Scottish Highers, you will have had your results for more than a week by the time the A-level grades are published. If you missed your grades, there is no need to wait for A-levels before you begin approaching universities. Admissions staff at English universities may not wish to commit themselves before they see results from south of the border, but Scottish universities will be filling places immediately.

Adjustment was the system for "trading up" if results turned out better than expected, but having never attracted many users this was cancelled from 2022 entry. Instead, students can use the "Decline My Place" function to enter Clearing, and if they use Clearing Plus, they will be signposted to universities with spaces whose entry requirements match their results.

### Clearing
If results morning did not elicit a "yay, I got in!" moment, put plan B into action and find a university place through Clearing. There will be plenty of options at a good range of

universities. Commenting on the record numbers of applicants who used Clearing in 2024, the head of UCAS Dr Jo Saxton said "There has also been a high number of applicants using Clearing, with students seemingly motivated by plenty of choice this cycle, giving the opportunity to pursue an alternative option they may not have previously considered or thought was out of reach."

In 2023 a record 39,620 students got a place through Clearing – a rise of nearly 14% on the previous year. Of these, the single largest group of students – 22,400 – were those who had already secured a place at university but chose to switch through Clearing, having changed their mind about their institution or course. The figures highlight the abundance of options in Clearing, as well as how students are using it as means of re-evaluating their choices.

Contrary to popular belief Clearing does not open for the first time on A-level results day, it begins on July 5, International Baccalaureate results day, and runs until October 19. The busiest day, however, will be August 18, when A-level students find out their grades. As long as you are not holding any offers and you have not withdrawn your application, you are eligible automatically. You will be sent a Clearing number via Track to quote to universities.

With recruitment restrictions lifted, universities that used to regard their absence from Clearing as a point of pride are appearing in its vacancy lists, and candidates will see options at the coveted research-led institutions included. Certain courses have more availability than others though, and some subjects, such as medicine and dentistry, do not show up in Clearing as they are so oversubscribed. Only a handful of universities do not take part these days, including Oxford, Cambridge, Imperial, the London School of Economics, and St Andrews.

The most popular courses may fill up quickly, but many remain open up to and beyond the start of the academic year. And, at least at the start of the process, the range of courses with vacancies is much wider than in Extra. The first step is to trawl through the course vacancy lists on the UCAS website, and elsewhere, before ringing the university offering the course that appeals most (and where you have a realistic chance of a place – do not waste time on courses where the standard offer is far above your grades). Universities have all hands on deck running Clearing hotlines and are adept at dealing with lots of calls in a short period, but even so you can spend a long time trying the phone while the most desirable places are beginning to disappear.

If you can't get through, send an email setting out your grades and the course that interests you, but keep trying by phone, too. Schools and colleges open on Results Day, and teachers should be willing to help with these calls, especially if you are in a panic. A good way of managing the calls is to let the teacher ring, get through to the university and then pass the phone to the applicant. At the end of calls do a round-up of next steps, as in the melee it is possible to misunderstand or forget things, such as requests for more information or follow-up forms to be filled out.

Wise students will not have waited for Results Day to draw up a list of possible Clearing targets. They will have had their list researched and ready to deploy if the time comes in advance. Many universities publish lists of courses that are likely to be in Clearing on their websites from the start of August. Reconsider some of the courses you mulled over when making your original application, or others at your chosen universities that had lower entrance requirements. But beware of switching to another subject simply because you have the right grades – you still have to sustain your interest and be capable of succeeding over three or more years. Many of the students who drop out of degrees are those who chose the wrong course in a rush during Clearing. In short, start your search immediately if you find yourself in Clearing, and act decisively, but do not panic. You can make as many approaches as you like, until you are accepted on the course of your choice. Remember that if you changed your personal statement for applications in Extra, this will be the one that goes to any universities that you approach in Clearing, so it may be difficult to return to the subjects in your original application.

Most of the available vacancies will appear in Clearing lists, but some of the universities towards the top of the league tables may have a limited number of openings that they choose not to advertise – either for reasons of status or because they do not want the administrative burden of fielding large numbers of calls to fill a handful of places. If there is a course that you find particularly attractive – especially if you have good grades and are applying late – it may be worth making a speculative call. You may be on the spot at just the right moment.

## What are the alternatives?

If your results are lower than expected and there is nothing you want in Clearing, there are several things you can do. The first is to re-sit one or more subjects. The modular nature of most courses means that you will have a clear idea of what you need to do to get better grades. You can go back to school or college or try a "crammer". Although some colleges have a good success rate with retakes, you have to be highly focused and realistic about the likely improvements. And some of the most competitive courses, such as medicine, may demand higher grades for a second application.

Other options are to get a job and study part-time, or to take a break from studying and return later in your career. You may have considered an apprenticeship before applying to university; the number and variety are growing all the time, so it may be worth another look. The UCAS post-16 options web page provides information on apprenticeship opportunities post-16 and has a search tool for higher and degree apprenticeship vacancies (**ucas.com/further-education/post-16-qualifications/post-16-options/staying-education-or-training**).

The part-time route can be arduous – many young people find a job enough to handle without the extra burden of academic work. But others find it just the combination they need for a fulfilling life. It all depends on your job, your social life and your commitment to the subject you will study. A number of universities now have a majority of mature students, so you need not be out of place if this is your chosen route.

## Taking a gap year

The other popular option is to take a gap year. Aside from the pandemic years when deferred entries went up, historically about 7% of applicants defer their entry until the following year while they travel or do voluntary or paid work. The option is largely the domain of school-leavers, known as "gappers", and a whole industry has grown up around tailor-made activities for them, many in Asia, Africa or Latin America. Some have been criticised for doing more for the organisers than the underprivileged communities that they purport to assist, but there are programmes that are useful and character-building, as well as safe. Most of the overseas programmes are not cheap but raising the money can be part of the experience.

Various organisations can help you find voluntary work. Some examples include vInspired (**vinspired.com**) and Plan my Gap Year (**planmygapyear.co.uk**). Voluntary Service Overseas (**vsointernational.org**) works mainly with older volunteers but has an offshoot, run with five other volunteering organisations, International Citizen Service (**volunteerics.org**), that places 18–25-year-olds around the world.

The alternative is to stay closer to home and make your contribution through organisations like Volunteering Matters (**volunteeringmatters.org.uk**) or to take a job that will make higher education more affordable when the time comes. Work placements can be casual or structured, such as the Year in Industry Scheme (**etrust.org.uk**). Sponsorship is also available, mainly to those wishing to study science, engineering or business. Buyer beware: we cannot vouch for any of these and you need to be clear whether the aim is to make money or to plump up your CV. If it is the second, you may end up spending money, not saving it.

Many admissions staff are happy to facilitate gap years because they think it makes for more mature, rounded students. The longer-term benefits may also be an advantage in the graduate employment market. Both university admissions officers and employers look for evidence that candidates have more about them than academic ability. The experience you gain on a gap year can help you develop many of the attributes they are looking for, such as interpersonal, organisational and teamwork skills, leadership, creativity, experience of new cultures or work environments, and enterprise.

There are subjects – maths in particular – that discourage a break because it takes too long to pick up study skills where you left off. From the student's point of view, you should also bear in mind that a gap year postpones the moment at which you embark on a career. This may be important if your course is a long one, such as medicine or architecture.

If you are considering a gap year, it makes sense to apply for a deferred place, rather than waiting for your results before applying. The application form has a section for deferments. That allows you to sort out your immediate future before you start travelling or working and leaves you the option of changing your mind if circumstances change.

## Useful websites

The essential website for making an application is, of course, that of UCAS:
**ucas.com/undergraduate/applying-to-university**

For applications to music conservatoires: **ucas.com/conservatoires**

For advice on your personal statement:
**ucas.com/undergraduate/applying-university/writing-your-personal-statement/ new-personal-statement-2026-entry**

## Gap years

For links to volunteering opportunities in the UK: **doit.life**
For links to many gap year organisations: **yearoutgroup.org**

# **6** The Diversity Index

The fairness of admissions to university has long been high on the political agenda. The baton has been firmly picked up by the Rt Hon. Bridget Phillipson MP, Secretary of State for Education in the Labour government elected in 2024. Referencing her own experience, the Oxford graduate from Washington in Tyne and Wear said: "Despite growing up in a deeply disadvantaged area, I had the opportunity to go to university – but I was one of the lucky ones. Breaking the link between where a young person grows up and the opportunities they have is central to our mission." And when setting out the government's headline priorities for reform of higher education, the Secretary of State put access at the top of the list, noting that the government expects "higher education providers to play a stronger role in expanding access and improving outcomes, especially for disadvantaged students. Such institutions should make a stronger contribution to their communities and to economic growth."

The education secretary is not alone in benefitting from the upward trajectory presented by higher education. Traditionally universities have been viewed as engines of social justice through the opportunities they afford for social mobility – a role which has been in sharper focus since the cap on student numbers was abolished in 2015, allowing universities for the first time to recruit as many students as they felt capable of educating. No longer elitist institutions for the few, universities invest heavily in widening participation among communities with low participation in higher education. Such measures go some way to levelling the unequal opportunities experienced by people early in life which make them less likely to benefit from a university education. The disadvantages they experienced may have impacted their level of knowledge or limited the skills they have accrued and their outlook on what is achievable. But headway is being made on widening access to higher education – as evidenced by admissions figures to UK universities across recent years.

Across all UK universities, UCAS data shows the second highest number of home 18-year-olds from the most disadvantaged backgrounds securing a place at university or college in 2023. A total of 31,590 UK 18-year-olds from POLAR4 Quintile 1 were accepted – down 2.5% from the record of 32,415 in 2022 but a significant increase on 26,535 in 2019 (up 19%). In Scotland, a record number of Scottish 17 and 18-year-olds from the 20% most disadvantaged postcodes secured a place at university or college in 2024, up 9% on 2023 and 46% higher than in 2019 – highlighting sustained effort to widen access to university in Scotland.

A glance at the number of offers made by Oxbridge in 2023 provides a headline snapshot of progress at these sought-after academic big hitters of ancient lineage: with 69 offers each Westminster School (an independent school) and state-maintained Hills Road Sixth Form College lead a top ten equally split between state and independent schools. This shows how far these universities have evolved their admissions in recent years: as recently as 2018, a report by the Sutton Trust found that just eight top independent schools had as many Oxbridge acceptances as three-quarters of all schools.

Meanwhile, UCAS has made a number of changes to encourage more students from low-income families to apply to university, waiving the £28.50 application fee for students in receipt of free school meals, replacing the personal statement with a series of questions, and providing historic entry grades data and offer rates for each course on its web pages – meaning school leavers can potentially make more ambitious choices. As one 17-year-old university applicant from Lincolnshire in receipt of free school meals said in a Times article in 2024: "Waiving the UCAS application fee will mean it's less of a burden when finances can be stretched. As one of five children in my family, I work a part-time job as I don't like asking my mum for money." Vivienne Stern, chief executive of Universities UK, which represents vice-chancellors, said: "The university sector has made great strides towards expanding opportunity but there is much further to go and it is clear that affordability is a real barrier."

Contextual offers, which undercut published requirements for students who meet widening participation criteria, are now offered by most universities. Evidently, universities' efforts to implement access and participation plans which improve equality of opportunity for students from disadvantaged backgrounds are producing change in the sector. Social and cultural diversity in higher education nurtures innovation and creativity and creates more choice for students and for graduate employers. Their diversity is one of the biggest attractions of UK universities for students from abroad. Universities transform lives and shift the dial on social mobility, as the Sutton Trust educational charity sums up: "Young people from less well-off backgrounds who attend university are more likely to become socially mobile into higher income brackets, and income gaps are lower between graduates from disadvantaged backgrounds and their peers compared to non-graduates."

The distance travelled on increasing diversity among student populations on campuses thus far is commendable, but as the dip among 2023's Quintile 1 entrants shows, it is not a straightforward upward curve. Additionally, the entry rate gap between the most disadvantaged students (Quintile 1) and the least disadvantaged (Quintile 5) students has slightly widened to 2.16 in 2023, compared to 2.09 in 2022.

There also remains work do be done on ensuring students recruited from disadvantaged and minority backgrounds thrive in their studies and succeed after graduation. Dropout rates are higher among disadvantaged students than for those from more privileged backgrounds. Figures published by the Student Loans Company showed a 28% rise over five years in students who signed up for a loan before dropping out of a course. The number went from 32,491 in 2018–19 to 41,630 in 2022–23 – a rise of 9,139. Such an attrition rate is costly not just in terms of money but also in wasted time and shattered ambitions. It is likely to affect a disproportionate number of students drawn from disadvantaged backgrounds – those also hit hardest by the impacts of the pandemic and the cost of living crisis.

Increased demand and competition for places coming down the track provides another lens through which inclusion and diversity is framed. With university applications projected to reach one million by 2030, it is feared that progress on widening participation may stall, as contracting offer rates effect disadvantaged students hardest. Research by UCAS, published in June 2023, put a positive spin on the boom in student numbers by showing the application gap between the most and least advantaged applying to university or college is forecast to narrow slightly. UCAS, though, has suggested that if universities adapt their offer-making – by including targeted offer-making strategies, minimum entry requirements for underrepresented cohorts and outreach work – the potential for those at the lower end of the attainment spectrum being squeezed out may be mitigated.

Time will tell. Whatever the fluctuations, the relevance for would-be students to access detailed information on how diverse and inclusive the institutions they are considering applying to remains constant.

### The table

Seven editions on from its introduction, therefore, our social inclusion ranking is more pertinent than ever. As well as providing a benchmark by which to measure change going forward, it also shines a light on admissions from some of the underrepresented groups on campuses and their subsequent prospects and performance. Today's applicants want to know about the composition of the student body they will be joining, and the tables on pages 100–103 help them in that quest.

We have two social inclusion rankings; one for England and Wales, with Scottish institutions ranked separately on account of a different measure of social deprivation – the Scottish Index of Multiple Deprivation (SIMD) – which better captures the position in the 15 Scottish universities than the POLAR4 (Participation of Local Areas) measure used for England and Wales. SIMD and POLAR4 are not directly comparable: one measures deprivation across several criteria, the other participation in higher education only. The two universities in Northern Ireland, Queen's Belfast and Ulster, are excluded from the ranking owing to differences in the country's school system which has a high proportion of selective grammar schools, making comparisons with the rest of the UK on social mix invalid via the methodology adopted in this *Guide*.

### THE DIVERSITY INDEX

We have once again resisted the suggestion to include some or all the measures contained within the social inclusion tables as part of our wider academic ranking. There is good reason for this: a university with a poor record for social inclusion may still have an excellent record for teaching and research. It might be a very good university with an outstanding global and national reputation, but with a socially narrow recruitment profile. By using the two multi-indicator, multi-institution tables that we publish together (alongside the relevant subject table) prospective students can identify the universities which are the best fit for them academically and where they might feel most at home socially.

The full list of equally-weighted indicators used in *The Times* and *The Sunday Times* social inclusion ranking for England and Wales is:

» recruitment from non-selective state schools
» recruitment from all ethnic minorities
» a measurement of the black awarding gap
» recruitment of white, working-class males
» recruitment from deprived areas (using POLAR4)
» a measurement of the deprived areas dropout gap
» recruitment of first-generation students
» recruitment of disabled students
» recruitment of mature students (those 21 or older on admission)

For Scottish institutions, there is no measure of the deprived areas dropout gap and the deprived areas measure is based on SIMD, rather than POLAR4, as outlined above.

With the exception of the admissions data for non-selective state schools, all the other indicators are in the public domain. The uniqueness of this social inclusion ranking is in combining these several strands of data together to build an overall picture of the social mix at each institution, and to measure university performance in two key areas: the gap between the proportion of white students awarded top grades in their degrees than black, Asian and ethnic minority students (known as the black awarding gap), and whether more students from the most deprived areas fail to complete their courses than those recruited from more advantaged districts.

The table is presented in a format that displays the raw data in all instances. No adjustment is made for university location, so a university with a strong, local recruitment pattern in an area of low ethnic minority population is unlikely do well on the measure covering the ethnicity of the intake. This was most notably the case with Wrexham University, which is for the seventh successive year the most socially inclusive university in the UK according to our ranking but had just 5.8% of its 2021–22 intake drawn from ethnic minorities.

However, by combining the indicators using a common statistical technique known as z-scoring, we have ensured no single indicator has a disproportionate effect on the overall total for each university. The totals for each university were transformed to a scale with 1,000 for the top score and the performance of all universities measured relative to that of the university ranked No 1.

Just as with our academic ranking, the organisations providing the raw data for the table are not involved in the process of aggregation, and are not responsible for any conclusion or inferences we have made. Every care has been taken to ensure the accuracy of the table and accompanying analysis, but no responsibility can be taken for errors or omissions.

The indicators used and what can be learned from them are outlined in turn below.

**Non-selective state school admissions**
For many years, the Higher Education Statistics Agency (HESA) has published as part of its annual performance indicators, the proportion of students admitted to universities from all state schools.

Among the entrants included in this proportion are those attending the 163 state grammars in England and the voluntary grammars in Northern Ireland. However, state school admissions to all universities stripped of the academically-selective grammar school sector are not published elsewhere. Removing the grammar school sector from the equation reveals the proportion of students admitted to each university in 2021–22 (the latest available data) from the largely non-selective state secondary schools (comprehensives and most academies) attended by around 80% of university applicants.

This is the indicator that has seen greatest change over the seven editions of the social inclusion ranking. There are now just three universities where fewer than half the students admitted came from comprehensives and academies: Imperial College London (43.5%, down 2 percentage points on the year before's data), Durham (48.4%, down 0.7 of a percentage point) and Cambridge (49.5%, up one percentage point). At the other end of the non-selective state school admissions ranking, Bedfordshire admitted 99.7% of its students from this educational background, closely followed by West of Scotland (99.4%), Middlesex (98.7%), Teesside (98.6%) and Wrexham (98.4%).

Over the seven editions of this ranking, the number of universities where less than half the students are recruited from non-selective state schools has halved, and Oxford has left that cohort completely for the third time this year, with 53.5% of students drawn from comprehensives and academies in 2021–22. This figure is up 1.3 percentage points since the year before, 11 percentage points over two years, and 14.1 percentage points from our first ranking in 2018 – a sharply accelerating rate of change. Cambridge, which admitted 40.1% of its students from non-selective state schools in our 2018 table, has increased the proportion by a still significant 9.4 percentage points over the intervening period, but now lags behind its principal domestic rival. The rate of change in the school backgrounds of entrants to Oxbridge is vastly outstripping most of its highly-selective rivals – and arguably directly impacting upon them, as the academically capable applicants turned down by Oxbridge find places elsewhere. The much vaunted "brain drain" to American universities – though significant among a clutch of private schools – represents barely a statistical trickle, with most students naturally put off by the much higher costs of studying across the Atlantic.

When Dorothy Byrne, president of Murray Edwards College, Cambridge, said in 2021 that the proportion of state-educated students admitted to Cambridge should match their distribution in UK schools (where the state/independent split is 93%/7%, aged 11–16), it was catnip to those who felt privately educated applicants were suddenly getting a rum deal at our two oldest universities. Despite the recent successes at increasing the numbers of students admitted from the maintained sector at Oxbridge, the reality remains nowhere near proportional parity between state and independent school admissions. Since beating the targets from its previous five-year access plan Cambridge has dropped its state school undergraduate admission targets, but says it will still take applicants' schools into account. Parents of privately educated Oxbridge hopefuls wishing to "game the system" have for a number of years been moving them to top state sixth form colleges and grammar schools for their A-levels.

Our latest data appears to back up the wider trend towards admitting more students from the non-selective state sector at our most selective universities. Just 16 universities (one fewer than in the previous year's figures and six fewer than the year before) now take less than 70% of their students from non-selective state schools; 12 of the 16 are members of the highly selective research-led Russell Group. The vast majority of universities (86 in all) admit more than 80% of their students from this demographic.

### Ethnic minority admissions

Data gathered from the 2021–22 admissions cycle shows the proportion of entrants to each university drawn from black, Asian, mixed and other ethnic minorities.

Eight London universities feature in the top 10, all with at least 65.1% of their students drawn from ethnic minorities but Aston is the most ethnically diverse university in England and Wales, recruiting 83.8% of its students from ethnic minorities. Following it are City, University of London (79.7%), Brunel London (77.4%) and SOAS (77.3%). Queen Mary, London is by some distance the most ethnically diverse of the Russell Group student communities and continues to lead the way in the social inclusion ranking overall among the 24-member group.

The least ethnically diverse university is Harper Adams, based in Newport, Shropshire, where 3.2% of the intake was drawn from ethnic minorities, followed by Royal Agricultural (3.6%), Highlands and Islands (5%), Plymouth Marjon (5.4%) and Wrexham (5.8%). Two of the bottom four on this measure are institutions offering largely land-based courses, traditionally attracting low ethnic minority participation. All four universities are in areas of the country with relatively small ethnic minority populations.

### Black awarding gap

One of the two university output measures in the social inclusion ranking, the data here is among the most arresting in the survey. We were unable to create a reliable measure of the black awarding gap in 15 universities – Aberystwyth, Arts Bournemouth, Bangor, Bath Spa, Bishop Grosseteste, Chichester, Harper Adams, Hartpury, Leeds Arts, Leeds Trinity, Norwich Arts, Plymouth Marjon, Royal Agricultural, Wrexham and York St John – because there were simply too few black graduates for effective analysis in 2021–22.

Where we could compare the proportions of white and black students gaining first-class or 2.1 degrees, the negative gap in achievement between the groups was at least 20 percentage points in 44 institutions. While this is one less than in the previous year's data, and a significant improvement over the year before when 60 universities saw a greater than 20 percentage point discrepancy, we need more data before we can be confident of a trend rather than a quirk arising from the relatively small numbers of students involved in the measure of black awarding in all institutions.

The gap was commendably narrow (less than 10 percentage points) in 16 institutions, one less than in the previous year's figures. In just one of them – Queen Mary, University of London – black students were awarded a higher proportion of top grades than their white counterparts.

The universities with the widest negative percentage point gap for black awarding (showing low proportions of firsts and 2.1s awarded to students from black backgrounds) were Stirling (-47.4%), Worcester (-45.8%), Falmouth (-40.2%), Buckingham (-38.5%), Gloucestershire (-37.2%), and Canterbury Christ Church (-37%).

Universities where black students were awarded the most favourable proportions of top-class grades in relation to their white counterparts were Queen Mary, London (+1.9%), Teesside (-1.3%), Suffolk (-2.2%), Buckinghamshire New (-3.0%) and Cambridge (-4.0%). Two of the top five places here are taken by Russell Group institutions, so often lagging in other areas of the social inclusion ranking, offering evidence that while the numbers ticking a social inclusion box in our highly selective universities might be lower, once admitted their levels of achievement are hard to tell apart from those drawn from more traditional university-going backgrounds.

### White working-class males

There have been countless reports in recent years about the educational underachievement of this group of children. It begins in primary school, accelerates in secondary school, and reaches its logical conclusion with significant underrepresentation at university. As with other measures in our social inclusion ranking, it is not fair to expect universities to correct the systemic failings of the wider education system.

Nevertheless, some universities offer significantly more opportunities to this often excluded social group. Those doing most are Plymouth Marjon (13% of entrants in 20222), Sheffield Hallam (11.8%), Liverpool Hope (11.4%), Abertay (11.3%), Highlands and Islands (10.9%), Staffordshire (10.6%) and Liverpool John Moores (10.3%). These are the only universities where white working-class boys make up over one in 10 or more of the student population.

At the opposite end of the spectrum, at these seven institutions white male students with a working-class background make up between 1 in 100 and 1 in 59 of students on campus: Suffolk (1%), Buckingham (1.1%), University College London and City, London (both 1.5%), London School of Economics (1.6%), King's College London and St George's London (both 1.7%). White working-class students are a rare sighting here and at the 51 universities where they make up fewer than one in 25 of the student population. This group's access to higher education continues to be one of the more pressing areas in need of action.

## Low participation areas (England and Wales only) and deprived areas (Scotland only)

This data is drawn from 2021–22 and looks at the home postcode of all university recruits, putting them into one of five pots, according to the level of participation in higher education.

For England and Wales, this indicator records the proportion of students recruited from Quintile 1 (of POLAR4 data) – the 20% of areas that have the lowest participation rates in higher education. In Scotland, this indicator records the proportion of students recruited from postcodes which fall into the bottom 20% of postcodes with the highest levels of deprivation measured against the Scottish Index of Multiple Deprivation (SIMD20).

Like all indicators, this one has limitations, chief among which is that London overall has high participation rates in higher education relative to the rest of the UK, so very few London-based university entrants fall into Quintile 1 (Q1), meaning that London universities score relatively poorly across the board on this measure, even if they have a socially diverse intake of students. (The strength of performance of many London institutions in other indicators – for example, high recruitment from ethnic minorities and a narrow black awarding gap – confirms this to be the case.)

Sunderland (30.3%) and Teesside (29.4%) record the highest proportions of students recruited from Q1. Both institutions recruit heavily within their immediate surrounds, the northeast being the English region with the lowest participation rate in higher education. Hull (28.8%) is ranked third on this measure. Bishop Grosseteste (26.5%) and Staffordshire (25.6%) are also in the top five for Q1 recruitment.

At the other end of the scale, London universities account for all of the five institutions with the lowest recruitment from Q1, headed by City, University of London (2.2%) and followed by Brunel, London (3%), Queen Mary, London (3.7%), SOAS (3.8%) and Westminster (4.3%). Oxford, in particular, shows a sharp improvement on this measure with the proportion of Q1 students rising from 4.2% in the data two years before to 7.3% in the current figures, an increase of 3.1% albeit from a low base.

In Scotland, the highest rates of recruitment of students falling into SIMD20 are to be found at West of Scotland (30.7%) and Glasgow Caledonian (22.1%), while the two Aberdeen universities, Robert Gordon (6.2%) and Aberdeen (7.9%), have the lowest rates.

## Low participation areas dropout gap

This data is drawn from 2022–23 (English universities only) and used in the England and Wales social inclusion ranking only. There is a strong correlation between performing well on this measure and a high ranking for social inclusion overall. Drawing upon the same POLAR4 data as above, it measures student outcomes from each of the five social quintiles. The proportion of students dropping out who were recruited from Q1 (the one-fifth of postcodes where university participation is the lowest) is compared to the proportion dropping out who were recruited from Quintiles 2, 3, 4 and 5 (Q2–5). A negative score in this section of the ranking indicates a higher proportion of students is dropping out from Q1 than those recruited from areas where more children go to university.

Already underrepresented in the student population overall, this measure identifies those universities where Q1 students who do get in are more likely to fail to see their courses through. The universities with the biggest negative percentage point gap for deprived area dropouts – where a bigger proportion of students from the most deprived areas fail to complete their courses than among the rest of the student population – are SOAS (-20.6%), Bedfordshire (-12.7%), Harper Adams (-12%), London Metropolitan (-11.1%), and Bolton (-8.7%). This is especially concerning for Bolton, which admits the 13th-highest proportion of students from Q1.

The universities performing most strongly in this aspect of widening participation, where a smaller proportion of students from Q1 drop out compared to the rest of the student population as a whole, are Creative Arts (+11.4%), Hertfordshire (+5.1%), Westminster (4.8%), York St John (+3.1%), Cumbria and Royal Holloway, London (both +3%) – four out of six of them are in the top 30 of social inclusion ranking overall.

### First generation students
This measure records the proportion of students recruited from homes where neither parent attended university. This indicator is considered one of the most informative in assessing the overall inclusiveness of university recruitment strategies. Once again, performance varies considerably from those where 60% or more of their students identify as first generation – Wolverhampton (70.7%), Birmingham Newman (69.3%), Bradford (67.3%), Sunderland (61.7%), Staffordshire (61.6%) and Bolton (60.1%) – to those where fewer than a quarter of students come from homes where parents did not go to university – Cambridge (17.2%), Oxford (17.3%), St Andrews (18.7%), Edinburgh (19%), Durham (23%), Bath (23.2%) and Bristol (24.8%).

Among the universities admitting fewest first-generation students this year, only Edinburgh, Durham and Bath were admitting fewer than recorded in the previous year's social inclusion data. So, here again slow progress is being made. Of course, as more and more students attend university and, in turn, become parents themselves, the proportions of first- generation students will eventually go down across the board.

### Disabled students
This indicator measures the proportion of all students in higher education in receipt of Disability Support Allowance (DSA). It is part of the bigger HESA dataset on widening participation, published in 2023 and is based on data from the 2021–22 academic year.

As with the other indicators, there is a significant difference between the universities at the top – Wrexham where HESA records 19.1% of students as being in receipt of DSA, Arts London (18.3%) and Harper Adams (18%) – and those at the bottom – Southampton (2.3%), Leeds Trinity (2.8%) and Buckinghamshire New (2.9%).

### Mature students
Mature students are returners to education and often win places with "life" qualifications, rather than A-levels. This immediately makes the group more diverse than the young entrants, who come mostly straight from school or via a gap year.

The age of the student population can have a major impact on the social scene on campus. Older students, particularly those with partners (and quite possibly children) are less likely to be found clubbing or propping up the bar late into the evening. Universities with a very small proportion of mature undergraduates – the LSE (1.4%), Bath (2.3%), Loughborough (2.4%), Oxford (2.5%) and Durham (2.5%) – are likely to have a livelier campus social life than Suffolk (91.7% mature admissions), Canterbury Christ Church (85.3%), Buckinghamshire New (85%), Leeds Trinity (84.4%) and Wales Trinity St David (79.8%).

### The overall picture
Social inclusion in British universities is evolving and considered a priority in all institutions. However, because of the different starting points for each university, the picture on the ground varies considerably from place to place. Oxford and Cambridge are moving at pace on a number of our measures, but they are not shifting dramatically in our main ranking. This is because our table reflects relative performance and the whole university sector is making

strides in improving social diversity on campus. This is a good thing, and the widening use of contextual offers gives this process a chance of continuing despite the challenges presented by the pandemic which have impacted the academic achievement of the disadvantaged disproportionately.

So, what do this year's social inclusion rankings tell you? It is not possible to appear near the top of them if an institution is only achieving well on one or two of the measures of social inclusion that *The Times* and *The Sunday Times* have chosen. Success in the tables comes from broadly-based achievement in recruiting from areas of society least represented in higher education, and then seeing those students progress with their degrees and achieve well.

Appearing near the foot of the tables does not mean social diversity is a non-consideration, simply that the numbers recruited from underrepresented groups are vastly lower compared to institutions ranked higher.

A different set of metrics looking at the same subject matter might produce a very different looking table, which is why it is necessary to understand what is being measured here. Based on the measures we have chosen the top three in the academic rankings – London School of Economics, St Andrews, and Oxford – appear respectively 100th in England and Wales, bottom in Scotland, and bottom in England and Wales of our social inclusion rankings. Wrexham places 115th in our academic ranking of 131 institutions but it is top in England and Wales for social inclusion. Sixteen of the bottom 20 universities for social inclusion in England and Wales (and the bottom three in Scotland) are highly selective Russell Group universities.

Used in conjunction, our academic and social inclusion rankings provide an intriguing insight to likely academic and professional success, the quality of the student experience, and the social, ethnic and educational mix of students likely to be found in the university lecture theatres and the after-hours clubs and bars. But whatever the student recruitment profile of the university you are considering, don't decide where to apply on that basis alone. If applicants from non-traditional backgrounds don't apply to universities ranked lower for social inclusion, then it only makes it easier for the status quo to prevail.

## Social Inclusion Ranking for England and Wales

| Ranking | Last year's rank | Institution | State schools (non-selective) (%) | Ethnic minorities (%) | Black awarding gap (%) | White working-class males (%) | Low participation areas (%) | Low participation areas dropout (%) | First generation students (%) | Disabled (%) | Mature (%) | Total |
|---|---|---|---|---|---|---|---|---|---|---|---|---|
| 1 | 1 | Wrexham | 98.4 | 5.8 | n/a | 5.6 | 20.0 | n/a | 58.3 | 19.1 | 68.3 | 1000 |
| 2 | 3 | Teesside | 98.6 | 11.8 | -1.3 | 9.2 | 29.4 | -0.6 | 57.3 | 8.9 | 52.4 | 970 |
| 3 | 4 | Plymouth Marjon | 95.3 | 5.4 | n/a | 13.0 | 19.0 | -2.1 | 54.8 | 16.6 | 34.6 | 945 |
| 4 | 11 | Staffordshire | 97.0 | 21.0 | -23.9 | 10.6 | 25.6 | 2.2 | 61.6 | 7.5 | 46.1 | 902 |
| 5 | 2 | Birmingham Newman | 98.3 | 49.1 | -15.8 | 3.3 | 18.5 | -2.1 | 69.3 | 14.1 | 43.9 | 898 |
| 6 | 9 | Wolverhampton | 96.9 | 53.1 | -24.6 | 4.1 | 23.0 | 2.1 | 70.7 | 8.0 | 48.9 | 884 |
| 7 | 5 | Suffolk | 97.8 | 33.9 | -2.2 | 1.0 | 25.0 | 1.6 | 57.8 | 3.8 | 91.7 | 881 |
| 8 | 7 | Sunderland | 95.4 | 30.6 | -15.1 | 7.4 | 30.3 | -3.6 | 61.7 | 4.4 | 65.9 | 868 |
| 9 | 14 | Bishop Grosseteste | 93.0 | 6.7 | n/a | 6.9 | 26.5 | -3.1 | 57.3 | 14.7 | 37.1 | 864 |
| 10 | 12 | Hull | 93.7 | 15.7 | -10.6 | 8.1 | 28.8 | 0.1 | 55.1 | 7.5 | 33.5 | 853 |
| 11 | 24 | Cumbria | 95.7 | 13.2 | -8.9 | 3.9 | 18.4 | 3.0 | 55.6 | 7.6 | 67.2 | 825 |
| 12 | 28 | Creative Arts | 94.3 | 25.9 | -12.7 | 3.4 | 14.1 | 11.4 | 44.0 | 7.2 | 56.6 | 816 |
| 13 | 21 | Sheffield Hallam | 95.9 | 23.4 | -21.8 | 11.8 | 24.0 | -2.7 | 52.2 | 9.0 | 21.6 | 815 |

| | | | | | | | | | | | | |
|---|---|---|---|---|---|---|---|---|---|---|---|---|
| 14 | 26 | Leeds Trinity | 96.7 | 51.0 | n/a | 2.1 | 21.2 | -1.6 | 57.9 | 2.8 | 84.4 | 795 |
| 15 | 8 | Bradford | 94.7 | 74.1 | -5.6 | 2.0 | 10.4 | -7.6 | 67.3 | 10.6 | 27.0 | 774 |
| 16 | 48 | York St John | 94.9 | 8.2 | n/a | 8.2 | 19.0 | 3.1 | 45.7 | 9.6 | 22.0 | 770 |
| 17 | 13 | Chester | 95.2 | 9.9 | -17.8 | 8.3 | 20.3 | -1.4 | 54.4 | 8.2 | 34.8 | 764 |
| =18 | =21 | Derby | 97.1 | 27.4 | -29.6 | 6.2 | 25.4 | -2.1 | 53.1 | 9.4 | 36.9 | 758 |
| =18 | 18 | Wales Trinity St David | 97.7 | 23.9 | -9.8 | 3.1 | 13.2 | n/a | 48.8 | 6.7 | 79.8 | 758 |
| 20 | 23 | Greenwich | 95.3 | 58.4 | -16.6 | 5.2 | 7.5 | 1.9 | 57.1 | 6.5 | 31.3 | 749 |
| 21 | =15 | Buckinghamshire New | 94.6 | 41.3 | -3.0 | 5.6 | 10.3 | -4.6 | 48.4 | 2.9 | 85.0 | 747 |
| =22 | =50 | Anglia Ruskin | 94.1 | 39.0 | -25.0 | 5.1 | 18.2 | 1.0 | 50.7 | 5.4 | 61.4 | 744 |
| =22 | 31 | Huddersfield | 97.0 | 46.6 | -18.9 | 5.0 | 14.7 | -0.5 | 57.1 | 7.8 | 25.1 | 744 |
| 24 | =43 | Canterbury Christ Church | 89.1 | 31.7 | -37.0 | 6.1 | 18.8 | 1.6 | 53.0 | 4.7 | 85.3 | 734 |
| 25 | 32 | De Montfort | 97.1 | 52.4 | -24.2 | 4.0 | 16.1 | -1.5 | 52.0 | 10.7 | 23.7 | 733 |
| 26 | 17 | Central Lancashire | 96.6 | 32.2 | -24.5 | 6.2 | 13.4 | -0.8 | 52.4 | 8.9 | 38.8 | 722 |
| 27 | 36 | Hertfordshire | 96.9 | 56.7 | -18.6 | 3.7 | 7.7 | 5.1 | 51.7 | 6.0 | 27.3 | 721 |
| 28 | 20 | Bath Spa | 92.0 | 31.4 | n/a | 6.2 | 13.8 | -5.0 | 43.5 | 8.5 | 71.7 | 720 |
| =29 | =33 | Essex | 92.7 | 41.9 | -12.0 | 5.2 | 16.5 | -0.6 | 47.3 | 6.2 | 25.5 | 712 |
| =29 | 37 | Lincoln | 93.2 | 12.0 | -20.5 | 8.5 | 18.1 | -2.5 | 49.8 | 10.9 | 14.7 | 712 |
| 31 | 30 | South Wales | 96.0 | 11.8 | -27.1 | 6.8 | 23.7 | n/a | 41.9 | 9.0 | 40.8 | 711 |
| 32 | 6 | West London | 97.0 | 41.5 | -11.4 | 2.0 | 8.4 | -2.8 | 53.6 | 5.9 | 75.1 | 710 |
| 33 | 29 | Middlesex | 98.7 | 61.4 | -19.1 | 2.4 | 4.8 | 1.9 | 56.9 | 5.7 | 43.9 | 707 |
| 34 | =15 | London South Bank | 97.1 | 68.5 | -24.3 | 2.9 | 6.2 | -1.5 | 51.8 | 9.7 | 39.8 | 700 |
| =35 | 35 | Bangor | 93.6 | 8.6 | n/a | 7.8 | 14.3 | n/a | 43.6 | 10.1 | 30.6 | 699 |
| =35 | 50 | Roehampton | 97.2 | 68.8 | -25.6 | 2.6 | 4.7 | 2.4 | 52.5 | 8.3 | 35.5 | 699 |
| 37 | 52 | Coventry | 94.3 | 55.2 | -18.1 | 4.2 | 15.7 | 1.3 | 46.5 | 4.7 | 27.7 | 698 |
| =38 | 10 | Bolton | 98.2 | 40.3 | -32.7 | 3.3 | 21.1 | -8.7 | 60.1 | 8.4 | 64.3 | 696 |
| =38 | 25 | Liverpool Hope | 91.6 | 13.0 | -27.1 | 11.4 | 20.2 | -5.4 | 48.6 | 9.6 | 18.0 | 696 |
| 40 | 52 | Birmingham City | 96.5 | 62.8 | -32.4 | 3.2 | 17.1 | 1.4 | 56.0 | 6.4 | 21.2 | 695 |
| =41 | 64 | Solent | 96.2 | 20.7 | -31.2 | 8.2 | 19.5 | 1.3 | 48.2 | 5.2 | 34.6 | 693 |
| =41 | 72 | Norwich Arts | 94.8 | 13.2 | n/a | 7.5 | 16.9 | -2.2 | 42.3 | 11.8 | 12.7 | 693 |
| 43 | =33 | Edge Hill | 96.9 | 8.9 | -15.8 | 7.3 | 19.3 | -1.4 | 51.0 | 5.2 | 26.7 | 691 |
| 44 | =43 | Westminster | 96.1 | 69.9 | -21.3 | 3.2 | 4.3 | 4.8 | 56.5 | 5.1 | 17.2 | 689 |
| 45 | 65 | Salford | 96.8 | 36.4 | -25.3 | 5.7 | 16.9 | -1.6 | 47.9 | 7.5 | 30.9 | 687 |
| 46 | 40 | Aberystwyth | 90.9 | 8.5 | n/a | 9.5 | 14.1 | n/a | 37.3 | 12.2 | 12.3 | 684 |
| 47 | =59 | Winchester | 92.5 | 12.3 | -23.7 | 6.2 | 16.1 | -0.6 | 47.7 | 11.1 | 23.2 | 680 |
| 48 | 39 | Arts London | 86.9 | 32.3 | -15.7 | 3.9 | 8.7 | -1.9 | 37.3 | 18.3 | 14.3 | 679 |
| 49 | 47 | Liverpool John Moores | 90.6 | 13.0 | -21.6 | 10.3 | 17.2 | -3.3 | 50.6 | 6.7 | 17.5 | 672 |
| 50 | =55 | Northampton | 97.4 | 38.6 | -33.7 | 4.1 | 18.1 | 0.2 | 51.7 | 5.5 | 45.2 | 671 |
| 51 | 19 | East London | 96.5 | 63.1 | -17.1 | 2.6 | 11.4 | -5.6 | 51.7 | 6.5 | 38.3 | 661 |
| 52 | =59 | Portsmouth | 92.3 | 27.8 | -27.6 | 7.4 | 17.8 | -1.4 | 45.4 | 8.7 | 14.3 | 659 |
| 53 | =43 | Keele | 86.2 | 38.4 | -18.1 | 5.5 | 18.9 | -4.0 | 42.7 | 9.7 | 15.4 | 657 |
| 54 | =57 | St Mary's, Twickenham | 95.6 | 37.8 | -29.7 | 5.2 | 6.5 | 1.7 | 43.4 | 10.7 | 26.8 | 648 |
| 55 | 77 | Goldsmiths, London | 90.4 | 50.7 | -19.4 | 4.3 | 5.1 | 1.6 | 45.0 | 7.7 | 27.1 | 646 |
| 56 | =57 | Cardiff Metropolitan | 93.6 | 14.6 | -27.7 | 8.2 | 16.3 | n/a | 45.0 | 8.3 | 20.9 | 645 |
| 57 | =55 | Hartpury | 90.8 | 6.0 | n/a | 6.4 | 12.3 | -0.8 | 45.2 | 11.8 | 12.8 | 644 |
| 58 | 68 | Brunel London | 93.3 | 77.4 | -22.1 | 3.9 | 3.0 | 2.4 | 50.3 | 5.2 | 11.6 | 640 |
| 59 | =43 | Chichester | 92.9 | 9.4 | n/a | 6.3 | 17.1 | -4.3 | 43.9 | 10.1 | 21.4 | 638 |
| 60 | =66 | Leeds Arts | 95.1 | 13.9 | n/a | 4.6 | 15.4 | -0.8 | 40.7 | 11.5 | 8.9 | 635 |
| 61 | 41 | Gloucestershire | 94.8 | 12.2 | -37.2 | 8.6 | 15.3 | -2.5 | 47.1 | 8.9 | 33.6 | 633 |

# Social Inclusion Ranking for England and Wales cont.

| Ranking | Last year's rank | Institution | State schools (non-selective) (%) | Ethnic minorities (%) | Black awarding gap (%) | White working-class males (%) | Low participation areas (%) | Low participation areas dropout (%) | First generation students (%) | Disabled (%) | Mature (%) | Total |
|---|---|---|---|---|---|---|---|---|---|---|---|---|
| =62 | 54 | Brighton | 91.2 | 21.2 | -24.0 | 6.8 | 13.9 | -3.5 | 44.3 | 9.8 | 22.5 | 630 |
| =62 | =62 | Northumbria | 89.1 | 10.7 | -18.9 | 7.8 | 18.0 | -4.8 | 49.8 | 7.0 | 18.3 | 630 |
| 64 | 82 | Manchester Metropolitan | 94.5 | 35.6 | -20.4 | 5.2 | 14.3 | -0.8 | 49.3 | 4.8 | 11.0 | 621 |
| 65 | =69 | Leicester | 82.0 | 64.4 | -6.5 | 3.0 | 11.4 | -1.7 | 39.1 | 6.8 | 8.0 | 620 |
| =66 | 49 | Aston | 87.6 | 83.8 | -12.1 | 1.9 | 11.6 | -2.9 | 53.4 | 3.0 | 5.0 | 617 |
| =66 | 61 | Leeds Beckett | 92.8 | 22.2 | -25.0 | 7.5 | 17.3 | -4.3 | 44.8 | 7.8 | 13.7 | 617 |
| 68 | =62 | Kingston | 95.2 | 65.1 | -26.3 | 3.1 | 6.6 | -3.4 | 51.4 | 8.2 | 20.4 | 614 |
| 69 | 73 | West of England | 93.0 | 18.9 | -34.5 | 6.7 | 16.1 | 0.8 | 41.3 | 8.0 | 24.2 | 613 |
| 70 | =69 | Bournemouth | 93.3 | 17.3 | -31.3 | 7.6 | 13.0 | -1.5 | 46.5 | 8.7 | 16.5 | 609 |
| 71 | 76 | Worcester | 95.8 | 12.6 | -45.8 | 6.2 | 13.8 | -4.2 | 50.6 | 12.6 | 40.3 | 607 |
| 72 | 74 | Plymouth | 87.5 | 14.2 | -33.3 | 7.5 | 14.5 | -2.4 | 44.6 | 9.6 | 27.6 | 600 |
| =73 | =66 | City, London | 89.7 | 79.7 | -15.4 | 1.5 | 2.2 | -0.5 | 56.4 | 3.1 | 10.1 | 586 |
| =73 | 27 | London Metropolitan | 97.3 | 51.9 | -17.5 | 1.8 | 7.0 | -11.1 | 51.9 | 4.4 | 74.9 | 586 |
| 75 | 42 | Queen Mary, London | 82.3 | 75.5 | 1.9 | 2.3 | 3.7 | -5.2 | 46.5 | 5.0 | 6.4 | 584 |
| 76 | 80 | Kent | 83.3 | 46.9 | -19.3 | 5.1 | 10.7 | -1.8 | 45.0 | 6.2 | 10.0 | 583 |
| 77 | 78 | Swansea | 92.7 | 17.2 | -14.5 | 7.0 | 12.0 | n/a | 36.3 | 5.4 | 19.0 | 581 |
| 78 | 79 | St George's, London | 72.3 | 62.8 | -4.3 | 1.7 | 5.4 | n/a | 37.4 | 7.4 | 31.4 | 579 |
| 79 | =69 | East Anglia | 84.4 | 23.4 | -11.0 | 6.2 | 13.0 | -4.5 | 39.0 | 7.1 | 14.4 | 578 |
| 80 | 84 | Surrey | 83.0 | 37.7 | -18.1 | 3.7 | 7.2 | 2.3 | 40.0 | 7.0 | 15.2 | 569 |
| 81 | 38 | Bedfordshire | 99.7 | 48.3 | -26.0 | 2.0 | 9.7 | -12.7 | 58.0 | 4.2 | 72.1 | 568 |
| 82 | 83 | Royal Holloway, London | 80.3 | 49.4 | -21.5 | 3.1 | 5.7 | 3.0 | 41.4 | 8.0 | 4.4 | 558 |
| 83 | 88 | Arts Bournemourh | 93.2 | 12.2 | n/a | 4.0 | 11.4 | -2.2 | 37.6 | 9.7 | 9.2 | 536 |
| 84 | 85 | Nottingham Trent | 89.3 | 32.7 | -28.2 | 5.0 | 13.5 | -3.7 | 40.8 | 7.6 | 9.7 | 535 |
| 85 | 89 | Oxford Brookes | 70.9 | 21.8 | -17.3 | 3.9 | 8.5 | 1.8 | 34.9 | 8.8 | 18.3 | 526 |
| 86 | 91 | Lancaster | 78.8 | 26.8 | -8.3 | 4.7 | 9.0 | -1.6 | 32.8 | 7.1 | 4.1 | 523 |
| 87 | 87 | Sheffield | 77.7 | 23.3 | -21.2 | 4.9 | 10.6 | -1.9 | 31.9 | 10.8 | 8.7 | 521 |
| 88 | 86 | King's College London | 67.2 | 62.1 | -14.7 | 1.7 | 5.9 | -0.5 | 39.2 | 6.9 | 13.2 | 511 |
| 89 | 97 | Falmouth | 92.2 | 7.6 | -40.2 | 7.3 | 11.7 | -3.5 | 32.1 | 11.8 | 16.0 | 507 |
| 90 | 90 | Sussex | 83.7 | 27.1 | -19.7 | 4.1 | 10.0 | -0.9 | 36.8 | 5.7 | 8.6 | 498 |
| 91 | 92 | York | 75.9 | 13.1 | -16.4 | 5.3 | 10.3 | -0.8 | 31.1 | 7.8 | 6.1 | 487 |
| 92 | 94 | Warwick | 62.0 | 45.6 | -7.3 | 3.0 | 6.5 | -0.9 | 31.0 | 6.9 | 7.2 | 478 |
| 93 | 98 | Manchester | 71.3 | 32.8 | -16.3 | 3.0 | 8.5 | -2.0 | 32.1 | 8.3 | 5.4 | 461 |
| 94 | 81 | Harper Adams | 78.2 | 3.2 | n/a | 4.3 | 8.3 | -12.0 | 34.8 | 18.0 | 13.0 | 457 |
| 95 | 93 | Reading | 78.7 | 37.6 | -28.3 | 3.4 | 8.3 | -2.2 | 35.7 | 7.3 | 8.3 | 451 |
| 96 | 95 | Loughborough | 68.2 | 24.4 | -13.5 | 4.8 | 6.5 | -2.1 | 31.4 | 7.4 | 2.4 | 445 |
| 97 | 96 | Birmingham | 71.3 | 43.5 | -18.9 | 2.6 | 9.2 | -2.7 | 33.8 | 6.2 | 3.7 | 438 |
| 98 | 99 | Cardiff | 78.1 | 19.0 | -16.4 | 3.9 | 9.8 | n/a | 31.2 | 5.7 | 9.2 | 428 |
| 99 | 100 | Nottingham | 65.7 | 34.5 | -15.6 | 2.8 | 7.9 | -2.5 | 30.0 | 7.2 | 5.9 | 422 |
| 100 | 101 | London School of Economics | 53.4 | 63.6 | -5.7 | 1.6 | 7.1 | n/a | 32.2 | 5.4 | 1.4 | 419 |
| 101 | 104 | Bristol | 61.3 | 20.0 | -7.3 | 2.9 | 6.9 | -0.4 | 24.8 | 7.3 | 5.4 | 415 |
| 102 | =102 | Liverpool | 75.7 | 18.8 | -29.5 | 4.3 | 10.5 | -4.8 | 38.4 | 7.1 | 7.4 | 409 |

| Rank | Last year's rank | Institution | | | | | | | | | | |
|---|---|---|---|---|---|---|---|---|---|---|---|---|
| 103 | 75 | SOAS, London | 84.4 | 77.3 | -15.5 | 1.8 | 3.8 | -20.6 | 48.0 | 7.4 | 12.4 | 407 |
| 104 | =102 | Newcastle | 66.8 | 15.6 | -19.2 | 4.5 | 10.1 | -2.7 | 32.1 | 5.8 | 4.6 | 400 |
| 105 | 108 | Leeds | 71.1 | 22.5 | -24.0 | 3.6 | 10.0 | -4.2 | 33.6 | 6.7 | 5.8 | 395 |
| 106 | 110 | Southampton | 72.6 | 33.4 | -22.0 | 4.1 | 7.9 | -1.6 | 31.9 | 2.3 | 7.9 | 390 |
| 107 | 105 | University College London | 52.5 | 56.0 | -8.7 | 1.5 | 5.3 | -2.3 | 26.9 | 5.2 | 3.9 | 380 |
| 108 | 106 | Bath | 55.5 | 20.3 | -9.7 | 3.5 | 6.8 | -1.3 | 23.2 | 6.8 | 2.3 | 373 |
| 109 | 107 | Exeter | 57.6 | 13.0 | -12.2 | 3.2 | 6.3 | -3.8 | 25.9 | 8.7 | 5.3 | 361 |
| 110 | 112 | Royal Agricultural | 55.6 | 3.6 | n/a | 3.9 | 4.5 | n/a | 34.6 | 9.6 | 20.2 | 329 |
| 111 | 109 | Oxford | 53.5 | 24.6 | -14.9 | 2.1 | 7.3 | -4.3 | 17.3 | 10.3 | 2.5 | 328 |
| 112 | 111 | Imperial College London | 43.5 | 60.1 | -19.2 | 1.9 | 5.2 | -0.6 | 25.8 | 3.3 | 8.8 | 323 |
| 113 | 115 | Durham | 48.4 | 15.0 | -11.4 | 3.1 | 8.8 | -3.0 | 23.0 | 6.5 | 2.5 | 320 |
| 114 | 114 | Buckingham | 69.8 | 60.0 | -38.5 | 1.1 | 6.0 | n/a | 26.9 | 3.6 | 35.3 | 316 |
| 115 | 113 | Cambridge | 49.5 | 30.8 | -4.0 | 1.8 | 5.3 | n/a | 17.2 | 5.0 | 4.9 | 283 |

## Social Inclusion Ranking for Scotland

| Rank | Last year's rank | Institution | State schools (non-selective) (%) | Ethnic minorities (%) | Black awarding gap (%) | White working-class males (%) | Deprived areas (%) | First generation students (%) | Disabled (%) | Mature (%) | Total |
|---|---|---|---|---|---|---|---|---|---|---|---|
| 1 | 2 | West of Scotland | 99.4 | 11.9 | -11.2 | 7.2 | 30.7 | 48.8 | 1.6 | 57.4 | 1000 |
| 2 | 1 | Abertay | 95.8 | 8.4 | - | 11.3 | 18.7 | 47.1 | 3.5 | 35.6 | 865 |
| 3 | 7 | Highlands and Islands | 98.3 | 5.0 | - | 10.9 | 12.1 | 49.5 | 3.6 | 59.9 | 846 |
| 4 | 4 | Glasgow Caledonian | 96.5 | 12.8 | -28.2 | 7.7 | 22.1 | 43.0 | 2.2 | 38.4 | 788 |
| 5 | 3 | Queen Margaret, Edinburgh | 95.0 | 6.4 | - | 5.1 | 13.8 | 47.4 | 7.6 | 41.0 | 759 |
| 6 | 5 | Edinburgh Napier | 94.7 | 9.3 | -23.5 | 6.8 | 13.4 | 40.7 | 5.2 | 36.7 | 713 |
| 7 | 8 | Strathclyde | 90.5 | 13.4 | -15.4 | 6.7 | 17.7 | 37.6 | 2.7 | 15.2 | 685 |
| 8 | 10 | Heriot-Watt | 83.0 | 14.2 | -18.0 | 7.6 | 11.5 | 34.5 | 5.4 | 18.9 | 684 |
| 9 | 6 | Dundee | 87.1 | 11.4 | -28.2 | 5.7 | 16.0 | 38.0 | 6.1 | 26.9 | 667 |
| 10 | 12 | Robert Gordon | 95.0 | 9.9 | -27.8 | 7.0 | 6.2 | 35.5 | 5.5 | 39.8 | 637 |
| 11 | 9 | Stirling | 91.5 | 6.0 | -47.4 | 6.4 | 12.9 | 38.1 | 8.8 | 28.7 | 579 |
| 12 | 11 | Aberdeen | 85.7 | 13.8 | -28.6 | 6.7 | 7.9 | 29.9 | 6.4 | 14.2 | 575 |
| 13 | 13 | Glasgow | 80.7 | 12.3 | -9.8 | 4.5 | 16.7 | 25.8 | 2.6 | 11.4 | 527 |
| 14 | 15 | Edinburgh | 61.7 | 14.3 | -13.7 | 2.9 | 10.2 | 19.0 | 5.7 | 6.5 | 395 |
| 15 | 14 | St Andrews | 56.2 | 17.4 | - | 3.3 | 14.9 | 18.7 | 5.4 | 8.8 | 388 |

# 7 Finding Somewhere to Live

There's no place like home, especially when it's your first since flying the nest. Finding safe, affordable, and comfortable student digs is inextricably bound to benefitting from all that university offers, whether that's getting a good night's sleep before a long day's learning, or diving into halls parties with corridors of new best friends. To help create a soft landing into undergraduate life most UK universities promise to house all first-year students in halls or in private accommodation partnered with the institution. There are Ts and Cs, of course, notably around firming the university as first choice and meeting housing application deadlines (detailed with university profiles in Chapter 12).

For fledgling undergraduates, the availability of housing often influences decision making, not least because of the financial outlay it represents. Paying the rent – always the heftiest financial outlay for students, after tuition fees – is an increasingly big deal. With maintenance loans inching up at a lower rate than inflation, and not all students getting the full amount anyway, student rents not only swallow up virtually all of the average maintenance loan, they outstrip it entirely for some. Students – and their families – have always had to dig deep to cover accommodation costs, even before the latest pressures. Plugging the financial hole falls most commonly to parents, who on average stump up £214 per month for their student's accommodation, according to money advice website Save the Student's National Student Accommodation Survey 2024. This is a huge increase from the 2023 survey, which found students had been receiving £145 per month from parents. Student part-time work is on the rise too. A survey of 10,000 full-time UK undergraduates by the Higher Education Policy Institute (HEPI) found a record 56% had paid employment while they were studying, working an average of 14.5 hours each week. Before 2021, roughly two-thirds of students had no paid employment in term time.

"In the end, affordability must be an educational issue. Living away from home opens up more study options and provides a more immersive study environment, where commuting to a local university may not," commented Martin Blakey, former chief executive of student housing charity Unipol, in HEPI's *Student Accommodation: The State of the Nation in 2024* report.

Students are not only feeling the pinch in their pockets. In an evolving student housing landscape, the accommodation supply is being squeezed too. The traditional choice for

**Rental breakdown across the 10 major regional cities**

| City | Annual average rent 2023/24 | Average % increase since 2021/22 |
|---|---|---|
| Bournemouth | £7,396 | 11.2% |
| Bristol | £9,200 | 9.0% |
| Cardiff | £6,632 | 11.1% |
| Exeter | £8,559 | 16.1% |
| Glasgow | £7,548 | 20.4% |
| Leeds | £7,627 | 14.7% |
| Liverpool | £6,467 | 6.7% |
| Nottingham | £8,427 | 15.5% |
| Portsmouth | £7,183 | 9.4% |
| Sheffield | £6,451 | 10.2% |
| 10 cities | £7,475 | 14.6% |

**Source:** Accommodation Costs Survey by HEPI/Unipol

second and subsequent years of study, private rentals known as "off-street" housing are home to around 44% of students (down from around 50% five years ago). Though the situation varies locally, their supply in general has shortened in recent years as private landlords move out of the student sector for complex reasons including rising borrowing and running costs and increasing overheads.

Meanwhile students are increasingly opting for purpose-built student accommodation (PBSA) developments for their second and third year. Though typically more expensive than house shares they pose an attractive alternative – with ensuite rooms, coffee bars, communal study areas with bean bags, on-site gyms and cinema rooms to recommend them. The latest Knight Frank/UCAS Student Accommodation Survey predicts that by the end of the decade, PBSA will become the choice for the majority of second and third-year students, who will turn their backs on shared houses owned by private landlords. But having served the sector since the turn of the millennium, the pipeline of PBSA is under pressure too, as developers contend with higher interest rates and increased construction costs. Having added around 30,000 bed spaces a year across much of the previous decade, the number of new PBSA additional bed spaces that became available in summer 2024 was the lowest this century at only 8,692 new rooms. Another 2,500 were due to come online during the academic year, according to Unipol/ANUK (Accreditation Network of UK).

There were no student accommodation horror stories to emerge among 2024's intake of new students. Memories remain fresh of the years of "covid bulge" recruitment, though, when students at universities in cities including Bristol and Glasgow were among those billeted in halls located long distances from their university. Others queued overnight for off-street rentals or signed for houses they had not even viewed. Even without such instances in the most recent recruitment cycles, students are still increasingly starting the search for a second year home almost a year in advance, adding stress to their settling in period as freshers and forcing them to sign up to live with people they may only have known for a few weeks.

Applicants concerned about unfavourable supply-and-demand housing situations may take some comfort in the flat university admission numbers of 2022/23, and there will likely be fewer international students looking for accommodation in 2025/26 due to the changes in visa regulations. But it is worth bearing in mind that higher tariff universities still registered an uplift in undergraduate numbers in 2024 unmatched by lower or medium-tariff universities.

A constant in student accommodation are the teething problems associated with shared living. Being met by the spectre of someone else's dirty dishes in the communal kitchen sink is a rude awakening for most students. It is up there as the No 1 niggle for student house-sharers, results of the Student Accommodation Survey 2024 revealed, followed by shortcomings with cleaning in general and then leaving lights/appliances on and being excessively loud. Aside from toxic housemate behaviour there may be issues with property maintenance as well. Damp was the most common problem, Save the Student's survey found, followed by the hot water/heating going on the blink, and disruptive building work.

## New legislation

Housing Minister Matthew Pennycook has said the Renters' Rights Bill (formerly called 'renters reform'), could be enacted "within the first half or around summer next year [2025]". So, the changes proposed will affect students looking to rent houses for 2025/26. Under the bill, all tenants will now be able to give two months' notice to leave their tenancy at any stage: "This will end the injustice of tenants being trapped paying rent for substandard properties and offer more flexibility to both parties to respond to changing circumstances," the government explains. The Bill also stipulates that rent can only be charged one month in advance – which is the norm for much of the private rented sector, but many students are charged rent termly and this will stop. It will no longer be possible to sync rent payment dates with maintenance loan payments and this change may well result in the increasing use of guarantors and / or large deposits being levied to try and offset the increased risk of rental default.

Students renting off-street properties will benefit from the increased flexibility and regulation that this Act will bring, but commentators have noted that in the longer term it is likely to mean more landlords exiting the student market and renting to professional tenants instead, who stay longer and do not leave annually or all at once.

New students are advised to plan their accommodation as early as they can, and to know their rights. The NUS says: "A nationwide housing shortage is pushing students into ever more desperate situations, and rogue landlords might exploit inexperienced students who have never rented before by acting illegally. The NUS believes that every student has the right to affordable and secure housing." Advice and support on all things housing is listed at **www.nus.org.uk/student-renters-rights-hub**.

## Living away from home

Most who can afford it see moving away to study as an integral rite of passage. There is no other option for those whose chosen course is at a university further than commuting distance. Others look forward to broadening their experiences in a new, unexplored location. For the fortunate majority, the search for accommodation will be over quickly because the university can offer a place in one of its halls of residence or self-catering flats. But for others, there will be an anxious search for a room in a strange city. Most universities will help with this if they cannot offer accommodation of their own. Save the Student's National Student Accommodation Survey 2024 found that 39% of students were living in properties owned by private landlords, 24% were in university halls, 16% were in private halls, 15% lived with their parents and 3% owned their own property.

## Halls of residence

Encouragingly, the majority of students reported that they are satisfied with their accommodation in the Student Accommodation Survey 2024 by UCAS and Knight Frank, with those living in private PBSA or university-run halls the most satisfied. The chances are that for most parents their child's university digs will bear little resemblance to the standard of room they lived in when studying. Student accommodation has evolved enormously over the years. Private providers now dominate the market and represented 70% of the bed spaces surveyed in the 2021 Unipol/NUS report. As ambitious refurbishments modernise campuses up and down the country, en-suite and studio rooms are replacing cheaper, older stock in university-owned halls, too.

First-years are guaranteed a room in halls by most universities, but even before the current squeeze on availability spaces have usually been limited so it pays to meet application deadlines. Applying early might help you get first pick of the different types of room available, too. Any rooms left over are allocated to postgraduates, international students in any year of study and some returning, non-first-year students. Institutions that recruit significant numbers in Clearing have rooms available late in the admissions cycle, but this is not always the case by any means and those gaining their places by Clearing have often been the ones affected by the recent housing shortages. Some universities reserve a small proportion of accommodation for students with families.

While halls are generally the preferred option for freshers, they are also the priciest – not only in private developments but in many cases in university-owned accommodation, too, making affordability a sticking point – as discussed earlier. Some private blocks come with high-spec interiors and swanky extras. Most developments are in big complexes, but there are also niche providers such as Student Cribs, which converts properties to a more luxurious standard than usual digs. The firm now operates in 24 cities.

Unite Students is one of the country's biggest providers. It owns and manages rooms for 68,000 students in 151 purpose-built blocks across 23 university towns and cities nationwide. UPP has around 35,000 residential places in complexes built for 16 universities, usually on campus, and where rents are negotiated with the university, often in consultation with the students' union.

Price and location are likely to be more important to students than who owns the property, but when it comes to student accommodation: caveat emptor! Standards can be variable, prices may leave little to live on and private halls are not without negative reviews. Flat Justice, a not-for-profit tenants' rights group, supported legal actions by 346 dissatisfied students against Unite, following experiences living in halls in Liverpool, London, Coventry and Birmingham. Rats and mice and dust from long-term building work are among the complaints, along with broken radiators, bed bugs, lifts broken for weeks, and students arriving to find an uncleaned flat.

Cladding has been a particular concern in recent years. An incident in Bolton raised safety concerns as fire ripped through a relatively new hall of residence with cladding, though it appeared to have met building regulations and not to be the type used on Grenfell Tower. The removal of cladding is another issue, as it can mean scaffolding being up for prolonged periods.

### Purpose Built Student Accommodation (PBSA)
At the top end of the market, private firms usually lead the way, at least in the bigger student cities. Rooms in these complexes are nearly always en-suite and with internet access, and may include other facilities such as your own phone line and satellite TV. Shared kitchens are top-quality and fitted out with the latest equipment. This kind of accommodation naturally comes at a higher price but offers the advantages of flexibility both in living arrangements, inclusive bills and through a range of payment options.

| Term-time accommodation of full-time and sandwich students 2020–21 | | | | Top Tenancy Problems for Students | |
| --- | --- | --- | --- | --- | --- |
| Provider maintained property | 342,790 | 15% | 1 | Damp | 36% |
| Private-sector halls | 190,590 | 8% | 2 | Lack of water or heating | 29% |
| Parental/guardian home | 417,445 | 18% | 3 | Disruptive building work | 18% |
| Own residence | 387,535 | 16% | 4 | Rodents and pests | 18% |
| Other rented accommodation | 731,790 | 31% | 5 | Inappropriate/unannounced landlord visits | 13% |
| Other | 126,670 | 5% | 6 | Smoke or carbon monoxide alarms not working | 9% |
| Not available | 160,095 | 7% | 7 | Dangerous living conditions | 8% |
| Total | 2,356,915 | | 8 | Bed bugs | 6% |
| | | | 9 | Break-ins or burglaries | 5% |
| | | | 10 | Other | 4% |

Source: HESA 2022 (adapted)

Source: National Student Accommodation Survey 2024/
www.savethestudent.org
Based on 1,000 responses

## University halls of residence

Many new or recently refurbished university-owned halls offer a standard of accommodation that is not far short of the privately-built residences. This is partly because rooms in these halls can be offered to conference delegates during vacations. You will probably find them to be in great demand and most students need to get their names down quickly to secure their choice of room. That said, you can often get a guarantee of accommodation if you give a firm acceptance of an offered place by a certain date in the summer. In light of the cost of living crisis, many universities have reported an increased preference for lower-cost accommodation from home and international students. Keen that this does not deter applicants, they are striving to maintain a "rent ladder" in their housing supply, with some lower cost accommodation being available to students who need it.

If you have gained your place through Clearing, this option may not exist, although rooms in private halls might still be on offer at this stage. There have been delays experienced in development completions in recent years and it is wise to ensure, as far as possible, that any new-builds are on time and approved for students to move into.

While a few halls are single-sex most are mixed, and often house over 500 students. In student villages, the numbers are now counted in thousands and are great environments for making friends and becoming part of the social scene.

One possible downside is that big student housing developments can also be noisy places where it can be difficult at times to get down to some work. Surveys of students have revealed that for those who found noise a problem, peace and quiet was a higher priority than access to public transport or good nightlife. Many university libraries, especially new ones, are now open 24 hours a day.

## Self-catering

Very few universities offer catered halls of residence and self-catering is the norm. Invest in sturdy crockery and basic utensils – the sort of kit that will survive novice cookery and shared kitchens – and that won't be missed should it get lost in a shared kitchen. To avoid reliance on instant noodles and takeaways it is wise to master at least a few culinary basics, and sharing meals with housemates can be a sociable way of settling in.

## Catering in university accommodation

Many universities have responded to a general increase in demand from students for a more independent lifestyle by providing more flexible catering facilities. A range of eateries, from fast food outlets to more traditional refectories, can usually be found on campus or in student villages. Students in university accommodation may be offered pay-as-you-eat deals as an alternative to full-board packages.

## What to do after the first year?

After your first year of living in university residences you may wish, and will probably be expected, to move out to other accommodation. Of the undergraduates canvassed by the Save the Student National Student Accommodation Survey 2024, 30% said they started looking for their second-year housing in or before November – noticeably more than in 2023 when it had been 25%. The main exceptions are the collegiate universities, particularly Oxford and Cambridge, but also others. Students from outside the EU are also often guaranteed accommodation. At a growing number of universities, where there is a sufficiently large stock of residential accommodation, it is not uncommon for students to move back into halls for their final year. The autumn and winter months are the most common times to view properties for those planning to move.

## How much will it cost?

Rents vary so much across the UK that national averages can bear little resemblance to what you end up paying. The 2024 NatWest Student Living Index found a range from £481 a month in Sheffield (the cheapest) and £522 in Newcastle up to £924 in Bath and £1,032 in London – the dearest. Such figures conceal a wide range of actual rents, particularly in London. This was always the case but has become even more obvious with the rapid growth of a luxury market at the same time as many students are willing to accept sub-standard accommodation to keep costs down.

A series of recent reports suggest that the need for good wi-fi has overtaken reasonable rents as students' top priority in choosing accommodation. A survey by **mystudenthalls.com** found that a big, bright room, good wi-fi, friendly people, a clean kitchen and a good gym are the top things students say they value in a place to live.

Some student accommodation seems designed especially for the Instagram grid, featuring extras such as neon graphic art, or in one residence in Glasgow, a giant slide to take students from the first to the ground floor. Properties owned by Hello Student include St Mary's in Bristol, a converted hospital in Clifton with boardroom style study space with exposed brick walls (premium duplex rents £513 a week) and King's Stables in Edinburgh in the shadow of Edinburgh Castle with a chic slatted roof and studios for rent at £347 to £387 per week.

While it is true that going for the cheapest accommodation does not always mean good value if it leaves you cold and unhappy, there is a balance to strike. Being able to afford such top-end digs must be a priority. Many students will not receive the full maintenance loan, due to its means-testing against household income. Cash is needed upfront for deposits, and/or a guarantee, probably from your parents, that the rent will be paid. Most universities with a range of accommodation have traditionally found that their most expensive rooms fill up first, and that students appear to have higher expectations than they used to. Although there is a shift towards students applying for the cheaper rooms currently, these are being gradually developed out of the system as universities upgrade their estates.

Another consideration is that both living costs and potential earnings should be factored into calculations when deciding where to live. Taking account of both income and outgoings, the 2024 NatWest Student Living Index shows Belfast as the most affordable town or city, closely followed by Bath (where students have the highest monthly average income from sources including parental contributions, grants, bank loans and part-time work which counterbalance the city's high rents) and Derby. Perhaps surprisingly, the least affordable locations were Lincoln, followed by Coventry and then Cambridge.

## The choices you have

- » University hall of residence, with individual study bedrooms and a full catering service. Many will have en-suite accommodation.
- » University halls, flats or houses where you provide your own food.
- » Private, purpose-built student accommodation.
- » Rented houses or flats, shared with fellow students.
- » Living at home.
- » Living as a lodger in a private house.

## Living at home

If students live within commuting distance of a good university, the option of dodging hefty rent and household bills is tempting. In 2024 15% of students lived at home with their parents, according to data collected by Save the Student's annual National Student Accommodation Survey. This may be a permanent shift, given the rising costs of student housing and of living more broadly, coupled with the willingness of many young people, student or not, to live with their parents well into their twenties.

Stay-at-home students tend to have longer commutes to campus than those in their own digs, the extra journey time a worthwhile compromise. Not only school-leavers live at home; the proportion includes mature students, many of whom live in their own homes rather than with their parents. The trend is four times more common at post-1992 universities than at older universities, reflecting the larger numbers of mature students with family responsibilities at the newer universities and a generally younger and more affluent student population at the older ones.

Before opting to stay at home solely on the basis that it makes financial sense, it is important to consider the relationship with your parents and the availability of quiet space in which to study. You will still be entitled to a maintenance loan, although for 2024–25 it is a maximum of £8,610 in England, rather than £10,227 if you were living away from home outside London, or £13,348 in London. There is no higher rate for anyone living at home in London, which seems unreasonable given the high cost of transport and other essentials in the capital.

The downside is that you may miss out on a lot of the student experience, especially the social scene and the opportunity to make new friends. Research has found that students who live at home are less likely than others to say they are learning a lot at university, and a survey by the Student Engagement Partnership suggests that they find life unexpectedly "tiring, expensive and stressful". Issues affecting their quality of life include travel, security and the lack of their own space. But remember that you can always move on later. Many initially home-based students do so in their second year.

## Making your choice

Choosing somewhere cheap is a false economy if it ends up making you feel depressed and isolated. Most students who drop out of university do so in the first few months, when homesickness and loneliness can be felt most acutely. Being warm, rested and well-fed is likely to have a positive effect on your studies. University halls offer a convenient, safe and reliable standard of accommodation, along with a supportive community environment. The sheer number of students – especially first-years – in halls makes this form of accommodation an easy way of meeting people from a wide range of courses and making friends. If meals are included, this extra adds further peace of mind both for students and their parents. But only a tiny proportion of places are catered.

Wherever you choose to live, there are some general points you will need to consider, such as how safe the neighbourhood seems to be, and how long it might take you to travel to and from classes. A survey of travel time between term-time accommodation and university found that most students in London can expect a commute of at least 30 minutes and often over an hour, while students living in Wales are usually much less than 30 minutes away from their university.

In Chapter 12, we provide details of what accommodation each university offers, covering the number of places, the costs, and their policy towards first-year students.

## Practical details

Whether or not you are starting out in university halls of residence, you will probably be expected to sign an agreement to cover your rent. Contract lengths vary. They can be for around 40 weeks, which includes the Christmas and Easter holiday periods, or for just the length of the three university terms. These term-time contracts are common when a university uses its rooms for conferences during vacations. Check whether the university has secure storage space for you to leave your belongings. Otherwise, you will have to take everything home or store it between terms.

International students may be offered special arrangements to continue living in halls during the short holidays. Organisations like **hostuk.org** can arrange for international students to stay in a UK family home at holiday times such as Christmas.

## Parental purchases

An option for families with the means to do so, is to buy a house or flat and take in student lodgers. This might not be the safe financial bet it once appeared, but it is still tempting for many parents. Estate agents Knight Frank have had a student division since 2007. Those who are considering this route tend to do so from their first year of study to maximise the return on their investment.

## Being a lodger or staying in a hostel

A small number of students live as a lodger in a family home, an option most frequently taken up by international students. Students with certain religious affiliations or from a particular country may wish to consider living in a hostel run by a charity catering for a specific group. Most of these are in London. There are also specialist commercial providers such as Mansion Student India, which runs housing for Indian students in the UK (**mansionstudent.co.uk/internationals**).

## Renting from the private sector

The proportion of students renting "off-street" housing from private landlords declined from 46% in 2023 to 39% in 2024, according to Save the Student. As discussed earlier in the chapter, the student housing market is under pressure currently, though historically every university city or town has been awash with such accommodation, to the point where so-called "student ghettoes" have emerged. Into this traditional market for rented flats and houses have come the new private-sector complexes and residences, which are also experiencing growing demand (up 1% to represent 16% of student rentals in 2024).

## How to start looking for rented property

Start this process as soon as you have accepted a place. Contact your university's accommodation service and ask for its list of approved rented properties. Some have a Student Accommodation Accreditation Scheme, run in collaboration with the local council. To get onto an approved list under such schemes, landlords must show they are adhering to basic standards of safety and security, such as having an up-to-date gas and electric safety certificate.

University accommodation officers should also be able to advise you on any hidden charges. For instance, you may be asked to pay a booking or reservation fee, and there are sometimes fees for references or for drawing up a tenancy agreement. The practice of charging a "joining fee", however, has been outlawed.

Speak to older students with first-hand experience. Most universities have a clickable "Chat to a Student" icon on their website, and the online community of students nationwide is another helpful source for getting your ear to the ground (**thestudentroom.com**). Certain areas of town may be notorious, and you can try to avoid them. What I Wish I Knew About University, a Facebook group featuring over 75,000 members, is increasingly the go-to source of peer-to-peer advice for parents of students. Think Mumsnet, but for university-age young people.

## Making a choice

Once you have made an initial choice of the area you would like to live in and the size of property you are looking for, the next stage is to look at possible places. If you plan to share, it is important that you all have a look at the property. If you will be living by yourself, take a friend with you when you go to view a property, since they can help you avoid any irrational or rushed on-the-spot decisions. Don't let yourself be pushed into signing on the dotted line there and then, despite current market pressures. Take time to visit and consider options, as well as checking out the local facilities, transport and the general environment at various times of the day and on different days of the week.

If you are living in private rented accommodation, it is likely that at least some of your neighbours will not be students. Local people often welcome students, but resentment can build up, particularly in areas of towns and cities that are dominated by student housing. It is important to respect your neighbours' rights, and not to behave antisocially.

## Preparing for sharing

It helps to co-habit with people whose outlook on day-to-day living is not too far out of line with your own. There can be a bit of a rush to sign up for second-year houses, which some students do as early as October. While it is good to be ahead of the scrum, you may not yet have met your best friends at this stage. If you have not selected your own group of friends, universities and landlords can help by taking personal preferences and lifestyle into account when grouping tenants together.

Adopt good shared living etiquette from the start to prevent housemate drama further down the line. Organise a cleaning rota for everyone to share the chores, set boundaries around sharing items in communal areas such as bathrooms and kitchens, and be collectively clear about replacing essentials such as loo roll, milk and washing up liquid. Sort out broadband that suits everyone. Be thoughtful about noise levels, especially with regards to DJ decks or music equipment.

## Security in Student Housing

With multiple students all living under the same roof – each with a laptop, phone and other portable gadgets – student accommodation represents a quick win with big rewards for burglars, so it is worthwhile being security conscious.

» Make sure that your rental property has five-lever mortise locks as well as standard catch locks on the front and back doors. Without these, contents insurance may be invalid. And use them when you go out. Ask if the locks have been changed and, if not, if previous tenants have returned all keys.
» Check that furniture and furnishings provided comply with basic fire resistance standards, that there are working smoke alarms, and that you see up-to-date gas and electricity certificates.
» Be careful about letting anyone in behind you into the house or your halls of residence. People often leave their flat or bedroom doors unlocked. It's best to ask those seeking entry to buzz whomever they're visiting instead.
» Invest in a light-timer for when you're out and don't advertise your departure on social media.
» It might seem slightly over the top, but tuck away your laptop, electronics and any jewellery when you go out. Take valuables home if you're vacating your rooms for any length of time.
» If you prefer your desk at a window, make sure you move costly equipment out of sight when not in use.
» Hide packaging for your laptop, mobile and any other pricey purchases. Just dumping the box next to the bins is tantamount to advertising 'Expensive new gadgets here'.
» Call the taxi from down the street. That way, no one knows which house you've just left empty.
» Not getting contents insurance is a false economy. You may be able to add items to your parents' home insurance.
» Register valuables on the UK National Property Register at **www.immobilise.com**. And use a good bike lock.

Source: www.savethestudent.org and NUS (adapted)

## The practical details about renting

It is a good idea to ask whether your house is covered by an accreditation scheme or code of standards. Such codes provide a clear outline of what constitutes good practice as well as the responsibilities of both landlords and tenants. Adhering to schemes like the National Code of Standards for Larger Student Developments compiled by the Accreditation Network UK may well become a requirement for larger properties, including those managed by universities.

At the very least, make sure that if you are renting from a private landlord, you have their telephone number and home address. Some can be remarkably difficult to contact when repairs are needed or when deposits are due to be returned.

### Top 10 most annoying housemate problems

| | | |
|---|---|---|
| 1 | Leaving dirty dishes out | 65% |
| 2 | Not helping with cleaning | 55% |
| 3 | Leaving appliances on | 44% |
| 4 | Being excessively loud | 44% |
| 5 | Leaving food to rot | 41% |
| 6 | Leaving hair in plugholes | 31% |
| 7 | Stealing food | 26% |
| 8 | Not changing loo roll | 26% |
| 9 | Leaving windows open | 23% |
| 10 | Leaving the toilet seat up | 23% |

Source: National Student Accommodation Survey 2024
Based on more than 1,000 responses

## Multiple occupation

If you are renting a private house, it may be subject to the Housing Act 2004 in England and Wales (similar legislation applies in Scotland and Northern Ireland). Licenses are compulsory for all private houses in multiple occupation (HMOs) with three or more storeys and that house five or more unrelated residents. The provisions of the Act also allow local authorities to designate whole areas in which HMOs of all sizes must be licensed. This means that a house must be licensed, well-managed and must meet various health and safety standards, and its owner is subject to various financial regulations. There is more on this at **gov.uk** under Private Renting (**gov.uk/private-renting**).

## Tenancy agreements

Whatever kind of accommodation you go for, you must be sure to have all the paperwork in order and be clear about what you are signing up to. If you are taking up residence in a shared house, flat or bedsit, the first document you will have to grapple with is a tenancy agreement or lease offering you an "assured shorthold tenancy". Since this is a binding legal document, you should be prepared to go through every clause with a fine-tooth comb. Remember that it is much more difficult to make changes or overcome problems arising from unfair agreements once you are a tenant than before you become one.

For help with understanding some of the clauses, your university accommodation office or students' union is a good place to start. A Citizens Advice Bureau or Law Advice Centre should also be able to offer free advice.

In particular, watch out for clauses that may make you jointly responsible for the actions of others. If you name a parent as a guarantor to cover any costs not paid by you, they may also be liable for charges levied on all tenants for damage that was not your fault. A rent review clause could allow your landlord to increase the rent at will, whereas without such a clause, they are restricted to one rent rise a year. Make sure you keep a copy of all documents and get a receipt (and keep it somewhere safe) for anything you have had to pay for that is the landlord's responsibility.

Contracts with private landlords tend to be longer than for university accommodation. They will frequently commit you to paying rent for 52 weeks of the year. Leaving aside the cost, there are probably more advantages than disadvantages to this kind of arrangement. It means you don't have to move out during vacations. You can store your belongings in your room when you go away (but don't leave anything valuable behind if you can help it). You may be able to negotiate a rent discount for periods when you are not staying in the property. The other advantage, particularly important for cash-strapped students, is that you have a base from which to find work and hold down a job during the holidays.

## Deposits

On top of the agreed rent, you will need to provide a deposit or bond to cover any breakages or damage. This will probably set you back the equivalent of another month's rent. The deposit should be returned, minus any deductions, at the end of the contract. However, be warned that disputes over the return of deposits are common, with the question of what constitutes reasonable wear and tear often the subject of disagreements between landlord and tenant. About one in six student renters have struggled to get their deposit back, according to successive annual Save the Student surveys.

To protect students from unscrupulous landlords, the 2004 Housing Act introduced a National Tenancy Deposit Scheme under which deposits are held by an independent body. There are details at **citizensadvice.org.uk**. You may also be asked to find guarantors for your rent payments – in practice, usually your parents.

## Inventories and other paperwork

You should get an inventory and schedule of condition of everything in the property. This is another document that you should check carefully and make sure that everything listed is as described. Write on the document anything that is different. The NUS suggests taking photographs of rooms and equipment when you first move in (setting the correct date on your camera), to provide you with additional proof. If you are not offered an inventory, then make one of your own. You should have someone else witness and sign this, send it to your landlord, and keep your own copy. Keeping in contact with your landlord and developing a good relationship with them will also do you no harm.

You should ask your landlord for a recent gas safety certificate issued by a qualified Gas Safe Register engineer, a fire safety certificate covering the furnishings, and a record of current gas and electricity meter readings.

Being energy efficient has become a high stakes activity since the prices of gas and electricity have spiralled. Freshers who are in halls are likely to be sheltered from the worst of the energy bill rises. But many students in shared houses will be unaware that in most agreements with student letting agents, the energy included is typically subject to a fair use policy – a cap or allowance – that is often based not on units of energy consumed but on sums of money spent. These sums, which may have seemed generous in the past, are being rapidly eclipsed by the rising price of gas and electricity. In the current energy climate, it pays to read the small print regarding fair usage policies to mitigate any shocking bills later down the line.

Take your own readings of meters when you move in. This also applies to water meters if you are expected to pay water rates (although this isn't usually the case). To save money and cut down on carbon emissions, put lids on pans, don't overfill the kettle, layer up your warm clothes instead of turning up the radiators and switch off the lights. The NUS issues its own advice on how to keep down energy bills, at **studentswitchoff.org**.

Students are not liable for council tax. If you are sharing a house only with other full-time students, then you will not have to pay it. However, you may be liable to pay a proportion of the council tax bill if you are sharing with anyone who is not a full-time student. You may need to get a council tax exemption certificate from your university as evidence that you are not liable for it.

## Safety and security

Once you have arrived and settled in, remember to take care of your own safety and the security of your possessions. You are particularly vulnerable as a fresher, when you are still getting used to your new-found independence. This may help explain why so many students are burgled or robbed in the first six weeks of the academic year. Take care with valuable portable items such as mobile phones, tablets and laptops, all of which are desirably saleable items for thieves.

Ensure you don't have them obviously on display when you are out and about and that you have insurance cover. If your mobile phone is stolen, call your network or 08701 123 123 to immobilise it. Students' unions, universities and the police will provide plenty of practical guidance when you arrive.

**Useful websites**

For advice on a range of housing issues, visit: **readytorent.nus.org.uk** and **nus.org.uk/housing**

The Shelter website has separate sections covering different housing regulations in England, Wales, Scotland and Northern Ireland: **shelter.org.uk**

As examples of providers of private hall accommodation, visit: **upp-ltd.com unitestudents.com imperialhomesolutions.co.uk student-cribs.com**

A number of sites will help you find accommodation and/or potential housemates, including: **accommodationforstudents.com uniplaces.com sturents.com studentpad.co.uk studentcrowd.com student.spareroom.co.uk**

Accreditation Network UK is at: **anuk.org.uk**

**hostuk.org** helps international students meet British people and families in their homes

# 8 Staying Safe and Seeking Help on Campus

University drop-off season is a rite of passage for freshers and parents. The Ikea trips for plates, pans and fairy lights. Maybe a rug to make it homely, some scatter cushions just in case. Last minute life lessons involving spag bol practice and a laundry how-to. As terms begin through September, social media feeds fill with candid shots of family cars piled high with possessions, primed for the motorway odyssey to halls of residence up and down the country. Saying goodbye at university drop-off has always been a loaded moment, full of jubilation, tearful farewells, and excited ambitions for the future. An awkward hug and a "see you at Christmas" might have been an acceptable farewell in the past. But for today's generation of helicopter parents – au fait with class WhatsApp groups, AirTags and micromanaging their children's lives – letting go can be hard to do. Even if you are not the type of parent to pack your young adult off with "open when" envelopes ("...when you're sick" (paracetamol, vitamin C); "...when you need a coffee" (Starbucks voucher)) or fill their freezer with individual portions of batch-cooked favourites, concerns for how they will get on are likely to be near the surface. And not without reason: starting university is a time of huge change for students – one that brings unprecedented levels of personal freedom. Few school-leavers will be used to the autonomy around alcohol, drugs and relationships that university life opens up.

Students may also feel anxious at the prospect of degree-level academia, following the long and sometimes fraught build-up of getting into university in the first place. Confidence can wobble in the face of peers who are at least as clever and hardworking as they are. Or perhaps finding their feet socially is the challenge. On top of these established pressures, current cohorts of freshers have dealt with the pandemic during their schooling and are now faced with making ends meet in the grip of the cost of living crisis. With maintenance loans barely covering the rent, and huge increases to the price of bills, food and other living costs, some students are at risk of feeling lonely and isolated by not being able to afford to socialise. Such concerns seem paradoxical, given that traditional worries are about students socialising too much.

Navigating the rise of "cancel culture" on campuses is an added complication, with peer-on-peer policing about deemed misdemeanours – ranging from inappropriate sexual behaviour and rape culture to the misuse of pronouns and "offensive" views on Israel and Gaza – causing students to be shunned by each other.

Wrapping them in cotton wool is not an option and no good will come of following their every move on FindMyiPhone. Instead, parents are advised to give their child independence while also checking in with them around the major issues: drinking, taking drugs, sex and staying safe – physically and mentally – on campus.

The extent to which universities are "in loco parentis" is an issue of discussion within the higher education sector. The age of majority was lowered to 18 from 21 in 1970, meaning that universities could do away with rules around hall of residence curfews, restrictions on guests and dress codes. Constraints like that would seem ridiculous now. Universities are also too big to keep tabs on all students all the time.

But universities do provide support and guidance to students on issues of alcohol, drugs, sexual consent and respect, and all have services to support student wellbeing and mental health. Courses covering drugs and alcohol and mandatory sessions on sexual consent are increasingly becoming part of the university landscape, while guidance and support on sexual consent and respect can be found by students who seek it out themselves or who sign-up to training offered by the university and/or its students' union.

### From the first round to sobering thoughts

Stereotypes of student binge drinking abound, fuelled by university social scenes which revolve around campus or college bars and Freshers' Week itineraries packed with club nights and boozy social mixer events. This extends to accommodation, with pre-drinks a cheap alternative to paying bar prices, and students often aiming to get sozzled enough before they go to ensure they spend little once they do.

The long-term health conditions caused by regular over-consumption of alcohol are unlikely to be at the forefront of the minds of freshly independent 18-year-olds as they knock back another Jägerbomb, but those drinking to excess can find themselves missing deadlines, involved in antisocial behaviour or letting their guard down around personal safety. The Alcohol Impact programme is run by SOS-UK, a student-led education charity focusing on sustainability and social justice, which partners with universities to reduce harm. Originally set up to tackle drunk, antisocial behaviour, the programme had the knock-on effect of increasing student wellbeing, while making campuses more inclusive for non-drinkers. It recommends 50 different actions to reduce harm around drinking, from training bar staff to help intoxicated students, to working with the local community to ensure students get home safely from a night out.

### Last orders

The proportion of under-25s who say they are nondrinkers or have not had alcohol in the past year rose from 19% in 2011 to 38% in 2021 – and that grew to 42% among young women. The trend has led to the rise of sober societies and alcohol-free accommodation at universities. In the past, being sober during your studies could have felt isolating, but the imperative to drink to make friends on campus is less acute these days.

For anyone wanting to encourage moderation to their student offspring, preaching sobriety tends not to be the most effective approach. The team behind the NUS Alcohol Impact survey advise fostering an open chat about alcohol over-consumption. A good way to get the conversation going is by explaining how to take care of someone else who has drunk to excess.

A harm reduction approach is even more important when hall parties take over. Pack an alcohol measure with your student's kitchen equipment (some universities give them out to encourage drinking responsibly). If having one does not result in your child fastidiously keeping a drinks diary, it could slow down the sloshing of another huge glug.

Finally, trust them. The NUS Alcohol Impact survey revealed that 80% of respondents agreed that drinking too much can spoil a good night.

## Chasing the high

There are lots of assumptions about students' inclinations for taking drugs, but "essentially there's very little written about student drug use", says Professor Nic Beech, vice-chancellor at the University of Salford and chair of the Universities UK student drug use taskforce, which convened in 2022 to help universities understand and address student drug use and published its report in 2024. Summarising, Professor Beech said: "As educators, our priority is to see students succeed and we know that drug use can work against this, impacting students' health, wellbeing, education, and future careers. Around one in eight of those we surveyed said they had used drugs in the past twelve months, and almost half of those wanted to reduce their use – but the evidence also shows fear can be a big deterrent in students seeking help to change their drug behaviour. Universities need to take a proactive role in showing students the risks of using drugs, but also in providing support to both users and non-users."

The Dame Carol Black independent review of drug use for the government looked at the whole population – not just students – and showed that for the age range of the majority of students there had been a big increase, particularly in powder cocaine use – which has gone up 25% in the past decade. Taking the Hit, an NUS study (published in 2018 – nothing more recent has been conducted), surveyed 2,081 students at 151 institutions. It found that 39% said they currently used drugs, and a further 17% had used them in the past. Cannabis was the most popular, used at some point by 94% of respondents. It was closely followed by Ecstasy/MDMA, with cocaine and nitrous oxide also making the list.

"Study drugs" are also favourites, purportedly taken by students to improve concentration and keep them writing essays into the early hours. Substances such as Ritalin and Modafinil were taken by one in 10 of the respondents, utilising prescription-only medicines usually procured via other methods to keep them focused during deadlines.

## Just say no?

A solely punitive approach to drug use isolates students rather than aiding them. Four in ten of the respondents to Taking the Hit said they wouldn't feel comfortable disclosing their drug use to their university for fear of punishment. "The trouble is that as soon as people feel isolated their wellbeing goes down, they are hesitant to socialise and that puts them more into the position where drugs and alcohol are likely to be the sort of thing that they go to," notes Professor Beech.

The student drug use taskforce encompassed a survey of nearly 4,000 students. It found that 18% said they had used drugs in the past and, within this group, two-thirds had used drugs in the past twelve months – equating to around one in eight (12%) of those surveyed. This is notably lower than a rate of use identified by the Office for National Statistics, that 17.6% of 16–24-year-olds in England and Wales reported drug use in the year to March 2023. Meanwhile, in Scotland, the Scottish Crime and Justice Survey covering 2018–2020 found that 23.5% of individuals aged 16–24 reported using drugs in the year prior to being surveyed. One of the more commonly reported reasons for taking drugs was to deal with anxiety and mental health issues.

The taskforce's findings recommend moves away from a "zero-tolerance" approach to one focused on "harm reduction" with support and education prioritised over disciplining students who are using drugs. "As well as tackling supply and reducing demand, if we want to help students succeed in education, we need to make it easier for them to access help where they need it, to be effectively informed and to retain the hope of success, which is a foundational motivation for learning," said Professor Beech.

Similarly, the Drug and Alcohol Impact scheme (organised by SOS-UK) aims to refocus the conversation on drugs towards reducing harm, and building healthier, safer, more productive student communities. Students for Sensible Drug Policy (SSDP) is an international grassroots organisation, advocating a change in drug policy on campuses and an "end to the war on drugs" and acknowledgement of the many reasons behind drug use, including mental health management and peer pressure. The goal is to empower students to make informed decisions, stating that pastoral and medical needs will always be prioritised over disciplinary proceedings.

This is not to say that drugs will soon be permissible on campuses. Of the 151 institutions surveyed in the Taking the Hit report, more than half took a firmer line than the law, penalising students for technically legal drug use. Accommodation contracts often have an outright ban on drugs, threatening eviction.

### What can parents do?
Open dialogue equips your child with harm reduction knowledge. By discussing the effects of certain drugs, and what to do if someone has a bad reaction or overdoses, students will garner information that could end up saving a life. To facilitate such a potentially thorny chat, the NUS Alcohol and Drugs Impact scheme recommends taking a bystander approach. By saying "your friends may take drugs, these are the risks they are undertaking" you make sure that they get the information for themselves while not directly tackling them on it. This may help young people to understand the risks in a non-judgmental, safe space.

University drug policies vary, so read the fine print. Websites such as **talktofrank.com** and **Volteface.me** provide information on the effects that different substances can have and advice on how to talk to young people about drugs.

### Consent
Sexual assault and violence on UK campuses is a very real problem, as highlighted in 2020 by the website everyonesinvited.uk, which reported survivors' testimonies of sexual abuse in 93 institutions profiled in the *Good University Guide*. Through freedom of information requests, Eva Tutchell and John Edmonds, authors of *Unsafe Spaces: Ending Sexual Abuse in Universities*, estimate there are between 50,000 and 100,000 sexual assaults at British universities every year.

"The first thing that amazed us was that universities, research-based organisations, have made no real attempt to collect authoritative information about sexual assaults on campuses," Edmonds says. "If you haven't got the evidence, the specialist knowledge, how do you put together a programme that is likely to work? They rely on reports made by students and by junior staff, but everybody knows that these sexual assaults are massively underreported."

In a nationwide study, campaign group Revolt Sexual Assault and student website The Student Room polled 4,500 students from 135 universities in 2018. About 70% of women respondents said they experienced sexual violence at university; among males the figure was 26%; for non-binary 61% and for disabled respondents 73%. Just 6% reported it to the university. Reasons for this can include students not feeling they'll be heard or protected.

The NUS thinks that universities need to look at their reporting systems. Edmonds and Tutchell believe that universities hope to avoid legal cases, protect their reputation and "keep everybody quiet". A report by the BBC in 2019 showed that universities had spent £87million in 2017–18 on non-disclosure agreements to stop bullying, discrimination and sexual misconduct allegations being made public.

## Sex and relationships among students

Are any universities getting it right? Edmonds and Tutchell conclude that there are a few who "haven't always got it right, but are taking it seriously". Findings of a poll of students' personal lives by the Higher Education Policy Institute (HEPI) for its report Sex and Relationships Among Students, published in 2021, revealed that more than half of students think it should be compulsory to pass a sexual consent assessment before entering higher education. Most students (59%) reported that they were "very confident" about "what constitutes sexual consent" but only half as many (30%) said they were "very confident" about how to navigate sexual consent after alcohol has been consumed. Two-thirds of students said they knew how to challenge inappropriate sexual behaviour (with 23% saying they feel "very confident" in doing so and 43% "fairly confident").

Unfortunately, it often takes scandal and media pressure to instigate change. St Andrews was under the spotlight in 2020 after dozens of allegations of sexual assault, several against an American-style fraternity at the university. A freedom of information request found that 42 reports of sexual assault and harassment had been made in the five years to 2020. Responding, the university hired a sexual violence support worker to support survivors.

The Emily Test charity campaigns for better protection for students. Its chief executive is Fiona Drouet, whose daughter, Emily, was a law undergraduate at Aberdeen University when she was subjected to a campaign of gender-based violence by her boyfriend, a fellow student, which ended tragically in her taking her own life.

## Reframing the birds and the bees

Understanding the intricacies of consent is the key to helping your child protect themselves and others, advises Mandy Saligari, a therapist who specialises in treating teenagers and young adults "So, start off by saying, 'I know you are going to roll your eyes, but I need you to listen because this is important'. Do not get put off by your child saying, 'Oh, no!' – you have the right to fulfil your parental duty.

"Teenagers need to understand that there is no 'point of no return'. At any stage, either party can stop and say, 'I do not want to do this'. You are not a prick-tease if you go three-quarters of the way and then say you don't want to continue. And if you are a boy and you hear 'No', stop straight away. Tell your teenager they should not be afraid to assert their sexual boundaries."

The uncomfortable truth is that most people who experience sexual violence, experience it from someone close or known to them, or perhaps someone who doesn't actually understand what consent is. In retrospect, following Emily's suicide, Drouet thinks that she was a naive parent. She'd tell her daughter to mind her drink wasn't spiked and not be out alone, but never discussed coercion or abuse. "I never said: 'this is what you should do if you find yourself in a relationship where you feel you're not free to do the things that you want to do, you're being put down all the time, you're being blackmailed or asked to do things sexually that you're not comfortable with'", she said.

Another thing to do as a parent is to make sure your child feels able to talk to you without judgment or blame. According to Edmonds, until you start talking to victims, you don't realise "how little you know – the hurt, the secrecy, the guilt, the whole gamut is just awful." Sex education in schools rarely covers issues of consent, so equip your child with practical information about support services on offer. Universities are, though, increasingly providing a reporting function for anyone subjected to any kinds of abuse on campus. Finally, if your child is sexually active, make sure they know how to access contraceptive services and sign up to a GP as soon as possible.

## Cancel culture
We are used to public speakers being no-platformed on campuses from time to time but so-called "cancel culture" is adding another dimension to inter-student relations. Naming and blaming each other for misdemeanours, students act as judge, jury and executioner in their exclusion of others from social circles. Twenty-year-old University of Oxford student Alexander Rogers killed himself within a week of being shamed by university friends in 2024. His death followed a post-pub tryst, which the woman involved told friends had left her feeling "uncomfortable", though no formal complaint was lodged, while others explained he had "messed up" and they needed space from him. Shortly afterwards, the third-year material sciences student left a goodbye note describing an "unintentional but unforgivable" act.

The coroner, Nicolas Graham, thought the punishment of ostracization played an influential role in his suicide. He cited an independent review commissioned by Rogers' college, Corpus Christi, describing an "established and normalised" culture in which "students could rush to judgment without knowledge of all the facts, could shun those accused, and a 'pile-on' might occur where a group would form a negative view about another individual". According to the report, "This culture was not limited to Oxford University. It is an issue for the higher education sector as a whole." The coroner urged ministers to take cancel culture – "the exclusion of students from social circles based on allegations of misconduct, often without due process or a fair hearing" – seriously.

## Troubled minds
A survey of 4,500 university students, carried out by the National Union of Students in 2022, found that nine in in 10 said their mental health was impacted by the cost of living, and a quarter of students said financial worries were having a major impact on their mental health, as increasing numbers cut down on essentials. It's a lot to contend with when you are trying to find your way in life, with the added pressure to perform, to succeed and to not let your family down.

Jenny Smith, policy manager at Student Minds, is particularly concerned for new students. "The start of a new academic year is a key pressure point. Students may be worried about their academic capability, establishing new friendships, or making ends meet financially."

Anxiety, depression and suicidal feelings are the three most common mental health problems among students, according to Mind, the mental health charity. The onset of mental health conditions often overlaps with the age when most students go to university. Depression rates across the general public have doubled, according to the Office for National Statistics (ONS). The reporting of mental health problems is on the rise: UCAS revealed that those sharing a mental health condition on their applications rose to 36,000 in 2023, compared with 22,000 in 2022 – a huge increase of 63.6%.

## Tackling the load
There has been a lot of positive work to address mental health in universities and colleges. The Office for Students (OfS) distributed £15million to higher education providers in the 2022–23 academic year to fund student mental health support, with the aim of enabling them to develop joint working between their student support services and local NHS mental

health services. The funding was also to help universities meet the increasing demand for mental health services. University provision is diversifying, with the pandemic hastening a trend towards web-based counselling and therapy apps, while more traditional in-person appointments are still part of most offerings.

All universities profiled in our *Guide* offer mental health services to students, and although provision and funding levels vary by institution most have sharpened their focus on how best to support students. Many have a platform which allows students to self-refer for mental health help, so they do not have to go via the GP or any other channels. Therapies might be one-off counselling, or a course of sessions, or students might be referred to wellbeing self-help groups. Access to the Togetherall online mental health service is freely available to students throughout the country. Therapy pets have begun visiting campuses to lift people's spirits and some student welfare services prescribe physical exercise to improve students' overall wellbeing. Talks on managing procrastination or perfectionism are given by the welfare services at lots of universities and there are workshops available to help with study skills. Access to university-run mental health services is different to the NHS (though universities will refer students to the NHS if necessary) and many promise same-day triage appointments to anyone in need.

The diagnosis of neurodivergent conditions in students is another field that universities are increasingly on the ball about. At the Newcastle University, a Neurodevelopmental Assessment Service (NDAS) assesses and diagnoses attention deficit hyperactivity disorder (ADHD) and autism on campus. More than 200 students approached it for an assessment in 2023. Dr Fiona Gullon-Scott, a clinical psychologist who launched the service in 2022 describes how students make it as far as university without a formal diagnosis, because they are bright and have been well scaffolded at home and school, "But at university, where there's very little structure and they're managing the minefield of new social situations as well as independent learning, they've found themselves unravelling." An ADHD diagnosis can result in extra time in exams, funding for specialist mentoring and reasonable adjustments to work deadlines, as well as medication in some cases.

## How can parents help?

The role of a parent or guardian has never been more important. Family and friends are often the first to know when students are unwell. If your prospective student is worried about the future, tell them that they are not alone. Suggest that, while there are many things that are out of our control, they can always reach out to you with their concerns and other people at university. Research what support is available to your child and spend time brainstorming helpful strategies together. For those consumed by money worries, practical help with creating a budget can help with their burden.

Student Minds has launched Student Space, offering free wellbeing resources and support via phone, text, webchat or email to all university students in England and Wales. For parents and carers worried about their child's mental health, the Parents' Helpline at Young Minds offers free, confidential advice. For other resources and information visit the Student Minds parents' FAQ page at **www.studentminds.org.uk/supportforparents.html**

## Digital personas

Even post-pandemic, this generation of students is experiencing the most online-based higher education experience to date. In the past decade, universities have increasingly seen coursework set, essays handed in and gradings taking place digitally. Lectures are recorded and uploaded onto student interfaces.

Along with online learning, students should be aware of the impact their online persona has. Posting on social media and messaging online is not private, and many students have been exposed in supposedly confidential group chats, or by statuses on a private profile. Once posted online – be it a compromising photo, crass opinion or cruel "banter" – then it is there to stay. Digital footprints are permanent.

Students at Durham rightly fell foul of this in September 2020, when a group chat containing multiple misogynistic, racist and discriminatory views was leaked. One student had his offer withdrawn. In a similar online exposure, 11 students at Warwick were suspended for making rape jokes, racist statements and anti-Semitic slurs in an online conversation.

Remind your child that things they post today may be seen not only by their university but by future employers. Caution them not to post anything they wouldn't be comfortable having read back to them in an interview, or in front of a lecture hall of peers.

Universities have social media guidelines for students and your child will be seen as a representative of the university, whether posting on a private page or not. Clue them up on this before they go and remind them that nothing is truly private.

### Keeping an eye online

Your child is unlikely to accept you as a friend on social media sites or share everything with you. If you give them space, they are more likely to willingly talk to you when they want to. Encourage privacy settings so their posts can't be shared beyond the intended audience.

If you're concerned that they might be feeling isolated, stay in touch. The key is open dialogue and reserving your own judgment. Developing this relationship before your child goes to university will reap dividends as they navigate their time away.

### Useful websites

For alcohol information: **http://www.alcoholimpact.nus.org.uk/**
**www.drinkaware.co.uk**

For information about drugs: **www.talktofrank.com**
**www.ssdp.org**

For information around consent: **www.nusconnect.org.uk**
**www.revoltsexualassault.com**

For information about mental health services the first point of reference should be a university's student support services.

For more general information: **www.studentminds.org.uk**
**www.youngminds.org.uk**

# 9 Coming to the UK to Study

"Be in no doubt: international students are welcome in the UK," declared Secretary of State for Education Bridget Phillipson in a speech soon after Labour's 2024 election victory. "This new government values their contribution – to our universities, to our communities, to our country," she continued. Phillipson's reassurances followed government measures to tighten student visas, which came into force in January 2024, that prevent international students on undergraduate degrees or taught postgraduate courses from bringing family members on a student visa. The policy was introduced by the previous Conservative administration in a bid to curb rising immigration. The new education secretary has been keen to reiterate the many ways in which international students benefit British campuses: "Arts, music, culture, sport, food, language, humour – international students drive dynamism on so many levels. And of course, their contribution to the British economy is substantial."

The education secretary's stance reinforces an established pride in the strength of UK universities, which are widely considered one of the country's most important and successful exports: the UK is the second most popular global destination for international students after the US. Often hubs for students from over 100 countries UK universities are renowned for offering high-quality teaching and research. Added to their academic gravitas, life on campuses up and down the country is welcoming and diverse.

UNESCO data shows there were more than 600,000 international students studying in UK higher education in 2021, exceeding the target of 600,000 by 2030 set in the government's International Education Strategy ahead of time. Since the 1990s, the share of international students in the UK has steadily increased. In 2021/22, they comprised 24% of all students in UK higher education, compared to 17% in 2011/12 and just 12% in 2001/02. The Graduate Visa route introduced in 2021 allows students to live and work in the UK for two years after graduation, or three years for PhD graduates, and has likely added to the appeal of the UK as study destination.

The picture is not of a uniformly upward curve in international student numbers, however. Brexit triggered the withdrawal of home fee status for EU undergraduate students at UK universities, leading to a stark downturn in the footfall of European students on British campuses. In 2021–22, the first academic year under post-Brexit rules, there were 31,000 newly enrolled EU students, a fall of 53% compared with the previous year. In contrast, the number of new students from outside the EU grew by 32% over the same period, findings by the Migration Observatory at the University of Oxford revealed.

As the incoming Labour administration seeks to highlight its message of welcome to international students it is under pressure to lift restrictions on dependents. In September 2024, data showed a 17% drop in the number of overseas students applying for UK visas in the year to August compared to the same period in 2023. The government launched a review of the International Education Strategy, first published in 2019, which may bring new student enrolment targets.

India sent more students to the UK than any other overseas country in 2022/23, overtaking China, which had previously held this position since 2018/19, the latest data from the Higher Education Statistics Authority (HESA) shows. The figures include postgraduates (the fastest-growing group) as well as undergraduates (who are the focus of our *Guide*). Students from Nigeria represent the third-biggest group. Within the European Union, France sent more students to UK providers in 2022/23 than any other EU country, despite the sharp decline in new EU student numbers. It is hoped that online learning may help re-engage students from the EU. There is also the GREAT Scholarships system for postgraduate students from 18 countries around the world, including three in the EU.

The range of tuition fees for international students (which includes students from EU countries) charged by each university is listed with its dedicated university profile in Chapter 12 of our *Guide*. Most fall broadly between around £11,000 and £25,000, with classroom-based subjects such as the humanities at the cheaper end. Subjects such as the engineering disciplines can cost over £35,000 while medical and veterinary degrees can sometimes reach up to around £60,000.

International students boosted the UK economy by £41.9 billion in 2021–22 (£4.3 billion generated by EU students, and £37.6 billion generated by non-EU students) – up from £31.3 billion in 2018–19 – figures calculated by the Higher Education Policy Institute in conjunction with Universities UK International found. In her speech, Bridget Phillipson cited international students each adding about £100,000 to our national prosperity.

There are intangible benefits too. International students give institutions access to a wider pool of talent. As graduates, they either contribute to wealth creation here or return home with an attachment to Britain that can develop into trade, investment or political capital on the world stage later down the track. According to the most recent Soft-Power Index analysis by HEPI, 58 world leaders (defined as monarchs, presidents and prime ministers) studied in the UK; only the United States takes credit for more.

**Why study in the UK?**
There is much to recommend a degree in Britain. It is home to three of the world's top ten institutions and 17 in the top 100, as recognised by the QS 2024 World University Rankings and Times Higher Education's World University Rankings 2024 have Oxford in first place globally and include 25 British universities in the top 200. Global surveys have shown that British universities are seen to offer high quality in a relatively safe environment. London tops the QS Best Student Cities league table and students throughout UK universities benefit from being immersed in the English language. Degree courses here, both undergraduate and postgraduate, are shorter than the average length worldwide, which helps balance our relatively high living costs. The fall in the value of the pound recently has added to the country's appeal.

As well as the strong reputation of UK degrees and the opportunity to be taught in and soak up the English language, research shows that most international graduates are well-rewarded when they return home. A report by Universities UK, published in 2019, showed that international graduates of UK universities earn much higher salaries than those who studied in their own country. The starting salaries of UK graduates in China and India were more than twice as high as those for graduates educated at home, while even those returning to the USA saw a salary premium of more than 10%.

Students who take the plunge to travel abroad to study are likely to be bright and highly motivated, so some uplift in such students' outcomes is to be expected. And, unless they have government scholarships, most international students have to be from relatively wealthy backgrounds to afford the fees and other expenses involved. But the scale of increase demonstrated in the report suggests that a UK degree remains a good investment. Three years after graduation, 95% of the international graduates surveyed were in work or further study.

Added to career benefits, international students report high rates of student satisfaction: more than 90% of said that they had been satisfied with their learning experience and almost as many said they would recommend their university to others.

## The top countries for sending international students to the UK

| EU countries (top 20) | | % of international students | Non-EU countries (top 20) | | % of international students |
|---|---|---|---|---|---|
| Spain | 6,470 | 2 | China | 62,585 | 22 |
| France | 6,405 | 2 | India | 27,965 | 10 |
| Ireland | 5,565 | 2 | Hong Kong (Special Administrative | 13,385 | 5 |
| Romania | 5,230 | 2 | Region of China) | | |
| Italy | 5,200 | 2 | United States | 9,620 | 3 |
| Poland | 4,745 | 2 | Malaysia | 9,285 | 3 |
| Germany | 3,885 | 1 | Nigeria | 8,255 | 3 |
| Cyprus (European Union) | 3,675 | 1 | Pakistan | 7,640 | 3 |
| Portugal | 3,545 | 1 | United Arab Emirates | 5,295 | 2 |
| Greece | 3,300 | 1 | Kuwait | 4,785 | 2 |
| Bulgaria | 2,240 | 1 | Singapore | 4,695 | 2 |
| Lithuania | 1,535 | 1 | Canada | 3,925 | 1 |
| Sweden | 1,450 | 1 | Nepal | 3,835 | 1 |
| Belgium | 1,345 | 0 | Bangladesh | 3,510 | 1 |
| Czech Republic | 1,280 | 0 | Saudi Arabia | 3,375 | 1 |
| Hungary | 1,215 | 0 | Korea (South) | 3,265 | 1 |
| Netherlands | 1,180 | 0 | Switzerland | 2,580 | 1 |
| Slovakia | 940 | 0 | Thailand | 2,170 | 1 |
| Gibraltar | 775 | 0 | Turkey | 2,150 | 1 |
| Finland | 690 | 0 | Norway | 2,140 | 1 |
| | | | Russia | 1,960 | 1 |
| Total (all non-UK EU) | 64,435 | | Total (all non-EU) | 220,185 | |

**Note:** First degree non-UK students

### International student satisfaction

In the latest survey by i-graduate, the student polling organisation, 90% of international students declared themselves satisfied with their experience of UK universities, 80% said they would recommend their institution and 84% said their programme was good value for money (each metric slightly above the global benchmarks). Career and employability aspects featured strongly in their feedback. Satisfaction with advice and guidance on long-term job opportunities and careers from academic staff scored 83% in the survey, 7% higher than the global benchmark. All aspects of careers support – such as contacting employers on students' behalf, offering advice and guidance, or supporting them with CVs and applications – were noticeably higher for UK universities than the global benchmark.

Accommodation also fared positively, despite pressures on housing supply and rising rents, and the survey found that international students were, overall, more satisfied with their accommodation than in most other countries globally. The cost of living is on their radar, it found, but has not had a significant impact yet, and the positive career outcomes were driving their choice of study destination.

The number of students taking UK degrees through a local institution, distance learning or a full branch campus of a UK university was already growing even before the health pandemic heralded widespread blended online learning. The numbers grew by 70% in a decade and are likely to rise further due to post-Brexit fee changes. Over 30 UK universities have a physical presence overseas and the success of these international hubs has led to the formation of a UK University Overseas Campuses Network, representing institutions providing a British education to more than 60,000 students and employing upwards of 5,000 staff. Most branch campuses are in Asia or the Middle East. Coventry – among the most popular UK universities with international students – has a campus in Poland.

### Where to study in the UK

Most of the UK's universities and other higher education institutions are in England. Of the 134 universities profiled in this *Guide*, 110 are in England, 15 in Scotland, seven in Wales and two in Northern Ireland. Fee limits in higher education for UK and EU students are determined separately in each administrative area. All undergraduates from outside the UK are now charged the international rate of fees. Within the UK, the cost of living varies by geographical area. London is home to University College London, the most popular university with non-EU students in 2022, even though it is in the most expensive city. Incoming students should find out as much as they can about what living in Britain is like. Further advice and information are available through the British Council at its offices worldwide, at more than 40 university exhibitions that it holds around the world every year, or at its Education UK website: **https://study-uk.britishcouncil.org**. Also useful is the information provided by the UK Council for International Student Affairs (UKCISA) at **www.ukcisa.org.uk**.

Universities in all parts of the UK invest heavily in the best academic staff, buildings and equipment, and take part in rigorous quality assurance monitoring. The Office for Students is the chief regulatory body for higher education in England, overseeing organisations such as the Quality Assurance Agency for Higher Education (QAA), which remains the arbiter of standards. Professional bodies also play an important role in relevant subjects.

Although many people from outside the UK associate British universities with Oxford and Cambridge, the reality at most higher education institutions is quite different. Some universities do still maintain ancient traditions, but most are modern institutions that

## The universities most favoured by EU and non-EU students

| Institution (top 20) | EU students | Institution (top 20) | Non-EU students |
|---|---|---|---|
| University College London | 2,515 | University College London | 12,925 |
| King's College London | 2,135 | Manchester | 10,130 |
| Edinburgh | 1,730 | King's College London | 8,630 |
| Manchester | 1,445 | Edinburgh | 8,300 |
| Warwick | 1,445 | University of the Arts, London | 7,985 |
| University of the Arts, London | 1,410 | Coventry | 6,930 |
| Imperial College London | 1,165 | Leeds | 5,495 |
| Glasgow | 1,150 | Imperial College London | 5,470 |
| Ulster | 1,135 | Warwick | 5,440 |
| Bath | 1,130 | De Montfort | 5,075 |
| Coventry | 1,130 | Bristol | 4,970 |
| Queen Mary University of London | 1,100 | Sheffield | 4,735 |
| Westminster | 965 | Birmingham | 4,630 |
| De Montfort | 950 | Liverpool | 4,595 |
| West London | 950 | Glasgow | 4,300 |
| Essex | 940 | Durham | 4,280 |
| Anglia Ruskin | 905 | West of England | 4,060 |
| Aberdeen | 875 | Queen Mary University of London | 3,915 |
| Greenwich | 860 | Exeter | 3,855 |
| Bedfordshire | 850 | Nottingham | 3,825 |

**Note:** First degree non-UK students

place at least as much emphasis on teaching as on research and offer many vocational programmes, often with close links to business, industry and the professions. The table above shows the universities that are most popular with international students at undergraduate level. Although some are among the most famous names in higher education, others achieved university status only in the past 30 years.

### What subjects to study?
Strongly vocational courses are favoured by international students. Many of these in professional areas such as architecture, dentistry or medicine take one or two years longer to complete than most other degree courses. Traditional first degrees are mostly awarded at Bachelor level (BA, BEng, BSc, etc.) and last three to four years. There are also some "enhanced" first degrees (MEng, MChem, etc) that take four years to complete. The relatively new Foundation degree programmes are almost all vocational and take two years to complete as a full-time course, with an option to study for a further year to gain a full degree. The table below shows the most popular subjects studied by international students. You need to consider the details of the degree you wish to study and ensure that you have looked at the ranking of that university in our main league table in Chapter 1 and in the subject tables in Chapter 10.

## The most popular subjects for international students

| Subject of study | EU students | Non-EU students | Total students | % of all international students |
|---|---|---|---|---|
| Business and management | 13,055 | 63,150 | 333,455 | 27% |
| Design, and creative and performing arts | 7,365 | 16,700 | 150,705 | 8% |
| Social sciences | 6,335 | 18,405 | 194,685 | 9% |
| Engineering and technology | 5,175 | 24,730 | 123,130 | 11% |
| Subjects allied to medicine | 4,870 | 13,780 | 232,475 | 7% |
| Computing | 4,355 | 17,415 | 111,415 | 8% |
| Biological and sport sciences | 3,240 | 6,245 | 92,855 | 3% |
| Psychology | 3,080 | 5,905 | 100,380 | 3% |
| Law | 2,980 | 11,585 | 96,500 | 5% |
| Language and area studies | 2,250 | 3,345 | 60,860 | 2% |
| Physical sciences | 2,100 | 4,995 | 49,685 | 2% |
| Historical, philosophical and religious studies | 1,700 | 3,640 | 57,940 | 2% |
| Medicine and dentistry | 1,570 | 6,040 | 59,320 | 3% |
| Media, journalism and communications | 1,485 | 4,955 | 32,905 | 2% |
| Architecture, building and planning | 1,340 | 4,770 | 41,600 | 2% |
| Mathematical sciences | 1,275 | 6,885 | 33,840 | 3% |
| Combined and general studies | 600 | 1,010 | 19,170 | 1% |
| Geography, earth and environmental studies (natural sciences) | 570 | 1,740 | 24,085 | 1% |
| Education and teaching | 340 | 2,010 | 45,810 | 1% |
| Veterinary sciences | 295 | 1,660 | 9,505 | 1% |
| Agriculture, food and related studies | 295 | 765 | 9,780 | 0% |
| Geography, earth and environmental studies (social sciences) | 175 | 450 | 8,345 | 0% |
| **Total** | **64,435** | **220,185** | **1,888,450** | |

**Note:** First degree non-UK students

## English language proficiency

The universities maintain high standards partly by setting demanding entry requirements, including proficiency in English. For international students, this usually includes a score of at least 5.5 in the International English Language Testing System (IELTS). Under visa regulations introduced in 2011, universities are able to vouch for a student's ability in English. This proficiency will need to be equivalent to an "upper intermediate" level (level B2) of the CEFR (Common European Framework of Reference for Languages) for studying at an undergraduate level (roughly equivalent to an overall score of 5.5 in IELTS).

There are many private and publicly funded colleges throughout the UK that run courses designed to bring the English language skills of prospective higher education students up to the required standard. However, not all of these are government approved. Some private organisations such as INTO (**www.intostudy.com**) have joined with universities to create centres running programmes preparing international students for degree-level study. The British Council also runs English language courses.

Tougher student visa regulations were introduced in 2012 and have since been refined. Although under the current system, universities' international students should not be denied entry to the UK, as long as they are proficient in English and are found to have followed other immigration rules, some lower-level preparatory courses taken by international students have been affected. It is, therefore, doubly important to consult the official UK government list of approved institutions (web address given at the end of this chapter) before applying.

## How to apply

The information below is best read in conjunction with that provided in Chapter 5, which deals with the application process in some detail. Some international students apply directly to a UK university for a place on a course, and others make their applications via an agent in their home country. But most applying for a full-time, first-degree course do so through the Universities and Colleges Admissions Service (UCAS). If you take this route, you will need to fill in an online UCAS application form at home, at school or perhaps at your nearest British Council office. There is plenty of advice on the UCAS website about the process. Whichever way you apply, the deadlines for getting your application in are the same.

Under the regulations at the time this *Guide* went to press, for those applying from within an EU country, application forms for most courses starting in 2026 must be received at UCAS by January 15, 2024. Note that some art and design courses have a later deadline of March 24. Applications for Oxford and Cambridge and for all courses in medicine, dentistry and veterinary science have to be received at UCAS by October 15 each year.

If you are applying from a non-EU country to study in 2026, you can submit your application to UCAS at any time starting from September 1, 2025 to June 30, 2025. Most people will apply well before the June 30 deadline.

## Entry and employment regulations

As discussed above, visa regulations have been the subject of continuing controversy in the UK. Recent governments have been criticised for increasing visa fees, doubling the cost of visa extensions, and ending the right to appeal against refusal of a visa. The current points system for entry – known as Tier 4 – came into effect in 2009. Under this scheme, prospective students can check whether they are eligible for entry against published criteria, and so assess their points score. Universities are also required to provide a Confirmation of Acceptance for Studies (CAS) to their international student entrants, who must have secured an unconditional offer, and the institution must appear as a "Tier 4 Sponsor" on the Home Office's Register of Sponsors. Prospective students have to demonstrate that, as well as the necessary qualifications, they have English language proficiency and enough money for the first year of their specified course. This includes the full fees for the first year and, currently, living costs of £1,483 a month, up to a maximum of nine months, if studying in London (£1,136 a month in the rest of the UK). Under the current visa requirements, details of financial support are checked in more detail than before.

All students wishing to enter the UK to study are required to obtain entry clearance before arrival. The only exceptions are British nationals living overseas, British Overseas Territories citizens, British protected persons, British subjects, and non-visa national short-term students who may enter under a new Student Visitor route. All overseas students must now obtain a Tier 4 student visa, including those from EU countries, Iceland, Liechtenstein, Norway and Switzerland. Fees are currently £490 for applicants outside the country, plus an annual healthcare surcharge of £776 per year.

As part of the application process, biometric data will be requested and this will be used to issue you with a Biometric Residence Permit (BRP). You will need a BRP to open a UK bank account, rent accommodation or establish your eligibility for benefits and services or to work part-time, for example. The details of the regulations are continually reviewed by the Home Office. You can find more at **www.gov.uk/tier-4-general-visa.**

Irish nationals have the right to live and work in the UK, under the UK-Ireland Common Travel Area arrangements. Irish students will not need to apply for a student visa or the graduate immigration route.

### Bringing your family

Since 2010, international students on courses of six months or less have been forbidden to bring a partner or children into the UK. The latest reforms extend this prohibition much wider, to include all international students – other than those on postgraduate research courses. The family members these students are allowed to bring are their husband or wife, civil partner (a same-sex relationship that has been formally registered in the UK or your home country) or long-term partner and dependent children. It is important to check the latest information at **www.ukcisa.org.uk**.

### Support from British universities

Support for international students is more comprehensive than in many countries and begins long before you arrive in the UK. Many universities have advisers in other countries. Some will put you in touch with current students or graduates who can give you a first-hand account of what life is like at a particular university. Pre-departure receptions for students and their families, as well as meet-and-greet arrangements for newly-arrived students, are common. You can also expect an orientation and induction programme in your first week, and many universities now have "buddying" systems where current students are assigned to help new arrivals. Each university also has a students' union that organises social, cultural and sporting events and clubs. Both the university and the students' union are likely to have full-time staff whose job it is to look after the welfare of students from overseas.

International students with pre-settled/settled status under the EU Settlement Scheme and studying in the UK for six months or more have free access to the National Health Service (NHS). They also benefit from subsidised dental and optical care under NHS rules, plus access to a professional counselling service and a university careers service. Non-EU students have had to pay a healthcare surcharge to benefit from this.

Those international students coming into the UK on a student visa or any other visa which included paying the Immigration Health Surcharge as part of their visa application are then also entitled to free access to the NHS and can register with a GP as a permanent patient.

At university, you will naturally encounter people from a wide range of cultures and walks of life. Getting involved in student societies, sport, voluntary work, and any of the wide range of social activities on offer will help you gain first-hand experience of British culture, and, if you need it, will help improve your command of the English language.

**Useful websites**

The British Council, with its dedicated Study UK site designed for those wishing to find out more about studying in the UK: **https://study-uk.britishcouncil.org/**

The UK Council for International Student Affairs (UKCISA) provides a wide range of information on all aspects of studying in the UK: **www.ukcisa.org.uk**
UCAS, for full details of undergraduate courses available and an explanation of the application process: **www.ucas.com/international/international-students**

For the latest information on entry and visa requirements: **www.gov.uk/tier-4-general-visa**

Register of sponsors for Tier 4 educational establishments: **www.gov.uk/government/publications/register-of-licensed-sponsors-students**

For a general guide to Britain, available in many languages: **www.visitbritain.com**

# **10** Subject by Subject Guide

Knowing where a university stands in the pecking order is crucial for applicants, but the quality of the course is at least as important – especially for the duration of your studies. The extent to which a degree lives up to your expectations and strengths will determine what you get out it and ultimately how well you do. The 70 tables in this chapter drill down into the experience students are likely to have in their chosen subject area – evaluating entry standards, research quality, student satisfaction and graduate career prospects. Perhaps surprisingly, the best courses in certain subjects are not always at the universities with the highest league table positions or the oldest foundations. Some fairly modest universities are specialists in niche areas – as evidenced by their research outputs, graduate career successes and feedback from current students. Even famous universities can have mediocre departments. That said, it may also be the case that the best course is at a top-end, ancient university that may not have been on your radar.

By considering institution and subject rankings together, applicants can make tangible headway in narrowing down their options. The wealth of publicly available statistics can create a well-rounded picture of whether a certain subject – or course in that subject at a particular university – is likely to give you what you are looking for. Applicants are increasingly wise to how important subject rankings are and there is a groundswell towards them being used even more than institutional rankings in decision making.

The information included in our subject tables allows applicants to dig down into details. For example, employment prospects might seem dishearteningly poor in the subject you love – but a close look into the outcomes of previous graduates at individual universities may elicit the institutions that buck the wider trend and bring the best of both worlds within sight. Or perhaps a certain institution has especially high rates of student satisfaction in a particular subject.

This chapter offers pointers to the leading universities in a wide range of subjects. Many, such as dentistry or sociology, have their own table. Others are grouped together in broader categories, such as "subjects allied to medicine". Subject groupings are compiled based on curated groups of the third tier of the Common Aggregation Hierarchy (CAH3) and Research Excellence Framework units of assessment. Institutions are able to request custom groupings as necessary. If you see a dash (–) this denotes a score is not available because the number of students is too small for the outcome to be statistically reliable. Please also be aware that it is possible not all institutions listed in a particular area will be running courses in 2025–26, as university curriculums have always varied frequently. Added to this are the current course closures being rolled out by some universities due to financial pressures within the sector.

The subject tables include scores from the National Student Survey (NSS). These distil the views of final-year undergraduates on various aspects of their course, with the results presented in two columns. "Teaching Quality" reflects the average scores in the sections of the survey focusing on teaching, assessment and feedback, learning opportunities and academic support. "Student Experience" is derived from the average of the NSS sections covering organisation and management, learning resources, student voice and learning community, as well as the survey's final question: overall satisfaction.

The three other measures used in our tables are research quality, students' entry qualifications and graduate employment outcomes. The Education table uses a fifth indicator, Ofsted grades, a measure of the quality of teaching based on Ofsted inspections of teacher training courses. None of the measures are weighted. A full explanation of the measures is given on the next page.

Cambridge is again the most successful university among our subject rankings. It tops 19 of the 70 tables – one of them (History) jointly with St Andrews, which is No 1 in seven tables; Oxford heads six; Loughborough leads five subject tables; the LSE, Imperial, UCL and Glasgow each come top in four rankings; Queen's Belfast takes the top spot in three tables while Durham, Glasgow Caledonian, Strathclyde and Warwick are first in two tables each. Seven other universities top one table each.

## Teaching Quality and Student Experience

The student satisfaction measure is divided into two components that give students' views of the quality of their courses. Following consultation with our steering group, *The Times and Sunday Times Good University Guide 2026* used an average from the relaunched National Student Survey (NSS) 2023 and 2024 data.

   i)   Teaching quality: The NSS covers seven aspects of a course, which are grouped into themes. The teaching quality measure reflects the average scores of the teaching, learning opportunities, assessment and feedback, and academic support themes. Students answer on a scale from 1 (top) to 4 (bottom), and the score in the table is based on the percentage of positive responses (options 1 and 2).

   ii)  Student experience: The student experience measure is drawn from the average NSS scores in the organisation and management, learning resources, and student voice themes. Students answer on a scale from 1 (top) to 4 (bottom) and the score in the table is based on the percentage of positive responses (options 1 and 2).

Teaching quality is favoured over student experience and accounts for 67% of the overall score for student satisfaction, with student experience making up the remaining 33%.

## Research quality

This information is sourced from the 2021 Research Excellence Framework (REF), a peer review exercise used to evaluate the quality of research of UK higher education institutions, undertaken by the Higher Education Funding Bodies. The output of the REF gave each institution a profile in the following categories: 4* world-leading; 3* internationally excellent; 2* internationally recognised; 1* nationally recognised and unclassified. The funding bodies have directed more funds to the very best research by applying weightings. For the 2025 edition of our Guide, we used the weightings adopted by UK Research and Innovation (UKRI) and Research England, published in 2020. A 4* output was weighted by a factor of 4, and 3* was weighted by a factor of 1. Outputs of 2* and 1* carry zero weight.

The score was weighted to account for the number of staff in each unit of assessment. The score is presented as a percentage of the maximum possible score of 3.

To achieve the maximum score, all staff would need to be at 4* world-leading level.

There are no scores in this category for Buckingham (as a private university it fell outside of the REF 2021).

**Entry standards**
Average mean tariff point scores on entry for first-year, first-degree students under 21 years of age based on A- and AS-levels, and Highers and Advanced Highers, and other equivalent qualifications (for example, the international baccalaureate). Tariff points refer to the score assigned by UCAS to grades from A-levels and equivalent qualifications that are used by

---

**The subjects listed below are covered in the tables in this chapter:**

Accounting and Finance
Aeronautical and
    Manufacturing Engineering
Agriculture and Forestry
American Studies
Anatomy and Physiology
Animal Science
Anthropology
Archaeology and Forensic
    Science
Architecture
Art and Design
Bioengineering and Biomedical
    Engineering
Biological Sciences
Building
Business, Management and
    Marketing
Celtic Studies
Chemical Engineering
Chemistry
Civil Engineering
Classics and Ancient History
Communication and Media
    Studies
Computer Science
Creative Writing
Criminology
Dentistry

Drama, Dance, Cinematics and
    Photography
East and South Asian Studies
Economics
Education
Electrical and Electronic
    Engineering
English
Food Science
French
General Engineering
Geography and Environmental
    Sciences
Geology
German
History
History of Art, Architecture and
    Design
Hospitality, Leisure, Recreation
    and Tourism
Iberian Languages
Information Systems and
    Management
Italian
Land and Property
    Management
Law
Liberal Arts
Linguistics

Materials Technology
Mathematics
Mechanical Engineering
Medicine
Middle Eastern and African
    Studies
Music
Natural Sciences
Nursing
Pharmacology and Pharmacy
Philosophy
Physics and Astronomy
Physiotherapy
Politics
Psychology
Radiography
Russian and East European
    Languages
Social Policy
Social Work
Sociology
Sports Science
Subjects Allied to Medicine
Theology and Religious Studies
Town and Country Planning
    and Landscape
Veterinary Medicine

universities to determine if their entry requirements have been met. Entrants with zero tariffs were excluded from the calculation. International A-level outcomes are not included in the HESA-sourced tariff point calculations. Two years of data were used to partially offset the inflation in tariff due to pandemic disruption. The first pandemic year 2019–20 was double weighted to balance out the teacher assessed grades given for university entry in 2021–2022.

This is the average mean tariff UCAS tariff score for new students under the age of 21, based on A- and AS-levels and Scottish Highers and Advanced Highers, and other equivalent qualifications (including the International Baccalaureate). International A-level outcomes are not included in the HESA-sourced tariff point calculations. Two years of data were used to partially offset the inflation in tariff due to pandemic disruption. The first pandemic year 2019–20 was double weighted to balance out the teacher assessed grades given for university entry in 2021–2022. Each student's examination grades were converted to a numerical score using the UCAS tariff. The points used in the tariff appear on pa6e 33.

## Graduate prospects

This is the percentage of graduates in high-skilled jobs or undertaking graduate-level study 15 months after graduation, recorded in the Graduate Outcomes survey published in June 2024 and based on 2021–2022 graduates. Graduate prospects scores are published for medicine, dentistry, and veterinary medicine for information but they do not inform the rankings. Education includes a fifth indicator: the latest teaching training assessments by Ofsted. These were combined using a Z-score transformation with equal weighting for the indicators, and the totals were transformed to a scale, with 100 for the top score. A low score on this measure does not necessarily indicate unemployment – some graduates may have taken jobs that are not categorised as professional work. The averages for each subject are given at the foot of each subject table in this chapter and in two tables in Chapter 3, see pages 54–57. Note that in the tables that follow, when a figure is followed by a *, it refers to data from a previous year.

Average graduate salaries are published at the foot of the tables but these are not a component of the rankings' methodology.

# Accounting and Finance

For the third year running, the London School of Economics takes first place in our Accounting and Finance table. It outdoes all 97 other universities for the quality of its research and claims the best graduate prospects, while LSE's student satisfactions rankings fall within the upper third for both teaching quality and the wider experience. Runner-up Warwick fares well in the eyes of its accounting and finance students, placing in the top 15 for teaching quality and the student experience, while City comes out second in research. Led by Glasgow, Scottish universities dominate for entry standards, while UCL attracts the highest grades south of the border (183 UCAS points).

"Often taken together, accounting and finance share a focus on matters monetary, business and management," Alnoor Bhimani, professor of management accounting and director of the South Asia Centre, London School of Economics says. "The field is no longer about just debits and credits, cost of capital determination or investment return calculations – it's about shaping tomorrow through insightful decision-making today."

Maths A-level is useful but not an essential requirement, except by a few leading universities. Business, economics and statistics are among the other A-levels that universities look for. Entry standards vary considerably by institution, from 30 universities averaging over 144 UCAS points (equal to three As at A-level) down to Canterbury Christ Church and London Met averaging just 85 UCAS points among their accounting and finance entrants.

Universities with more modest overall rankings in the table lead for student satisfaction – with Edge Hill (50th overall) top for students' evaluation of teaching quality, followed by Worcester and Central Lancashire. Aberystwyth, in =41st overall, achieves the best rates of student satisfaction with the wider experience.

Following the LSE for graduate prospects is Bristol, with 92.7% of graduates in high-skilled jobs or further study 15 months after degrees, then Queen's, Belfast – which has been in the top three for the metric in this table for the past three years. More than 90% of graduates from Exeter, Bath, Sheffield and Warwick had also achieved these career outcomes when surveyed. But, perhaps surprisingly, accounting and finance overall do not set our graduate prospects measure alight, ranking 54th out of 70 subject areas.

| Accounting and Finance | Teaching quality % | Student experience % | Research quality % | Entry standards (UCAS points) | Graduate prospects % | Overall score |
|---|---|---|---|---|---|---|
| 1 London School of Economics | 86.4 | 85.8 | 69 | 171 | 96.9 | 100 |
| 2 Warwick | 89.7 | 90.6 | 65.2 | 165 | 90 | 99.4 |
| 3 University College London | 84.6 | 88.3 | 62.3 | 183 | — | 98.3 |
| 4 Strathclyde | 83.8 | 83.2 | 52.5 | 209 | 83.6 | 97.6 |
| 5 City | 85.3 | 87.4 | 67.2 | 154 | 85.3 | 96.7 |
| 6 King's College London | 85.3 | 87.6 | 63 | 161 | — | 96.5 |
| 7 Bath | 83.3 | 83.5 | 65.2 | 156 | 90.7 | 96.4 |
| 8 Glasgow | 72.3 | 77.4 | 57.2 | 225 | 84.7 | 95.7 |
| 9 Durham | 85.2 | 85.2 | 55.8 | 150 | 89.8 | 95.4 |
| 10 Liverpool | 89 | 90.6 | 58 | 144 | 79.5 | 95.2 |
| =11 Leeds | 79.6 | 83.7 | 62.3 | 167 | 84.9 | 95 |
| =11 Manchester | 79.4 | 81.3 | 66.2 | 166 | 85 | 95 |
| 13 Queen's, Belfast | 85.3 | 86 | 40.5 | 156 | 92.2 | 94.6 |
| 14 Exeter | 81 | 78.3 | 63.5 | 148 | 91.2 | 94.5 |

| | | | | | | |
|---|---|---|---|---|---|---|
| **15** Loughborough | 84.4 | 86.7 | 49.2 | 149 | 87.7 | 94.2 |
| **16** Edinburgh | 73.8 | 78.9 | 59 | 187 | 85.5 | 94 |
| **17** Lancaster | 84.5 | 85.5 | 59.2 | 131 | 86.2 | 93.8 |
| **18** Dundee | 90.9 | 88.1 | 28.5 | 174 | 77.8 | 93.7 |
| **19** Bristol | 80.2 | 80.8 | 46 | 158 | 92.7 | 93.4 |
| **20** Aberdeen | 85.6 | 87.3 | 32.2 | 180 | 79 | 93.3 |
| **21** Ulster | 90.6 | 89.3 | 45.8 | 124 | 82.9 | 93.2 |
| **22** Surrey | 87.5 | 90.3 | 54.8 | 127 | 76.2 | 92.8 |
| **23** Newcastle | 84.1 | 83.3 | 40.5 | 145 | 87.9 | 92.4 |
| **24** Birmingham | 77.1 | 80 | 55.2 | 147 | 87.5 | 92.1 |
| **25** Southampton | 81.6 | 82.1 | 52 | 146 | 78.8 | 91.6 |
| **=26** Sheffield | 79.7 | 83 | 48.8 | 129 | 90.3 | 91.5 |
| **=26** Heriot-Watt | 77.2 | 79.2 | 38.2 | 184 | 80.9 | 91.5 |
| **28** Reading | 83.9 | 84.3 | 46.2 | 126 | 84.3 | 91.3 |
| **29** Stirling | 77.5 | 78.2 | 38.2 | 173 | 84.3 | 91.2 |
| **=30** East Anglia | 81.8 | 82.5 | 57.8 | 131 | 76.1 | 90.9 |
| **=30** Edinburgh Napier | 90.4 | 87.4 | 20 | 159 | 74.1 | 90.9 |
| **32** Nottingham | 77.2 | 78.1 | 46.8 | 148 | 86.9 | 90.8 |
| **33** Cardiff | 76.8 | 79.1 | 56 | 147 | 75.9 | 90.1 |
| **34** Aston | 82.8 | 82.6 | 43.5 | 131 | 79.2 | 90 |
| **35** Northumbria | 86.9 | 83.8 | 28.2 | 137 | 77.3 | 89.5 |
| **36** Royal Holloway | 85.8 | 85.7 | 43 | 126 | 70.5 | 89.4 |
| **=37** Nottingham Trent | 90.4 | 87.8 | 34.2 | 116 | 71.8 | 89.3 |
| **=37** Swansea | 84.9 | 83.4 | 38.8 | 131 | 74.5 | 89.3 |
| **39** Glasgow Caledonian | 83.4 | 83.9 | 25.8 | 178 | 65.2 | 89.2 |
| **40** Robert Gordon | 90.6 | 88.2 | 19 | 165 | 60.3 | 89.1 |
| **=41** Aberystwyth | 92.6 | 93.7 | 22.8 | 109 | 73.7* | 89 |
| **=41** Portsmouth | 91.4 | 89.6 | 37.8 | 105 | 69 | 89 |
| **43** Leicester | 82 | 83.7 | 45.8 | 122 | 75.1 | 88.9 |
| **44** Sussex | 79.6 | 81 | 50.7 | 131 | 72.9 | 88.8 |
| **45** Chester | 91.1 | 89.7 | 25.2 | 117 | 72.3 | 88.7 |
| **46** Liverpool John Moores | 89.6 | 89 | 21 | 129 | 72.4 | 88.6 |
| **=47** Queen Mary, London | 76.3 | 76 | 53.2 | 153 | 68.8 | 88.5 |
| **=47** Central Lancashire | 93.1 | 90.7 | 28.2 | 118 | 64.3 | 88.5 |
| **49** Kent | 82.6 | 79.9 | 37.2 | 123 | 77.9 | 88.1 |
| **50** Edge Hill | 94.3 | 92 | 21 | 125 | 60 | 87.9 |
| **51** Manchester Metropolitan | 86.7 | 86.3 | 42.8 | 124 | 60.3 | 87.8 |
| **=52** Hull | 85.1 | 89 | 29.5 | 118 | 67.4 | 86.9 |
| **=52** Worcester | 93.5 | 89.3 | 12.5 | 110 | — | 86.9 |
| **54** Bangor | 88.8 | 88.6 | 32.2 | 105 | 61.4 | 86.3 |
| **55** Greenwich | 86.6 | 88.2 | 33.2 | 110 | 58.5 | 85.7 |
| **56** Oxford Brookes | 79.8 | 82 | 26 | 115 | 75.8 | 85.4 |
| **57** Essex | 79.8 | 83.7 | 39.8 | 110 | 65.1 | 85.2 |
| **58** Coventry | 85.9 | 86.3 | 33.2 | 104 | 59.7 | 85 |
| **59** Plymouth | 84 | 83.4 | 28.7 | 109 | 65.4 | 84.9 |
| **60** York St John | 84.3 | 83.5 | 9.8 | 100 | 81.2 | 84.7 |
| **61** Keele | 78.4 | 80.6 | 24.8 | 112 | 74.1 | 84.2 |
| **=62** Hertfordshire | 85.3 | 85.5 | 29 | 100 | 59.8 | 84 |

## Accounting and Finanace cont.

| | Teaching quality % | Student experience % | Research quality % | Entry standards (UCAS points) | Graduate prospects % | Overall score |
|---|---|---|---|---|---|---|
| =62 Brunel | 80.7 | 82.3 | 30.2 | 117 | 61.2 | 84 |
| =64 Westminster | 79 | 80.4 | 37.5 | 120 | 57.4 | 83.8 |
| =64 Kingston | 87.5 | 87.8 | 24 | 103 | 55.6 | 83.8 |
| =64 Winchester | 86.2 | 81.1 | 22.2 | 104 | 64.2 | 83.8 |
| =67 Salford | 85.9 | 85.6 | 24.8 | 118 | 51.8 | 83.6 |
| =67 Lincoln | 83.2 | 79.8 | 25 | 106 | 65.8 | 83.6 |
| =67 West of England | 81.3 | 78.7 | 27.3 | 109 | 66.5 | 83.6 |
| =70 Wolverhampton | 88.1 | 84.5 | 20.2 | 88 | 64.9 | 83.5 |
| =70 Derby | 87.7 | 85.6 | 18 | 102 | 60.4 | 83.5 |
| 72 SOAS London | 73.4 | 69.2 | 44.2 | 127 | — | 83.3 |
| 73 Bolton | 86.8 | 86.3 | 0 | 116 | 66 | 83.1 |
| 74 Bradford | 80.1 | 81.6 | 38.2 | 112 | 52.1 | 82.9 |
| 75 Middlesex | 81.4 | 80.8 | 46.2 | 97 | 50.9 | 82.8 |
| 76 Sheffield Hallam | 76.8 | 74.7 | 23.5 | 110 | 73.5 | 82.7 |
| =77 Huddersfield | 78.8 | 80.5 | 23.2 | 114 | 62.2 | 82.4 |
| =77 West London | 91.9 | 92.3 | — | 107 | 52.3 | 82.4 |
| =79 Roehampton | 79.9 | 78.9 | 32.8 | 93 | — | 82.2 |
| =79 Leeds Beckett | 87.2 | 81.8 | 8.2 | 99 | 64.4 | 82.2 |
| =81 Teesside | 89.4 | 87.9 | — | 92 | 63.7 | 82 |
| =81 Gloucestershire | 79.3 | 72.3 | 8.8 | 103 | 80.6 | 82 |
| 83 Brighton | 77.7 | 73.1 | 28.5 | 97 | 68.9 | 81.7 |
| 84 South Wales | 80.9 | 77.6 | 9 | 112 | 67.8 | 81.6 |
| =85 East London | 86.5 | 84.7 | 11 | 94 | 58 | 81.3 |
| =85 West of Scotland | 81.8 | 78.7 | 10.5 | 133 | 53.2 | 81.3 |
| 87 De Montfort | 83.6 | 81.8 | 19 | 96 | 56.9 | 81.2 |
| 88 Birmingham City | 85.5 | 85.4 | 11.2 | 110 | 47.8 | 80.7 |
| 89 Cardiff Metropolitan | 82.2 | 81.3 | 14 | 106 | 54.5 | 80.4 |
| 90 London South Bank | 81.1 | 82.2 | 21.5 | 100 | 49.9 | 80 |
| 91 London Metropolitan | 81.1 | 80.2 | 22 | 85 | 55.8 | 79.7 |
| =92 Northampton | 84.2 | 84.4 | 1.2 | 93 | 53.8 | 78.8 |
| =92 Bedfordshire | 77.7 | 79.8 | 22 | 93 | 52.2 | 78.8 |
| =92 Bournemouth | 67 | 70.8 | 23 | 98 | 73.3 | 78.8 |
| 95 Anglia Ruskin | 73.9 | 75 | 45.8 | 89 | 42.7 | 78.3 |
| 96 Staffordshire | 69.7 | 62.1 | 38.8 | — | 60 | 77.7 |
| 97 Canterbury Christ Church | 75.5 | 73.5 | 13.2 | 85 | 62.2 | 77.5 |
| 98 Sunderland | 77.9 | 75.6 | — | 101 | 53.8 | 76.6 |

| | | | |
|---|---|---|---|
| Employed in high-skilled job | 43% | Employed in lower-skilled job | 26% |
| Employed in high-skilled job and studying | 10% | Employed in lower-skilled job and studying | 3% |
| Studying | 3% | Unemployed | 6% |
| High-skilled work (median) salary | £26,750 | Low/medium skilled salary | £20,000 |

# Aeronautical and Manufacturing Engineering

Imperial tops the table for the fourth year running, its position boosted by having the top research rating in the subjects as well as the highest entry standards. Bristol takes third place this year, having swapped positions with Cambridge which is second overall and in front for graduate prospects and for the broad student experience. Aston (15th overall) is top for student satisfaction with teaching quality while Sheffield (fourth overall) is in the top five for both measures of student satisfaction.

The courses under this category focus predominantly on aeronautical or manufacturing engineering (often called production engineering) but the table also contains some courses with the mechanical title. Entry standards can be stiff: over a third of the universities in our table average over 150 UCAS points, although there are still some places to be found with more modest grades. Ulster, in 21st place, is the highest-ranked post-1992 university, closely followed by South Wales (23rd), Teesside (24th) and Coventry (25th).

Subjects categorised by UCAS as aeronautical and aerospace engineering have attracted rising demand, which edged over to 23,800 in 2023, when nearly 18,000 students gained offers. Production and manufacturing engineering drew nearly 11,000 applications in the same admissions cycle, and just under 9,000 received offers.

Most courses require maths and physics, other desirable subjects include further maths, chemistry, computer science, and design technology. An awareness of AI methods is also increasingly useful, notes Professor Ian Craddock, head of the School of Civil, Aerospace and Design Engineering, University of Bristol, who says: "Never forget that engineering always impacts society, so an understanding of global politics, the environment, and relevant law and regulation is just as valuable."

With average starting salaries of £30,000 the subjects rank =5th and they place 20th in our graduate prospects measure, with almost two-thirds of graduates in high-skilled jobs when surveyed 15 months after their degree and around one in ten engaged in further study.

| Aeronautical and Manufacturing Engineering | Teaching quality % | Student experience % | Research quality % | Entry standards (UCAS points) | Graduate prospects % | Overall score |
|---|---|---|---|---|---|---|
| 1 Imperial College | 81.6 | 82.5 | 81 | 211 | 98.1 | 100 |
| 2 Cambridge | 86.4 | 89.8 | 77.2 | — | 95.8* | 98.6 |
| 3 Bristol | 80.4 | 75.5 | 68 | 190 | 94.6 | 94.9 |
| 4 Sheffield | 89.2 | 88.7 | 66.8 | 157 | 86.2 | 93.9 |
| 5 Southampton | 76.5 | 72.8 | 70 | 177 | 94.3 | 92.9 |
| 6 Bath | 82.3 | 77.2 | 49.5 | 184 | 94.4 | 92.8 |
| 7 Glasgow | 70.7 | 66.2 | 61.5 | 207 | 91.4 | 91.6 |
| 8 Nottingham | 78.7 | 76.1 | 59 | 151 | 91.5 | 89.7 |
| 9 Loughborough | 83.3 | 80.3 | 46.5 | 156 | 89.2 | 89.6 |
| 10 Manchester | 74.9 | 69.3 | 63 | 165 | 89.7 | 89.3 |
| 11 Queen's, Belfast | 83 | 78.4 | 51 | 152 | 86.2 | 89 |
| 12 Surrey | 80.3 | 78.6 | 55.2 | 143 | 88.2 | 88.6 |
| =13 Leeds | 77.1 | 76.8 | 64.8 | 176 | 72.6 | 88.4 |
| =13 Heriot-Watt | 75.7 | 64 | 55.5 | 178 | — | 88.4 |
| 15 Aston | 92.2 | 83.7 | 35.2 | 126 | 84.6 | 87.4 |
| 16 Strathclyde | 68.8 | 67.2 | 52.8 | — | 100 | 87 |
| 17 Liverpool | 74.4 | 74.9 | 57 | 141 | 87.9 | 86.8 |

**Aeronautical and Manufacturing Engineering** cont.

| | Teaching quality % | Student experience % | Research quality % | Entry standards (UCAS points) | Graduate prospects % | Overall score |
|---|---|---|---|---|---|---|
| **18** Swansea | 81.2 | 80.2 | 48.8 | 132 | 79.7 | 85.6 |
| **19** Queen Mary, London | 72 | 71.9 | 66 | 143 | 76.1 | 84.9 |
| **20** Leicester | 78.4 | 73.4 | 39.8 | 133 | 85.5 | 84.3 |
| **21** Ulster | 73.7 | 71.4 | 49.8 | 132 | 85.4 | 84.2 |
| **22** Sussex | 81.8 | 80.6 | 29.5 | 129 | 84.6 | 84.1 |
| **23** South Wales | 91.2 | 86.9 | 26.8 | 125 | 63.8 | 82.1 |
| **24** Teesside | 85.2 | 79.2 | 18.8 | 128 | 77.8 | 82 |
| **25** Coventry | 79.7 | 72.9 | 23.5 | 127 | 84.3 | 81.9 |
| **26** City | 85.3 | 86.2 | 32.5 | 115 | 69.2 | 81.7 |
| **27** West of Scotland | 83.8 | 78.8 | 16.5 | 131 | — | 81.6 |
| **28** Portsmouth | 88.9 | 81.1 | 21 | 105 | 77.2 | 81.4 |
| **=29** Sheffield Hallam | 78.1 | 71.9 | 30 | 114 | 85.1 | 81.3 |
| **=29** Wales Trinity St David | 90.3 | 82.9 | — | 121 | 80.8* | 81.3 |
| **31** Central Lancashire | 82.1 | 77.4 | 23 | 127 | 73.5 | 80.7 |
| **32** Salford | 72.7 | 67.8 | 33.2 | 128 | 79.7 | 80.1 |
| **33** West of England | 71.3 | 63.6 | 30.8 | 128 | 84.2 | 79.8 |
| **34** De Montfort | 82.4 | 83.2 | 21.8 | 102 | — | 79.5 |
| **35** Birmingham City | 82.3 | 79.7 | 17.5 | 118 | 70.3 | 78.9 |
| **36** Brighton | 73.2 | 68.5 | 36.5 | 99 | 80.2 | 78.4 |
| **37** Brunel | 63.5 | 68 | 33 | 133 | 80 | 78.3 |
| **38** Huddersfield | 72.7 | 70.1 | 32.5 | 119 | — | 78.2 |
| **39** Bolton | 77.6 | 74.1 | 22 | 106 | — | 77.3 |
| **40** Hertfordshire | 74.3 | 69.9 | 33 | 103 | 70.9 | 76.9 |
| **41** Kingston | 80.7 | 74.6 | 17.2 | 109 | 67 | 76.6 |
| **42** Sunderland | 78.1 | 70.9 | 29.2 | — | 60.9 | 76 |
| **43** Staffordshire | 75.4 | 68.2 | 25.5 | 117 | 55.7 | 74 |
| **=44** Derby | 75.2 | 64.1 | 14 | 111 | 49.2 | 70.4 |
| **=44** Wolverhampton | 61.6 | 59.7 | 18.2 | 97 | 70.6 | 70.4 |

| | | | |
|---|---|---|---|
| Employed in high-skilled job | 65% | Employed in lower-skilled job | 13% |
| Employed in high-skilled job and studying | 2% | Employed in lower-skilled job and studying | 0% |
| Studying | 8% | Unemployed | 5% |
| High-skilled work (median) salary | £30,000 | Low/medium skilled salary | £22,000 |

# Agriculture and Forestry

Queen's, Belfast retains the lead in our Agriculture and Forestry table for the fourth year in a row, its position buoyed by the top score for research – based on results of the Research Excellence Framework 2021, and the highest entry standards. The most satisfied students are at Bangor, which leads on both measures derived from the National Student Survey: teaching quality and wider undergraduate experience – helping it move into third place overall. Nottingham, which topped the table four years ago, settles for seventh place this year, while Aberystwyth moves up to second. Ranking fifth, Harper Adams (which comes top for graduate outcomes) is ahead of the other two specialist institutions in the table, Hartpury and Royal Agricultural.

Agriculture and its related disciplines involve developing solutions for sustainably feeding the growing population while protecting the environment. "The scientific evidence is unequivocal: we have exceeded our planetary boundaries in terms of climate change, biodiversity loss and natural nutrient cycles," comments Professor Michael Lee, deputy vice-chancellor, Harper Adams University.

After three years of rising demand for agriculture degrees, applications decreased a little in 2023 – to just over 6,000, and 1,800 students were accepted onto courses – also down compared with the three years prior. Forestry and arboriculture attract much smaller numbers, with just 210 applicants and 70 new undergraduates in 2023.

The two subjects place =41st out of the 70 subjects in our graduate prospects ranking (where they tie perhaps surprisingly with law), based on more than six in ten graduates working in high-skilled jobs and/or furthering their studies 15 months after degrees. Average early career salaries of £26,000 compare more favourably still – ranking agriculture and forestry =28th.

| Agriculture and Forestry | Teaching quality % | Student experience % | Research quality % | Entry standards (UCAS points) | Graduate prospects % | Overall score |
|---|---|---|---|---|---|---|
| 1 Queen's, Belfast | 79.9 | 72.5 | 69.2 | 148 | 70.2 | 100 |
| 2 Aberystwyth | 81.2 | 81.5 | 48.8 | 141 | — | 96.6 |
| 3 Bangor | 93 | 87.6 | 67.5 | — | 54.8* | 96.2 |
| 4 Newcastle | 81.3 | 79.7 | 42.8 | 129 | 70 | 94.3 |
| 5 Harper Adams | 85.8 | 77 | 19.5 | 127 | 75.1 | 93.3 |
| 6 Reading | 82.7 | 79.8 | 42.5 | 128 | — | 92.8 |
| 7 Nottingham | 76.7 | 75.4 | 52 | 133 | 62.5 | 92.6 |
| 8 Hartpury | 89.3 | 84.6 | — | 110 | 64.3 | 85.8 |
| 9 Royal Agricultural University | 63.6 | 63.3 | 24.2 | 115 | 59.6 | 81.7 |

| | | | |
|---|---|---|---|
| Employed in high-skilled job | 53% | Employed in lower-skilled job | 32% |
| Employed in high-skilled job and studying | 5% | Employed in lower-skilled job and studying | 0% |
| Studying | 5% | Unemployed | 3% |
| High-skilled work (median) salary | £26,500 | Low/medium skilled salary | £24,500 |

# American Studies

Combining disciplines including history, politics and literature, American studies degrees concentrate on the United States, as well as Latin America and the Caribbean. Students are often offered the opportunity of spending a year at a university across the pond as part of a four-year course. The subject helps students to understand key global challenges such as inequality, climate crisis, international security and migration. Universities look for English language, English literature and history A-levels, while politics is also considered useful.

University College London is the leading institution for American Studies for the third consecutive year, while former winner Sussex settles for second once more. UCL's lead is boosted by the highest entry standards by a clear margin, with entrants averaging 174 UCAS points, followed by Manchester (in fourth place overall) where entrants averaged 143 points. Results of the Research Excellence Framework 2021 place Birmingham (seventh overall) in front. Powered by the top scores for student satisfaction with teaching quality and the wider experience, Manchester Met, the only post-1992 university in our table, has overtaken its neighbour institution, Manchester, to take third place this year.

"When you graduate, the degree sets you up for a range of careers, working at home and abroad, in business, government, the civil service, NGOs and charities or education," says Dr Nick Witham, associate professor of United States history and head of the Institute of the Americas, UCL. Placing =62nd out of 70 subject areas, American studies has lost ground in our graduate prospects table, where it ranked 45th last year. Fifteen months after finishing their degree 52% of graduates were in high-skilled jobs and/or engaged in further study, but more than three in ten were employed in jobs deemed "lower-skilled" and 6% were unemployed. For starting salaries, American studies places =53rd, with graduates attracting average early career incomes of £24,000 per year. Demand for the subject has waned: applications and enrolments declined for the fourth year running in 2023, but the subject remains offered by 51 higher education providers on the UCAS website, often in combination with another.

| American Studies | Teaching quality % | Student experience % | Research quality % | Entry standards (UCAS points) | Graduate prospects % | Overall score |
|---|---|---|---|---|---|---|
| 1 University College London | 80.8 | 79.3 | 65.7 | 174 | — | 100 |
| 2 Sussex | 81.7 | 75 | 65.1 | 132 | 83.4 | 98.3 |
| 3 Manchester Metropolitan | 87.7 | 82.8 | 61.8 | 119 | — | 97.9 |
| 4 Manchester | 81.7 | 71.4 | 66.5 | 143 | 79.8 | 97.7 |
| 5 Nottingham | 82.4 | 77 | 63.7 | 133 | 77.2 | 96.6 |
| 6 East Anglia | 83.7 | 76.6 | 63 | 126 | 76.3 | 96.1 |
| 7 Birmingham | 78.9 | 74.5 | 68.8 | — | 75.5* | 95.3 |
| 8 Hull | 84.9 | 81.1 | 55.5 | 131 | 73.2* | 95 |
| 9 Swansea | 83.7 | 81.1 | 45.2 | 118 | 77.6 | 93.9 |

| | | | |
|---|---|---|---|
| Employed in high-skilled job | 38% | Employed in lower-skilled job | 31% |
| Employed in high-skilled job and studying | 1% | Employed in lower-skilled job and studying | 0% |
| Studying | 12% | Unemployed | 6% |
| High-skilled work (median) salary | £25,000 | Low/medium skilled salary | £20,000 |

## Anatomy and Physiology

Very few courses in this table actually have the title of anatomy or physiology – far more common are degrees titled biomedical science. The subject involves studying the structure and function of the human body, covering molecular and cellular mechanisms. A two-science minimum at A-level usually means biology and chemistry, although physics is also an option. The leading universities look for maths too. Demand for the subject area has increased lately, and courses within biomedical science, anatomy and physiology attracted over 58,000 applications and around 11,000 new student admissions in 2023. It is a good idea to attend university open days and look at websites to find a particular course of interest, as their content may differ across institutions. In terms of jobs, "Anatomy and physiology provides good grounding for careers in relevant research, clinical scientist roles or scientific or medical information, marketing or sales," says Dr Katherine Brooke-Wavell, senior lecturer in human biology, Loughborough University.

In a table dominated by the older institutions, Edinburgh moves up one place to the top spot, its rank driven by strong performances across all metrics without coming first in any individually. Aberdeen, the winner for the past two years and now in second place, leads for student satisfaction with the wider experience and teaching quality and Dundee is in front for research. Queen's, Belfast has risen six places to rank third overall, while the best graduate prospects were achieved for the second year running by Swansea – where almost all (97.8%) of graduates in the subject were in high-skilled jobs or further study 15 months after their degree. Oxford and Cambridge tied at No 1 in this table only three years ago, but neither university have sufficient data for the subjects to be included in our current edition.

Anatomy and physiology rank 35th out of 70 subject areas in our graduate employment index, while average starting salaries of £25,900 put the subjects 36th.

| Anatomy and Physiology | Teaching quality % | Student experience % | Research quality % | Entry standards (UCAS points) | Graduate prospects % | Overall score |
|---|---|---|---|---|---|---|
| 1 Edinburgh | 79.3 | 79 | 69.2 | 186 | 89.4 | 100 |
| 2 Aberdeen | 91.1 | 88.8 | 33.2 | 206 | 90 | 98.4 |
| 3 Queen's, Belfast | 88.1 | 82.2 | 69.2 | 159 | 84.4* | 98 |
| 4 Glasgow | 86 | 78.7 | 55.8 | 217 | 74.9 | 96.5 |
| =5 Dundee | 83.7 | 73.3 | 78 | 181 | 73.9 | 96.4 |
| =5 Loughborough | 81.4 | 86.5 | 66.8 | 162 | 83.1 | 96.4 |
| 7 Swansea | 75.4 | 63.4 | 66.8 | 132 | 97.8 | 95.8 |
| 8 Newcastle | 87 | 82.7 | 58.8 | 151 | — | 95.4 |
| 9 Bristol | 81.9 | 77.5 | 57.4 | 156 | 83.5 | 93.7 |
| 10 Liverpool | 76.5 | 80.9 | 46.8 | 144 | 88.2 | 91.6 |
| 11 Nottingham | 88.2 | 86.8 | 54 | 130 | 79.2 | 91.4 |
| 12 Manchester Metropolitan | 75.2 | 74.5 | 51.2 | 133 | 86.4 | 90.1 |
| 13 St George's, London | 83.9 | 76.7 | 50.2 | 128 | — | 89.3 |
| 14 Leicester | 78.7 | 79.7 | 53.5 | 127 | — | 88.9 |
| 15 Leeds | 77.6 | 73.3 | 52 | 153 | 76 | 88.8 |
| 16 Essex | 88.4 | 88 | 42.5 | 106 | 82.2 | 88.4 |
| 17 Bangor | 78.6 | 77.9 | 59.8 | 122 | 70.8* | 86.4 |
| =18 West of England | 82.2 | 83.5 | 42.8 | 117 | 74.2 | 85.1 |
| =18 Westminster | 84.5 | 87.5 | 36.8 | 109 | — | 85.1 |
| 20 Sunderland | 82.1 | 79 | 30.2 | 124 | — | 83.7 |
| 21 Huddersfield | 81.6 | 78.3 | 22.5 | 133 | — | 82.6 |
| 22 Ulster | 47.5 | 37.5 | 53.5 | 129 | 73.5 | 77.6 |

| | | | | |
|---|---|---|---|---|
| Employed in high-skilled job | 42% | Employed in lower-skilled job | | 16% |
| Employed in high-skilled job and studying | 5% | Employed in lower-skilled job and studying | | 2% |
| Studying | 19% | Unemployed | | 5% |
| High-skilled work (median) salary | £27,000 | Low-/medium-skilled salary | | £20,000 |

## Animal Science

This is the tenth edition of our Animal Science table, which was first launched to reflect the growing interest in the subject area and is extracted from the agriculture category – with courses ranging from veterinary nursing and equine science to animal behaviour. Students learn about animal physiology, behaviour and welfare, which Dr Beth Nicholls, senior research fellow in ecology and evolution at the School of Life Sciences, University of Sussex explains is "critical for sustainable farming, wildlife preservation and understanding zoonotic diseases." Transferable skills include data analysis, report writing, and delivering effective presentations. High roller starting salaries are not what draws animal science students, however. The subject ties with creative writing at the foot of our salaries ranking, with annual average wages of £22,000 for graduates. Early career prospects more broadly also fare poorly, relative to other subjects, ranking 68th out of 70 – with just under half of graduates employed in high-skilled jobs or postgraduate study 15 months on from their degrees. After two bumper years of applications, demand cooled in 2023 when just over 8,430 applied and 2,010 students were accepted onto courses.

Led by Glasgow at No 1 the top three of our table is unchanged this year from last. Glasgow's rank is boosted by the highest entry standards by some distance, with new entrants averaging 204 UCAS points. Manchester, in third place overall, is top for research. Middlesex, the table's highest-ranked modern university, moves into the top 10 (seventh), its performance enhanced by the best graduate outcomes – with 100% of graduates in high-skilled jobs or further study 15 months on from their degrees. Conversely, at Plymouth only 29.4% of graduates had achieved these outcomes. The Royal Veterinary College, in =15th place overall and with the second-best graduate prospects, leads the four specialist institutions, followed by Harper Adams (17th). Lincoln, in 14th place overall, is top for both measures of student satisfaction: teaching quality and the wider experience, while the Royal Agricultural College is bottom for each of them.

| Animal Science | Teaching quality % | Student experience % | Research quality % | Entry standards (UCAS points) | Graduate prospects % | Overall score |
|---|---|---|---|---|---|---|
| 1 Glasgow | 83.9 | 75.2 | 64.8 | 204 | 73.5 | 100 |
| 2 Bristol | 83.2 | 78.5 | 60.2 | 148 | 82.7 | 94.2 |
| 3 Manchester | 77.4 | 74.8 | 69.5 | 156 | 64.9 | 91.7 |
| 4 Liverpool | 76.1 | 76.9 | 68.2 | 145 | 73.5 | 91.3 |
| 5 Nottingham | 78 | 75.6 | 52 | 137 | 82.3 | 90.3 |
| 6 Reading | 86 | 80.9 | 42.5 | 138 | — | 89.8 |
| 7 Middlesex | 88.1 | 80 | — | 128 | 100 | 89.2 |
| 8 Aberystwyth | 83.7 | 82.1 | 48.8 | 126 | 66.3 | 88.2 |
| 9 Newcastle | 72.6 | 77.7 | 58.8 | 135 | 71.9 | 88.1 |
| 10 Queen's, Belfast | 69.7 | 71.9 | 69.2 | 138 | 69.2 | 87.8 |
| 11 Sussex | 77.2 | 71.8 | 49.8 | 137 | 69 | 87.3 |
| 12 Bangor | 81.2 | 78.2 | 67.5 | 122 | 53.6 | 86.8 |
| 13 Liverpool John Moores | 84.6 | 82.9 | 28.7 | 141 | 50 | 85.8 |
| 14 Lincoln | 90.5 | 85.7 | — | 127 | 65.7 | 85.2 |
| =15 Plymouth | 82.2 | 76 | 58.2 | 135 | 29.4 | 83.7 |
| =15 Royal Veterinary College | 75.1 | 66.6 | — | 135 | 88.9 | 83.7 |
| 17 Harper Adams | 85.1 | 73.4 | — | 128 | 73.2 | 83.6 |
| 18 Anglia Ruskin | 88.4 | 79.2 | 17.8 | 120 | 54.2 | 83.2 |
| 19 Oxford Brookes | 74.2 | 71.7 | 39.5 | 125 | 59.3 | 82.5 |
| 20 Hartpury | 86.1 | 75.8 | 15.8 | 123 | 53.1 | 82.2 |
| 21 Chester | 76.5 | 75.1 | 6.2 | 126 | 64.5 | 80.9 |
| 22 Nottingham Trent | 84.8 | 77.1 | — | 129 | 42.9 | 79.6 |
| 23 Greenwich | 77.2 | 76.5 | — | 123 | 58.3 | 79.3 |
| 24 Canterbury Christ Church | 87 | 83 | 9.5 | 98 | — | 79.2 |
| 25 Derby | 79.8 | 73.2 | — | 118 | 54.8 | 78.3 |
| 26 Cumbria | 77.2 | 59.2 | — | 116 | 54.4 | 75.7 |
| 27 Royal Agricultural University | 61.6 | 58.2 | — | 118 | 46.1 | 71 |

| | | | | |
|---|---|---|---|---|
| Employed in high-skilled job | 35% | Employed in lower-skilled job | 36% |
| Employed in high-skilled job and studying | 3% | Employed in lower-skilled job and studying | 2% |
| Studying | 10% | Unemployed | 5% |
| High-skilled work (median) salary | £23,400 | Low-/medium-skilled salary | £20,000 |

# Anthropology

St Andrews takes the top spot in our new Anthropology table, boosted by the highest entry standards and third-best rates of student satisfaction in both categories. Former No 1 London School of Economics (LSE) has slipped to fifth – though still comes top for research. Oxford is steady in the runner-up spot overall (and top for graduate outcomes). Durham is up five places to sit third. East Anglia, in tenth place overall, is only marginally behind LSE for its research quality. The study of humans and human society, from the physical evolution of the human body and brain, to the political, cultural and linguistic practices of modern societies, anthropology has tended to be the preserve of old universities. Brunel (founded in the 1960s) leads on student satisfaction across teaching quality and the wider experience and moves up to ninth place overall, where it ties with Cambridge this year. Plymouth, in 17th is the top-ranked post-1992 university.

Over half of the table (13 universities) averaged over 144 UCAS points (equivalent to AAA at A-level). The subject attracts small numbers of students: 1,120 were accepted onto courses in 2023. Anthropologists investigate wide-ranging fields such as religion, gender, geopolitics, climate change, robotics and AI, human rights, social media, and capitalism. When last surveyed 15 months after finishing their degrees, around six in ten graduates were working in high-skilled jobs, furthering their studies, or doing both – ranking anthropology 47th (up from 55th) in the employment table of 70 subject areas. For average starting salaries, annual earnings of £25,200 place it 44th.

| Anthropology | Teaching quality % | Student experience % | Research quality % | Entry standards (UCAS points) | Graduate prospects % | Overall score |
|---|---|---|---|---|---|---|
| 1 St Andrews | 90.5 | 86.8 | 49.2 | 199 | — | 100 |
| 2 Oxford | 82.7 | 74.3 | 54.2 | 189 | 94.1* | 98.6 |
| 3 Durham | 88.2 | 81.3 | 54.8 | 168 | 87.8 | 97.8 |
| 4 Aberdeen | 92 | 88.1 | 42.2 | 177 | — | 96.6 |
| 5 London School of Economics | 82.6 | 80.2 | 73.2 | 172 | 68.8 | 96.2 |
| 6 Birmingham | 85.9 | 83.8 | 67 | 133 | — | 95.6 |
| 7 University College London | 79 | 77.5 | 52.2 | 169 | 87.5 | 94.7 |
| 8 East Anglia | 81.9 | 78.6 | 70.8 | 131 | 78.5 | 94.2 |
| =9 Brunel | 98.3 | 98.6 | 34.8 | — | 70.6 | 94.1 |
| =9 Cambridge | 83.2 | 65.3 | 40.8 | 193 | 86.9 | 94.1 |
| 11 Exeter | 83.9 | 81 | 46.8 | 156 | 84.3 | 93.5 |
| 12 SOAS London | 82.6 | 67.9 | 61.8 | 151 | — | 93 |
| 13 Manchester | 82.3 | 77.3 | 61.3 | 153 | 71.7 | 92.7 |
| 14 Edinburgh | 73.3 | 71.8 | 51.7 | 174 | 76.8 | 90.8 |
| 15 Sussex | 82.2 | 81.8 | 53.8 | 139 | 69.3 | 90 |
| 16 Bristol | 74.4 | 71.4 | 58.8 | 146 | 73.1 | 89.3 |
| 17 Plymouth | 82.9 | 79.1 | 47.1 | 115 | — | 87.1 |
| 18 Liverpool John Moores | 84.1 | 81.4 | 28.7 | 140 | — | 85.7 |
| =19 Goldsmiths, London | 81.7 | 74.6 | 51.5 | 122 | 56.2 | 84.8 |

| Anthropology cont. | Teaching quality % | Student experience % | Research quality % | Entry standards (UCAS points) | Graduate prospects % | Overall score |
|---|---|---|---|---|---|---|
| **=19** Queen's, Belfast | 77.4 | 67.3 | 41.5 | 139 | — | 84.8 |
| **21** Bournemouth | 80.6 | 78.2 | 50.5 | 106 | 61.1 | 84.4 |
| **22** King's College London | 74.5 | 71.1 | — | 179 | 83.3 | 83 |
| **23** Oxford Brookes | 80.5 | 75.9 | 34.8 | 104 | 68.8 | 82.6 |

| | | | |
|---|---|---|---|
| Employed in high-skilled job | 43% | Employed in lower-skilled job | 24% |
| Employed in high-skilled job and studying | 5% | Employed in lower-skilled job and studying | 1% |
| Studying | 12% | Unemployed | 6% |
| High-skilled work (median) salary | £26,775 | Low-/medium-skilled salary | £19,000 |

# Archaeology and Forensic Science

Tenure at the top of our Archaeology and Forensic Science table has shifted to Oxford this year, its position buoyed by strong performance across all measures – including the second-highest entry standards and graduate prospects. Last year's No 1 – Durham – is in third place. Reading ranks seventh overall but it is top for research quality, based on outcomes of the most recent Research Excellence Framework in 2021, and also tops the table for both measures of student satisfaction: teaching quality and the wider experience, derived from the National Student Survey. London South Bank ranks =36th overall but places second for each of the NSS-based metrics, followed by Central Lancashire.

While most archaeology courses have no subject requirements, the leading universities will usually want a science. Geography and History are also relevant A-levels. Single honours archaeology degrees attracted 990 new students in 2023, while 2,430 students were accepted onto courses classified by UCAS as forensic and archaeological sciences. "Archaeology and heritage isn't just about the past; this is an exciting, evolving field in which skills traditionally used to uncover historical secrets are increasingly being applied to help us better understand our present and future," says Karina Croucher, professor of archaeology, heritage and wellbeing at the University of Bradford, who adds: "Archaeology and forensic sciences involves geophysics, drones, analytical chemistry, CT scanning, the use of augmented and virtual reality to present and analyse data, and an array of scientific and humanities research approaches, leading to multiple career pathways."

In our graduate employment table of 70 subject areas, archaeology and forensic sciences rank 56th, based on over 56% of graduates working in high-skilled jobs and/or furthering their studies 15 months on from their degrees. More than a quarter (27%) were employed in jobs deemed "low-skilled", however. Starting salaries of £22,585 put the subjects third from bottom in the pay index, in 67th place out of 70 subject areas.

| Archaeology and Forensic Science | Teaching quality % | Student experience % | Research quality % | Entry standards (UCAS points) | Graduate prospects % | Overall score |
|---|---|---|---|---|---|---|
| **1** Oxford | 85.1 | 69.6 | 61.8 | 186 | 88.7* | 100 |
| **2** University College London | 89.3 | 81.8 | 55.8 | 154 | 95.7 | 99.9 |
| **3** Durham | 87 | 78.4 | 70.2 | 158 | 82.5 | 98.1 |
| **4** Cambridge | 80.4 | 56.4 | 71 | 188 | — | 96.7 |

| | | | | | | | |
|---|---|---|---|---|---|---|---|
| 5 | Exeter | 86.8 | 86.6 | 58.8 | 147 | 77.5 | 95.1 |
| 6 | Leicester | 84.5 | 78.1 | 70 | — | 77.4* | 95 |
| 7 | Reading | 94.4 | 92.1 | 76.5 | 117 | 65.3* | 93.9 |
| 8 | York | 87 | 78.5 | 63 | 137 | 73.6 | 93 |
| 9 | Birmingham | 89.2 | 81.1 | 54.2 | 134 | — | 92.6 |
| 10 | Southampton | 84.9 | 67.6 | 69.8 | 133 | 73.7 | 92 |
| 11 | Queen's, Belfast | 89.6 | 83.3 | 51.2 | 130 | — | 91.9 |
| 12 | Nottingham | 89 | 84.6 | 51.5 | 127 | 72.9* | 91.5 |
| 13 | Glasgow Caledonian | 70.6 | 71.2 | 61 | 163 | 75.8 | 91.2 |
| 14 | Edinburgh | 67.5 | 67.3 | 59.1 | 183 | — | 91.1 |
| 15 | Keele | 82.9 | 75 | 48 | 138 | 76.6 | 90.5 |
| 16 | Newcastle | 88.5 | 82.9 | 47.8 | 121 | 74.1 | 90.4 |
| 17 | Cardiff | 82.6 | 69.8 | 58 | 125 | 72.7 | 89 |
| 18 | Lincoln | 85.8 | 84.9 | 27.8 | 116 | 81.8 | 88.7 |
| 19 | Central Lancashire | 92.2 | 90 | 32.8 | 125 | 66.4 | 88.6 |
| 20 | West of Scotland | 87.6 | 77.1 | 28.7 | 138 | — | 87.8 |
| =21 | Robert Gordon | 84.3 | 76.2 | — | 161 | 77.4 | 87.4 |
| =21 | Northumbria | 73.9 | 68.6 | 53.5 | 140 | 71.6 | 87.4 |
| 23 | Glasgow | 86.4 | 82.7 | 54.2 | — | 56.5 | 86.9 |
| 24 | Hull | 87.7 | 81.1 | 55.5 | 119 | 56.6 | 86.7 |
| 25 | Liverpool | 76.2 | 72.6 | 43.5 | 130 | 72.8 | 86.5 |
| 26 | Kent | 87.4 | 86.5 | — | 138 | 74.6 | 86.1 |
| 27 | Nottingham Trent | 86.2 | 76.4 | — | 135 | 78.9 | 85.7 |
| =28 | Bournemouth | 80.6 | 72.1 | 50.5 | 113 | 67.3 | 85.4 |
| =28 | Liverpool John Moores | 73.6 | 75.6 | 28.7 | 144 | 72.2 | 85.4 |
| =30 | Huddersfield | 82.8 | 86.7 | 24 | 128 | — | 85.3 |
| =30 | Bradford | 85.2 | 79.2 | 38.2 | 111 | — | 85.3 |
| =32 | Kingston | 83.4 | 73.4 | 38.5 | 107 | 67.7 | 84.2 |
| =32 | Wales Trinity St David | 87.7 | 72.2 | 31 | 113 | — | 84.2 |
| 34 | Teesside | 87.3 | 83.5 | 18.8 | 125 | 60.7 | 83.7 |
| 35 | Anglia Ruskin | 84 | 79.8 | 33.8 | 115 | 60.4 | 83.3 |
| =36 | London South Bank | 92.8 | 90 | — | 100 | 69.0* | 82.7 |
| =36 | West London | 86.7 | 78.8 | — | 115 | 73.7 | 82.7 |
| 38 | Staffordshire | 77.9 | 70.2 | 31 | 117 | 67.7 | 82.5 |
| 39 | De Montfort | 87.8 | 82.1 | — | 108 | 72.4 | 82.4 |
| 40 | Winchester | 90.2 | 79 | 16 | 101 | 64.6 | 82.2 |
| 41 | Canterbury Christ Church | 88 | 83.9 | 17.8 | 90 | 68.1 | 81.9 |
| =42 | Chester | 89.6 | 77.8 | 22.5 | 108 | 57.9 | 81.8 |
| =42 | Coventry | 92 | 89 | — | 112 | 61.6 | 81.8 |
| 44 | Derby | 80.2 | 73.5 | — | 119 | 72.1 | 80.7 |
| 45 | West of England | 82.4 | 76.1 | — | 129 | 63.9 | 80.6 |
| 46 | Greenwich | 83.3 | 79.7 | — | 121 | 54.5 | 78.1 |
| 47 | South Wales | 70.9 | 58.1 | — | 116 | 69.6 | 76 |
| 48 | Wolverhampton | 81.1 | 67.4 | — | 118 | 47.8 | 74.6 |

| | | | |
|---|---|---|---|
| Employed in high-skilled job | 40% | Employed in lower-skilled job | 27% |
| Employed in high-skilled job and studying | 4% | Employed in lower-skilled job and studying | 2% |
| Studying | 10% | Unemployed | 6% |
| High-skilled work (median) salary | £23,500 | Low-/medium-skilled salary | £19,000 |

# Architecture

Loughborough tops the Architecture table for the second year running, its position boosted by the top graduate prospects – with 100% of graduates securing high-skilled jobs or furthering their studies 15 months on from their degrees. Loughborough also has the second-best research quality rating and top 10 rates of student satisfaction with both teaching quality and the wider experience. Up two places this year, runner-up Sheffield is unbeaten for student satisfaction with the wider experience and fifth for teaching quality. Cardiff retains third place in the table for the third consecutive year. The highest entry standards are at Strathclyde and Cambridge, which also leads the field in research within architecture but has slipped to fourth place overall this year due to rates of student satisfaction which rank in the lower half of the table. In our latest National Student Survey (NSS) analysis Nottingham Trent (24th overall) is first for students' evaluation of teaching quality, where it is followed by Wolverhampton. The University for the Creative Arts is in the top three for both NSS-derived measures. At the other end of the scale, architecture students at Brighton and Lincoln reported the lowest rates of satisfaction with teaching quality.

There are usually no essential subjects required to study architecture, although the leading universities will look for a mixture of art and science, and a portfolio is essential. Entry standards range from the 99 UCAS tariff points averaged by entrants to Hertfordshire up to the 202 points averaged at Cambridge and Strathclyde. It takes most architects seven years to fully qualify, of which a degree is the first step. Such a timeframe asks a lot of students' dedication to the profession and of their financial wherewithal to support themselves. Course materials add to costs. Study time is spent drawing, making and researching through design.

"This is a deeply interdisciplinary subject, combining humanities, arts, social sciences and technology," says Professor Flora Samuel, head of the Department of Architecture, University of Cambridge. Early career trajectories are positive; two-thirds of graduates were in professional jobs 15 months after their degrees according to the latest data, which combined with around 10% in postgraduate study and/or a professional-grade job ranks the subject 19th out of 70 areas. Early career salaries compare less favourably however, with average annual earnings of £23,000 putting the subject in the bottom ten.

| Architecture | Teaching quality % | Student experience % | Research quality % | Entry standards (UCAS points) | Graduate prospects % | Overall score |
|---|---|---|---|---|---|---|
| 1 Loughborough | 89.5 | 86.9 | 72 | 166 | 100 | 100 |
| 2 Sheffield | 90 | 89.2 | 71.8 | 173 | 89.4 | 97.8 |
| 3 Cardiff | 89.5 | 80.2 | 67.5 | 170 | 92.1 | 96.8 |
| 4 Cambridge | 80.5 | 73.1 | 74.8 | 202 | 88 | 96.3 |
| 5 Bath | 86.9 | 81 | 49.5 | 195 | 92.1 | 95.9 |
| 6 Edinburgh | 85.1 | 79.1 | 59 | 183 | 92.2 | 95.7 |
| 7 Liverpool | 90 | 85.6 | 55.2 | 153 | 88.6 | 93.6 |
| 8 Nottingham | 85.4 | 74.4 | 59 | 154 | 91.5 | 93 |
| 9 Strathclyde | 87.2 | 72 | 50.2 | 202 | 81.7 | 92.7 |
| 10 Queen's, Belfast | 90.1 | 79.9 | 36.5 | 147 | 96.3 | 92.5 |
| 11 Newcastle | 83 | 76 | 56 | 168 | 85.5 | 91.5 |
| 12 Manchester School of Architecture | 80.7 | 73.5 | 53.2 | 168 | 88.5 | 91.3 |
| =13 Liverpool John Moores | 88.8 | 86.3 | 38.2 | 148 | 89.8 | 91.2 |
| =13 University College London | 82.5 | 68 | 61 | 177 | 82.8 | 91.2 |

| | | | | | | |
|---|---|---|---|---|---|---|
| **15** University of the Arts London | 76.3 | 72.5 | 46 | 159 | 91.2 | 89.5 |
| **16** Coventry | 84.6 | 81.9 | 54.2 | 111 | 88 | 88.9 |
| **=17** Oxford Brookes | 86.3 | 77.9 | 33.2 | 136 | 91.3 | 88.8 |
| **=17** Sheffield Hallam | 86.9 | 76.6 | 43.2 | 117 | 91.2 | 88.8 |
| **19** Robert Gordon | 88.9 | 82.5 | 14 | 159 | 89.5 | 88.5 |
| **20** Plymouth | 87.1 | 76.3 | 49 | 117 | 87.3 | 88.4 |
| **=21** University for the Creative Arts | 90.1 | 88.6 | 41.2 | 128 | 81.1 | 88.2 |
| **=21** Kent | 78.5 | 74.2 | 61 | 135 | 83.7 | 88.2 |
| **23** Ulster | 85.7 | 78.8 | 54.2 | 129 | 81.1 | 88.1 |
| **24** Nottingham Trent | 90.7 | 85.5 | 38 | 119 | 84.5 | 88 |
| **25** West of England | 85.3 | 78.2 | 40.8 | 152 | 80.9 | 87.8 |
| **26** Birmingham City | 88 | 78.8 | 31.2 | 136 | 85.7 | 87.4 |
| **27** Reading | 79.8 | 71.2 | 53.5 | 131 | — | 87.3 |
| **28** Westminster | 89.9 | 84.6 | 38.2 | 130 | 80.2 | 87.2 |
| **29** Dundee | 83.5 | 59.6 | — | 179 | 97 | 87 |
| **30** Greenwich | 86.7 | 78.6 | 30 | 125 | 87.1 | 86.6 |
| **31** Northumbria | 88.2 | 81.7 | 25 | 141 | 82.5 | 86.3 |
| **32** Kingston | 82.4 | 75.4 | 63 | 128 | 73.6 | 85.9 |
| **33** Salford | 74.8 | 73.4 | 43.5 | 127 | 87.5 | 85.6 |
| **34** London South Bank | 83.5 | 66.2 | 35 | 115 | 85.7 | 84.3 |
| **35** Leeds Beckett | 81.1 | 70.1 | 24.5 | 106 | 92.5 | 84.1 |
| **36** Edinburgh Napier | 71.1 | 71.2 | 38 | 140 | 83.1 | 83.6 |
| **37** Brighton | 63.6 | 67.2 | 53 | 118 | 87.1 | 83.1 |
| **=38** East London | 88 | 83.7 | 25 | 103 | 78.8 | 82.7 |
| **=38** Wolverhampton | 90.5 | 79.2 | 20 | 100 | — | 82.7 |
| **=40** De Montfort | 77.4 | 69.2 | 40.5 | 105 | 80 | 81.7 |
| **=40** Portsmouth | 79.3 | 71.9 | 41.8 | 115 | 75 | 81.7 |
| **42** Huddersfield | 83.3 | 67.3 | 36.5 | 127 | 71.8 | 81.4 |
| **43** Anglia Ruskin | 81.4 | 77.8 | 23.8 | 103 | — | 80.8 |
| **44** Hertfordshire | 80.2 | 73.4 | 24.2 | 99 | 79.2* | 79.9 |
| **45** Lincoln | 60.1 | 59.9 | 12.2 | 115 | 94.1 | 78.3 |
| **=46** Arts University, Bournemouth | 79.7 | 68.7 | 23 | 121 | 70.4 | 78.2 |
| **=46** Derby | 78.6 | 65.8 | — | 106 | 86.3* | 78.2 |
| **48** London Metropolitan | 82.9 | 69.4 | — | 117 | 68.3 | 75.1 |

| | | | | |
|---|---|---|---|---|
| Employed in high-skilled job | 67% | Employed in lower-skilled job | | 9% |
| Employed in high-skilled job and studying | 5% | Employed in lower-skilled job and studying | | 0% |
| Studying | 5% | Unemployed | | 8% |
| High-skilled work (median) salary | £23,000 | Low-/medium-skilled salary | | £20,000 |

## Art and Design

Oxford remains at the top of the Art and Design table for the fourth year running, its ranking boosted by results of the latest Research Excellence Framework 2021, which put it comfortably in front of all other universities in the table. Behind Oxford on research quality is Westminster, which sits 38th overall. Oxford also attracts by far the highest entry standards, with entrants averaging a staggering 248 UCAS points – among the highest tariff scores of any subject table in our *Guide*. Newcastle (which topped the table four years ago) and Glasgow also averaged over 200 UCAS points. At the other end of the scale only two universities (Bedfordshire and East London) have entry standards below 100 tariff points, on average.

Most art and design courses are at the post-1992 universities and/or the specialist arts institutions, but the older universities dominate the top 10 of our table due largely to their higher entry standards – although most artists would argue that entry grades are less significant than in other subjects. Selection rests primarily on the quality of candidates' portfolios and many undergraduates enter via a one-year Art Foundation course. Even the research-led Russell Group of universities do not require any essential A-levels, although they do advise that art and design subjects are preferred. Several renowned art schools are now part of the Russell Group and other high-tariff universities: such as the Ruskin School of Art (Oxford), Slade School of Fine Art (at this year's runner-up University College London) and the Duncan Jordanstone College of Art and Design (Dundee). Fine art has long been a strength at Newcastle, in fifth place.

In sixth place, Kingston is the highest-ranked modern university while Falmouth, at 36th, places the highest of the six specialist institutions, just ahead of Arts London (37th). Bangor leads for student satisfaction with teaching quality and comes second for students' evaluation of the wider experience. Otherwise, our National Student Survey (NSS) analysis found modern universities to have the edge over their older peers for satisfaction rates, with Suffolk top for the broad student experience and Canterbury Christ Church third for both NSS-derived measures. Art and design are among the biggest recruiters in higher education, with more than 126,300 applications in 2023 and over 23,600 new students starting courses. Design studies is much the largest area while fine art – though it accounts for a far smaller proportion of students – still attracted nearly 4,400 new starters in 2023. The subjects usually feature in the lower reaches of employment tables, though there are 11 subject areas below them in our latest ranking of 70. For salaries the subjects are =61st, based on average early career incomes of £24,000. The trend for graduates to not necessarily proceed straight into high-skilled jobs tends not to be a surprise to artists and designers, who accept they may have a period in low-paid self-employment early in their career. Based on the latest Graduate Outcomes survey, Winchester (70th overall) is top, followed by Loughborough (third) and University College London – which each had at least 80% of graduates already in professional jobs or further study 15 months after their degrees.

| Art and Design | Teaching quality % | Student experience % | Research quality % | Entry standards (UCAS points) | Graduate prospects % | Overall score |
|---|---|---|---|---|---|---|
| 1 Oxford | 81.5 | 74.6 | 88.8 | 248 | — | 100 |
| 2 University College London | 89.1 | 84.2 | 64.7 | 194 | 80.8 | 96.7 |
| 3 Loughborough | 87.4 | 84 | 51.7 | 174 | 81.2 | 93.7 |
| 4 Goldsmiths, London | 90 | 85.6 | 57.5 | 179 | 72.9 | 93.2 |
| 5 Newcastle | 87.7 | 81.2 | 61 | 212 | 62.7 | 92.1 |
| 6 Kingston | 86.1 | 77.6 | 63 | 171 | 69.2 | 90.5 |
| 7 Lancaster | 80.1 | 78 | 59.5 | 156 | 78.0* | 90 |
| 8 Leeds | 80.6 | 77.1 | 54.8 | 165 | 76 | 89.7 |
| =9 Manchester | 83.8 | 82.9 | 63 | 157 | 68.4 | 89.3 |
| =9 Reading | 85.9 | 82.7 | 51.8 | 132 | 77.3 | 89.3 |
| 11 Dundee | 84.4 | 76.6 | 57.2 | 180 | 66 | 89.1 |
| 12 Sunderland | 89.5 | 82.4 | 49.8 | 121 | 76.2 | 88.9 |
| =13 Northumbria | 86.9 | 79.2 | 45.8 | 149 | 73.7 | 88.7 |
| =13 Bournemouth | 92.1 | 88.2 | 38.5 | 108 | 78.7 | 88.7 |

| | | | | | | |
|---|---|---|---|---|---|---|
| =15 | Bangor | 96.6 | 92.6 | 40.2 | 127 | 66.7 | 88.5 |
| =15 | Nottingham Trent | 85.1 | 81.8 | 53 | 141 | 72.5 | 88.5 |
| =15 | Glasgow | 70.5 | 62.3 | 68.8 | 209 | — | 88.5 |
| 18 | Manchester Metropolitan | 82.3 | 77.4 | 51.7 | 155 | 72.7 | 88.2 |
| 19 | Southampton | 86.4 | 77 | 56.5 | 149 | 67.8 | 88 |
| 20 | Edinburgh Napier | 86.5 | 77 | 23.5 | 177 | 73 | 87.8 |
| 21 | Coventry | 85.4 | 78.6 | 54.2 | 127 | 72.7 | 87.5 |
| =22 | Robert Gordon | 91.9 | 83.9 | 13.8 | 166 | 70.1 | 87.2 |
| =22 | Sheffield Hallam | 87.9 | 82.9 | 57 | 122 | 67.9 | 87.2 |
| =24 | Staffordshire | 89.2 | 81.7 | 53.5 | 130 | 65.8 | 87 |
| =24 | Cardiff Metropolitan | 84.4 | 75.9 | 56.2 | 132 | 70.8 | 87 |
| 26 | Canterbury Christ Church | 96.3 | 90.5 | 38 | 104 | — | 86.8 |
| 27 | Teesside | 92.3 | 82.9 | 49.2 | 116 | 63.2 | 85.8 |
| 28 | Edinburgh | 80.7 | 72.5 | 54 | 172 | 61.5 | 85.7 |
| 29 | Central Lancashire | 92.8 | 87.2 | 35.2 | 126 | 63.3 | 85.6 |
| =30 | Ulster | 83.7 | 75.3 | 54.5 | 127 | 67.9 | 85.5 |
| =30 | Aberystwyth | 89.8 | 79 | 41 | 138 | 63.9 | 85.5 |
| =32 | Portsmouth | 85.5 | 77.8 | 41.8 | 121 | 71.8 | 85.4 |
| =32 | Lincoln | 90.1 | 81.6 | 43.8 | 126 | 63.8 | 85.4 |
| =32 | Glasgow Caledonian | 84.8 | 80.1 | 13.8 | 177 | 68.3 | 85.4 |
| 35 | Falmouth | 85.5 | 79.4 | 48.8 | 143 | 62 | 85.2 |
| 36 | University of the Arts London | 80.9 | 74.7 | 46 | 154 | 65.5 | 85 |
| 37 | West of England | 85.1 | 77.9 | 36 | 152 | 63.9 | 84.8 |
| 38 | Westminster | 80 | 75.9 | 75.5 | 142 | 55 | 84.5 |
| 39 | Liverpool John Moores | 80.1 | 74.2 | 38.2 | 178 | 61 | 84.4 |
| 40 | De Montfort | 86.5 | 81.1 | 32 | 125 | 68.3 | 84.3 |
| 41 | Gloucestershire | 82.9 | 73.4 | 45 | 125 | 67.4 | 83.9 |
| =42 | Norwich University of the Arts | 83.6 | 78.8 | 38.8 | 133 | 63.8 | 83.5 |
| =42 | South Wales | 90 | 83.1 | 35.8 | 121 | 60.8 | 83.5 |
| =44 | Buckinghamshire New | 90.2 | 81.4 | 41.2 | 115 | 60.1 | 83.4 |
| =44 | Middlesex | 85.2 | 81.5 | 41.2 | 115 | 64.8 | 83.4 |
| 46 | Suffolk | 96.5 | 94.9 | — | 122 | 63.3 | 83.2 |
| =47 | Oxford Brookes | 88.1 | 76.2 | 25.5 | 128 | 64.7 | 82.8 |
| =47 | Worcester | 82.4 | 76.3 | 19.2 | 117 | 75.2 | 82.8 |
| 49 | Huddersfield | 82.4 | 75.1 | 30.8 | 127 | 68.3 | 82.7 |
| =50 | Greenwich | 77 | 66.7 | 30 | 124 | 76.9 | 82.6 |
| =50 | London Metropolitan | 86.3 | 79.1 | 42.2 | 121 | 59.5 | 82.6 |
| =52 | Brighton | 76.1 | 68.6 | 53 | 143 | 62.6 | 82.5 |
| =52 | Abertay | 82.5 | 73.7 | — | 154 | 73.3 | 82.5 |
| =52 | Heriot-Watt | 79.6 | 68 | 34.2 | 166 | 61.2 | 82.5 |
| 55 | Birmingham City | 85.3 | 80.8 | 31.2 | 130 | 60.9 | 82.3 |
| 56 | Leeds Beckett | 83.5 | 78.4 | 29.2 | 110 | 67.3 | 81.8 |
| 57 | York St John | 83.2 | 76.3 | 5.8 | 118 | 75.6 | 81.7 |
| 58 | University for the Creative Arts | 83.3 | 73.4 | 41.2 | 140 | 56 | 81.6 |
| 59 | Wales Trinity St David | 86.2 | 74.2 | 20.8 | 155 | 56.9 | 81.5 |
| =60 | Plymouth | 77 | 70.3 | 26.5 | 128 | 70.4 | 81.1 |
| =60 | Salford | 87.4 | 81.2 | — | 136 | 64.9 | 81.1 |
| 62 | Arts University, Bournemouth | 82.2 | 77.6 | 23 | 150 | 57.7 | 80.9 |

| | Teaching quality % | Student experience % | Research quality % | Entry standards (UCAS points) | Graduate prospects % | Overall score |
|---|---|---|---|---|---|---|
| **63** Northampton | 88.9 | 83.3 | 12.2 | 115 | 61.7 | 80.6 |
| **64** Wolverhampton | 83.3 | 76.6 | 35.2 | 115 | 59.5 | 80.5 |
| **65** Leeds Arts | 82.5 | 78.6 | 6.2 | 154 | 59.1 | 79.9 |
| **66** Chester | 81.1 | 73.6 | 26.2 | 125 | 61.1 | 79.8 |
| **67** Bolton | 87 | 75.9 | 17.8 | 116 | 59.8 | 79.6 |
| **68** Liverpool Hope | 88.4 | 85 | 12.5 | 131 | 53.2 | 79.5 |
| **69** Derby | 81.2 | 70.4 | 19.5 | 120 | 64.8 | 79.4 |
| **70** Winchester | 75.4 | 65.4 | — | 112 | 81.5 | 79.3 |
| **71** London South Bank | 83.6 | 74.1 | — | 107 | 70.6 | 79 |
| **72** Wrexham | 86.7 | 80.8 | 3.2 | 130 | 56.9 | 78.7 |
| **=73** East London | 90.1 | 85.7 | 14.8 | 91 | 55.2 | 78.1 |
| **=73** Bath Spa | 77.8 | 68.1 | 18.5 | 127 | 62.3 | 78.1 |
| **75** Cumbria | 71.1 | 64.2 | 23.2 | 135 | 65.8 | 78 |
| **76** Anglia Ruskin | 76 | 67 | 31.2 | 121 | 57.3 | 77.1 |
| **77** Hertfordshire | 82 | 72.4 | 24.2 | 112 | 51.6 | 76.3 |
| **=78** Bedfordshire | 79.7 | 70.3 | — | 89 | 68 | 75.7 |
| **=78** West London | 77.3 | 65.5 | — | 113 | 65.8 | 75.7 |
| **=80** Chichester | 79.2 | 70.3 | — | 134 | 54.2* | 75 |
| **=80** Solent, Southampton | 81.6 | 74 | — | 106 | 57.6 | 75 |
| **82** Kent | 80.2 | 71.6 | — | 119 | 55.9 | 74.8 |

| | | | |
|---|---|---|---|
| Employed in high-skilled job | 50% | Employed in lower-skilled job | 30% |
| Employed in high-skilled job and studying | 2% | Employed in lower-skilled job and studying | 1% |
| Studying | 3% | Unemployed | 8% |
| High-skilled work (median) salary | £24,000 | Low-/medium-skilled salary | £20,000 |

# Bioengineering and Biomedical Engineering

Dundee takes the lead in our dedicated Bioengineering and Biomedical Engineering table, now in its fourth year of publication and extending to 23 universities this year, nine more than last year. Dundee's win is based on strong performance across the table's metrics, without coming top in any individually. The highest entry standards are at Strathclyde (eighth overall), while runner-up Imperial achieved the best results in the subjects in the latest Research Excellence Framework 2021.

Ageing populations, the demand for new treatments for chronic conditions and the need to respond rapidly to evolving disease challenges have brought about growth in biomedical engineering and bioengineering among universities worldwide over the past two decades. The discipline collectively involves a range of engineering and scientific skills, including some of the newest areas of science in genomics imaging and computing to meet those challenges. "We apply maths and physics in context, bringing everything together in a practical way. We measure human signals to better understand the body, focusing on preventing and curing diseases, healthy ageing, and enhancing human potential," says Dr Markus Pakleppa, senior lecturer in biomedical engineering, School of Science and Engineering, University of Dundee.

For student satisfaction with both teaching quality and the wider experience Reading does best, followed by Sheffield and King's College London respectively. At the opposite end of the scale, students at Aston expressed much lower rates of satisfaction in our latest National Student Survey analysis, and the university comes bottom for the wider experience and second-from-bottom for teaching quality, only Queen Mary London fares more poorly. In 12th place Nottingham Trent is the highest-ranked post-1992 university.

Graduate bioengineers may go on to develop prosthetics and biomedical implants, 3D medical imaging or image-guided and robot-assisted surgery – among a range of career pathways. Some biomedical graduates apply for places on the Graduate Entry into Medicine programmes. There is insufficient employment data so far for seven out of the 23 universities in our table, of which Imperial stands out for achieving the highest rate (98.1%) of graduates in high-skilled work or further study 15 months on from their degrees, closely followed by Aston and Reading (both 96%). In our graduate prospects ranking of 70 subject areas, bioengineering and biomedical engineering sit 18th. Full-time further study accounts for a sizeable proportion (15.4%) of the 77.3% of graduates who were in high-skilled jobs and/or studying 15 months on from their degrees. The subjects rank 20th for starting salaries.

| Bioengineering and Biomedical Engineering | Teaching quality % | Student experience % | Research quality % | Entry standards (UCAS points) | Graduate prospects % | Overall score |
|---|---|---|---|---|---|---|
| 1 Dundee | 81.7 | 77.5 | 78 | 194 | — | 100 |
| 2 Imperial College | 76.3 | 72.7 | 81 | 198 | 98.1 | 99 |
| 3 Oxford | 80.8 | 76.1 | 69.5 | 216 | 94 | 98.9 |
| 4 Sheffield | 87.4 | 85.7 | 66.8 | 164 | 92 | 97.1 |
| 5 Leeds | 78.1 | 77 | 64.8 | 194 | — | 95.5 |
| 6 Reading | 93.5 | 96.9 | 54 | 123 | 96 | 95.4 |
| 7 Loughborough | 78.2 | 81.7 | 66.8 | 163 | 92.5 | 94.3 |
| 8 Strathclyde | 80.5 | 74.4 | 52.8 | 218 | 84.3 | 93.9 |
| 9 King's College London | 86.9 | 90.5 | 50 | 153 | 83.8 | 92.1 |
| 10 University College London | 74.4 | 72.7 | 64 | 164 | — | 90.6 |
| 11 Cardiff | 82.2 | 78.5 | 54 | 149 | — | 90.3 |
| 12 Nottingham Trent | 84.7 | 82 | 59 | 118 | 80.8 | 89.4 |
| 13 Ulster | 83.4 | 79 | 49.8 | 128 | 89.1 | 89.3 |
| 14 Surrey | 83.2 | 82 | 55.2 | 116 | — | 88.4 |
| 15 Essex | 85.5 | 83.4 | 42.5 | 135 | — | 88 |
| 16 Birmingham | 77.9 | 77 | 55 | 128 | — | 87 |
| 17 Queen Mary, London | 66.9 | 67.9 | 50.5 | 144 | 88.9 | 85.1 |
| 18 Swansea | 75.8 | 77.2 | 48.8 | 140 | 72.4* | 84.7 |
| 19 Aston | 72 | 54.5 | 46 | 127 | 96.0* | 84.5 |
| 20 Salford | 74 | 74.6 | 37 | 127 | 74.8 | 81.3 |
| 21 City | 77.8 | 79.7 | 32.5 | 114 | — | 80.4 |
| 22 Birmingham City | 80 | 75.3 | — | 114 | 65.2 | 73.5 |
| 23 Bradford | 78.9 | 79.8 | — | 125 | 57.1 | 72.9 |

| | | | | |
|---|---|---|---|---|
| Employed in high-skilled job | 58% | Employed in lower-skilled job | | 10% |
| Employed in high-skilled job and studying | 4% | Employed in lower-skilled job and studying | | 0% |
| Studying | 15% | Unemployed | | 5% |
| High-skilled work (median) salary | £28,000 | Low-/medium-skilled salary | | £22,000 |

# Biological Sciences

For the 20th year, Cambridge tops the Biological Sciences table, its tenure strengthened once more by fiercely high entry standards – with new undergraduates averaging 222 UCAS tariff points. Cambridge also boasts the best graduate prospects and second-highest research quality rating. But based on the outcomes of the Research Excellence Framework 2021, it is Dundee that tops all 94 universities in our table for its strength in biological sciences research, while tying with Edinburgh overall in fourth place. Performing strongly across all measures, Oxford is in second position for the third year running, while St Andrews moves up seven places into third position.

The upper reaches of our table are dominated by universities with old foundations across the UK. In 17th place, Leeds Beckett is the top-ranked modern university, while Ulster in Northern Ireland (29th overall) claims rates of employment second only to Cambridge – with 91.3% of its biological sciences graduates in high-skilled jobs and/or further study 15 months on from their degrees. The post-1992 universities do best on rates of student satisfaction: Canterbury Christ Church is top for the wider experience, followed by Leeds Beckett, and the same universities swap places for students' evaluation of teaching quality, both measures derived from the National Student Survey.

"This is a broad degree that unlocks the mysteries of all living things, from microbes and plants to animals and humans. It offers a solid foundation on the living world and essential skills sought by employers in addition to exploring areas of biology that interest you," notes Dr Tara Pirie, lecturer in ecology and conservation, School of Biosciences, University of Surrey.

Nearly one in five (19.1%) of biological sciences graduates were engaged in further study 15 months after the undergraduate degrees, according to the most recent Graduate Outcomes survey, while 39.1% were in high-skilled jobs and 4% were combining work with studying – placing the biological sciences in the lower half (44th) of our 70-subject employment index. For starting salaries, they place =46th.

Of the specialisms within the grouping, biology is the most popular – with applications over 24,700 and nearly 3,900 new students in 2023 – slightly more than the year before and halting three prior consecutive years of declining demand. It is closely followed by molecular biology, biophysics and biochemistry, which had over 3,700 enrolments in the same admissions round, while zoology attracted almost 1,800 new students.

There has been growing interest in the study of ecology and environmental biology, although three years of increasing applications and enrolments came to an end in 2023's admissions cycle, when numbers dipped to just over 10,400 applications and just under 2,100 new student enrolments. Many of the leading universities will demand two sciences at A-level, or the equivalent – usually biology and chemistry – for any of the biological sciences.

| Biological Sciences | Teaching quality % | Student experience % | Research quality % | Entry standards (UCAS points) | Graduate prospects % | Overall score |
|---|---|---|---|---|---|---|
| 1 Cambridge | 86.9 | 81.2 | 73.5 | 222 | 94.3 | 100 |
| 2 Oxford | 83.1 | 69.8 | 69.5 | 197 | 89.4 | 94.8 |
| 3 St Andrews | 85.7 | 81.5 | 49.5 | 206 | 88.7 | 94.7 |
| =4 Dundee | 84.7 | 78.2 | 78 | 175 | 82.4 | 94.1 |
| =4 Edinburgh | 79.2 | 80.4 | 69.2 | 196 | 86.2 | 94.1 |
| 6 Durham | 89.2 | 82.1 | 44 | 180 | 89.6 | 93.5 |
| =7 Bristol | 85.3 | 85.4 | 67.2 | 164 | 83.2 | 93.2 |

| | | | | | | |
|---|---|---|---|---|---|---|
| =7 | Bath | 86.8 | 86.8 | 49.2 | 166 | 89.8 | 93.2 |
| 9 | Imperial College | 77.5 | 74 | 63.2 | 192 | 89.9 | 92.9 |
| =10 | Glasgow | 84 | 75.5 | 55.8 | 204 | 82.2 | 92.8 |
| =10 | Loughborough | 84.6 | 88.1 | 66.8 | 151 | 84.9 | 92.8 |
| 12 | York | 83.5 | 82.6 | 66 | 155 | 86.8 | 92.6 |
| =13 | Strathclyde | 80.3 | 74 | 65.8 | 210 | 78.8 | 92.5 |
| =13 | Sheffield | 84.7 | 82.7 | 70.2 | 154 | 82.9 | 92.5 |
| 15 | Queen's, Belfast | 81.1 | 82.8 | 69.2 | 146 | 87.4 | 92 |
| 16 | University College London | 77.9 | 81.5 | 64 | 180 | 84.6 | 91.9 |
| 17 | Leeds Beckett | 93 | 92.1 | 38 | — | 82.6* | 91.8 |
| 18 | Surrey | 87.7 | 86.4 | 58 | 131 | 83.3 | 90.8 |
| 19 | Lancaster | 86.3 | 86.1 | 59.1 | 150 | 75.6 | 90 |
| 20 | Manchester | 75.8 | 70.4 | 69.5 | 167 | 82.8 | 89.7 |
| 21 | Liverpool | 79.2 | 78.1 | 68.2 | 146 | 80.9 | 89.5 |
| 22 | Exeter | 82.5 | 81.6 | 60.5 | 159 | 75.3 | 89.3 |
| 23 | King's College London | 78.6 | 80.7 | 50 | 162 | 84.3 | 89.2 |
| =24 | Warwick | 82.5 | 80.1 | 46.5 | 157 | 82.4 | 88.9 |
| =24 | Aston | 86.9 | 85.4 | 46 | 114 | 87.1 | 88.9 |
| 26 | Cardiff | 78.1 | 76.4 | 53.5 | 150 | 86.6 | 88.8 |
| 27 | Birmingham | 79.9 | 79.5 | 57 | 150 | 81.1 | 88.7 |
| 28 | Aberdeen | 85.6 | 84.3 | 33.2 | 177 | 76.7 | 88.6 |
| 29 | Ulster | 80.9 | 80.8 | 53.5 | 109 | 91.3 | 88.5 |
| =30 | Stirling | 82.3 | 83.5 | 45.8 | 175 | 73.7 | 88.3 |
| =30 | Southampton | 78.3 | 79.7 | 53.5 | 145 | 84 | 88.3 |
| 32 | East Anglia | 83.6 | 81.4 | 56 | 127 | 80.1 | 88.1 |
| 33 | Leeds | 76.3 | 74.6 | 52 | 155 | 85.1 | 87.9 |
| 34 | Swansea | 85.3 | 81.8 | 64.2 | 131 | 70.3 | 87.6 |
| 35 | Queen Mary, London | 79.4 | 79.7 | 50.5 | 138 | 82.6 | 87.5 |
| 36 | Glasgow Caledonian | 85.9 | 81.1 | 61 | 151 | 65.4 | 87.4 |
| 37 | Reading | 88.1 | 83.9 | 54 | 120 | 72.6 | 87.2 |
| 38 | Leicester | 79.9 | 79.1 | 53.5 | 128 | 81.6 | 87.1 |
| 39 | Essex | 86.5 | 85.4 | 42.5 | 107 | 82.2 | 86.9 |
| 40 | Liverpool John Moores | 86.4 | 84.1 | 28.7 | 126 | 83.8 | 86.6 |
| 41 | Nottingham | 78.4 | 75.8 | 50.2 | 139 | 80.5 | 86.4 |
| 42 | Aberystwyth | 88.2 | 87.3 | 48.8 | 117 | 70.4 | 86.3 |
| 43 | Gloucestershire | 91.3 | 87.9 | 25.8 | 103 | 82.4 | 86.2 |
| 44 | Portsmouth | 84.9 | 80.2 | 41.2 | 109 | 82.2 | 86 |
| 45 | Northumbria | 75.4 | 76.9 | 53.5 | 134 | 80.1 | 85.7 |
| 46 | Newcastle | 75.1 | 77.1 | 58.8 | 140 | 75.3 | 85.6 |
| 47 | Bangor | 77.5 | 70.8 | 67.5 | 114 | 77.5* | 85.4 |
| =48 | Plymouth | 83.3 | 78.9 | 42.9 | 130 | 75 | 85.3 |
| =48 | Manchester Metropolitan | 84.7 | 85.6 | 44.8 | 121 | 71.9 | 85.3 |
| =50 | St George's, London | 72.6 | 65.6 | 50.2 | 141 | 85.7 | 85.2 |
| =50 | Sussex | 78.8 | 77.6 | 49.8 | 145 | 72.3 | 85.2 |
| =50 | Abertay | 87.2 | 81.5 | — | 142 | 88.2 | 85.2 |
| =53 | Royal Holloway | 77.2 | 79 | 43.5 | 123 | 82.4 | 85 |
| =53 | Kent | 82.6 | 77.5 | 50 | 121 | 73.9 | 85 |
| =55 | West of England | 88.7 | 87.6 | 42.8 | 114 | 67.3 | 84.8 |

**Biological Sciences** cont.

| | | Teaching quality % | Student experience % | Research quality % | Entry standards (UCAS points) | Graduate prospects % | Overall score |
|---|---|---|---|---|---|---|---|
| =55 | Keele | 79.5 | 80.3 | 39.2 | 122 | 80.5 | 84.8 |
| 57 | Oxford Brookes | 82.6 | 82.3 | 39.5 | 115 | 77 | 84.6 |
| 58 | Heriot-Watt | 76 | 73.8 | 32.8 | 164 | 77.5 | 84.4 |
| 59 | Coventry | 85.6 | 79 | 47.2 | 81 | 77.7 | 83.9 |
| 60 | Brighton | 85.5 | 78.6 | 50.5 | 100 | 68.3 | 83.4 |
| 61 | Nottingham Trent | 87 | 80.9 | 43.5 | 116 | 63.8 | 83.1 |
| 62 | Staffordshire | 83.9 | 63.2 | 30.8 | — | 80 | 82.9 |
| =63 | Salford | 85.1 | 79.4 | 37 | 124 | 66.3 | 82.8 |
| =63 | Hull | 82.8 | 78.4 | 42 | 115 | 69.4 | 82.8 |
| =65 | Lincoln | 92.2 | 87.1 | — | 116 | 76.2 | 82.7 |
| =65 | Teesside | 78.2 | 71.9 | 35 | 105 | 83.3* | 82.7 |
| 67 | West of Scotland | 89.9 | 84.3 | 30.8 | 139 | 55.7 | 82.3 |
| 68 | Edinburgh Napier | 87 | 85.4 | — | 155 | 68.5 | 81.9 |
| 69 | Robert Gordon | 79.3 | 74 | — | 165 | 78.9 | 81.8 |
| 70 | Sheffield Hallam | 85.5 | 81.3 | 16.8 | 103 | 76.2 | 81.6 |
| 71 | Hertfordshire | 75.8 | 64.9 | 48 | 100 | 78.8 | 81.5 |
| =72 | Bournemouth | 84.3 | 81.3 | 29.2 | 102 | 69.7 | 81.3 |
| =72 | Royal Veterinary College | 84.4 | 83 | — | 122 | 79.1 | 81.3 |
| 74 | Anglia Ruskin | 92.3 | 87.9 | 33.8 | 93 | 56.5 | 81 |
| 75 | Kingston | 78.8 | 79.6 | 38.5 | 106 | 68.6 | 80.8 |
| 76 | Huddersfield | 76.6 | 74.8 | 24 | 119 | 76.8 | 80.7 |
| =77 | Liverpool Hope | 81.6 | 81 | — | 119 | 80.3* | 80.6 |
| =77 | Bedfordshire | 89.1 | 89.5 | — | 97 | 74.4* | 80.6 |
| 79 | Canterbury Christ Church | 92.4 | 92.3 | 9.5 | 72 | 70.8 | 80.5 |
| 80 | Edge Hill | 79.2 | 72.5 | 13.8 | 113 | 79 | 80 |
| 81 | Cardiff Metropolitan | 79.8 | 72.6 | — | 119 | 82.9 | 79.8 |
| 82 | Worcester | 81.9 | 78 | 7.8 | 104 | 75.8 | 79.3 |
| 83 | Derby | 79.7 | 77.7 | — | 110 | 80.5 | 79.2 |
| 84 | Bath Spa | 86.7 | 84.9 | — | 97 | 72.5 | 79.1 |
| 85 | Roehampton | 78.1 | 74.9 | 37.5 | 88 | — | 79 |
| 86 | Greenwich | 77.6 | 77.5 | — | 108 | 82.3 | 78.9 |
| 87 | Westminster | 78.5 | 80.3 | 36.8 | 110 | 58.9 | 78.7 |
| 88 | Brunel | 79.9 | 77.6 | — | 119 | 70.8 | 77.6 |
| 89 | Bradford | 78.7 | 81.3 | — | 114 | 70.2 | 77.3 |
| 90 | Cumbria | 85.2 | 75.6 | — | 119 | 59.2 | 76.1 |
| 91 | Wolverhampton | 81.9 | 72.2 | — | 106 | 56.7 | 73.6 |
| 92 | Chester | 63.1 | 67.3 | 6.2 | 113 | 72.6 | 73.1 |
| 93 | Northampton | 68.6 | 66.4 | 14 | 88 | 62.5 | 71.6 |
| 94 | South Wales | 77.4 | 55.2 | 16.2 | 105 | 51 | 71.4 |

| | | | |
|---|---|---|---|
| Employed in high-skilled job | 39% | Employed in lower-skilled job | 19% |
| Employed in high-skilled job and studying | 3% | Employed in lower-skilled job and studying | 1% |
| Studying | 19% | Unemployed | 6% |
| High-skilled work (median) salary | £26,000 | Low-/medium-skilled salary | £21,000 |

# Building

Building courses include surveying, construction, building services engineering and construction management. They have attracted growing numbers of new students, and in 2023 nearly 6,000 undergraduates were accepted onto degrees. Applicants may be drawn by the firm foundations offered by the subject's career prospects: building ranks ninth for the second consecutive year in our employment table, based on more than four in five graduates being employed in high-skilled jobs and/or furthering their studies within fifteen months of finishing their degrees. Rates of pay are also encouraging too, the £28,500 average annual incomes earned by building graduates tying the subject with civil engineering at =17th place in our salaries index. Degree apprenticeships, although not included in our table, offer an increasingly popular route into the construction industry.

Loughborough moves into the top spot of the Building table this year, from third place in our previous edition, boosted by the best graduate prospects – with almost all (98%) of graduates achieving the desired outcomes of a high-skilled job and/or further study within 15 months of finishing their degrees. Loughborough also leads for research, based on outcomes of the Research Excellence Framework 2021. Nottingham and Ulster are steady in second and fourth place respectively this year, as they were last year. Heriot Watt, which led the Building table's previous edition, slips to third place overall but still has the highest entry standards (158 UCAS points).

Students at the University of the West of England (UWE) were the most satisfied with their teaching quality, our National Student Survey analysis shows, followed by those at Nottingham, Robert Gordon and Nottingham Trent. For the wider experience, UWE and Nottingham claim the highest rates of student satisfaction again, with Liverpool John Moores and Nottingham Trent following them.

"You'll master the art and science of constructing buildings that make people happy and healthy, and, importantly, are inclusive and sustainable," says Dr Chaitali Basu, associate director of digital construction, University of the West of England.

| Building | Teaching quality % | Student experience % | Research quality % | Entry standards (UCAS points) | Graduate prospects % | Overall score |
|---|---|---|---|---|---|---|
| 1 Loughborough | 73.8 | 72.9 | 72 | 140 | 98.8 | 100 |
| 2 Nottingham | 86.7 | 85.5 | 59 | 133 | 87.5 | 99 |
| 3 Heriot-Watt | 75 | 72.9 | 59 | 158 | 89.6 | 98.3 |
| 4 Ulster | 81.7 | 81.2 | 54.2 | 142 | 87.4 | 97.8 |
| 5 Reading | 82.4 | 79.3 | 53.5 | 122 | 95.7 | 97.5 |
| 6 West of England | 86.8 | 87.2 | 40.8 | 119 | 92.9 | 96.8 |
| 7 University College London | 83.3 | 80.6 | 61 | — | 79.2 | 95.2 |
| =8 Liverpool John Moores | 81.7 | 84.1 | 28.7 | 133 | 90.6 | 94.8 |
| =8 Northumbria | 82.7 | 80.7 | 25 | 144 | 88 | 94.8 |
| 10 Robert Gordon | 86.6 | 78.6 | 14 | 131 | 95.5 | 94.6 |
| 11 Plymouth | 77 | 71.7 | 49 | 122 | 92 | 94.1 |
| 12 Edinburgh Napier | 79.1 | 75.8 | 38 | 139 | 85.7 | 93.8 |
| =13 Nottingham Trent | 84.3 | 81.3 | 38 | 110 | 90.7 | 93.7 |
| =13 Glasgow Caledonian | 74.9 | 75.1 | 30.2 | 151 | 87.5 | 93.7 |
| =13 Sheffield Hallam | 82.1 | 75.7 | 43.2 | 115 | 90.8 | 93.7 |
| 16 Salford | 76.5 | 77.1 | 43.5 | 122 | 90.7 | 93.5 |
| 17 Coventry | 83.8 | 76.1 | 23.5 | 112 | 95.8 | 92.8 |

| Building cont. | Teaching quality % | Student experience % | Research quality % | Entry standards (UCAS points) | Graduate prospects % | Overall score |
|---|---|---|---|---|---|---|
| **18** Oxford Brookes | 79.8 | 75.4 | 33.2 | 113 | 91.3 | 92 |
| **19** Aston | 77 | 76.3 | 35.2 | 125 | 83.3 | 90.9 |
| **20** Portsmouth | 79.4 | 74.5 | 21 | 111 | 93 | 90.5 |
| **21** Anglia Ruskin | 82 | 77.8 | 23.8 | 110 | 82.6 | 88.9 |
| **22** London South Bank | 69.3 | 66 | 35 | 126 | 83.3 | 88.2 |
| **23** Birmingham City | 82.8 | 78.3 | 34.8 | 118 | 70.1 | 88.1 |
| **24** Westminster | 74.4 | 76.8 | 38.2 | 121 | 74.2 | 87.9 |
| **25** Leeds Beckett | 75.7 | 73.6 | 24.5 | 104 | 86.5 | 87.5 |
| **26** Wolverhampton | 82.2 | 77.5 | 20 | 100 | — | 87.3 |
| **27** Brighton | 77.2 | 71.5 | 36.5 | 93 | 82.5 | 86.8 |
| **28** Central Lancashire | 81.2 | 75.8 | — | 126 | 79.4 | 86.6 |
| **29** Greenwich | 65.5 | 61.9 | 30 | 108 | 83.3 | 84.2 |
| **30** Kingston | 72.9 | 72.1 | 17.2 | 103 | 76.9 | 83.2 |
| **31** Derby | 68.9 | 68 | — | 102 | 83.3 | 81.4 |

| | | | |
|---|---|---|---|
| Employed in high-skilled job | 75% | Employed in lower-skilled job | 8% |
| Employed in high-skilled job and studying | 8% | Employed in lower-skilled job and studying | 0% |
| Studying | 0% | Unemployed | 4% |
| High-skilled work (median) salary | £29,000 | Low-/medium-skilled salary | £24,450 |

## Business, Management and Marketing

Warwick has returned to the top of our Business, Management and Marketing table this year, buoyed by strong performance across all measures – including high rates of student satisfaction – without leading on any individually. Warwick has swapped places with last year's No 1 and this year's runner-up, Oxford – which is still top for graduate prospects (almost all graduates (99.6%) were employed in high-skilled jobs or continuing their studies within 15 months) and attracts the highest entry standards (213 UCAS points). St Andrews, which previously ranked at No 1 for several years running, settles for fourth place on this occasion, and places fifth for both measures of student satisfaction derived from our National Student Survey analysis: teaching quality and the wider experience. The London School of Economics, in fifth place overall, achieved the best results in the REF 2021 and therefore tops our research quality rating, in which it is followed by City (=15th), Oxford and Manchester (11th). The universities that nailed the highest scores for satisfaction with teaching quality rank in the middle to lower reaches of the table overall. Buckinghamshire New (in 88th place overall) came top for this measure, followed by East London (=85th) and West London (=91st) – the same two London universities swap positions to take first and second place in our measure for student satisfaction with the wider experience.

The wide choice of institutions offering courses within our Business, Management and Marketing table reflects the popularity of the various branches of the subjects and ranks 118 universities this year. Demand in these fields has been growing recently, and in 2023's admissions cycle there were 64,485 applications to business and management degrees (the fourth consecutive increase and up from 61,380 in 2022) and 78,440 to business studies (an increase from 77,730). Management studies degrees (73,810 applications in 2023) and marketing courses (40,530) experienced small year-on-year dips in demand, but applications remained well above the years prior to 2022. The huge number of options means there should also be plenty of opportunities to secure a place through Clearing. Some of the most famous business schools are absent from this table because they only offer postgraduate qualifications such as MBAs, whereas our *Guide* details undergraduate provision.

But graduate prospects are the most closely correlated aspect of the business ranking to the complete result. Seven of the top 10 for this measure rank in the top 10 for business, management and marketing overall. Our analysis of graduate employment in high-skilled jobs or postgraduate study 15 months on from degrees showed that following Oxford are LSE (98.3%), Bath (92.1%) and Durham (91.8%). By contrast, Suffolk (118th overall) is at the foot of our employment ranking with 48.5% of graduates in high-skilled work or study after 15 months.

"There are more than 5.5 million private-sector businesses in the UK, which offer four out of five jobs, so it's no wonder that business and management graduates are in demand. A degree in these subjects provides knowledge and skills that are specific to core careers in important industries, such as banking, finance, consumer goods, accounting and consulting," says Juan López-Cotarelo, associate professor in the Organisation and Human Resource Management group, University of Warwick. As a subject area overall however, business, management and marketing manage only 48th place in our 70-subject table, but they compare more favourably in our earnings index (=28th).

| Business, Management and Marketing | Teaching quality % | Student experience % | Research quality % | Entry standards (UCAS points) | Graduate prospects % | Overall score |
|---|---|---|---|---|---|---|
| 1 Warwick | 86.9 | 88.1 | 65.2 | 192 | 89.5 | 100 |
| 2 Oxford | 79 | 75.7 | 66.2 | 213 | 98.2 | 99.6 |
| 3 Bath | 86 | 86.4 | 65.2 | 173 | 92.1 | 98.7 |
| 4 St Andrews | 89.3 | 87.2 | 48.2 | 198 | 85.8 | 98.4 |
| 5 London School of Economics | 81.9 | 80.2 | 69 | 177 | 96.4 | 98.3 |
| 6 Strathclyde | 85.1 | 83.9 | 52.5 | 204 | 84.2 | 97.5 |
| 7 King's College London | 78.3 | 80.9 | 63 | 191 | 90.9 | 96.7 |
| 8 University College London | 80.7 | 83.6 | 62.3 | 176 | 91.3 | 96.6 |
| 9 Exeter | 79.8 | 83.3 | 63.5 | 157 | 87.7 | 94.5 |
| 10 Loughborough | 80.8 | 86.6 | 49.2 | 155 | 90.3 | 93.9 |
| 11 Manchester | 78.7 | 79.5 | 66.2 | 161 | 84.1 | 93.7 |
| =12 Edinburgh | 72.6 | 76.1 | 59 | 186 | 88.4 | 93.4 |
| =12 Durham | 78.2 | 78.9 | 55.8 | 157 | 91.8 | 93.4 |
| 14 Liverpool | 82.7 | 83.9 | 58 | 142 | 85.5 | 93.3 |
| =15 Leeds | 76.9 | 81.7 | 62.3 | 156 | 84.1 | 92.7 |
| =15 City | 74.9 | 75 | 67.2 | 180 | 78.7 | 92.7 |
| =15 Aberdeen | 82.7 | 85.1 | 32.2 | 176 | 84.4 | 92.7 |
| =15 Lancaster | 81.3 | 81.5 | 59.2 | 144 | 84.1 | 92.7 |
| 19 Glasgow | 72.4 | 74.9 | 57.2 | 194 | 80.6 | 92.2 |
| 20 Surrey | 85.6 | 87.7 | 54.8 | 134 | 77.3 | 92.1 |
| 21 Bristol | 76.4 | 79.7 | 46 | 161 | 88.9 | 91.7 |
| 22 Southampton | 78.6 | 80.3 | 52 | 147 | 82.5 | 90.9 |
| 23 Birmingham | 74.5 | 77 | 55.2 | 148 | 88.2 | 90.8 |
| 24 Reading | 81.4 | 83 | 46.2 | 129 | 84.5 | 90.4 |
| 25 Heriot-Watt | 77.5 | 80.4 | 38.2 | 170 | 79.2 | 90.1 |
| 26 Ulster | 84.8 | 82.7 | 45.8 | 127 | 78.3 | 90 |

# Business, Management and Marketing cont.

| | Teaching quality % | Student experience % | Research quality % | Entry standards (UCAS points) | Graduate prospects % | Overall score |
|---|---|---|---|---|---|---|
| =27 Nottingham | 77.8 | 79.8 | 46.8 | 145 | 81.7 | 89.8 |
| =27 East Anglia | 80.5 | 80 | 57.8 | 132 | 75.5 | 89.8 |
| =27 Cardiff | 74.4 | 76.9 | 56 | 147 | 82.5 | 89.8 |
| 30 Aston | 80.4 | 81 | 43.5 | 130 | 83.8 | 89.6 |
| 31 Sheffield | 76.4 | 80.6 | 48.8 | 142 | 81.7 | 89.4 |
| =32 Sussex | 79.5 | 80.7 | 50.7 | 133 | 78.3 | 89.3 |
| =32 Stirling | 79 | 79.3 | 38.2 | 165 | 75.1 | 89.3 |
| 34 Newcastle | 76.4 | 80.9 | 40.5 | 146 | 83.4 | 89.2 |
| 35 Queen's, Belfast | 75.9 | 75.8 | 40.5 | 145 | 86.6 | 89 |
| 36 Dundee | 79.4 | 76.1 | 28.5 | 179 | 74.6 | 88.9 |
| 37 Manchester Metropolitan | 85.9 | 84.4 | 42.8 | 123 | 71.9 | 88.8 |
| 38 York | 74.9 | 74.4 | 50.5 | 144 | 81.9 | 88.7 |
| 39 Swansea | 82.3 | 81 | 38.8 | 133 | 77.4 | 88.6 |
| 40 Royal Holloway | 80.9 | 81.4 | 43 | 134 | 75.6 | 88.5 |
| 41 Robert Gordon | 88.6 | 85.9 | 19 | 158 | 65.9 | 88.4 |
| 42 Nottingham Trent | 85.5 | 84.6 | 34.2 | 124 | 75.2 | 88.3 |
| 43 Bangor | 84.3 | 80.6 | 32.2 | 126 | 78.5* | 88.1 |
| 44 Leicester | 78.3 | 81.8 | 45.8 | 126 | 75.4 | 87.6 |
| 45 Aberystwyth | 86.1 | 84.2 | 22.8 | 129 | 74.7 | 87.5 |
| =46 Central Lancashire | 87.5 | 85.1 | 28.2 | 121 | 68.8 | 86.9 |
| =46 Falmouth | 87 | 78.8 | 48.8 | 114 | 62.9 | 86.9 |
| =48 Northumbria | 79.1 | 78.5 | 28.2 | 135 | 79.3 | 86.8 |
| =48 Liverpool John Moores | 84.2 | 85.3 | 21 | 134 | 72.5 | 86.8 |
| =48 Edinburgh Napier | 80.6 | 80 | 20 | 148 | 76.1 | 86.8 |
| =48 Hull | 82.6 | 81.1 | 29.5 | 122 | 77.2 | 86.8 |
| =52 Chester | 85.2 | 79.8 | 25.2 | 123 | 75.4 | 86.7 |
| =52 Glasgow Caledonian | 82 | 83.1 | — | 176 | 73 | 86.7 |
| =52 Kent | 80.5 | 76.8 | 37.2 | 125 | 75.9 | 86.7 |
| 55 Queen Mary, London | 75.9 | 75.9 | 53.2 | 156 | 61.2 | 86.6 |
| 56 Portsmouth | 81.5 | 79.4 | 37.8 | 115 | 74.6 | 86.3 |
| 57 Plymouth | 81.1 | 80.8 | 28.7 | 120 | 76.4 | 86 |
| =58 Keele | 81.3 | 80.2 | 24.8 | 113 | 78.9 | 85.5 |
| =58 Lincoln | 81.3 | 80 | 25 | 117 | 77.4 | 85.5 |
| 60 West of England | 82.8 | 81.8 | 27.3 | 115 | 72.9 | 85.4 |
| 61 Oxford Brookes | 79.5 | 78.9 | 26 | 115 | 79.9 | 85.3 |
| =62 University of the Arts London | 76.3 | 73.1 | 46 | 140 | 64.6 | 85.1 |
| =62 Derby | 84.4 | 82.5 | 18 | 114 | 74.2 | 85.1 |
| 64 Coventry | 86.5 | 85.2 | 33.2 | 111 | 59.8 | 85 |
| =65 Edge Hill | 81.1 | 78.9 | 21 | 128 | 73.2 | 84.9 |
| =65 Bradford | 81.9 | 84.7 | 38.2 | 117 | 61.6 | 84.9 |
| =67 Gloucestershire | 85.1 | 81.9 | 8.8 | 116 | 76.6 | 84.7 |
| =67 Queen Margaret, Edinburgh | 82.3 | 77.5 | 7.5 | 145 | 72.4 | 84.7 |
| =67 Hertfordshire | 86.6 | 85.8 | 29 | 103 | 63.9 | 84.7 |
| 70 Worcester | 82.9 | 81.7 | 12.5 | 109 | 79.2 | 84.5 |

| | | | | | | |
|---|---|---|---|---|---|---|
| =71 | Brunel | 81.4 | 83 | 30.2 | 122 | 63.5 | 84.4 |
| =71 | Middlesex | 83.2 | 81.8 | 46.2 | 103 | 59.2 | 84.4 |
| =73 | Sheffield Hallam | 83.4 | 78.7 | 23.5 | 112 | 70.5 | 84.2 |
| =73 | Teesside | 77 | 70.8 | 49.2 | 111 | 69.7 | 84.2 |
| =75 | Wolverhampton | 88.7 | 85.8 | 20.2 | 97 | 65.2 | 84.1 |
| =75 | South Wales | 90.3 | 84.4 | 9 | 114 | 64.1 | 84.1 |
| 77 | Huddersfield | 84.3 | 83.2 | 23.2 | 123 | 60.4 | 84 |
| 78 | Essex | 80.6 | 83.7 | 39.8 | 110 | 58.5 | 83.6 |
| =79 | University for the Creative Arts | 76.6 | 71 | 41.2 | 119 | 67.9 | 83.5 |
| =79 | Cardiff Metropolitan | 81.4 | 77.7 | 14 | 111 | 76.6 | 83.5 |
| =79 | Salford | 82.2 | 80.5 | 24.8 | 122 | 62.5 | 83.5 |
| 82 | Canterbury Christ Church | 81.2 | 76.7 | 38 | 93 | 68.3 | 83.3 |
| =83 | Westminster | 79.6 | 81.5 | 37.5 | 118 | 56.4 | 83 |
| =83 | Bath Spa | 82.8 | 78.1 | 23.8 | 103 | 68.7 | 83 |
| =85 | East London | 91.5 | 89.5 | 11 | 108 | 53.1 | 82.9 |
| =85 | SOAS London | 71.5 | 64.2 | 44.2 | 137 | — | 82.9 |
| 87 | Brighton | 78.3 | 74.6 | 28.5 | 107 | 72.1 | 82.8 |
| 88 | Buckinghamshire New | 92.2 | 86.5 | — | 117 | 56.4 | 82.7 |
| =89 | Greenwich | 81.4 | 80.3 | 33.2 | 116 | 55.2 | 82.5 |
| =89 | Bournemouth | 73.9 | 73.5 | 23 | 111 | 79.5 | 82.5 |
| =91 | West London | 90.5 | 90.5 | — | 114 | 55.5 | 82.3 |
| =91 | Wales Trinity St David | 87.9 | 86 | — | 138 | 52.7 | 82.3 |
| =91 | London South Bank | 82.2 | 79.9 | 21.5 | 100 | 67.2 | 82.3 |
| =94 | Anglia Ruskin | 78.2 | 76.2 | 45.8 | 99 | 59.9 | 82.2 |
| =94 | West of Scotland | 81 | 73 | 10.5 | 131 | 67.4 | 82.2 |
| 96 | London Metropolitan | 84.3 | 78.7 | 22 | 100 | 63.3 | 82.1 |
| 97 | Birmingham City | 81.8 | 79.8 | 11.2 | 117 | 64.8 | 81.9 |
| 98 | Leeds Beckett | 80.6 | 78.1 | 8.2 | 105 | 74.6 | 81.8 |
| 99 | Roehampton | 83 | 82.7 | 32.8 | 100 | 53.5 | 81.7 |
| =100 | Liverpool Hope | 86.2 | 83.4 | — | 110 | 63.7 | 81.5 |
| =100 | Kingston | 79.3 | 78.2 | 24 | 110 | 62.6 | 81.5 |
| =100 | De Montfort | 81.1 | 80.6 | 19 | 97 | 66.5 | 81.5 |
| =103 | Solent, Southampton | 82.8 | 77.8 | — | 107 | 71.9 | 81.1 |
| =103 | Abertay | 79.4 | 77.7 | — | 138 | 64.4 | 81.1 |
| 105 | Chichester | 77.6 | 65.9 | 1.2 | 107 | 83.3 | 80.6 |
| 106 | Leeds Trinity | 84.8 | 81.4 | — | 99 | 64.7 | 80.3 |
| =107 | Goldsmiths, London | 71.7 | 66.8 | 29.7 | 127 | 63.5 | 80.1 |
| =107 | Sunderland | 88.2 | 86.8 | — | 104 | 52.8 | 80.1 |
| 109 | Cumbria | 81.9 | 77.5 | 7.8 | 108 | 61.5 | 80 |
| 110 | Winchester | 71.3 | 65.1 | 22.2 | 114 | 73.1 | 79.8 |
| 111 | Bolton | 84.8 | 79.5 | 0 | 111 | 57.7 | 79.7 |
| 112 | St Mary's, Twickenham | 77.7 | 78.3 | — | 98 | 73.8 | 79.6 |
| 113 | York St John | 74.1 | 67.8 | 9.8 | 101 | 78.7 | 79.5 |
| 114 | Northampton | 81.2 | 76.2 | 13.2 | 100 | 58.2 | 79.1 |
| 115 | Staffordshire | 70 | 62.2 | 38.8 | 109 | 60.9 | 78.5 |
| 116 | Bedfordshire | 77.2 | 73.2 | 22 | 100 | 52.9 | 77.7 |
| 117 | Royal Agricultural University | 65.6 | 65.3 | — | 113 | 70.2 | 75.2 |
| 118 | Suffolk | 76.4 | 57.6 | — | 108 | 48.5 | 73.1 |

| Employed in high-skilled job | 53% | Employed in lower-skilled job | 26% |
| Employed in high-skilled job and studying | 4% | Employed in lower-skilled job and studying | 1% |
| Studying | 3% | Unemployed | 7% |
| High-skilled work (median) salary | £27,000 | Low-/medium-skilled salary | £21,800 |

## Celtic Studies

Cardiff retains the No 1 spot in a table where each university's rank is unmoved this year compared with last. attracts the highest entry standards and has the strongest graduate prospects, along with the best results in the Research Excellence Framework 2021. The content of courses within this grouping caters largely to each university's host Celtic nation. Universities in Wales focus predominantly on degrees in Welsh history, culture and language, and those in Scotland and Ireland cover similar themes but with the focus on Gaelic, Scottish or Irish studies. The subject encompasses topics including history, mythology and folklore, modern literature, linguistics, and contemporary struggles for the revitalisation of languages such as Welsh, Scottish Gaelic and Irish. Most students become fluent in at least one of the languages. Students who opt for Celtic studies report high levels of student satisfaction at the majority of universities in our table, led by Cardiff, which does best for both measures derived from the National Student Survey (NSS): teaching quality and the wider experience. At the other end of the satisfaction scale is Glasgow, which places bottom for both NSS-derived metrics.

The subject area attracts a select group of students, and just 155 new undergraduates began Celtic studies degrees in 2023 – the most populated specialism being Welsh studies degrees which accounted for nearly a third of the year's intake. Small student numbers in the subject mean there is not always sufficient data to include every university that offers courses in our table, which has shrunk from six universities two years ago to just four. Cambridge, for instance, has topped our Celtic Studies table eight times in the past and still offers its Anglo-Saxon, Norse and Celtic degree, accepting around 25–30 undergraduates each year. But Cambridge did not have a tariff score in the data relevant to this year's *Guide*, hence its absence from our table.

Nevertheless, career prospects for those with a Celtic studies degree have tended to be positive. The subject ranks 31st in our employment ranking of 70 subject areas and places =32nd in our salaries index, based on average annual earnings of £26,500.

| Celtic Studies | Teaching quality % | Student experience % | Research quality % | Entry standards (UCAS points) | Graduate prospects % | Overall score |
|---|---|---|---|---|---|---|
| 1 Cardiff | 93 | 91.3 | 55.5 | 170 | — | 100 |
| 2 Swansea | 90.5 | 85.4 | 40.8 | 146 | — | 87 |
| 3 Queen's, Belfast | 90.5 | 89.6 | 37 | 148 | — | 86.5 |
| 4 Glasgow | 76 | 69.9 | 40.8 | — | 52.9 | 81.9 |

| Employed in high-skilled job | 35% | Employed in lower-skilled job | 17% |
| Employed in high-skilled job and studying | 13% | Employed in lower-skilled job and studying | 5% |
| Studying | 17% | Unemployed | 0% |
| High-skilled work (median) salary | £27,000 | Low-/medium-skilled salary | N/A |

# Chemical Engineering

Creating useful products from raw materials, chemical engineering combines natural sciences with life sciences, maths and economics. Dr Farnaz Mohsenpour, global head of chemical and process engineering, Heriot-Watt University explains: "Our chemical engineers are working on research that includes developing new materials to store carbon from the atmosphere and using waste from whisky distilling and other industries to produce green hydrogen, a type of sustainable fuel." Chemical engineering graduates are in demand; four in five were employed in high-skilled jobs and/or postgraduate study when surveyed 15 months on from their degrees – only 11 subjects do better in our employment ranking. Average early career salaries of £30,000 compare even more favourably, ranking =5th out of 70 subject areas.

Cambridge has extended its lead in our Chemical Engineering table, having last year toppled Oxford from No 1 by the narrowest of margins (0.1%) it is now ahead of this year's joint runners-up Oxford and Imperial by 2.9%. Cambridge claims the highest entry standards in the subject (222 UCAS tariff points, on average) and also leads for graduate prospects. Imperial is unbeaten for research quality, based on its results in the latest Research Excellence Framework in 2021. Chemical engineering students throughout the table tend to arrive with good grades; almost half of the universities have entry standards that equate to AAA or above at A-level (144 UCAS points). But less highly qualified applicants should not be put off as there are plenty of institutions with more accessible entry standards too, such as Swansea, which ranks 14th overall and averaged 128 UCAS points. Almost all Cambridge graduates in the subject were employed in high-skilled jobs or furthering their studies when surveyed 15 months on from their degrees, while even at the lowest end of the scale at Queen Mary, more than three-quarters of graduates had achieved the most desired outcomes.

The highest levels of student satisfaction with teaching quality were found at Sheffield, based on our latest National Student Survey analysis, followed by Portsmouth. For student evaluation of teaching quality, Bradford is top, followed by London South Bank and then Imperial.

Applicants will need maths, which is essential for chemical engineering degrees, and while chemistry or physics are required the leading universities will usually expect both. Most courses offer industry placements in the final year and lead to Chartered Engineer status. Applications and enrolments increased in 2023's admissions cycle, halting three years of declines, and over 2,400 students started courses.

| Chemical Engineering | Teaching quality % | Student experience % | Research quality % | Entry standards (UCAS points) | Graduate prospects % | Overall score |
|---|---|---|---|---|---|---|
| 1 Cambridge | 87.9 | 77.6 | 77.2 | 222 | 97.1 | 100 |
| =2 Oxford | 80.8 | 76.1 | 77.5 | 216 | 94 | 97.1 |
| =2 Imperial College | 89.7 | 89.8 | 81 | 203 | 86.8 | 97.1 |
| 4 Bath | 88.6 | 83.8 | 49.5 | 169 | 93.8 | 93.8 |
| 5 Nottingham | 87.5 | 83 | 59 | 161 | 92 | 93.4 |
| =6 Birmingham | 81.9 | 81.6 | 63.7 | 174 | 91.6 | 93.3 |
| =6 Edinburgh | 78.6 | 75.3 | 55.5 | 198 | 93.8 | 93.3 |
| 8 University College London | 76.8 | 75.9 | 70 | 176 | 91.4 | 92.5 |
| 9 Strathclyde | 81.2 | 77 | 52.8 | 209 | 88.8 | 92.4 |
| 10 Heriot-Watt | 89 | 85.5 | 55.5 | 168 | 86.1 | 91.8 |
| 11 Leeds | 75.9 | 71.5 | 64.8 | 165 | 93.6 | 91.6 |

## Chemical Engineering cont.

| | | Teaching quality % | Student experience % | Research quality % | Entry standards (UCAS points) | Graduate prospects % | Overall score |
|---|---|---|---|---|---|---|---|
| 12 | Sheffield | 82.3 | 84.3 | 66.8 | 148 | 84.9 | 90.1 |
| 13 | Loughborough | 77.8 | 80.6 | 46.5 | 146 | 92.7 | 89.6 |
| 14 | Swansea | 86.2 | 87.2 | 48.8 | 128 | 85.7 | 88.5 |
| 15 | Manchester | 73.6 | 75.1 | 63 | 167 | 84.2 | 88.1 |
| =16 | Newcastle | 76.5 | 72.3 | 58.5 | 132 | 88.3 | 87.5 |
| =16 | Surrey | 85.6 | 82.6 | 55.2 | 130 | 82.2 | 87.5 |
| 18 | Aston | 86 | 84.2 | 35.2 | 119 | 88.3 | 87.2 |
| 19 | Queen's, Belfast | 67.5 | 65.4 | 51 | 152 | 91.4 | 86.5 |
| 20 | Hull | 86.4 | 85.2 | 36.2 | 114 | 85.1 | 86.1 |
| =21 | Ulster | 76.2 | 74.7 | 49.8 | 133 | — | 85.7 |
| =21 | Brunel | 84.8 | 83.4 | 33 | 120 | — | 85.7 |
| 23 | Portsmouth | 88.5 | 89 | 21 | — | 80.8* | 84.6 |
| 24 | Queen Mary, London | 74.9 | 73 | 66 | 135 | 77.8 | 84.4 |
| =25 | Aberdeen | 65 | 67.1 | 35.8 | 185 | 85.4 | 84.2 |
| =25 | Bradford | 92.1 | 87.5 | 27 | 103 | 80.4 | 84.2 |
| 27 | Teesside | 80.4 | 80.4 | 18.8 | — | 85.7 | 83.6 |
| 28 | London South Bank | 90.5 | 86 | 27.3 | 100 | 79.4 | 83.2 |
| 29 | Huddersfield | 87.5 | 81.2 | 18.5 | 106 | — | 83.1 |
| 30 | Sheffield Hallam | 79 | 78.5 | 30 | 114 | 80.8 | 81.9 |
| 31 | Lancaster | 72.3 | 68.6 | 44.8 | 138 | 78.4 | 81.7 |
| 32 | Chester | 74.1 | 61.3 | 15.8 | 106 | 91.3 | 81.3 |
| 33 | Greenwich | 78.4 | 73.1 | 31.5 | 93 | — | 80.8 |

| | | | |
|---|---|---|---|
| Employed in high-skilled job | 68% | Employed in lower-skilled job | 8% |
| Employed in high-skilled job and studying | 4% | Employed in lower-skilled job and studying | 0% |
| Studying | 8% | Unemployed | 6% |
| High-skilled work (median) salary | £30,000 | Low-/medium-skilled salary | £23,000 |

# Chemistry

Entry standards are generally high to study chemistry, and 22 universities average over 144 UCAS tariff points (equivalent to AAA at A-level). They are led by Cambridge, which tops our table overall once again this year and where entrants arrived with 222 UCAS points on average. Bristol, in 13th place overall, pips Cambridge to first place for research, based on the results of the latest Research Excellence Framework 2021. In a table traditionally dominated by the older universities at its upper end, Northumbria is the top-ranked modern institution in 18th place, down from third last year and 10th the year before. In our new National Student Survey analysis, Central Lancashire (47th overall) is top for student satisfaction with teaching quality, followed by Plymouth (19th) and Lincoln (=30th). Aston (=27th overall) leads for students' evaluation of the wider experience, with Lincoln and Plymouth again in the top three as well. In contrast, chemistry students at De Montfort (52nd in the table) reported the lowest rates of satisfaction with the broad student experience and teaching quality.

Chemistry A-level, or equivalent qualification, is almost always a prerequisite and the leading universities will also look for maths and/or at least one other science – it is worth checking which second science individual institutions ask for, as these may differ. Courses include laboratory and experimentation work, alongside independent and group research projects and industry experience or placements. Dr Kate Nicholson, deputy head of applied sciences, Northumbria University, says studying chemistry "is the gateway to careers in healthcare, environment and food security, or driving future developments in sustainable technologies and materials."

Nearly a fifth of chemistry graduates (18.7%) had progressed to postgraduate study when surveyed 15 months after their degrees, the latest data shows, while more than half were working full-time in high-skilled jobs and 4.4% were combining study and jobs – which combine to rank chemistry 24th out of 70 subject areas for graduate prospects. The subject places in the top 25 for early career earnings too. Chemistry received 29,350 applications in 2023, returning demand to its former heights after declining numbers in the two years before, and over 5,200 new chemistry students were accepted onto courses – reflecting an uplift in new starters as well. Options for aspiring undergraduates are broad: with 124 universities and colleges offering courses in 2025–26.

| Chemistry | Teaching quality % | Student experience % | Research quality % | Entry standards (UCAS points) | Graduate prospects % | Overall score |
|---|---|---|---|---|---|---|
| 1 Cambridge | 86.9 | 81.2 | 80 | 222 | 94.3 | 100 |
| 2 St Andrews | 88.6 | 82.2 | 66.8 | 216 | 100 | 99.9 |
| 3 Oxford | 83.7 | 67.9 | 74 | 198 | 94.4 | 95.8 |
| 4 Imperial College | 83.2 | 84 | 75.5 | 198 | 85.4 | 94.8 |
| 5 York | 84.7 | 82.9 | 71 | 172 | 91.4 | 94.5 |
| 6 Strathclyde | 89.5 | 87.6 | 56.8 | 202 | 85 | 94.1 |
| 7 Edinburgh | 76.5 | 73 | 66.8 | 199 | 94.3 | 93.9 |
| 8 Liverpool | 83.3 | 82.7 | 72.8 | 146 | 93.7 | 93.4 |
| 9 Durham | 84.8 | 75.6 | 55 | 187 | 91.4 | 92.7 |
| 10 Bath | 82.8 | 85.1 | 64.5 | 162 | 89.8 | 92.3 |
| 11 Queen's, Belfast | 84.2 | 80.7 | 48.8 | 159 | 97.4 | 92.1 |
| 12 University College London | 78.4 | 80.5 | 76 | 173 | 83.7 | 91.5 |
| 13 Bristol | 79.1 | 73.8 | 80.5 | 159 | 86.1 | 91.4 |
| 14 Birmingham | 89.7 | 87.8 | 53.5 | 155 | 87.2 | 91.3 |
| 15 Glasgow | 78.9 | 70.4 | 55.5 | 200 | 85.7 | 90.2 |
| 16 Warwick | 78.8 | 73.7 | 63.2 | 157 | 90.2 | 90.1 |
| 17 Sheffield | 83.4 | 84.1 | 62.7 | 142 | 87 | 90 |
| 18 Northumbria | 78.1 | 77.4 | 53.5 | — | 94.1* | 89.8 |
| 19 Plymouth | 95 | 91 | 40.8 | 114 | 91.2 | 89.6 |
| 20 Southampton | 86.3 | 76.3 | 61.8 | 149 | 84.4 | 89.5 |
| 21 Leicester | 90.7 | 88.3 | 51.2 | 118 | 89 | 89.4 |
| 22 King's College London | 72.4 | 62.8 | 74.2 | 153 | 91 | 89.3 |
| 23 Manchester | 72.9 | 71.3 | 72.2 | 166 | 83.2 | 88.5 |
| 24 Loughborough | 90.2 | 85 | 34.8 | 142 | 87.9 | 88.1 |
| 25 Surrey | 89.3 | 84.1 | 55.2 | 134 | 80.8 | 88 |
| 26 Cardiff | 75.3 | 70.3 | 57.8 | 128 | 91.3 | 86.8 |
| =27 Aston | 93.2 | 93.2 | 35.2 | 116 | — | 86.7 |
| =27 Aberdeen | 81.5 | 80.7 | 39.5 | 181 | 80 | 86.7 |
| =27 Heriot-Watt | 87.6 | 83.4 | 32.8 | 169 | 80.7 | 86.7 |
| =30 Nottingham | 76.9 | 75.2 | 58.2 | 140 | 85 | 86.6 |

## Chemistry cont.

| | | Teaching quality % | Student experience % | Research quality % | Entry standards (UCAS points) | Graduate prospects % | Overall score |
|---|---|---|---|---|---|---|---|
| =30 | Lincoln | 94.2 | 91.9 | 42.2 | 113 | 80.9 | 86.6 |
| 32 | Swansea | 90.5 | 87.1 | 43 | 126 | 81.2 | 86.5 |
| =33 | Newcastle | 77.5 | 73.7 | 62.7 | 131 | 84.2 | 86.4 |
| =33 | Leeds | 77.2 | 75.5 | 50.2 | 151 | 85.3 | 86.4 |
| 35 | Queen Mary, London | 81.7 | 79.7 | 62.5 | 133 | 78.7 | 86.3 |
| 36 | East Anglia | 73.4 | 67.5 | 54 | 129 | 93.2 | 86.2 |
| 37 | Manchester Metropolitan | 87.7 | 84.2 | 45.5 | 122 | 82.4 | 86 |
| 38 | Keele | 87.6 | 85 | 48 | 115 | 82.2 | 85.9 |
| 39 | Sussex | 84.6 | 61.3 | 43.5 | 141 | 86 | 85.3 |
| 40 | Nottingham Trent | 86 | 79.7 | 59 | 111 | 78.1 | 85.2 |
| 41 | Lancaster | 87.3 | 79.5 | 30.2 | 134 | 82.1 | 84.2 |
| 42 | Hull | 89.6 | 84.2 | 35.2 | 110 | 81.2 | 83.9 |
| 43 | Greenwich | 83.7 | 80 | 32.8 | 122 | — | 82.6 |
| 44 | Kent | 82.9 | 80.5 | 40.2 | 107 | 79.7 | 82.3 |
| 45 | Huddersfield | 88.9 | 81.8 | 18.5 | 125 | 80.2 | 82.1 |
| 46 | Sheffield Hallam | 88.7 | 84.5 | — | 106 | 91.5 | 81.8 |
| 47 | Central Lancashire | 96.7 | 90.1 | — | 119 | 80 | 81.5 |
| 48 | Bradford | 84.8 | 79.1 | 25 | 106 | 76.0* | 79.4 |
| 49 | Kingston | 84 | 83.4 | 38.5 | 99 | 68.6 | 78.9 |
| 50 | Reading | 73 | 65.4 | 36 | 118 | 78.4 | 78.7 |
| 51 | Salford | 77.8 | 80.3 | 37 | 119 | 64.7 | 77.2 |
| 52 | De Montfort | 62.5 | 60.2 | — | 96 | 68.8 | 67 |

| | | | |
|---|---|---|---|
| Employed in high-skilled job | 51% | Employed in lower-skilled job | 11% |
| Employed in high-skilled job and studying | 4% | Employed in lower-skilled job and studying | 0% |
| Studying | 19% | Unemployed | 6% |
| High-skilled work (median) salary | £27,000 | Low-/medium-skilled salary | £20,000 |

# Civil Engineering

Leading a shake-up of the top 10 of our Civil Engineering table, Cambridge has swapped places with Oxford to take the No 1 spot, from third place last year. Cambridge's lead returns it to the position it held for 16 years until three years ago, and its civil engineering students average an eyewatering 227 UCAS tariff points – the highest entry standards. Runner-up Imperial occupies the same position this year as last and has a peerless research quality rating, based on the results of the Research Excellence Framework 2021.Strathclyde and Bath sit fourth jointly, while Bristol loses five places to rank ninth and University College London has fallen 11 places to 20th. While the older institutions dominate the upper end of our rankings, the highest rates of student satisfaction with teaching (as derived from our latest National Student Survey analysis) are found at modern university Hertfordshire (29th overall), while West London comes top for students' evaluations of the broader experience and ranks 42nd overall. Abertay, Nottingham and Sheffield also place in the top three for student satisfaction measures, while civil engineering students at Anglia Ruskin place the university bottom for satisfaction with the wider experience, a position Sheffield Hallam holds for teaching quality.

As the future brains behind the design, construction and maintenance of roads, bridges, pipelines, processing plants, buildings and harbours, civil engineering students learn how to apply physics, maths and mechanics to structural design. Professor Carlo Prato, head of the School of Civil Engineering, University of Leeds, notes that civil engineers are also "integral to the provision of everything from clean air and water to renewable energy and carbon reduction." As well as A-levels and Scottish Highers, BTEC qualifications are a popular means of entry into a civil engineering undergraduate degree, but applicants should check with individual universities as to their preferred entry requirements.

Some degrees in the subject are four year courses leading to an MEng; others are sandwich courses that include a work placement.

A regular among the top 10 subjects for graduate prospects, civil engineering ranks seventh this year. When surveyed 15 months on from their degrees, more than 85% of graduates were working in high-skilled jobs and/or furthering their studies. Promising average starting salaries of £28,500 put civil engineering =17th out of 70 subject areas for earnings. But a decrease in demand brought applications under 22,700 in 2023 and fewer than 3,900 undergraduates were accepted onto courses.

| Civil Engineering | Teaching quality % | Student experience % | Research quality % | Entry standards (UCAS points) | Graduate prospects % | Overall score |
|---|---|---|---|---|---|---|
| 1 Cambridge | 81.6 | 80.9 | 77.2 | 227 | 97.2 | 100 |
| 2 Imperial College | 81.5 | 82.4 | 81 | 192 | 100 | 98.8 |
| 3 Oxford | 80.8 | 76.1 | 77.5 | 216 | 94 | 97.7 |
| =4 Bath | 86.7 | 84.6 | 49.5 | 179 | 98 | 95.3 |
| =4 Strathclyde | 84.4 | 82.9 | 52.8 | 191 | 95.9 | 95.3 |
| 6 Sheffield | 90.6 | 87.5 | 66.8 | 157 | 92.2 | 95.2 |
| 7 Leeds | 86.8 | 85 | 64.8 | 178 | 91 | 95 |
| 8 Southampton | 88.2 | 84.5 | 70 | 160 | 91.2 | 94.7 |
| 9 Bristol | 83.3 | 79.9 | 68 | 182 | 91.2 | 94.4 |
| 10 Edinburgh | 77.3 | 76.1 | 55.5 | 184 | 100 | 94 |
| 11 Glasgow | 76.6 | 72.5 | 61.5 | 207 | 93.2 | 93.9 |
| 12 Dundee | 87.6 | 83.9 | 50.2 | 180 | 91.2 | 93.8 |
| 13 Nottingham | 90.8 | 90.5 | 59 | 143 | 89.7 | 93 |
| 14 Manchester | 79.5 | 74.6 | 63 | 154 | 96.9 | 92.3 |
| 15 Surrey | 81.7 | 83.4 | 55.2 | 129 | 100 | 91.8 |
| =16 Loughborough | 78.9 | 77.9 | 72 | 140 | 93.5 | 91.4 |
| =16 Liverpool | 84.2 | 82.8 | 57 | 140 | 93.1 | 91.4 |
| 18 Heriot-Watt | 78.5 | 74.3 | 55.5 | 167 | 94.2 | 91.3 |
| 19 Birmingham | 75.1 | 74.1 | 63.7 | 148 | 98.2 | 91.2 |
| 20 University College London | 74.7 | 73.4 | 70 | 163 | 91.3 | 90.8 |
| 21 Queen's, Belfast | 78.6 | 69.3 | 51 | 149 | 98.7 | 90.5 |
| =22 Cardiff | 81.3 | 82.3 | 54 | 143 | 92.6 | 90.4 |
| =22 Abertay | 89.6 | 90.7 | 24.2 | — | 92.9 | 90.4 |
| =24 Swansea | 83.2 | 82.4 | 48.8 | 141 | 92.5 | 90.1 |
| =24 Ulster | 84.6 | 81.8 | 49.8 | 131 | 93.6 | 90.1 |
| 26 Brighton | 83.2 | 89 | 36.5 | 121 | 96.3* | 89.1 |
| 27 Northumbria | 84.4 | 87.3 | 43 | 144 | 87.5 | 89 |
| 28 Newcastle | 76.1 | 73.3 | 58.5 | 131 | 93.5 | 88.4 |
| 29 Hertfordshire | 92.2 | 87.6 | 33 | 110 | — | 88.3 |

| | | Teaching quality % | Student experience % | Research quality % | Entry standards (UCAS points) | Graduate prospects % | Overall score |
|---|---|---|---|---|---|---|---|
| 30 | Aberdeen | 75.3 | 74.9 | 35.8 | 155 | 95.7 | 88.1 |
| 31 | Exeter | 78.1 | 72.9 | 47 | 145 | 91.4 | 87.9 |
| 32 | Edinburgh Napier | 83.8 | 82.8 | 22.8 | 132 | 93.1 | 87 |
| 33 | Birmingham City | 90.5 | 87.5 | 17.5 | 118 | 91.2 | 86.9 |
| 34 | Greenwich | 81.5 | 85.2 | 31.5 | 123 | 91.9 | 86.7 |
| 35 | Nottingham Trent | 80.9 | 78.2 | 38 | 121 | 90.6 | 86.1 |
| 36 | Central Lancashire | 84.7 | 82 | 23 | 128 | — | 85.6 |
| 37 | West of England | 77.6 | 72.3 | 30.8 | 130 | 93 | 85.3 |
| 38 | Glasgow Caledonian | 80.6 | 78.1 | 12.8 | 164 | 86.2 | 85.1 |
| 39 | Liverpool John Moores | 73.3 | 70.4 | 45.5 | 129 | 90.6 | 85 |
| 40 | West of Scotland | 81 | 77 | 16.5 | — | 91.3 | 84.6 |
| 41 | Aston | 74.2 | 74.2 | 35.2 | 138 | — | 84.2 |
| 42 | West London | 87.8 | 91.1 | 13.8 | 110 | 83.8 | 83.6 |
| =43 | City | 72.2 | 70.1 | 32.5 | 122 | 92.9 | 83.5 |
| =43 | Bradford | 83.3 | 82.8 | 27 | 115 | 83.3 | 83.5 |
| =43 | Portsmouth | 83.7 | 81.1 | 21 | 112 | 86.6 | 83.5 |
| =46 | Plymouth | 71 | 69.8 | 32.5 | 122 | 92 | 83 |
| =46 | Derby | 84.5 | 77.6 | 14 | 120 | — | 83 |
| 48 | Salford | 76.6 | 72.6 | 33.2 | 129 | 83.3 | 82.6 |
| 49 | Coventry | 76.7 | 69.9 | 23.5 | 118 | 88.9 | 82.2 |
| 50 | Wolverhampton | 83.8 | 75.7 | 18.2 | 92 | — | 80.6 |
| 51 | Brunel | 71.8 | 75.2 | 33 | 137 | 76.6 | 80.4 |
| 52 | Teesside | 71 | 67.9 | 18.8 | 116 | 88.5 | 79.9 |
| 53 | London South Bank | 79.2 | 72.9 | 27.3 | 123 | 73.8 | 79.5 |
| 54 | Leeds Beckett | 82.3 | 82.1 | 24.5 | 105 | 72.5 | 79.2 |
| =55 | Kingston | 81 | 76.8 | 17.2 | 113 | 74.1 | 78.6 |
| =55 | Bolton | 72.4 | 73.1 | 22 | 106 | — | 78.6 |
| 57 | East London | 88.7 | 88.3 | 21.2 | 104 | 64 | 78.3 |
| 58 | Sheffield Hallam | 64.8 | 53.6 | 30 | 128 | — | 77.3 |
| 59 | Anglia Ruskin | 66.4 | 50.9 | 23.8 | 119 | — | 75.7 |

| | | | |
|---|---|---|---|
| Employed in high-skilled job | 77% | Employed in lower-skilled job | 6% |
| Employed in high-skilled job and studying | 5% | Employed in lower-skilled job and studying | 1% |
| Studying | 4% | Unemployed | 4% |
| High-skilled work (median) salary | £28,800 | Low-/medium-skilled salary | £21,000 |

## Classics and Ancient History

St Andrews takes the lead in our new Classics and Ancient History table, ousting Oxford into second place after two years at the top. St Andrews' win is resounding: it is top for graduate prospects – with 96.5% of graduates engaged in high-skilled jobs and/or further study within 15 months of their degree, boasts peerless rates of student satisfaction with teaching quality and the wider experience, and also has the highest entry standards. After its 16-year reign at the top of the table came to an end three years ago, Cambridge sits fifth this year. For research quality in the subjects, Warwick ranks No 1, based on results of the latest Research Excellence Framework 2021, where it is closely followed by King's College London and Manchester, which tie in our analysis. After those at St Andrews, students at Birmingham and Swansea reported the second and third highest rates of satisfaction with teaching quality, while for the wider experience Swansea is followed by Leicester in the top three. Conversely, Manchester finishes bottom for each of these student-led measures. Independent schools dominate provision of Latin and Greek at A-level, producing some of the highest average grades of any subject (at more than half of the universities in our table entrants averaged over 144 UCAS points, equal to three As at A-level).

Classics takes in the broad literature, history and culture of Ancient Greek and Roman societies spanning 1,500 years, and can include architecture, religion and philosophy. Some courses will want Latin or Greek A-level, while others will allow students to learn the languages from scratch once they have enrolled. Several universities teach the subjects as part of modular courses, but not on their own. "Almost all classics departments welcome students with qualifications in any subject and make language study optional. Employers will love you; my former students run museums, civil service departments, schools, pop groups, theatres, banks, advertising agencies, and travel, data analysis and broadcasting companies. One is now an MP," says Professor Edith Hall, Department of Classics and Ancient History, University of Durham.

Classics and ancient history rank =56th in our new employment table of 70 subject areas, based on 56.1% of graduates working in high-skilled jobs and/or studying when surveyed 15 months after their degrees. Although not an ingredient of our subject ranking overall, in our pay index the subjects fare a little more strongly, placing =46th. The demand for classics courses continued an upward trend in 2023, when the subject attracted nearly 8,200 applications, while the numbers enrolling increased more modestly and just under 1,400 students were accepted onto degrees.

| Classics and Ancient History | Teaching quality % | Student experience % | Research quality % | Entry standards (UCAS points) | Graduate prospects % | Overall score |
|---|---|---|---|---|---|---|
| 1 St Andrews | 97.2 | 92.9 | 42.5 | 204 | 96.5 | 100 |
| 2 Oxford | 86.2 | 65.5 | 60 | 193 | 91.3 | 97.3 |
| 3 Durham | 84.9 | 77.7 | 57.8 | 179 | 86.8 | 95.6 |
| 4 Glasgow | 84.7 | 76.6 | 62.5 | 176 | — | 95.5 |
| 5 Cambridge | — | — | 48.8 | 187 | 84.2 | 94.8 |
| 6 Warwick | 89.3 | 82.4 | 65.8 | 141 | 77.8 | 94.4 |
| 7 Exeter | 86.7 | 82.9 | 61.5 | 164 | 76.4 | 94.2 |
| 8 King's College London | 79.5 | 67.8 | 65.5 | 147 | 77.2 | 91 |
| 9 Nottingham | 89.4 | 83.6 | 51.5 | 136 | 78.6 | 90.9 |
| 10 Leeds | 85.9 | 82.9 | 52 | 146 | 77.9 | 90.7 |
| 11 Birmingham | 93.8 | 85.4 | 54.2 | 137 | 66.7 | 90.6 |
| 12 Manchester | 76 | 63.3 | 65.5 | 144 | 82.3 | 90.5 |
| 13 Royal Holloway | 84.5 | 78.1 | 53.5 | 126 | 84.7 | 90.2 |
| 14 University College London | 83.2 | 78.5 | 44.2 | 172 | 73.9 | 88.9 |
| 15 Kent | 88.3 | 74.6 | 58.8 | 109 | 73.8 | 88.7 |
| 16 Bristol | 82.5 | 76.6 | 52.8 | 147 | 71.3 | 88.3 |
| 17 Edinburgh | 76.3 | 70.9 | 51.5 | 168 | 69.3 | 87.2 |
| 18 Swansea | 92.5 | 88.2 | 45.2 | 113 | 65.1 | 86.3 |
| 19 Liverpool | 79.3 | 69.3 | 43.5 | 130 | 81.4 | 85.4 |

**Classics and Ancient History** cont.

| | | Teaching quality % | Student experience % | Research quality % | Entry standards (UCAS points) | Graduate prospects % | Overall score |
|---|---|---|---|---|---|---|---|
| **20** | Newcastle | 84.1 | 80 | 42 | 129 | 71.6 | 85.2 |
| **21** | Reading | 87.1 | 84.9 | 43.2 | 120 | 66.3 | 84.9 |
| **22** | Cardiff | 80.2 | 71.5 | 42.2 | 126 | 63 | 81.6 |
| **23** | Leicester | 88 | 86.2 | — | 119 | 51.6* | 71.9 |

| | | | |
|---|---|---|---|
| Employed in high-skilled job | 36% | Employed in lower-skilled job | 23% |
| Employed in high-skilled job and studying | 4% | Employed in lower-skilled job and studying | 1% |
| Studying | 15% | Unemployed | 5% |
| High-skilled work (median) salary | £27,000 | Low-/medium-skilled salary | £20,000 |

## Communication and Media Studies

Loughborough returns to the top of our Communication and Media Studies table this year, having held the same spot for a four-year run until three years ago. It is also No 1 for the student experience, followed by Keele (38th overall) and Sheffield – which is up four places to rank third in the overall table. Students' evaluation of teaching quality puts Gloucester (=11th) in the lead, with Central Lancashire (=18th) and London South Bank (54th) second and third respectively. For research, sixth-place Cardiff achieves the top score in our analysis of the Research Excellence Framework 2021, followed by Goldsmiths, Loughborough and Southampton. Led by Strathclyde, which topped the table's previous edition, Stirling and Glasgow Caledonian, the Scottish universities average the highest entry standards (benefitting from the favourable tariff conversion for Scottish secondary qualifications), with Leeds attracting the highest grades south of the border. Entry grades span a broad spectrum, from 202 UCAS points at Strathclyde down to 80 points at Bedfordshire – one of six universities to average below 100 points in the UCAS tariff.

This subject table covers a wide range of courses; some focus on the history and theory of media and culture in society, while others range from practical production for TV, film and radio to script-writing or journalism. "The creative and cultural industries are of immense economic value, but it's not just about the money. There is so much in popular culture that deserves to be valued and analysed. Media and communication programmes offer an exciting interdisciplinary field of study that puts you at the heart of these critical debates," says Professor David Deacon, head of the Department of Communication and Media, Loughborough University. After years of rising applications to the subjects, demand for them cooled in 2023's admissions cycle, when just over 62,300 applied (down 4% year on year), while around 11,600 students started courses (a 10% dip compared with the year before).

Low starting salaries tend to be the norm in media industries, and average annual pay of £23,000 for those with communication and media studies degrees rank the subjects in the bottom ten of our pay index. They do better in our graduate prospects table, placing 52nd out of 70 subject areas this year, based on 59.5% of graduates having found high-skilled jobs and/or furthering their studies within 15 months of finishing degrees. Most communication and media studies students will be wise to the dearth of "professional"-grade roles upon graduation, but career prospects vary considerably by university. At least four in five of those who studied at 11 universities had achieved the desired career outcomes 15 months after graduating, led by Gloucester, City (10th place overall), Newcastle (5th) and Leeds (9th). At the opposite end of the scale, less than half of those with degrees in the subjects from Northampton (86th overall) and London Metropolitan (88th) had achieved the same outcomes within the same timeframe.

## Communication and Media Studies

| | | Teaching quality % | Student experience % | Research quality % | Entry standards (UCAS points) | Graduate prospects % | Overall score |
|---|---|---|---|---|---|---|---|
| 1 | Loughborough | 88.9 | 93.5 | 71.8 | 149 | 84.6 | 100 |
| 2 | Strathclyde | 81.7 | 78.8 | 58.8 | 202 | 80 | 98.9 |
| 3 | Sheffield | 86.7 | 87.9 | 59.5 | 148 | 84.8 | 97.3 |
| 4 | Warwick | 86.7 | 80.4 | 68.8 | 155 | 79.3 | 97.1 |
| 5 | Newcastle | 83.8 | 83.1 | 60.8 | 148 | 86.8 | 96.5 |
| 6 | Cardiff | 79.3 | 77.3 | 77 | 144 | 84.5 | 95.9 |
| 7 | Leicester | 86.5 | 85.7 | 68.6 | 130 | 78.6 | 95.2 |
| 8 | Exeter | 85.3 | 80.4 | 55.9 | 150 | 77.6 | 94.4 |
| 9 | Leeds | 78.4 | 77.1 | 50.2 | 160 | 85.5 | 94 |
| 10 | City | 85.1 | 84.1 | 42.8 | 129 | 88.5 | 93.4 |
| =11 | Glasgow Caledonian | 83 | 72.6 | 38.5 | 174 | 78.7 | 93.2 |
| =11 | Gloucestershire | 92.5 | 87.4 | 23.8 | 119 | 92.7 | 93.2 |
| =13 | Lancaster | 84.4 | 83.6 | 60.2 | 137 | 72.7 | 92.8 |
| =13 | Edinburgh Napier | 86.5 | 81.1 | 38.8 | 152 | 77.1 | 92.8 |
| 15 | Stirling | 83.1 | 78.2 | 44.5 | 177 | 67 | 92.4 |
| 16 | Robert Gordon | 89.5 | 83.4 | 26 | 154 | 76 | 92.1 |
| 17 | King's College London | 76.2 | 75.3 | 64.5 | 157 | 71.6 | 91.9 |
| =18 | Central Lancashire | 92.3 | 85.3 | 31.8 | 116 | 79.7 | 91 |
| =18 | Royal Holloway | 82.3 | 72.7 | 63.7 | 141 | 67.9 | 91 |
| =18 | Liverpool | 77.4 | 77.6 | 55.2 | 135 | 80.1 | 91 |
| =21 | Salford | 85.6 | 78.9 | 49.8 | 123 | 75.3 | 90.5 |
| =21 | Swansea | 89.7 | 86.2 | 31.5 | 135 | 71.4 | 90.5 |
| 23 | Nottingham Trent | 86.8 | 83.3 | 42.5 | 116 | 78.3 | 90.4 |
| 24 | Coventry | 87.8 | 82.8 | 54.2 | 117 | 68.1 | 90.1 |
| 25 | Sussex | 81.2 | 78.6 | 61.8 | 136 | 64.6 | 89.9 |
| 26 | Essex | 81.3 | 73.5 | 49.8 | 125 | 78.9 | 89.8 |
| 27 | Manchester Metropolitan | 84.4 | 78.1 | 51.7 | 120 | 72.3 | 89.5 |
| 28 | Edge Hill | 91.1 | 84.5 | 39.8 | 120 | 66.9 | 89.4 |
| 29 | East Anglia | 83.4 | 75.2 | 50.2 | 126 | 71.8 | 89.2 |
| 30 | Southampton | 79.2 | 71.7 | 69.2 | 141 | 59.1 | 89 |
| =31 | West London | 85 | 86.5 | 45.5 | 114 | — | 88.9 |
| =31 | Northumbria | 80 | 78.6 | 45.8 | 134 | 72.2 | 88.9 |
| =33 | Liverpool John Moores | 89.2 | 86.4 | 22.2 | 137 | 68 | 88.7 |
| =33 | Bournemouth | 81.8 | 74.1 | 47.2 | 114 | 79 | 88.7 |
| =35 | Nottingham | 78.3 | 76 | 54.8 | 130 | 69.8 | 88.5 |
| =35 | Teesside | 84.8 | 79.9 | 49.2 | 115 | 69.2 | 88.5 |
| 37 | Ulster | 85.1 | 77.1 | 35 | 127 | 73.1 | 88.3 |
| 38 | Keele | 91.2 | 88 | 54.8 | 107 | 55.6 | 88.2 |
| 39 | Goldsmiths, London | 74.6 | 67.6 | 72.8 | 125 | 67.5 | 88 |
| =40 | Canterbury Christ Church | 85.7 | 81.2 | 38 | 106 | 75.9 | 87.9 |
| =40 | Westminster | 85.9 | 87.9 | 50 | 112 | 62.2 | 87.9 |
| 42 | University of the Arts London | 81.7 | 76.4 | 46 | 126 | 67.2 | 87.4 |
| 43 | Queen Margaret, Edinburgh | 78.9 | 72.2 | 33 | 160 | 63.5 | 87.1 |
| 44 | West of England | 79.9 | 73.6 | 48.2 | 118 | 70.6 | 86.9 |

## Communication and Media Studies
cont.

| | | Teaching quality % | Student experience % | Research quality % | Entry standards (UCAS points) | Graduate prospects % | Overall score |
|---|---|---|---|---|---|---|---|
| 45 | Leeds Beckett | 90.2 | 84.5 | 26.5 | 101 | 71.9 | 86.8 |
| 46 | Staffordshire | 81.2 | 76.1 | 31.5 | 116 | 77.9 | 86.7 |
| 47 | Portsmouth | 87.7 | 81.9 | 30.2 | 109 | 68.9 | 86.5 |
| 48 | Sunderland | 88.4 | 82.1 | 25.5 | 109 | 70.3 | 86.4 |
| 49 | Birmingham City | 83.8 | 75.1 | 40.8 | 121 | 65.1 | 86.3 |
| =50 | Sheffield Hallam | 81.3 | 73.8 | 46 | 113 | 68.6 | 86.2 |
| =50 | East London | 84.6 | 80.8 | 34.2 | 107 | 70.7 | 86.2 |
| 52 | Huddersfield | 81.4 | 74.5 | 49.8 | 115 | 64.3 | 86.1 |
| 53 | Hertfordshire | 82.9 | 79.9 | 24.2 | 98 | 82.7 | 86 |
| 54 | London South Bank | 91.3 | 80.9 | 35.8 | 93 | 65.5 | 85.8 |
| 55 | Lincoln | 85.3 | 77.3 | 33.5 | 117 | 65.3 | 85.7 |
| 56 | Hull | 87.4 | 81.6 | 35 | 124 | 54.4 | 85.4 |
| 57 | Oxford Brookes | 84.9 | 80 | 21.5 | 115 | 70.6 | 85.3 |
| 58 | Derby | 81.6 | 79.6 | 24 | 112 | 74.1 | 85.1 |
| 59 | Bangor | 87 | 83.9 | 33.2 | 123 | 53.3 | 84.9 |
| 60 | Leeds Trinity | 89.6 | 81.1 | — | 102 | 80.4 | 84.7 |
| 61 | Bath Spa | 85 | 76 | 42 | 109 | 59 | 84.6 |
| 62 | York | 78.4 | 72.9 | — | 148 | 76.9* | 84.5 |
| 63 | West of Scotland | 86.1 | 75 | 19.2 | 131 | 61 | 84.4 |
| 64 | Kingston | 75.1 | 65.9 | 45 | 118 | 69.3 | 84.2 |
| 65 | Solent, Southampton | 90.2 | 85.6 | 9.5 | 107 | 65.4 | 84.1 |
| 66 | Liverpool Hope | 90.8 | 79.4 | — | 116 | 69.4 | 84 |
| 67 | Roehampton | 81.5 | 73.7 | 53 | 98 | 59.6 | 83.9 |
| 68 | Queen Mary, London | 80.9 | 71.8 | — | 147 | 69.4 | 83.4 |
| =69 | Kent | 84.4 | 82.5 | — | 120 | 69.5* | 83 |
| =69 | Falmouth | 76.6 | 63.1 | 48.8 | 125 | 57.4 | 83 |
| 71 | York St John | 90.5 | 84.3 | — | 111 | 64.3 | 82.9 |
| =72 | Winchester | 78.2 | 73.1 | 29.2 | 108 | 67.5 | 82.5 |
| =72 | Aberystwyth | 89.4 | 85 | — | 125 | 57.0* | 82.5 |
| =72 | Anglia Ruskin | 80 | 73.9 | 53.8 | 101 | 53.1* | 82.5 |
| =75 | Worcester | 85.2 | 79.6 | 5.8 | 106 | 69.9 | 82.4 |
| =75 | Brighton | 74.5 | 64.8 | 44.2 | 109 | 66.5 | 82.4 |
| =75 | South Wales | 79.8 | 70.1 | 35.8 | 108 | 62.6 | 82.4 |
| 78 | De Montfort | 82.5 | 78.9 | 24 | 106 | 61.2 | 82.1 |
| 79 | Chester | 81.1 | 67.7 | 21 | 121 | 60.9 | 81.6 |
| =80 | Middlesex | 75.5 | 71.3 | 26 | 109 | 66.7* | 81.1 |
| =80 | Wolverhampton | 80.3 | 82.5 | 31.5 | 87 | — | 81.1 |
| 82 | St Mark and St John | 79.9 | 66.8 | — | 119 | 73.5* | 80.9 |
| 83 | Brunel | 77.4 | 75.2 | — | 105 | 71.6 | 79.4 |
| 84 | St Mary's, Twickenham | 79.6 | 72.1 | — | 104 | 54.8* | 76.2 |
| 85 | Bedfordshire | 78.6 | 64.4 | 27 | 80 | 52.9 | 75.9 |
| 86 | Northampton | 83.2 | 70.5 | — | 99 | 48.7 | 75.3 |
| 87 | Chichester | 73.6 | 65.5 | — | 105 | 50.0* | 73 |
| 88 | London Metropolitan | 72.6 | 64.1 | — | 109 | 49.2 | 72.9 |

| Employed in high-skilled job | 53% | Employed in lower-skilled job | 26% |
| Employed in high-skilled job and studying | 2% | Employed in lower-skilled job and studying | 1% |
| Studying | 3% | Unemployed | 8% |
| High-skilled work (median) salary | £23,000 | Low-/medium-skilled salary | £19,300 |

# Computer Science

The fastest-growing subject area in the UK, the interest in computing degrees comes amid the rise in the popularity of AI and gaming, and with advances such as ChatGPT coming to the market. As a UCAS subject group computing received 195,690 applications in 2023, up 9% on 2022 and up 26% on 2021. Courses encompass a broad area, taking in everything from computer science and software engineering to AI, video games design and animation.

Job security in an evolving industrial landscape is part of the appeal. Thirty universities report at least 90% of their computer science graduates as being in high-skilled jobs or postgraduate study within 15 months. Oxford, in first place of our table, achieves a perfect 100%. Job prospects for computer science graduates are pretty good throughout the table, with only 17 of the 114 universities registering rates of high-skilled work/postgraduate study beneath 70%. As a whole, computer sciences ranks 26th out of our employment ranking's 70 subject areas. Although earnings are not an ingredient of our main subject rankings, part of the appeal of degrees within computer science is their promise of enticing graduate pay cheques and starting salaries of £29,860 rank the subject 14th out of 70 in our pay index.

Cambridge, which topped the table for the past two years, sits third. Imperial secured the best results in computer science in our analysis of the Research Excellence Framework 2021, followed by Oxford. Led by Cambridge and St Andrews, which each averaged 220 UCAS points among entrants, there are six universities where entry standards tip over 200 UCAS points. Students at Bolton (in =66th place overall) expressed the highest rates of satisfaction with teaching quality, while those at East London (=95th) were the most satisfied with the broad experience.

Tom Curtin, industrial liaison officer, Department of Computing, Imperial College London notes: "Computer scientists have provided the digital systems at the heart of everything we do, driven the technology sector providing the basis for almost every trillion-dollar company to emerge over the past decade and, in the near future, will be at the helm of the next industrial revolution, driven by AI." Applicants are advised to ensure their maths skills are up to scratch, keep abreast of technology and data science news, and experiment with new computing technologies. Computing as a whole remains a male-dominated field, with only 18% of all UK 18-year-olds' applications made by females – although this is higher than the 17% in 2022 and 16% in 2021.

| Computer Science | Teaching quality % | Student experience % | Research quality % | Entry standards (UCAS points) | Graduate prospects % | Overall score |
|---|---|---|---|---|---|---|
| 1 Oxford | 89.1 | 80.8 | 85.8 | 207 | 100 | 100 |
| 2 Imperial College | 81.4 | 81.3 | 94.8 | 208 | 97 | 98.5 |
| 3 Cambridge | 84.8 | 76.5 | 78.2 | 220 | 94.8 | 97.6 |
| 4 St Andrews | 85 | 86 | 41.2 | 220 | 99.1 | 96 |
| 5 Birmingham | 84.1 | 84.6 | 82.8 | 169 | 97.2 | 95.5 |
| 6 Glasgow | 77.8 | 74.3 | 71.8 | 209 | 91.4 | 93.6 |
| 7 Sheffield | 86.4 | 87.7 | 69.8 | 156 | 92.5 | 93.3 |
| 8 Warwick | 75.4 | 74.8 | 81.8 | 190 | 93 | 92.9 |

**Computer Science** cont.

| | | Teaching quality % | Student experience % | Research quality % | Entry standards (UCAS points) | Graduate prospects % | Overall score |
|---|---|---|---|---|---|---|---|
| 9 | Bath | 83.8 | 88.9 | 52.2 | 175 | 93.1 | 92.6 |
| 10 | Manchester | 73.7 | 74.5 | 71.2 | 190 | 97.5 | 92.4 |
| =11 | Bristol | 76 | 74.6 | 76 | 180 | 94.7 | 92.1 |
| =11 | Edinburgh | 68.8 | 71 | 81.2 | 210 | 92 | 92.1 |
| 13 | University College London | 70.6 | 69 | 82.2 | 190 | 95.2 | 91.6 |
| 14 | King's College London | 76.2 | 74.5 | 68 | 175 | 96 | 91.3 |
| 15 | Strathclyde | 82.5 | 78.6 | 46.2 | 197 | 87.6 | 91.1 |
| 16 | Dundee | 83.8 | 85.7 | 53.5 | 174 | 86.8 | 91 |
| 17 | Durham | 74.2 | 66.5 | 59 | 192 | 96.6 | 90.4 |
| 18 | Southampton | 73.4 | 69.5 | 70.8 | 172 | 92.4 | 89.4 |
| 19 | Nottingham | 77 | 79.4 | 63.5 | 160 | 89.7 | 89.2 |
| 20 | Loughborough | 81.6 | 83.1 | 46.5 | 155 | 90.3 | 88.8 |
| =21 | Queen Mary, London | 78 | 77.1 | 74.2 | 150 | 84.9 | 88.6 |
| =21 | Lancaster | 76 | 78.8 | 64.8 | 146 | 92.4 | 88.6 |
| 23 | Liverpool | 77.3 | 78.5 | 61 | 140 | 94.2 | 88.4 |
| 24 | Royal Holloway | 79.7 | 76.5 | 65 | 134 | 91.8 | 88.3 |
| 25 | Exeter | 78.9 | 77.3 | 45.5 | 154 | 93.8 | 88.1 |
| 26 | Sussex | 78.7 | 82 | 59.2 | 137 | 88.6 | 87.6 |
| 27 | Surrey | 79.1 | 81.1 | 50.5 | 133 | 92.4 | 87.2 |
| 28 | Aberystwyth | 86.8 | 87.5 | 43.8 | 125 | 84 | 86.9 |
| 29 | Queen's, Belfast | 73.4 | 76.8 | 51 | 147 | 92.3 | 86.4 |
| =30 | Swansea | 80.7 | 75.5 | 46.5 | 133 | 90.7 | 86.3 |
| =30 | Aberdeen | 75.3 | 77.4 | 44 | 167 | — | 86.3 |
| =32 | York | 66.1 | 67.1 | 72.5 | 150 | 93.5 | 86.1 |
| =32 | Edinburgh Napier | 81.2 | 75.6 | 47.2 | 150 | 82.6 | 86.1 |
| =34 | Leicester | 78.2 | 83.3 | 41.8 | 133 | 89.4 | 85.8 |
| =34 | Leeds | 62 | 60.2 | 72 | 174 | 92.1 | 85.8 |
| 36 | Cardiff | 69.9 | 71.2 | 57.8 | 149 | 91.7 | 85.7 |
| 37 | Newcastle | 70.4 | 72.1 | 60.5 | 142 | 91.9 | 85.6 |
| 38 | Ulster | 82.5 | 79.9 | 38 | 128 | 87.2 | 85.4 |
| 39 | Robert Gordon | 90.9 | 86.6 | 16 | 143 | 77.5 | 85.1 |
| 40 | Northumbria | 81.6 | 79.4 | 25.8 | 140 | 87.6 | 84.8 |
| =41 | Essex | 77.7 | 75.9 | 53.5 | 125 | 85.7 | 84.7 |
| =41 | Aston | 78.6 | 78.4 | 29.2 | 140 | 89.5 | 84.7 |
| 43 | Reading | 79.9 | 77.2 | 39.8 | 126 | 87 | 84.4 |
| =44 | Manchester Metropolitan | 82.7 | 79.5 | 29.2 | 133 | 83.6 | 84.2 |
| =44 | Brunel | 83.1 | 81.8 | 37.5 | 131 | 78.7 | 84.2 |
| 46 | East Anglia | 73.6 | 73.5 | 41.8 | 139 | 88.7 | 83.9 |
| 47 | Abertay | 83.5 | 83.4 | — | 159 | 82.8 | 83.7 |
| 48 | Hull | 81.1 | 82.6 | 31.2 | 128 | 81.8 | 83.6 |
| =49 | Heriot-Watt | 65.5 | 67.1 | 39.5 | 169 | 90 | 83.5 |
| =49 | Kent | 74.3 | 71.9 | 57.2 | 134 | 81.1 | 83.5 |
| 51 | City | 72.2 | 74.8 | 47.5 | 127 | 86.7 | 83 |
| 52 | Portsmouth | 82.7 | 81.6 | 32.8 | 116 | 80.7 | 82.9 |

| | | | | | | |
|---|---|---|---|---|---|---|
| =53 Worcester | 87.7 | 82.8 | 12.5 | 106 | 86 | 82.6 |
| =53 Liverpool John Moores | 81.9 | 79.8 | 26 | 145 | 74.1 | 82.6 |
| 55 West of England | 78.1 | 74.9 | 32.2 | 128 | 83.8 | 82.5 |
| 56 Birmingham City | 85.4 | 84.1 | 23.2 | 122 | 75.6 | 82.3 |
| 57 Bangor | 83 | 76.5 | 40.2 | 111 | 77.1 | 82.1 |
| 58 Glasgow Caledonian | 79.7 | 75.3 | 13.8 | 146 | 81.2 | 81.9 |
| 59 Stirling | 75.6 | 73.7 | 24 | 146 | 81.1 | 81.7 |
| 60 University of the Arts London | 83.4 | 79.4 | 46 | 113 | 68.3 | 81.4 |
| 61 Huddersfield | 74.4 | 74.2 | 26.5 | 132 | 83.8 | 81.2 |
| =62 Nottingham Trent | 79.5 | 73.1 | 26 | 129 | 79 | 81.1 |
| =62 Staffordshire | 80.4 | 72.7 | 25.5 | 124 | 79.7 | 81.1 |
| =64 Oxford Brookes | 80.4 | 78.3 | 24.2 | 114 | 80.8 | 81 |
| =64 Coventry | 80.7 | 77.4 | 23.5 | 116 | 80.5 | 81 |
| =66 South Wales | 84.5 | 78.8 | 18.8 | 122 | 74.3 | 80.8 |
| =66 Chester | 79.1 | 74.6 | 13.2 | 127 | 83.9 | 80.8 |
| =66 Bolton | 91.3 | 85.9 | — | 115 | 73.8 | 80.8 |
| 69 West of Scotland | 84.4 | 77.1 | 18 | 137 | 69.1 | 80.5 |
| 70 Teesside | 88 | 82.6 | 18.8 | 124 | 65.3 | 80.4 |
| 71 Bournemouth | 77.3 | 72 | 22.2 | 121 | 82.7 | 80.3 |
| 72 Plymouth | 72 | 67 | 32 | 125 | 85.4 | 80.2 |
| 73 Middlesex | 88.7 | 87.8 | 20.2 | 111 | 63.9 | 80.1 |
| =74 Lincoln | 66.3 | 68.7 | 44 | 126 | 84.5 | 80 |
| =74 Buckinghamshire New | 86.7 | 79 | — | 107 | 81.6 | 80 |
| =76 Roehampton | 80.6 | 76.5 | 53 | — | 58.5 | 79.9 |
| =76 Sunderland | 83.5 | 79.4 | 14.5 | 102 | 80 | 79.9 |
| 78 Sheffield Hallam | 80.4 | 74.2 | 17 | 119 | 78.1 | 79.7 |
| =79 Greenwich | 79.7 | 80.5 | 28 | 120 | 69.6 | 79.6 |
| =79 Bedfordshire | 82.6 | 80.4 | 15.2 | 115 | 74.2 | 79.6 |
| 81 Kingston | 82.1 | 81.8 | 23.5 | 110 | 70.8 | 79.4 |
| 82 Bradford | 78.8 | 74.3 | 20.5 | 123 | 75 | 79.3 |
| 83 West London | 85 | 85.7 | 20 | 118 | 63 | 79.2 |
| 84 Wales Trinity St David | 79.7 | 75.1 | — | 162 | 68 | 79.1 |
| 85 Falmouth | 75.3 | 67 | 48.8 | 124 | 67.4 | 79 |
| 86 Edge Hill | 71.4 | 72.6 | 20 | 131 | 79.4 | 78.7 |
| 87 Hertfordshire | 72.8 | 72.5 | 41.2 | 115 | 72.3 | 78.6 |
| 88 Leeds Beckett | 79 | 75.8 | 18.2 | 113 | 74.7 | 78.5 |
| 89 Bath Spa | 82.8 | 70.1 | — | 105 | 84 | 78.4 |
| 90 De Montfort | 74.8 | 74.2 | 25 | 109 | 77.2 | 78.2 |
| =91 York St John | 75.5 | 66.1 | — | 106 | 93.2 | 78.1 |
| =91 Westminster | 78 | 78.9 | 24 | 114 | 69 | 78.1 |
| 93 Keele | 70.6 | 69.5 | 20.8 | 120 | 81.8 | 77.9 |
| 94 Wolverhampton | 77.4 | 74.2 | 12.5 | 89 | 85.3 | 77.8 |
| =95 Brighton | 72.7 | 68.1 | 32.5 | 98 | 80.9 | 77.7 |
| =95 East London | 90.2 | 90.9 | 28.7 | 88 | 52.7 | 77.7 |
| 97 Goldsmiths, London | 70 | 60.1 | 28.5 | 132 | 77.2 | 77.5 |
| =98 Salford | 70.9 | 69.3 | 28.2 | 127 | 71.4 | 77.2 |
| =98 Anglia Ruskin | 78.5 | 75.8 | 10 | 108 | 74.3 | 77.2 |
| =98 London South Bank | 80 | 80 | — | 100 | 78 | 77.2 |

## Computer Science cont.

| | | Teaching quality % | Student experience % | Research quality % | Entry standards (UCAS points) | Graduate prospects % | Overall score |
|---|---|---|---|---|---|---|---|
| **101** | Central Lancashire | 73.5 | 67.3 | 17.8 | 130 | 72 | 76.9 |
| **=102** | Gloucestershire | 75.1 | 67.1 | 6.2 | 118 | 79.3 | 76.7 |
| **=102** | Northampton | 77.7 | 70.1 | 8.5 | 107 | 77.3 | 76.7 |
| **104** | London Metropolitan | 81.5 | 79.2 | 13.2 | 90 | 68.8 | 76.1 |
| **=105** | Derby | 71 | 65.5 | 15.8 | 116 | 77.8 | 76 |
| **=105** | Liverpool Hope | 75 | 69.7 | 19.5 | 113 | 69.6 | 76 |
| **107** | Norwich University of the Arts | 80 | 75.1 | — | 131 | 61.2 | 75.5 |
| **108** | Canterbury Christ Church | 79.3 | 74 | 16.8 | 95 | 66.4 | 75.3 |
| **109** | Solent, Southampton | 76.5 | 70.4 | — | 108 | 71.7 | 74.6 |
| **110** | Cardiff Metropolitan | 71.8 | 68.4 | — | 120 | 72.9 | 74.3 |
| **111** | Winchester | 66.4 | 57.6 | — | 108 | 87.8 | 74 |
| **112** | Suffolk | 69.5 | 58.8 | — | 117 | 72 | 72.3 |
| **113** | Wrexham | 73.9 | 63.9 | 1.5 | 112 | 64.3 | 72.2 |
| **114** | University for the Creative Arts | 79.2 | 64.5 | — | 127 | 41.3 | 69.9 |

| | | | |
|---|---|---|---|
| Employed in high-skilled job | 65% | Employed in lower-skilled job | 11% |
| Employed in high-skilled job and studying | 4% | Employed in lower-skilled job and studying | 1% |
| Studying | 4% | Unemployed | 9% |
| High-skilled work (median) salary | £30,000 | Low-/medium-skilled salary | £20,000 |

# Creative Writing

Taking the lead in our new Creative Writing table, Newcastle has the top research in the field, based on results of the Research Excellence Framework 2021. After two years at No 1, Warwick takes second place but continues to claim the highest entry standards of 165 UCAS points. Creative writing students tend to enjoy their studies, as represented in our latest National Student Survey analysis, which shows high rates of satisfaction with teaching quality throughout the table. These are topped at Anglia Ruskin, which places 15th overall. Arts University, Bournemouth does best for students' evaluation of the broader experience.

"Creative writing provides an opportunity to study literature by creating your own work. You'll learn to read and write with attention to themes and ideas and an eye on technique, structure and more. You will create work that interacts with the world around you, exploring and understanding yourself and other people," says Dr Douglas Cowie, senior lecturer in the Department of English, Royal Holloway, University of London.

Applicants to creative writing courses may not be motivated by immediate professional full-time employment upon graduation, which is perhaps why only 25 of the 43 universities tabled a postgraduate prospects score. Of these, Bournemouth does best based on 83.3% of its graduates being employed in high-skilled work and/or further study within 15 months – a proportion which falls to 48.8% at Chichester. As a whole, creative writing has lost five places to sit at the foot of our employment ranking of 70 subject areas this year. More than four in ten graduates were in high-skilled work and/or further study when surveyed 15 months after their degrees, but three in ten were in jobs deemed "low-skilled" and around one in ten were unemployed – the highest unemployment rate of any subject group. Creative writing is also bottom of the salaries table, jointly with animal science.

Even so, the demand for creative writing courses registered a second consecutive uplift in 2022, when more than 8,100 applied for degrees. New student enrolments went marginally in the opposite direction however, and just under 1,800 undergraduates were accepted onto creative writing programmes. In 2025–26, 113 universities and colleges are offering the subject.

| Creative Writing | Teaching quality % | Student experience % | Research quality % | Entry standards (UCAS points) | Graduate prospects % | Overall score |
|---|---|---|---|---|---|---|
| 1 Newcastle | 86 | 80.3 | 83.8 | 143 | — | 100 |
| 2 Warwick | 86.2 | 74.5 | 64.8 | 165 | — | 99.6 |
| 3 Royal Holloway | 87.2 | 82.3 | 60.5 | 149 | — | 98.2 |
| 4 Birmingham | 82.6 | 74.6 | 68.8 | 152 | 74.6 | 97.4 |
| 5 Leeds | 79.6 | 75.9 | 73.2 | 157 | — | 97.3 |
| 6 East Anglia | 79.8 | 74.2 | 67 | 150 | 75.5 | 96.3 |
| 7 Liverpool John Moores | 89.2 | 81.3 | 58 | 142 | 63.2 | 96 |
| 8 Manchester Metropolitan | 89.3 | 83.1 | 61.8 | 124 | 70.1 | 95.8 |
| 9 Kent | 85.6 | 74.1 | 64.5 | 127 | 77.9* | 95.6 |
| 10 Lancaster | 85.8 | 79.8 | 48 | 148 | — | 95.4 |
| 11 Keele | 91.7 | 86.3 | 54.8 | 111 | — | 94.5 |
| 12 Plymouth | 88.4 | 74.8 | 60.5 | 124 | — | 94.1 |
| 13 Lincoln | 92.4 | 88.4 | 36 | 120 | — | 93.6 |
| 14 Nottingham Trent | 90.7 | 78.5 | 39.2 | 129 | — | 93.3 |
| 15 Anglia Ruskin | 93.2 | 84.8 | 46 | 103 | — | 92.5 |
| 16 Canterbury Christ Church | 89.2 | 82.1 | 53.2 | 109 | — | 92.3 |
| 17 Greenwich | 92.6 | 84.1 | 26.5 | 123 | — | 92.1 |
| 18 York St John | 92.9 | 90.2 | 22.8 | 104 | 72.7 | 91.9 |
| 19 Bangor | 84.8 | 77.8 | 44.2 | 125 | 67.4 | 91.8 |
| 20 Salford | 92.3 | 83.5 | 26.5 | 118 | 65.3 | 91.6 |
| 21 West of England | 86.1 | 79.3 | 32.2 | 114 | 77.2 | 91.4 |
| 22 Essex | 83.5 | 79.2 | 49.8 | 124 | — | 91.3 |
| 23 Aberystwyth | 86.4 | 82.5 | 25.5 | 130 | 66.2 | 91.1 |
| 24 Portsmouth | 92.5 | 85.7 | 30.8 | 103 | 65.7 | 90.8 |
| 25 Falmouth | 87.6 | 75.4 | 48.8 | 120 | 58.1* | 90.7 |
| 26 Brighton | 85.5 | 78 | 44.2 | 101 | 74.5 | 90.6 |
| =27 Kingston | 88.6 | 74.3 | 47 | 111 | — | 90.4 |
| =27 Arts University, Bournemouth | 87.4 | 91.4 | 23 | 120 | — | 90.4 |
| =29 De Montfort | 86.2 | 80.7 | 54.5 | 115 | 51.7 | 90 |
| =29 Brunel | 84.9 | 76.3 | 42.8 | 111 | 67.4 | 90 |
| 31 Birmingham City | 80.7 | 71.7 | 65.5 | 113 | — | 89.9 |
| 32 Bournemouth | 81.7 | 71.5 | 22.5 | — | 83.3* | 89.5 |
| 33 Edge Hill | 85.1 | 78.1 | 32.8 | 124 | 60.8 | 89.4 |
| 34 Derby | 91.7 | 87 | — | 118 | 64.5* | 88.9 |
| =35 Sheffield Hallam | 83.3 | 74.8 | 50.7 | 108 | — | 88.5 |
| =35 Central Lancashire | 91.6 | 84.4 | 33.8 | 119 | 41.0* | 88.5 |
| 37 Roehampton | 88.6 | 70.4 | 50.5 | 107 | 52.4* | 88.4 |
| 38 Bath Spa | 85.7 | 74.5 | 51.7 | 106 | 50.9 | 87.8 |
| 39 Gloucestershire | 86.6 | 76.6 | 32.8 | 101 | 59.2 | 87.1 |

| | Teaching quality % | Student experience % | Research quality % | Entry standards (UCAS points) | Graduate prospects % | Overall score |
|---|---|---|---|---|---|---|
| **40** Chichester | 88.9 | 79.2 | 37.2 | 109 | 44.8 | 87 |
| **41** Westminster | 76.2 | 72.7 | 55.5 | 107 | — | 86.1 |
| **42** Winchester | 84.3 | 77.3 | 16.2 | 116 | 56.1 | 85.8 |
| **43** Worcester | 84.4 | 74.4 | 19.2 | 105 | 60.7* | 85.5 |

| | | | |
|---|---|---|---|
| Employed in high-skilled job | 36% | Employed in lower-skilled job | 30% |
| Employed in high-skilled job and studying | 3% | Employed in lower-skilled job and studying | 2% |
| Studying | 6% | Unemployed | 10% |
| High-skilled work (median) salary | £24,000 | Low-/medium-skilled salary | £19,000 |

# Criminology

"What is crime? Why does it occur? And what are the best ways to address it?" asks Dr Donna Marie Brown, associate professor in criminology, Durham University. Covering topics including policing, prisons and youth justice, criminology students learn about criminological theory, the roles of criminal justice agencies and the impact of crimes on victims and communities. Now in its ninth year and stretching to 88 universities, our Criminology table reflects this growing undergraduate field, offered by 159 universities and colleges across 1,225 courses for 2025-26, either by itself, as part of a joint honours degree, or within a broader social science degree. Sociology and psychology are welcomed by some university departments, but there are no specific entry requirements for criminology degrees, apart possibly from GCSE maths, since the course is likely to involve the use of statistics.

Loughborough has ousted Durham at the top of our Criminology table, a position it last held three years ago. Loughborough performs strongly across all metrics without coming first in any individually. In second place overall Sheffield does best for graduate job prospects – based on 82.8% of its criminology graduates being in high-skilled work and/or further study within 15 months. Kent comes out top for research in our analysis of the latest Research Excellence Framework 2021. Wrexham, in 10th place overall, has the most satisfied criminology students for the second year running – outdoing all others in the table for teaching quality and the broader experience – both measures derived from the National Student Survey. Surrey, Worcester and Bedfordshire also feature in the top three for these student-led measures.

Career opportunities further down the line include in the police force, prison service, Home Office, charities or law practice. But overall, criminology comes second from bottom of our employment index (though this represents a one-place improvement on the last two years), where it is held back by the almost equal proportion of graduates that start out in low-skilled jobs (36.2%) as in high- skilled employment (37.2%). Average early career salaries of £23,000 compare more favourably with other subject areas, and criminology ranks =61st out of 70.

| Criminology | Teaching quality % | Student experience % | Research quality % | Entry standards (UCAS points) | Graduate prospects % | Overall score |
|---|---|---|---|---|---|---|
| **1** Loughborough | 85.5 | 87.3 | 55.8 | 149 | 82.5 | 100 |
| **2** Sheffield | 82 | 82.2 | 55 | 147 | 82.8 | 98.3 |

| | | | | | | |
|---|---|---|---|---|---|---|
| 3 | University College London | 79.6 | 75.5 | 61.5 | 154 | — | 95.4 |
| 4 | Durham | 81.2 | 76.7 | 53 | 154 | 70.7 | 95.1 |
| 5 | Bath | 80.3 | 78.3 | 59.5 | 148 | — | 94.9 |
| 6 | Lancaster | 84.3 | 79.9 | 48 | 146 | 69.7 | 94.8 |
| 7 | York | 79.9 | 77.2 | 58 | 143 | 72.2 | 94.7 |
| 8 | Southampton | 75 | 75 | 66.8 | 144 | 71.1 | 94.1 |
| 9 | Exeter | 78.8 | 78.9 | 46.8 | 152 | 70.8 | 93.9 |
| =10 | Wrexham | 95.6 | 91.1 | 20.5 | — | 66.7 | 93.8 |
| =10 | Nottingham | 84.2 | 82 | 54 | 137 | 65.3 | 93.8 |
| =12 | Bedfordshire | 91.8 | 89.2 | 50.2 | 104 | — | 93.1 |
| =12 | Stirling | 74 | 71.4 | 47.5 | 178 | 64.6 | 93.1 |
| =12 | Cardiff | 75.6 | 78.1 | 54 | 149 | 69 | 93.1 |
| 15 | Leicester | 83.4 | 83.8 | 52.2 | 125 | 67.3 | 92.8 |
| 16 | City | 78.5 | 78.6 | 64 | 136 | 64.2 | 92.7 |
| 17 | Birmingham | 78.4 | 79.8 | 61 | 143 | 61.5 | 92.6 |
| 18 | Queen's, Belfast | 74.7 | 72 | 56.5 | 147 | 69.8 | 92.5 |
| 19 | Plymouth | 83.5 | 80.7 | 50.5 | 119 | 69.7 | 92.2 |
| 20 | Huddersfield | 87.5 | 85.6 | 43.5 | 114 | 65.3 | 91.4 |
| 21 | Surrey | 90.2 | 89.9 | — | 140 | 67.7 | 90.7 |
| 22 | Worcester | 93.4 | 89.7 | 12.8 | 124 | 64.3 | 90.6 |
| =23 | Sussex | 80.6 | 79.8 | 41 | 132 | 63.8 | 90.2 |
| =23 | Central Lancashire | 79.2 | 77.7 | 51.5 | 124 | 64.6 | 90.2 |
| 25 | Kent | 81 | 79.8 | 72.2 | 111 | 56.1 | 90.1 |
| 26 | Essex | 79.3 | 79.9 | 62.5 | 118 | 59.3 | 90 |
| =27 | Swansea | 79 | 77.2 | 27.8 | 132 | 72.2 | 89.9 |
| =27 | Portsmouth | 84 | 81 | 33 | 124 | 65.9 | 89.9 |
| 29 | Bangor | 83.3 | 76.6 | 33.2 | 134 | — | 89.7 |
| 30 | Hull | 83.2 | 78 | 53.8 | 119 | 57.9 | 89.5 |
| =31 | Royal Holloway | 76.1 | 74.4 | 38 | 129 | 70.9 | 89.4 |
| =31 | Manchester Metropolitan | 85 | 85.3 | 32.8 | 122 | 61.5 | 89.4 |
| =31 | West London | 83.5 | 79.1 | 39 | 117 | 65.4 | 89.4 |
| 34 | Manchester | 78.4 | 75.3 | 40.8 | 151 | 55.8 | 89.2 |
| 35 | Ulster | 85.3 | 80.6 | 53.8 | 127 | 47.7 | 88.8 |
| 36 | Lincoln | 76.9 | 74.5 | 51 | 117 | 62.9 | 88.1 |
| 37 | Newman | 86.7 | 82.3 | 13.8 | 94 | 76.8 | 88 |
| =38 | Abertay | 86.6 | 84 | — | 148 | 58.5 | 87.8 |
| =38 | Aberystwyth | 80.6 | 80.4 | 34.2 | 120 | 61.9 | 87.8 |
| =38 | Edinburgh Napier | 80.7 | 77.4 | 35.2 | 167 | 42.2 | 87.8 |
| =41 | Keele | 82 | 79 | 33.2 | 116 | 62 | 87.5 |
| =41 | Liverpool | 70.5 | 70.6 | 55 | 131 | 61.3 | 87.5 |
| =43 | West of England | 75 | 73.3 | 35.2 | 116 | 69.7 | 87.1 |
| =43 | Sunderland | 86.5 | 81.1 | 39.5 | 104 | 56 | 87.1 |
| 45 | Nottingham Trent | 84.3 | 81 | 29.5 | 114 | 58.7 | 86.9 |
| =46 | Staffordshire | 87.1 | 78.8 | 18.2 | 101 | 66.4 | 86.6 |
| =46 | Middlesex | 82.2 | 79.5 | 27.8 | 103 | 66.1 | 86.6 |
| =48 | Liverpool John Moores | 79.9 | 77.1 | 15.8 | 133 | 62.1 | 86.5 |
| =48 | Bournemouth | 80.7 | 77.7 | 10.2 | 110 | 73.4 | 86.5 |
| =50 | Northumbria | 69.9 | 64.5 | 42 | 139 | 63.1 | 86.4 |

# Criminology cont.

| | Teaching quality % | Student experience % | Research quality % | Entry standards (UCAS points) | Graduate prospects % | Overall score |
|---|---|---|---|---|---|---|
| =50 Westminster | 79.8 | 76.9 | -31.5 | 111 | 63.4 | 86.4 |
| 52 Suffolk | 87 | 82 | 21.8 | 106 | – | 86.3 |
| =53 Salford | 81.3 | 79.1 | 44.5 | 117 | 51 | 86.2 |
| =53 Birmingham City | 83.2 | 78.9 | 25.8 | 116 | 58.6 | 86.2 |
| 55 Sheffield Hallam | 84.5 | 79.4 | 26.2 | 110 | 58.7 | 86 |
| 56 Edge Hill | 82.2 | 77.9 | 17.5 | 127 | 56.6 | 85.5 |
| 57 South Wales | 76.6 | 70.1 | 33.5 | 113 | 64.2 | 85.4 |
| =58 Liverpool Hope | 84 | 79.8 | 21.2 | 112 | 57 | 85.2 |
| =58 Greenwich | 76.1 | 71.8 | 37 | 119 | 58.6 | 85.2 |
| 60 Coventry | 86.4 | 87.1 | – | 104 | 64.4 | 85 |
| 61 East London | 85.1 | 75.2 | 40 | 93 | 53.2 | 84.4 |
| 62 Derby | 80.4 | 77 | 25.5 | 111 | 56.7 | 84.3 |
| 63 Leeds Beckett | 83.6 | 83.2 | 17.8 | 102 | 56 | 83.8 |
| 64 Cumbria | 86.4 | 80 | 8.2 | 107 | – | 83.7 |
| 65 Roehampton | 79.8 | 70.5 | 40.2 | 96 | 56.9 | 83.6 |
| 66 Goldsmiths, London | 70 | 63.3 | 48 | 118 | – | 83.3 |
| =67 De Montfort | 77.4 | 75.7 | 43.2 | 98 | 52.5 | 83.2 |
| =67 York St John | 86.7 | 84.7 | – | 105 | 56.6 | 83.2 |
| 69 Winchester | 77.9 | 74.2 | 16.5 | 107 | 61.3 | 82.9 |
| 70 Kingston | 81.1 | 80.6 | 27 | 102 | 50.2 | 82.7 |
| 71 Leeds Trinity | 85 | 79.3 | – | 110 | 56.2 | 82.6 |
| 72 Solent, Southampton | 80.4 | 76.2 | 9.5 | 107 | 57.2 | 82 |
| 73 Hertfordshire | 78.4 | 76.2 | – | 99 | 66.2 | 81.8 |
| 74 Teesside | 81.3 | 70.6 | 18.2 | 108 | 52.7 | 81.7 |
| 75 St Mary's, Twickenham | 83 | 77.6 | 10.5 | 99 | – | 81.6 |
| =76 London South Bank | 78.9 | 74.3 | 27.8 | 96 | 52.8 | 81.5 |
| =76 Anglia Ruskin | 75.4 | 66.7 | 35.5 | 108 | 51.4 | 81.5 |
| =76 Oxford Brookes | 80.1 | 78.2 | 28.2 | 111 | 42.9 | 81.5 |
| 79 London Metropolitan | 82.6 | 80.3 | – | 87 | 63.5 | 81.4 |
| 80 Chester | 85.6 | 80.8 | 12.8 | 119 | 38.5 | 81.2 |
| 81 Brighton | 72.9 | 65.1 | 34 | 105 | 55.4 | 81.1 |
| 82 Buckinghamshire New | 83.9 | 83.4 | 12.5 | 82 | – | 80.8 |
| 83 Gloucestershire | 75.6 | 72.1 | – | 115 | 60.3 | 80.7 |
| 84 Bath Spa | 79.5 | 74.5 | – | 97 | 58.9 | 79.9 |
| 85 Wolverhampton | 81.3 | 72.5 | 12.2 | 93 | – | 79.6 |
| 86 Canterbury Christ Church | 78.7 | 77.2 | – | 95 | 56.6 | 79.3 |
| 87 Northampton | 82.6 | 81.3 | 4.2 | 97 | 39.6 | 77.5 |
| 88 Bradford | 62.6 | 59 | – | 111 | 51.4 | 73.5 |

| | | | |
|---|---|---|---|
| Employed in high-skilled job | 37% | Employed in lower-skilled job | 36% |
| Employed in high-skilled job and studying | 4% | Employed in lower-skilled job and studying | 2% |
| Studying | 6% | Unemployed | 5% |
| High-skilled work (median) salary | £24,700 | Low-/medium-skilled salary | £20,500 |

# Dentistry

The increasing demand for dentistry degrees continued to climb in 2023 when applications were up 18% year on year, to over 23,100. The number of dental school places available is capped by the government, as with medicine, and in 2023 1,505 dentistry students began courses. Career prospects are reliably positive. Dentistry remains the No 1 most lucrative option for graduates, with a median starting salary of £42,000 according to the latest figures. Although graduate outcomes are not as consistently high as for medicine, most graduates (88.4%) from five-year dentistry courses are in a high-skilled job as a dentist or enrolled on postgraduate study within 15 months – which ranks dentistry sixth in our employment index (down three places this year).

Queen's, Belfast retains the lead in our new Dentistry table for the second year running, while Glasgow – which topped it for seven years before – is steady in the runner-up spot again this year. With just 15 undergraduate dental schools across the country, this is one of the smaller and more stable subject rankings and this year's table differs very little from our previous edition, albeit with some reshuffling, such as Bristol moving up to third place from fifth, and Birmingham shifting down from =10th to 14th.

The dental school at Queen's has been delivering dental education in Northern Ireland since 1920. It has the highest average entry grades in the UK (179 UCAS points), sits fourth for research and second for student satisfaction with the broad experience, as well as fourth for teaching quality – both measures derived from our National Student Survey analysis. Dundee and Liverpool each achieve perfect 100% rates of graduate employment in high-skilled jobs and/or further study 15 months after degrees. King's College London is top for research but bottom for student satisfaction with teaching quality, while Manchester students expressed the lowest rates of satisfaction with the wider experience. The table is dominated by older universities, with only Plymouth and Central Lancashire representing the modern university sector.

"With growing evidence linking oral and general health, a sound understanding of biological sciences – in addition to practical skills – is essential to diagnose and manage dental conditions," comments Professor Ewen McColl, head of the Peninsula Dental School, University of Plymouth.

| Dentistry | Teaching quality % | Student experience % | Research quality % | Entry standards (UCAS points) | Graduate prospects % | Overall score |
|---|---|---|---|---|---|---|
| 1 Queen's, Belfast | 92.8 | 88.3 | 66.2 | 179 | 93.4 | 100 |
| 2 Glasgow | 95.2 | 85.7 | 63.5 | — | 97.4 | 97.6 |
| 3 Bristol | 90.6 | 82.6 | 70.9 | 168 | 95.5 | 97.4 |
| 4 Dundee | 95.4 | 93.6 | 60.8 | — | 100 | 97.3 |
| 5 Newcastle | 92.1 | 86.4 | 65.8 | 168 | 97.3 | 96.6 |
| 6 Cardiff | 86.2 | 71.7 | 58.8 | 174 | 96.2 | 95.1 |
| 7 Sheffield | 88.9 | 75.2 | 63.7 | 166 | 94.8 | 94.6 |
| 8 King's College London | 54.5 | 45.1 | 76.2 | 176 | 94.2 | 93.6 |
| 9 Liverpool | 93.3 | 85.2 | 63.2 | 155 | 100 | 92.5 |
| 10 Queen Mary, London | 78.1 | 64.7 | 54.8 | 173 | 96.8 | 92.3 |
| = 11 Leeds | 79.4 | 71.8 | 65 | 159 | 95.2 | 91.3 |
| = 11 Manchester | 62 | 44.5 | 71.2 | 168 | 96.8 | 91.3 |
| 13 Plymouth | 91.7 | 88.2 | 39.5 | 170 | 95.6 | 91 |
| 14 Birmingham | 82.1 | 59.1 | 55 | 166 | 95.7 | 90.6 |
| 15 Central Lancashire | 85.1 | 69.7 | 35.5 | 145 | 97.7 | 80.9 |

| | | |
|---|---|---|
| Employed in high-skilled job | 81% | |
| Employed in high-skilled job and studying | 7% | |
| Studying | 1% | |
| High-skilled work (median) salary | £42,000 | |

| | |
|---|---|
| Employed in lower-skilled job | 0% |
| Employed in lower-skilled job and studying | 0% |
| Unemployed | 3% |
| Low-/medium-skilled salary | N/A |

## Drama, Dance, Cinematics and Photography

Courses are broad-based within our Drama, Dance, Cinematics and Photography table, covering the four disciplines (although UCAS pairs photography with cinematics under the same grouping), and ranging from acting, theatre studies and performing arts to professional and commercial dance, film studies and photography. Joint honours courses, such as drama studies and English, are also incorporated.

Glasgow tops our new table, its rank boosted by the highest entry standards. In second place overall and last year's No 1 in the table Manchester is in front for research quality, based on results of the Research Excellence Framework 2021, where it is closely followed by the Central School of Speech and Drama – which, in =21st place overall, ranks fourth among the six specialist institutions, behind Guildhall (12th), Royal Conservatoire of Scotland (19th) and Trinity Laban (20th), and ahead of LAMDA (60th) and Rose Bruford (61st).

Students at Coventry expressed the highest rates of satisfaction with teaching quality and the wider experience in our latest National Student Survey (NSS) analysis. Conversely, those at Newcastle (in 69th place overall) gave the least positive reviews of teaching quality, while St Mary's Twickenham is bottom for student satisfaction with the wider experience.

Three universities: Surrey (11th in the table), Suffolk (38th) and East Anglia (35th) registered over 80% of their graduates employed in high-skilled jobs and/or furthering their studies within 15 months of their degrees. Around half that proportion (41.8%) had achieved the same outcomes among graduates of Brighton – one of five universities with less than half of its graduates achieving these outcomes 15 months on, along with West of Scotland, Bedfordshire, Hertfordshire, and Liverpool Hope. The subjects as a whole are up three places to rank 65th out of the 70 in our new employment ranking.

Although 19 institutions averaged over 144 UCAS points among their entrants (equivalent to AAA), performance or portfolio are often more important criteria for entry and there are plenty of courses with accessible entry standards.

| Drama, Dance, Cinematics and Photography | Teaching quality % | Student experience % | Research quality % | Entry standards (UCAS points) | Graduate prospects % | Overall score |
|---|---|---|---|---|---|---|
| 1 Glasgow | 84.2 | 74.6 | 60.5 | 195 | 68.5 | 100 |
| 2 Manchester | 78.3 | 69.4 | 80.5 | 167 | 73.3 | 98 |
| 3 Queen Mary, London | 85 | 77.5 | 76.4 | 138 | 77 | 97.6 |
| 4 Birmingham | 90.9 | 82.9 | 50.2 | 158 | 70.2 | 97.4 |
| 5 Exeter | 80.8 | 77.7 | 62.3 | 154 | 77.1 | 97 |
| 6 Warwick | 85 | 76 | 68.8 | 148 | 70.4 | 96.1 |
| 7 York | 80.3 | 70.1 | 58.2 | 158 | 74.4 | 95.5 |
| 8 Lancaster | 84.6 | 82.9 | 59.5 | 156 | 63.8 | 95 |
| 9 Essex | 90.2 | 76.8 | 34.2 | 158 | 70.1 | 94.9 |
| 10 Coventry | 93.6 | 87.8 | 55.5 | 125 | 68.5 | 94.8 |
| 11 Surrey | 76 | 67.6 | 43.8 | 157 | 83 | 94.7 |

| | | | | | | |
|---|---|---|---|---|---|---|
| 12 Guildhall School of Music and Drama | 84.2 | 71.6 | 61.3 | 137 | 74.6 | 94.4 |
| 13 Royal Holloway | 81.1 | 72.2 | 78.5 | 148 | 64.2 | 94.3 |
| 14 Bristol | 76.3 | 68 | 64.2 | 162 | 65.4 | 93.1 |
| 15 Manchester Metropolitan | 84.2 | 72.5 | 61.8 | 140 | 65.7 | 92.7 |
| 16 Edinburgh Napier | 87.2 | 72.4 | 8.5 | 174 | 68.1 | 92.4 |
| 17 Leeds | 76.9 | 72.8 | 56.8 | 158 | 61.8 | 91.6 |
| 18 Aberystwyth | 88 | 82.8 | 44.5 | 128 | 65.9 | 91.4 |
| 19 Royal Conservatoire of Scotland | 89 | 77 | 35.2 | 152 | 59.3 | 91.3 |
| 20 Trinity Laban | 78.3 | 74.2 | 38 | 138 | 75.6 | 91.2 |
| =21 Nottingham Trent | 86.9 | 77.5 | 53 | 136 | 60 | 91 |
| =21 Central School of Speech and Drama | 72.4 | 57.1 | 79.8 | 141 | 68.3 | 91 |
| 23 West of England | 82.6 | 76.2 | 48.2 | 142 | 62.6 | 90.8 |
| 24 Northumbria | 81.2 | 78.2 | 45.8 | 143 | 63.7 | 90.7 |
| 25 Kent | 85.2 | 77.4 | 74.8 | 124 | 55.1 | 90.3 |
| 26 Kingston | 81 | 74.7 | 45 | 143 | 63.2 | 90.1 |
| 27 Queen Margaret, Edinburgh | 86.2 | 74.1 | — | 184 | 57.6 | 90 |
| 28 Anglia Ruskin | 84 | 76.8 | 61.8 | 129 | 57.7 | 89.8 |
| 29 Queen's, Belfast | 81.3 | 75.4 | 46.8 | 144 | 59.5 | 89.6 |
| =30 De Montfort | 83.4 | 76.2 | 45 | 121 | 68.1 | 89.4 |
| =30 Edinburgh | 73.4 | 65 | 59.2 | 161 | 56.9 | 89.4 |
| 32 Sunderland | 87.1 | 83.4 | 49.8 | 124 | 57.3 | 89.3 |
| 33 Ulster | 87 | 77.1 | 49 | 122 | 60.4 | 89.1 |
| 34 Birmingham City | 82.6 | 67.2 | 46.5 | 132 | 63.1 | 88.6 |
| =35 West London | 86.8 | 71.1 | 32.2 | 128 | 65.3 | 88.5 |
| =35 East Anglia | 81.2 | 68.1 | — | 136 | 81.8 | 88.5 |
| 37 Goldsmiths, London | 70.8 | 60.1 | 46.8 | 130 | 76.8 | 88.3 |
| 38 Suffolk | 88.8 | 76.5 | — | 107 | 82.6 | 88.1 |
| 39 Liverpool John Moores | 85.5 | 81.1 | 22.2 | 142 | 57.6 | 87.9 |
| =40 Salford | 84 | 78 | 30.2 | 132 | 61.3 | 87.8 |
| =40 Central Lancashire | 87.6 | 78.3 | 19 | 130 | 63.3 | 87.8 |
| =40 Oxford Brookes | 89.3 | 82.6 | 21.5 | 125 | — | 87.8 |
| 43 Portsmouth | 84.5 | 78.6 | 30.2 | 125 | 63.2 | 87.6 |
| 44 Roehampton | 76.1 | 59.4 | 68.8 | 114 | 66.7 | 87.4 |
| 45 Falmouth | 81.3 | 76.9 | 48.8 | 127 | 56.4 | 87.2 |
| 46 Lincoln | 85.5 | 75.6 | 37.2 | 126 | 57.7 | 87 |
| =47 Sussex | 78.8 | 70.4 | 48 | 141 | 54.1 | 86.9 |
| =47 Gloucestershire | 83.9 | 70.7 | 45 | 122 | 59.4 | 86.9 |
| =49 Chester | 86.2 | 80.1 | 21 | 130 | 59.3 | 86.8 |
| =49 Leeds Arts | 85.1 | 78.4 | 2.8 | 139 | 64.7 | 86.8 |
| 51 Edge Hill | 84.7 | 79.1 | — | 134 | 67.8 | 86.7 |
| 52 Canterbury Christ Church | 86.9 | 78.2 | 38.5 | 111 | 59.4 | 86.5 |
| =53 Westminster | 67.4 | 63.3 | 75.5 | 131 | 58.9 | 86.4 |
| =53 Hull | 80 | 70.4 | 35 | 120 | 66.2 | 86.4 |
| 55 Plymouth | 77.1 | 67.7 | 49.8 | 126 | 60 | 86.1 |
| 56 Arts University, Bournemouth | 79.8 | 71.7 | 23 | 145 | 56.6 | 85.7 |
| =57 University of the Arts London | 77.2 | 68.9 | 46 | 135 | 54.8 | 85.6 |
| =57 Bath Spa | 87.3 | 75.4 | 26 | 121 | 57.7 | 85.6 |
| 59 Staffordshire | 84.3 | 77 | 31.5 | 121 | 57.1 | 85.5 |

# Drama, Dance, Cinematics and Photography cont.

| | | Teaching quality % | Student experience % | Research quality % | Entry standards (UCAS points) | Graduate prospects % | Overall score |
|---|---|---|---|---|---|---|---|
| 60 | LAMDA | 89.4 | 82.8 | — | 116 | 64.5 | 85.3 |
| 61 | Rose Bruford | 84.6 | 65 | 19 | 129 | 61.9 | 85.2 |
| =62 | Reading | 72.3 | 68.9 | 59 | 124 | 57 | 85.1 |
| =62 | Greenwich | 84.5 | 72.7 | — | 131 | 65.5 | 85.1 |
| 64 | Buckinghamshire New | 88.2 | 76.8 | — | 111 | 68.9 | 84.9 |
| 65 | Bolton | 88 | 74.8 | — | 120 | 65.1 | 84.7 |
| 66 | Wolverhampton | 87.9 | 76.3 | 6.8 | 115 | 63.4 | 84.5 |
| 67 | Northampton | 80.3 | 65.2 | 30.2 | 123 | 60.7 | 84.4 |
| 68 | University for the Creative Arts | 74.3 | 64.4 | 41.2 | 136 | 55.4 | 84.2 |
| =69 | East London | 91.1 | 70.8 | 13 | 116 | 57.5 | 84.1 |
| =69 | Newcastle | 63.9 | 63.5 | 59.2 | 136 | — | 84.1 |
| =69 | South Wales | 79.5 | 65.7 | 35.8 | 126 | 56.3 | 84.1 |
| =69 | Brunel | 81.8 | 71 | 38 | 122 | 53.2 | 84.1 |
| 73 | Liverpool Hope | 89.3 | 82.1 | 17.5 | 122 | 49.3 | 83.9 |
| 74 | Chichester | 77.2 | 62 | 13.2 | 131 | 64.9 | 83.5 |
| =75 | Wales Trinity St David | 85.5 | 69.6 | — | 149 | 50.5 | 83.3 |
| =75 | Derby | 84.9 | 77.5 | — | 119 | 61.8 | 83.3 |
| =75 | Solent, Southampton | 85.8 | 79.2 | — | 120 | 59.6 | 83.3 |
| =78 | Norwich University of the Arts | 82.4 | 73.3 | — | 130 | 60.1 | 83.2 |
| =78 | West of Scotland | 85.1 | 76.5 | 19.2 | 142 | 42.9 | 83.2 |
| =80 | London Metropolitan | 90.7 | 86 | — | 120 | 51.9 | 83.1 |
| 80 | Bournemouth | 77.6 | 68.2 | 38.5 | 119 | 55.3 | 83.1 |
| 82 | Middlesex | 82 | 76.9 | 26 | 114 | 54.4 | 82.9 |
| =83 | York St John | 82.3 | 71.9 | 33.2 | 114 | 52.8 | 82.8 |
| =83 | Worcester | 84.3 | 74 | 5.8 | 116 | 60.5 | 82.8 |
| 85 | Hertfordshire | 81.7 | 73.4 | 42.5 | 112 | 48.1 | 82.3 |
| =86 | Huddersfield | 78 | 68.6 | 20 | 127 | 55.4 | 82.2 |
| =86 | Winchester | 78.8 | 67.9 | 32.5 | 110 | 57.6 | 82.2 |
| 88 | Sheffield Hallam | 83.7 | 76 | — | 119 | 56.5 | 81.5 |
| 89 | London South Bank | 84.5 | 71.9 | — | 112 | 55 | 80.2 |
| 90 | Cumbria | 79.1 | 69.8 | — | 111 | 57.4 | 79.1 |
| 91 | Leeds Beckett | 69.9 | 59.2 | 15.8 | 116 | 58.6 | 78.4 |
| 92 | Bedfordshire | 88.5 | 74.8 | — | 103 | 45.1 | 77.8 |
| 93 | St Mary's, Twickenham | 74.7 | 55.7 | — | 120 | 57.1 | 77.6 |
| 94 | Brighton | 67.6 | 62.3 | 44.2 | 113 | 41.8 | 76.5 |

| | | | |
|---|---|---|---|
| Employed in high-skilled job | 45% | Employed in lower-skilled job | 33% |
| Employed in high-skilled job and studying | 2% | Employed in lower-skilled job and studying | 1% |
| Studying | 3% | Unemployed | 8% |
| High-skilled work (median) salary | £24,000 | Low-/medium-skilled salary | £20,000 |

# East and South Asian Studies

This subject table encompasses Chinese studies, Japanese studies and South Asian studies. The subjects are offered by only a small number of universities in the UK, among them SOAS in London (in fifth place of our table overall), which also offers a range of languages including Burmese, Indonesian, Thai, Tibetan and Vietnamese. Degrees in these subjects are afforded extra protection by the government because of their small size and their economic and cultural significance.

Most undergraduates learn their chosen language from scratch, although universities expect to see evidence of potential in other modern language qualifications.

Oxford leads the table for the third consecutive year. Its rank is boosted by the top research quality rating, based on results of the Research Excellence Framework 2021, where it is followed by Edinburgh (fourth overall) – which achieved the top graduate outcomes in the subjects according to the latest figures. Runner-up Cambridge has the edge on entry standards – with entrants averaging 196 UCAS points, only marginally ahead of the 194 points at Oxford.

In our new National Student Survey analysis, the best rates of student satisfaction with teaching quality are found at Oxford Brookes, while Durham props up the opposite end of the teaching quality scale. The same two universities top-and-tail our measure for student satisfaction with the broader experience.

Student numbers, which were already modest, have declined for the past five years. In 2023, there were 3,390 applications to the subjects (down 20% year on year) and 675 new undergraduates were accepted onto courses (down 22%).

East and South Asian studies rank 60th in our graduate employment list of 70 subject areas, while starting salaries of £25,000 compare more favourably, =46th place of our pay index.

| East and South Asian Studies | Teaching quality % | Student experience % | Research quality % | Entry standards (UCAS points) | Graduate prospects % | Overall score |
|---|---|---|---|---|---|---|
| 1 Oxford | 81.6 | 54 | 62.3 | 194 | 80.8* | 100 |
| 2 Cambridge | 87 | 67 | 45.2 | 196 | — | 96.6 |
| 3 Nottingham | 81.5 | 70.9 | 62 | 142 | — | 94.7 |
| 4 Edinburgh | 71.9 | 67.3 | 45.8 | 189 | 83.0* | 93.9 |
| 5 SOAS London | 72.1 | 60.6 | 60 | 147 | 80.8 | 92.9 |
| 6 Leeds | 77.4 | 76.6 | 52 | 149 | 77.9 | 92.3 |
| 7 Cardiff | 84.5 | 78.2 | 55.5 | 130 | — | 92 |
| 8 Sheffield | 87.2 | 83.7 | 48.8 | 152 | 64 | 91.2 |
| 9 Manchester | 76.3 | 66.7 | 52.5 | 149 | 72 | 90.2 |
| 10 Durham | 57 | 44.2 | 46 | 177 | 83.3 | 87.7 |
| 11 Oxford Brookes | 92.3 | 85 | 36 | 120 | 46.7* | 81.1 |
| 12 Central Lancashire | 80.8 | 75.5 | 31.8 | 114 | 58 | 78.5 |

| | | | |
|---|---|---|---|
| Employed in high-skilled job | 36% | Employed in lower-skilled job | 29% |
| Employed in high-skilled job and studying | 3% | Employed in lower-skilled job and studying | 2% |
| Studying | 12% | Unemployed | 9% |
| High-skilled work (median) salary | £27,500 | Low-/medium-skilled salary | £20,000 |

# Economics

Warwick ranks No 1 in our Economics table for the third consecutive year. Warwick's performance is driven by strength in all five areas measured in our ranking – including top-15 finishes for both measures of student satisfaction and the second-best score for research quality – without being unbeaten on any individually. In runner-up position overall, the London School of Economics (LSE) topped our Economics table three years ago and claims the best graduate prospects this year jointly with Cambridge and King's College London. The LSE also leads for research in the field, based on results of the Research Excellence Framework 2021, but sits second to Warwick due largely to being outdone on rates of student satisfaction, for which LSE ranks in the top 35 for teaching quality and the wider experience, measures derived from the National Student Survey.

Cambridge, steady in third place overall, leads on entry standards with 223 UCAS points averaged by its new entrants. St Andrews and Oxford also registered above 200 points. Economics students at Hertfordshire (in =41st place overall) are by a clear margin the most satisfied with their teaching quality and the wider experience for the second year running. Those at Huddersfield, Ulster and Liverpool registered in the top three across these metrics. Conversely, economics undergraduates at Cardiff and Leicester expressed the lowest rates of contentment with teaching quality, positions held by Goldsmiths and Cambridge for the wider experience.

Applications to study economics soared past 100,000 in 2023 (up 8% year on year) and new student enrolments increased too, though less steeply by around 5%, and nearly 13,900 undergraduates were accepted onto economics courses.

Maths A-level (or equivalent qualification) is usually required by the leading universities, while philosophy, sociology, government and politics, further maths and economics may be useful. Dr Michael Gmeiner and Professor Dimitra Petropoulou, Department of Economics, London School of Economics and Political Science (LSE), advise applicants to "become comfortable with mathematics because it's used extensively in economics," and say: "An economics degree is rigorous and highly applicable to the real world, equipping students with the skills to analyse the important issues of our time."

Economics graduates are among the best paid, commanding median salaries of £30,000 – only four of the 70 subjects in our earnings index place higher. Economics sits 25th in our employment ranking (down five places), with the latest data showing just under three-quarters of graduates in high-skilled jobs and/or postgraduate study within 15 months of degrees.

| Economics | Teaching quality % | Student experience % | Research quality % | Entry standards (UCAS points) | Graduate prospects % | Overall score |
|---|---|---|---|---|---|---|
| 1 Warwick | 84.7 | 85.5 | 76.5 | 191 | 93.3 | 100 |
| 2 London School of Economics | 80.1 | 79.4 | 80.8 | 193 | 96.2 | 99.3 |
| 3 Cambridge | 82.9 | 71.6 | 68.2 | 223 | 96.2 | 99.1 |
| 4 Oxford | 83.5 | 74.5 | 62 | 208 | 94.8 | 97.8 |
| 5 St Andrews | 89.1 | 88.6 | 31.2 | 219 | 91 | 97.1 |
| 6 University College London | 74.2 | 79.6 | 72.5 | 188 | 94.8 | 96.3 |
| 7 Strathclyde | 84.8 | 84 | 52.5 | 196 | 86.6 | 95.8 |
| 8 Durham | 79.9 | 77.1 | 55.8 | 184 | 92.9 | 94.8 |
| 9 Nottingham | 76.6 | 79.2 | 64.5 | 170 | 91.1 | 94.1 |
| 10 Lancaster | 84.7 | 83.7 | 59.2 | 142 | 88.7 | 94 |
| 11 Liverpool | 85.4 | 88.9 | 58 | 139 | 84.4 | 93.7 |

| | | | | | | | |
|---|---|---|---|---|---|---|---|
| 12 | Loughborough | 85.7 | 87 | 49.2 | 153 | 85.7 | 93.5 |
| 13 | Leeds | 74.5 | 80.2 | 62.3 | 168 | 91.2 | 93.4 |
| 14 | Glasgow | 73 | 75.3 | 57.2 | 195 | 87.8 | 92.7 |
| =15 | Exeter | 79.3 | 82.1 | 44.8 | 164 | 91.4 | 92.5 |
| =15 | Sheffield | 83.2 | 86.3 | 48.8 | 147 | 85.9 | 92.5 |
| =15 | Surrey | 86.3 | 88.6 | 54.2 | 131 | 81.8 | 92.5 |
| =18 | Bristol | 72.8 | 76.2 | 60.2 | 170 | 90.4 | 92.2 |
| =18 | Birmingham | 78 | 78.7 | 55.2 | 150 | 91.2 | 92.2 |
| 20 | Ulster | 90.8 | 90.5 | 45.8 | 117 | 81.3 | 91.9 |
| 21 | Queen Mary, London | 77.2 | 76.4 | 60.5 | 154 | 87.4 | 91.8 |
| 22 | Edinburgh | 71.6 | 75.1 | 50.2 | 184 | 92.8 | 91.7 |
| 23 | Hull | 87.9 | 83.3 | 29.5 | — | 88.6 | 91.5 |
| 24 | Bath | 78.7 | 83.2 | 25.2 | 174 | 94.4 | 91.3 |
| 25 | East Anglia | 82.2 | 83.3 | 46.2 | 130 | 87.8 | 91 |
| 26 | Manchester | 75.6 | 75.7 | 54.5 | 159 | 87.6 | 90.9 |
| 27 | Aston | 83.3 | 85.4 | 43.5 | 119 | 89 | 90.7 |
| =28 | York | 75.6 | 74.2 | 48.8 | 146 | 90.2 | 89.8 |
| =28 | Heriot-Watt | 77.2 | 78 | 38.2 | 166 | 86.4 | 89.8 |
| 30 | Stirling | 82.6 | 78.8 | 38.2 | 152 | 82.4 | 89.7 |
| 31 | Queen's, Belfast | 74.7 | 77.3 | 40.5 | 143 | 93 | 89.4 |
| 32 | Southampton | 77.2 | 80.6 | 42 | 140 | 87.4 | 89.3 |
| 33 | Cardiff | 69 | 74.8 | 56 | 141 | 90.7 | 89 |
| 34 | Newcastle | 74.2 | 79.9 | 40.5 | 149 | 86.8 | 88.7 |
| 35 | Reading | 79.8 | 82.2 | 46.2 | 118 | 82.9 | 88.6 |
| 36 | Sussex | 77.5 | 78.6 | 52 | 130 | 79.6 | 88.3 |
| =37 | Essex | 81.6 | 84.7 | 59.5 | 106 | 71.2 | 88 |
| =37 | King's College London | 77.6 | 77 | — | 183 | 96.2 | 88 |
| 39 | Brighton | 85 | 87.4 | 28.5 | 91 | 87.6* | 87.8 |
| 40 | Royal Holloway | 76 | 78.4 | 53.8 | 119 | 78.9 | 87.3 |
| 41 | Hertfordshire | 96.9 | 97.6 | 29 | 87 | 63.7 | 87.2 |
| 42 | Oxford Brookes | 83.2 | 86.2 | 26 | 116 | 81.8 | 87.1 |
| =43 | Aberdeen | 79.8 | 79.1 | 32.2 | 172 | 70 | 87 |
| =43 | Nottingham Trent | 84.3 | 84.1 | 34.2 | 117 | 75.9 | 87 |
| 45 | Keele | 83.2 | 82.7 | 24.8 | 100 | 88.3 | 86.9 |
| 46 | Portsmouth | 86.2 | 83.8 | 37.8 | 110 | 70.2 | 86.4 |
| 47 | Swansea | 83 | 79.7 | 38.8 | 117 | 73.6 | 86.3 |
| 48 | Manchester Metropolitan | 79 | 78.4 | 42.8 | 116 | 76.1 | 86 |
| 49 | Kent | 79.7 | 77.6 | 29.5 | 121 | 80.8 | 85.7 |
| 50 | Huddersfield | 91.6 | 88.5 | 23.2 | 111 | 64.2 | 85.5 |
| 51 | Plymouth | 77.5 | 79.9 | 28.7 | 109 | 80 | 84.6 |
| 52 | Dundee | 72.1 | 73.7 | — | 176 | 88.9 | 84.4 |
| 53 | Greenwich | 85.2 | 84.1 | 33.2 | 97 | 67.2 | 84.3 |
| 54 | Lincoln | 80.3 | 81.2 | — | 113 | 86.2 | 83.4 |
| 55 | Bournemouth | 77.9 | 75.3 | 23 | 105 | 77.5 | 82.7 |
| 56 | City | 72 | 75.8 | 32.5 | 121 | 73.5 | 82.5 |
| 57 | Coventry | 74.4 | 74.8 | 33.2 | 97 | 75.9 | 82.2 |
| =58 | London South Bank | 87 | 83 | — | 84 | 75.9 | 81.6 |
| =58 | Sheffield Hallam | 82.5 | 79.8 | — | 104 | 77.6 | 81.6 |

| Economics cont. | | Teaching quality % | Student experience % | Research quality % | Entry standards (UCAS points) | Graduate prospects % | Overall score |
|---|---|---|---|---|---|---|---|
| 60 | SOAS London | 74.8 | 73.2 | — | 141 | 78.6 | 81.1 |
| 61 | West of England | 74.5 | 72.2 | 27.3 | 107 | 72 | 81 |
| 62 | Leeds Beckett | 77.4 | 75.6 | 8.2 | 98 | 80 | 80.9 |
| 63 | Leicester | 70.9 | 74 | — | 122 | 86.3 | 80.6 |
| 64 | Kingston | 78.5 | 78.6 | 24 | 89 | 66 | 80.2 |
| 65 | Westminster | 74.7 | 77.7 | 37.5 | 105 | 54.5 | 79.5 |
| 66 | De Montfort | 76.9 | 75.4 | — | 90 | 76.7 | 78.6 |
| 67 | Middlesex | 86.1 | 84.5 | — | 88 | 57.6 | 78.3 |
| 68 | Birmingham City | 82.1 | 77.1 | 11.2 | 107 | 54.9 | 78.2 |
| =69 | Brunel | 72 | 73.1 | 16 | 109 | 62.1 | 77.3 |
| =69 | Goldsmiths, London | 76.9 | 71 | — | 105 | 68.4 | 77.3 |
| 71 | Northampton | 73.8 | 72.4 | 1.2 | 81 | — | 74.7 |

| | | | |
|---|---|---|---|
| Employed in high-skilled job | 58% | Employed in lower-skilled job | 13% |
| Employed in high-skilled job and studying | 9% | Employed in lower-skilled job and studying | 1% |
| Studying | 6% | Unemployed | 5% |
| High-skilled work (median) salary | £31,000 | Low-/medium-skilled salary | £22,500 |

# Education

Durham takes the lead in our new Education table, boosted by the top research rating in the field – based on results of the latest Research Excellence Framework in 2021 – as well as strong performance across the other five metrics. Our Education table includes inspection data by Ofsted for universities in England, adding an extra column which distinguishes it from the other 69 subject rankings in our *Guide*. Fourteen universities tie for the top score (four) from Ofsted, most of which also place within our table's top 30. These are, in descending order: Durham, Bristol, Cambridge, Bristol, Nottingham, Birmingham, Warwick, Brighton, University College London, Winchester, St Mary's, Twickenham, Chichester and Edge Hill, and Brunel. Only Chester at 42nd and Worcester at 43rd – both with Ofsted's highest rating – rank outside our top 30.

Applications to teaching training BEd degrees – the most common route into primary teaching – declined sharply in 2023 when 43,695 applied – a 17% decrease on 2022 and 22% lower than 2021's boom year for applications to teacher training. The number of students who gained places declined less steeply – by 11% year on year – and 8,935 undergraduates were accepted onto courses in 2023. Academic Studies in Education degrees are also encompassed in our ranking, and the subject attracted 27,180 applications in 2023, while 6,315 new undergraduates began courses.

"Informed by cutting-edge research, policy and practice and supported by the latest learning technologies, you will be empowered to implement change and transform people's lives for the better," say Dr Trevor Grimshaw, Dr Ioannis Costas Batlle and Dr Sam Carr, Department of Education, University of Bath, who advise applicants to "Find the recommended reading lists and start training yourself to analyse the literature critically, noting down your key questions as you read."

Secondary school teachers are more likely to take the Postgraduate Certificate in Education, or to train through the Teach First or Schools Direct programmes, which are not included in our table's statistics. Our focus exclusively on undergraduate provision explains the absence of some of the best-known education departments, which only offer postgraduate courses. Cambridge, where degrees combine the academic study of education with other subjects but do not offer Qualified Teacher Status, is down one place to tie in the runner-up spot with Bristol this year. The Royal Conservatoire of Scotland, a former leader of our Education table, sits in fifth place overall but has the highest entry standards of 216 UCAS points. The top six for entry standards are exclusively Scottish universities, which benefit from the favourable tariff conversion for Scottish secondary qualifications, while also performing strongly across our table's other measures.

For student satisfaction with teaching quality, South Wales is in first place, while Warwick leads for student satisfaction with the broader experience. At the foot of the same ranking is Oxford Brookes and for teaching quality Cumbria students express the lowest rates of satisfaction, our National Student Survey analysis shows.

Education sits 28th in our employment ranking of 70 subject areas (up five places). The demands for new primary and secondary teachers vary across the country, creating differing graduate outcomes scores at universities. Royal Conservatoire Scotland tops our ranking this year, with 96.6% of graduates in high-skilled work and/or postgraduate study 15 months after their degrees.

St Mary's, Twickenham and Durham also had over 90% of graduates achieving these outcomes. Though not an ingredient of our ranking, teachers' pay is of interest to many. Median graduate salaries of £25,714 for those in high-skilled jobs place education just outside the upper half of subject areas, at =38th.

| Education | Teaching quality % | Student experience % | Ofsted rating | Research quality % | Entry standards (UCAS points) | Graduate prospects % | Overall score |
|---|---|---|---|---|---|---|---|
| 1 Durham | 82 | 78.2 | 73.2 | 4 | 152 | 92.5 | 100 |
| =2 Bristol | 86.9 | 84.6 | 67.5 | 4 | 153 | 85.7 | 99.7 |
| =2 Cambridge | 83.8 | 65.6 | 67.8 | 4 | 179 | 88 | 99.7 |
| 4 Edinburgh | 81.4 | 75.8 | 51 | — | 195 | 88.8 | 99 |
| 5 Royal Conservatoire of Scotland | 82.3 | 70.1 | — | — | 216 | 96.6 | 98.6 |
| 6 Glasgow | 81.7 | 73.6 | 64.5 | — | 191 | 83.6 | 98.4 |
| 7 Nottingham | 88 | 84 | 61.5 | 4 | 132 | — | 98.1 |
| 8 Aberdeen | 90.2 | 89.5 | 23 | — | 177 | 85.9 | 97.7 |
| =9 Dundee | 87 | 78.8 | 35.2 | — | 178 | 87 | 97.3 |
| =9 Warwick | 92.8 | 91.6 | 55.8 | 4 | 136 | 75.3 | 97.3 |
| 11 Sussex | 88.6 | 81.4 | 64.8 | 3.4 | 136 | 87.8 | 97 |
| 12 Brighton | 92.1 | 87 | 37.5 | 4 | 123 | 84.9 | 96.4 |
| 13 Stirling | 76 | 67.6 | 53.2 | — | 196 | 85.7 | 96 |
| =14 Birmingham | 84.1 | 83 | 70.5 | 3.5 | 139 | 81.1 | 95.5 |
| =14 Strathclyde | 85.2 | 78.1 | 20.8 | — | 203 | 80.7 | 95.5 |
| =14 West of Scotland | 90.2 | 82.5 | 17.5 | — | 193 | 77.7 | 95.5 |
| 17 Leeds | 84 | 85.4 | 44.2 | — | 150 | 84.8 | 95.1 |
| 18 Cardiff | 79.8 | 76.5 | 72 | — | 154 | 80.4 | 95 |
| =19 University College London | 81.5 | 84.8 | 68.8 | 4 | 157 | 65.4 | 94.4 |
| =19 St Mary's, Twickenham | 91.4 | 87.8 | — | 4 | 112 | 93.4 | 94.4 |
| =19 Winchester | 83.5 | 80.5 | 28 | 4 | 126 | 89.6 | 94.4 |
| 22 Northumbria | 84.8 | 80.3 | 42 | 3 | 151 | 89.9 | 94 |
| 23 Bath | 81 | 75.6 | 47.8 | — | 145 | 86.8 | 93.7 |
| =24 Suffolk | 87.1 | 86.1 | 21.8 | — | — | 85.7 | 93.3 |

**Education** cont.

| | | Teaching quality % | Student experience % | Ofsted rating | Research quality % | Entry standards (UCAS points) | Graduate prospects % | Overall score |
|---|---|---|---|---|---|---|---|---|
| =24 | Southampton | 78.3 | 79.9 | 41 | 4 | 157 | 75.9* | 93.3 |
| 26 | Sheffield | 85.7 | 87.7 | 62 | 3 | 155 | 74.1 | 93.2 |
| 27 | Reading | 88.1 | 81.7 | 41.8 | 3 | 134 | 87 | 93.1 |
| 28 | Roehampton | 87.5 | 83.1 | 53.5 | 3.5 | 115 | 79.6 | 92.9 |
| 29 | Sheffield Hallam | 84.9 | 77.6 | 39.2 | 3.7 | 127 | 81.7 | 92.5 |
| =30 | Chichester | 87 | 83.5 | 5.2 | 4 | 123 | 85 | 92.4 |
| =30 | Edge Hill | 80.9 | 74.9 | 30.8 | 4 | 134 | 82.4 | 92.4 |
| 32 | Bangor | 83 | 71.3 | 42 | — | 148 | 82.1 | 92.2 |
| 33 | West of England | 87.5 | 83.2 | 48.5 | 3 | 129 | 81.3 | 92 |
| =34 | East Anglia | 84.4 | 79 | 41.2 | 3 | 131 | 87.7 | 91.9 |
| =34 | Newcastle | 88.5 | 85.4 | 36.8 | 3.2 | 123 | 82.6* | 91.9 |
| =36 | Derby | 84.3 | 80.4 | 29.2 | 3.5 | 127 | 84.5 | 91.8 |
| =36 | St Mark and St John | 91.8 | 85.9 | 14 | 3.3 | 122 | 84.2 | 91.8 |
| 38 | Bedfordshire | 92.9 | 86.9 | 21 | 3.1 | 111 | 83.7 | 91 |
| 39 | Wolverhampton | 92.6 | 85.3 | 10.5 | 3 | 127 | 84.5 | 90.8 |
| =40 | Nottingham Trent | 86.5 | 81.8 | 29.5 | 3 | 129 | 83.1 | 90.5 |
| =40 | Keele | 85.8 | 82.5 | 33.2 | — | 118 | 81.1 | 90.5 |
| 42 | Chester | 77.8 | 73.5 | 16.2 | 4 | 128 | 82.7 | 90.2 |
| 43 | Worcester | 82.3 | 78.7 | 10.8 | 4 | 125 | 78.7 | 90 |
| 44 | Manchester Metropolitan | 83.9 | 78.5 | 42.8 | 3 | 135 | 77.7 | 89.9 |
| 45 | South Wales | 94.2 | 84 | — | — | 123 | 77.6 | 89.8 |
| 46 | Coventry | 85.8 | 78.2 | 54.2 | 3 | 126 | 73.1 | 89.7 |
| =47 | Anglia Ruskin | 86.5 | 81.4 | 16.2 | — | 115 | 84.8 | 89.6 |
| =47 | Northampton | 86.2 | 83.1 | 28.2 | 3 | 115 | 83.5 | 89.6 |
| =47 | Kingston | 86.5 | 82.2 | 28.5 | 3 | 126 | 80.2 | 89.6 |
| =50 | York | 75 | 77.1 | 70.8 | 3.3 | 132 | 69.7 | 89.4 |
| =50 | York St John | 84.2 | 80.7 | 24.5 | 3.2 | 126 | 80.9 | 89.4 |
| 52 | Bishop Grosseteste | 91 | 86.7 | 10.2 | 3 | 118 | 81.2 | 89.2 |
| 53 | Bath Spa | 79.7 | 71.2 | 31.5 | 3.7 | 110 | 82.2 | 89.1 |
| =54 | Staffordshire | 89.1 | 82.5 | 18.2 | 3 | 133 | 76 | 88.9 |
| =54 | Liverpool John Moores | 84.9 | 81.1 | 21.8 | 3 | 146 | 75.5 | 88.9 |
| =54 | Huddersfield | 88.9 | 85 | 31.2 | 3.1 | 129 | 69.5 | 88.9 |
| =54 | Hertfordshire | 92.7 | 90.1 | 9.5 | 3 | 114 | 78.3 | 88.9 |
| 58 | Wales Trinity St David | 90.9 | 84.8 | 11.8 | — | 143 | 69.7 | 88.8 |
| 59 | Cardiff Metropolitan | 84.9 | 84.7 | 17.5 | — | 125 | 77.9 | 88.6 |
| =60 | Liverpool Hope | 87.6 | 79.7 | 23.8 | 3 | 127 | 76.3 | 88.4 |
| =60 | Swansea | 79.9 | 75.7 | 46.5 | — | 137 | 71.9 | 88.4 |
| 62 | Brunel | 88.4 | 87.2 | 20.8 | 3 | 119 | 75 | 88.2 |
| 63 | Gloucestershire | 85.7 | 82.5 | 16.2 | 3 | 122 | 79.6 | 88 |
| 64 | East London | 88.8 | 82 | 11.2 | 3 | 119 | 78.4 | 87.8 |
| =65 | Bolton | 83.6 | 83.5 | 7.8 | 3 | 108 | 86.7 | 87.6 |
| =65 | Lincoln | 87.7 | 78.1 | 28.5 | — | 121 | 71.3 | 87.6 |
| 67 | Plymouth | 80.2 | 75.6 | 39.2 | 3 | 125 | 75 | 87.3 |
| 68 | Central Lancashire | 91.5 | 87.1 | — | — | 125 | 68.8 | 87 |

| | | | | | | | |
|---|---|---|---|---|---|---|---|
| 69 | Middlesex | 87.8 | 84.7 | 15.5 | 3 | 114 | 74.3 | 86.9 |
| 70 | Aberystwyth | 87.8 | 85.2 | — | — | 122 | 73.3 | 86.7 |
| 71 | Greenwich | 81.3 | 76.2 | 17 | 3 | 124 | 79.2 | 86.6 |
| 72 | Newman | 84.3 | 80.1 | 4.8 | 3 | 123 | 79.2 | 86.5 |
| =73 | Sunderland | 82.1 | 73.6 | 9.2 | 3 | 132 | 78.1 | 86.3 |
| =73 | Teesside | 88.7 | 79.5 | 18.2 | 3 | 110 | 72.8 | 86.3 |
| 75 | Portsmouth | 77 | 78.7 | 51.7 | 3.5 | 115 | 62.7 | 86.2 |
| =76 | Leeds Beckett | 84.5 | 76.5 | 17.2 | 3 | 116 | 75.5 | 86 |
| =76 | Canterbury Christ Church | 81.3 | 72 | 29.5 | 3 | 109 | 78.3 | 86 |
| 78 | Leeds Trinity | 81 | 71.3 | 8 | 3 | 111 | 83.4 | 85.5 |
| 79 | Birmingham City | 79.7 | 75.9 | 11.8 | 3 | 127 | 76.6 | 85.4 |
| 80 | London Metropolitan | 90.1 | 77.7 | 6.5 | 3 | 101 | 73.9 | 85.2 |
| =81 | Hull | 80.4 | 72.1 | 31.5 | 2.2 | 129 | 76.5 | 84 |
| =81 | Oxford Brookes | 75.7 | 60.1 | 36 | 2.3 | 119 | 84.5 | 84 |
| 83 | London South Bank | 77.4 | 76.5 | — | 3 | 108 | 79.6 | 83.4 |
| 84 | Cumbria | 72.5 | 63 | 8.5 | 3 | 127 | 79.3 | 83 |
| 85 | West London | 91.9 | 91 | — | — | 125 | 52.5 | 82.7 |
| 86 | Buckinghamshire New | 80.7 | 77.6 | 6.5 | — | — | 70.5 | 81.9 |
| 87 | Goldsmiths, London | 78.7 | 70 | 29.5 | 3 | 113 | 60.9 | 81.7 |
| 88 | De Montfort | 76.7 | 76.9 | — | — | 110 | 72.5 | 81 |

| | | | | |
|---|---|---|---|---|
| Employed in high-skilled job | 64% | Employed in lower-skilled job | | 17% |
| Employed in high-skilled job and studying | 4% | Employed in lower-skilled job and studying | | 1% |
| Studying | 5% | Unemployed | | 4% |
| High-skilled work (median) salary | £26,000 | Low-/medium-skilled salary | | £19,000 |

# Electrical and Electronic Engineering

"Electrical and electronic engineering is pivotal to modern innovation, driving advancements in renewable energy, telecommunications and electric vehicles," says Dr Mohamed K Darwish, course director for MSC in advanced electronic and electrical engineering, and Dr Konstantinos Banitsas, lecturer and researcher, Department of Electronic and Computer Engineering, Brunel University.

Maths is a required subject, along with a second science such as physics, electronics or chemistry. Electrical and electronic engineering attracts the second highest number of applications and enrolments among the engineering disciplines (behind mechanical engineering). In 2023 there were 30,550 applications and just under 5,000 undergraduates were accepted onto courses.

Entry standards at the leading institutions are high. Led by our table's overall frontrunner Cambridge, where entrants averaged an extraordinary 227 UCAS tariff points, 32 universities recorded over 144 points (equivalent to AAA at A level).

Imperial, in third place overall, has the edge for research quality – based on results of the Research Excellence Framework 2021. Oxford sits second for research, as it does overall. The QS world rankings 2025 put Cambridge and Oxford in the top 10 for the subject, and Imperial 11th.

The best graduate prospects are found at Cambridge where nearly all (97.2%) graduates were working in high-skilled jobs and/or enrolled in postgraduate study within 15 months. It is one of 16 universities to register at least 90% for this measure. The subject as a whole ranks =5th in our salaries index and compares almost as favourably in our employment table – where it ranks ninth.

Modern universities fare more positively in the eyes of their students than those with older foundations: in our National Student Survey analysis Leeds Beckett (=45th overall) is top for student satisfaction with the broad experience, followed by London South Bank (56th) and De Montfort (42nd). For students' evaluation of teaching quality, Birmingham City (43rd) comes top, followed by London South Bank and Manchester Metropolitan (=23rd).

| Electrical and Electronic Engineering | Teaching quality % | Student experience % | Research quality % | Entry standards (UCAS points) | Graduate prospects % | Overall score |
|---|---|---|---|---|---|---|
| 1 Cambridge | 81.6 | 80.9 | 77.2 | 227 | 97.2 | 100 |
| 2 Oxford | 80.8 | 76.1 | 77.5 | 216 | 94 | 97.8 |
| 3 Imperial College | 77.4 | 70.6 | 81 | 203 | 95 | 96.2 |
| 4 Southampton | 82.4 | 78.8 | 70 | 173 | 95.5 | 95 |
| 5 Strathclyde | 82.4 | 78 | 52.8 | 212 | 90.9 | 94.6 |
| 6 University College London | 82.7 | 82.1 | 70 | 172 | 90.0* | 94.2 |
| 7 Sheffield | 83.7 | 86 | 66.8 | 154 | 94.1 | 94.1 |
| 8 Leeds | 77.9 | 77.1 | 64.8 | 174 | 96.8 | 93.4 |
| 9 Nottingham | 84.2 | 83.1 | 59 | 153 | 94.3 | 93 |
| =10 Manchester | 79.9 | 77.5 | 63 | 167 | 92.5 | 92.4 |
| =10 Glasgow | 70.1 | 65.3 | 61.5 | 212 | 96.1 | 92.4 |
| 12 Queen Mary, London | 82.3 | 83.6 | 66 | 139 | 93.8 | 92.3 |
| 13 Queen's, Belfast | 83.2 | 84.9 | 51 | 158 | 92.7 | 92 |
| 14 Heriot-Watt | 77.4 | 76.5 | 55.5 | 179 | 93.2 | 91.8 |
| 15 Liverpool | 80.7 | 83.4 | 57 | 137 | 95.9 | 91.2 |
| 16 Edinburgh | 72.4 | 75.4 | 55.5 | 196 | — | 90.9 |
| =17 Exeter | 83.4 | 80.3 | 47 | 147 | 92.7 | 90.4 |
| =17 Bristol | 74.1 | 74.6 | 72.8 | 165 | 86.5 | 90.4 |
| 19 Cardiff | 84.2 | 83.6 | 54 | 131 | 90.9 | 90.2 |
| 20 Surrey | 82.1 | 81.9 | 55.2 | 137 | 88.1 | 89.5 |
| 21 Bath | 77.8 | 75.2 | 49.5 | 162 | 89.2 | 89 |
| 22 Newcastle | 80.2 | 80.4 | 58.5 | 137 | 84.7 | 88.5 |
| =23 Manchester Metropolitan | 84.8 | 83.9 | 45.5 | 124 | 87.5 | 88.3 |
| =23 Birmingham | 80.5 | 79.6 | 63.7 | 151 | 76.2 | 88.3 |
| 25 Loughborough | 77.2 | 73.4 | 46.5 | 148 | 93.1 | 88.2 |
| 26 Swansea | 78.2 | 76.8 | 48.8 | 134 | 89.7 | 87.4 |
| 27 Aberdeen | 75.3 | 74.9 | 35.8 | 156 | 93.3 | 87.2 |
| 28 Essex | 80.8 | 82.6 | 53.5 | 128 | 81.4 | 87 |
| 29 Ulster | 83.6 | 82.9 | 49.8 | 125 | 80.6* | 86.9 |
| 30 Northumbria | 81 | 83.7 | 43 | 140 | 76.5 | 85.7 |
| 31 King's College London | 66.4 | 70.6 | 62 | 163 | 79.4* | 85.1 |
| 32 Lancaster | 71.8 | 71.5 | 44.8 | 156 | — | 84.8 |
| =33 Royal Holloway | 82.9 | 84 | 33 | 109 | — | 84.2 |
| =33 Robert Gordon | 77.6 | 66.6 | 20.5 | 140 | 93.8 | 84.2 |
| 35 Plymouth | 76.6 | 69.4 | 32.5 | 120 | 93.2 | 84.1 |
| 36 Greenwich | 82.6 | 79.5 | 31.5 | 117 | — | 83.9 |
| 37 Glasgow Caledonian | 83.3 | 79.5 | 12.8 | 160 | 77 | 83.8 |
| 38 Liverpool John Moores | 77.1 | 73.1 | 45.5 | 136 | 76.7 | 83.7 |
| 39 Huddersfield | 80.3 | 82.2 | 32.5 | 115 | — | 83.6 |

| | | | | | | | |
|---|---|---|---|---|---|---|---|
| 40 | Brunel | 79.6 | 77.4 | 33 | 136 | 77.3 | 83.5 |
| 41 | York | 70.5 | 64.1 | 49.8 | 132 | 85.1 | 83.2 |
| 42 | De Montfort | 84.1 | 86 | 21.8 | 110 | — | 83.1 |
| 43 | Birmingham City | 87.1 | 80.7 | 17.5 | 132 | 74.4 | 83 |
| 44 | Aston | 75.3 | 73.2 | 35.2 | 127 | 82.9* | 82.8 |
| =45 | Coventry | 80.3 | 81.8 | 23.5 | 119 | 81.2 | 82.7 |
| =45 | Leeds Beckett | 83.6 | 87.5 | 18.2 | 110 | — | 82.7 |
| =45 | Salford | 74.9 | 69.4 | 33.2 | 126 | 86.2 | 82.7 |
| 48 | Nottingham Trent | 84.7 | 73.9 | 59 | 123 | 58.3 | 82.5 |
| =49 | Kent | 74.8 | 71.5 | 41.5 | 121 | 79.5 | 82.1 |
| =49 | West of England | 78 | 72.8 | 30.8 | 125 | — | 82.1 |
| 51 | City | 76.9 | 79.3 | 32.5 | 115 | — | 82 |
| 52 | Portsmouth | 82.7 | 78.8 | 21 | 104 | 80.8 | 81.5 |
| 53 | Edinburgh Napier | 72.7 | 65.5 | 22.8 | 140 | 85.7 | 81.4 |
| 54 | Teesside | 78.8 | 78.5 | 18.8 | 118 | 77.8 | 80.6 |
| 55 | Westminster | 82.9 | 82.2 | 24 | 126 | 63.9 | 80.2 |
| 56 | London South Bank | 86.2 | 86.6 | 27.3 | 109 | 58.7 | 79.6 |
| 57 | Sheffield Hallam | 73.6 | 72.5 | 30 | 113 | 76.4 | 79.3 |
| 58 | Derby | 79.4 | 70.9 | 14 | 122 | 72.1 | 78.5 |
| 59 | South Wales | 77.1 | 63.3 | 26.8 | 111 | 71.4 | 77.6 |
| 60 | Brighton | 59 | 60 | 36.5 | 107 | 88.0* | 77.1 |
| 61 | Hertfordshire | 62.1 | 60.9 | 33 | 103 | — | 73.4 |

| | | | |
|---|---|---|---|
| Employed in high-skilled job | 72% | Employed in lower-skilled job | 8% |
| Employed in high-skilled job and studying | 3% | Employed in lower-skilled job and studying | 0% |
| Studying | 6% | Unemployed | 5% |
| High-skilled work (median) salary | £30,000 | Low-/medium-skilled salary | £21,000 |

# English

St Andrews returns to the top of our English table, following two years in second place. Averaging 200 UCAS points among its English degree entrants St Andrews has the highest entry standards. In a table which commonly experiences changes at the top, Oxford – No 1 for the past two years – is this year's runner-up. Cambridge and University College London are steady in third and fourth place respectively. Newcastle sits 15th overall but is peerless for its research in the subject, while Edinburgh (24th) achieves the second-best research quality score. At more than a quarter (25) of the universities listed, students arrived with upwards of 144 UCAS points (equivalent to three As at A level) but there are also plenty of much lower-tariff options, with 11 universities registering 100 points or less. Newman, in 46th place overall, has the third-lowest entry standards (93 UCAS points) but comes top for student satisfaction with teaching quality, behind Derby (54th in the main table).

English literature is usually required for entry. Some English degrees offer an equal balance of literature and language, while others specialise in one or the other – a distinction usually clear in the course title. English is also frequently paired with other subjects in joint honours degrees. "An English degree offers a unique opportunity for you to engage with the rich global heritage of creativity in the English language and to enhance your own linguistic, critical and creative abilities. The skills and knowledge you will acquire are so fundamental, they will prepare you not just for any career but for any future you care to make for yourself," says Professor Peter D McDonald, tutor in English, St Hugh's College, University of Oxford.

English has not been immune to the declining popularity of humanities subjects, but despite some universities making the controversial decision to drop their degrees in English literature (amid pressure from government to ensure graduates go straight into well-paid jobs) applications and enrolments to English literature degrees edged up by around 4% in 2023, to around 21,500 and 3,800 respectively – although demand was still lower than four years earlier. Applications and enrolments in English language and English studies degrees decreased in 2023, however, and compared with four years earlier English language attracted a third fewer new starters in 2023 and English studies admissions were down by 17%. Our analysis of the latest Graduate Outcomes survey shows almost six in ten English graduates (59.5%) employed in high-skilled jobs and/or postgraduate study 15 months on, ranking the subject =52nd out of 70. These outcomes vary considerably by university, ranging from 91.5% in high-skilled jobs/postgraduate study at Aston to 60.8% at Hertfordshire. Average graduate salaries of £24,500 put English 52nd.

There remain plenty of universities to study English. The UCAS website showed 965 courses in English literature at 110 universities and colleges for 2025-26. For English degrees more broadly, there were 1,666 courses offered by 130 providers.

| English | Teaching quality % | Student experience % | Research quality % | Entry standards (UCAS points) | Graduate prospects % | Overall score |
|---|---|---|---|---|---|---|
| 1 St Andrews | 90.2 | 88.5 | 61.8 | 200 | 84.3 | 100 |
| 2 Oxford | 92.6 | 71.7 | 69.8 | 191 | 83.3 | 99.2 |
| 3 Cambridge | 86.2 | 75.1 | 65 | 188 | 88.3 | 98.6 |
| 4 University College London | 85.9 | 82.1 | 61.5 | 183 | 83.2 | 96.9 |
| 5 Strathclyde | 87.5 | 83.9 | 58.8 | 199 | 76.5 | 96.3 |
| 6 Aberdeen | 91.2 | 89.2 | 53.8 | 173 | 80.2 | 96.1 |
| 7 Warwick | 86.6 | 83.4 | 64.8 | 156 | 84.6 | 96 |
| 8 Durham | 83.9 | 72.5 | 55.5 | 186 | 85.6 | 95.7 |
| 9 Southampton | 88.5 | 84.1 | 69.2 | 142 | 82.4 | 95.5 |
| 10 Leicester | 87.8 | 87.6 | 67.8 | 124 | 86.9 | 95.4 |
| 11 Surrey | 94 | 89.7 | 63 | 122 | 83.4 | 95.3 |
| 12 York | 83.5 | 81.4 | 70.2 | 157 | 81.9 | 95.2 |
| 13 Nottingham | 86.9 | 82.4 | 70.5 | 146 | 81.4 | 95.1 |
| 14 Exeter | 86.5 | 82.5 | 59.5 | 161 | 82.5 | 95 |
| 15 Newcastle | 84 | 79.7 | 83.8 | 141 | 78 | 94.7 |
| 16 Leeds | 81.1 | 78.4 | 73.2 | 160 | 79.4 | 94.2 |
| 17 Edinburgh Napier | 93.7 | 87.6 | 48.2 | 155 | 75.5 | 93.2 |
| =18 Liverpool | 86 | 82.8 | 65.5 | 135 | 80 | 93.1 |
| =18 Liverpool John Moores | 92.1 | 90 | 58 | 131 | 77.3 | 93.1 |
| =18 Birmingham | 84.6 | 78.3 | 68.8 | 150 | 77.1 | 93.1 |
| 21 Glasgow | 81.7 | 73.8 | 61.8 | 188 | 73.2 | 92.7 |
| 22 Sheffield | 87.8 | 86.8 | 62.3 | 150 | 73.2 | 92.6 |
| 23 Aston | 88 | 85.4 | 38 | 123 | 91.5 | 92.5 |
| =24 Loughborough | 88.2 | 86.9 | 54.5 | 149 | 75.1 | 92.1 |
| =24 Edinburgh | 70.5 | 66.6 | 74.5 | 178 | 79.1 | 92.1 |
| =26 Manchester | 81.2 | 72.3 | 66.5 | 166 | 75 | 92 |
| =26 King's College London | 78 | 69.8 | 70.8 | 157 | 78.9 | 92 |
| =28 Birmingham City | 86 | 80.7 | 65.5 | 111 | 82.6 | 91.9 |

| | | | | | | |
|---|---|---|---|---|---|---|
| =28 | Royal Holloway | 81.1 | 77.1 | 60.5 | 139 | 82.9 | 91.9 |
| =30 | Lancaster | 90.1 | 84.2 | 48 | 149 | 75.9 | 91.7 |
| =30 | Cardiff | 83.1 | 78.5 | 67.2 | 139 | 77 | 91.7 |
| 32 | City | 91.9 | 89.3 | 43.8 | 109 | 84.0* | 91.4 |
| 33 | Reading | 87.6 | 83.8 | 51 | 122 | 81.4 | 91.1 |
| =34 | East Anglia | 83.9 | 80.2 | 67 | 141 | 73.1 | 91 |
| =34 | Falmouth | 89.7 | 83.4 | 48.8 | — | 77.4* | 91 |
| =36 | Bath Spa | 88.6 | 83.3 | 51.7 | 110 | 82.8 | 90.9 |
| =36 | Sussex | 83.9 | 79.1 | 67 | 135 | 74.6 | 90.9 |
| 38 | Bristol | 78.3 | 72.9 | 54.5 | 167 | 77.7 | 90.6 |
| 39 | Manchester Metropolitan | 85.4 | 81.1 | 61.8 | 116 | 78.1 | 90.4 |
| 40 | Queen's, Belfast | 83.5 | 78.8 | 47.5 | 148 | 78.5 | 90.3 |
| =41 | Swansea | 90.4 | 85.4 | 60 | 134 | 67.3 | 89.9 |
| =41 | Huddersfield | 85.3 | 75.3 | 60 | 111 | 80 | 89.9 |
| =43 | Hull | 90.8 | 88.8 | 55.5 | 118 | 71.6 | 89.8 |
| =43 | Dundee | 85.9 | 78.6 | 40.8 | 170 | 72.6 | 89.8 |
| 45 | Northumbria | 87 | 82.2 | 54 | 128 | 74.1 | 89.6 |
| =46 | Stirling | 84.1 | 79.8 | 47.5 | 177 | 67.4 | 89.4 |
| =46 | Newman | 97 | 94.4 | 43.8 | 93 | — | 89.4 |
| 48 | Keele | 87.9 | 83.7 | 54.8 | 114 | 74.4 | 89 |
| =49 | Oxford Brookes | 90 | 79.5 | 72.8 | 105 | 66.5 | 88.7 |
| =49 | Kent | 85.3 | 77 | 64.5 | 121 | 70.7 | 88.7 |
| 51 | Canterbury Christ Church | 91.1 | 85.1 | 53.2 | 106 | 72.3 | 88.6 |
| 52 | Plymouth | 87 | 79.9 | 60.5 | 128 | 68.1 | 88.5 |
| 53 | Ulster | 94.1 | 90.7 | 41 | 114 | 71 | 88.3 |
| 54 | Derby | 96.2 | 95.2 | — | 118 | 83.9 | 87.7 |
| =55 | Queen Mary, London | 81.8 | 74.9 | 59.5 | 124 | 71.4 | 87.4 |
| =55 | Northampton | 96.8 | 91.3 | 30.2 | 101 | — | 87.4 |
| 57 | Goldsmiths, London | 83 | 68.1 | 46 | 117 | 80.1 | 87.2 |
| 58 | De Montfort | 84.1 | 78.6 | 54.5 | 98 | 76.3 | 87.1 |
| 59 | Edge Hill | 81.9 | 76.8 | 32.8 | 124 | 81.6 | 86.9 |
| 60 | Essex | 88.5 | 84.3 | 49.8 | 112 | 68.4* | 86.7 |
| =61 | Sheffield Hallam | 83.2 | 80.4 | 50.7 | 106 | 74.2 | 86.5 |
| =61 | Teesside | 88 | 79.2 | 49.2 | 100 | — | 86.5 |
| =61 | Westminster | 84.5 | 76.5 | 55.5 | 103 | 72.7 | 86.5 |
| 64 | Coventry | 85 | 75.9 | 54.2 | 106 | 71.8 | 86.4 |
| 65 | Central Lancashire | 91.8 | 88.7 | 33.8 | 112 | 70.1 | 86.3 |
| 66 | Worcester | 88.4 | 78.7 | 19.2 | 106 | 82.9* | 85.9 |
| =67 | Nottingham Trent | 91.3 | 86.1 | 39.2 | 108 | 68 | 85.7 |
| =67 | Anglia Ruskin | 87.3 | 82.7 | 46 | 99 | 71.2 | 85.7 |
| 69 | Brunel | 84.5 | 81.6 | 42.8 | 104 | 73.3 | 85.5 |
| =70 | Lincoln | 88.8 | 83.9 | 36 | 116 | 68.8 | 85.3 |
| =70 | Liverpool Hope | 92.6 | 83.7 | 36 | 107 | 67.6 | 85.3 |
| 72 | Bangor | 90 | 82.8 | 44.2 | 117 | 63 | 85.1 |
| =73 | Brighton | 83 | 76.5 | 44.2 | 100 | 74.7 | 85 |
| =73 | Wolverhampton | 87 | 80.8 | 44 | 100 | 70 | 85 |
| =73 | Greenwich | 91.3 | 83.6 | 26.5 | 111 | 71.3 | 85 |
| 76 | Aberystwyth | 88.3 | 88.1 | 25.5 | 119 | 70.2 | 84.7 |

| | Teaching quality % | Student experience % | Research quality % | Entry standards (UCAS points) | Graduate prospects % | Overall score |
|---|---|---|---|---|---|---|
| =77 Portsmouth | 91.2 | 88.5 | 30.8 | 108 | 66.7 | 84.4 |
| =77 West of England | 89.9 | 85.7 | 32.2 | 115 | 66.1 | 84.4 |
| =77 Hertfordshire | 93.9 | 90.5 | 42.5 | 98 | 60.8 | 84.4 |
| =80 Roehampton | 89 | 80.9 | 50.5 | 103 | 62.5 | 84.3 |
| =80 Chester | 93.1 | 83 | 25 | 113 | 67.6 | 84.3 |
| 82 Salford | 84.2 | 78.5 | 26.5 | 110 | 75.7 | 84.1 |
| 83 York St John | 90.6 | 87.1 | 22.8 | 103 | 69.7 | 83.6 |
| =84 Kingston | 91.1 | 87.5 | 47 | 98 | 56.1* | 82.8 |
| =84 Leeds Beckett | 92.7 | 88.3 | 30.8 | 96 | 62.8 | 82.8 |
| =84 Leeds Trinity | 88.4 | 74.1 | 32.5 | 98 | — | 82.8 |
| 87 Bishop Grosseteste | 93.8 | 79.5 | 19 | 96 | — | 82.6 |
| 88 Bournemouth | 81 | 70.4 | 22.5 | 105 | 70.8 | 80.3 |
| =89 Gloucestershire | 80.3 | 65.5 | 32.8 | 110 | 65.2 | 79.8 |
| =89 Chichester | 69.8 | 76.9 | 37.2 | 116 | — | 79.8 |
| 91 Winchester | 85 | 82 | 16.2 | 117 | 61.9 | 79.7 |
| 92 Sunderland | 57.5 | 34.5 | 40.5 | — | 87.5 | 77.6 |

| | | | |
|---|---|---|---|
| Employed in high-skilled job | 43% | Employed in lower-skilled job | 23% |
| Employed in high-skilled job and studying | 4% | Employed in lower-skilled job and studying | 1% |
| Studying | 12% | Unemployed | 6% |
| High-skilled work (median) salary | £25,000 | Low-/medium-skilled salary | £19,500 |

# Food Science

Queen's, Belfast takes the lead in our new Food Science table's tightly packed top three, where it is followed by Glasgow Caledonian (No 1 for the past two years) and Surrey – which maintains its long-held top three record in the ranking. Queen's, Belfast is in front for research quality, based on its results in food science areas in the Research Excellence Framework 2021. For metrics of student satisfaction Nottingham Trent ranks first for teaching quality and St Mary's, Twickenham leads for students' evaluation of the broad experience.

Nottingham Trent, in 17th place overall, is top for student satisfaction with teaching quality while St Mary's, Twickenham (27th in the main table) is unbeaten for the wider experience in our National Student Survey analysis. At the other end of scale, students at Liverpool Hope reported the lowest rates of satisfaction with both teaching quality and the wider experience.

Degrees under this grouping encompass a broad range of courses, from nutrition and dietetics – which offer opportunities to study alongside doctors, nurses and other health professionals in hospitals – to food manufacturing and professional cookery. There is even a BSc in Baking Science and Technology offered by London South Bank at its National Bakery School. "Never has there been a more critical time for our global society to comprehend the importance of what we feed our bodies and how nutrients (fat, protein, vitamins and minerals, etc) affect our short and long-term health. Understanding our human metabolic demands for nutrients and improving health through optimal, safe and appropriate food is exactly what is studied in the subject areas of nutrition science and food science," says Professor Susan Lanham-New, head of the Department of Nutritional Sciences, University of Surrey. Applicants are advised to ensure that courses are approved by the accrediting bodies – for nutrition science degrees it is the Association for Nutrition and for food science degrees it's the Institute of Food Science and Technology. Food science courses usually feature in the top 30 of our employment and salaries rankings, as they do this year in 29th and =28th place respectively.

| Food Science | Teaching quality % | Student experience % | Research quality % | Entry standards (UCAS points) | Graduate prospects % | Overall score |
|---|---|---|---|---|---|---|
| 1 Queen's, Belfast | 86.9 | 92.4 | 69.2 | 151 | 92.6 | 100 |
| 2 Glasgow Caledonian | 80.4 | 79.1 | 61 | 190 | 90 | 99.6 |
| 3 Surrey | 90.6 | 91.1 | 58 | 149 | 95.1 | 99.4 |
| 4 Plymouth | 88.3 | 80.5 | 58.2 | 149 | 87.8 | 96.4 |
| 5 Hertfordshire | 86.1 | 83.2 | 42.5 | — | 100 | 95.8 |
| 6 Nottingham | 84.6 | 79.2 | 52 | 146 | 88.6 | 94.3 |
| 7 Reading | 89.9 | 86.7 | 42.5 | 134 | 90.9 | 94 |
| 8 Ulster | 86.1 | 83.4 | 53.5 | 135 | 87.3 | 93.9 |
| 9 Leeds | 80.2 | 81.7 | 45.5 | 155 | 87 | 93.1 |
| 10 Northumbria | 89.5 | 85.9 | 53.5 | — | 70.8* | 92.5 |
| 11 Oxford Brookes | 91.8 | 93 | 39.5 | 125 | — | 92.4 |
| 12 Abertay | 92 | 88.5 | 28.2 | 155 | 76.9 | 92.2 |
| 13 Nottingham Trent | 92.7 | 90.2 | 30.8 | 127 | — | 90.8 |
| 14 Westminster | 87.3 | 80.4 | 36.8 | — | 73.5 | 88.3 |
| 15 Coventry | 85 | 76.4 | 24.8 | 134 | 82.4 | 87.6 |
| 16 Manchester Metropolitan | 84 | 76.6 | 36 | 127 | 76.5 | 87.3 |
| 17 Chester | 76.8 | 72 | 31 | 121 | 95 | 87 |
| 18 Bournemouth | 85.1 | 83.8 | 29.2 | 119 | 79.4 | 86.8 |
| 19 Harper Adams | 87.1 | 78.1 | 19.5 | 103 | 92.7 | 86.1 |
| 20 Newcastle | 73.9 | 69.2 | 42.8 | 148 | 68.6 | 85.9 |
| 21 Robert Gordon | 72.6 | 69.9 | — | 174 | 83.3 | 84.7 |
| 22 Liverpool Hope | 89.6 | 85.4 | 15 | 116 | — | 84.3 |
| 23 Bath Spa | 91.5 | 91.1 | — | 105 | 84 | 84 |
| 24 Sheffield Hallam | 85.4 | 81.3 | — | 127 | 82 | 83.6 |
| 25 Leeds Beckett | 84.5 | 83.5 | — | 114 | 85.1 | 82.8 |
| 26 Queen Margaret, Edinburgh | 77.3 | 81.6 | — | 155 | 70 | 82.4 |
| 27 St Mary's, Twickenham | 91.8 | 93.3 | — | 104 | 73.5 | 82.3 |
| 28 Cardiff Metropolitan | 75.9 | 68.8 | — | 128 | 81.2 | 80 |
| 29 London South Bank | 92.4 | 80.4 | — | 129 | 50 | 79.6 |
| 30 Liverpool John Moores | 71.3 | 68.7 | 26.5 | 135 | 54.2* | 78.8 |
| 31 Edge Hill | 83.2 | 77.8 | — | 117 | 62.5 | 78.1 |

| | | | |
|---|---|---|---|
| Employed in high-skilled job | 60% | Employed in lower-skilled job | 18% |
| Employed in high-skilled job and studying | 2% | Employed in lower-skilled job and studying | 1% |
| Studying | 8% | Unemployed | 3% |
| High-skilled work (median) salary | £26,325 | Low-/medium-skilled salary | £21,000 |

# French

"Studying French allows students to become fluent users of a world language while training them to engage, communicate and interact with people from diverse cultural and linguistic backgrounds. By developing linguistic proficiency and critical-thinking skills in tandem, this unique combination of analytic, transcultural and communicative competencies ensures that French students are highly sought-after graduates," notes Dr Angela O'Flaherty, lecturer in French, Department of Language and Linguistic Science, University of York – which ranks 10th overall in our table and No 1 for research quality in the subject.

Led by St Andrews – which has ousted Cambridge from the top of this year's French ranking – degrees attract high entry standards: 22 out of the 29 universities tabled average upwards of 144 UCAS points (equivalent to AAA at A-level). Unusually, there are no universities with post-1992 foundations – reflecting the long decline in the popularity of studying modern languages. Applications and enrolments continued their downward trend in 2023, when 4,240 applied and 770 undergraduates were accepted onto courses. But those with French in their sights still have options; the UCAS website showed 919 courses in French offered by 67 colleges and universities in 2024–25, many offered as part of dual honours courses in conjunction with a wide variety of other subjects. Applicants are advised to listen, watch or read about their interests (culture, sport, history, music etc) in French.

French sits 40th in our employment index of 70 subject areas (up five places) and 45th for graduate salaries.

| French | Teaching quality % | Student experience % | Research quality % | Entry standards (UCAS points) | Graduate prospects % | Overall score |
|---|---|---|---|---|---|---|
| 1 St Andrews | 90.4 | 86.8 | 51.5 | 214 | — | 100 |
| 2 Cambridge | 92.2 | 73.7 | 61 | 190 | 91.5 | 99.3 |
| 3 Lancaster | 90.8 | 84.5 | 68.5 | 157 | — | 97.6 |
| 4 Oxford | 86.6 | 70.2 | 51.2 | 188 | 83.8 | 94.3 |
| 5 Bristol | 84.1 | 76.9 | 64 | 165 | 81.3 | 94.1 |
| 6 Warwick | 89.3 | 83 | 46.2 | 160 | 85.5 | 94 |
| 7 Aberdeen | 93.1 | 82.7 | 32.5 | 186 | — | 93.8 |
| 8 Durham | 85.9 | 71.8 | 46 | 181 | 85.6 | 93.4 |
| 9 Newcastle | 82.4 | 80.7 | 61.8 | 150 | 83.6 | 93.2 |
| 10 York | 83.2 | 70.5 | 74.8 | 144 | 80.0* | 93 |
| 11 University College London | 85.1 | 70.9 | 56 | 164 | 83.3* | 92.9 |
| 12 Royal Holloway | 87.1 | 82.3 | 60 | 137 | — | 92.6 |
| 13 Manchester | 82.9 | 74.4 | 59.5 | 155 | 82.1 | 92.4 |
| 14 Nottingham | 82.3 | 73.3 | 62 | 141 | 85.7* | 92.3 |
| =15 Queen's, Belfast | 88.2 | 84.8 | 37 | 151 | 83.4 | 91.4 |
| =15 Stirling | 82.9 | 73.3 | 47.5 | 178 | — | 91.4 |
| 17 Exeter | 83.7 | 78.1 | 50 | 149 | 82.9 | 91.3 |
| 18 Bath | 85.3 | 80.8 | 31.8 | 153 | 89.1 | 90.9 |
| 19 Liverpool | 82 | 77 | 59 | 131 | 81.0* | 90.4 |
| 20 Leeds | 83.6 | 78.4 | 52 | 154 | 74.9 | 90.2 |
| 21 Cardiff | 83 | 79.1 | 55.5 | 136 | 77.3 | 89.9 |
| 22 Birmingham | 79 | 74.5 | 54.8 | 149 | 79.8 | 89.8 |
| 23 Southampton | 86.6 | 72.5 | 47.8 | 156 | 70.6* | 88.9 |

| | | Teaching quality % | Student experience % | Research quality % | Entry standards (UCAS points) | Graduate prospects % | Overall score |
|---|---|---|---|---|---|---|---|
| 24 | King's College London | 74.8 | 69.4 | 51.2 | 157 | 81.1 | 88.6 |
| 25 | Edinburgh | 73.4 | 69.2 | 45.8 | 185 | 73.2 | 87.7 |
| 26 | Queen Mary, London | 87.6 | 78.9 | 51.1 | 130 | 66.7 | 87.6 |
| 27 | Kent | 87.8 | 82.6 | 57.5 | 117 | 62.9* | 87.2 |
| 28 | Glasgow | 78.4 | 70.2 | 25.5 | 208 | 66.8 | 86.2 |
| 29 | Sheffield | 87.6 | 80.9 | 35.8 | — | 66.1* | 86.1 |

| | | | |
|---|---|---|---|
| Employed in high-skilled job | 50% | Employed in lower-skilled job | 21% |
| Employed in high-skilled job and studying | 2% | Employed in lower-skilled job and studying | 1% |
| Studying | 11% | Unemployed | 6% |
| High-skilled work (median) salary | £26,000 | Low-/medium-skilled salary | £23,000 |

# General Engineering

Students opting for the general strand of engineering gain the flexibility that the breadth of the subject allows in their future careers, while degrees also provide opportunities to specialise in a specific area of interest. "This approach equips graduates with versatile problem-solving skills and a holistic understanding of engineering, making them highly adaptable and sought-after. By engaging with cutting-edge research and innovative projects, students gain hands-on experience and a competitive edge in the job market," says Dr Andy Nichols, general engineering course director, University of Sheffield.

Up four places to No 1 in our General Engineering table, Imperial's rank is boosted by the top research quality rating as well as student satisfaction scores which put it second for the broad experience and third for teaching quality in our National Student Survey analysis. After the past two years at the top of the table Cambridge is this year's runner-up but still claims the highest entry standards – its general engineering students averaging an extraordinary 227 UCAS points upon entry. Bristol led this table for the three years before Cambridge's recent run, and tops the graduate prospects ranking this year – with a perfect 100% of general engineering students employed in high-skilled jobs and/or further study within 15 months.

Fifth-place Sheffield is hitting all the right notes with its general engineering students, whose feedback in the National Student Survey ranks it top for the broad experience in our analysis, while Exeter is unbeaten for teaching quality.

Four universities (Cambridge, Oxford, Durham and Bristol) average 200-plus UCAS tariff points among their new entrants, and entry standards are higher than 144 points (equivalent to AAA) at 13 universities. But the subject can also be accessed with more modest grades, such as the 132 UCAS points averaged by general engineering students at Aston, which places 12th overall.

General engineering makes a convincing choice for careers prospects. It ranks eighth in our employment index and =5th for starting salaries. Having followed an upward curve for a decade or so applications have levelled out and in 2023 the subject attracted 21,255 applications and just under 4,000 new undergraduates were accepted onto courses.

| General Engineering | | Teaching quality % | Student experience % | Research quality % | Entry standards (UCAS points) | Graduate prospects % | Overall score |
|---|---|---|---|---|---|---|---|
| 1 | Imperial College | 90.5 | 89.7 | 81 | 196 | 95.9 | 100 |
| 2 | Cambridge | 81.6 | 80.9 | 77.2 | 227 | 97.2 | 99.4 |
| 3 | Bristol | 85.1 | 71.1 | 68 | 200 | 100 | 97.8 |

| General Engineering cont. | Teaching quality % | Student experience % | Research quality % | Entry standards (UCAS points) | Graduate prospects % | Overall score |
|---|---|---|---|---|---|---|
| 4 Oxford | 80.8 | 76.1 | 77.5 | 216 | 94 | 97 |
| 5 Sheffield | 93.7 | 88.6 | 66.8 | 179 | 89.7 | 95.9 |
| 6 Durham | 81.2 | 74 | 52.8 | 202 | 95.4 | 94.3 |
| 7 University College London | 81 | 61.5 | 70 | 194 | — | 93.4 |
| 8 Exeter | 93.2 | 90.5 | 47 | 144 | 91.3 | 92.5 |
| 9 Strathclyde | 86.1 | 77.5 | 52.8 | 187 | 88.9 | 92.3 |
| 10 Loughborough | 82.2 | 75.9 | 46.5 | 154 | 90.9 | 89.6 |
| 11 Warwick | 75.9 | 76.3 | 56.2 | 162 | 88.2 | 88.7 |
| 12 Aston | 89.3 | 81.7 | 35.2 | 132 | — | 88.4 |
| 13 Ulster | 81.5 | 79.1 | 49.8 | 132 | 89.4 | 88.1 |
| 14 Queen Mary, London | 72.6 | 66.1 | 66 | 152 | — | 87.8 |
| 15 Liverpool John Moores | 86.7 | 78.2 | 45.5 | 138 | 83.3 | 86.8 |
| 16 Aberdeen | 75.3 | 74.9 | 35.8 | 167 | — | 86.7 |
| 17 Brunel | 81.4 | 72.1 | 33 | 131 | 90 | 86.1 |
| 18 Cardiff | 65.5 | 74.4 | 54 | 134 | — | 83.8 |
| 19 West of Scotland | 80.8 | 76.4 | 16.5 | — | 85.3 | 83.1 |
| 20 Coventry | 82.7 | 78.1 | 23.5 | 121 | 81.4 | 82.1 |
| 21 Glasgow Caledonian | 80.6 | 72.2 | 12.8 | — | 82 | 80.5 |
| 22 London South Bank | 71.2 | 66 | 27.3 | 127 | — | 80.4 |
| 23 Bournemouth | 77.9 | 73.6 | 14 | 116 | 79.8 | 79.1 |
| 24 Northampton | 70.1 | 48.4 | 8.5 | 90 | — | 72.9 |

| | | | |
|---|---|---|---|
| Employed in high-skilled job | 78% | Employed in lower-skilled job | 6% |
| Employed in high-skilled job and studying | 3% | Employed in lower-skilled job and studying | 0% |
| Studying | 4% | Unemployed | 4% |
| High-skilled work (median) salary | £30,000 | Low-/medium-skilled salary | £23,000 |

## Geography and Environmental Sciences

"Are you fascinated with finding out how nature works – and how people interact with it?" asks Dr Hannah Cloke, professor of hydrology, University of Reading. "Geography and environmental science helps to find patterns and make sense of the mess. Most of the biggest issues the world faces, like climate change, biodiversity loss or war, need both human and physical solutions, which is why geographers see the world in this way."

Our table incorporates the different strands of geography – physical and human. The former focuses on physical processes and natural environments, the latter concerns human societies and the links between people and the planet. Environmental science studies the earth's physical, chemical and biological processes and looks at what impacts the planet in terms of social, political and cultural developments.

In a shake-up to the top ten of our Geography and Environmental Sciences table only Loughborough holds the same position (eighth) this year as last. Durham has gained four places to take the No 1 spot from Oxford, which held it for the past two years, and St Andrews is up one place to rank third. The London School of Economics has fallen six places to rank ninth, Edinburgh is down ten places to 16th and Exeter has declined 11 places to 21st. Going in the opposite direction, Royal Holloway has been boosted by strong rates of student satisfaction to gain 15 places and rank joint fifth with Southampton. But East Anglia, in 26th place overall, has the edge for research, the Research Excellence Framework 2021 results showed, followed by Bristol, which ranks second for research quality and 13th overall.

In 40th place overall, Gloucester outdoes all other institutions for student satisfaction with teaching quality and Chester is top for students' evaluation of teaching quality, our National Student Survey analysis shows.

The subjects rank 43rd out of 70 for starting salaries and compare a little more favourably for employment more widely, in 36th place, based on nearly seven in ten (67.9%) graduates employed in high-skilled work or furthering their studies within 15 months. Performance in achieving these outcomes varies considerably by institution from 94.9% at Durham down to 57.3% at Kingston (66th overall).

Entry standards do not reach the heights of some other subjects, with no universities averaging higher than the 198 UCAS points at third-place St Andrews, and seven averaging 100 or less. Geography at A-level or equivalent is a requirement for geography degrees. For environmental science, the leading universities look for two subjects from geology, maths, psychology, physics, geography, biology or chemistry. The demand for places varies between the disciplines, with human geography attracting the highest numbers (17,105 applications and 3,110 enrolments in 2023 – both up year on year), followed by physical geographical sciences (13,290 and 2,395). Though still attracting a smaller cohort of students, applications to environmental science degrees have risen by a third between 2019 and 2023, when 7,920 applications and 1,370 new students gained places.

| Geography and Environmental Sciences | Teaching quality % | Student experience % | Research quality % | Entry standards (UCAS points) | Graduate prospects % | Overall score |
|---|---|---|---|---|---|---|
| 1 Durham | 87 | 81.6 | 68.8 | 173 | 94.4 | 100 |
| 2 Oxford | 88.6 | 79.8 | 66 | 191 | 89 | 99.8 |
| =3 St Andrews | 87.9 | 83.4 | 48.2 | 198 | 83.7 | 97.1 |
| =3 Cambridge | 81.3 | 67.7 | 59.2 | 186 | 94 | 97.1 |
| =5 Southampton | 88.1 | 81.9 | 67.5 | 144 | 87.2 | 96.1 |
| =5 Royal Holloway | 94 | 92.8 | 64 | 125 | 84.6 | 96.1 |
| 7 University College London | 82.9 | 81.3 | 59.2 | 175 | 86.7 | 96 |
| 8 Loughborough | 89.6 | 91.8 | 54.2 | 143 | 86.9 | 95.9 |
| 9 London School of Economics | 77.3 | 75.7 | 63 | 168 | 92.7 | 95.7 |
| 10 Glasgow | 77.9 | 73.3 | 65.5 | 189 | 83.3 | 94.9 |
| 11 Lancaster | 83.9 | 81.3 | 68.2 | 145 | 84.8 | 94.6 |
| 12 Aberdeen | 91.4 | 83.2 | 41.5 | 184 | 77.8 | 94.5 |
| 13 Bristol | 79.6 | 76.9 | 70 | 159 | 84.1 | 94.2 |
| 14 Sheffield | 87.5 | 86.8 | 51 | 146 | 83.2 | 93.7 |
| 15 King's College London | 83.6 | 83.1 | 58.8 | 148 | 82.2 | 93.2 |
| 16 Edinburgh | 74.5 | 72.9 | 63.2 | 174 | 84.3 | 93 |
| 17 Dundee | 79.8 | 76.6 | 46.2 | 177 | 83 | 92.6 |
| 18 Reading | 86.2 | 84.6 | 68.5 | 120 | 79.9 | 92.3 |
| 19 Birmingham | 80 | 79.2 | 49.2 | 145 | 87.1 | 92 |
| 20 Leeds | 74.7 | 74.7 | 66 | 152 | 83.9 | 91.8 |
| 21 Exeter | 79.8 | 80.5 | 67.2 | 153 | 75.9 | 91.7 |
| 22 Aberystwyth | 89.2 | 85.5 | 47 | 118 | 83.2 | 91.5 |

**Geography and Environmental Sciences** cont.

| | | Teaching quality % | Student experience % | Research quality % | Entry standards (UCAS points) | Graduate prospects % | Overall score |
|---|---|---|---|---|---|---|---|
| =23 | Nottingham | 80.5 | 81.9 | 58.5 | 136 | 81.4 | 91.2 |
| =23 | York | 81.7 | 79 | 65.5 | 137 | 78.1 | 91.2 |
| =23 | Manchester | 80.3 | 76.2 | 49 | 155 | 82.1 | 91.2 |
| 26 | East Anglia | 82.1 | 80 | 73.8 | 126 | 76.2 | 91 |
| 27 | Northumbria | 92.2 | 86.6 | 49 | 126 | 74.2 | 90.7 |
| 28 | Stirling | 82.2 | 78.4 | 45.8 | 170 | 73.5 | 90.2 |
| 29 | Queen's, Belfast | 87.4 | 83.7 | 35.5 | 134 | 80.8 | 90.1 |
| 30 | Swansea | 82.2 | 80.2 | 51.7 | 129 | 80.8 | 90 |
| =31 | Ulster | 88.5 | 84.8 | 43 | 120 | 79.4 | 89.9 |
| =31 | Warwick | 80.7 | 75.4 | — | 175 | 92.6 | 89.9 |
| 33 | Newcastle | 77.8 | 78.2 | 53.8 | 134 | 81.5 | 89.6 |
| 34 | Sussex | 83.7 | 83.3 | 57.2 | 131 | 73.7 | 89.5 |
| 35 | Keele | 90.1 | 82.6 | 35.2 | 111 | 82.4 | 89.4 |
| =36 | Northampton | 95.1 | 85.2 | 12 | — | 80.3 | 89.1 |
| =36 | Bangor | 83.7 | 81 | 67.5 | 114 | 73.5 | 89.1 |
| 38 | Liverpool | 81.2 | 80.7 | 45.2 | 129 | 79.9 | 88.9 |
| 39 | Liverpool John Moores | 91.7 | 86.7 | 28.7 | 119 | 77.8 | 88.8 |
| 40 | Gloucestershire | 96 | 92.2 | 25.8 | 105 | 75 | 88.2 |
| =41 | Cardiff | 81.2 | 80.6 | 38.2 | 134 | 78.5 | 88 |
| =41 | Salford | 93.1 | 91.6 | 41 | 105 | 70.4 | 88 |
| 43 | West of England | 93.9 | 91 | 40.8 | 108 | 68.3 | 87.7 |
| 44 | Leicester | 90.6 | 86.3 | 28.7 | 117 | 72.5 | 86.9 |
| 45 | SOAS London | 80.1 | 70 | 29.8 | 158 | — | 86.8 |
| =46 | Nottingham Trent | 87 | 83 | 30.8 | 103 | 77.6 | 86.3 |
| =46 | Queen Mary, London | 77.7 | 75.5 | 52.5 | 125 | 73.6 | 86.3 |
| 48 | Worcester | 93.8 | 86.3 | 12.2 | 101 | 77.8 | 86 |
| =49 | Manchester Metropolitan | 80.6 | 77.4 | 44.8 | 110 | 74.7 | 85.6 |
| =49 | Edge Hill | 89.6 | 84.4 | 15.2 | 116 | 75 | 85.6 |
| 51 | Portsmouth | 86.5 | 83.8 | 26.8 | 102 | 76.5 | 85.5 |
| 52 | Leeds Beckett | 89.5 | 89.6 | 24.5 | 106 | 70.9* | 85.3 |
| =53 | Huddersfield | 89.8 | 76.2 | 24 | 105 | — | 84.7 |
| =53 | Chester | 92.8 | 93.2 | 7.2 | 112 | 70 | 84.7 |
| 55 | Hull | 84.7 | 61.2 | 42 | 108 | 75 | 84.5 |
| 56 | Plymouth | 82.6 | 82 | 31 | 116 | 70.7 | 84.3 |
| 57 | Lincoln | 84.6 | 78.4 | 14 | 113 | 77.8 | 84.2 |
| 58 | Coventry | 92.2 | 85.1 | 17 | 103 | 68.6 | 83.8 |
| 59 | Derby | 86.7 | 78.5 | — | 116 | 79.2 | 83.7 |
| 60 | Hertfordshire | 89.4 | 84.7 | 42.5 | 94 | 62.4 | 83.6 |
| 61 | York St John | 86.7 | 81.2 | 14 | 92 | 76.1 | 83 |
| 62 | Oxford Brookes | 82.6 | 77.1 | 34.8 | 101 | 69.1 | 82.7 |
| 63 | Brighton | 89.7 | 81.6 | 31.8 | 93 | 62.3 | 82.1 |
| 64 | Liverpool Hope | 83.1 | 85.6 | 9.5 | 107 | — | 81.9 |
| 65 | Bath Spa | 77.5 | 70.9 | 19.2 | 94 | 76 | 80.5 |
| 66 | Kingston | 92 | 84.9 | 17.2 | 98 | 57.3 | 80.4 |

| | | | | | | |
|---|---|---:|---:|---:|---:|---:|---:|
| 67 | Bournemouth | 81.3 | 83.1 | 31.2 | 97 | 60.9 | 80.1 |
| 68 | Cumbria | 74.5 | 61.3 | 16.5 | 116 | — | 77.9 |
| 69 | Sheffield Hallam | 81.2 | 73.6 | — | 102 | 67.3 | 77.8 |
| 70 | Winchester | 63.2 | 59.9 | — | 100 | 69 | 72.5 |

| | | | |
|---|---:|---|---:|
| Employed in high-skilled job | 52% | Employed in lower-skilled job | 19% |
| Employed in high-skilled job and studying | 4% | Employed in lower-skilled job and studying | 1% |
| Studying | 11% | Unemployed | 5% |
| High-skilled work (median) salary | £26,000 | Low-/medium-skilled salary | £20,779 |

## Geology

Cambridge tops our Geology table for the fifth year running while St Andrews is runner-up for the second consecutive year. Exeter is up two places to rank third – boosted by the top rating for teaching quality and the second-best for the wider experience in our new National Student Survey analysis. Imperial has slipped one place to rank fourth but still has the lead for research, based on the results of the Research Excellence Framework, and also tops the table for student satisfaction with the broad undergraduate experience. Geology students in general tend to enjoy their degrees: even at the bottom end of the scale, Keele scores more than 75% for teaching quality.

The study of how the earth was formed and shaped, geology degrees at the leading universities require any two subjects from: biology, chemistry, economics, further maths, geography, geology, maths, physics and psychology. "Geology is practical: discover your own fossil and mineral collection and make friends for life in small classes. Or, it's mathematical: for example, computer simulations of mining heat, and future climates. Relevant jobs in the UK and worldwide are in natural resources, energy supply, environmental protection, planetary exploration, and local and national government," explains Professor Stuart Haszeldine, School of Geosciences, University of Edinburgh.

Entry standards can be high; led by Cambridge – where entrants averaged 222 UCAS points – more than half of the universities listed attracted over 144 points in the UCAS tariff (equivalent to AAA at A-level). Life after an undergraduate geology degree can often include postgraduate study, which over one in five graduates was engaged in either full-time or combined with a job 15 months on from their courses. More than half had already secured high-skilled full-time jobs. Overall, geology places 27th in our employment ranking of 70 subject areas. Rates of pay for those with a geology degree average at £26,000 and place =28th.

| Geology | Teaching quality % | Student experience % | Research quality % | Entry standards (UCAS points) | Graduate prospects % | Overall score |
|---|---:|---:|---:|---:|---:|---:|
| 1 Cambridge | 86.9 | 81.2 | 79.5 | 222 | 94.3 | 100 |
| 2 St Andrews | 84.9 | 76.6 | 68.2 | 206 | 100 | 98 |
| 3 Exeter | 95.6 | 89.4 | 69.8 | 149 | 92.9 | 97.6 |
| 4 Imperial College | 89.7 | 90.2 | 81 | 167 | 87.2 | 97.3 |
| 5 Oxford | 82 | 73.4 | 71.2 | 203 | 100 | 97.1 |
| 6 East Anglia | 90.2 | 80.5 | 73.8 | 141 | — | 94.8 |
| 7 Durham | 88.8 | 79 | 60.2 | 158 | 92.9 | 94.1 |
| 8 Edinburgh | 80.7 | 75.1 | 63.2 | 205 | 89.1 | 93.7 |
| 9 Leeds | 81 | 81.3 | 68.2 | 156 | 90.9 | 92.7 |
| =10 Bristol | 84.6 | 80.4 | 75.2 | 153 | 83.3 | 92.6 |

**Geology** cont.

| | Teaching quality % | Student experience % | Research quality % | Entry standards (UCAS points) | Graduate prospects % | Overall score |
|---|---|---|---|---|---|---|
| =10 Birmingham | 79.1 | 73.8 | 74.8 | 144 | 95.3 | 92.6 |
| 12 Glasgow | 84.5 | 77.2 | 39.5 | 200 | 87.9 | 91.5 |
| 13 Leicester | 89.1 | 82.6 | 50.5 | 119 | 92.7 | 91.2 |
| 14 Southampton | 86.1 | 74.4 | 71 | 143 | 80.8 | 90.8 |
| 15 Liverpool | 85.2 | 81.1 | 57 | 133 | 87.7 | 90.5 |
| =16 University College London | 80.7 | 79.9 | 63 | 151 | 84.6* | 90.2 |
| =16 Aberdeen | 94.5 | 85 | 41.5 | 155 | 76.5* | 90.2 |
| 18 Cardiff | 80.9 | 75.4 | 67.8 | 124 | 86.7 | 89.4 |
| 19 Bangor | 84.8 | 84.4 | 67.5 | 115 | 71.7 | 87.6 |
| 20 Manchester | 79.1 | 68.7 | 69.8 | 153 | 75 | 87.5 |
| 21 Hull | 84.3 | 76.7 | 42 | 106 | 91.3 | 87.3 |
| 22 Plymouth | 85.9 | 83.4 | 40.8 | 117 | 83.9 | 87.2 |
| 23 Royal Holloway | 84.8 | 77.5 | 42 | 125 | 83.9 | 86.9 |
| 24 Newcastle | 77.2 | 70.8 | 58.5 | 120 | — | 85 |
| 25 Portsmouth | 89.5 | 84.7 | 40.8 | 106 | 64.8 | 83.5 |
| 26 Derby | 81.3 | 76.2 | 28 | — | 78.4* | 82.1 |
| 27 Keele | 76.9 | 62.3 | 35.2 | 110 | 81.9 | 81.3 |

| | | | |
|---|---|---|---|
| Employed in high-skilled job | 52% | Employed in lower-skilled job | 13% |
| Employed in high-skilled job and studying | 3% | Employed in lower-skilled job and studying | 0% |
| Studying | 18% | Unemployed | 5% |
| High-skilled work (median) salary | £26,000 | Low-/medium-skilled salary | £19,000 |

# German

The small student numbers that German degrees attract usually create fluctuations in the table, but this year's top four buck trend: led by St Andrews at No 1 all four occupy the same places this year as last. In third overall, Bristol is in front for research quality in our analysis of the Research Excellence Framework 2021 results. In our National Student Survey analysis Cambridge is top for teaching quality and St Andrews leads for the broad experience. Students of German tend to enjoy their studies whichever university they attend – returning positive ratings for teaching quality which go no lower than 75.7% at Edinburgh.

Entry standards to German degrees are high: at 16 out of the 19 universities in our table German degree new students enrolled with over 144 UCAS points, on average (equivalent to three As at A-level). As with modern languages more broadly, demand for the subject continued its ongoing decline in the 2023 recruitment cycle. German studies degrees are now grouped with Scandinavian studies within UCAS data, and just 1,115 students started courses in the subjects in 2023, down from 1,205 in 2022 and almost half the number of new starters four years before. While no post-1992 universities feature in our table, there are still plenty of places to study German, either as a single honours degree or in combination with a wide range of subjects including law, film, accountancy and other languages. Most universities in the table offer German from scratch, as well as catering for those who took it at A-level.

"Germany is the UK's biggest trading partner after the US and as such, German, which is spoken by millions worldwide, has been identified by the British Council as one of the five languages consistently most important to the UK's strategic interests," note Dr Mark Allinson, Dr Anna Havinga and Dr Benedict Schofield, Department of German, University of Bristol. The latest data shows that almost seven in ten (69.1%) German graduates were employed in high-skilled jobs and/or furthering their studies 15 months on from their degrees – outcomes that place the subject 32nd in our employment ranking of 70. For average starting salaries it ranks =38th.

| German | Teaching quality % | Student experience % | Research quality % | Entry standards (UCAS points) | Graduate prospects % | Overall score |
|---|---|---|---|---|---|---|
| 1 St Andrews | 91.5 | 89.2 | 51.5 | 198 | — | 100 |
| 2 Cambridge | 92.2 | 73.7 | 61 | 190 | 91.5 | 99.3 |
| 3 Bristol | 86.7 | 78.4 | 64 | 168 | 87 | 96.3 |
| 4 Oxford | 85.5 | 66.4 | 51.2 | 185 | 88.2 | 94.2 |
| 5 Liverpool | 91.6 | 83.2 | 59 | 133 | — | 93.8 |
| 6 Manchester | 85.2 | 72.4 | 59.5 | 165 | — | 93.7 |
| =7 King's College London | 86.5 | 81.1 | 51.2 | 161 | — | 93.1 |
| =7 Nottingham | 85.3 | 81.1 | 62 | 143 | — | 93.1 |
| =7 Durham | 85.9 | 71.8 | 46 | 181 | 85.6 | 93.1 |
| =7 Warwick | 87.9 | 81.5 | 46.2 | 163 | 84.8 | 93.1 |
| 11 Newcastle | 82.9 | 80.5 | 61.8 | 147 | 79.0* | 92.1 |
| 12 University College London | 83.5 | 72.1 | 56 | 161 | — | 91.9 |
| 13 Exeter | 83.7 | 78.1 | 50 | 149 | 82.8 | 90.9 |
| 14 Birmingham | 79.1 | 74.6 | 54.8 | 149 | 79.8 | 89.6 |
| 15 Leeds | 79.9 | 73.1 | 52 | 155 | — | 89.3 |
| 16 Edinburgh | 75.7 | 70.2 | 45.8 | 180 | — | 88.9 |
| 17 Cardiff | 82.1 | 75.8 | 55.5 | 126 | — | 88 |
| 18 Bath | 78.9 | 77.4 | 31.8 | 159 | — | 85.5 |
| 19 Glasgow | 80.4 | 73.7 | 25.5 | 196 | 57.8* | 85 |

| | | | |
|---|---|---|---|
| Employed in high-skilled job | 56% | Employed in lower-skilled job | 18% |
| Employed in high-skilled job and studying | 2% | Employed in lower-skilled job and studying | 1% |
| Studying | 10% | Unemployed | 4% |
| High-skilled work (median) salary | £27,000 | Low-/medium-skilled salary | N/A |

## History

"There are so many good reasons to study history," says Peter Frankopan, professor of global history, University of Oxford, and Unesco professor of Silk Roads studies, University of Cambridge: "First, learning how to handle, evaluate and understand complex sources is an important skill in its own right. Second, these days it is possible to investigate the past in ways that have never been possible before — from using climate archives and genomics to studying bone isotopes and big data."

At No 1 in our History table, St Andrews leads a top three which is unchanged this year from last. St Andrews' position is strengthened by the highest entry standards – 197 points in the UCAS tariff. The best job prospects are at the London School of Economics (up three places to rank fourth overall), with the latest data showing 93% of its history graduates employed in professional-level jobs and/or further study 15 months after their degrees. The rest of the top 15 features largely the same universities in our new ranking as in our previous edition, albeit reshuffled, aside from Aston's appearance in eighth place – up from 44th – in a rise powered by superb rates of student satisfaction which rank it top for the student experience and second for teaching quality. Derby (=46th overall) does equally well in these National Student Survey-derived metrics, where it swaps places with Aston in each. Kent (in 17th place overall) leads for research quality, based on results of the latest Research Excellence Framework 2021, where it is followed by Leicester and University College London.

Applications and enrolments to the subject showed a small 2% upturn in 2023. The modest surge is not sufficient to stem the downward flow in demand for history more widely, however. The subject has experienced repeated declines in successive admissions years – in line with the pattern among the humanities – as university applicants look for greater career certainty in their undergraduate choices. But the lessening interest in history degrees seems confined to the lower- and medium-tariff institutions and in 2023 the subject still attracted 52,345 applications and 9,610 new undergraduates.

Graduate prospects vary considerably across the table, from those at LSE down to Essex, where only 53.3% of history graduates had secured the desired outcomes of a high-skilled job and/or postgraduate study 15 months after their degrees. Placing 55th out of 70 subjects for graduate prospects, history is not a degree with an immediate utilitarian use. When surveyed 15 months after their degrees less than four in ten graduates (37.1%) were employed full-time in high-skilled jobs, while around half that proportion had progressed to postgraduate study – either full-time or in conjunction with working. Meanwhile more than a quarter (25.9%) were working in jobs deemed "low-skilled". Graduate pay fares slightly better compared with other subjects; history ranking =46th and graduates in high-skilled jobs command £25,000 salaries.

| History | Teaching quality % | Student experience % | Research quality % | Entry standards (UCAS points) | Graduate prospects % | Overall score |
|---|---|---|---|---|---|---|
| =1 St Andrews | 91.3 | 87.1 | 62 | 197 | 82.9 | 100 |
| =1 Cambridge | — | — | 54.5 | 193 | 83.4 | 100 |
| 3 Oxford | 87.4 | 73.5 | 61.3 | 192 | 89.1 | 98.6 |
| 4 London School of Economics | 85.3 | 82.9 | 59.8 | 171 | 93 | 98.2 |
| 5 University College London | 86.5 | 79.8 | 67.8 | 178 | 85.4 | 98 |
| =6 Warwick | 87.2 | 83.5 | 61.3 | 156 | 86 | 96.3 |
| =6 Durham | 82.5 | 69.1 | 59.2 | 189 | 88.6 | 96.3 |
| 8 Aston | 98.6 | 98 | 49 | 122 | — | 95.2 |
| 9 Strathclyde | 89.9 | 85.6 | 49 | 195 | 70.5 | 94.9 |
| =10 Exeter | 82.8 | 78.1 | 66 | 163 | 81.1 | 94.6 |
| =10 Leicester | 89.4 | 87.2 | 71.5 | 122 | 78.5 | 94.6 |
| 12 Loughborough | 91.4 | 91.2 | 45 | 141 | 80.9 | 94 |
| 13 Glasgow | 83.6 | 77 | 62.5 | 189 | 70.4 | 93.7 |
| 14 York | 81.9 | 73.6 | 64.8 | 156 | 82 | 93.5 |
| 15 Sheffield | 88 | 84.8 | 49 | 151 | 79.7 | 93.4 |
| 16 Birmingham | 82.6 | 74.8 | 60.2 | 151 | 82.4 | 93 |
| 17 Kent | 89.4 | 78.8 | 77.2 | 127 | 69.7 | 92.9 |
| 18 King's College London | 79.1 | 71.6 | 62.7 | 167 | 80.2 | 92.6 |
| 19 Bristol | 78.7 | 72.2 | 56.5 | 167 | 81.6 | 92.2 |
| 20 Queen Mary, London | 85.8 | 77.9 | 67.2 | 127 | 76.2 | 92 |
| 21 Manchester | 79.9 | 71.4 | 67 | 162 | 75 | 91.9 |
| 22 Southampton | 84.5 | 77.2 | 59.5 | 140 | 77.1 | 91.7 |

| | | | | | | |
|---|---|---|---|---|---|---|
| 23 Nottingham | 84.3 | 80.2 | 52.5 | 142 | 78.9 | 91.6 |
| =24 Lancaster | 86.8 | 76.1 | 51.7 | 147 | 75.5 | 91.4 |
| =24 Lincoln | 91.8 | 84.5 | 66 | 111 | 68.9 | 91.4 |
| =26 Leeds | 79.8 | 77.1 | 49.2 | 162 | 79.1 | 91.1 |
| =26 East Anglia | 86.8 | 74.7 | 67.5 | 126 | 72.7 | 91.1 |
| 28 Stirling | 87.6 | 80.4 | 51.7 | 179 | 60.8 | 90.9 |
| 29 Royal Holloway | 88.1 | 82.3 | 53.5 | 134 | 71.7 | 90.8 |
| 30 Hull | 91.2 | 86.4 | 60.8 | 108 | 69.8 | 90.7 |
| 31 Aberdeen | 85.3 | 82.8 | 38.5 | 173 | 70.2 | 90.5 |
| 32 Coventry | 97.6 | 96.3 | 33.2 | 111 | 70.6 | 90.3 |
| 33 Teesside | 95.6 | 88 | 49.2 | 110 | 66.7 | 90 |
| 34 Liverpool | 84.3 | 78.6 | 52.8 | 135 | 73.3 | 89.8 |
| =35 Sussex | 82.8 | 78.8 | 62.7 | 131 | 70.2 | 89.7 |
| =35 Plymouth | 94.7 | 91.2 | 42.8 | 109 | 68.7 | 89.7 |
| 37 Northumbria | 88.2 | 82.4 | 49.5 | 128 | 69.8 | 89.5 |
| 38 Edinburgh | 72.5 | 69.6 | 55.8 | 177 | 75 | 89.3 |
| 39 Cardiff | 80.7 | 72.8 | 42.2 | 134 | 84.1 | 89.2 |
| 40 Bournemouth | 92.2 | 81.4 | 47.2 | 106 | 72 | 89.1 |
| 41 Aberystwyth | 89.4 | 86.5 | 36.8 | 119 | 74.4 | 89 |
| =42 Swansea | 90.4 | 87.1 | 45.2 | 126 | 65.6 | 88.9 |
| =42 Queen's, Belfast | 83.6 | 80.1 | 54.2 | 140 | 67.3 | 88.9 |
| 44 Reading | 87.5 | 83.6 | 42.2 | 119 | 74.1 | 88.8 |
| 45 Central Lancashire | 95.2 | 91.7 | 24.5 | 102 | 75 | 88.4 |
| =46 Huddersfield | 91.9 | 77.1 | 33.5 | 112 | 74.4 | 87.9 |
| =46 Derby | 98.8 | 96.8 | — | 106 | 78.4 | 87.9 |
| 48 Worcester | 88.8 | 85.2 | 30.2 | 110 | 76.4 | 87.7 |
| 49 Salford | 93.6 | 83.2 | 51.7 | 110 | 58.3 | 87.5 |
| 50 Nottingham Trent | 88 | 76.9 | 51.5 | 104 | 67.2 | 87 |
| =51 Manchester Metropolitan | 86.9 | 78.9 | 41 | 115 | 69.4 | 86.7 |
| =51 Portsmouth | 88.3 | 87 | 51.7 | 95 | 64 | 86.7 |
| =53 Brighton | 92.7 | 69.3 | 44.2 | 98 | — | 86.4 |
| =53 Roehampton | 87.9 | 64.8 | 42.8 | 98 | 76.9* | 86.4 |
| =53 Hertfordshire | 87.3 | 76.7 | 49 | 100 | — | 86.4 |
| 56 City | 88.7 | 81.8 | 40.8 | 101 | — | 86.3 |
| =57 Dundee | 81.5 | 71.6 | 23.8 | 178 | 66.9 | 86.1 |
| =57 Ulster | 88.7 | 85.1 | 34 | 115 | 65.9 | 86.1 |
| 59 Newman | 95.3 | 91.1 | 15 | 93 | 71.4 | 85.8 |
| 60 Liverpool John Moores | 88.8 | 84.6 | 19.8 | 128 | 67.9 | 85.7 |
| =61 De Montfort | 86.1 | 80.7 | 37.5 | 93 | 71.6 | 85.3 |
| =61 Newcastle | 77.6 | 75.1 | 33.5 | 143 | 71.8 | 85.3 |
| 63 Liverpool Hope | 90.2 | 82.1 | 24.2 | 110 | 67.9 | 85.2 |
| 64 Brunel | 93.3 | 89 | — | 102 | 77.4 | 85.1 |
| 65 Northampton | 92.5 | 80.6 | 31.2 | 96 | 64.8 | 84.9 |
| 66 Bangor | 87.3 | 80.7 | 33.2 | 120 | 60.8 | 84.5 |
| 67 Leeds Beckett | 97.2 | 94.7 | 13.8 | 95 | 61 | 84.3 |
| =68 York St John | 92.5 | 86.8 | 18 | 99 | 64.7 | 84 |
| =68 SOAS London | 78.6 | 62.6 | 47.5 | 138 | 63.5* | 84 |
| 70 Anglia Ruskin | 85.2 | 75.1 | 47 | 90 | 64.4 | 83.9 |

## History cont.

| | | Teaching quality % | Student experience % | Research quality % | Entry standards (UCAS points) | Graduate prospects % | Overall score |
|---|---|---|---|---|---|---|---|
| 71 | Bishop Grosseteste | 93.2 | 87.5 | 16 | 94 | — | 83.8 |
| 72 | Goldsmiths, London | 85.2 | 62.7 | 41.5 | 113 | 65.2 | 83.7 |
| 73 | Chichester | 88.5 | 75.8 | 33 | 106 | 61.6 | 83.6 |
| 74 | Gloucestershire | 93.7 | 85.5 | 8.2 | 91 | 69.6 | 83.5 |
| 75 | Oxford Brookes | 82.3 | 79.7 | 28.2 | 103 | 70.7 | 83.4 |
| 76 | Edge Hill | 80 | 76.1 | 27.8 | 106 | 73.6 | 83.3 |
| 77 | Sheffield Hallam | 85.7 | 77.1 | 25.2 | 102 | 68.9 | 83.2 |
| 78 | Keele | 84.2 | 78.7 | 41.5 | 112 | 55.8 | 82.9 |
| =79 | Wales Trinity St David | 85.8 | 75.9 | 31 | — | 62.7* | 82.8 |
| =79 | Essex | 86.4 | 81.2 | 40.2 | 109 | 53.5 | 82.8 |
| 81 | Canterbury Christ Church | 88.8 | 82.5 | 17.8 | 89 | 67.7 | 82.5 |
| 82 | Winchester | 88.4 | 75.8 | 18.8 | 102 | 64.9 | 82.2 |
| 83 | Wolverhampton | 87.7 | 77.8 | 23.8 | 99 | 60 | 81.5 |
| 84 | Chester | 85.7 | 75.6 | 28.7 | 103 | 57.6 | 81.1 |
| 85 | Westminster | 85.8 | 83.3 | 23 | 100 | 54.3 | 80.2 |
| 86 | West of England | 85.9 | 79.4 | 15 | 106 | 57.7 | 80 |
| 87 | South Wales | 92.2 | 85.2 | 30.5 | — | 39.7* | 79.4 |
| 88 | Bath Spa | 81.4 | 78.4 | 25 | 104 | 54.3 | 79.1 |
| 89 | Greenwich | 79.2 | 66.6 | 25.5 | 107 | 58.2 | 78.5 |

| | | | |
|---|---|---|---|
| Employed in high-skilled job | 37% | Employed in lower-skilled job | 26% |
| Employed in high-skilled job and studying | 4% | Employed in lower-skilled job and studying | 2% |
| Studying | 14% | Unemployed | 5% |
| High-skilled work (median) salary | £26,000 | Low-/medium-skilled salary | £20,000 |

## History of Art, Architecture and Design

Cambridge returns to the lead in our new History of Art, Architecture and Design table, boosted by the best graduate outcomes and the highest entry standards. No 1 for the past two years, St Andrews is runner-up overall but still in front for research quality. The university where the Princess of Wales studied history of art, St Andrews also achieves the top rates of student satisfaction with teaching quality as well as the broader experience, measures derived from the National Student Survey.

"Art history matters because art matters. Great works of art offer profound distillations of the human experience; they help us to understand our relationship with the world and with one another," says Professor Mark Hallett, Märit Rausing director, Courtauld Institute of Art, "It gives you skills – of analysis, argument, presentation and collaboration – that will enable you to flourish in a wide variety of professions." In ninth place overall the Courtauld is a self-governing college of the University of London based in Somerset House and has previously topped our table – the only specialist institution to have done so in any ranking.

Demand for places to study history of art, architecture and design degrees has been consistent over recent years, and in 2023 the subject attracted 6,265 applications and 1,145 new students. Career prospects may not be immediately gratifying; the subject ranks in the bottom ten (=62nd) of our new employment index of 70 areas, where its position is held back by the similar numbers of graduates employed full-time in high-skilled jobs (four in ten) as jobs deemed "low-skilled" (three in ten). The subject compares more favourably in our pay ranking, where starting salaries commanded by graduates rank it =53rd.

| History of Art, Architecture and Design | Teaching quality % | Student experience % | Research quality % | Entry standards (UCAS points) | Graduate prospects % | Overall score |
|---|---|---|---|---|---|---|
| 1 Cambridge | | | 65.8 | 191 | 79.2* | 100 |
| 2 St Andrews | 93.9 | 92.3 | 78.2 | 173 | 71.4 | 99 |
| 3 University College London | 87.7 | 85.2 | 64.7 | 172 | 76.5* | 96.2 |
| 4 Oxford | 87 | 72.2 | 61.3 | 198 | — | 95.1 |
| 5 Sussex | 91.1 | 89.1 | 70 | 146 | — | 94.6 |
| 6 Birmingham | 84.2 | 75.8 | 70.2 | 158 | — | 92.3 |
| 7 East Anglia | 92 | 82.7 | 67 | 132 | — | 91.9 |
| 8 York | 81.1 | 77.7 | 77 | 142 | 67.3 | 91 |
| 9 Courtauld | 86 | 68.9 | 63.5 | 159 | 68.3 | 90.9 |
| 10 Nottingham | 93.6 | 82.4 | 54.8 | 131 | — | 89.7 |
| 11 Glasgow | 86.5 | 74.2 | 68.8 | 176 | 54.3 | 89.6 |
| 12 Exeter | 83.1 | 81.8 | 55.9 | 155 | — | 89.3 |
| =13 Leeds | 83.2 | 77.5 | 54.8 | 159 | 66.9 | 89.2 |
| =13 Goldsmiths, London | 82.8 | 77.7 | 57.5 | 160 | 65.5 | 89.2 |
| 15 Bristol | 78 | 75 | 59.8 | 152 | 69.7 | 88.8 |
| 16 Warwick | 85.6 | 68.7 | 55 | 158 | 66.2 | 88.7 |
| 17 Manchester Metropolitan | 84.4 | 77.5 | 51.7 | 151 | — | 87.9 |
| 18 Manchester | 75.6 | 66.8 | 70.8 | 156 | 62.7* | 87.7 |
| 19 Edinburgh | 76.4 | 72.4 | 54 | 158 | 67.2 | 87.1 |
| 20 Oxford Brookes | 91.5 | 86.1 | 25.5 | 112 | 74 | 85.3 |
| 21 Brighton | 90.3 | 85.6 | 53 | 105 | 60.3* | 84.9 |

| | | | |
|---|---|---|---|
| Employed in high-skilled job | 41% | Employed in lower-skilled job | 31% |
| Employed in high-skilled job and studying | 1% | Employed in lower-skilled job and studying | 3% |
| Studying | 7% | Unemployed | 6% |
| High-skilled work (median) salary | £25,000 | Low-/medium-skilled salary | £20,000 |

## Hospitality, Leisure, Recreation and Tourism

A wide variety of courses are incorporated in our Hospitality, Leisure, Recreation and Tourism table, all of them directed towards management in the leisure and tourism industries. They include degrees in international hospitality management, and adventure tourism management. "Studying tourism takes a multidisciplinary perspective and equips students with a range of core skills, such as planning, logistics and marketing, while encouraging entrepreneurialism and leadership," says Dr Laura Dixon, principal lecturer, events management and international tourism management, Liverpool John Moores University.

Modern universities dominate the ranking, representing all but four of the 49 institutions tabled, but Birmingham – founded at the turn of the 20th century – is No 1 for the ninth year running. Helping secure its overall rank is the top-rated research in the area and third-highest entry standards in the UK. Ahead for entry standards are Glasgow Caledonian and Edinburgh, where students arrived with averages of 164 and 163 UCAS points respectively

(Scottish universities benefitting from the favourable tariff conversion for Scottish secondary qualifications). The top 10 features most of the same universities this year as last, such as Glasgow Caledonian and Liverpool John Moores, each occupying the same rank for the second year running. Surrey, also commonly found in the upper reaches of our table, is fourth this year.

Arts University, Bournemouth – in 20th place overall – has the top rates of student satisfaction with teaching quality, followed by Central Lancashire (27th) and Lincoln (7th), while for students' evaluation of the wider experience Lincoln leads the field. Conversely, students at Staffordshire expressed the lowest rates of satisfaction with both teaching quality and the wider experience, our National Student Survey analysis shows. The top career destinations were found at Winchester when the latest Graduate Outcomes survey took its census 15 months on from degrees, by which point 74.1% of the university's graduates in the subjects were in high-skilled jobs and/or further study.

As a whole, though, the subjects have moved up seven places in our employment ranking, to 61st out of 70 areas. The subject area continues to be held back in our ranking by the high proportion (36.7%) of graduates working in jobs classified as "low-skilled". Salaries compare better: with hospitality, leisure, recreation and tourism ranked =53rd out of 70, based on average graduate salaries of £24,000.

| Hospitality, Leisure, Recreation and Tourism | Teaching quality % | Student experience % | Research quality % | Entry standards (UCAS points) | Graduate prospects % | Overall score |
|---|---|---|---|---|---|---|
| 1 Birmingham | 81.3 | 68.8 | 73.2 | 161 | — | 100 |
| 2 Glasgow Caledonian | 85.1 | 80.9 | 38.5 | 164 | 68.5 | 95.8 |
| 3 Liverpool John Moores | 86.9 | 85.6 | 60.8 | 140 | 62.6 | 95.3 |
| 4 Surrey | 86.5 | 87.8 | 57 | 137 | 65.2 | 95.2 |
| 5 Edinburgh | 78.4 | 79.6 | 55 | 163 | 61.5* | 94.9 |
| 6 Manchester Metropolitan | 88.2 | 86.3 | 42.8 | 132 | 65 | 92.4 |
| 7 Lincoln | 93 | 91.4 | 30.8 | 127 | 66.7 | 91.8 |
| 8 Edinburgh Napier | 88.9 | 87.3 | 23.5 | 147 | 63.8 | 91.4 |
| 9 Brighton | 85.8 | 82.4 | 45.5 | 112 | 73.6 | 91.3 |
| 10 Leeds Beckett | 86 | 83.8 | 49.2 | 106 | 71.1 | 90.7 |
| 11 Winchester | 89.9 | 84.7 | 20.8 | 122 | 74.1 | 90 |
| 12 Ulster | 91.9 | 91.4 | 45.8 | 125 | 51.2 | 89.9 |
| 13 Chester | 88.6 | 86.4 | 25.2 | 130 | 64.8 | 89.5 |
| 14 Falmouth | 92.3 | 84.3 | 48.8 | 119 | 52.2 | 89.2 |
| 15 Sheffield Hallam | 81.3 | 76.4 | 45.2 | 115 | 69.4 | 89.1 |
| 16 Cardiff Metropolitan | 78.5 | 76 | 43.8 | 121 | 65.4 | 88.1 |
| =17 Northumbria | 82.2 | 87.2 | 28.2 | 142 | 54.2* | 87.7 |
| =17 Essex | 92.1 | 86 | 32.5 | 110 | — | 87.7 |
| 19 Bournemouth | 78.4 | 75.6 | 41.8 | 120 | 65.3 | 87.5 |
| 20 Arts University, Bournemouth | 94.9 | 90.2 | 23 | 112 | — | 87.4 |
| 21 Coventry | 89.1 | 87.5 | 24.8 | 122 | 59.7 | 87.3 |
| 22 Canterbury Christ Church | 87.9 | 84.2 | 38 | 102 | 64.7 | 87.2 |
| 23 West of Scotland | 90.9 | 85.2 | 29 | — | 54.8 | 87.1 |
| 24 Westminster | 77.3 | 78.7 | 37.5 | 127 | — | 86.5 |
| 25 Robert Gordon | 91.3 | 86 | — | 141 | 60 | 86.4 |
| 26 London South Bank | 84.2 | 73.7 | 32.2 | 108 | 66.7 | 85.9 |
| 27 Central Lancashire | 93.3 | 91.2 | 19.2 | 128 | 45.7 | 85.1 |

| | | | | | | | |
|---|---|---|---|---|---|---|---|
| 28 | Oxford Brookes | 84.2 | 83.1 | — | 120 | 73.8 | 85 |
| =29 | West London | 90.5 | 90.1 | 24.2 | 121 | 47.7 | 84.8 |
| =29 | Birmingham City | 87.9 | 80.6 | — | 125 | 67.7 | 84.8 |
| 31 | Huddersfield | 79.8 | 83.3 | 23.2 | 133 | 53.7* | 84.7 |
| 32 | West of England | 86.1 | 83.2 | — | 120 | 68.3 | 84.2 |
| 33 | Plymouth | 74.8 | 72.5 | 28.7 | 128 | 59.4 | 84.1 |
| 34 | Gloucestershire | 75.5 | 70.3 | 24.5 | 118 | 67.6 | 84 |
| 35 | Solent, Southampton | 80.3 | 76.5 | 18.5 | 117 | 64.6 | 83.8 |
| 36 | Buckinghamshire New | 80.2 | 70.8 | 22.8 | 108 | 66.9 | 83.3 |
| 37 | Anglia Ruskin | 78.9 | 77.4 | 18.5 | — | 63.5 | 83.2 |
| 38 | Sunderland | 90 | 87.4 | 22 | 118 | 42 | 82.3 |
| 39 | Hertfordshire | 78.9 | 74.6 | 29 | 104 | 60 | 82.2 |
| =40 | East London | 90.8 | 89.1 | — | 92 | 68.8 | 82.1 |
| =40 | Wales Trinity St David | 90.1 | 86.5 | — | 130 | 49.3 | 82.1 |
| 42 | Northampton | 83.5 | 77.7 | 13.2 | 116 | 56.6 | 81.8 |
| =43 | Derby | 88.4 | 81 | — | 122 | 54.7 | 81.4 |
| =43 | York St John | 75 | 73.5 | 27.5 | 117 | — | 81.4 |
| =45 | Greenwich | 85 | 84.8 | — | 120 | 53.5 | 80.6 |
| =45 | Queen Margaret, Edinburgh | 72.6 | 70.9 | — | 143 | 57.9 | 80.6 |
| 47 | Bedfordshire | 86.8 | 83.2 | 22 | — | 34.4 | 77.6 |
| 48 | Chichester | 70.6 | 62.8 | 33.2 | 103 | — | 77.3 |
| 49 | Staffordshire | 68.7 | 59.3 | — | 115 | 63.9 | 76.4 |

| | | | | |
|---|---|---|---|---|
| Employed in high-skilled job | 45% | Employed in lower-skilled job | | 37% |
| Employed in high-skilled job and studying | 2% | Employed in lower-skilled job and studying | | 1% |
| Studying | 4% | Unemployed | | 6% |
| High-skilled work (median) salary | £25,000 | Low-/medium-skilled salary | | £21,300 |

# Iberian Languages

Cambridge swaps places with St Andrews to take the lead in our new Iberian Languages table. They lead a ranking which is accustomed to fluctuations due to the small student numbers the languages of Spanish and Portuguese attract. Lancaster is up ten places to rank third while University College London is down ten places to sit 14th, for instance. Just three of the 34 institutions listed are post-1992 universities and entry standards tend to be high: at 23 out of the 24 universities tabled entrants averaged over 144 UCAS points (equal to three As at A level). Cambridge benefits from strong performance across all five measures – including the top graduate prospects and second-best teaching quality score – derived from our National Student Survey analysis. Sheffield (20th overall) does even better for student satisfaction, topping the table for teaching quality, while Reading (seventh) is in front for students' evaluation of the broad experience.

York (in =9th place overall) achieved the top results in the subjects in the Research Excellence Framework 2021 while Strathclyde (29th overall) is out in front for graduate prospects, with more than nine in 10 (91.2%) employed in high-skilled jobs or further study 15 months after their degrees.

The Iberian languages sit 46th in our 70-subject employment ranking this year, down from 38th, with six in ten (61.9%) graduates in high-skilled jobs and/or further study within 15 months of graduating. Average early careers salaries of £26,000 rank the subjects in the upper half of our pay index, at =28th.

"Studying Iberian languages (the languages of Spain and/or Portugal) allows students to communicate fluently in two major global languages, which means graduates can work across the world. Studying a language and the cultures associated with it allows you to experience the world in a distinctive way," says Dr Eamon McCarthy, senior lecturer in Spanish and Latin American studies, University of Stirling.

In line with other modern language degrees, the demand for places to study Spanish and Portuguese continued to decline in the 2023 admissions cycle however, when Iberian studies attracted 4,505 applications and 820 new students (a third fewer than four years before in 2019). But there were still 61 universities and colleges offering Spanish on the UCAS website for 2025-26, however. Many students take Spanish as part of a broader modern language degree or paired with diverse subjects as part of a joint honours programme rather than as a single honours programme. Though no longer tracked individually by UCAS, Portuguese had been registering zero single honours students since 2012 – but it can still be studied, and 23 institutions were offering the language for 2025-26, mostly as part of joint honours degrees or combined modern or Latin languages courses.

| Iberian Languages | Teaching quality % | Student experience % | Research quality % | Entry standards (UCAS points) | Graduate prospects % | Overall score |
|---|---|---|---|---|---|---|
| 1 Cambridge | 92.2 | 73.7 | 61 | 190 | 91.5 | 100 |
| 2 St Andrews | 88.6 | 84.9 | 51.5 | 201 | — | 98.5 |
| 3 Lancaster | 87.9 | 77.5 | 68.5 | 145 | — | 95.8 |
| 4 Warwick | 88.8 | 82 | 46.2 | 161 | 88.7 | 95.3 |
| 5 Oxford | 88.4 | 69.6 | 51.2 | 188 | 83.7 | 95.2 |
| 6 Stirling | 84.1 | 81.5 | 47.5 | 190 | — | 94.8 |
| 7 Reading | 87.4 | 88.8 | 54.5 | — | 79.2* | 94.7 |
| 8 Durham | 85.9 | 71.8 | 46 | 181 | 85.6 | 94 |
| =9 Newcastle | 82.3 | 79.4 | 61.8 | 149 | 83.1 | 93.5 |
| =9 York | 80.6 | 72.8 | 74.8 | 138 | — | 93.5 |
| =11 Queen's, Belfast | 89.5 | 87.2 | 37 | 145 | 83.7 | 92.4 |
| =11 Nottingham | 84.7 | 77.1 | 62 | 146 | 77.6 | 92.4 |
| =11 Aberdeen | 90.5 | 72.3 | 32.5 | 186 | — | 92.4 |
| 14 University College London | 79.1 | 67.6 | 56 | 166 | 84.1* | 92.1 |
| 15 Exeter | 83.7 | 78.1 | 50 | 149 | 82.9 | 92 |
| 16 Leeds | 83.2 | 82.4 | 52 | 155 | 78.7 | 91.9 |
| 17 Southampton | 88.8 | 76.5 | 47.8 | 154 | 78.0* | 91.8 |
| 18 King's College London | 83.9 | 76.8 | 51.2 | 152 | 80.4 | 91.7 |
| 19 Bristol | 83.9 | 78.7 | 64 | 159 | 68.8 | 91.3 |
| 20 Sheffield | 94.8 | 84.7 | 35.8 | — | 73.8 | 91.1 |
| =21 Royal Holloway | 82.6 | 79.4 | 60 | 125 | — | 91 |
| =21 Edinburgh | 71.8 | 68.3 | 45.8 | 181 | 88.8 | 91 |
| =23 Liverpool | 87.4 | 84.5 | 59 | 131 | 70.7* | 90.7 |
| =23 Manchester | 79.2 | 67.5 | 59.5 | 152 | 80.2 | 90.7 |
| 25 Bath | 82.8 | 78.7 | 31.8 | 153 | 87.7 | 90.6 |
| 26 Birmingham | 79.1 | 74.6 | 54.8 | 149 | 80.1 | 90.5 |
| 27 Manchester Metropolitan | 88 | 83.1 | 51.7 | 107 | — | 90.2 |
| 28 Aberystwyth | 86.7 | 81.4 | 41.2 | 119 | — | 88.4 |
| 29 Strathclyde | 85.5 | 77.5 | — | 194 | 84.4* | 88.2 |
| 30 Cardiff | 80.4 | 74.7 | 55.5 | 126 | 73.1 | 87.7 |
| 31 Queen Mary, London | 77.4 | 67.8 | 51.1 | 124 | — | 85.9 |

| | | | | | | |
|---|---|---|---|---|---|---|
| **32** Chester | | 76.9 | 71.6 | 31.2 | 98 | 87.5 | 84.8 |
| **33** Glasgow | | 78.9 | 70.6 | 25.5 | 203 | 61.7 | 84.6 |
| **34** Westminster | | 84.4 | 81.6 | 24.5 | 114 | — | 84.1 |

| | | | |
|---|---|---|---|
| Employed in high-skilled job | 49% | Employed in lower-skilled job | 21% |
| Employed in high-skilled job and studying | 4% | Employed in lower-skilled job and studying | 0% |
| Studying | 9% | Unemployed | 8% |
| High-skilled work (median) salary | £26,900 | Low-/medium-skilled salary | £23,000 |

# Information Systems and Management

Our table includes all subjects to do with information curation and management. Formerly titled Librarianship and Information Management, this is the fourth appearance of our broadened and renamed subject grouping. The courses encompassed range from information systems, data management and curatorial studies to bioinformatics, museum studies and systems analysis and design. The ranking also still takes in librarianship, which requires some postgraduate training after a first degree in order to enter the profession and has practically disappeared at undergraduate level.

University College London (UCL) tops our Information Systems and Management table by a clear margin and for the fourth consecutive year. It was the top scorer in the Research Excellence Framework 2021 and it has the highest entry standards by far. Northumbria, which moves up to third place overall from eight last year, is top for student satisfaction with teaching quality as well as the broader experience in our National Student Survey analysis.

Runner-up Ulster had the best-employed graduates when canvassed by the latest Graduate Outcomes survey, which showed more than four in five (82.6%) working in highskilled jobs and/or enrolled in postgraduate study 15 months on from their degrees.

The subject group as a whole features in the upper half of our 70-subject employment, at 33rd position. It compares even better on earnings (though pay is not an ingredient of our table) placing =21st, with graduates commanding salaries of £27,000, on average. At UCL, Edyta Kostanek, deputy programme director for BSc information management for business says "Students are equipped with cutting-edge knowledge that is supported by the latest research in innovation and entrepreneurship. With a curriculum that includes real-world projects and hands-on experience, graduates are ready to succeed in diverse sectors."

| Information Systems and Management | Teaching quality % | Student experience % | Research quality % | Entry standards (UCAS points) | Graduate prospects % | Overall score |
|---|---|---|---|---|---|---|
| **1** University College London | 76.6 | 84.8 | 56.8 | 186 | — | 100 |
| **2** Ulster | 83 | 81 | 45.8 | 132 | 82.6 | 96.5 |
| **=3** Edge Hill | 80.9 | 78.7 | 39.8 | 143 | — | 93.2 |
| **=3** Northumbria | 90.4 | 87.1 | 25.8 | 141 | 76.7 | 93.2 |
| **=5** Manchester Metropolitan | 87.8 | 85.1 | 29 | 134 | 74.2 | 91.2 |
| **=5** Coventry | 87 | 77 | 23.5 | 131 | 77.4 | 91.2 |
| **7** West London | 76.1 | 77.7 | 45.5 | 123 | — | 90.8 |
| **8** Anglia Ruskin | 71.9 | 56.8 | 53.8 | 131 | — | 90.4 |
| **9** Portsmouth | 87.3 | 84 | 32.8 | 105 | 74.6 | 89.4 |
| **10** Huddersfield | 81.1 | 85.3 | 26.5 | 126 | 74.2 | 89 |
| **11** South Wales | 88.5 | 77.5 | — | 121 | 76.8* | 87.4 |

| Employed in high-skilled job | 62% | Employed in lower-skilled job | 17% |
| Employed in high-skilled job and studying | 4% | Employed in lower-skilled job and studying | 0% |
| Studying | 2% | Unemployed | 8% |
| High-skilled work (median) salary | £27,000 | Low-/medium-skilled salary | £23,000 |

# Italian

Led by Cambridge at No 1, the top three of our table is unchanged for the third consecutive year. Cambridge has the edge for graduate prospects, and it is also hitting the right notes with its students of Italian, coming top for teaching quality in our National Student Survey analysis. Leeds (fourth overall) is in front for student satisfaction with the wider experience. In a generally high-tariff subject and a table without any post-1992 universities, Glasgow leads on entry standards, its new students averaging 195 UCAS points. No universities averaged below the 149 points (equal to AAA at A-level) at Exeter and Birmingham.

To study Italian at undergraduate level, one modern language at A-level is required by the leading universities. Some require Italian specifically, while others allow it to be learned from scratch. Degree courses often include time spent abroad studying or teaching. Describing the merits of the subject, Katrin Wehling-Giorgi, professor in Italian studies, Durham University says "Studying Italian will provide you with a plurilingual, intercultural mindset. You will become fluent in the language of a vibrant, top-ten world economy, the lingua franca of fashion, music and architecture. Italy is the birthplace of lyric opera, Renaissance art, neorealist cinema, literary giants from Dante to Ferrante and a transnational diaspora, and studying Italian opens worldwide opportunities from the civil service to the cultural sector."

However, the downward trend in demand for Italian degrees (along with modern languages more broadly) brought new student numbers to 135 in 2023 – ten more than in 2022 but 27% fewer than four years before in 2019. The UCAS website showed 37 colleges and universities offering 550 courses for 2025-26, most them as part of joint honours degrees or as part of a wider modern languages programme. Only three were offering Italian as a single honours degree.

A five-place rise for Italian brings it closer to the upper half of our 70 subject areas (39th place), based on 63.8% of those with an Italian degree working in high-skilled jobs and/or postgraduate study 15 months on. Average early career salaries of £25,715 rank the subject 37th.

| Italian | Teaching quality % | Student experience % | Research quality % | Entry standards (UCAS points) | Graduate prospects % | Overall score |
|---|---|---|---|---|---|---|
| 1 Cambridge | 92.2 | 73.7 | 61 | 190 | 91.5 | 100 |
| 2 Durham | 85.9 | 71.8 | 46 | 181 | 85.6 | 93.8 |
| 3 Warwick | 88.7 | 81.7 | 46.2 | 162 | 85.6 | 93.5 |
| 4 Leeds | 90.1 | 84.4 | 52 | 153 | — | 93.4 |
| 5 Oxford | 85.5 | 66.4 | 51.2 | 179 | — | 93 |
| 6 Bristol | 85.2 | 82.9 | 64 | 155 | 67.3 | 92.2 |
| 7 University College London | 77.8 | 73.8 | 56 | 167 | — | 91.2 |
| 8 Exeter | 83.7 | 78.1 | 50 | 149 | 82.8 | 90.8 |
| 9 Edinburgh | 77.6 | 77.7 | 45.8 | 174 | — | 90.3 |
| 10 Manchester | 78.4 | 70.1 | 59.5 | 155 | — | 90 |
| 11 Birmingham | 79.1 | 74.6 | 54.8 | 149 | 79.3 | 89.7 |
| 12 Glasgow | 76.8 | 72.7 | 25.5 | 195 | 60.5* | 85.9 |

| Employed in high-skilled job | 45% | Employed in lower-skilled job | 22% |
| Employed in high-skilled job and studying | 5% | Employed in lower-skilled job and studying | 1% |
| Studying | 12% | Unemployed | 6% |
| High-skilled work (median) salary | £26,000 | Low-/medium-skilled salary | N/A |

## Land and Property Management

Graduate employment levels in land and property management are among the best of any subject group outside the health professions and engineering disciplines. The latest Graduate Outcomes survey showed almost 80% of graduates employed in high-skilled jobs and/or furthering their studies 15 months on, ranking the subjects 13th out of our employment index's 70 areas. At Sheffield Hallam, which ranks fifth overall in our table, a perfect 100% of graduates achieved these outcomes. Average early career salaries of £26,265 also compare positively with other subjects albeit less strongly, in 27th place.

In a diverse subject grouping that includes programmes in woodland ecology, surveying and conservation, real-estate degrees are the biggest recruiters. In third place of the table Reading runs a Pathways to Property widening participation programme at its Henley Business School to attract greater numbers of state-school-educated applicants into studying real estate.

Cambridge's lead in the table remains unchallenged, its land economy degree attracts the highest entry standards by far and the university leads the field in research quality too, based on results of the latest Research Excellence Framework (REF) 2021. Runner-up in the table for the third consecutive year, Manchester is second for entry standards and third for research. Eleventh-placed Kingston also performed strongly in the REF 2021 and sits second to Cambridge for research quality.

Anthony Goodier, principal lecturer in built environment, Sheffield Hallam University says: "This subject encapsulates diverse aspects of property and real estate. It can offer you an interesting, varied and rewarding global career. There are huge opportunities to work in the public and private sectors because land and property professionals have a crucial role to play in addressing the challenges we face, from meeting the housing need to improving the performance of urban and rural real estate as we progress towards net zero."

| Land and Property Management | Teaching quality % | Student experience % | Research quality % | Entry standards (UCAS points) | Graduate prospects % | Overall score |
|---|---|---|---|---|---|---|
| 1 Cambridge | 83.5 | 68 | 74.8 | 191 | — | 100 |
| 2 Manchester | 79.8 | 81.4 | 59.2 | 153 | — | 93.4 |
| 3 Reading | 80.9 | 82.5 | 53.5 | 130 | 94.4 | 91.4 |
| 4 Ulster | 88.5 | 85.9 | 54.2 | 128 | 75.0* | 88.7 |
| 5 Sheffield Hallam | 80.3 | 69 | 43.2 | 107 | 100 | 88.3 |
| 6 Liverpool John Moores | 84.6 | 86.8 | 28.7 | 129 | — | 87.5 |
| 7 Salford | 83.3 | 81.9 | 43.5 | — | 82.8 | 87.2 |
| 8 Nottingham Trent | 84.9 | 80.3 | 38 | 109 | 85.7 | 86.3 |
| 9 Birmingham City | 83.1 | 81.4 | 34.8 | 115 | — | 86 |
| 10 Westminster | 79.4 | 81.2 | 37.5 | 115 | 86 | 85.4 |
| 11 Kingston | 73.8 | 65.4 | 63 | 100 | — | 84.6 |
| 12 Leeds Beckett | 77.6 | 73.3 | 24.5 | 112 | — | 81 |
| 13 Royal Agricultural University | 67.6 | 63.5 | — | 115 | 90.3 | 77 |

| | | | | |
|---|---|---|---|---|
| Employed in high-skilled job | 68% | Employed in lower-skilled job | 10% |
| Employed in high-skilled job and studying | 9% | Employed in lower-skilled job and studying | 0% |
| Studying | 2% | Unemployed | 4% |
| High-skilled work (median) salary | £26,500 | Low-/medium-skilled salary | £20,000 |

## Law

University College London takes the No 1 spot in our new Law table, bringing an end to Cambridge's long-held run at the top. UCL's research quality within law is peerless, based on results of the latest Research Excellence Framework 2021 and it outdoes Cambridge on student satisfaction with the broad undergraduate experience. In second place overall, Cambridge still has the edge for graduate prospects – with 96.9% of graduates employed in high-skilled jobs and/ or postgraduate study within 15 months. Further reshuffles among the upper ranks of the table include London School of Economics rising to fourth place (from ninth) while Durham is up three places to fifth. Oxford has slipped three places to rank seventh. Climbing six places to sit 13th, Ulster is the top-ranked modern university in the table. Modern universities more broadly do best for students' evaluation of teaching quality, with our National Student Survey analysis showing Cumbria (68th overall) in front, followed by Gloucestershire (=44th) and Edinburgh Napier (31st). But for students' ratings of the broader experience Surrey – founded in the 1960s – comes top, followed by West London (=69th in the main table) and Edinburgh Napier.

One of the most popular choices for higher education, law continues to attract record applications. In 2023, 157,680 applied to study law, 14% more than in 2019 after successive years of rising demand. Interest from 18-year-old applicants has seen the sharpest increase of 27% between 2019 and 2023. The number of places available has risen too but has not kept pace with applications, and 28,195 law students were accepted onto courses in 2023 (up 7% since 2019). More encouragingly for school leavers, however, the number of places going to 18-year-olds has increased more steeply by 22% across the same timeframe.

Entry standards reflect the fierce demand for places: seven of the 102 universities in our table average more than 200 points in the UCAS tariff and more than a third average over 144 points (equivalent to three As at A-level). Led by Glasgow, four Scottish universities (which benefit from the favourable tariff conversion for Scottish secondary qualifications) claim the highest entry tariffs among their law entrants. King's College London attracted the highest tariff score south of the border. But there are so many places to study law that there are still 11 universities where entrants averaged below 100 points.

Law graduates who want to become solicitors in England progress to the legal practice course, while those aiming to be barristers take the bar vocational course. In Scotland, most law courses are based on the distinctive Scottish legal system, which also has different professional qualifications. About half of law graduates do not go into practice and, perhaps surprisingly, law ranks only =41st out of the 70 subject areas in our employment ranking, with 63.1% of graduates in high-skilled work or postgraduate study 15 months on from degrees.

"If you want to enter the legal profession, a law degree teaches you the principles applied in legal practice. A law degree will also provide you with a rigorous training in critical thinking, which will prepare you for a number of professions," advises Dr Peter Candy, assistant professor in civil law, University of Cambridge.

Training contracts for those going into law keep pay in graduate-level jobs relatively austere, and the subject ranks a lowly 60th out of the 70 in our pay index. But the average starting salary of £23,500 earned by legal graduates across all universities bears little resemblance to the packets likely later down the line, and there is a strong case for the delayed career gratification posed by law.

There are not normally specific subject requirements for law, but A-levels of use include history, English, politics, classics and philosophy. Applicants are advised to read widely and to be curious about the law and its relationship with other areas of society.

| Law | Teaching quality % | Student experience % | Research quality % | Entry standards (UCAS points) | Graduate prospects % | Overall score |
|---|---|---|---|---|---|---|
| 1 University College London | 82.2 | 79.1 | 74.5 | 199 | 93.1 | 100 |
| 2 Cambridge | 83.8 | 76 | 59.2 | 200 | 96.9 | 99.3 |
| 3 Glasgow | 77 | 74.8 | 66.8 | 224 | 88.7 | 97.9 |
| 4 London School of Economics | 84.3 | 78.5 | 61.3 | 190 | 87 | 97 |
| 5 Durham | 81.2 | 74.1 | 59.5 | 191 | 90.5 | 96.4 |
| 6 Strathclyde | 83.7 | 83.2 | 45.8 | 210 | 84.4 | 96.3 |
| 7 Oxford | 80.1 | 64.5 | 62 | 200 | 91.8 | 96.2 |
| 8 Edinburgh | 75.2 | 69.7 | 64.2 | 211 | 90.5 | 96.1 |
| 9 King's College London | 80.6 | 73.7 | 56.2 | 203 | 86.9 | 95.8 |
| 10 Sheffield | 83.6 | 82.7 | 55 | 154 | 91.7 | 95.6 |
| 11 Aberdeen | 82.5 | 82.3 | 43.2 | 198 | 85.4 | 95.2 |
| 12 Warwick | 78.8 | 78.5 | 62 | 166 | 88.1 | 94.5 |
| 13 Ulster | 85.4 | 83.1 | 55 | 132 | 87.5 | 93.8 |
| 14 Bristol | 72.7 | 71.5 | 67.5 | 178 | 88.4 | 93.6 |
| =15 Exeter | 77.9 | 78.7 | 54.8 | 159 | 90 | 93.5 |
| =15 Lancaster | 87.8 | 87.8 | 48 | 143 | 81.9 | 93.5 |
| =15 Surrey | 88.5 | 89 | 41.5 | 126 | 88 | 93.5 |
| =18 Queen Mary, London | 76.7 | 77 | 57 | 172 | 86.9 | 93.4 |
| =18 York | 80.9 | 81.3 | 49.2 | 165 | 85.9 | 93.4 |
| =20 Dundee | 82 | 81.7 | 29.2 | 188 | 85.8 | 92.9 |
| =20 Queen's, Belfast | 72.7 | 73.7 | 62.3 | 160 | 91.8 | 92.9 |
| 22 Glasgow Caledonian | 87.7 | 85.6 | 25.8 | 204 | 74.2 | 92.7 |
| =23 Nottingham | 79.2 | 79.5 | 53.5 | 162 | 83.9 | 92.6 |
| =23 Cardiff | 76.3 | 77.7 | 60.5 | 152 | 87.3 | 92.6 |
| 25 Southampton | 78.9 | 76.6 | 46.5 | 147 | 91.3 | 92.3 |
| 26 Aston | 84.8 | 88.1 | 43.5 | 130 | 84.7 | 92.2 |
| 27 Kent | 81.4 | 78.5 | 69.8 | 137 | 78.4 | 92 |
| 28 Birmingham | 73.2 | 73.6 | 61.5 | 155 | 88.4 | 91.9 |
| 29 Leeds | 71.4 | 73.6 | 66.5 | 166 | 83.3 | 91.4 |
| 30 Stirling | 80.7 | 75.2 | 38.5 | 187 | 78.2 | 91 |
| 31 Edinburgh Napier | 89.5 | 88.2 | 5.5 | 168 | 82.4 | 90.9 |
| 32 Newcastle | 76.9 | 76.9 | 41.8 | 152 | 87.6 | 90.7 |
| 33 Liverpool | 75.2 | 78.2 | 51.5 | 144 | 85.4 | 90.5 |
| 34 Abertay | 87.3 | 85.1 | 5 | 149 | 87.8 | 90 |
| =35 Northumbria | 84.1 | 79.9 | 30.8 | 133 | 85.1 | 89.9 |
| =35 Leicester | 81.4 | 82.3 | 32 | 134 | 86.1 | 89.9 |
| 37 East Anglia | 78.4 | 79.1 | 32.5 | 136 | 88.4 | 89.5 |
| 38 Nottingham Trent | 83.5 | 80.1 | 53 | 116 | 77.5 | 89.4 |
| 39 Manchester | 73.6 | 69 | 40.8 | 165 | 86 | 89.2 |
| 40 Sussex | 78.7 | 80.3 | 44.8 | 131 | 80.2 | 88.9 |

**Law** cont.

| | | Teaching quality % | Student experience % | Research quality % | Entry standards (UCAS points) | Graduate prospects % | Overall score |
|---|---|---|---|---|---|---|---|
| 41 | Swansea | 81.7 | 80.9 | 27.8 | 133 | 83.2 | 88.6 |
| 42 | Essex | 80.6 | 79.8 | 56 | 114 | 74.6 | 88.2 |
| 43 | Reading | 79 | 79.2 | 33.8 | 124 | 84 | 88.1 |
| =44 | Manchester Metropolitan | 81.6 | 80.5 | 42.8 | 119 | 77.4 | 88 |
| =44 | Gloucestershire | 91.6 | 84.1 | 8.8 | 103 | 84.8 | 88 |
| 46 | Royal Holloway | 73.4 | 73.1 | 38 | 130 | 87.2 | 87.5 |
| =47 | City | 81 | 80.1 | 34.8 | 133 | 76 | 87.4 |
| =47 | Bournemouth | 82.2 | 82.4 | 26 | 104 | 84.7 | 87.4 |
| 49 | Portsmouth | 83.7 | 78.8 | 26.8 | 121 | 78.9 | 87.1 |
| 50 | West of England | 80.2 | 78.9 | 46.5 | 110 | 75.7 | 87 |
| 51 | South Wales | 83.7 | 74.9 | 33.5 | 115 | 78.6 | 86.9 |
| 52 | Plymouth | 78.9 | 77.5 | 37.2 | 115 | 79.7 | 86.7 |
| 53 | Robert Gordon | 79.8 | 70.8 | — | 162 | 87.2 | 86.6 |
| =54 | Kingston | 82.5 | 81.9 | 27 | 99 | 80 | 86.1 |
| =54 | Keele | 79 | 79.5 | 29.5 | 113 | 80.3 | 86.1 |
| =54 | SOAS London | 64.9 | 58.5 | 58.8 | 142 | 84.6 | 86.1 |
| =57 | Hertfordshire | 82.8 | 80.9 | 29 | 98 | 78.9 | 86 |
| =57 | Greenwich | 80 | 75.7 | 37 | 112 | 77.1 | 86 |
| 59 | Liverpool John Moores | 84.5 | 83.9 | 9 | 129 | 76.8 | 85.9 |
| =60 | Wolverhampton | 89.5 | 84 | 27.8 | 95 | 70.7 | 85.8 |
| =60 | Solent, Southampton | 88.3 | 83.4 | — | 105 | 82.9 | 85.8 |
| =60 | Coventry | 86.3 | 82 | 33.2 | 105 | 70 | 85.8 |
| 63 | Edge Hill | 83.8 | 79.9 | 36 | 121 | 67.5 | 85.6 |
| =64 | Lincoln | 79.1 | 76.6 | 32.8 | 114 | 77.2 | 85.5 |
| =64 | Hull | 84.6 | 82 | 11.2 | 122 | 76.6 | 85.5 |
| 66 | Bangor | 82.2 | 77.8 | — | 126 | 84 | 85.1 |
| 67 | Oxford Brookes | 77.9 | 75.3 | 32.5 | 102 | 79 | 84.7 |
| 68 | Cumbria | 92.4 | 86.3 | — | 116 | 68 | 84.4 |
| =69 | West London | 89.5 | 88.9 | — | 103 | 71.5 | 84 |
| =69 | Aberystwyth | 77.8 | 76.4 | 34.2 | 116 | 71.3 | 84 |
| 71 | Leeds Beckett | 85.6 | 84.7 | 11.8 | 106 | 71.2 | 83.9 |
| =72 | Middlesex | 83.6 | 80.9 | 26 | 99 | 69.4 | 83.7 |
| =72 | Winchester | 81.5 | 74.9 | 11.5 | 107 | 79.3 | 83.7 |
| =74 | St Mary's, Twickenham | 86.2 | 80.4 | — | 91 | 80.5 | 83.5 |
| =74 | Derby | 85.8 | 76.7 | — | 118 | 75.7 | 83.5 |
| 76 | Salford | 76.9 | 72.3 | 24.8 | 119 | 74.9 | 83.4 |
| =77 | Buckingham | 82.5 | 70.9 | — | 109 | 83.7 | 83.3 |
| =77 | Westminster | 81.7 | 79.7 | 29 | 112 | 65.8 | 83.3 |
| 79 | Sunderland | 88.2 | 83.9 | — | 106 | 71.1 | 83.2 |
| =80 | Central Lancashire | 83.6 | 80.5 | 13.2 | 123 | 66.5 | 83 |
| =80 | De Montfort | 81.2 | 81 | 13.5 | 95 | 75.9 | 83 |
| 82 | Huddersfield | 79.3 | 79.7 | 15.2 | 121 | 71 | 82.9 |
| 83 | Roehampton | 81.8 | 78.2 | 40.2 | 94 | 63.2 | 82.8 |
| 84 | Worcester | 82.6 | 74.5 | 12.8 | 103 | 74.4 | 82.7 |

| | | | | | | | |
|---|---|---|---|---|---|---|---|
| 85 | Bradford | 82.6 | 83.1 | — | 116 | 71.9 | 82.4 |
| 86 | York St John | 80.9 | 78.2 | — | 108 | 77.6 | 82.3 |
| 87 | Chester | 84 | 75.4 | 12.8 | 116 | 67 | 82.1 |
| =88 | Liverpool Hope | 78.4 | 66.1 | — | 107 | 84.1 | 81.7 |
| =88 | Bedfordshire | 87.7 | 85.6 | — | 109 | 63.8 | 81.7 |
| 90 | London South Bank | 80 | 75 | — | 101 | 79 | 81.6 |
| 91 | Brunel | 68.1 | 70.3 | 34.5 | 118 | 73.5 | 81.5 |
| 92 | Brighton | 73.6 | 67.8 | 28.5 | 101 | 73.2 | 80.9 |
| 93 | Sheffield Hallam | 79.9 | 72.9 | — | 111 | 73.8 | 80.7 |
| 94 | London Metropolitan | 83.1 | 82.2 | — | 99 | 67.5 | 80.4 |
| 95 | Anglia Ruskin | 81.5 | 77.9 | 9.8 | 97 | 67 | 80.3 |
| 96 | Birmingham City | 75.9 | 75.4 | 9 | 116 | 67.1 | 79.7 |
| 97 | West of Scotland | 80.9 | 73.6 | — | 122 | 62.9 | 79.2 |
| 98 | East London | 83.6 | 78.1 | 17.8 | 98 | 55.3 | 79.1 |
| 99 | Northampton | 76.2 | 71.1 | — | 102 | 73.5 | 79 |
| =100 | Canterbury Christ Church | 78.8 | 74.9 | 16.8 | 92 | 63 | 78.9 |
| =100 | Teesside | 79.3 | 74.5 | 18.2 | 107 | 58.2 | 78.9 |
| 102 | Staffordshire | 59.9 | 51.6 | 18.2 | 107 | 65 | 72.9 |

| | | | | |
|---|---|---|---|---|
| Employed in high-skilled job | 45% | Employed in lower-skilled job | | 20% |
| Employed in high-skilled job and studying | 6% | Employed in lower-skilled job and studying | | 2% |
| Studying | 10% | Unemployed | | 5% |
| High-skilled work (median) salary | £24,500 | Low-/medium-skilled salary | | £20,000 |

## Liberal Arts

Now in its fourth year, our Liberal Arts table is topped for the third time in a row by University College London (UCL), while its inaugural No 1, Warwick, is runner-up once more. UCL's lead is secured by the top research quality rating in the subject, while its entrants average by far the highest entry standards (198 UCAS points) and its graduates secured the best outcomes – the latest data showing 92.5% in high-skilled jobs and/or postgraduate study within 15 months. Warwick, though, has the most satisfied students, topping both measures derived from the National Student Survey: teaching quality and the broader experience. At the opposite end of the scale, students at Leeds (ninth overall) and Birmingham (joint fifth) recorded the lowest rates of satisfaction with teaching quality and the wide experience respectively.

Interdisciplinary by design, liberal arts degrees encompass the arts, humanities and social sciences, although there is no set formula. They provide undergraduates with opportunities to hone their analysis, communication skills and critical thinking. As students progress through the courses they begin to specialise in areas of particular interest. Dr George Legg, senior lecturer in liberal arts and head of the Department of Interdisciplinary Humanities, King's College London says: "Concerns around climate, technology, conflict and identity require multiple disciplinary perspectives if they are to be solved. Rather than focusing on a single subject, students specialise – or major – in a certain discipline while also taking courses in other subject areas. This flexible thinking means liberal arts students are well equipped for the complex world that awaits them after graduation."

Career paths include roles in the media, communications, PR, politics and art galleries. Job prospects for the subject as a whole rank 38th this year (down nine places) with 64.3% of graduates employed in high-skilled jobs and/or furthering their studies 15 months on. Salaries

compare more favourably with other subject areas, with early career earnings of £27,000 per
year placing the subject 21st out of 70 areas.

| Liberal Arts | Teaching quality % | Student experience % | Research quality % | Entry standards (UCAS points) | Graduate prospects % | Overall score |
|---|---|---|---|---|---|---|
| 1 University College London | 79.4 | 76 | 67.8 | 198 | 92.5 | 100 |
| 2 Warwick | 91.6 | 88.2 | 61.3 | 164 | — | 98.8 |
| 3 King's College London | 80 | 73.3 | 62.7 | 179 | 90.3 | 96.8 |
| 4 East Anglia | 83.3 | 78.6 | 67.5 | 148 | — | 95.5 |
| =5 Birmingham | 81.2 | 72.5 | 56.8 | 176 | 86.5 | 94.4 |
| =5 Nottingham | 86 | 82.3 | 58.2 | 155 | 83.8 | 94.4 |
| 7 Exeter | 80.3 | 79.1 | 58.3 | 167 | 80.3 | 92.9 |
| 8 Bristol | 78.5 | 73.4 | 58.7 | 175 | 77.8 | 92.1 |
| 9 Leeds | 76.2 | 74.9 | 47 | 178 | 80.8* | 90.2 |
| 10 Royal Holloway | 79.4 | 75.2 | 53.5 | 134 | — | 88.4 |

| | | | |
|---|---|---|---|
| Employed in high-skilled job | 49% | Employed in lower-skilled job | 22% |
| Employed in high-skilled job and studying | 5% | Employed in lower-skilled job and studying | 0% |
| Studying | 10% | Unemployed | 4% |
| High skilled work (median) salary | £27,500 | Low-/medium-skilled salary | N/A |

## Linguistics

Cambridge retains the lead in our Linguistics table, which has otherwise been thoroughly reshuffled
this year. University College London (UCL) is up six places to take the runner-up spot while
Lancaster is down one place in third. Oxford, formerly a regular incumbent at the top of the table,
has slipped seven places to sit 10th this year. At 204 UCAS points, Cambridge attracts the highest
entry standards among its linguistics students while fifth-place York leads the field in research,
based on results of the Research Excellence Framework 2021. In our latest National Student
Survey Swansea is top for teaching quality, followed by UCL and the two swap places for students'
evaluations of the wider experience. In 13th place, Manchester Metropolitan remains the highest-
ranked modern university despite a seven-place decline this year. It is one of only four universities
with post-1992 foundations in a subject ranking dominated by older universities.

The scientific study of language, linguistics analyses how language is put together and how
it functions, involving its form and meaning as well as how it works in context. "Linguistics is
a frontier science that embodies psychology, sociology, neuroscience, computer science and
many others. Studying linguistics will give you the skills to pursue many types of careers,"
says Dr Emma Nguyen, lecturer in child language acquisition, School of English Literature,
Language and Linguistics, Newcastle University.

The degree can lead to careers in speech therapy or in the field of teaching English as a
foreign language. The subject ranks =58th in our employment index, based on 56% of graduates
being in high-skilled jobs and/or further study within 15 months, and =53rd in our pay scale.

Within this category are some degrees in English language, and large numbers that pair
linguistics with other subjects. The leading universities require English or English literature at
A level, while drama and theatre studies is also considered useful. There were 15 universities and
colleges offering 62 courses in the subject for 2025–26. In 2023 there were, 4,900 applications to

linguistics degrees and 780 students were accepted onto courses, 14% fewer than the year before.

| Linguistics | Teaching quality % | Student experience % | Research quality % | Entry standards (UCAS points) | Graduate prospects % | Overall score |
|---|---|---|---|---|---|---|
| 1 Cambridge | 87.8 | 63.4 | 61 | 209 | 91.3 | 100 |
| 2 University College London | 89.3 | 89.7 | 56 | 158 | – | 96.6 |
| 3 Lancaster | 84.8 | 83.7 | 68.5 | 145 | 82.2 | 96 |
| 4 Swansea | 94.5 | 87.9 | 60 | 119 | – | 95.4 |
| 5 York | 86.1 | 82.7 | 74.8 | 142 | 72.4 | 95.1 |
| =6 Southampton | 84.2 | 81.3 | 47.8 | – | 92.1 | 94.8 |
| =6 Sheffield | 85.5 | 87.2 | 62.3 | 141 | – | 94.8 |
| 8 Warwick | 89.2 | 84.5 | 46.2 | 155 | 82.0* | 94.1 |
| 9 Newcastle | 84.4 | 78.8 | 61.8 | 155 | 74.1* | 93.3 |
| 10 Oxford | 85.3 | 69.1 | 44 | 194 | – | 93.2 |
| 11 King's College London | 85.5 | 80.6 | 51.2 | 158 | – | 93 |
| 12 Queen Mary, London | 88.1 | 83 | 51.1 | 125 | 83.3 | 92.7 |
| 13 Manchester Metropolitan | 87.6 | 77.8 | 61.8 | 115 | 78.8 | 92.1 |
| 14 Leeds | 87.5 | 84.2 | 52 | 146 | 71.7 | 91.8 |
| 15 Cardiff | 86.9 | 83.4 | 55.5 | 123 | – | 91.5 |
| 16 Reading | 85.4 | 82.8 | 54.5 | 127 | – | 91 |
| 17 Manchester | 82.3 | 79.8 | 59.5 | 161 | 64 | 90.7 |
| 18 Edinburgh | 76.2 | 74.5 | 45.8 | 183 | 76.7 | 90.5 |
| 19 Essex | 82.9 | 81.8 | 65 | 120 | 62.7 | 88.9 |
| 20 York St John | 81.5 | 76.7 | 30.5 | 108 | 76.9 | 84.2 |
| 21 West of England | 80.4 | 76.9 | 32.2 | 114 | – | 82.2 |
| 22 Ulster | 69.8 | 66.2 | 37 | 123 | 64.7 | 79.8 |

| | | | |
|---|---|---|---|
| Employed in high-skilled job | 38% | Employed in lower-skilled job | 28% |
| Employed in high-skilled job and studying | 3% | Employed in lower-skilled job and studying | 1% |
| Studying | 14% | Unemployed | 6% |
| High-skilled work (median) salary | £25,000 | Low-/medium-skilled salary | £20,000 |

# Materials Technology

Courses in this table cover four distinct areas: materials science, mining engineering, textiles technology and printing, and marine technology. These highly specialised subjects attract relatively small student numbers. The prominent research-led universities require maths and physics at A-level, or equivalent.

"With graduate skills in materials technology you could be working on complex projects in space technologies, the future of aerospace advancements or medical applications," says Dr Leigh Fleming, head of the Department of Engineering, University of Huddersfield.

The subject does well in the national salaries table, securing =5th place this year. It is only eight places lower in our employment index, with nearly eight in ten graduates (78.2%) in professional level jobs and/or furthering their studies 15 months on.

Cambridge's lead at the top of our Materials Technology table is ensured again this year, boosted by far the highest entry standards at 222 UCAS points on average – even in a subject where high grades are the norm among the leading universities. Cambridge is also one of six universities (more than half the table) where over 90% of graduates were employed in high-skilled jobs and/or postgraduate study 15 months on from their degrees. It is outdone on this measure by Imperial – where 100% of graduates had achieved the desired career outcomes, Oxford (96.4%) and Queen Mary, London (95.6%).

In third place overall, down from second last year, Imperial is in front for research quality in materials technology, based on results of the Research Excellence Framework 2021. For rates of student satisfaction Birmingham, in 11th place overall, outdoes all others for teaching quality and Swansea does best for the wider experience – metrics derived from the National Student Survey. Conversely, Imperial comes bottom for both.

QS ranks Cambridge =3rd in the world for materials science, with Oxford four places below it and Imperial 11th

| Materials Technology | Teaching quality % | Student experience % | Research quality % | Entry standards (UCAS points) | Graduate prospects % | Overall score |
|---|---|---|---|---|---|---|
| 1 Cambridge | 86.9 | 81.2 | 77.2 | 222 | 94.3 | 100 |
| 2 Oxford | 83.9 | 74.6 | 77.5 | 213 | 96.4 | 98.1 |
| 3 Imperial College | 77.9 | 72 | 81 | 187 | 100 | 95.3 |
| 4 Sheffield | 86.5 | 86.3 | 66.8 | 158 | 91.1 | 95.2 |
| 5 Loughborough | 90.2 | 85.6 | 46.5 | 158 | 93.3 | 94.4 |
| 6 Manchester | 83.5 | 79.4 | 63 | 169 | 82.1 | 92.6 |
| 7 Queen Mary, London | 78.6 | 73.4 | 66 | — | 95.6* | 92 |
| 8 Swansea | 90 | 90 | 48.8 | 123 | 84.6 | 91.9 |
| 9 Birmingham | 80 | 77.9 | 63.7 | 147 | 87.3 | 90.9 |
| 10 Huddersfield | 88.1 | 78.9 | 32.5 | 138 | 48.4* | 84.7 |
| 11 Birmingham City | 90.9 | 78 | 17.5 | 122 | 59.9* | 84.3 |

| | | | |
|---|---|---|---|
| Employed in high-skilled job | 53% | Employed in lower-skilled job | 10% |
| Employed in high-skilled job and studying | 3% | Employed in lower-skilled job and studying | 1% |
| Studying | 21% | Unemployed | 5% |
| High-skilled work (median) salary | £30,000 | Low-/medium-skilled salary | N/A |

## Mathematics

"Studying mathematics gives you a window into a fascinating world of ideas, ranging from exotic and beautiful pure maths through to some of the theory and concrete methods needed to tackle the biggest challenges facing humanity, including climate change and pandemics. Pursuing maths at university level will give you problem-solving and communication skills, critical and creative thinking, and analytical and data wrangling skills – and employers love a mathematician," say Professor Julia Gog, Claire Metcalfe and Rachel Thomas, Millennium Mathematics Project, University of Cambridge.

Imperial has the edge in our new Mathematics table, where it has taken the lead from Cambridge by virtue of a 0.3% lead. There is less than one percentage point between the top four, with runner-up Cambridge just 0.1% ahead of Oxford, which in turn is 0.2% in front of St Andrews. In its latest global rankings by subject, QS puts Cambridge second in the world for mathematics, Oxford fourth and Imperial ninth.

The leading universities will usually look for extra maths as well as maths at A-level, or equivalent. Courses tend to combine pure and applied maths, but some universities allow for specialising in one or the other. In a high-tariff table St Andrews has the top entry standards, its entrants averaging an extraordinary 238 UCAS points. Nine universities average over 200 UCAS points and 32 of the 68 universities tabled average 144 or higher (equal to three As at A-level). The high tariffs are due to the two maths A-levels – plus two or three others – taken by the most successful candidates at the top universities. But there are still plenty of places to be found with a broader spread of entry scores: 14 universities averaged 120 points or lower.

Oxford is in front for research, based on results of the Research Excellence Framework 2021 and also comes out top for graduate prospects this year – with 93.6% of its graduates employed in high-skilled jobs and/or postgraduate study 15 months after their degrees. In second place for graduate prospects is Wolverhampton (=52nd overall), with 92.6% of graduates achieving the desired outcomes within 15 months.

In 11th place, South Wales is the top-ranked modern university and has leapt 25 places up the table. Its rank is boosted by having the most satisfied maths students – whose National Student Survey (NSS) feedback has resulted in perfect 100% scores for teaching quality and the wider experience in our NSS analysis. Hull (56th overall) and Aberystwyth (39th) share second and third place for these measures, while at the opposite end of the scale Edge Hill (67th overall) and Aston (63rd) take the bottom two places for them.

The demand for places has been fairly consistent in recent years, and in 2023 maths attracted 34,705 applications and 8,795 new students. The subject adds up to a promising career for most, ranking comfortably inside the top 25 of our employment table, with three-quarters (74.7%) of mathematics graduates in high-skilled employment or postgraduate study 15 months after finishing their degrees. Such expertise commands average graduate salaries of £29,000 – the 16th highest earnings in our pay index of 70 subject areas.

| Mathematics | Teaching quality % | Student experience % | Research quality % | Entry standards (UCAS points) | Graduate prospects % | Overall score |
|---|---|---|---|---|---|---|
| 1 Imperial College | 87.9 | 86 | 76.8 | 207 | 89.8 | 100 |
| 2 Cambridge | 88 | 81.3 | 78 | 221 | 87.2 | 99.7 |
| 3 Oxford | 84.8 | 72.2 | 83.2 | 209 | 93.6 | 99.6 |
| 4 St Andrews | 88.4 | 87.8 | 57.5 | 238 | 88.5 | 99.4 |
| 5 Warwick | 85.9 | 85 | 73.5 | 201 | 87.9 | 98.3 |
| 6 Bristol | 84.2 | 81.3 | 77 | 180 | 91 | 97.5 |
| =7 Heriot-Watt | 82.8 | 83.3 | 66 | 189 | 90 | 96.4 |
| =7 Bath | 84.4 | 84.4 | 61.5 | 188 | 90.2 | 96.4 |
| 9 Glasgow | 80.7 | 76.9 | 74.5 | 213 | 84.6 | 96.1 |
| 10 University College London | 81.8 | 83.6 | 57.5 | 192 | 87.4 | 94.8 |
| 11 South Wales | 100 | 100 | 24.5 | — | 82.8 | 94.6 |
| 12 Lancaster | 85.5 | 83.9 | 70 | 159 | 83.7 | 94.3 |
| 13 Durham | 81.9 | 76 | 48.8 | 206 | 88.9 | 94.1 |
| 14 Edinburgh | 74.1 | 73.6 | 66 | 214 | 86.3 | 93.7 |
| =15 Birmingham | 83.3 | 79.7 | 58.8 | 169 | 87 | 93.5 |
| =15 Aberdeen | 89.9 | 86.5 | 40 | 178 | — | 93.5 |
| 17 London School of Economics | 73.7 | 74.6 | 64 | 181 | 92.2 | 93.3 |
| 18 Manchester | 79.2 | 77.8 | 66 | 181 | 85 | 93.2 |

**Mathematics** cont.

| | Teaching quality % | Student experience % | Research quality % | Entry standards (UCAS points) | Graduate prospects % | Overall score |
|---|---|---|---|---|---|---|
| =19 Nottingham | 80.9 | 78.8 | 57.5 | 170 | 87.5 | 92.9 |
| =19 Sheffield | 84.6 | 84.8 | 59.2 | 147 | 85.9 | 92.9 |
| =21 Dundee | 89.9 | 86 | 55.2 | 185 | 73.3 | 92.5 |
| =21 Strathclyde | 84.2 | 83 | 43.2 | 206 | 80.5 | 92.5 |
| 23 Southampton | 83.4 | 80.4 | 61.5 | 164 | 80.6 | 92 |
| =24 Loughborough | 84.7 | 86.3 | 46.5 | 161 | 83.8 | 91.9 |
| =24 Swansea | 86.3 | 84.3 | 58.2 | 140 | 82.7 | 91.9 |
| =26 Exeter | 80.9 | 77.5 | 64.1 | 157 | 82.7 | 91.5 |
| =26 Queen's, Belfast | 81.2 | 79.5 | 44.5 | 165 | 88.2 | 91.5 |
| 28 York | 84.9 | 82.1 | 55 | 154 | 81.4 | 91.4 |
| 29 Leicester | 80.9 | 79.1 | 51.7 | 129 | 91.8 | 91.2 |
| 30 Stirling | 83.7 | 76.5 | 41.8 | 178 | 84.2 | 91 |
| =31 Leeds | 75.2 | 77.1 | 55.2 | 163 | 85.4 | 90.3 |
| =31 Cardiff | 79.8 | 80.6 | 45.5 | 144 | 88.2 | 90.3 |
| 33 Hertfordshire | 88.5 | 79.9 | 45.5 | — | 78.6 | 89.9 |
| =34 Nottingham Trent | 86.8 | 82.3 | 59 | 109 | 80.4 | 89.7 |
| =34 Kent | 86.4 | 85.5 | 46.5 | 129 | 80.9 | 89.7 |
| 36 Surrey | 83.1 | 88.2 | 33.5 | 139 | 85.5 | 89.5 |
| =37 King's College London | 78.5 | 76.7 | 59.5 | 170 | 75.8 | 89.2 |
| =37 Newcastle | 77.6 | 79.1 | 48 | 142 | 85.9 | 89.2 |
| 39 Aberystwyth | 92.8 | 91 | 22.5 | 139 | 79.2 | 89.1 |
| =40 Plymouth | 91 | 87 | 22.5 | 132 | 82.8 | 88.8 |
| =40 East Anglia | 83.1 | 83.4 | 44.5 | 145 | 78.8 | 88.8 |
| 42 Reading | 86.4 | 83.5 | 51.5 | 126 | 75.7 | 88.6 |
| 43 Manchester Metropolitan | 86.3 | 84.9 | 45.5 | 117 | 79.2 | 88.4 |
| 44 Sussex | 82 | 81.7 | 50 | 138 | 76.5 | 88 |
| 45 Royal Holloway | 83.1 | 77.9 | 30.2 | 135 | 85.3 | 87.7 |
| 46 Coventry | 80.9 | 83.7 | 36.8 | 110 | 83.6 | 86.9 |
| 47 Huddersfield | 90.5 | 83.3 | 26.5 | 114 | — | 86.6 |
| 48 Queen Mary, London | 76 | 77.7 | 51.5 | 138 | 76.6 | 86.4 |
| 49 Liverpool | 80.7 | 81.4 | 43.2 | 144 | 72.3 | 86.1 |
| 50 Lincoln | 91.3 | 89.6 | 17.5 | 120 | 75.2 | 86 |
| 51 Liverpool John Moores | 87.3 | 82.3 | 26 | 122 | 77.4 | 85.9 |
| =52 Wolverhampton | 90 | 76.6 | — | 102 | 92.6 | 85.8 |
| =52 Essex | 80.8 | 83.7 | 29 | 124 | 80.1 | 85.8 |
| 54 City | 76 | 76 | 52 | 113 | 79.3 | 85.7 |
| 55 Salford | 81.8 | 81.1 | 33.2 | 127 | — | 85.6 |
| 56 Hull | 93.4 | 89.6 | — | 121 | 79.2 | 85.5 |
| 57 Brunel | 80.9 | 77.8 | 32.2 | 111 | 78.2 | 84.4 |
| 58 Portsmouth | 86.2 | 87.8 | 37.2 | 108 | 66.1 | 83.9 |
| 59 Keele | 83 | 77.6 | 27.3 | 121 | 74.7 | 83.8 |
| 60 Brighton | 91.3 | 87.7 | 32.5 | 101 | 63.8 | 83.5 |
| =61 Sheffield Hallam | 88.5 | 81.1 | — | 103 | 81.5 | 83.1 |
| =61 Greenwich | 86.4 | 85.2 | 28 | 101 | 69.4 | 83.1 |

| | | | | | | |
|---|---|---|---|---|---|---|
| **63** Aston | | 68.4 | 69.8 | 35.2 | 116 | 84.9 | 83 |
| **64** West of England | | 84.6 | 82.1 | 32.2 | 117 | 65.4 | 82.6 |
| **65** Northumbria | | — | — | 49 | 137 | 61.5 | 82.3 |
| **66** Chester | | — | — | 18.8 | 128 | 73.5* | 81.3 |
| **67** Edge Hill | | 69.1 | 62.2 | — | 128 | 83.7 | 78.6 |

| | | | |
|---|---|---|---|
| Employed in high-skilled job | 56% | Employed in lower-skilled job | 11% |
| Employed in high-skilled job and studying | 7% | Employed in lower-skilled job and studying | 1% |
| Studying | 11% | Unemployed | 7% |
| High-skilled work (median) salary | £30,000 | Low-/medium-skilled salary | £20,000 |

# Mechanical Engineering

Mechanical engineering is the most popular strand of engineering by a clear margin, as reflected in the size of our table – which reaches to 67 universities. "Student numbers in the subject have stayed consistently buoyant across the past decade-plus, and in 2023 it attracted over 34,600 applications and just under 7,700 new undergraduates. UCAS showed 140 universities and colleges offering courses in mechanical engineering for 2025–26. Most of the leading universities require maths – preferably with a strong component of mechanics – and another science (usually physics) at A-level, or equivalent.

At No 1 in our new ranking Imperial has taken the lead from Oxford, which settles for third place, while Cambridge – which topped the table two years ago – is runner-up. Imperial outdoes both for research quality, based on results of the national Research Excellence Framework 2021 assessment, and is second for graduate prospects – with 96% in high-skilled jobs and/ or postgraduate study within 15 months. Only Cambridge did better – with 97.2% of graduates achieving these outcomes, and 16 universities in the table tallied at least 90%. In fourth place overall Sheffield is top for the broad undergraduate experience in our new National Student Survey analysis while Teesside (39th overall) is unbeaten for students' evaluation of teaching quality. London South Bank (46th) also did well in both of these measures, as did Imperial. Entry standards are some of the highest of any subject, with five universities averaging more than 200 UCAS points among entrants, led by Cambridge whose mechanical engineering students averaged 227 UCAS points. Even so, there are places to be found with more modest qualifications, and at four universities (Hertfordshire, in 56th place overall, Brighton, 45th, East London, 65th, and Northampton, 66th) students arrived with under 100 UCAS points

A top-20 rank (16th) in our employment table adds to the subject's appeal and graduates command starting salaries of £30,000 on average, which put mechanical engineering =5th in this year's pay index.

| **Mechanical Engineering** | Teaching quality % | Student experience % | Research quality % | Entry standards (UCAS points) | Graduate prospects % | Overall score |
|---|---|---|---|---|---|---|
| **1** Imperial College | 85.4 | 86.7 | 81 | 219 | 96 | 100 |
| **2** Cambridge | 81.6 | 80.9 | 77.2 | 227 | 97.2 | 99 |
| **3** Oxford | 80.8 | 76.1 | 77.5 | 216 | 94 | 96.8 |
| **4** Sheffield | 88.1 | 90.3 | 66.8 | 161 | 89.2 | 93.6 |
| **5** Bristol | 77.9 | 76.1 | 68 | 188 | 93.3 | 92.9 |
| **6** Bath | 85.5 | 79.7 | 49.5 | 187 | 93 | 92.6 |

## Mechanical Engineering cont.

| | | Teaching quality % | Student experience % | Research quality % | Entry standards (UCAS points) | Graduate prospects % | Overall score |
|---|---|---|---|---|---|---|---|
| 7 | Strathclyde | 77.1 | 73.3 | 52.8 | 214 | 90.9 | 91.7 |
| 8 | Southampton | 82.2 | 79.2 | 70 | 170 | 85.8 | 91.3 |
| 9 | Loughborough | 83.8 | 83.3 | 46.5 | 158 | 94.4 | 90.5 |
| 10 | Nottingham | 80.4 | 78.9 | 59 | 147 | 93.6 | 89.9 |
| 11 | Leeds | 74.1 | 74.1 | 64.8 | 182 | 87.5 | 89.6 |
| 12 | Birmingham | 74.2 | 73.3 | 63.7 | 152 | 94.4 | 89 |
| 13 | Glasgow | 66 | 63.8 | 61.5 | 207 | 90.9 | 88.8 |
| 14 | Manchester | 77 | 73.9 | 63 | 175 | 83.5 | 88.6 |
| =15 | University College London | 72 | 69.4 | 70 | 184 | 83.2 | 88.3 |
| =15 | Edinburgh | 72.1 | 69.8 | 55.5 | 193 | 87.4 | 88.3 |
| 17 | Surrey | 83.3 | 81.8 | 55.2 | 129 | 88.7 | 88 |
| 18 | Liverpool | 81.3 | 82.4 | 57 | 139 | 86.4 | 87.9 |
| 19 | Queen's, Belfast | 78.5 | 81.2 | 51 | 148 | 89.7 | 87.8 |
| 20 | Heriot-Watt | 71.6 | 69.7 | 55.5 | 173 | 90.3 | 87.5 |
| 21 | Swansea | 83.5 | 82.5 | 48.8 | 135 | 86.7 | 87.2 |
| 22 | Aberdeen | 75.1 | 78.3 | 35.8 | 171 | 92 | 87.1 |
| 23 | Cardiff | 76.3 | 75.4 | 54 | 140 | 90.6 | 86.8 |
| 24 | Edinburgh Napier | 86.3 | 81.3 | 22.8 | 143 | 88.2 | 85.5 |
| =25 | Ulster | 80.9 | 76.1 | 49.8 | 128 | 85.8 | 85.4 |
| =25 | Lancaster | 79.6 | 70.7 | 44.8 | 144 | 87.4 | 85.4 |
| 27 | Nottingham Trent | 80.8 | 73.5 | 59 | 116 | 85.3 | 85.3 |
| 28 | Exeter | 75.5 | 72.5 | 47 | 154 | 84.8 | 85 |
| 29 | Queen Mary, London | 69.7 | 72.5 | 66 | 142 | 82.3 | 84.5 |
| =30 | Newcastle | 68.8 | 67.6 | 58.5 | 135 | 89.3 | 84.2 |
| =30 | Liverpool John Moores | 81.5 | 78.5 | 45.5 | 125 | 82.4 | 84.2 |
| 32 | Leicester | 78.1 | 71.7 | 39.8 | 128 | 88.4 | 83.8 |
| 33 | Sussex | 75.3 | 76.8 | 29.5 | 134 | 90.8 | 83.3 |
| 34 | Greenwich | 83.5 | 81 | 31.5 | 121 | — | 82.8 |
| =35 | Northumbria | 77.7 | 77.7 | 43 | 139 | 77.4 | 82.7 |
| =35 | Dundee | 68 | 55.6 | 50.2 | 175 | 81.8 | 82.7 |
| 37 | Robert Gordon | 74.2 | 70.5 | 20.5 | 148 | 90 | 82.2 |
| 38 | Manchester Metropolitan | 83.6 | 80 | 45.5 | 126 | 69.7 | 81.8 |
| 39 | Teesside | 91.8 | 87.9 | 18.8 | 127 | 70.8 | 81.6 |
| 40 | Hull | 77.9 | 77.7 | 36.2 | 125 | 79.6 | 81.5 |
| 41 | Coventry | 82.9 | 80.6 | 23.5 | 118 | 80.4 | 81.1 |
| 42 | Aston | 74.5 | 73.5 | 35.2 | 129 | 81.7 | 81 |
| =43 | Glasgow Caledonian | 78.6 | 76.4 | 12.8 | 153 | 80.3 | 80.8 |
| =43 | Plymouth | 76.8 | 64.9 | 32.5 | 123 | 85.6 | 80.8 |
| 45 | Brighton | 73.6 | 71.9 | 36.5 | 96 | 90.2 | 80.6 |
| 46 | London South Bank | 88.4 | 84.9 | 27.3 | 113 | 70.4 | 80.5 |
| 47 | West of England | 73.7 | 72.3 | 30.8 | 135 | 78.6 | 79.8 |
| 48 | Portsmouth | 82.8 | 82.7 | 21 | 114 | 75.4 | 79.5 |
| 49 | Derby | 78.9 | 70.2 | 14 | 116 | 84.9 | 79 |
| 50 | Oxford Brookes | 79.4 | 69.9 | 18 | 114 | 81.5 | 78.5 |

| | | | | | | |
|---|---|---|---|---|---|---|
| **51** Kingston | | 85 | 80.7 | 17.2 | 108 | 73.1 | 78.4 |
| **=52** Brunel | | 75.7 | 71 | 33 | 132 | 69.2 | 77.9 |
| **=52** Bradford | | 87.1 | 79.8 | 27 | 106 | 65.2* | 77.9 |
| **54** Bournemouth | | 80 | 82 | 14 | 106 | 73.5 | 76.9 |
| **55** Huddersfield | | 74.6 | 72.4 | 32.5 | 103 | 73.3 | 76.8 |
| **=56** De Montfort | | 77.5 | 76.4 | 21.8 | 100 | 74.5 | 76.6 |
| **=56** Hertfordshire | | 78.6 | 75.3 | 33 | 99 | 68.6 | 76.6 |
| **58** West of Scotland | | 75.7 | 74.8 | 16.5 | — | 73.9 | 76.2 |
| **59** Central Lancashire | | 74.9 | 73.7 | 23 | 111 | 71.4 | 75.9 |
| **60** Salford | | 64.7 | 63.7 | 33.2 | 137 | 72 | 75.7 |
| **61** City | | 71.9 | 68.2 | 32.5 | 114 | 69 | 75.4 |
| **=62** Lincoln | | 66.6 | 61.2 | 24 | 115 | 79 | 75 |
| **=62** Birmingham City | | 77.2 | 73.1 | 17.5 | 116 | 67.5 | 75 |
| **64** Sheffield Hallam | | 67.5 | 62.4 | 30 | 115 | 71.1 | 74.1 |
| **65** East London | | 87.9 | 84.3 | 21.2 | 88 | 48.1 | 72.5 |
| **66** Northampton | | 70.1 | 48.4 | 8.5 | 83 | — | 67.2 |
| **67** Chichester | | 53 | 51.7 | 12.5 | 108 | — | 65.2 |

| | | | |
|---|---|---|---|
| Employed in high-skilled job | 68% | Employed in lower-skilled job | 10% |
| Employed in high-skilled job and studying | 4% | Employed in lower-skilled job and studying | 0% |
| Studying | 5% | Unemployed | 6% |
| High-skilled work (median) salary | £30,000 | Low-/medium-skilled salary | £24,000 |

# Medicine

Oxford's long reign at the top of our table remains unchallenged, but Dundee has ousted Glasgow from its formerly established runner-up spot. Boosted by the distinction of offering guaranteed work at the end of the course, the subject carries unique prestige. Medicine occupies second place in our graduate employment table, a step down from its usual first place – outdone by 0.4% by veterinary medicine on this occasion. Starting salaries of £35,000 on average are second only to those offered by dentistry degrees. Twelve medical schools report 100% graduate employment, and St Andrews, with the lowest rate, still reports 95% of medicine graduates in high-skilled jobs or further study after 15 months. The consistency of graduate prospects means we do not use the measure to help calculate our rankings to avoid small differences distorting positions (although the percentages are shown for guidance).

In such a compressed ranking, with just three medical schools scoring less than 80 points overall, success in our table's other four metrics is spread around. Our latest National Student Survey analysis shows Oxford to have the highest rates of student satisfaction with teaching quality, followed by Leicester. St Andrews is third for teaching quality and top for students' evaluation of the wider experience, where Leicester (fifth overall) ranks second again, and Sunderland (=24th) sits third. At the opposite end of the scale, students at Nottingham (36th overall) and Buckingham (39th) reported the lowest rates of satisfaction with the broad experience.

Occupying seventh place in the main table, Cambridge was the top scorer in the Research Excellence Framework 2021, followed by Bristol (ninth overall), University College London (12th) and Leicester. The Scottish universities dominate our Medicine table's entry standards measure, led by Dundee with 244 points in the UCAS tariff. Seven of the schools in the table average over 200 UCAS points.

Applications to study medicine were around 10% lower in 2023 than the year before, UCAS figures show, as numbers return to pre-pandemic levels. Commentators have also suggested the shift may be due to pay levels, highlighted by a series of strikes, and the gruelling depiction of doctors' working lives in memoirs and TV dramas. But the downturn has only marginally dented the subject's otherwise upward trajectory in demand, and applications in 2023 were still around 20% higher than four years before in 2019. Reapplicants account for significant numbers, as would-be trainee doctors take a year out to improve their applications by doing more work experience, building on their personal statement and resitting the UCAT or BMAT specialist aptitude tests (see chapter 2). Such volume of demand is despite only four medical schools being allowed per application, with the fifth space left for a back-up subject – which most use for a related course requiring lower grades such as biomedical science.

The number of places available to study medicine remains capped by the government. A clutch of medical schools has opened since 2019 to increase capacity, including at Sunderland, Lincoln, Edge Hill, Kent/Canterbury Christ Church and Anglia Ruskin universities. In 2023 9,500 medical students were accepted onto courses, in line with government regulations.

Nearly all schools demand chemistry and most biology. Physics or maths is required by some, either as an alternative or in addition to biology. Universities want to see a commitment to the subject through work experience in hospitals, GP surgeries, a hospice or similar medical setting. Medical schools interview most candidates before making an offer. Undergraduates must be prepared to work long hours, particularly towards the end of the course, which will usually be five years long. Many students are now opting for the postgraduate route into the profession instead, though this is even longer. "The discipline and attributes medicine instils in you lay the foundation for your success as a unique future leader. Medical training equips you to manage change and develops your problem-solving abilities through learning to diagnose, consider and recommend treatment," notes Professor Amir Sam, head of the School of Medicine, Imperial College London.

| Medicine | Teaching quality % | Student experience % | Research quality % | Entry standards (UCAS points) | Graduate prospects % | Overall score |
|---|---|---|---|---|---|---|
| 1 Oxford | 91.6 | 81.6 | 67.5 | 206 | 99.4 | 100 |
| 2 Dundee | 81.9 | 69.2 | 57 | 244 | 100 | 97.7 |
| 3 Glasgow | 76.2 | 63.1 | 68.5 | 240 | 99.6 | 97.2 |
| 4 Imperial College | 85.2 | 84.3 | 68.5 | 192 | 99.2 | 96.9 |
| 5 Leicester | 90.3 | 87.4 | 70.2 | 167 | 99.6 | 96.4 |
| 6 St Andrews | 88.8 | 88 | 45.5 | 214 | 95.7 | 96.1 |
| =7 Cambridge | 76.1 | 61.6 | 76.2 | 212 | 99.5 | 95.6 |
| =7 Edinburgh | 75.9 | 66.7 | 64 | 231 | 100 | 95.6 |
| 9 Bristol | 84.9 | 70.8 | 71.8 | 184 | 99.6 | 95.3 |
| 10 Aberdeen | 88.2 | 80.8 | 30.5 | 242 | 98.8 | 95.1 |
| 11 Queen's, Belfast | 84.4 | 76.5 | 66.2 | 188 | 100 | 95 |
| 12 University College London | 77 | 72.2 | 70.8 | 190 | 99.7 | 93.4 |
| 13 Cardiff | 81.9 | 75.4 | 55.5 | 188 | 100 | 91.9 |
| 14 Queen Mary, London | 79.4 | 74.1 | 58 | 192 | 98.4 | 91.8 |
| 15 Lancaster | 87.1 | 77.4 | 55 | 167 | 100 | 91.3 |
| 16 Hull-York Medical School | 83.1 | 64.4 | 61.2 | 167 | 99.3 | 90 |
| =17 Exeter | 82.1 | 69.8 | 53.2 | 178 | 100 | 89.8 |
| =17 Keele | 84.9 | 75.6 | 49 | 172 | 99.3 | 89.8 |
| 19 Swansea | 74.6 | 58.4 | 66.8 | — | 98.9 | 89.5 |

| | | | | | | | |
|---|---|---|---|---|---|---|---|
| 20 | Newcastle | 82.1 | 69 | 50.7 | 176 | 99.2 | 88.9 |
| 21 | Manchester | 76 | 61.2 | 61.3 | 178 | 99.4 | 88.6 |
| =22 | Birmingham | 74.5 | 66.3 | 59.8 | 174 | 99.4 | 87.9 |
| =22 | King's College London | 71.6 | 59.3 | 65.5 | 177 | 99.4 | 87.9 |
| =24 | Sunderland | 88.1 | 86.9 | 30.2 | 164 | — | 87.1 |
| =24 | East Anglia | 78.5 | 71.4 | 50 | 169 | 99.4 | 87.1 |
| 26 | Sheffield | 76.5 | 65.5 | 51 | 174 | 100 | 86.7 |
| 27 | Leeds | 80.5 | 71.2 | 39.5 | 178 | 99.1 | 86.6 |
| 28 | St George's, London | 75.1 | 62.3 | 50.2 | 176 | 99.3 | 86 |
| 29 | Southampton | 76.7 | 67.4 | 49.5 | 166 | 99.6 | 85.7 |
| 30 | Aston | 77.4 | 71.4 | 46 | 162 | — | 85.3 |
| 31 | Liverpool | 72.3 | 70.5 | 46.8 | 170 | 99.2 | 84.6 |
| 32 | Sussex | 82.2 | 67.7 | 32 | 169 | 100 | 84.3 |
| 33 | Anglia Ruskin | 78.4 | 68.9 | 33.8 | 159 | — | 82.4 |
| 34 | Plymouth | 71.7 | 62.4 | 38.2 | 169 | 100 | 81.7 |
| 35 | Warwick | 82.4 | 70.9 | 23.2 | — | 99.5 | 81.5 |
| 36 | Nottingham | 64.8 | 40.6 | 54 | 167 | 99.6 | 80.4 |
| 37 | Brighton | 82.2 | 67.7 | — | 169 | 100 | 77.6 |
| 38 | Central Lancashire | 82.8 | 72.5 | — | 141 | 78.8 | 75.2 |
| 39 | Buckingham | 71.1 | 56.3 | — | 133 | 100 | 69.1 |

| | | | |
|---|---|---|---|
| Employed in high-skilled job | 81% | Employed in lower-skilled job | 0% |
| Employed in high-skilled job and studying | 8% | Employed in lower-skilled job and studying | 0% |
| Studying | 5% | Unemployed | 0% |
| High-skilled work (median) salary | £35,000 | Low-/medium-skilled salary | N/A |

## Middle Eastern and African Studies

"Curious about the world's major religions or the key languages of Arabic, Hebrew, Persian and Turkish, not to mention the environment, arts, history, music and literature?" ask Dr Seyed Ali Alavi and Narguess Farzad, School of Languages, Cultures and Linguistics, SOAS University of London. "Then Middle Eastern studies is for you. The Middle East, the cradle of ancient civilisations and birthplace of writing, is pivotal to contemporary global issues, connecting regions and serving as the hub for energy resources."

One of the smallest categories in this *Guide*, Middle Eastern and African studies degrees attract tiny – and shrinking – student numbers. Just 140 undergraduates began programmes in the subjects in 2022, ten fewer than the year before and down from 250 in 2019, continuing a longer-term downward trend. But modules from the courses in this grouping will have been taken by many students as part of broader area studies courses.

A reshuffle of the table puts Oxford in the lead, its position secured by the second-highest entry standards and the second-best research quality rating. Exeter – which topped the ranking for the past two years – slips to third overall but remains top for research, based on results of the Research Excellence Framework 2021. Cambridge claims the highest rates of student satisfaction with teaching quality and Leeds is in front for students' evaluations of the broad experience. In a high-tariff subject grouping no universities average beneath 145 points (where three As at A-level is equivalent to 144 points) among their new entrants, while the standards are highest at Cambridge.

The absence of graduate prospects scores in the majority of universities in our table is due to student cohorts being insufficient to meet the response threshold for our employment ranking. As a grouping, however, the subjects place 37th this year, with almost two-thirds of graduates (65.1%) in high-skilled employment and/or furthering their studies within 15 months. Those with a degree in Middle Eastern and African studies degrees earn £28,000 graduate salaries, on average, ranking the subject in the top 20 of our pay index.

| Middle Eastern and African Studies | Teaching quality % | Student experience % | Research quality % | Entry standards (UCAS points) | Graduate prospects % | Overall score |
|---|---|---|---|---|---|---|
| 1 Oxford | 80 | 52.5 | 62.3 | 193 | — | 100 |
| 2 Cambridge | 87 | 67 | 45.2 | 196 | — | 98.6 |
| 3 Exeter | 83.7 | 78.1 | 65.8 | 146 | 77.2 | 97.6 |
| 4 SOAS London | 79.5 | 70.7 | 60 | 145 | 84.8* | 97 |
| 5 Leeds | 79.8 | 78.7 | 52 | 150 | — | 94.4 |
| 6 Edinburgh | 75.7 | 70.8 | 51.7 | 162 | — | 93.5 |
| 7 Manchester | 74.7 | 64.4 | 52.5 | 154 | — | 91.9 |

| | | | |
|---|---|---|---|
| Employed in high-skilled job | 49% | Employed in lower-skilled job | 17% |
| Employed in high-skilled job and studying | 5% | Employed in lower-skilled job and studying | 1% |
| Studying | 10% | Unemployed | 10% |
| High-skilled work (median) salary | £30,000 | Low-/medium-skilled salary | N/A |

# Music

"Studying music as a performer or creator means learning to be playful in your work every day. It means collaborating, problem-solving, listening – and really hearing. It means fast reactions and dedicated repetition. These are all skills associated with play, but also with the best of leaders," says Armin Zanner, vice-principal and director of music, Guildhall School of Music & Drama.

Reflecting music's many contrasting genres, courses in our subject ranking vary considerably in style and content – from the practical and vocational programmes in conservatoires to the more theoretical degrees in older universities, via sonic arts, creative sound design and everything in between elsewhere. After three years of rising applications, demand cooled a little in 2023's admissions cycle and 37,345 applied to music courses. The number of students enrolling dropped more steeply to 8,955 – down 5% on the year before and 11% lower than four years before in 2019.

In 16th place overall, Guildhall School of Music and Drama ranks first out of the seven specialist institutions, followed by the Royal College of Music in =21st place, Royal Conservatoire of Scotland (23rd), Royal Academy of Music (36th), Royal Northern College of Music (41st), Trinity Laban (47th), and Leeds Conservatoire (66th).

But Cambridge's strength in undergraduate music provision is the most eminent this year, its rank buoyed by strong performance across all five metrics in our table without topping any of them individually. Last year's No 1, Manchester, has slipped to sixth place. King's College London is up seven places to tie in the runner-up position with Durham, formerly a regular in the No 1 spot. Royal Holloway, in fourth place overall, achieved the best results in music in the Research Excellence Framework 2021, while Westminster (57th in our main table) is not far behind it for research quality. Entry standards tip over the 200 UCAS tariff point mark at three universities – Glasgow, Edinburgh and Durham – though there are also plenty of places to be found with a broad spectrum of entry standards, which reach down to 99 points at Canterbury Christ Church.

The best rates of student satisfaction are often found at post-1992 universities – in music's case this year at De Montfort (26th overall) which comes top for both metrics in our new National Student Survey analysis. Following it on each measure is Oxford Brookes (32nd overall), while Surrey (11th) is third for teaching quality and York (=12th) is third for the wider experience. At the opposite end of the student satisfaction scale is Anglia Ruskin.

King's College London had the best-employed graduates when surveyed 15 months after their degrees, with 96.5% in high-skilled jobs and/or further study. Five of the seven specialist institutions rank in the top 20 for graduate prospects: the Royal College of Music, Royal Academy of Music, Royal Northern College of Music, Royal Conservatoire of Scotland and Guildhall School of Music and Drama. Music invariably ranks above the other performing arts in our employment table, as it does this year in 49th place. In the earnings table music ties with art and design (and another four subjects) in =61st place out of 70 subject areas.

| Music | Teaching quality % | Student experience % | Research quality % | Entry standards (UCAS points) | Graduate prospects % | Overall score |
|---|---|---|---|---|---|---|
| 1 Cambridge | 87.1 | 64.3 | 71 | 196 | 87.8 | 100 |
| =2 King's College London | 83.9 | 77.2 | 72.2 | 163 | 96.5* | 99.5 |
| =2 Durham | 84.7 | 74.5 | 59.5 | 202 | 88.1 | 99.5 |
| 4 Royal Holloway | 81.6 | 74.2 | 78.5 | 172 | 90.6 | 99 |
| 5 Bristol | 88.8 | 84 | 64.2 | 165 | 86.6 | 98.4 |
| 6 Manchester | 78 | 70 | 66.5 | 199 | 88.7 | 98.1 |
| 7 Oxford | 86.6 | 66.3 | 49.2 | 191 | 88.7 | 97 |
| 8 Sheffield | 81 | 76.8 | 57 | 164 | 88.5* | 95.1 |
| =9 Glasgow | 74.9 | 69.3 | 60.5 | 208 | 78.4 | 94.9 |
| =9 Birmingham | 86.8 | 78.5 | 50.2 | 171 | 81.2 | 94.9 |
| 11 Surrey | 93.2 | 87.5 | 43.8 | 155 | 79.3 | 94.8 |
| =12 York | 91.8 | 88.9 | 54.8 | 152 | 73.7 | 94.4 |
| =12 Leeds | 78.1 | 72.5 | 65.2 | 182 | 78.6 | 94.4 |
| 14 Cardiff | 85.8 | 83.1 | 50.5 | 153 | 84 | 94.1 |
| 15 Southampton | 86.3 | 78.3 | 58.8 | 170 | 73.3 | 94 |
| 16 Guildhall School of Music and Drama | 85.8 | 74.6 | 61.3 | 147 | 82 | 93.7 |
| =17 Huddersfield | 87.9 | 85.6 | 71.5 | 124 | 77.6 | 93.6 |
| =17 Edinburgh | 79.9 | 72.3 | 59.2 | 204 | 67.2 | 93.6 |
| 19 City | 85.6 | 71.9 | 66.5 | 147 | — | 93.2 |
| 20 Liverpool | 89.1 | 84.5 | 43.8 | 157 | 76 | 92.9 |
| =21 Royal College of Music | 86 | 76.5 | 45.5 | 125 | 93.9 | 92.5 |
| =21 Nottingham | 84.3 | 75.4 | 62.7 | 137 | 81.2 | 92.5 |
| 23 Royal Conservatoire of Scotland | 81.8 | 70.2 | 35.2 | 172 | 82.5 | 91.3 |
| 24 Coventry | 87.7 | 83.8 | 55.5 | 119 | 79.2 | 91.2 |
| 25 Brighton | 91.3 | 85.5 | 53 | 117 | — | 91 |
| 26 De Montfort | 97.3 | 94.5 | 45 | 120 | 65.3 | 90.4 |
| 27 Birmingham City | 86.3 | 71.3 | 46.5 | 145 | 75.8 | 90.1 |
| 28 Newcastle | 82.6 | 70 | 59.2 | 155 | 68.4 | 90 |
| 29 Edinburgh Napier | 89.1 | 85.3 | 8.5 | 191 | 68.6 | 89.8 |
| =30 Plymouth | 86.8 | 83.5 | 49.8 | 124 | — | 89.5 |
| =30 Bangor | 81.8 | 74.2 | 42 | — | 80 | 89.5 |
| 32 Oxford Brookes | 95 | 91.3 | 21.5 | — | 68.6* | 89.4 |

**Music** cont.

| | | Teaching quality % | Student experience % | Research quality % | Entry standards (UCAS points) | Graduate prospects % | Overall score |
|---|---|---|---|---|---|---|---|
| =33 | Sussex | 84.6 | 77 | 48 | 136 | — | 89 |
| =33 | Queen's, Belfast | 81.9 | 76.7 | 46.8 | 152 | 71 | 89 |
| 35 | Ulster | 86.2 | 85.3 | 49 | 121 | 72.9 | 88.9 |
| 36 | Royal Academy of Music | 84.6 | 70.6 | 20 | 134 | 92 | 88.8 |
| 37 | West of England | 92.5 | 86.1 | 48.2 | 117 | 65.2 | 88.5 |
| 38 | Salford | 84 | 77.2 | 30.2 | 143 | 78.4 | 88.4 |
| 39 | Kingston | 88.7 | 78.3 | 45 | 121 | — | 88.3 |
| 40 | Aberdeen | 84.2 | 75.1 | 31 | 172 | 64.4 | 87.8 |
| 41 | Royal Northern College of Music | 80.6 | 67.9 | 34 | 135 | 82.8 | 87.4 |
| 42 | Goldsmiths, London | 76.6 | 61 | 46.8 | 136 | 81.1 | 87 |
| 43 | Lincoln | 91.9 | 79.6 | 37.2 | 122 | 62.9 | 86.3 |
| 44 | Portsmouth | 88.5 | 85.2 | 30.2 | 127 | 63.8 | 85.6 |
| =45 | Winchester | 90.9 | 82.2 | 32.5 | 123 | 61.4 | 85.4 |
| =45 | South Wales | 86.2 | 74.4 | 35.8 | 127 | 66.7 | 85.4 |
| 47 | Trinity Laban | 81.9 | 65.4 | 38 | 125 | 73.7 | 85 |
| 48 | West London | 79.6 | 68.7 | 32.2 | 131 | 74.6 | 84.8 |
| 49 | Canterbury Christ Church | 89.9 | 83.2 | 38.5 | 99 | 65.3 | 84.7 |
| =50 | Nottingham Trent | 91.4 | 84.5 | — | 126 | 72.5 | 84.3 |
| =50 | Chester | 84.7 | 66.5 | 21 | 143 | 68.8 | 84.3 |
| 52 | Chichester | 85.4 | 70.4 | 13.2 | 140 | 71.9 | 84.2 |
| 53 | Staffordshire | 85 | 75.3 | 31.5 | 130 | 63.1 | 84.1 |
| =54 | Falmouth | 83.8 | 77.9 | 48.8 | 110 | 60 | 83.7 |
| =54 | Greenwich | 88.9 | 82.2 | — | 142 | 67 | 83.7 |
| 56 | Hull | — | — | 35 | 124 | 67.3 | 83.4 |
| =57 | York St John | 84.4 | 69.8 | 33.2 | 116 | 66.2 | 83.1 |
| =57 | Westminster | 65.1 | 63.1 | 75.5 | 126 | 63.6 | 83.1 |
| =59 | Bath Spa | 80.8 | 74.9 | 26 | 119 | 71.3 | 83 |
| =59 | East London | 86.2 | 78.4 | 13 | 127 | 67.4 | 83 |
| 61 | Bedfordshire | 87.5 | 71.5 | — | 128 | 75 | 82.8 |
| 62 | Leeds Beckett | 85.7 | 82.9 | 15.8 | 117 | 64.4 | 82.1 |
| 63 | Hertfordshire | 85.8 | 77.2 | 24.2 | 111 | 63 | 81.8 |
| 64 | West of Scotland | 80.6 | 76 | 19.2 | 152 | 55.7 | 81.7 |
| 65 | Bournemouth | 81.4 | 66.5 | 38.5 | 108 | 62.5 | 81.1 |
| 66 | Leeds Conservatoire | 85.7 | 69.9 | — | 138 | 64.4 | 80.8 |
| 67 | Anglia Ruskin | 64.7 | 53.4 | 61.8 | — | 65.7* | 80.1 |
| 68 | Gloucestershire | 72.6 | 61.9 | 23.8 | 122 | 69.6 | 79.3 |
| 69 | Solent, Southampton | 88.9 | 83 | — | 119 | 52.5 | 78.5 |
| 70 | Middlesex | 79.1 | 68.2 | 26 | 102 | — | 78.2 |
| =71 | Wolverhampton | 83.5 | 63.4 | 6.8 | 123 | 58.6 | 77.8 |
| =71 | Leeds Arts | 79.2 | 61.4 | 2.8 | 138 | — | 77.8 |
| 73 | Northampton | 76.1 | 62.7 | 12.2 | 124 | — | 76.8 |
| 74 | Liverpool Hope | 80.7 | 73.7 | 17.5 | 118 | 44.9 | 75.9 |
| 75 | Central Lancashire | 71.6 | 56.9 | 19 | 124 | 59 | 75.8 |
| 76 | Edge Hill | 71.3 | 65.6 | — | 134 | 57.4 | 74.6 |

| Employed in high-skilled job | 49% | Employed in lower-skilled job | 26% |
| Employed in high-skilled job and studying | 4% | Employed in lower-skilled job and studying | 1% |
| Studying | 6% | Unemployed | 6% |
| High-skilled work (median) salary | £25,000 | Low-/medium-skilled salary | £20,000 |

## Natural Sciences

Natural sciences degrees give students the benefit of studying across different scientific disciplines as well as the flexibility to specialise in areas of specific interest as programmes progress. Some universities offer the opportunity to transfer to a single science after a year, if a student decides their interests lie in one particular direction. "As scientists we want to explore the universe and everything in it, but the universe isn't divided into biology, chemistry and physics," explains Professor Geoffrey Nash, head of natural sciences, University of Exeter. "Through studying natural sciences we look for the connections between areas of science, allowing us to harness their power to make a difference to people's lives, to make the world a better place."

Now in its fourth year, the Natural Sciences table is topped by Cambridge for the fourth time. In a convincing lead overall, Cambridge is first for research quality, entry standards and graduate prospects. Runner-up Exeter is in front for student satisfaction – topping the table for teaching quality and the wider experiences in our latest National Student Survey analysis. Natural sciences attracts high grades throughout the table: entry standards are no lower than 165 points (at Loughborough). The subject's interdisciplinary approach provides a breadth of knowledge and practical skills likely to serve graduates well in their careers in industry or postgraduate research. Four of the 11 universities tabled had at least 90% of graduates employed in high-skilled jobs and/or further study within 15 months and none had less than 80% achieving these outcomes. As a subject, natural sciences ranks 15th out the 70 groupings in our employment index and at =5th place for salaries, it compares more favourably still for earnings.

| Natural Sciences | Teaching quality % | Student experience % | Research quality % | Entry standards (UCAS points) | Graduate prospects % | Overall score |
|---|---|---|---|---|---|---|
| 1 Cambridge | 86.9 | 81.2 | 73.5 | 222 | 94.3 | 100 |
| 2 Exeter | 93.8 | 89.9 | 59.3 | 179 | 90 | 94.9 |
| 3 Durham | 81.6 | 74.6 | 53 | 207 | 89.4 | 92.7 |
| 4 University College London | 76.6 | 71.4 | 64 | 188 | 92.6 | 92.6 |
| 5 York | 81.4 | 73.5 | 66 | 188 | 83 | 91 |
| =6 Lancaster | 88 | 82 | 68.2 | 170 | 80 | 90.7 |
| =6 Leeds | 82.2 | 71.4 | 50.2 | 181 | 91.7 | 90.7 |
| 8 Bath | 85.9 | 81.1 | 49.2 | 189 | 85.3 | 90.6 |
| 9 Nottingham | 79.5 | 75.9 | 57.9 | 174 | 86.7 | 89.6 |
| 10 Loughborough | 89.9 | 85 | 41 | 165 | 85 | 88.4 |
| 11 East Anglia | 78.3 | 73 | 56 | 173 | — | 88.2 |

| Employed in high-skilled job | 50% | Employed in lower-skilled job | 7% |
| Employed in high-skilled job and studying | 6% | Employed in lower-skilled job and studying | 0% |
| Studying | 22% | Unemployed | 6% |
| High-skilled work (median) salary | £30,700 | Low-/medium-skilled salary | N/A |

# Nursing

Applications to nursing and midwifery courses at UK universities were at their lowest in five years for admissions in the 2024–25 academic year. UCAS figures at the June 2024 deadline showed 41,520 nursing applications, representing a 5.5% decrease from 2023 and down 26.7% from the post-pandemic boom of 2021. The figures for midwifery painted a similar picture, with 8,760 applications by the June 2024 deadline – down 9.9% compared with the previous year and 34.4% lower than the 2021 peak. Only in Wales did higher education institutions register an upturn in nursing applications, which rose from 3,330 in 2023 to 3,870 for 2024 entry. Royal College of Nursing general secretary and chief executive Professor Nicola Ranger said financial insecurity, high student debt and a lack of investment in nursing education could be behind the fall in applications.

But there are plenty of options available to those considering nursing courses – as evidenced by our Nursing table, which stretches to 76 universities – and the NHS Long Term Workforce pledge has set ambitious targets for student nursing intakes. "Nursing is about delivering safe, evidence-based care, which in the 21st century means student nurses will need a diverse range of skills and an ability to solve complex problems on an almost daily basis," says Susan Ward, head of nursing, School of Healthcare Sciences, Cardiff University.

As a degree, nursing offers a near guarantee of employment on graduation and three universities in our table – Birmingham, Edinburgh and Wrexham – record a perfect 100% rate of graduates being employed in professional-level jobs or postgraduate study within 15 months of graduating. No universities registered lower than the 80.9% of graduates achieving these outcomes at Anglia Ruskin. Nursing is third in the employment table of 70 subjects, down from second last year and behind only veterinary medicine and medicine. Pay, though not an ingredient of our subject ranking, is a topic of especially hot debate in nursing. Average graduate salaries of £25,665 rank the subject 41st out the 70 featured in our *Guide*, a big drop from 27th place two editions ago.

Glasgow retains the lead in our subject ranking for the third consecutive year. It has the highest entry standards by some distance: 212 UCAS points and scores highly with its students, placing in the top ten for teaching quality and the broader experience – based on their responses to the National Student Survey (NSS). Edinburgh, No 1 for nursing three years ago, is runner-up for the second year running, just as Sheffield is in third place. Up 14 places to tie with Queen's, Belfast in =5th place Wrexham is the top-ranked modern university, its position boosted by having the top scores for teaching quality and the wider university experience in our new National Student Survey analysis. Conversely, Gloucester comes bottom for each of these student-led metrics.

Results of the Research Excellence Framework 2021 assessment show that King's College London (=27th overall) leads for research quality in nursing, followed by Manchester (=34th) and Southampton (=16th). In the QS World University Rankings by Subject, which focus on research and academic reputation and do not include measures for student satisfaction, King's College is top in Europe for nursing and second in the world.

| Nursing | Teaching quality % | Student experience % | Research quality % | Entry standards (UCAS points) | Graduate prospects % | Overall score |
|---|---|---|---|---|---|---|
| 1 Glasgow | 86.7 | 84.4 | 63.5 | 212 | 97.2 | 100 |
| 2 Edinburgh | 84 | 76 | 55.2 | 198 | 100 | 98.8 |
| 3 Sheffield | 91.4 | 88.2 | 63.7 | 152 | 97.5 | 96.1 |
| 4 Keele | 83.9 | 76.4 | 66.2 | 141 | 99.4 | 94.8 |
| =5 Wrexham | 97.9 | 97 | 1.5 | — | 100 | 93.6 |

| | | | | | | | |
|---|---|---|---|---|---|---|---|
| =5 | Queen's, Belfast | 85.8 | 81.6 | 66.2 | 135 | 97 | 93.6 |
| 7 | Surrey | 81.4 | 76.4 | 58 | 148 | 97.6 | 93.4 |
| 8 | Glasgow Caledonian | 81.6 | 75.9 | 61 | 139 | 98.2 | 93.3 |
| 9 | Northumbria | 79.9 | 76.1 | 53.5 | 143 | 98.9 | 93.2 |
| =10 | Birmingham | 75.8 | 65.4 | 55 | 147 | 100 | 93 |
| =10 | Leeds | 74.7 | 68.8 | 65 | 150 | 98.1 | 93 |
| =12 | Swansea | 66.9 | 58.7 | 66.8 | 157 | 99.4 | 92.8 |
| =12 | Hull | 80.2 | 71.2 | 55.5 | 141 | 98.7 | 92.8 |
| =14 | Ulster | 89.5 | 87.6 | 53.5 | 135 | 95.4 | 92.7 |
| =14 | Coventry | 84.4 | 74.9 | 47.2 | 135 | 99.2 | 92.7 |
| =16 | Southampton | 76 | 69.2 | 69.8 | 148 | 96.3 | 92.6 |
| =16 | Cardiff | 74.2 | 66.9 | 58.8 | 163 | 96.4 | 92.6 |
| 18 | Nottingham | 78.5 | 71.6 | 66.8 | 139 | 96.6 | 92.2 |
| 19 | Dundee | 77.6 | 65.3 | 60.8 | 130 | 99.7 | 92.1 |
| 20 | Exeter | 76.4 | 58.7 | 54.5 | 153 | — | 92 |
| 21 | Hertfordshire | 86.7 | 82 | 48 | 117 | 98.8 | 91.8 |
| =22 | East Anglia | 80.9 | 75.4 | 55.5 | 134 | 97.1 | 91.7 |
| =22 | York | 78.2 | 75.2 | 65 | 141 | 95.2 | 91.7 |
| 24 | Lincoln | 74.6 | 68.1 | 55.8 | 138 | 98.4 | 91.5 |
| =25 | Derby | 84.9 | 80.3 | 24 | 142 | 97.8 | 91.2 |
| =25 | Edinburgh Napier | 81.4 | 78.3 | 40.5 | 136 | 97.4 | 91.2 |
| =27 | King's College London | 78 | 71.2 | 76.2 | 141 | 92.7 | 91 |
| =27 | Bangor | 65.4 | 55.9 | 59.8 | 150 | 98.7 | 91 |
| =27 | Kingston | 81.1 | 76.8 | 38.5 | 135 | 97.7 | 91 |
| 30 | Queen Margaret, Edinburgh | 88.6 | 85.4 | 36.5 | 151 | 92.3 | 90.9 |
| =31 | Stirling | 75.3 | 68.3 | 44 | 135 | 98.9 | 90.8 |
| =31 | Oxford Brookes | 86 | 77.2 | 37.8 | 128 | 97.3 | 90.8 |
| 33 | West London | 86.1 | 78.7 | 29.5 | 134 | 97.2 | 90.7 |
| =34 | Plymouth | 75.8 | 65.3 | 39.5 | 143 | 98.1 | 90.5 |
| =34 | Manchester | 72.1 | 65.2 | 71.2 | 147 | 93.7 | 90.5 |
| =36 | Liverpool John Moores | 78.7 | 72.6 | 26.5 | 148 | 97.3 | 90.4 |
| =36 | Robert Gordon | 82.4 | 72.5 | 24.5 | 131 | 99.7 | 90.4 |
| 38 | Liverpool | 87.1 | 82.4 | 46.8 | 137 | 92.7 | 90.3 |
| 39 | South Wales | 77.4 | 65.7 | 25.2 | 149 | 97.6 | 89.9 |
| =40 | Portsmouth | 75.5 | 69.8 | 41.2 | 130 | 98.2 | 89.8 |
| =40 | Salford | 76.1 | 66.1 | 37 | 141 | 97.3 | 89.8 |
| =40 | Roehampton | 92.7 | 88 | 37.5 | 102 | — | 89.8 |
| =40 | Greenwich | 88.3 | 80.7 | 32.3 | 117 | 96.9 | 89.8 |
| 44 | Staffordshire | 80.6 | 72.8 | 30.8 | 123 | 98.9 | 89.7 |
| 45 | Central Lancashire | 77.7 | 72.7 | 35.5 | 140 | 96 | 89.6 |
| =46 | Brighton | 71.8 | 63.4 | 50.5 | 130 | 97.9 | 89.5 |
| =46 | City | 73.1 | 67.7 | 58 | 139 | 94.4 | 89.5 |
| 48 | Birmingham City | 74.9 | 68.5 | 37.8 | 133 | 97.4 | 89.3 |
| 49 | Sunderland | 82.7 | 75.2 | 30.2 | 124 | 96.7 | 89.1 |
| 50 | West of Scotland | 79.3 | 67.7 | 30.8 | 142 | 95.3 | 89 |
| 51 | Chester | 77.2 | 66.5 | 31 | 129 | 98.1 | 88.9 |
| =52 | Essex | 83 | 76.3 | 28.5 | 114 | 97.3 | 88.5 |
| =52 | West of England | 70.7 | 60 | 42.8 | 133 | 97 | 88.5 |

## Nursing cont.

| | | Teaching quality % | Student experience % | Research quality % | Entry standards (UCAS points) | Graduate prospects % | Overall score |
|---|---|---|---|---|---|---|---|
| =52 | Sheffield Hallam | 70.7 | 62.8 | 29.8 | 128 | 99.5 | 88.5 |
| 55 | London South Bank | 83.9 | 77.4 | 34.5 | 126 | 93.9 | 88.4 |
| =56 | Teesside | 77.3 | 68 | 35 | 126 | 96.3 | 88.3 |
| =56 | Huddersfield | 73.4 | 69.3 | 22.5 | 136 | 97.5 | 88.3 |
| =56 | Canterbury Christ Church | 78.6 | 65 | 31.8 | 124 | 97.1 | 88.3 |
| =59 | Wolverhampton | 77.7 | 68.3 | 24.2 | 137 | 96 | 88.2 |
| =59 | Manchester Metropolitan | 78.1 | 72.3 | 36 | 138 | 93.3 | 88.2 |
| =61 | East London | 85 | 74.2 | 25.5 | 117 | 96.1 | 88.1 |
| =61 | Leeds Beckett | 70.8 | 65.9 | 38 | 126 | 97.5 | 88.1 |
| =63 | Middlesex | 85.2 | 79.9 | 22.5 | 115 | 96.1 | 88 |
| =63 | Bolton | 80.1 | 74.4 | 2 | 140 | 97 | 88 |
| 65 | Bournemouth | 77.3 | 67.1 | 29.2 | 114 | 98.5 | 87.9 |
| 66 | Bedfordshire | 81.1 | 71.8 | 22.5 | 125 | 95.2 | 87.4 |
| 67 | Northampton | 81.1 | 75 | 5 | 136 | 94.7 | 86.9 |
| 68 | Buckinghamshire New | 86.9 | 80 | 16.8 | 110 | 94.6 | 86.7 |
| 69 | Edge Hill | 68.7 | 66.5 | 22.2 | 138 | 95.2 | 86.5 |
| =70 | Worcester | 72.6 | 68.7 | 24.2 | 126 | 95.3 | 86.4 |
| =70 | Bradford | 66.9 | 58.1 | 33.8 | 141 | 94.2 | 86.4 |
| 72 | De Montfort | 72.8 | 62.5 | 20.8 | 126 | 96.3 | 86.3 |
| 73 | Cumbria | 72.4 | 70.7 | 18.5 | 128 | 94.1 | 85.6 |
| 74 | Suffolk | 75.9 | 67.4 | — | 120 | 95.7 | 84.6 |
| 75 | Gloucestershire | 61.4 | 52.4 | 16.2 | 129 | 95.2 | 83.6 |
| 76 | Anglia Ruskin | 80.2 | 68.6 | 33.8 | 121 | 80.9 | 80.5 |

| | | | |
|---|---|---|---|
| Employed in high-skilled job | 89% | Employed in lower-skilled job | 2% |
| Employed in high-skilled job and studying | 4% | Employed in lower-skilled job and studying | 0% |
| Studying | 1% | Unemployed | 1% |
| High-skilled work (median) salary | £25,675 | Low-/medium-skilled salary | N/A |

# Pharmacology and Pharmacy

No 1 for the fourth consecutive year, Strathclyde in Glasgow's eminence in our Pharmacology and Pharmacy table is secured by the highest entry standards (224 points in the UCAS tariff) along with strong performances across all other measures in our ranking. Strathclyde offers degrees in all three of the subjects encompassed in this grouping: pharmacology – which is a branch of medicine concerned with drugs, their uses, effects and how they interact with the human body; pharmacy – which trains and licenses individuals to dispense prescription medicines as pharmacists; and toxicology – which is similar to pharmacology but focuses on the toxic rather than healing properties of venoms, poisons and drugs. Most English universities offer only one or the other, and courses are evenly split among institutions.

"Pharmacologists look for answers to viral pandemics, tropical diseases such as malaria and sleeping sickness, and venomous snake bites. Thanks to pharmacologists we can treat many conditions that used to be fatal. There are many more that still need research," explains Dr Andrew Fielding, senior lecturer in cancer research, Lancaster University.

King's College London (in 20th place overall) has the edge for research quality in our analysis of the Research Excellence Framework 2021 results. In our latest National Student Survey (NSS) analysis 24th-place St George's, London (now City St George's) achieves the highest rates of satisfaction with teaching quality and the broader experience, while third-place Ulster, the table's highest-ranked modern university, comes second for teaching quality and third for the student experience. At the opposite end of the scale, the least satisfied students for both NSS-based measures were at Central Lancashire (42nd overall).

The four-year MPharm degree is a direct route to professional registration as a pharmacist and the most popular option, or students can study three-year degrees in pharmaceutical science or as part of a broader degree. Pharmacology is available as a three-year BSc or as an extended course. Biology and chemistry are usually required by the leading universities, while maths, further maths and physics may also be useful. Applications to pharmacology and pharmacy degrees have rocketed since before the pandemic. There were 31,745 applications to pharmacy in 2023 (up by around 73% since 2019) and 10,100 applications to pharmacology (nearly 50% higher than in 2019). The spike in interest is timely; the NHS Long Term Workforce Plan, published in 2023, has pledged to expand training places for pharmacists in England by 29% by 2028–29.

Solid career prospects are in store for graduates. The subjects are usually in the top ten of our employment table but have slipped to 22nd out of 70 subject areas this year. The latest Graduate Outcomes survey found three-quarters of those with pharmacology and pharmacy degrees employed in professional-level jobs and/or furthering their studies within 15 months. Pay offers early career rewards: the subjects tie with veterinary science in third place of our pay index (behind only dentistry and medicine), based on average graduate salaries of £33,000.

| Pharmacology and Pharmacy | Teaching quality % | Student experience % | Research quality % | Entry standards (UCAS points) | Graduate prospects % | Overall score |
|---|---|---|---|---|---|---|
| 1 Strathclyde | 83 | 80.3 | 65.8 | 224 | 93.1 | 100 |
| 2 Glasgow | 80.3 | 79.3 | 63.5 | 197 | — | 97.5 |
| 3 Ulster | 95.7 | 90.5 | 53.5 | 155 | 95.8 | 97 |
| 4 Queen's, Belfast | 83.5 | 81.3 | 66.2 | 161 | 97.7 | 96.7 |
| 5 Dundee | 93.9 | 92.8 | 60.8 | — | 88 | 95.7 |
| 6 Cardiff | 86.7 | 75.5 | 58.8 | 161 | 97 | 95.6 |
| 7 Newcastle | 85 | 82.5 | 65.8 | 139 | 97.5 | 95.2 |
| 8 Nottingham | 85.2 | 81.5 | 66.8 | 151 | 92.7 | 94.6 |
| 9 Bath | 82.6 | 84.9 | 63.7 | 147 | 92.3 | 93.6 |
| 10 Liverpool | 87.9 | 84.2 | 46.8 | 149 | 95.3 | 93.5 |
| 11 Leeds | 78 | 77.3 | 52 | 159 | 95.7* | 92.7 |
| 12 Aberdeen | 89.6 | 87.3 | 30.5 | 164 | 91.4* | 91.9 |
| 13 Manchester | 74.7 | 66 | 71.2 | 154 | 91.1 | 91.7 |
| 14 University College London | 83.2 | 80.1 | 57.8 | 158 | 86.9 | 91.6 |
| =15 Sunderland | 89.7 | 79.7 | 30.2 | 130 | 100 | 91.4 |
| =15 Robert Gordon | 83.8 | 74.4 | 24.5 | 192 | 92.1 | 91.4 |
| =17 Birmingham | 86.9 | 80.4 | 55 | 140 | 89 | 91.2 |
| =17 Swansea | 76.4 | 75.6 | 66.8 | 145 | — | 91.2 |
| 19 King's College London | 76.6 | 73.5 | 76.2 | 146 | 85.8 | 90.9 |
| 20 Keele | 77.7 | 71.6 | 66.2 | 137 | 88.5 | 89.9 |
| 21 Glasgow Caledonian | 84.6 | 78.3 | 61 | 160 | 79.3 | 89.8 |

**Pharmacology and Pharmacy** cont.

| | | Teaching quality % | Student experience % | Research quality % | Entry standards (UCAS points) | Graduate prospects % | Overall score |
|---|---|---|---|---|---|---|---|
| 22 | Reading | 83.8 | 77.8 | 54 | 122 | 90.9 | 89.6 |
| 23 | Bristol | 75 | 70 | 57.5 | 150 | 86.4 | 88.5 |
| 24 | St George's, London | 96.5 | 93 | 50.2 | 120 | 78.1 | 88.3 |
| 25 | Brighton | 72.3 | 71.1 | 50.5 | 125 | 94 | 87.7 |
| 26 | East Anglia | 79.3 | 70.3 | 55.5 | 130 | 86.9 | 87.6 |
| 27 | Bradford | 81.5 | 75.2 | 33.8 | 139 | 88.8 | 86.9 |
| 28 | Liverpool John Moores | 80.3 | 79.9 | 26.5 | 133 | 91.1 | 86.5 |
| 29 | Aston | 76.3 | 76.7 | 46 | 123 | 88.9 | 86.4 |
| 30 | Queen Mary, London | 79.1 | 81.6 | 54.8 | 142 | 76.7 | 86 |
| 31 | Westminster | 84.5 | 87.5 | 36.8 | 109 | — | 85.5 |
| 32 | Huddersfield | 81.5 | 77.2 | 22.5 | 132 | 89.5 | 85.3 |
| 33 | Lincoln | 69.3 | 65.3 | 55.8 | 130 | 86.3 | 85.1 |
| 34 | Nottingham Trent | 88.3 | 84.4 | 43.5 | 112 | 79.4 | 85 |
| 35 | Portsmouth | 84.1 | 81 | 41.2 | 108 | 84.3 | 84.9 |
| 36 | Hertfordshire | 81.9 | 77.9 | 48 | 113 | 81.8 | 84.7 |
| 37 | Greenwich | 86.7 | 82.8 | 32.3 | 121 | 80.3 | 84.1 |
| =38 | Kingston | 79 | 77.5 | 38.5 | 117 | 84 | 83.9 |
| =38 | De Montfort | 81.4 | 77.9 | 20.8 | 113 | 90 | 83.9 |
| 40 | Kent | 76.2 | 66.9 | 36.8 | 128 | 84.5 | 83.4 |
| 41 | Wolverhampton | 72.6 | 68.6 | 24.2 | 120 | 85.2 | 80.8 |
| 42 | Central Lancashire | 58.2 | 54.8 | 35.5 | 135 | 82.7 | 78.8 |

| | | | | |
|---|---|---|---|---|
| Employed in high-skilled job | 59% | Employed in lower-skilled job | | 7% |
| Employed in high-skilled job and studying | 7% | Employed in lower-skilled job and studying | | 0% |
| Studying | 9% | Unemployed | | 6% |
| High-skilled work (median) salary | £33,000 | Low-/medium-skilled salary | | £20,500 |

# Philosophy

Students of philosophy engage with the ideas of great thinkers, examining their arguments and expressing their own opinions. Social science and humanities subjects (English, religious studies, psychology, politics, sociology) are useful in an application, while some of the leading universities may also look for maths – as degrees involve more mathematical skills than many candidates expect, especially when the syllabus has an emphasis on logic. "Philosophy is honest, self-reflective and fresh. Its abstractness and rigour produce the most transferable skills of any university degree. Philosophy students go on to be politicians, lawyers, business people, medical professionals, journalists and, more importantly, good parents, partners, citizens and friends," says Dr Michael T Stuart, lecturer in philosophy, University of York. In 51st place philosophy has moved nine places down our employment ranking of 70 subject areas, based on six in ten graduates (59.8%) being in high-skilled jobs and/or furthering their studies within 15 months. Graduate salaries compare more favourably in =38th place. After two years of rising demand, applications levelled out in 2023 and 16,760 applied. The numbers of students starting courses has remained remarkably consistent across the past four admissions years and in 2023 there were 3,555 new philosophy undergraduates.

The LSE recorded a perfect 100% of graduates in professional jobs and/or further study

15 months after their degrees, helping secure the No 1 spot for LSE in our Philosophy table, overtaking St Andrews after three years at the top. Oxford, which led the table four years ago, attracts the highest entry standards – with entrants averaging 203 points in the UCAS tariff. But there is a wide range of entry standards across the table, from the heights at Oxford to 99 points at its neighbouring university, Oxford Brookes. Cardiff, in 21st place overall, was the top scorer in the Research Excellence Framework 2021. The upper end of our Philosophy table is remarkably stable year on year, and nine of this year's top 10 universities appeared in last year's top 10 too. Exeter is a new arrival in eighth place – up three places this year while Durham has slipped the same number of places to sit 11th. In our latest National Student Survey analysis, West of England (=37th) outdoes the rest of the table for the broad student experience and Aberdeen (15th) is unbeaten for teaching quality, followed by Hull (23rd) and Oxford Brookes (24th) in each metric.

| Philosophy | Teaching quality % | Student experience % | Research quality % | Entry standards (UCAS points) | Graduate prospects % | Overall score |
|---|---|---|---|---|---|---|
| 1 London School of Economics | 83.3 | 80.8 | 60 | 188 | 100 | 100 |
| =2 St Andrews | 90.6 | 87.7 | 55 | 199 | 76.4 | 97.1 |
| =2 Warwick | 86.7 | 84.2 | 55.8 | 176 | 88.7 | 97.1 |
| 4 Oxford | 84.4 | 70.8 | 50.7 | 203 | 90.6 | 96.8 |
| 5 University College London | 79.4 | 78.3 | 66.8 | 180 | 86.9 | 96.2 |
| 6 Cambridge | 84.5 | 67.4 | 59 | 196 | 86.2 | 96.1 |
| 7 York | 86.3 | 82.1 | 66.2 | 142 | 83.7 | 94.8 |
| 8 Birmingham | 84.6 | 80.4 | 66 | 148 | 83 | 94.4 |
| =9 Durham | 79.7 | 70.7 | 47.8 | 182 | 88.9 | 93.4 |
| =9 King's College London | 79.1 | 75.2 | 52.2 | 175 | 87.1 | 93.4 |
| =11 Southampton | 89.2 | 86.4 | 59 | 138 | 75 | 92.7 |
| =11 Newcastle | 88.5 | 84.5 | 61.8 | 134 | 76 | 92.7 |
| 13 Exeter | 80.3 | 79.3 | 46.8 | 165 | 85.5 | 92.3 |
| 14 Sheffield | 85.6 | 85.8 | 45.5 | 148 | 81.9 | 92 |
| 15 Aberdeen | 92.9 | 89.2 | 22.8 | 169 | — | 91.7 |
| 16 Essex | 91.6 | 86.2 | 46.5 | 113 | 79.6 | 90.7 |
| 17 Bristol | 79.8 | 74.6 | 54.8 | 165 | 75 | 90.4 |
| 18 Liverpool | 85.5 | 83.4 | 45.2 | 133 | 78.2 | 89.8 |
| 19 Glasgow | 79.3 | 77.2 | 51 | 172 | 69.5 | 89.3 |
| 20 Lancaster | 86.2 | 80.8 | 49 | 144 | 70.2 | 89.2 |
| 21 Cardiff | 82.9 | 79.7 | 67.2 | 129 | 66.7 | 89.1 |
| 22 Nottingham | 82.5 | 80.1 | 41.5 | 138 | 79.7 | 88.9 |
| 23 Hull | 93.6 | 88.9 | 31.5 | — | 66.4* | 88.3 |
| 24 Oxford Brookes | 94.4 | 88.4 | 28.2 | 99 | 80 | 88.1 |
| 25 Sussex | 81.1 | 79.5 | 49 | 131 | 72.8 | 87.6 |
| 26 Bangor | 88.6 | 83.9 | 33.2 | 141 | 69.8 | 87.5 |
| =27 Edinburgh | 73.5 | 69.6 | 49 | 171 | 72.3 | 87.4 |
| =27 Manchester | 75.6 | 68.4 | 55.5 | 160 | 69.8 | 87.4 |
| 29 Stirling | 82.3 | 82 | 36 | 141 | — | 87.2 |
| 30 Leeds | 72.4 | 74.3 | 47 | 153 | 76.7 | 87.1 |
| 31 Reading | 86.8 | 82 | 36.2 | 123 | 73.3 | 86.9 |

## Philosophy cont.

| | | Teaching quality % | Student experience % | Research quality % | Entry standards (UCAS points) | Graduate prospects % | Overall score |
|---|---|---|---|---|---|---|---|
| 32 | Dundee | 83.6 | 71.5 | 17.8 | 171 | — | 85.5 |
| 33 | Manchester Metropolitan | 86.5 | 80.1 | 41 | 108 | 69.2 | 85.3 |
| 34 | East Anglia | 83.2 | 77 | 38.2 | 125 | 69.6 | 85.1 |
| 35 | Royal Holloway | 84.1 | 79.6 | 26.5 | 130 | 70.7 | 84.5 |
| 36 | Keele | 88.8 | 86.6 | 9.5 | 111 | 78.8* | 84.4 |
| =37 | West of England | 95.4 | 82.2 | 35.2 | 107 | 53.6 | 83.2 |
| =37 | Queen's, Belfast | 75.4 | 68.1 | 33 | 149 | — | 83.2 |
| 39 | Lincoln | 90.5 | 85.5 | — | 102 | 74.1 | 81.6 |
| 40 | Hertfordshire | 79 | 67.4 | 35 | 102 | — | 80.3 |

| | | | |
|---|---|---|---|
| Employed in high-skilled job | 42% | Employed in lower-skilled job | 22% |
| Employed in high-skilled job and studying | 5% | Employed in lower-skilled job and studying | 1% |
| Studying | 11% | Unemployed | 6% |
| High-skilled work (median) salary | £28,000 | Low-/medium-skilled salary | £20,600 |

# Physics and Astronomy

Famous physicists and astronomers from Galileo Galilei to Marie Curie, Albert Einstein to Stephen Hawking, have helped earn the subjects a reputation for being the rarefied preserves of boffins, but Dr Patrick Parkinson, UK Research and Innovation Future Leaders fellow in physics and astronomy, University of Manchester believes "Everyone is born a physicist – as babies we explore how things move, how things get hot or cold and periodic day and night," he says. "It is a global pursuit using experiments and theory, along the way developing revolutionary technologies: transistors, the internet, GPS positioning, MRI scanners, fusion energy and quantum computing. Graduates apply the skills they learn in the fields of research, policy, engineering, computer science, finance and beyond."

Rising student numbers – in astronomy in particular – have been attributed at least in part to Brian Cox, the University of Manchester particle physicist, whose television work has injected some accessibility and cool to the field. But demand cooled a little in 2023 and just under 3,500 applied to the subject while 705 were accepted onto courses. Physics – much the larger field – attracted 20,660 applications (down by about 7% year on year) and 7,770 new undergraduates gained places (down 4%).

Stiff entry standards at the leading universities remain a constant, though, with the Physics and Astronomy table attracting some of the highest in our *Guide*. Seven of the 49 universities tabled average over 200 UCAS points among entrants, led by Cambridge, where new undergraduates averaged 222 points. Only 18 averaged under 144 points (equivalent to three As at A-level) and just two universities dropped below 110 points, the equivalent of BBC at A-level.

Most degrees in both physics and astronomy demand physics and maths at A-level, as well as good grades overall.

The top two in the table are unchanged, with Cambridge heading St Andrews for the third successive year. Oxford is third in our UK rankings and third in the world for physics and astronomy according to QS, which also has Cambridge in fifth. Manchester is up one place to sixth this year, its rank buoyed by the top scores in the Research Excellence Framework 2021, where it is closely followed by Sheffield (21st overall) and Birmingham – up one place to fourth this year.

In a remarkable achievement, Northumbria (37th overall) has outdone all other universities in the table for student satisfaction with both teaching quality and the wider undergraduate experience. Central Lancaster (36th), Lancaster (fifth), Lincoln (43rd) and Aberdeen (24th) also perform strongly in these student-led measures. At the opposite end of the scale, Imperial College London ranks bottom for teaching quality and third from bottom for the student experience – which hold back its overall ranking to =11th place, despite the second-best graduate prospects in the table. Oxford has the edge for graduate employment – with 97.1% in high-skilled jobs and/or furthering their studies within 15 months.

The subjects translate into positive career potential, ranking 21st in our employment index and 15th for pay.

| Physics and Astronomy | Teaching quality % | Student experience % | Research quality % | Entry standards (UCAS points) | Graduate prospects % | Overall score |
|---|---|---|---|---|---|---|
| 1 Cambridge | 86.9 | 81.2 | 72.8 | 222 | 94.3 | 100 |
| 2 St Andrews | 91.7 | 88.8 | 65.8 | 221 | 88.4 | 98.6 |
| 3 Oxford | 80.6 | 66.1 | 66.5 | 217 | 97.1 | 97.1 |
| 4 Birmingham | 81.5 | 79.3 | 73.2 | 189 | 91.3 | 96 |
| 5 Lancaster | 93.3 | 87 | 58.5 | 166 | 91.2 | 95.4 |
| 6 Manchester | 78 | 72.8 | 74 | 197 | 89.5 | 94.7 |
| 7 Durham | 83.2 | 75.1 | 57.2 | 211 | 89.7 | 94.3 |
| 8 Warwick | 86.3 | 79.4 | 59.8 | 186 | 89.7 | 94.2 |
| 9 Bristol | 83.7 | 76.4 | 70.5 | 176 | 87.7 | 93.9 |
| 10 Strathclyde | 88.7 | 80.3 | 63.2 | 192 | 83 | 93.6 |
| =11 Exeter | 85.6 | 81.7 | 59.2 | 167 | 90.5 | 93.3 |
| =11 Imperial College | 69.7 | 67 | 60.8 | 212 | 95.7 | 93.3 |
| 13 Bath | 82.7 | 81.1 | 55.5 | 179 | 91.5 | 93.2 |
| 14 Glasgow | 75.2 | 73.1 | 64.5 | 216 | 86.7 | 93 |
| 15 Heriot-Watt | 85.5 | 84.5 | 65.5 | 164 | 84.4 | 92.4 |
| 16 Nottingham | 84.5 | 78 | 68.8 | 165 | 84.5 | 92.3 |
| 17 Queen's, Belfast | 86.8 | 87 | 46.8 | 166 | 88.8 | 91.6 |
| 18 Edinburgh | 75.8 | 67 | 62.7 | 213 | 84.5 | 91.5 |
| 19 Cardiff | 90.8 | 85.4 | 59.2 | 151 | 82.7 | 91.3 |
| 20 Surrey | 89.1 | 86.2 | 45.5 | 141 | 91.2 | 91.1 |
| 21 Sheffield | 84.9 | 84.4 | 73.8 | 152 | 78.2 | 90.9 |
| 22 Portsmouth | 87.6 | 83.8 | 68.5 | 102 | 88.2 | 90.8 |
| 23 Leeds | 78 | 77.6 | 64.5 | 159 | 86.5 | 90.5 |
| 24 Aberdeen | 85.8 | 90.2 | 40 | 177 | — | 90 |
| =25 York | 79.5 | 75.8 | 62.7 | 158 | 84.2 | 89.6 |
| =25 Southampton | 84.9 | 80.9 | 52.2 | 154 | 85.1 | 89.6 |
| 27 University College London | 72.3 | 72.1 | 55.5 | 177 | 86.3 | 88.5 |
| 28 Swansea | 88 | 86.2 | 46.5 | 138 | 83.1 | 88.3 |
| =29 Sussex | 87 | 85.4 | 55 | 143 | 77.1 | 87.7 |
| =29 Nottingham Trent | 88.5 | 85.5 | 59 | 110 | 80.2 | 87.7 |
| 31 Royal Holloway | 88 | 83 | 48 | 143 | 80.2 | 87.6 |
| 32 Loughborough | 86.7 | 83.6 | 39.2 | 150 | 83.5 | 87.5 |
| 33 Dundee | 74.5 | 81.3 | 50.2 | 167 | — | 87.3 |

| | Teaching quality % | Student experience % | Research quality % | Entry standards (UCAS points) | Graduate prospects % | Overall score |
|---|---|---|---|---|---|---|
| =34 Leicester | 87.5 | 88.2 | 44 | 134 | 81.2 | 87.2 |
| =34 Liverpool | 79.8 | 72.9 | 61.5 | 140 | 81 | 87.2 |
| 36 Central Lancashire | 94.6 | 79.3 | 41.2 | – | 77.8* | 87.1 |
| 37 Northumbria | 94.7 | 98.1 | 43 | 144 | 72 | 87 |
| 38 King's College London | 73.1 | 70.4 | 49.2 | 161 | 86.4 | 86.7 |
| 39 Hull | 92 | 89.7 | 45.5 | 112 | 78.3 | 86.2 |
| 40 Queen Mary, London | 81.8 | 80.1 | 48.8 | 139 | 78.7 | 85.5 |
| 41 West of Scotland | 88.1 | 80.4 | 31 | 145 | – | 85.2 |
| 42 Newcastle | 70.1 | 68.3 | 48 | 140 | 88 | 85 |
| 43 Lincoln | 91.9 | 92.1 | 28.2 | 113 | – | 84.6 |
| =44 Salford | 83.4 | 79.4 | 33.2 | 125 | 80 | 83 |
| =44 Aberystwyth | 89.3 | 87.6 | 21 | 118 | 81.1 | 83 |
| 46 Keele | 82.5 | 71.6 | 49.5 | 124 | 73.9 | 82.7 |
| 47 Kent | 79.9 | 72.4 | 32.5 | 122 | 77.4 | 80.6 |
| 48 East Anglia | 78.3 | 73 | – | 128 | 86.8 | 78.8 |
| 49 Hertfordshire | 72.7 | 61.3 | 45.5 | 98 | 67.6 | 75.7 |

| | | | |
|---|---|---|---|
| Employed in high-skilled job | 51% | Employed in lower-skilled job | 10% |
| Employed in high-skilled job and studying | 4% | Employed in lower-skilled job and studying | 0% |
| Studying | 20% | Unemployed | 6% |
| High-skilled work (median) salary | £30,000 | Low-/medium-skilled salary | £20,000 |

# Physiotherapy

Formerly part of the "Subjects Allied to Medicine" grouping, the Physiotherapy table is now in its 12th year. Modern universities feature prominently, occupying half of the top ten. Glasgow Caledonian retains the lead for the third consecutive year, its rank boosted by the top entry standards of 209 UCAS points. For research quality, King's College London (=13th place overall) leads the field, having achieved the best results in the field in the REF 2021, where it is followed by Southampton – the table's former No 1 and this year's runner-up. In third place overall, Robert Gordon in Aberdeen has the highest rates of student satisfaction with teaching quality and the wider experience – measures derived from our new National Student Survey analysis. Salford (21st overall) and Leeds Beckett (seventh) place second and third for each. At the opposite end of the scale, the physiotherapy students least satisfied with their teaching were at Coventry (31st), Wolverhampton (34th) and 39th-place St George's, London (now City St George's), while the lowest rates of satisfaction with the wider experience were at London South Bank (40th), followed by Coventry and St George's, London (City St George's). For research quality, King's College London (=13th place overall) leads the field, having achieved the best results in the field in the REF 2021, where it is followed by Southampton – the table's former No 1 and this year's runner-up.

Lindsay O'Connor, senior teaching fellow in neurological physiotherapy, University of Southampton, says physiotherapists "work with individuals across the lifespan to achieve their goals and optimise function, from sitting up for the first time in critical care to rehabilitation after a sporting injury."

Graduate employment outcomes are reliably strong, and at four of the 40 universities listed 100% of physiotherapy graduates were employed in professional jobs and/or postgraduate study within 15 months. Only at two universities, London South Bank and East London, does this proportion fall below 90% and the subject ranks fifth in the employment table, behind veterinary medicine, medicine, nursing and radiography. For salaries, though not an ingredient of our ranking, physiotherapy compares less strongly but still features comfortably in the upper half of subjects, at =28th.

The subject's popularity has been gathering pace, and UCAS figures show applications and enrolments to be about a third higher in 2023 than they were four admissions years before, in 2019. Candidates need biology A-level, while physics, chemistry and maths are also useful, as are sociology and PE A-levels.

| Physiotherapy | Teaching quality % | Student experience % | Research quality % | Entry standards (UCAS points) | Graduate prospects % | Overall score |
|---|---|---|---|---|---|---|
| 1 Glasgow Caledonian | 82.3 | 77.7 | 61 | 209 | 98.1 | 100 |
| 2 Southampton | 91.3 | 88 | 69.8 | 162 | 100 | 99.6 |
| 3 Robert Gordon | 94.3 | 92.4 | 24.5 | 207 | 100 | 99.4 |
| 4 Queen Margaret, Edinburgh | 90.5 | 86.2 | 36.5 | — | 100.0* | 95.6 |
| 5 Northumbria | 85.7 | 80.2 | 60.5 | 147 | 97.9 | 95 |
| 6 Liverpool | 87.1 | 84.5 | 46.8 | 156 | 98.2 | 94.9 |
| 7 Leeds Beckett | 92.4 | 89.6 | 38 | 157 | 96.4 | 94.4 |
| 8 Cardiff | 74.9 | 71.7 | 58.8 | 160 | 98.1 | 93.9 |
| 9 Keele | 85.3 | 81.7 | 66.2 | 150 | 92 | 93.4 |
| =10 East Anglia | 76.6 | 74.4 | 55.5 | 169 | 94.9 | 93.3 |
| =10 Brighton | 88.9 | 83.2 | 50.5 | 139 | 96.4 | 93.3 |
| 12 Birmingham | 76.6 | 68.1 | 55 | 171 | 95.2 | 93.2 |
| =13 King's College London | 72.8 | 66.3 | 76.2 | 162 | 93 | 93.1 |
| =13 West of England | 89.9 | 88.6 | 42.8 | 153 | 94.1 | 93.1 |
| 15 Plymouth | 89.7 | 81.6 | 39.5 | 156 | 93.7 | 92.4 |
| 16 Ulster | 77.6 | 63.2 | 53.5 | 150 | 97.9 | 92.2 |
| 17 Central Lancashire | 87 | 77 | 35.5 | — | 96.3 | 91.9 |
| 18 Manchester Metropolitan | 75.8 | 75.4 | 51.2 | 151 | 96 | 91.8 |
| 19 Essex | 82.7 | 80.5 | 32.5 | — | 97.5 | 91.5 |
| 20 Bradford | 80.3 | 68.8 | 33.8 | 150 | 98.4 | 91.1 |
| 21 Salford | 93.4 | 89.6 | 37 | 140 | 91.7 | 90.9 |
| 22 Nottingham | 78 | 69.6 | 56 | 148 | 92.7 | 90.6 |
| 23 Hertfordshire | 87.8 | 85.8 | 48 | 129 | 92.7 | 90.5 |
| 24 Teesside | 78.3 | 77.2 | 35 | 137 | 98 | 90.1 |
| 25 Brunel | 88.8 | 81 | 47.2 | 129 | 92.2 | 90 |
| 26 Huddersfield | 85.5 | 81.6 | 22.2 | 136 | 97.7 | 89.9 |
| 27 Bournemouth | 82.8 | 78.4 | 29.2 | 130 | 97.4 | 89.4 |
| 27 Worcester | 82.2 | 78 | 24.2 | 136 | 97.7 | 89.4 |
| 29 Oxford Brookes | 83.7 | 72 | 37.8 | 145 | 92.3 | 89.2 |
| 30 York St John | 90 | 83.8 | 13.8 | 146 | 94 | 89.1 |
| 31 Coventry | 66.4 | 57.1 | 47.2 | 145 | 97 | 88.7 |
| 32 Cumbria | 84.7 | 81.3 | 18.5 | 132 | 95.8 | 88.2 |

**Physiotherapy** cont.

| | teaching quality % | Student experience % | Research quality % | Entry standards (UCAS points) | Graduate prospects % | Overall score |
|---|---|---|---|---|---|---|
| **33** Sheffield Hallam | 72.3 | 66.2 | 29.8 | 145 | 96.7 | 88.1 |
| **34** Wolverhampton | 70.6 | 63.3 | 24.2 | 139 | 100 | 88 |
| **=35** Leicester | 88.8 | 86.8 | — | 135 | 94.4 | 86.8 |
| **=35** Gloucestershire | 76.6 | 68.6 | 24.5 | 146 | — | 86.8 |
| **37** Winchester | 83.7 | 78.6 | — | 123 | 98.4 | 86.2 |
| **38** East London | 86.5 | 74.9 | 25.5 | 134 | 88.9 | 86 |
| **39** St George's, London | 70.9 | 59.3 | — | 153 | 97.9 | 85.6 |
| **40** London South Bank | 73.6 | 55.2 | 34.5 | 125 | 79.5 | 79 |

| | | | |
|---|---|---|---|
| Employed in high-skilled job | 87% | Employed in lower-skilled job | 2% |
| Employed in high-skilled job and studying | 4% | Employed in lower-skilled job and studying | 0% |
| Studying | 1% | Unemployed | 3% |
| High-skilled work (median) salary | £26,000 | Low-/medium-skilled salary | N/A |

# Politics

The UK government has been led by four different prime ministers in the same timeframe that St Andrews has led our Politics table. In its sixth year at the top, St Andrews continues to attract the highest average entry standards, of 208 UCAS points, and performs strongly across all other metrics in the table – placing in the top three for graduate outcomes and top 11 for both measures of student satisfaction: teaching quality and the wider experience. There is stability at the upper end of the table more widely, with most of the top 15 featuring in successive annual tables – albeit reshuffled to an extent. Oxford has ousted Warwick from the runner-up spot this year and the London School of Economics (LSE) is up two places in third. Sheffield has gained four places to rank tenth while Exeter is down six to place 15th. Strathclyde, fifth overall, was the top scorer in politics in the Research Excellence Framework 2021, where its results are followed by those of Royal Holloway (11th), Edinburgh (17th) and the LSE.

Northumbria – in 33rd place – is the top-ranked modern university. Another, Salford (in 22nd place overall), has outdone all others for student satisfaction with teaching quality while 20th-place Surrey does best for students' evaluation of the wider experience.

"There is no one way to study politics at university. Whatever you decide to focus on, you'll confront some of the biggest challenges facing contemporary society and develop a set of skills, including critical thought, data analysis and self-expression, that can be applied to a wide range of career paths, such as in journalism, public service or the world of business," says Dr Rod Dacombe, reader in politics, department of political economy, King's College London. The leading universities look for humanities and social sciences A-levels in general – English, economics, sociology and history among them – without demanding any specifically. Dr Rod Dacombe advises that "To get the most out of studying politics you need to find out what it is you really care about. Read about what is going on in the world, form opinions and be prepared to be challenged."

Average starting salaries for politics graduates rank the subject =28th in our pay index of 70 areas. In 43rd place of the employment table it compares less favourably with other subject groupings. When surveyed 15 months after their degrees, 62.4% of graduates were employed in professional-level jobs and/or furthering their studies, but over a fifth were working in jobs classified as "low-skilled". These figures vary widely by institution – from Oxford, the LSE and

St Andrews where more than 90% of graduates achieved the desired career outcomes within 15 months, down to four universities (West of England, Westminster, Canterbury Christ Church and Winchester) where under 60% had reached the same professional goals. Demand for the subject boomed in the decade up to 2019, and after a dip in 2020 applications climbed again – to over 49,300 in 2023 – and 11,175 students were accepted onto courses.

### Politics

| | | Teaching quality % | Student experience % | Research quality % | Entry standards (UCAS points) | Graduate prospects % | Overall score |
|---|---|---|---|---|---|---|---|
| 1 | St Andrews | 88.7 | 85.5 | 47 | 208 | 90 | 100 |
| 2 | Oxford | 83.3 | 70.4 | 61.3 | 205 | 91.9 | 99.2 |
| 3 | London School of Economics | 81.5 | 77.3 | 65.8 | 177 | 91.4 | 98.1 |
| 4 | Warwick | 85.6 | 85.8 | 60.5 | 172 | 82.6 | 96.9 |
| 5 | Strathclyde | 83.7 | 76 | 70.5 | 202 | 75.6 | 96.8 |
| 6 | University College London | 75.3 | 76.8 | 64.5 | 183 | 89.5 | 96.1 |
| 7 | Cambridge | 84.3 | 67.8 | 50.2 | 192 | 85.4 | 95.3 |
| 8 | Glasgow | 82.1 | 77.1 | 50.2 | 203 | 80 | 95 |
| 9 | Durham | 83.3 | 77.1 | 42.5 | 176 | 88.6 | 94.8 |
| 10 | Sheffield | 81.9 | 76.4 | 58 | 154 | 84.6 | 94 |
| 11 | Royal Holloway | 83.9 | 80.2 | 67.2 | 126 | 82.7 | 93.9 |
| 12 | King's College London | 78.8 | 72.8 | 52.2 | 185 | 81.9 | 93.4 |
| 13 | York | 79.6 | 76.6 | 57.5 | 148 | 85.3 | 93.2 |
| 14 | Birmingham | 81.1 | 74.6 | 51.5 | 147 | 87 | 92.9 |
| 15 | Exeter | 79.4 | 75.8 | 57.5 | 158 | 82 | 92.8 |
| 16 | SOAS London | 79.2 | 70.6 | 55.5 | 156 | 84.5 | 92.5 |
| 17 | Edinburgh | 69.8 | 66.1 | 66.5 | 189 | 79.8 | 91.8 |
| 18 | Aston | 84.6 | 83.1 | 49 | 116 | 83.5 | 91.6 |
| 19 | Loughborough | 88.1 | 87.2 | 29.5 | 140 | 81.9 | 91.5 |
| 20 | Surrey | 92.3 | 90.2 | 40.2 | 121 | 75 | 91.4 |
| 21 | Aberdeen | 87 | 83.9 | 23.5 | 180 | 76.6 | 91.3 |
| 22 | Salford | 94.2 | 87.2 | 51.7 | 104 | 71.3 | 91.2 |
| 23 | Stirling | 84.3 | 81.7 | 28.7 | 178 | 77.4 | 91.1 |
| 24 | Lancaster | 82.2 | 77.9 | 49 | 143 | 79.1 | 91 |
| 25 | Swansea | 90.9 | 86.6 | 31.5 | 122 | 80.2 | 90.9 |
| =26 | Bristol | 76.2 | 72.1 | 50.7 | 168 | 79.4 | 90.7 |
| =26 | Nottingham | 81 | 79.3 | 46 | 146 | 79.3 | 90.7 |
| =28 | Aberystwyth | 90.5 | 87.6 | 42.8 | 120 | 73.4 | 90.6 |
| =28 | Reading | 87.3 | 80.2 | 49.2 | 119 | 77 | 90.6 |
| 30 | Bath | 78.6 | 76.9 | 31.8 | 160 | 85.6 | 90.4 |
| 31 | Manchester | 76.9 | 70.3 | 60.5 | 158 | 74.7 | 90.2 |
| 32 | Queen Mary, London | 77.3 | 70.5 | 61.3 | 142 | 76.3 | 89.8 |
| 33 | Northumbria | 83.2 | 81.4 | 42 | 127 | 78.8 | 89.7 |
| 34 | Newcastle | 78.8 | 81.4 | 39.5 | 143 | 78.6 | 89.1 |
| 35 | Cardiff | 79.4 | 77.8 | 49 | 137 | 74.7 | 88.8 |
| 36 | City | 82.7 | 80.7 | 40.8 | 116 | 78.7 | 88.6 |
| 37 | Brunel | 90.8 | 89.9 | 35 | 92 | 74.2 | 88.4 |
| =38 | Sussex | 79.6 | 76.7 | 55.7 | 134 | 70.2 | 88.3 |

| Politics cont. | teaching quality % | Student experience % | Research quality % | Entry standards (UCAS points) | Graduate prospects % | Overall score |
|---|---|---|---|---|---|---|
| =38 Plymouth | 83.8 | 80.5 | 37.9 | 107 | 80.1 | 88.3 |
| 40 Essex | 84.4 | 84.2 | 60.5 | 112 | 64.4 | 88.2 |
| 41 Leicester | 84 | 80.8 | 36.8 | 119 | 76.6 | 88.1 |
| 42 Southampton | 76.7 | 70.7 | 39.8 | 136 | 82.4 | 88 |
| =43 Queen's, Belfast | 76.9 | 71.9 | 40.8 | 142 | 79.2 | 87.9 |
| =43 Liverpool | 81.4 | 76.3 | 39.8 | 132 | 75.7 | 87.9 |
| 45 Portsmouth | 84.3 | 82.3 | 51.7 | 102 | 70.3 | 87.7 |
| 46 East Anglia | 79.2 | 72.6 | 56.2 | 123 | 70.6 | 87.3 |
| 47 Leeds | 73.6 | 73.4 | 35.8 | 154 | 78.8 | 87.2 |
| 48 Bournemouth | 80.6 | 70.5 | 47.2 | 103 | 77.6 | 86.8 |
| 49 Chester | 92.3 | 84.5 | 12.8 | 101 | 77.2* | 86.6 |
| 50 Coventry | 91.1 | 89 | 39.5 | 96 | 63.6 | 86.5 |
| 51 Nottingham Trent | 85.1 | 81.2 | 29.5 | 103 | 75.9 | 86.4 |
| 52 Kent | 82.5 | 78 | 41 | 112 | 69.8 | 85.8 |
| 53 Ulster | 83.9 | 80.4 | 53.8 | 109 | 60.4 | 85.6 |
| 54 Manchester Metropolitan | 86.6 | 79.6 | 29 | 114 | 68.3 | 85.3 |
| =55 Brighton | 85.4 | 60.9 | 44.2 | 95 | 71.7 | 84.8 |
| =55 Leeds Beckett | 89.9 | 86.8 | 15.5 | 93 | 71.9 | 84.8 |
| 57 Lincoln | 82.6 | 74.5 | 34 | 109 | 69.6 | 84.4 |
| 58 Hull | 88.6 | 80.8 | 11.2 | 117 | 69.9 | 84.2 |
| 59 Sheffield Hallam | 89.7 | 75 | — | 102 | 78.9 | 83.8 |
| 60 Westminster | 85.3 | 80.3 | 41.5 | 108 | 57.8 | 83.6 |
| 61 West of England | 85.4 | 83.1 | 35.2 | 108 | 56.9 | 83 |
| =62 West of Scotland | 88 | 78.4 | 13.2 | — | 66.1 | 82.7 |
| =62 Dundee | 80.9 | 71.2 | — | 179 | 65.8 | 82.7 |
| 64 Oxford Brookes | 81 | 76 | 27.5 | 103 | 67.7 | 82.4 |
| =65 Canterbury Christ Church | 93.4 | 85.7 | 13.2 | 89 | 58.3 | 81.7 |
| =65 De Montfort | 88 | 76.2 | — | 97 | 73 | 81.7 |
| 67 Northampton | 79.5 | 71.4 | 1.2 | — | 81.0* | 81.6 |
| 68 Keele | 78.6 | 73.4 | 28 | 110 | 64.8 | 81.3 |
| =69 Greenwich | 81.3 | 76.7 | — | 105 | 71.4 | 80.1 |
| =69 Liverpool Hope | 86.4 | 76.1 | 5.5 | 107 | 63 | 80.1 |
| 71 Goldsmiths, London | 71.4 | 62.8 | 29 | 108 | 67.9 | 79.1 |
| 72 Winchester | 77.3 | 52.7 | 19.8 | 101 | 59.7 | 76 |

| | | | |
|---|---|---|---|
| Employed in high-skilled job | 46% | Employed in lower-skilled job | 22% |
| Employed in high-skilled job and studying | 5% | Employed in lower-skilled job and studying | 1% |
| Studying | 10% | Unemployed | 7% |
| High-skilled work (median) salary | £27,500 | Low-/medium-skilled salary | £20,352 |

# Psychology

The London School of Economics (LSE) is No 1 out of the 115 universities in our Psychology table. It is the third year running that LSE has topped the ranking, where its eminence is secured with the top research rating by a clear margin, based on our analysis of the Research Excellence Framework 2021, as well as rates of student satisfaction which place the LSE third for teaching quality and fourth for the wider experience. St Andrews, in second place overall, is top for graduate prospects and one of only 11 universities where at least 80% of graduates were in high-skilled jobs or postgraduate study 15 months after their degrees. While the older institutions dominate the upper ranks of the main table, Cumbria (in 59th place overall) outdoes all others for students' evaluation of teaching quality, followed by Wales Trinity (32nd). Cumbria also leads for the wider student experience, followed by Bath (fifth overall). Conversely, Northampton gets the lowest ratings for both of these student-led metrics and places 115th overall.

Most undergraduate programmes are accredited by the British Psychological Society, which ensures that key topics are covered, but the clinical and biological content of courses varies considerably. Some courses require maths and/or biology A-levels among three high grade passes, while others are much less demanding. The contrast is evident in the table, with 35 universities averaging at least 144 points in the UCAS tariff (equivalent to three As at A-level) and another 24 falling below 110 points.

Professor Peter Fonagy, head of the Division of Psychology and Language Sciences, UCL explains that "Psychologists ask fundamental questions about consciousness, memory, language and other aspects of people that are not yet fully understood. They address mental health issues that pervade society, from day-to-day wellbeing to treatment of clinical disorders. They use their knowledge of how to change human behaviour to respond to global challenges such as climate change, pandemic disease and artificial intelligence."

The numbers of psychology students accepted onto courses grew by 50% in the decade up to 2018 and have continued their incline more recently. Even after a 3% decline in 2023, psychology still received over 126,000 applications and 26,775 new students were accepted onto courses. Immediate career prospects are unlikely to be what is attracting so many students: psychology ranks 67th in our 70-subject employment table, based on only half of graduates being employed in professional-level jobs and/or studying within 15 months of finishing their degrees. The proportion working in "low-skilled" jobs at this point after graduation (31.9%) is not far below the proportion that had secured full-time professional jobs (34.2%). Explaining this, commentators within psychology suggest that graduates may benefit from a more gradual transition into complex psychological roles, such as those involving direct work with clients and service users, and that experience gained in non-graduate jobs can help to build confidence and serve as stepping stones to putting their university-acquired skills into practice. Average graduate salaries of £23,000 rank the subject =61st out of 70.

| Psychology | Teaching quality % | Student experience % | Research quality % | Entry standards (UCAS points) | Graduate prospects % | Overall score |
|---|---|---|---|---|---|---|
| 1 London School of Economics | 91.3 | 90.9 | 86.2 | 197 | — | 100 |
| 2 St Andrews | 85.2 | 84.8 | 61.8 | 201 | 90.6 | 97 |
| 3 Cambridge | 86.6 | 70.7 | 75 | 188 | 83.3 | 94.3 |
| 4 Oxford | 87.6 | 68.9 | 75.5 | 195 | — | 94 |
| 5 Bath | 85.4 | 91.3 | 37.2 | 185 | 83.4 | 92.8 |
| 6 University College London | 77.3 | 78.9 | 73.2 | 180 | 84.2 | 92.6 |
| 7 Strathclyde | 82.5 | 79.9 | 65.8 | 195 | 76.4 | 92.5 |
| =8 Glasgow | 82.5 | 79.2 | 65.8 | 205 | 73.4 | 92.4 |
| =8 York | 87.2 | 87.3 | 69.2 | 159 | 76.5 | 92.4 |
| 10 King's College London | 82.7 | 81 | 69 | 176 | 79.3 | 92.3 |

| Psychology cont. | Teaching quality % | Student experience % | Research quality % | Entry standards (UCAS points) | Graduate prospects % | Overall score |
|---|---|---|---|---|---|---|
| 11 Loughborough | 82.2 | 86.3 | 66.8 | 157 | 81.1 | 91.7 |
| 12 Warwick | 85.4 | 85.9 | 57.5 | 154 | 79.1 | 90.9 |
| =13 Cardiff | 76.9 | 77.8 | 68.8 | 166 | 80.9 | 90.3 |
| =13 Exeter | 77.9 | 80.2 | 62.7 | 166 | 81.4 | 90.3 |
| 15 Surrey | 88.1 | 90.1 | 58 | 134 | 76.6 | 90.2 |
| 16 Durham | 78.2 | 77.3 | 50 | 172 | 84.4 | 90 |
| 17 Glasgow Caledonian | 85.3 | 83.6 | 61 | 179 | 63.1 | 89 |
| 18 Royal Holloway | 78.5 | 80 | 74 | 143 | 75.1 | 88.5 |
| 19 Sheffield | 81.9 | 84.6 | 62.7 | 144 | 70.8 | 87.9 |
| 20 Birmingham | 76.3 | 76 | 64 | 151 | 77.7 | 87.8 |
| 21 Newcastle | 78.7 | 77.7 | 55.2 | 154 | 76.5 | 87.7 |
| 22 Reading | 79 | 81.2 | 56.2 | 131 | 79.6 | 87.3 |
| =23 Bristol | 74.7 | 74.3 | 57.8 | 167 | 74.9 | 87.1 |
| =23 Edinburgh | 67.5 | 70.6 | 76.8 | 194 | 68.4 | 87.1 |
| 25 Aberdeen | 83.5 | 82.8 | 49 | 171 | 61.7 | 86.6 |
| =26 Lancaster | 78.6 | 78.9 | 48.8 | 150 | 74.2 | 86.4 |
| =26 Chichester | 90.7 | 87.2 | 8 | 114 | 84.9 | 86.4 |
| 28 Manchester | 74.5 | 75.9 | 62.7 | 157 | 71.9 | 86.3 |
| 29 Aston | 84.8 | 86.2 | 46 | 124 | 72.2 | 86.2 |
| =30 East Anglia | 76 | 79.7 | 60.8 | 134 | 75.1 | 86.1 |
| =30 Nottingham | 76.1 | 78.4 | 52.2 | 153 | 73.7 | 86.1 |
| 32 Wales Trinity St David | 93.5 | 88.3 | 1.2 | 128 | 77.5 | 85.9 |
| =33 Queen's, Belfast | 83.6 | 83.7 | 31 | 155 | 69.6 | 85.8 |
| =33 Leeds | 77.5 | 76.3 | 53.2 | 157 | 70 | 85.8 |
| 35 Liverpool | 74.5 | 77.5 | 65.5 | 141 | 71.3 | 85.5 |
| 36 Southampton | 77.3 | 80.2 | 60.5 | 147 | 66.6 | 85.4 |
| 37 Leicester | 80.6 | 86 | 55 | 125 | 68.7 | 85.3 |
| =38 Stirling | 78.5 | 77 | 47.2 | 166 | 65.6 | 85.1 |
| =38 Heriot-Watt | 75.8 | 78.7 | 13.5 | 162 | 81.8 | 85.1 |
| 40 Ulster | 83.1 | 82.6 | 41.8 | 126 | 71.1 | 84.9 |
| =41 Portsmouth | 86.4 | 85.6 | 40.8 | 121 | 68.1 | 84.8 |
| =41 Suffolk | 90.2 | 87.7 | — | 105 | 84 | 84.8 |
| =41 Sussex | 77.2 | 77.9 | 59.5 | 139 | 68.2 | 84.8 |
| =41 Edinburgh Napier | 84.5 | 83.5 | — | 165 | 74 | 84.8 |
| =41 Bangor | 82.9 | 80.4 | 47 | 121 | 71.5 | 84.8 |
| 46 Staffordshire | 90.2 | 84.1 | 30.8 | 111 | 70.7 | 84.5 |
| 47 Dundee | 80 | 77 | 39 | 173 | 61.7 | 84.3 |
| =48 City | 82.7 | 86.6 | 36 | 137 | 65.4 | 84.2 |
| =48 Northumbria | 83.1 | 83.5 | 28 | 139 | 69.3 | 84.2 |
| 50 Lincoln | 81 | 81 | 39.5 | 125 | 71.9 | 84.1 |
| 51 Abertay | 92.8 | 89.5 | 21 | 144 | 56.4 | 83.9 |
| 52 Essex | 79.9 | 80.6 | 56 | 117 | 67.4 | 83.8 |
| 53 Kent | 71.8 | 72.6 | 50.7 | 138 | 73.6 | 83.3 |
| =54 Manchester Metropolitan | 83.9 | 83 | 36 | 125 | 63.8 | 82.9 |

| | | | | | | | |
|---|---|---|---|---|---|---|---|
| =54 | Nottingham Trent | 81.7 | 81.2 | 39.2 | 120 | 67.2 | 82.9 |
| =54 | Hull | 82.6 | 79.8 | 40.5 | 119 | 66.8 | 82.9 |
| =57 | Oxford Brookes | 82 | 81.7 | 39 | 115 | 68.1 | 82.8 |
| =57 | Swansea | 77.7 | 77.5 | 30 | 131 | 73 | 82.8 |
| 59 | Cumbria | 96.2 | 93.5 | — | 118 | 61.9 | 82.7 |
| 60 | Sunderland | 85.6 | 74.5 | 30.2 | 112 | 71.4 | 82.6 |
| 61 | Teesside | 88.8 | 87.3 | 7.2 | 107 | 70.7 | 82.2 |
| 62 | Plymouth | 77.4 | 76.4 | 40.5 | 125 | 68.5 | 82.1 |
| =63 | Bolton | 89.4 | 83.4 | 1.8 | 116 | 69.9 | 81.9 |
| =63 | Liverpool John Moores | 84.2 | 83.6 | 16.2 | 138 | 63.2 | 81.9 |
| 65 | Coventry | 80.9 | 79.1 | 47 | 113 | 63.4 | 81.8 |
| 66 | Edge Hill | 79.2 | 81.5 | 18.8 | 130 | 69.3 | 81.6 |
| 67 | South Wales | 88.1 | 86.6 | — | 114 | 69 | 81.4 |
| =68 | West of England | 78.8 | 76.8 | 35.2 | 124 | 66 | 81.3 |
| =68 | Canterbury Christ Church | 85.3 | 88.3 | 24 | 103 | 64.1 | 81.3 |
| 70 | Central Lancashire | 78.4 | 78.3 | 30 | 120 | 68.3 | 81.2 |
| 71 | Derby | 87.8 | 88.3 | 10.2 | 115 | 62.8 | 81.1 |
| 72 | Keele | 75.4 | 78.7 | 35.2 | 115 | 69.6 | 81 |
| 73 | Aberystwyth | 85.7 | 85 | 12.5 | 120 | 63.3 | 80.9 |
| 74 | Newman | 90 | 89 | 3.5 | 96 | 66.6 | 80.7 |
| 75 | St Mary's, Twickenham | 85.5 | 85.4 | — | 107 | 70.4 | 80.5 |
| 76 | Huddersfield | 85 | 82.9 | 22 | 117 | 60.1 | 80.4 |
| =77 | York St John | 83 | 81.2 | 20.5 | 114 | 63.6 | 80.3 |
| =77 | Bournemouth | 76.5 | 81.2 | 22.8 | 109 | 71 | 80.3 |
| =79 | Wolverhampton | 90.4 | 86.3 | 12.5 | 99 | 58.8 | 79.7 |
| =79 | Birmingham City | 82.6 | 82.3 | 18.2 | 115 | 61.6 | 79.7 |
| =81 | Gloucestershire | 81.8 | 80.5 | 5 | 117 | 67 | 79.5 |
| =81 | Anglia Ruskin | 80.7 | 78.2 | 25 | 101 | 66.2 | 79.5 |
| =81 | Liverpool Hope | 79.9 | 77.2 | 32 | 112 | 61.3 | 79.5 |
| =84 | East London | 80.4 | 76.3 | 23.2 | 103 | 67.1 | 79.4 |
| =84 | Leeds Beckett | 84.3 | 84 | 21.5 | 105 | 59.2 | 79.4 |
| =86 | West London | 86.7 | 83.9 | — | 111 | 63.5 | 79.3 |
| =86 | Middlesex | 79.7 | 80.6 | 30.2 | 104 | 62.1 | 79.3 |
| 88 | Worcester | 78.7 | 79.3 | 19.2 | 112 | 64.9 | 79.1 |
| =89 | Hertfordshire | 80.2 | 79.3 | 39.8 | 102 | 57.9 | 79 |
| =89 | Queen Margaret, Edinburgh | 75.6 | 70.6 | 21 | 158 | 57.5 | 79 |
| 91 | Chester | 81.6 | 80.5 | 13 | 120 | 60.8 | 78.9 |
| =92 | Greenwich | 73.7 | 75.4 | 32.3 | 115 | 64.4 | 78.8 |
| =92 | Sheffield Hallam | 78.5 | 76.9 | 26.8 | 111 | 62.2 | 78.8 |
| 94 | Westminster | 79.4 | 80.5 | 24.8 | 110 | 60.1 | 78.7 |
| 95 | Leeds Trinity | 79.9 | 78.7 | 9.2 | 106 | 67.4 | 78.5 |
| 96 | Queen Mary, London | 76.7 | 79.3 | — | 145 | 61.8 | 78.4 |
| =97 | Salford | 78 | 79.1 | 37 | 117 | 53.7 | 78.3 |
| =97 | London South Bank | 80.2 | 74.5 | 18 | 105 | 65 | 78.3 |
| 99 | London Metropolitan | 87.3 | 86.7 | — | 90 | 62.5 | 78.1 |
| 100 | Winchester | 80.8 | 81.8 | 16.2 | 110 | 57.7 | 77.8 |
| =101 | Brunel | 75.3 | 76.7 | 23.2 | 109 | 61.8 | 77.5 |
| =101 | Bradford | 77.8 | 78.6 | 8.2 | 114 | 63 | 77.5 |

**Psychology** cont.

| | | Teaching quality % | Student experience % | Research quality % | Entry standards (UCAS points) | Graduate prospects % | Overall score |
|---|---|---|---|---|---|---|---|
| 103 | Roehampton | 78.5 | 73.3 | 37.5 | 101 | 56.7 | 77.4 |
| 104 | Goldsmiths, London | 70.7 | 65.1 | 35.5 | 117 | 64.2 | 77.3 |
| 105 | Bedfordshire | 81.1 | 77.7 | — | 103 | 63.8 | 76.8 |
| 106 | West of Scotland | 81.9 | 76.1 | 13.2 | 131 | 49.5 | 76.7 |
| 107 | Brighton | 73.5 | 68.8 | 34 | 110 | 57.8 | 76.3 |
| 108 | Cardiff Metropolitan | 79.7 | 82.1 | — | 120 | 53.7 | 75.9 |
| 109 | Bath Spa | 74 | 69.4 | 7.2 | 103 | 67.6 | 75.8 |
| =110 | Solent, Southampton | 81.7 | 77.5 | — | 111 | 55 | 75.5 |
| =110 | De Montfort | 73.7 | 73.9 | 20.5 | 102 | 59.2 | 75.5 |
| 112 | Kingston | 74.5 | 74.4 | 20.5 | 103 | 57.1 | 75.3 |
| 113 | Buckinghamshire New | 91.2 | 87 | — | 89 | 42.4* | 74.4 |
| 114 | Bishop Grosseteste | 74.3 | 66.4 | 6.2 | 103 | 60 | 73.7 |
| 115 | Northampton | 64.3 | 64.9 | 8.5 | 108 | 51.4 | 69.8 |

| | | | |
|---|---|---|---|
| Employed in high-skilled job | 34% | Employed in lower-skilled job | 32% |
| Employed in high-skilled job and studying | 5% | Employed in lower-skilled job and studying | 2% |
| Studying | 9% | Unemployed | 5% |
| High-skilled work (median) salary | £24,800 | Low-/medium-skilled salary | £20,000 |

# Radiography

"There are two radiography disciplines – diagnostic and therapeutic," explains Dr Jane Harvey-Lloyd, associate professor in diagnostic radiography, School of Medicine, University of Leeds. "Diagnostics uses a range of imaging modalities to diagnose illness and disease. Therapeutics uses methods like ionising radiation to treat mainly cancer. New technology is continuously emerging, providing new ways to diagnose and treat illness and disease. If you are considering a dynamic career that combines cutting-edge technology with caring for others, radiography is for you."

Diagnostic courses usually involve two years of studying anatomy, physiology and physics, followed by further training in oncology, psycho-social studies and other modules. Candidates need at least one science A-level, or equivalent, usually biology. Graduates of radiography can rest assured that professional-level work is on the horizon soon after university, with radiography invariably featuring in the top 10 of our employment ranking – where it is up four places to rank fourth this year. Exeter, Leeds, Robert Gordon, Canterbury Christ Church, Teesside and Derby achieved perfect 100% graduate prospects scores, due to every one of their radiography graduates being employed in professional jobs and/or postgraduate study within 15 months. Only one university, St George's, London (now City St George's), had fewer than nine in ten graduates achieving the desired career outcomes at the same point of survey, and it still tallied a respectable 84% rate. For pay, radiography compares less strongly with other subjects, but is comfortably in the upper half of our 70-subject salaries index.

For the third consecutive year, Glasgow Caledonian leads our dedicated ranking for radiography degrees, now in its 12th edition having previously been listed among "Subjects Allied to Medicine" in the *Guide*. It does best in both measures derived from the National Student Survey (NSS): teaching quality and the wider undergraduate experience and its radiography entrants average the highest entry standards. Former winner Leeds takes fourth place this year, while Queen Margaret, Edinburgh is runner-up for the second year in a row. Strength in research is unbeaten at Keele (=14th overall) which achieved the top scores in the recent Research Excellence Framework 2021, followed by Leeds. Our National Student Survey analysis shows the two universities of St George's, London and City – which have since merged to form City St George's University – to share second and third place for teaching quality and the wider experience. Conversely, Plymouth comes bottom for the student experience and Keele is at the foot of the table for teaching quality.

| Radiography | Teaching quality % | Student experience % | Research quality % | Entry standards (UCAS points) | Graduate prospects % | Overall score |
|---|---|---|---|---|---|---|
| 1 Glasgow Caledonian | 90.4 | 88.9 | 61 | 186 | 95.9 | 100 |
| 2 Queen Margaret, Edinburgh | 87.5 | 83.2 | 36.5 | 172 | — | 96.2 |
| 3 Exeter | 85.3 | 80.1 | 53.2 | 138 | 100 | 94.8 |
| 4 Leeds | 67.9 | 61.2 | 65 | 152 | 100 | 93.9 |
| 5 Liverpool | 84.2 | 80.8 | 46.8 | 137 | 98.5 | 93.2 |
| 6 Ulster | 82.1 | 74.1 | 53.5 | 145 | 96.1 | 93 |
| 7 Cardiff | 70.6 | 60.6 | 58.8 | 149 | 96.7 | 91.8 |
| 8 Bradford | 84.1 | 74.7 | 33.8 | 147 | 97 | 91.5 |
| 9 Robert Gordon | 71 | 66.7 | 24.5 | 170 | 100 | 91.3 |
| 10 City | 88.2 | 85.4 | 58 | 125 | 91.3 | 91.2 |
| 11 Portsmouth | 86.8 | 82.3 | 41.2 | 126 | 95.5 | 90.5 |
| 12 Canterbury Christ Church | 84.9 | 77.4 | 31.8 | 121 | 100 | 90.2 |
| 13 Salford | 75.9 | 75.4 | 37 | 149 | 95.2 | 90.1 |
| =14 Hertfordshire | 86.5 | 84.4 | 48 | 114 | 94.8 | 90 |
| =14 Keele | 66.2 | 58.8 | 66.2 | 134 | — | 90 |
| 16 Birmingham City | 79 | 74.9 | 37.8 | 142 | 94.6 | 89.7 |
| 17 Cumbria | 86.7 | 82.3 | 18.5 | 133 | 98.2 | 89.5 |
| 18 Teesside | 77.5 | 73.3 | 35 | 122 | 100 | 89.3 |
| =19 London South Bank | 85.1 | 79.1 | 34.5 | 140 | 90.9 | 88.7 |
| =19 West of England | 77.4 | 69.5 | 42.8 | 128 | 95.3 | 88.7 |
| 21 Derby | 73 | 69.5 | 24 | 138 | 100 | 88.6 |
| 22 Sheffield Hallam | 73.6 | 70.3 | 29.8 | 140 | 90.7 | 85.7 |
| 23 Suffolk | 86.5 | 85.2 | — | 114 | 98.6 | 85.6 |
| 24 Plymouth | 71 | 48.2 | 39.5 | 130 | — | 85.1 |
| 25 St George's, London | 88.2 | 86.3 | — | 130 | 83.9 | 81.3 |

| | | | | |
|---|---|---|---|---|
| Employed in high-skilled job | 88% | Employed in lower-skilled job | | 3% |
| Employed in high-skilled job and studying | 3% | Employed in lower-skilled job and studying | | 0% |
| Studying | 2% | Unemployed | | 2% |
| High-skilled work (median) salary | £26,404 | Low-/medium-skilled salary | | N/A |

# Russian and Eastern European Languages

Dr Ruth Coates, associate professor in Russian religious thought, Department of Russian, University of Bristol says "Russia's devastating war against Ukraine has shown the extent of its will to strengthen its geopolitical position in the world. In this context, specialists familiar with Russia's language, politics, history and culture, who are able to provide context and interpret its actions, are more needed than ever. Studying Russian opens up a world of amazing cultural diversity with a dramatic past."

Unusually among our subject rankings, there are no post-1992 universities in the Russian and Eastern European Languages table, which is populated exclusively by institutions with older foundations. The subjects attract tiny student cohorts on single honours programmes, though many others learn Russian as part of a broader modern languages degree. Now grouped by UCAS as "Slavic studies", the languages attracted just 570 applications in 2023 (down from 605 in 2022) and 155 new students were accepted onto courses (five fewer than the year before). For 2025-26, only 12 providers are offering programmes in Russian, some as part of broader modern language degrees, and five providers are listing 14 courses that include Eastern European studies. Most undergraduates learn Russian or another Eastern European language from scratch, and while there are no required subjects for entry to degrees, a language is useful.

Cambridge returns to the top of the Russian and Eastern European Languages table this year, where it enjoyed an eight-year run until Bristol took No 1 for the past two editions. Cambridge's rank is buoyed by the highest rates of student satisfaction with teaching quality and the top graduate prospects. Bristol's research in the field remains unsurpassed however, our analysis of the Research Excellence Framework 2021 shows, while Nottingham is not far behind it on this measure, and Cambridge ranks third.

Despite the small numbers, entry standards are high throughout the table, and in a tightly packed grouping they go no lower than 134 points at Queen Mary, London. The highest, of 192 UCAS points, are claimed by third-place Oxford. Russian and Eastern European languages have fallen from the midpoint to 50th of our 70-subject employment ranking, based on six in ten graduates being in high-skilled jobs and/or further study within 15 months. They rank higher in the pay index, at =28th.

| Russian and Eastern European Languages | Teaching quality % | Student experience % | Research quality % | Entry standards (UCAS points) | Graduate prospects % | Overall score |
|---|---|---|---|---|---|---|
| 1 Cambridge | 92.2 | 73.7 | 61 | 190 | 91.5 | 100 |
| 2 Bristol | 89.1 | 77.8 | 64 | 164 | — | 97 |
| 3 Oxford | 85.5 | 66.4 | 51.2 | 192 | — | 95.4 |
| 4 University College London | 83 | 80.7 | 56 | 165 | 91.3 | 94 |
| 5 Durham | 85.9 | 71.8 | 46 | 181 | 85.6 | 92.4 |
| 6 Manchester | 80.5 | 74.8 | 59.5 | 154 | — | 91.1 |
| 7 Exeter | 83.7 | 78.1 | 50 | 149 | 82.8 | 88.8 |
| 8 Birmingham | 78.9 | 74.5 | 54.8 | 149 | — | 87.9 |
| 9 Queen Mary, London | 80.9 | 71.5 | 51.1 | 134 | — | 83.6 |
| 10 Edinburgh | 57.3 | 53.4 | 45.8 | 175 | — | 82.3 |
| 11 Glasgow | 79.4 | 74.5 | 25.5 | 187 | 42.1 | 81.1 |
| 12 Leeds | 55.2 | 51.1 | 52 | 157 | — | 80.4 |

| | | | |
|---|---|---|---|
| Employed in high-skilled job | 42% | Employed in lower-skilled job | 29% |
| Employed in high-skilled job and studying | 8% | Employed in lower-skilled job and studying | 2% |
| Studying | 9% | Unemployed | 3% |
| High-skilled work (median) salary | £26,500 | Low-/medium-skilled salary | N/A |

# Social Policy

The London School of Economics (LSE) occupies its accustomed place at the top of our Social Policy table this year, its rank helped by an established research strength in the field: LSE leads in our analysis of the Research Excellence Framework (REF) 2021, just as it did in the previous REF 2014 exercise. LSE is also in front for graduate prospects, with the latest data showing 88.2% working in high-skilled jobs and/or further study within 15 months. Bath, which toppled LSE from the No 1 spot two years ago and ranked third last year, has slipped to 17th place. It is held back by lower rates of student satisfaction in our new National Student Survey analysis, in which Swansea (fourth overall) ranks top for the student experience and second for teaching quality – outdone by Staffordshire, in fifth place of the table and the top-ranked modern university. The highest entry standards are at Glasgow, the only university to average more than 200 UCAS tariff points. Eleven universities averaged upwards of 144 UCAS points (equivalent to three As at A-level) and there are usually no required subjects for entry.

Social policy students analyse how societies respond to the challenges of social, demographic and economic change. "How effectively do societies ensure that everyone has what they need to lead a good life? How could we do better?" asks Kitty Stewart, professor of social policy, LSE. "Education, health, housing, employment, poverty and inequality are all core subjects for social policy students. We also think about the new challenges posed by migration, an ageing population and the climate crisis."

Many undergraduates take joint honours degrees – such as pairings with politics or modern languages – or within wider social sciences programmes. Having remained steady for around a decade or so, demand for the subject has dipped, and in 2023 it attracted 6,120 applications and 1,135 undergraduates were accepted onto courses – the lowest numbers in four years.

Not all social policy graduates progress immediately into top careers, however, and the subject overall ranks only 64th in our employment table – down five places this year. When surveyed 15 months after their degrees more than a third of social policy graduates were working full-time in jobs classified as "low-skilled" and only marginally more (40.1%) were employed in full-time professional-level jobs. The trend is reflected in our table, where at three universities (Northampton, Bedfordshire and West of Scotland) only a little over half of the graduates had found professional work or continued studying 15 months after their degrees. At one, Ulster, this proportion falls to 41.6%. Earnings compare better with other subjects, ranking =53rd in our pay index.

| Social Policy | Teaching quality % | Student experience % | Research quality % | Entry standards (UCAS points) | Graduate prospects % | Overall score |
|---|---|---|---|---|---|---|
| 1 London School of Economics | 83.5 | 81.3 | 86.2 | 165 | 85.2 | 100 |
| 2 Glasgow | 78.5 | 71.9 | 62 | 206 | 71.7 | 95.1 |
| 3 Strathclyde | 85.2 | 81.9 | 43.8 | 199 | 69.1 | 93.9 |
| 4 Swansea | 91.8 | 91.3 | 46.5 | 131 | — | 91.6 |
| =5 Kent | 86.3 | 83.9 | 72.2 | 108 | — | 91 |
| =5 Staffordshire | 92.6 | 85.8 | 18.2 | — | 84.9 | 91 |
| 7 Nottingham | 87 | 86.1 | 54 | 131 | — | 90.7 |
| 8 Bristol | 75.4 | 77.3 | 77.8 | 145 | 66 | 90.6 |
| 9 University College London | 78.7 | 72.6 | 61.5 | 156 | — | 90.5 |
| 10 Edinburgh | 72 | 70.1 | 55.2 | 180 | — | 89.7 |
| 11 Queen's, Belfast | 79.9 | 77.3 | 56.5 | 146 | — | 89.5 |

| | Teaching quality % | Student experience % | Research quality % | Entry standards (UCAS points) | Graduate prospects % | Overall score |
|---|---|---|---|---|---|---|
| 12 Leeds | 79.2 | 79.1 | 48.5 | 151 | 72.5 | 89.3 |
| 13 Birmingham | 75.8 | 71.3 | 61 | 144 | 73.1 | 89 |
| 14 York | 75 | 69.3 | 58 | 134 | 77.9 | 88.2 |
| 15 Nottingham Trent | 91.5 | 86.5 | 29.5 | 136 | – | 88 |
| 16 Sheffield | 86.4 | 81.4 | 36.8 | 135 | 69.9 | 87.6 |
| 17 Bath | 69.8 | 70.3 | 59.5 | 157 | – | 87.1 |
| 18 Salford | 89.5 | 88.1 | 44.5 | 109 | 65.3 | 86.9 |
| 19 Stirling | 73.8 | 72.1 | 47.5 | 161 | – | 86.7 |
| =20 Cardiff | 79.6 | 75.1 | 54 | 124 | – | 86 |
| =20 Plymouth | 79.7 | 76.7 | 50.5 | 119 | 69.7 | 86 |
| 22 Wales Trinity St David | 87.1 | 77.3 | 11.8 | – | 75 | 84 |
| 23 Aston | 77.9 | 77.5 | 42.5 | 121 | – | 83.1 |
| 24 Liverpool | 69.2 | 71.2 | 55 | 127 | – | 82.6 |
| 25 Lincoln | 76.9 | 75.3 | 51 | 107 | – | 82.5 |
| 26 Bedfordshire | 83.8 | 78.2 | 50.2 | 102 | 51.6 | 81.9 |
| 27 Hertfordshire | 78.4 | 76.2 | 48 | 99 | – | 81.6 |
| 28 Bangor | 84 | 73.4 | 33.2 | 138 | 48.0* | 81.4 |
| 29 Central Lancashire | 69.5 | 69.1 | 51.5 | 117 | – | 80.6 |
| 30 Edge Hill | 80.4 | 77.1 | 17.5 | 126 | – | 79.7 |
| 31 West of Scotland | 87.6 | 73.8 | 13.2 | 134 | 50 | 79.4 |
| =32 South Wales | 75.8 | 67.5 | 33.5 | 107 | 59.1* | 78.4 |
| =32 East London | 80.8 | 80.1 | 40 | 74 | – | 78.4 |
| 34 De Montfort | 67 | 54.2 | 43.2 | 111 | 67.4 | 78.3 |
| 35 Northampton | 84.5 | 78.9 | – | 111 | 52.9 | 75.8 |
| 36 Wolverhampton | 83.3 | 74.9 | 12.2 | 92 | 54.0* | 75.5 |
| 37 Ulster | 63.3 | 56.4 | 53.8 | 112 | 41.6 | 73.9 |

| | | | |
|---|---|---|---|
| Employed in high-skilled job | 40% | Employed in lower-skilled job | 33% |
| Employed in high-skilled job and studying | 4% | Employed in lower-skilled job and studying | 1% |
| Studying | 7% | Unemployed | 5% |
| High-skilled work (median) salary | £25,000 | Low-/medium-skilled salary | £21,000 |

# Social Work

In a table often characterised by universities rising and falling in the rankings, Lancaster takes over at the top, swapping places with the university that has been No 1 for the past two years, Edinburgh, now in third place. Lancaster performs strongly across the board – it has the third-highest entry standards, rates of student satisfaction which put it fifth for teaching quality and 11th for the wider experience, and places in the top five for research. Bristol, in tenth place in the table, was the top scorer in the field in the Research Excellence Framework 2021, followed by Kent (this year's runner-up overall) and then East Anglia (14th). Teesside outdoes all 74 other universities in the Social Work table for the warm reviews by its social work students, placing top for teaching quality and for the broad undergraduate experience in our latest National Student Survey analysis. At the opposite end of the scale, West of England (in =51st) fares worst for both teaching quality and the broader experience.

Led by Glasgow Caledonian, which registered 97.7% of graduates in professional-level jobs and/or furthering their studies within 15 months, 18 universities had over 90% of graduates achieving these looked-for career outcomes. The Frontline programme, modelled on Teach First, aims to attract graduates of other subjects to train in the profession, and degree apprenticeships offer another social work route (though these are not profiled here), but social work degrees are still the main pathway to careers. Even so, applications declined by around 19% in 2023 and the numbers accepted onto courses decreased by 16%.

It comes as a surprise to some that graduate salaries for those with a social work degree compare very favourably with other subject areas. Average early career salaries of £29,885 rank social work 13th in our 70-subject pay index. It is comfortably in the upper half of the graduate table too, in 30th place. Added to the relative job security is a sense of purpose, as explained by Professor Anne Campbell, programme director of the master's in substance use and substance use disorders, School of Social Sciences, Education and Social Work, Queen's University, Belfast: "A career in social work will make a positive difference in the lives of children, young people, adults and older people. You will promote social justice in health and social care settings, and in education, criminal justice and the voluntary sector. You will be supported in practice and with continuous personal and professional development opportunities throughout your career."

| Social Work | Teaching quality % | Student experience % | Research quality % | Entry standards (UCAS points) | Graduate prospects % | Overall score |
|---|---|---|---|---|---|---|
| 1 Lancaster | 89.5 | 87.7 | 60.2 | 153 | 86.2 | 100 |
| 2 Kent | 87.2 | 76.6 | 72.2 | 134 | 97.1 | 99.5 |
| 3 Edinburgh | 78.5 | 70 | 55.2 | 171 | — | 99.4 |
| 4 Nottingham | 92.1 | 87.5 | 54 | 140 | 91.4 | 99 |
| 5 Strathclyde | 81.4 | 75 | 43.8 | 179 | 84.1 | 98.4 |
| 6 Queen's, Belfast | 83.8 | 79.2 | 56.5 | 144 | 94.8 | 98 |
| 7 Hertfordshire | 92.2 | 89.2 | 48 | 138 | 88.6 | 97.6 |
| =8 Bath | 84.2 | 81.1 | 59.5 | 140 | 92.1 | 97.5 |
| =8 Glasgow Caledonian | 89.4 | 82 | 26 | 152 | 97.7 | 97.5 |
| 10 Bristol | 81.4 | 85.1 | 77.8 | 139 | 80.8 | 97 |
| 11 Hull | 93.1 | 88.7 | 53.8 | 140 | 79.5 | 96.8 |
| 12 Essex | 88.7 | 83 | 62.5 | 118 | 95.6 | 96.5 |
| 13 Salford | 85.9 | 78.8 | 44.5 | 141 | 95.1 | 96.4 |
| 14 East Anglia | 72.6 | 68.2 | 69.8 | 134 | 95.8 | 94.9 |
| 15 Manchester Metropolitan | 92.2 | 89.3 | 32.8 | 142 | 81.9 | 94.8 |
| 16 Dundee | 87.8 | 80.3 | 28.5 | 137 | 94.3 | 94.3 |
| 17 Plymouth | 82.7 | 78.8 | 50.5 | 134 | 85.7 | 93.6 |
| 18 Central Lancashire | 85 | 78 | 51.5 | 131 | 83.5 | 93.2 |
| 19 Middlesex | 91 | 87.2 | 27.8 | 123 | 92.8 | 93.1 |
| 20 Ulster | 87.8 | 84.1 | 53.8 | 123 | 80.3 | 92.9 |
| 21 Sussex | 84.4 | 77.7 | 41 | 137 | 83.3 | 92.5 |
| =22 Robert Gordon | 91.5 | 85.6 | — | 141 | 93.1 | 92.3 |
| =22 Teesside | 93.9 | 90.8 | 18.2 | 124 | 89.1 | 92.3 |
| =24 Portsmouth | 87.2 | 81.2 | 33 | 128 | 88.3 | 92.2 |
| =24 Northumbria | 82.1 | 77.2 | 42 | 150 | 74.3 | 92.2 |

## Social Work cont.

| | Teaching quality % | Student experience % | Research quality % | Entry standards (UCAS points) | Graduate prospects % | Overall score |
|---|---|---|---|---|---|---|
| =26 Bournemouth | 87.5 | 84.8 | 10.2 | 140 | 91.4 | 92.1 |
| =26 Huddersfield | 86 | 84.3 | 43.5 | 135 | 76.6 | 92.1 |
| =28 Lincoln | 88.5 | 76.8 | 51 | 128 | 76.9 | 92 |
| =28 Bangor | 86.3 | 77 | 59.8 | 113 | — | 92 |
| 30 Brighton | 87.6 | 81.7 | 34 | 116 | 92 | 91.5 |
| 31 Keele | 86.9 | 80.8 | 33.2 | 125 | 87 | 91.4 |
| 32 Swansea | 85.8 | 84 | 46.5 | 127 | 75.6 | 91.1 |
| 33 Anglia Ruskin | 85 | 75.9 | 30 | 122 | 93.4 | 91 |
| =34 West of Scotland | 88.6 | 80.3 | 13.2 | 140 | 83.5 | 90.7 |
| =34 Kingston | 92.3 | 84.5 | 38.5 | 116 | 79.4 | 90.7 |
| 36 York | 69.1 | 61.8 | 58 | 138 | — | 89.5 |
| 37 Chester | 88.4 | 80.6 | 12.8 | 128 | 85 | 89.2 |
| 38 Greenwich | 82 | 74.4 | 17 | 146 | 78.4 | 89 |
| 39 Gloucestershire | 81.8 | 70.5 | 16.2 | 122 | 97.2 | 88.9 |
| =40 De Montfort | 83.7 | 77 | 43.2 | 109 | 83.2 | 88.4 |
| =40 Wrexham | 89.1 | 78 | 20.5 | — | 79.3 | 88.4 |
| =40 Suffolk | 82.8 | 65.2 | 21.8 | — | 91.1 | 88.4 |
| 43 South Wales | 83.8 | 76.1 | 33.5 | 116 | 84 | 88.3 |
| 44 Worcester | 88.7 | 81.7 | 12.8 | 128 | — | 88.2 |
| 45 Liverpool Hope | 80.5 | 76.7 | 21.2 | 126 | 85.3 | 87.9 |
| =46 Nottingham Trent | 87.6 | 83.3 | 29.5 | 117 | 75.5 | 87.8 |
| =46 Solent, Southampton | 86.6 | 74.6 | 9.5 | 117 | 93.2 | 87.8 |
| =48 Birmingham City | 84.2 | 79.9 | 25.8 | 120 | 80.3 | 87.6 |
| =48 Coventry | 88.7 | 84.7 | — | 130 | 81.4 | 87.6 |
| 50 Sunderland | 90.1 | 82.7 | 39.5 | 122 | 58.7 | 86.7 |
| =51 Staffordshire | 82.3 | 78.3 | 18.2 | 123 | 80.4 | 86.6 |
| =51 West of England | 59.2 | 52.1 | 35.2 | 138 | 96.4 | 86.6 |
| 53 East London | 80 | 65.7 | 40 | 113 | 81.2 | 86.3 |
| =54 Sheffield Hallam | 69.3 | 62 | 26.2 | 142 | 81.6 | 86.2 |
| =54 Edge Hill | 78.7 | 75.8 | 17.5 | 135 | 75.4 | 86.2 |
| 56 London South Bank | 76.6 | 64.6 | 27.8 | 120 | 86.7 | 86 |
| 57 Oxford Brookes | 76.7 | 64.6 | 37.8 | 113 | 80.6 | 85.2 |
| 58 Chichester | 88.8 | 75.3 | 3 | 110 | 83.7 | 84.6 |
| 59 Goldsmiths, London | 67.1 | 52.1 | 48 | 111 | 88.9 | 84.4 |
| 60 Leeds Beckett | 83.4 | 81.7 | 17.8 | 112 | 73.8 | 84.1 |
| 61 Cardiff Metropolitan | 81 | 73 | — | 124 | 82.2 | 84 |
| 62 Bedfordshire | 85.4 | 76.9 | 50.2 | 111 | 52.7 | 83.8 |
| 63 Canterbury Christ Church | 85.8 | 76.8 | 31.8 | 102 | 69.6 | 83.6 |
| 64 Derby | 82 | 71.6 | 25.5 | 121 | 64.8 | 83.3 |
| 65 Winchester | 85.1 | 72.2 | 16.5 | 114 | 70.1 | 82.9 |
| 66 West London | 72.8 | 60.5 | 39 | 109 | 73.3 | 81.9 |
| 67 Liverpool John Moores | 88.5 | 84.5 | 15.8 | — | 56.0* | 81.8 |
| 68 Buckinghamshire New | 91.9 | 79.4 | 12.5 | 101 | 63.7 | 81.5 |
| 69 Leeds Trinity | 83.5 | 78.8 | — | 109 | 70.7 | 80.5 |

| | | | | | | | |
|---|---|---|---|---|---|---|---|
| **70** | Newman | 87 | 86 | 13.8 | 109 | 52.5 | 80 |
| **71** | Northampton | 81.1 | 78.6 | — | 112 | 68.5 | 79.9 |
| **72** | London Metropolitan | 83.7 | 75.6 | — | 113 | 65.6 | 79.8 |
| **73** | Wolverhampton | 77.5 | 70.9 | 12.2 | 107 | 69.1 | 79.3 |
| **74** | Cumbria | 68.7 | 58.3 | 8.2 | 111 | — | 75.2 |

| | | | |
|---|---|---|---|
| Employed in high-skilled job | 61% | Employed in lower-skilled job | 19% |
| Employed in high-skilled job and studying | 4% | Employed in lower-skilled job and studying | 1% |
| Studying | 4% | Unemployed | 4% |
| High-skilled work (median) salary | £30,007 | Low-/medium-skilled salary | £20,838 |

# Sociology

The most applied-to subject within the social sciences grouping, sociology attracted over 80,000 applications in 2023 and more than 15,700 new undergraduates were accepted onto courses. Such levels are despite a year-on-year decline in applications and the third successive downturn in new starter numbers. There are not usually any required subjects, though the leading universities look for a broad selection of humanities A-levels – from classics and ancient history to English and psychology. The study of human social relationships and institutions, "Sociology encourages a profound and creative examination of the world," explains Professor Sam Friedman, associate professor of sociology, LSE. "It trains you to question assumptions that are taken for granted, delve beneath the surface and think critically about how society is organised and how we experience our lives. In particular it enables an exploration of the multiple forms of power and inequality that shape the world today, and how they affect the lives of all of us."

With entry standards across our table of 88 universities ranging from 200 UCAS tariff points at Glasgow to 24 institutions where entrants averaged 110 points and under, there are broad options for applicants. Cambridge is the top-ranked university to study sociology for the fifth consecutive year, its rank boosted by strong performances across the five measures in our ranking without topping any individually. For graduate prospects Cambridge is just behind Durham – which registered 88.7% of sociology graduates in high-skilled jobs and/or further study within 15 months. Entry standards are highest at Glasgow, followed by Cambridge, while sixth-place Loughborough has the edge for research in the field – based on results of the Research Excellence Framework 2021.

Glasgow Caledonian is the top-ranked post-1992 university, tying in 18th place with Birmingham and Manchester, with Lancaster in 14th place, while Worcester (40th overall) has the highest rates of student satisfaction with teaching quality and is behind only Surrey (joint eighth overall) for students' evaluation of the broader undergraduate experience.

Courses cover topics such as gender roles, multiculturalism, media and culture, and can include options to study criminology or social policy. The subject's academic breadth may be the source of its popularity, as it tends to offer little immediate gratification in terms of graduate prospects. In the new employment table, sociology ranks 64th out of 70 subject areas and it places =53rd in our salaries ranking. The latest data shows 43% of graduates were employed in professional-level jobs 15 months after their degrees, only 11% more than were employed in roles deemed "low-skilled".

# Sociology

| | | Teaching quality % | Student experience % | Research quality % | Entry standards (UCAS points) | Graduate prospects % | Overall score |
|---|---|---|---|---|---|---|---|
| 1 | Cambridge | 83.7 | 66.9 | 69.2 | 193 | 87 | 100 |
| 2 | Durham | 81.7 | 76.2 | 53 | 181 | 88.7 | 98.2 |
| 3 | Oxford | 81.8 | 73.6 | 70.5 | 189 | — | 98.1 |
| 4 | Glasgow | 79.1 | 78.1 | 62 | 200 | 75.7 | 97.2 |
| 5 | King's College London | 82.5 | 78.9 | 57 | 154 | 82.6 | 95.7 |
| 6 | Loughborough | 85.5 | 87.3 | 71.8 | 145 | 70 | 95.4 |
| 7 | Aberdeen | 89.2 | 88.3 | 37 | 181 | 69.1 | 95.2 |
| =8 | Surrey | 90.2 | 89.9 | 48 | 129 | 76.9 | 94.7 |
| =8 | Warwick | 83.8 | 77.7 | 53.8 | 147 | 81.1 | 94.7 |
| 10 | Lancaster | 84.3 | 79.9 | 60.2 | 146 | — | 93.9 |
| 11 | Bath | 80.1 | 77.9 | 59.5 | 153 | 76.3 | 93.7 |
| 12 | London School of Economics | 81.4 | 76.6 | 61 | 159 | 69.5* | 92.9 |
| 13 | Nottingham | 84.2 | 82 | 54 | 135 | 74.2 | 92.8 |
| 14 | York | 79.9 | 77.2 | 68.5 | 140 | 70.4 | 92.2 |
| =15 | Bristol | 81.6 | 78.6 | 49 | 153 | 71 | 91.8 |
| =15 | Exeter | 78.8 | 78.9 | 46.8 | 152 | 75.8 | 91.8 |
| 17 | Suffolk | 87.1 | 85.4 | 21.8 | — | 77.6 | 91.4 |
| =18 | Glasgow Caledonian | 84.7 | 79.5 | 26 | 183 | 65.5 | 91.2 |
| =18 | Birmingham | 78.4 | 79.8 | 61 | 144 | 68.8 | 91.2 |
| =18 | Manchester | 78.4 | 75.3 | 67.2 | 151 | 65.5 | 91.2 |
| =21 | Sheffield | 82.2 | 82.3 | 36.8 | 136 | 74.8 | 90.5 |
| =21 | Aston | 84.9 | 81.9 | 42.5 | 121 | 74.1 | 90.5 |
| =23 | University College London | 79 | 75 | — | 174 | 85.7 | 90.2 |
| =23 | Sussex | 80.6 | 79.8 | 55 | 134 | 68.3 | 90.2 |
| 25 | Plymouth | 83.5 | 80.7 | 50.5 | 109 | 74.6 | 90.1 |
| 26 | City | 78.5 | 78.6 | 64 | 125 | 68.9 | 90 |
| 27 | Southampton | 75 | 75 | 66.8 | 138 | 68.5 | 89.9 |
| 28 | Edinburgh | 70.7 | 70.6 | 53.5 | 185 | 65.5 | 89.8 |
| 29 | Cardiff | 77.2 | 78.7 | 54 | 141 | 67.3 | 89.4 |
| 30 | Essex | 79.3 | 79.9 | 62.5 | 122 | 65.8 | 89.3 |
| =31 | Leicester | 83.4 | 83.8 | 48 | 118 | 65.8 | 88.9 |
| =31 | Queen's, Belfast | 74.7 | 72 | 56.5 | 136 | 71.7 | 88.9 |
| 33 | Hull | 83.2 | 78 | 53.8 | 113 | — | 88.8 |
| 34 | Northumbria | 69.9 | 64.5 | 42 | 136 | 86.7 | 88.6 |
| 35 | Swansea | 79 | 77.2 | 46.5 | 135 | — | 88.5 |
| =36 | Stirling | 74 | 71.4 | 47.5 | 175 | 61.5 | 88.4 |
| =36 | Huddersfield | 87.5 | 85.6 | 43.5 | 114 | 61.7 | 88.4 |
| =38 | Leeds | 73.5 | 71.9 | 48.5 | 146 | 69.6 | 88 |
| =38 | Nottingham Trent | 84.3 | 81 | 29.5 | 112 | 73.6 | 88 |
| 40 | Worcester | 93.4 | 89.7 | 12.8 | 112 | — | 87.9 |
| =41 | Portsmouth | 84 | 81 | 33 | 102 | 71.3 | 87 |
| =41 | Newcastle | 78.2 | 81.9 | 42.5 | 138 | 60.6 | 87 |
| =41 | Coventry | 86.4 | 87.1 | 39.5 | 98 | 63.4 | 87 |
| 44 | Abertay | 86.4 | 83.9 | 13.5 | — | 68.2 | 86.9 |

| | | | | | | | |
|---|---|---|---|---|---|---|---|
| **45** | Bangor | 83.3 | 76.6 | 33.2 | 124 | — | 86.8 |
| **46** | Royal Holloway | 76.6 | 75 | 38 | 118 | 71.3 | 86.2 |
| **=47** | Liverpool | 70.5 | 70.6 | 55 | 130 | 66.6 | 85.9 |
| **=47** | Ulster | 85.3 | 80.6 | 53.8 | 111 | 52 | 85.9 |
| **49** | Manchester Metropolitan | 85.2 | 85.7 | 29 | 123 | 57 | 85.8 |
| **=50** | West of Scotland | 87.4 | 78 | 13.2 | 125 | 65 | 85.7 |
| **=50** | Edinburgh Napier | 83.5 | 78.8 | — | 150 | 66.9 | 85.7 |
| **52** | Chester | 85.6 | 80.8 | 12.8 | 120 | 66.9* | 85.6 |
| **53** | Robert Gordon | 88.6 | 84.4 | — | 144 | 59.3 | 85.5 |
| **54** | York St John | 86.7 | 84.7 | 10 | 106 | 67.4 | 85 |
| **=55** | Bournemouth | 80.7 | 77.7 | 10.2 | 110 | 76 | 84.9 |
| **=55** | Bedfordshire | 92.5 | 87.5 | — | 108 | 63.1 | 84.9 |
| **=55** | Brunel | 89.6 | 85.3 | 30.8 | 104 | 53.8 | 84.9 |
| **58** | Liverpool John Moores | 79.9 | 77.1 | 22.2 | 119 | 66.7 | 84.6 |
| **59** | Keele | 82 | 79 | 33.2 | 113 | 59.5 | 84.5 |
| **=60** | Salford | 81.3 | 79.1 | 44.5 | 109 | 54.2 | 84 |
| **=60** | Oxford Brookes | 80.1 | 78.2 | 27.5 | 106 | 65.2 | 84 |
| **62** | Roehampton | 79.8 | 70.5 | 40.2 | 93 | 66 | 83.6 |
| **63** | Leeds Beckett | 83.6 | 83.2 | 17.8 | 101 | 62 | 83.3 |
| **64** | Derby | 80.4 | 77 | — | 107 | 74.7 | 83.1 |
| **65** | Edge Hill | 83.1 | 78.7 | — | 124 | 64.3 | 82.9 |
| **66** | Kingston | 81.1 | 80.6 | 27 | 97 | — | 82.8 |
| **67** | Gloucestershire | 74.4 | 71.8 | 24.5 | 113 | 65.2 | 82 |
| **68** | East London | 85.1 | 75.2 | 26.8 | 96 | 55.4 | 81.9 |
| **69** | Central Lancashire | 80.3 | 78.5 | — | 112 | 66.8 | 81.8 |
| **=70** | Sheffield Hallam | 84.5 | 79.4 | — | 107 | 62.7 | 81.7 |
| **=70** | Birmingham City | 82.3 | 78 | 21 | 116 | 52.6 | 81.7 |
| **=70** | Kent | 81.2 | 79.5 | — | 114 | 63.6 | 81.7 |
| **73** | Goldsmiths, London | 70 | 63.1 | 52.5 | 115 | 58.6 | 81.6 |
| **=74** | Liverpool Hope | 84 | 79.8 | — | 117 | 56.7 | 81.1 |
| **=74** | West of England | 75 | 73.3 | 35.2 | 115 | 54 | 81.1 |
| **=76** | Teesside | 81.3 | 70.6 | 18.2 | 105 | — | 81 |
| **=76** | Canterbury Christ Church | 78.7 | 77.2 | 13.2 | 97 | 64.2 | 81 |
| **78** | Winchester | 77.9 | 74.2 | — | 109 | 67.1 | 80.6 |
| **79** | Greenwich | 76.1 | 71.8 | — | 108 | 70.3 | 80.5 |
| **80** | Northampton | 82.6 | 81.3 | 4.2 | 93 | 58.2 | 79.8 |
| **=81** | Anglia Ruskin | 75.4 | 66.7 | 35.5 | 111 | 50.7 | 79.4 |
| **=81** | Middlesex | 85.3 | 81.9 | — | 106 | 50.7 | 79.4 |
| **83** | Queen Margaret, Edinburgh | 67 | 57 | 7.8 | 148 | 65.4 | 79.2 |
| **84** | Westminster | 79.8 | 76.9 | — | 104 | 58.7 | 79.1 |
| **85** | Lincoln | 76.9 | 74 | — | 114 | 59.8 | 79 |
| **86** | Bath Spa | 80.4 | 75 | — | 100 | 58.9 | 78.7 |
| **87** | South Wales | 76.6 | 70.1 | — | 101 | 56.9 | 76.8 |
| **88** | Brighton | 72.9 | 65.4 | 34 | 103 | 44.9 | 76.5 |

| | | | |
|---|---|---|---|
| Employed in high-skilled job | 36% | Employed in lower-skilled job | 32% |
| Employed in high-skilled job and studying | 4% | Employed in lower-skilled job and studying | 1% |
| Studying | 9% | Unemployed | 7% |
| High-skilled work (median) salary | £25,500 | Low-/medium-skilled salary | £21,000 |

# Sports Science

Fittingly, sports science is one of our more competitive subject rankings, with ranks changing hands regularly. Success in this context is based on universities' performance in sports degree courses and research, rather than the standard of their sports facilities or their teams' victories. Since 2017, the table has been led by Birmingham, Bath – twice, Exeter and Loughborough. But for a fifth successive year Glasgow lifts the cup in our Sports Science table, its rank boosted by the highest entry standards of 216 UCAS points along with strong performances across the rest of the metrics in the ranking. Bath is runner-up, also for the fifth consecutive year, and benefits from top ten rates of student satisfaction with the broad undergraduate experience and a top 15 finish for teaching quality as well as graduate prospects that rank in the top four universities.

Third-place overall, Exeter leads the field for research in sports science by a clear margin, based on results of the Research Excellence Framework 2021. Following it for research quality are King's College London (11th in the table) and Bangor (24th).

The best sports facilities do not always equate to top outcomes in the academic discipline of sport science – but they can help, such as the laboratories in which performance, endurance and recovery are closely monitored. Loughborough, the most famous name in university sport, podiums in fourth place of our table overall. Though not an ingredient of our ranking, Loughborough's superb facilities are the training hub for countless elite sportspeople, and with Loughborough-linked athletes returning home from the Paris 2024 Olympics with 16 medals, if Loughborough University were a country, it would have outperformed nations including Brazil, Austria and South Africa.

Nottingham has placed second to Loughborough in the British Universities and Colleges Sport (BUCS) points table for the three years up to 2023–24. It has staged a spectacular return to form in our academic ranking too, where it places sixth this year (having plummeted to fourth from bottom last year) – lifted by much improved rates of student satisfaction, including a top-15 finish for students' evaluation of the broad experience. In our new National Student Survey analysis Lancaster (eighth overall), Teesside (=17th) and Buckinghamshire New ( 30th) are the top three universities for teaching quality, in descending order. For the wider experience Aberystwyth (=17th overall), Buckinghamshire New (30th) and Surrey (5th) lead the table.

Dr Adam Brazil, lecturer in sports biomechanics, University of Bath, says sports science connects learning to real world settings and "provides an exciting framework to explore scientific disciplines such as human physiology, biomechanics and psychology. Career prospects are vast and varied and you may find yourself pursuing a career as an elite sport practitioner, exercise rehabilitation specialist or academic researcher."

Sport and exercise sciences have been one of the big growth areas of UK higher education over the past 15 years or so, and despite a 10% decline in applications to the subject in 2023, 74,810 still applied to it (20% more than four years before). The number of students accepted onto courses in 2023 declined less sharply, by 8%, and 16,170 enrolled on degrees. Many courses involve more science and less physical activity than some candidates expect, and the leading universities look for the sciences and maths at A-level. Having shot up our previous edition's 70-subject employment table to place 21st, sports science has sunk to 45th this year, based on 62.2% of graduates being in high-skilled jobs and/or furthering their studies within 15 months. Salaries stack up less favourably, in =53rd place.

## Sports Science

| | | Teaching quality % | Student experience % | Research quality % | Entry standards (UCAS points) | Graduate prospects % | Overall score |
|---|---|---|---|---|---|---|---|
| 1 | Glasgow | 83 | 78.8 | 68.5 | 217 | — | 100 |
| 2 | Bath | 89.9 | 89.9 | 73.2 | 161 | 84.7 | 98.3 |
| 3 | Exeter | 81.8 | 84.9 | 84 | 161 | 81.2 | 96.1 |
| 4 | Loughborough | 81.2 | 85.3 | 66.8 | 161 | 86.6 | 95.7 |
| 5 | Surrey | 90 | 91.3 | 58 | 137 | 84.4 | 95 |
| 6 | Nottingham | 84.2 | 87 | 61 | 142 | 82.8 | 93.5 |
| 7 | Liverpool John Moores | 86.4 | 85.2 | 60.8 | 154 | 76.8 | 93.2 |
| =8 | Lancaster | 94 | 90.7 | 55 | 142 | 72.7 | 92.9 |
| =8 | Coventry | 92.3 | 89.5 | 24.8 | 135 | 87.3 | 92.9 |
| 10 | Durham | 83.1 | 80.4 | 61 | 168 | 75.5 | 92.8 |
| 11 | King's College London | 77.6 | 76.1 | 80.2 | 154 | — | 92.7 |
| 12 | Manchester Metropolitan | 86.5 | 83.2 | 51.2 | 137 | 83.9 | 92.6 |
| =13 | Birmingham | 79.7 | 78.9 | 73.2 | 150 | 78.7 | 92.4 |
| =13 | Swansea | 85.6 | 87.2 | 48.2 | 136 | 83.8 | 92.4 |
| 15 | Chichester | 89.9 | 84.5 | 33.2 | 129 | 87.6 | 92.3 |
| 16 | Northumbria | 86.4 | 85.4 | 60.5 | 150 | 74.5 | 92.2 |
| =17 | Teesside | 94 | 90.6 | 35 | 136 | 78.6 | 92.1 |
| =17 | Aberystwyth | 92.4 | 93.7 | 48.8 | 121 | — | 92.1 |
| 19 | Aberdeen | 82.8 | 78.9 | 30.5 | 187 | — | 92 |
| 20 | St Mary's, Twickenham | 89.2 | 85.2 | 46 | 118 | 83.1 | 91.3 |
| 21 | Edge Hill | 87.6 | 84 | 32.5 | 143 | 80.3 | 90.7 |
| =22 | Cardiff Metropolitan | 85.8 | 82.8 | 43.8 | 139 | 79.2 | 90.6 |
| =22 | Leeds | 72 | 70.8 | 65.8 | 150 | 84.5 | 90.6 |
| 24 | Bangor | 86.4 | 85.7 | 73.8 | 127 | 69.5 | 90.3 |
| 25 | Portsmouth | 85.5 | 82.3 | 57.5 | 126 | 76.8 | 90.1 |
| 26 | Abertay | 91.4 | 89.9 | 19.8 | 157 | 72.5 | 90 |
| 27 | Brunel | 81.8 | 81.9 | 50.5 | 132 | 79.5 | 89.8 |
| 28 | Newcastle | 80.3 | 78.7 | 50.7 | 145 | 77.5 | 89.7 |
| 29 | Stirling | 81.3 | 79.1 | 36.5 | 172 | 73.2 | 89.6 |
| 30 | Buckinghamshire New | 93.4 | 91.4 | 22.8 | 113 | 80.5 | 89.5 |
| 31 | Brighton | 86.5 | 82.6 | 45.5 | 119 | 79.5 | 89.4 |
| 32 | Nottingham Trent | 88 | 86.7 | 36.8 | 131 | 75.5 | 89.3 |
| =33 | Edinburgh | 70.4 | 70.5 | 55 | 193 | 70.8 | 89.1 |
| =33 | Strathclyde | 87.2 | 84.7 | — | 196 | 70 | 89.1 |
| =33 | Hertfordshire | 88.5 | 82.4 | 48 | 112 | 77.7 | 89.1 |
| =33 | Ulster | 82.3 | 79.6 | 43.2 | 143 | 76.6 | 89.1 |
| =33 | South Wales | 89.6 | 83.7 | 45.8 | 117 | 75.9 | 89.1 |
| =38 | Greenwich | 84.4 | 75 | 32.3 | 129 | 83.9 | 88.9 |
| =38 | Leeds Beckett | 86.6 | 83.6 | 49.2 | 121 | 75.3 | 88.9 |
| =38 | Lincoln | 91 | 85.1 | 30.8 | 127 | 75.4 | 88.9 |
| =38 | Worcester | 88.5 | 86 | 15.2 | 122 | 84.1 | 88.9 |
| =42 | Oxford Brookes | 88.5 | 81.8 | 37.8 | 121 | 78 | 88.8 |
| =42 | York St John | 90.2 | 89.8 | 27.5 | 126 | 75.5 | 88.8 |
| =44 | Salford | 85.7 | 78.7 | 37 | 139 | 75.8 | 88.7 |

## Sports Science cont.

| | | Teaching quality % | Student experience % | Research quality % | Entry standards (UCAS points) | Graduate prospects % | Overall score |
|---|---|---|---|---|---|---|---|
| =44 | Roehampton | 88.9 | 85.6 | 37.5 | 106 | 80.5 | 88.7 |
| 46 | Sheffield Hallam | 84.1 | 80.6 | 45.2 | 126 | 77.1 | 88.6 |
| 47 | Bournemouth | 82.2 | 78.4 | 41.8 | 123 | 78.2 | 87.7 |
| 48 | Hartpury | 90.6 | 83.6 | 15.8 | 128 | 75.6 | 87.3 |
| =49 | Robert Gordon | 88.8 | 82.2 | — | 162 | 72 | 87.1 |
| =49 | Chester | 85.9 | 86.7 | 15.8 | 134 | 75.8 | 87.1 |
| 51 | Wolverhampton | 93.4 | 88.7 | 25.2 | 108 | 72.1 | 86.8 |
| =52 | Central Lancashire | 89 | 81.4 | 19.2 | 129 | 74 | 86.7 |
| =52 | Essex | 85.6 | 84.1 | 32.5 | 138 | 68.6 | 86.7 |
| 54 | Solent, Southampton | 88.9 | 84.7 | 18.5 | 125 | 73.1 | 86.5 |
| =55 | Staffordshire | 92.2 | 80.4 | 30.8 | 122 | 67.8 | 86.3 |
| =55 | West of Scotland | 85.4 | 79.7 | 29 | 145 | 67.9 | 86.3 |
| =55 | Hull | 86 | 78.8 | 47.2 | 140 | 62.7 | 86.3 |
| 58 | Bedfordshire | 84.9 | 79.8 | 22 | 112 | 80.2 | 86.2 |
| =59 | Gloucestershire | 81.9 | 71.6 | 24.5 | 124 | 80.7 | 86 |
| =59 | Edinburgh Napier | 74.8 | 75.2 | 23.5 | 158 | 75.4 | 86 |
| 61 | St Mark and St John | 89.8 | 86.2 | 20 | 122 | 70.1 | 85.9 |
| 62 | Newman | 92.2 | 87.9 | 13.2 | 112 | — | 85.8 |
| 63 | Canterbury Christ Church | 86 | 81.5 | 38 | 99 | 74.6 | 85.6 |
| 64 | Kingston | 92.1 | 85.9 | 38.5 | 116 | 61.8 | 85.4 |
| 65 | Derby | 89.7 | 85.3 | — | 122 | 75.4 | 85.3 |
| 66 | East Anglia | 88.9 | 89.9 | — | 143 | 67.4 | 85.1 |
| =67 | Wales Trinity St David | 86.6 | 79.9 | 11.8 | 136 | 70.6 | 85 |
| =67 | Liverpool Hope | 82.9 | 77.8 | 13.8 | 125 | 76.9 | 85 |
| 69 | Kent | 85 | 81.4 | 37.2 | 131 | 63.6 | 84.9 |
| 70 | Winchester | 84.8 | 79.6 | 20.8 | 113 | 75.3 | 84.8 |
| =71 | Birmingham City | 88.7 | 85.5 | — | 132 | 70.8 | 84.6 |
| =71 | Middlesex | 87.7 | 80.9 | 16 | 120 | 71.4 | 84.6 |
| 73 | Huddersfield | 83.3 | 73.4 | 22.2 | 130 | 70.9 | 84.2 |
| 74 | Bolton | 88.3 | 82.3 | — | 119 | 71.8 | 83.4 |
| 75 | Anglia Ruskin | 87.8 | 85.5 | 18.5 | 121 | 63.5 | 83.3 |
| 76 | Northampton | 89.3 | 84.9 | 5 | 107 | 69.7 | 82.9 |
| 77 | Leeds Trinity | 74.5 | 67.4 | 18 | 114 | 81.9 | 82.8 |
| 78 | London South Bank | 83.1 | 76.4 | 32.2 | 100 | — | 82.6 |
| 79 | Sunderland | 79.4 | 70.2 | 22 | 121 | 63.6 | 80.2 |
| 80 | Suffolk | 71.3 | 68 | — | 116 | 76.9 | 79.2 |
| 81 | East London | 83 | 75.2 | — | 114 | 57.3 | 77.3 |
| 82 | Cumbria | 80.3 | 63.9 | — | 121 | 61.1 | 77.1 |

| | | | |
|---|---|---|---|
| Employed in high-skilled job | 46% | Employed in lower-skilled job | 24% |
| Employed in high-skilled job and studying | 5% | Employed in lower-skilled job and studying | 1% |
| Studying | 9% | Unemployed | 3% |
| High-skilled work (median) salary | £25,000 | Low-/medium-skilled salary | £20,500 |

# Subjects Allied to Medicine

"Are you fascinated by the human body? A problem solver? A good communicator with a desire to change people's lives?" asks Dr Rachael Cubberley, head of the School of Allied Health and Social Care, Anglia Ruskin University. "From clinical to policy, strategic to education, allied health provides diversification opportunities throughout your career. A purpose-driven career, regulated by professional bodies, that can flex and adapt as your life changes is endlessly rewarding."

A wide range of degrees is encompassed within the Subjects Allied to Medicine table. They include audiology, complementary therapies, counselling, health services management, health sciences, nutrition, occupational therapy, optometry, ophthalmology, orthoptics, osteopathy, podiatry and speech therapy. Physiotherapy and radiography have rankings of their own. Not all the universities that feature in this table offer all of the subjects that fall under the broad "allied to medicine" heading, and performance in our ranking is naturally influenced by which specialisms are offered.

In a top three of Scottish universities Strathclyde returns to No 1 in the table, where it previously enjoyed a six-year run until two year ago. Strathclyde's strong performances across all five of the ranking's metrics include the third-highest entry standards and a top ten research rating. Last year's No 1, Dundee, slips to eighth place while Glasgow – which has the highest entry standards in the table with 205 points in the UCAS tariff – moves up one place into the runner-up spot.

The post-1992 universities represent more than half of the table, but only Glasgow Caledonian places in the top 10. King's College London sits 14th overall but its strength in research is unsurpassed, based on results of the Research Excellence Framework 2021. Manchester (ninth overall), Southampton (=22nd) and 16th-place Bristol follow it for research quality.

In our National Student Survey (NSS) analysis, Edinburgh Napier (=12th overall) is rated top for teaching quality by its students, in a ranking that sees Buckinghamshire New (35th in the table) and St Mary's Twickenham (=51st) fill second and third places respectively. For the wider undergraduate experience, also derived from the NSS, Buckinghamshire New is unbeaten, followed by St Mary's, Twickenham and Lancaster (fourth overall). Conversely, Brunel comes bottom for both.

Applications in 2022 saw a small increase in ophthalmics but after three years of increasing applications demand dipped in counselling, psychotherapy and occupational therapy. Applications also decreased within nutrition and dietetics, and in complementary and alternative medicine. The best rates of graduate employment are found jointly at Buckinghamshire New and Wrexham – where 97.4% of graduates were in high-skilled work or postgraduate study within 15 months – while 31 universities in total had at least nine in 10 graduates achieving the same outcomes. At just three, Middlesex, East London and Roehampton, this proportion falls below 70%. Their generally solid job prospects rank the subjects allied to medicine 10th in our 70-subject employment table (up from 24th last year) though pay falls outside the top half of subjects – with average graduate salaries of £25,655, placing the subjects 42nd.

| Subjects Allied to Medicine | Teaching quality % | Student experience % | Research quality % | Entry standards (UCAS points) | Graduate prospects % | Overall score |
|---|---|---|---|---|---|---|
| 1 Strathclyde | 82.6 | 80.9 | 65.8 | 190 | 87.4 | 100 |
| 2 Glasgow | 77.9 | 76.2 | 63.5 | 205 | 86.9 | 99.6 |
| 3 Glasgow Caledonian | 80.4 | 76 | 61 | 190 | 91.6 | 99.5 |
| 4 Lancaster | 88.8 | 89.2 | 55 | 147 | 91.1 | 97.6 |
| 5 City | 90.8 | 89 | 58 | 136 | 91.4 | 97.5 |

**Subjects Allied to Medicine** cont.

| | Teaching quality % | Student experience % | Research quality % | Entry standards (UCAS points) | Graduate prospects % | Overall score |
|---|---|---|---|---|---|---|
| 6 Cardiff | 80.5 | 76.3 | 58.8 | 154 | 97.1 | 97.2 |
| 7 University College London | 76.5 | 75.3 | 57.8 | 174 | 91.8 | 96.6 |
| 8 Dundee | 79.8 | 79.7 | 60.8 | 191 | 78.3 | 96.4 |
| 9 Manchester | 78.7 | 74.1 | 71.2 | 154 | 90.4 | 96.3 |
| 10 Swansea | 82.9 | 75.5 | 66.8 | 150 | 89.3 | 96.2 |
| 11 East Anglia | 83.6 | 80.3 | 55.5 | 139 | 94.5 | 95.7 |
| =12 Robert Gordon | 87 | 82.9 | 24.5 | 167 | 92 | 95.2 |
| =12 Edinburgh Napier | 94.1 | 88.6 | 40.5 | 141 | 86 | 95.2 |
| 14 King's College London | 77.9 | 76.6 | 76.2 | 160 | 79.8 | 94.9 |
| 15 Surrey | 82.1 | 81.5 | 58 | 146 | 87.9 | 94.8 |
| 16 Bristol | 75.4 | 72.5 | 68.7 | 175 | 80.5 | 94.6 |
| =17 Ulster | 85.4 | 81.1 | 53.5 | 142 | 87.3 | 94.5 |
| =17 Wrexham | 88.5 | 84.6 | 20.5 | — | 97.4 | 94.5 |
| 19 Exeter | 80.6 | 75.9 | 53.2 | 152 | 90 | 94.4 |
| 20 Birmingham | 80.4 | 76.8 | 59.8 | 152 | 85.1 | 94.1 |
| 21 Lincoln | 90.8 | 86.3 | 55.8 | 122 | 85.4 | 94 |
| =22 Liverpool | 84.6 | 84.9 | 46.8 | 134 | 90.8 | 93.9 |
| =22 Southampton | 76.4 | 69.4 | 69.8 | 140 | 90.9 | 93.9 |
| =24 Newcastle | 77.1 | 73.6 | 61.8 | 154 | 86.8 | 93.8 |
| =24 Queen Margaret, Edinburgh | 83.3 | 74.4 | 36.5 | 167 | 87.6 | 93.8 |
| 26 Hull | 87.6 | 82.3 | 55.5 | 127 | 86.7 | 93.7 |
| 27 West of England | 81.3 | 72.8 | 42.8 | 146 | 93.9 | 93.5 |
| 28 Reading | 85.3 | 83.3 | 56.2 | 128 | 86.5 | 93.4 |
| 29 Queen Mary, London | 80.1 | 79.8 | 54.8 | 148 | 85.1 | 93.2 |
| 30 Aston | 84.1 | 83.6 | 46 | 127 | 91 | 93 |
| 31 Nottingham | 80 | 73.6 | 57.9 | 144 | 84.8 | 92.5 |
| 32 Leeds | 74.5 | 71 | 65 | 152 | 83 | 92.2 |
| 33 Northumbria | 79.8 | 69.9 | 53.5 | 149 | 84.6 | 92.1 |
| 34 London South Bank | 88.3 | 80.5 | 34.5 | 116 | 93.9 | 91.9 |
| 35 Buckinghamshire New | 94.1 | 90.2 | 16.8 | 104 | 97.4 | 91.8 |
| 36 Cardiff Metropolitan | 83.1 | 79.3 | 20.5 | 151 | 90.9 | 91.7 |
| 37 Sussex | 82.6 | 82 | 54.2 | 136 | 80 | 91.5 |
| 38 Plymouth | 78.8 | 75 | 39.5 | 137 | 91.2 | 91.2 |
| 39 South Wales | 87.1 | 77 | 25.2 | 132 | 89.5 | 90.7 |
| 40 Huddersfield | 84.6 | 77.1 | 22.5 | 133 | 91 | 90.3 |
| =41 Northampton | 85.7 | 82.5 | 7.5 | 126 | 97.3 | 90.2 |
| =41 Sheffield | 78.4 | 75.1 | 63.7 | 145 | 73 | 90.2 |
| 43 Portsmouth | 84 | 81.1 | 41.2 | 122 | 84.2 | 89.9 |
| 44 Essex | 83.8 | 77.2 | 28.5 | 125 | 90.1 | 89.8 |
| =45 Salford | 82.9 | 78.3 | 37 | 128 | 85.3 | 89.7 |
| =45 Bradford | 77.7 | 71 | 33.8 | 145 | 87.3 | 89.7 |
| 47 Liverpool John Moores | 84.9 | 82 | 26.5 | 145 | 80 | 89.6 |
| =48 Oxford Brookes | 76 | 71.3 | 37.8 | 128 | 93 | 89.5 |
| =48 Bangor | 83.9 | 78.7 | 59.8 | 120 | 76 | 89.5 |

| | | | | | | | |
|---|---|---|---|---|---|---|---|
| 50 | St George's, London | 85.3 | 73.2 | — | 141 | 95.8 | 89.3 |
| =51 | St Mary's, Twickenham | 91.5 | 89.4 | — | 123 | 90.2 | 89.2 |
| =51 | Coventry | 75.2 | 70.8 | 47.2 | 133 | 86.1 | 89.2 |
| 53 | Staffordshire | 78.9 | 66.6 | 30.8 | 125 | 91.8 | 88.3 |
| =54 | Hertfordshire | 81 | 77.9 | 48 | 111 | 82.4 | 88.1 |
| =54 | Teesside | 79.1 | 69.1 | 35 | 122 | 89.3 | 88.1 |
| =56 | Keele | 74.9 | 77.2 | 66.2 | 125 | 72.5 | 87.8 |
| =56 | St Mark and St John | 89.7 | 81.9 | — | 120 | 90.8 | 87.8 |
| 58 | Central Lancashire | 78.5 | 74 | 35.5 | 132 | 81.9 | 87.7 |
| 59 | Bournemouth | 82.8 | 75 | 29.2 | 112 | 88.1 | 87.6 |
| 60 | Brighton | 77.1 | 67.3 | 50.5 | 115 | 84.7 | 87.5 |
| =61 | West of Scotland | 83.2 | 78.2 | 30.8 | 135 | 75.4 | 87.2 |
| =61 | Canterbury Christ Church | 72.4 | 61.8 | 31.8 | 124 | 95 | 87.2 |
| 63 | Derby | 88.6 | 84.6 | 24 | 125 | 73.5 | 86.8 |
| =64 | Edge Hill | 74.3 | 65.4 | 22.2 | 133 | 90.5 | 86.6 |
| =64 | Greenwich | 79 | 70.5 | 32.3 | 120 | 84.5 | 86.6 |
| =66 | Nottingham Trent | 73.5 | 70.9 | 43.5 | 126 | 80.3 | 86.2 |
| =66 | Chester | 77.5 | 73.9 | 31 | 119 | 84.1 | 86.2 |
| 68 | York St John | 81.9 | 74.9 | 13.8 | 121 | 86.8 | 86.1 |
| 69 | Leicester | 84 | 85.6 | — | 129 | 83.3 | 86 |
| 70 | Sunderland | 75.2 | 67 | 30.2 | 127 | 84.7 | 85.8 |
| =71 | Sheffield Hallam | 71.7 | 65.2 | 29.8 | 121 | 90.1 | 85.6 |
| =71 | Leeds Beckett | 82 | 77.2 | 38 | 111 | 76.3 | 85.6 |
| 73 | Manchester Metropolitan | 79.1 | 75.8 | 36 | 128 | 73.2 | 85.5 |
| 74 | Gloucestershire | 79.9 | 79.3 | 16.2 | 127 | — | 85.4 |
| =75 | Cumbria | 71.4 | 67.2 | 18.5 | 134 | 88.7 | 85.3 |
| =75 | Suffolk | 79.8 | 71.7 | — | 123 | 92.3 | 85.3 |
| 77 | Brunel | 59.2 | 53.9 | 47.2 | 126 | 94.1 | 85.2 |
| 78 | Bedfordshire | 73.9 | 59.9 | 22.5 | 123 | 89.9 | 84.8 |
| 79 | Anglia Ruskin | 73.9 | 69.1 | 33.8 | 107 | 86.3 | 84.6 |
| 80 | Worcester | 69.9 | 66.6 | 24.2 | 133 | 83.3 | 84.1 |
| 81 | London Metropolitan | 79.4 | 76.1 | 23.8 | 132 | 71.2 | 83.9 |
| 82 | Wolverhampton | 80.6 | 74.7 | 24.2 | 120 | 73 | 83.4 |
| 83 | Birmingham City | 72.7 | 69 | 37.8 | 126 | 72.6 | 83.1 |
| 84 | Bolton | 88.2 | 77.8 | 2 | 116 | 75.1 | 83 |
| 85 | Roehampton | 81.2 | 82.6 | 37.5 | 106 | 60.7 | 81.4 |
| =86 | Middlesex | 77.8 | 73.5 | 22.5 | 105 | 69.9 | 80.2 |
| =86 | East London | 86.9 | 77.6 | 25.5 | 96 | 62.2 | 80.2 |
| 88 | Westminster | 68 | 70 | 36.8 | 110 | 71.2 | 80.1 |
| 89 | De Montfort | 74 | 72.7 | 20.8 | 109 | 70 | 79.4 |

| | | | | |
|---|---|---|---|---|
| Employed in high-skilled job | 74% | Employed in lower-skilled job | | 8% |
| Employed in high-skilled job and studying | 4% | Employed in lower-skilled job and studying | | 1% |
| Studying | 4% | Unemployed | | 3% |
| High-skilled work (median) salary | £26,000 | Low-/medium-skilled salary | | £20,000 |

# Theology and Religious Studies

Looking at how different beliefs have influenced society historically and their roles within the contemporary world, Theology and Religious Studies courses draw on students' critical thinking and textual analysis, encouraging intellectual curiosity and articulate communication. There are usually no required subjects and it is not necessary to be a religious believer but it helps to have experience of essay-writing subjects such as history, English or politics – in which balancing arguments and analysing texts are to the fore.

Cambridge holds on to its accustomed lead in the Theology and Religious Studies table, boosted by its usual high entry standards along with the third-highest score for teaching quality, derived from our new National Student Survey analysis. At almost half of the universities tabled, new entrants averaged over 144 tariff points (equal to three As at A-level) but there are still four universities with 110 points and under. Runner-up Durham is unbeaten for graduate prospects, with 92.3% of graduates employed in professional-level jobs and/or postgraduate study 15 months after their degrees. Exeter leads the field for research, based on results of the Research Excellence Framework 2021, where it is followed by Birmingham and King's College London.

Birmingham Newman, in =17th overall, claims the best rates of student satisfaction in our new National Student Survey analysis, followed by St Andrews (fifth). For the wider experience Birmingham Newman is unbeaten again, while Liverpool Hope (16th) comes second.

Across successive admissions cycles, applications and enrolments in theology and religious studies have been following a similar pattern to the size of congregations filling pews on Sundays. But in 2023 demand nudged upwards, with the subjects registering 4,000 applications (up from 3,980 in 2022) and 835 undergraduates accepted onto courses (30 more than the year before). By no means do all who take theology or religious studies degrees go on to work for the Church; other career routes include the civil service, law, international development, the arts, banking, investment, teaching, research, the media and communications. But the vocation is among the career pathways that contribute to the subjects ranking 36th out of 70 in our employment table. For pay they place =46th.

"The study of theology and religious studies gives you the historical, critical and analytic tools to understand its place and role and to address some of the most profound questions of human existence. It helps to develop skills in writing, testing evidence, argument and working with complex concepts, which are valuable throughout life and across professional and academic domains," says Dr Alastair Lockhart, member of the Faculty of Divinity, University of Cambridge, and visiting senior research fellow in theology and religious studies, King's College London.

| Theology and Religious Studies | Teaching quality % | Student experience % | Research quality % | Entry standards (UCAS points) | Graduate prospects % | Overall score |
|---|---|---|---|---|---|---|
| 1 Cambridge | 94 | 70.9 | 58.5 | 187 | 87.2 | 100 |
| 2 Durham | 86.9 | 73 | 55 | 162 | 92.3 | 97.6 |
| 3 Glasgow | 86.3 | 83.6 | 62.5 | 177 | 79.3 | 97.1 |
| 4 Oxford | 84.9 | 74.7 | 44.8 | 186 | 87.6 | 96.7 |
| 5 St Andrews | 95.9 | 88.7 | 36.5 | 159 | — | 96.6 |
| 6 Exeter | 87.2 | 83.7 | 75 | 140 | 71.8 | 93.9 |
| 7 Birmingham | 80.2 | 80.8 | 67.2 | 142 | 81.2 | 93.8 |
| =8 Edinburgh | 81.4 | 79.4 | 51.2 | 161 | 78.4 | 92.7 |
| =8 Bristol | 80.9 | 72.7 | 48.5 | 148 | 86.2 | 92.7 |

| | | | | | | |
|---|---|---|---|---|---|---|
| 10 King's College London | 76.7 | 76.6 | 67 | 145 | 80.9 | 92.6 |
| 11 Cardiff | 85.5 | 79.7 | 42.2 | 131 | 86.1 | 92.3 |
| 12 Chester | 94 | 90.8 | 44.5 | 107 | 79.4 | 92.1 |
| 13 Leeds | 79.5 | 78.2 | 52 | 138 | 83.0* | 91.6 |
| 14 Manchester | 83.8 | 77.9 | 39.5 | 149 | 78.3* | 90.7 |
| 15 Nottingham | 82.8 | 77.3 | 51.5 | 132 | 76.9 | 90.2 |
| 16 Liverpool Hope | 88.6 | 93.8 | 30.5 | 110 | — | 88.9 |
| =17 Newman | 97.9 | 96.2 | 8.8 | 104 | — | 88 |
| =17 York St John | 87.4 | 83.1 | 15.8 | — | 79.4* | 88 |
| 19 Canterbury Christ Church | 85.6 | 82.2 | 25 | 101 | 76.1* | 85.5 |
| 20 Roehampton | 93.8 | 84.6 | 31.5 | — | 57.1* | 84.8 |

| | | | |
|---|---|---|---|
| Employed in high-skilled job | 49% | Employed in lower-skilled job | 21% |
| Employed in high-skilled job and studying | 5% | Employed in lower-skilled job and studying | 2% |
| Studying | 10% | Unemployed | 4% |
| High-skilled work (median) salary | £25,500 | Low-/medium-skilled salary | £19,000 |

# Town and Country Planning and Landscape

Courses under the rubric of town and country planning and landscape studies include urban studies, sustainable development and rural enterprise land management. "If you're interested in sustainability, cities and making the world a better place, town and country planning could be the degree for you," advises Dr Andy Inch, senior lecturer at the School of Geography and Planning, University of Sheffield. "Good planning is vital for tackling many of the 21st century's biggest challenges, from climate change and nature depletion to housing, health and inequality. A professionally accredited planning degree will push you beyond understanding the big issues to asking what can be done about them, opening up a range of exciting future careers. And one of the best things about studying planning is that you can learn by visiting interesting places and thinking about the ways they're changing."

Positive career outcomes place the subjects 17th out of 70 in our employment table, with the latest figures showing more than three-quarters of graduates had secured professional-level jobs and/or postgraduate study within 15 months. Pay is promising too: average early career salaries of £26,265 are in the top 25.

Loughborough is No 1 in this year's table, ousting University College London after two years at the top. Loughborough's record on graduate employment is unbeaten and it also leads for research quality, based on its performance in the Research Excellence Framework 2021, where it is closely followed by Sheffield (third overall). Averaging 184 points in the UCAS tariff, runner-up Edinburgh leads on entry standards by a clear margin. Students at 12th-place Queen's, Belfast report the highest rates of satisfaction with teaching quality and the broader undergraduate experience in our National Student Survey analysis.

There were 4,825 applications applied to planning courses in 2023 and 795 students were accepted onto degrees (marginally lower than the year before). Student numbers are lower on landscape design degrees, which accepted 160 new students in 2023 (up from 145 in 2022).

Cambridge, a former leader of the table, is now absent from it due to its land economy degree being included in our Land and Property Management table instead.

## Town and Country Planning and Landscape

| | | Teaching quality % | Student experience % | Research quality % | Entry standards (UCAS points) | Graduate prospects % | Overall score |
|---|---|---|---|---|---|---|---|
| 1 | Loughborough | 90.1 | 74.1 | 72 | 145 | 92 | 100 |
| 2 | Edinburgh | 80.1 | 76.9 | 59 | 184 | — | 99.1 |
| 3 | Sheffield | 87 | 84.1 | 71.8 | 152 | 87.3 | 98.7 |
| 4 | University College London | 79.4 | 79.9 | 61 | 164 | 88.9 | 97.4 |
| 5 | Heriot-Watt | 74.7 | 66.6 | 59 | 168 | 88.2 | 95.3 |
| 6 | Manchester | 75.6 | 77.5 | 59.2 | 153 | — | 94.9 |
| 7 | Liverpool | 88.4 | 83 | 45.2 | 123 | 89.7 | 94.7 |
| 8 | Birmingham | 83.1 | 82.7 | 49.2 | 132 | — | 93.7 |
| 9 | Cardiff | 79.6 | 80.5 | 38.2 | 133 | 89.4 | 92.7 |
| 10 | Ulster | 83.2 | 80.1 | 54.2 | 132 | 83.3* | 92.6 |
| 11 | Newcastle | 76.3 | 73 | 56 | 127 | 87.8 | 92.5 |
| 12 | Queen's, Belfast | 93.8 | 91 | 36.5 | 133 | 80.6* | 92.2 |
| 13 | Leeds Beckett | 92.9 | 85.4 | 24.5 | 114 | 86.7 | 91.4 |
| 14 | Oxford Brookes | 84.2 | 72.3 | 33.2 | 122 | 87.2 | 90.6 |
| 15 | Westminster | 90.6 | 77.1 | 38.2 | 100 | — | 90 |
| 16 | Gloucestershire | 78.1 | 78.4 | 24 | — | 87.5* | 89.1 |
| 17 | West of England | 83.6 | 80.8 | 40.8 | 127 | 77.8* | 88.4 |
| 18 | London South Bank | 77.1 | 59.5 | 35 | 112 | — | 85.7 |

| | | | |
|---|---|---|---|
| Employed in high-skilled job | 66% | Employed in lower-skilled job | 12% |
| Employed in high-skilled job and studying | 4% | Employed in lower-skilled job and studying | 1% |
| Studying | 6% | Unemployed | 4% |
| High-skilled work (median) salary | £27,000 | Low-/medium-skilled salary | £21,500 |

# Veterinary Medicine

Veterinary medicine student numbers are centrally controlled, and the subject is offered by very few universities; none of them in Northern Ireland and only one in Wales, at Aberystwyth – which is too new to have sufficient data for our table yet. The same goes for the joint vet school at Keele and Harper Adams and at Central Lancashire, which accepted its first intake of students in 2023. The norm for veterinary medicine degrees is five years, but the Cambridge course takes six and Bristol, Nottingham and the Royal Veterinary College offer a gateway year. Edinburgh, Bristol and the Royal Veterinary College also run four-year accelerated courses for graduates.

Liverpool secures the No 1 spot this year, ousting Glasgow after two years at the top. Liverpool's rank has been boosted by improved rates of student satisfaction which now rank it second for teaching quality and for the wider experience in our new National Student Survey (NSS) analysis. Liverpool was already the top-rated university for research in the subject, based on results of the Research Excellence Framework 2021.

"A degree in veterinary medicine leads to a broad spectrum of career opportunities, from work as a clinical veterinarian taking care of food and companion animals, to specialisation in a highly technical discipline like orthopaedic surgery or advanced imaging, to studying emerging and transboundary diseases in far flung corners of the earth – not to mention the sea," notes Professor Paul Lunn, dean of the School of Veterinary Science, University of Liverpool.

Entrants to Glasgow's veterinary medicine degree average 217 points in the UCAS tariff – the top entry standards in a high-tariff table – and the university is second for research. Sixth-place Nottingham has the most accessible entry standards, with its trainee vets entering an average of 157 points in the UCAS tariff. The university is hitting all the right notes with its students too, achieving unsurpassed scores for teaching quality and the broader student experience in these NSS-derived measures. Nottingham also has the edge for graduate prospects, with 97.9% of graduates employed in high-skilled jobs and/or postgraduate study 15 months after their degrees. But employment scores are so tightly bunched, going no lower than 93.1% achieving the same outcomes at Edinburgh, that they do not form part of the calculations that determine universities' positions. Veterinary medicine tops our 70-subject employment table this year, up from fourth last year. For graduate salaries, it ties with pharmacy and pharmacology.

Applicants are advised to focus on achieving top class performances in biology and chemistry. A third science may be required by some universities, others may allow another third subject. Applicants to institutions including Cambridge and the Royal Veterinary College may also be required to take an admissions test, while Surrey uses an online questionnaire. All vet schools require candidates to have proven their commitment to the course by completing some form of relevant work experience before applying. Ever a competitive subject, in the 2023 admissions cycle there were 11,935 applications for 1,720 places. The deadline for applications is October 15th, earlier than for most other subjects to allow extra time to process the high demand for courses.

| Veterinary Medicine | Teaching quality % | Student experience % | Research quality % | Entry standards (UCAS points) | Graduate prospects % | Overall score |
|---|---|---|---|---|---|---|
| 1 Liverpool | 93.9 | 84.2 | 68.2 | 176 | 96.9 | 100 |
| 2 Glasgow | 77.6 | 67 | 64.8 | 217 | 97.3 | 97.5 |
| 3 Edinburgh | 88.5 | 77 | 50.2 | 215 | 93.1 | 95.2 |
| 4 Cambridge | 83.1 | 64.2 | 60.2 | 200 | 96.1 | 95 |
| 5 Surrey | 87.3 | 77.3 | 58 | 168 | 96.4 | 92.8 |
| 6 Nottingham | 95.3 | 87.3 | 52 | 157 | 97.9 | 92 |
| 7 Bristol | 81.2 | 67.9 | 60.2 | 173 | 96.1 | 91.9 |
| 8 Royal Veterinary College | 79.6 | 61.4 | 55 | 178 | 97.4 | 89.4 |

| | | | |
|---|---|---|---|
| Employed in high-skilled job | 92% | Employed in lower-skilled job | 1% |
| Employed in high-skilled job and studying | 2% | Employed in lower-skilled job and studying | 0% |
| Studying | 1% | Unemployed | 2% |
| High-skilled work (median) salary | £33,000 | Low-/medium-skilled salary | N/A |

# 11 Applying to Oxbridge

Two ancient universities with one portmanteau moniker, Oxbridge is recognised as among the best in the world. For nearly three decades Oxford and Cambridge dominated at the top of our league table with an unbroken duopoly – until St Andrews first pipped them to the post four years ago. Settling for third and fourth place respectively this year, Oxford and Cambridge are behind both the London School of Economics and St Andrews – universities where high rates of student satisfaction are contributing to their soaring success.

In global rankings however, which take account of research profiles but not student reviews, Oxbridge remains unmatched in UK higher education: Oxford has been placed first in the world by *Times Higher Education (THE)* every year from 2017 to 2024, and it is third in the QS World University Rankings 2025. Cambridge also excels on the global stage: it is fifth in the QS World University Rankings 2025; fifth in the Times Higher Education World University Rankings 2024; and fourth in the Shanghai Ranking 2024, where it is the top-rated UK institution.

But it is their admissions arrangements, rather than their reputations, that warrant a separate chapter in our *Guide*. Oxford and Cambridge are part of the UCAS system but there are three significant peculiarities to the process of applying to them:

1. The deadline for applications is October 15 at 6pm – three months earlier than for other universities for entry in 2026 or deferred entry in 2027.
2. You can only apply to one or the other university in the same year, so you need to choose between the two.
3. Selection is in the hands of the colleges rather than the university centrally. Most candidates apply to a specific college, although open applications can be made if you are happy to go to any college.

## What are the chances of getting in?

This is the starter for ten for those with Oxbridge in their sights. There is little to choose between the two universities in terms of entry requirements. Cambridge typically receives six applications per place across all subjects, while Oxford receives over seven per place. But there are big differences by subject, as the tables on pages 275–78 and page 287 show. Competition is particularly fierce in degrees such as computer science, medicine and law, but those applying to read earth sciences or modern languages have a much better chance of success. In theory, all colleges are equally hard to get into, as Oxbridge "pools" students who they like but do not have space for, allowing other colleges to snap them up. But acceptance rates do vary from college to college. Analysis by The Tab youth news site showed acceptance rates in 2024 ranging from 42% at Murray Edwards to 15.1% at Downing at Cambridge and 18.9% at Jesus to 10.9% at Trinity – both Oxford colleges. Age and wealth tend to attract applications too: St John's, Oxford, and Trinity, Cambridge (both old colleges with big endowments) are among those to receive the highest numbers of applications.

The number of places available is fairly constant (pandemic-influenced fluctuations aside) and hovers around 3,300 at Oxford most years (3,260 undergraduates were accepted in 2023), from 24,230 applications (up by 0.6% from 24,080 in 2022). Cambridge received 21,445 applications in 2023 (down 4.6% from 22,470 in 2022), made 4,553 offers (an increase of 7.4% from 4,238), and accepted 3,557 new undergraduates (0.4% more than the year before).

Entry standards are famously formidable. While three A grades is Oxford's minimum standard offer, many courses – particularly in the sciences – require at least one A* grade. At Oxford, 53.0% of applicants and 84.1% of 2023's admitted students were awarded A*AA or better at A-level (down from 66.9% and 91.2% respectively in 2022). Nearly half (47%) of admitted students in 2023 got triple A* or better. The picture is very similar at Cambridge, where the typical conditional A-level offer is A*AA or A*A*A. Of home students accepted to Cambridge in the 2023 cycle 94.4% achieved the equivalent of A*AA, counting only their best three A-levels, excluding general studies and critical thinking (down from 97.9% in 2022 and 98.6% in 2021).

Although applicants' socioeconomic and educational background are considered, Oxbridge stops short of making contextual offers with lower grades. Instead using this information to give admissions tutors a rounded picture of an applicant and the context in which their achievements occurred.

Such statistics should not put bright, academically driven students off from applying. What is the worst that can happen? One wasted option out of five on a UCAS form, perhaps. One thing to be mindful of, though, is that selectors have to be confident that applicants will cope with the demands of an undergraduate course at Oxbridge. At only eight weeks long, Oxbridge terms are intensive. Admissions tutors are looking for genuine interest in the chosen subject, very high levels of academic ability and outstanding examination results, along with a capacity for hard work, independent learning and intellectual flexibility.

### Student satisfaction?
Oxbridge students have spoken, ending their boycott of the National Student Survey (NSS), which began in 2017. In our new NSS analysis Oxford ranks 19th for student satisfaction with teaching quality – and first among its Russell Group peers. For satisfaction with the wider undergraduate experience, however, the results are diametrically opposed – with Oxford ranking 124th, the worst result among Russell Group members. For teaching quality Cambridge is =30th in the UK and third among Russell Group members and also compares much less positively for student reviews of the wider undergraduate experience (=116th).

The reputation of both universities, like many, was dented by the marking and assessment boycott in 2023, part of long-running industrial action over pay by the national lecturers' union. This left thousands of students unable to graduate on time that summer because exams and dissertations had been unmarked. Cambridge, where only 59% of final year students in 2023 graduated on time, was one of the worst-affected universities.

But job prospects for those with Oxbridge degrees are reliably promising. The two universities tie in fourth place of our Graduate Outcomes survey analysis, with 90.4% of

## Cambridge: The Tompkins Table

The 2024 Tompkins table ranks by college the results of all Cambridge students in their end-of-year Tripos examinations each summer.

| College | 2024 | 2022* | 2019 | 2018 | College | 2024 | 2022* | 2019 | 2018 |
|---|---|---|---|---|---|---|---|---|---|
| Trinity | 1 | 2 | 2 | 3 | Magdalene | 16 | 18 | 18 | 18 |
| Christ's | 2 | 1 | 1 | 1 | Robinson | 17 | 17 | 21 | 24 |
| Corpus Christi | 3 | 9 | 11 | 15 | Jesus | 18 | 4 | 14 | 6 |
| Pembroke | 4 | 5 | 3 | 2 | Trinity Hall | 19 | 19 | 10 | 12 |
| Selwyn | 5 | 14 | 8 | 11 | Sidney Sussex | 20 | 16 | 13 | 17 |
| Churchill | 6 | 8 | 5 | 7 | Fitzwilliam | 21 | 20 | 17 | 19 |
| Queens' | 7 | 10 | 6 | 13 | Wolfson | 22 | 21 | 27 | 29 |
| St Catharine's | 8 | 3 | 9 | 10 | Lucy Cavendish | 23 | 29 | 29 | 28 |
| Emmanuel | 9 | 11 | 7 | 9 | King's | 24 | 22 | 12 | 5 |
| Gonville & Caius | 10 | 7 | 16 | 14 | Homerton | 25 | 26 | 26 | 27 |
| Downing | 11 | 13 | 23 | 20 | Murray Edwards | 26 | 27 | 19 | 26 |
| Clare | 12 | 12 | 24 | 16 | Newnham | 27 | 24 | 22 | 22 |
| St Edmund's | 13 | 28 | 28 | 21 | Girton | 28 | 25 | 20 | 23 |
| St John's | 14 | 6 | 15 | 8 | Hughes Hall | 29 | 23 | 25 | 25 |
| Peterhouse | 15 | 15 | 4 | 4 | | | | | |

Based on degree classifications: 1st = 5pts; 2.1 = 3pts; 2.2 = 2pts; 3rd = 1pt.
* The Tompkins Table was not published in 2020 or 2021 because of the pandemic.

graduates employed in high skilled jobs or engaged in postgraduate study 15 months on from their degrees.

### Diversity

Progress to widen access to Oxbridge is accelerating. In 2023, the proportion of students joining Oxford from state schools was 67.6%, slightly less than in the year before (68.1%) but up from 62.3% in 2019. Our records show that as far back as 2002 this proportion was just 54.3%. At Cambridge, 72.6% of the intake of home students in 2023 was from state schools in 2023 – down from 72.9% the year before and the first decline in the proportion of state school admissions in a decade. Even so, this still represented a rise from 68% in 2019 and an even bigger hike from 55.5% in 2002. But in our social inclusion index, which ranks universities according to their admissions from non-selective state schools only and does not include grammars, Cambridge sits 113th out of the 115 universities in England and Wales, with 49.5% from non-selective state schools. Only Imperial College London and Durham accepted more students from independent or selective state schools. Oxford fares a little better, ranking 110th for its proportion from non-selective schools (53.5%)

The universities compare better with others on ethnic diversity: the proportion of students from ethnic minorities (24.6%) ranks Oxford 64th and Cambridge 57th (30.8). Cambridge has shown improvement in the years since the Stormzy Scholarship was introduced in 2018 and expanded in 2021. More than 40 black British students have benefited so far from the £20,000 award, covering tuition fees and a maintenance grant. Thirty scholarships will be offered from 2024–26 through a partnership between Stormzy's #Merky Foundation and HSBC UK.

The universities continue to work hard to dispel their "champagne set" connotations and attract bright students from a broad range of backgrounds. In 2023, 21.2% of UK undergraduates admitted to Oxford came from the least advantaged backgrounds (up from 13.3% in 2018) and 7.6% were eligible for Free School Meals. At Cambridge 21.2% of 2023 admissions were from the least advantaged postcodes. The universities have both launched foundation years: Oxford's Astrophoria Foundation Year welcomed its first 22 UK state school students in 2023, while the Cambridge Foundation Year in arts, humanities and social sciences launched in 2022. Designed for disadvantaged students, the one-year courses are fully funded, with fees and living costs covered by the university and with lower grade requirements than for undergraduate programmes. Foundation year students who achieve the required level may progress to a full degree. Oxford has grown its bridging programme, Opportunity Oxford, in which 170 students participated in 2023. Among other outreach activities, Cambridge works with social mobility charities such as the Sutton Trust and Target Oxbridge, while individual colleges have links with different areas with low records of sending students to Russell Group universities.

Oxbridge is clearly making progress, but the universities continue to prop up the nether regions of our main social inclusion index of universities in England and Wales – which looks at nine measures of social inclusion: state school entrants (non-grammar); ethnic minorities; black attainment gap; white working-class males; low participation areas; low participation areas dropout gap; first-generation students; disabled students; mature students. Oxford ranks 111th out of 115 (down from 109th last year). Cambridge fares more poorly still, in bottom place (115th) a two-place drop from 113th in our previous edition.

## Stating the case: public or private

Professor Stephen Toope, the former vice-chancellor of the University of Cambridge made

---

### Oxford: The Norrington Table

The 2022 Norrington table ranks by college the performance of 3,052 undergraduates from the summer of 2021.

| College | 2022 | 2021 | 2020 | 2019 | College | 2022 | 2021 | 2020 | 2019 |
|---|---|---|---|---|---|---|---|---|---|
| Merton | 1 | 1 | 5 | 1 | Worcester | 16 | 7 | 14 | 24 |
| Lincoln | 2 | 3 | 10 | 21 | Oriel | 17 | 20 | 9 | 8 |
| Harris Manchester | 3 | 9 | 21 | 11 | University | 18 | 14 | 13 | 13 |
| Queen's | 4 | 11 | 3 | 7 | St Hilda's | 19 | 29 | 17 | 18 |
| St Peter's | 5 | 13 | 4 | 25 | Balliol | 20 | 8 | 16 | 9 |
| St Catherine's | 6 | 6 | 2 | 4 | Corpus Christi | 21 | 12 | 23 | 12 |
| Wadham | 7 | 18 | 6 | 20 | St Anne's | 22 | 10 | 22 | 28 |
| St John's | 8 | 2 | 8 | 6 | Christ Church | 23 | 21 | 28 | 15 |
| Somerville | 9 | 26 | 30 | 22 | St Edmund Hall | 24 | 24 | 25 | 29 |
| Pembroke | 10 | 28 | 19 | 17 | St Hugh's | 25 | 19 | 15 | 30 |
| Keble | 11 | 16 | 24 | 23 | Hertford | 26 | 27 | 11 | 14 |
| Magdalen | 12 | 22 | 20 | 3 | Trinity | 27 | 23 | 12 | 26 |
| Mansfield | 13 | 17 | 29 | 5 | Lady Margaret Hall | 28 | 30 | 27 | 27 |
| New College | 14 | 5 | 1 | 2 | Jesus | 29 | 15 | 18 | 10 |
| Brasenose | 15 | 4 | 7 | 16 | Exeter | 30 | 25 | 26 | 19 |

*Published by University of Oxford. Based on degree classifications: 1st=5pts; 2.1=3pts; 2.2=2pts; 3rd=1pt. Score shown is the percentage of total points available. Where tied, the overall number of first-class degrees and then 2.1s are used as separators.

## Oxford applications and acceptances by course

| Arts | Applications | | | Acceptances | | | Success rate % | | |
|---|---|---|---|---|---|---|---|---|---|
| | 2023 | 2022 | 2021 | 2023 | 2022 | 2021 | 2023 | 2022 | 2021 |
| Ancient and modern history | 98 | 81 | 98 | 20 | 14 | 26 | 20.4 | 17.3 | 26.5 |
| Archaeology and anthropology | 125 | 101 | 103 | 22 | 20 | 19 | 17.6 | 19.8 | 18.4 |
| Asian and Middle Eastern studies | 109 | 168 | 156 | 35 | 48 | 41 | 32.1 | 28.6 | 26.3 |
| Classical archaeology and ancient history | 152 | 67 | 121 | 25 | 19 | 29 | 16.4 | 28.4 | 24 |
| Classics | 313 | 293 | 252 | 100 | 123 | 106 | 31.9 | 42 | 42.1 |
| Classics and English | 60 | 30 | 35 | 13 | 8 | 13 | 21.7 | 26.7 | 37.1 |
| Classics and modern languages | 23 | 23 | 13 | 10 | 8 | 5 | 43.5 | 34.8 | 38.5 |
| Computer science and philosophy | 129 | 31 | 151 | 12 | 9 | 12 | 9.3 | 29 | 7.9 |
| Economics and management | 1542 | 1192 | 1,732 | 83 | 84 | 87 | 5.4 | 7 | 5 |
| English language and literature | 975 | 1142 | 942 | 212 | 240 | 229 | 21.7 | 21 | 24.3 |
| English and modern languages | 91 | 117 | 99 | 35 | 18 | 32 | 38.5 | 15.4 | 32.3 |
| European and Middle Eastern languages | 40 | 28 | 31 | 13 | 8 | 15 | 32.5 | 28.6 | 48.4 |
| Fine art | 255 | 189 | 264 | 28 | 28 | 29 | 11.0 | 14.8 | 11 |
| Geography | 339 | 371 | 458 | 70 | 77 | 79 | 20.6 | 20.8 | 17.2 |
| History | 958 | 1029 | 933 | 214 | 246 | 229 | 22.3 | 23.9 | 24.5 |
| History and economics | 158 | 99 | 172 | 18 | 13 | 17 | 11.4 | 13.1 | 9.9 |
| History and English | 104 | 89 | 121 | 12 | 7 | 13 | 11.5 | 7.9 | 10.7 |
| History and modern languages | 72 | 87 | 83 | 18 | 16 | 23 | 25.0 | 18.4 | 27.7 |
| History and politics | 381 | 279 | 463 | 48 | 39 | 49 | 12.6 | 14 | 10.2 |
| History of art | 107 | 137 | 121 | 14 | 12 | 18 | 13.1 | 8.8 | 14.9 |
| Law | 1858 | 1302 | 1,674 | 192 | 196 | 234 | 10.3 | 15.1 | 15 |
| Law with law studies in Europe | 341 | 317 | 304 | 26 | 31 | 31 | 7.6 | 9.8 | 10.9 |
| Mathematics and philosophy | 163 | 90 | 158 | 19 | 16 | 20 | 11.7 | 17.8 | 12.7 |
| Modern languages | 309 | 573 | 371 | 145 | 189 | 166 | 46.9 | 33 | 44.7 |
| Modern languages and linguistics | 91 | 72 | 86 | 39 | 27 | 34 | 42.9 | 37.5 | 39.5 |
| Music | 169 | 221 | 146 | 81 | 70 | 74 | 47.9 | 31.7 | 50.7 |
| Philosophy and modern languages | 56 | 51 | 63 | 21 | 13 | 16 | 37.5 | 25.5 | 25.4 |
| Philosophy and theology | 146 | 118 | 146 | 25 | 28 | 29 | 17.1 | 23.7 | 19.9 |
| Physics and philosophy | 139 | 146 | 174 | 12 | 16 | 14 | 8.6 | 11 | 8 |
| Philosophy, politics and economics (PPE) | 1864 | 1640 | 2,300 | 229 | 232 | 232 | 12.3 | 14.1 | 10.1 |
| Theology and religion | 116 | 91 | 112 | 46 | 28 | 43 | 39.7 | 30.8 | 38.4 |
| Religion and Asian and Middle Eastern studies | 3 | 4 | 11 | 1 | 1 | 3 | 33.3 | 25 | 27.3 |
| **Total Arts** | **11,286** | **10,178** | **11,893** | **1,838** | **1884** | **1,942** | **16.3** | **18.5** | **23.6** |

major efforts on widening access, overseeing the creation of the university's foundation year and stating: "We have to keep making it very, very clear we are intending to reduce over time the number of people who are coming from independent school backgrounds into places like Oxford or Cambridge." Since taking over as Cambridge's vice-chancellor, Deborah Prentice has reassured private school applicants who may "fear discrimination" that "we are open to talent from absolutely everywhere and it's more competitive because we're trying to get the applicant numbers up but there's no discrimination". Cambridge has said it is doing away

**Oxford applications and acceptances by course** cont.

| Sciences | Applications | | | Acceptances | | | Success rate % | | |
|---|---|---|---|---|---|---|---|---|---|
| | 2023 | 2022 | 2021 | 2023 | 2022 | 2021 | 2023 | 2022 | 2021 |
| Biochemistry | 875 | 399 | 738 | 100 | 90 | 107 | 11.4 | 22.6 | 14.5 |
| Biology | 742 | 428 | 677 | 109 | 111 | 99 | 14.7 | 25.9 | 14.6 |
| Biomedical sciences | 490 | 193 | 558 | 41 | 33 | 43 | 8.4 | 17.1 | 7.7 |
| Chemistry | 1015 | 638 | 862 | 175 | 180 | 183 | 17.2 | 28.2 | 2.2 |
| Computer science | 866 | 147 | 843 | 52 | 23 | 33 | 6.0 | 15.6 | 3.9 |
| Earth sciences (Geology) | 163 | 116 | 111 | 34 | 34 | 37 | 20.9 | 29.3 | 33.3 |
| Engineering science | 1031 | 720 | 1,097 | 163 | 157 | 172 | 15.8 | 21.8 | 15.7 |
| Experimental psychology | 379 | 212 | 469 | 43 | 50 | 57 | 11.3 | 23.6 | 12.2 |
| Human sciences | 193 | 155 | 233 | 26 | 31 | 29 | 13.5 | 20 | 12.4 |
| Materials science | 148 | 79 | 178 | 44 | 33 | 45 | 29.7 | 41.8 | 25.3 |
| Mathematics | 1807 | 917 | 1,849 | 179 | 161 | 169 | 9.9 | 17.6 | 9.1 |
| Mathematics and computer science | 593 | 119 | 603 | 51 | 28 | 46 | 8.6 | 23.5 | 7.6 |
| Mathematics and statistics | 142 | 172 | 262 | 3 | 22 | 9 | 2.1 | 12.8 | 3.4 |
| Medicine | 1712 | 1471 | 2,054 | 149 | 149 | 165 | 8.7 | 10.1 | 9 |
| Physics | 1494 | 1011 | 1,630 | 174 | 173 | 181 | 11.6 | 17.1 | 11 |
| Psychology and philosophy (PPL) | 275 | 161 | 281 | 38 | 29 | 30 | 13.8 | 18 | 10.7 |
| **Total Sciences** | **11,925** | **6,938** | **12,445** | **1,381** | **1314** | **1,342** | **12.7** | **18.7** | **11.9** |
| **Total Arts and Sciences** | **23,211** | **17,116** | **24,338** | **3,219** | **3,198** | **3,284** | **14.5** | **18.6** | **17.8** |

with its state-school admissions target, which had been set at 69.1% by 2024–25, having already surpassed it. The university is drawing up its next access plan, which will cover the years 2025–26 to 2028–29 and will focus on finding ways to increase the number of students from underprivileged backgrounds, underrepresented ethnicities and underrepresented regions.

At Oxford, Irene Tracey, the university's first state-educated vice-chancellor and the former warden of its Merton College refuted claims of a conspiracy against privately educated pupils, telling *The Times* in 2023: "I've done admissions for 25 years so I can absolutely speak at the coalface about how we do it. There are no quotas. There are no biases, it's so thorough and fair, and we work our socks off to make sure that we've got the best kids ... Inevitably, as we've opened up and done so much more on engagement, you're going to have more competition and that's going to be reflected in the numbers. That's the reality."

Of the 80 UK schools that sent the highest proportion of sixth-formers to Oxbridge in 2023, 29 were independent (down from 35 in 2021), 29 were grammars (up from 21), 17 were sixth-form colleges and five (down from six) were comprehensive or academies. Meanwhile the number of students admitted from Eton has halved from 99 in 2014 to 48 in 2023. Westminster, the London independent school, achieved the highest number of Oxbridge acceptances, 69 – a feat shared by Hills Road Sixth Form College in Cambridge. The vast majority of Britons are educated in state schools: 94% of the population and 83% of those who take A-levels. Although their share has fallen, the number of places occupied by private school pupils remains disproportionately large.

# Cambridge applications and acceptances by course

| Arts, Humanities and Social Sciences | Applications | | | Acceptances | | | Success rate % | | |
|---|---|---|---|---|---|---|---|---|---|
| | 2023 | 2022 | 2021 | 2023 | 2022 | 2021 | 2023 | 2022 | 2021 |
| Anglo-Saxon, Norse and Celtic | 62 | 54 | 45 | 19 | 22 | 24 | 30.6 | 40.7 | 53.3 |
| Archaeology | 82 | 60 | 39 | 32 | 21 | 20 | 39.0 | 35 | 51.3 |
| Architecture | 522 | 583 | 370 | 60 | 66 | 53 | 11.5 | 11.3 | 14.3 |
| Asian and Middle Eastern studies | 124 | 160 | 108 | 60 | 54 | 41 | 48.4 | 33.8 | 38 |
| Classics | 126 | 123 | 107 | 50 | 53 | 54 | 39.7 | 43.1 | 50.5 |
| Classics (four years) | 106 | 97 | 53 | 29 | 37 | 26 | 27.4 | 38.1 | 49 |
| Economics | 1336 | 1513 | 776 | 162 | 151 | 102 | 12.1 | 10 | 13.1 |
| Education | 190 | 268 | 62 | 34 | 41 | 26 | 17.9 | 15.3 | 41.9 |
| English | 756 | 776 | 654 | 187 | 185 | 172 | 24.7 | 23.8 | 26.3 |
| Geography | 524 | 491 | 386 | 99 | 96 | 88 | 18.9 | 19.6 | 22.8 |
| History | 607 | 580 | 522 | 164 | 171 | 172 | 27.0 | 29.5 | 33 |
| History and modern languages | 88 | 125 | 64 | 31 | 30 | 20 | 35.2 | 24 | 31.3 |
| History and politics | 342 | 335 | 225 | 67 | 49 | 51 | 19.6 | 14.6 | 22.7 |
| History of art | 87 | 96 | 67 | 31 | 20 | 28 | 35.6 | 20.8 | 41.8 |
| Human, social and political sciences | 1436 | 1482 | 819 | 166 | 168 | 129 | 11.6 | 11.3 | 15.8 |
| Land economy | 629 | 487 | 222 | 71 | 64 | 44 | 11.3 | 13.1 | 19.8 |
| Law | 1580 | 1845 | 1,097 | 230 | 217 | 169 | 14.6 | 11.8 | 15.4 |
| Linguistics | 119 | 143 | 80 | 26 | 31 | 34 | 21.8 | 21.7 | 42.5 |
| Modern and medieval languages | 254 | 336 | 319 | 128 | 144 | 148 | 50.4 | 42.9 | 46.4 |
| Music | 140 | 153 | 154 | 51 | 71 | 65 | 36.4 | 46.4 | 42.2 |
| Philosophy | 306 | 308 | 206 | 50 | 51 | 47 | 16.3 | 16.6 | 22.8 |
| Theology and religious studies | 105 | 107 | 91 | 37 | 43 | 37 | 35.2 | 40.2 | 40.7 |
| **Total Arts, Humanities and Social Sciences** | **9521** | **10122** | **6466** | **1784** | **1785** | **1,550** | **26.6** | **17.6** | **33.4** |

| Sciences | 2023 | 2022 | 2021 | 2023 | 2022 | 2021 | 2023 | 2022 | 2021 |
|---|---|---|---|---|---|---|---|---|---|
| Computer science | 1583 | 1,625 | 955 | 121 | 136 | 77 | 7.6 | 8.4 | 8.1 |
| Engineering | 2410 | 2,672 | 1,545 | 333 | 344 | 220 | 13.8 | 12.9 | 14.2 |
| Mathematics | 1588 | 1,515 | 921 | 258 | 252 | 140 | 16.2 | 16.6 | 15.2 |
| Medicine | 1754 | 1,971 | 1,369 | 273 | 271 | 246 | 15.6 | 13.7 | 18 |
| Medicine (graduate course) | 548 | 529 | 42 | 40 | 37 | 3 | 7.3 | 7 | 7.1 |
| Natural sciences | 2444 | 2,695 | 1,796 | 547 | 568 | 410 | 22.4 | 21.1 | 22.8 |
| Psychological and behavioural sciences | 891 | 939 | 476 | 81 | 87 | 65 | 9.1 | 9.3 | 13.7 |
| Veterinary medicine | 333 | 402 | 297 | 73 | 64 | 58 | 21.9 | 15.9 | 19.5 |
| **Total Science and Technology** | **11,551** | **12,348** | **7,401** | **1,726** | **1,759** | **1,219** | **14.2** | **14.2** | **14.8** |

| Total | 21,072 | 22,470 | 13,867 | 3,510 | 3,544 | 3,660 | 20.4 | 15.8 | 24.1 |

## Choosing the right college

Undergraduates at Cambridge are admitted to 29 colleges, each with its own distinctive history, atmosphere and location. It is worth visiting before applying to help you decide on a college that most suits, though it is possible to make an open application. Oxford has 30 colleges that accept undergraduates, and applicants should likewise do their research. That said, both universities work to find a college for those who either make an open application or who are not taken by their first choice. At Oxford, subject tutors put candidates into bands, using the results of admissions tests as well as exam results and references. Applicants may not be seen by their preferred college if the tutors think their chances are better elsewhere. The "pool" at Cambridge gives the most promising candidates a second chance if they were not offered a place at the college they applied to. Most Oxbridge applicants still apply direct to a particular college, in part because these are where they will live and socialise. Famously sporty colleges, for instance, might not suit quieter students. Cambridge still interviews around 80% of applicants, whereas Oxford interviews around 40% to 45% of candidates.

At both universities, teaching is in-college for most students, although those on science programmes branch out after their first year. One-to-one tutorials, Oxbridge's traditional strength for undergraduates, are not the only method of teaching and learning, but teaching groups remain much smaller than in most universities and tutors are an inspiration for many. The tables in this chapter give an idea of the relative strengths of the colleges, as well as the levels of competition for a place in different subjects. But only individual research will help you uncover where you will feel most at home

## The application process

Historically the application process has been viewed as one shrouded in myth and conspiracy, but both universities have worked hard to demystify it. Cambridge requires most applicants to take a written pre-interview admission assessment at the beginning of November. Some subjects administer tests at interview and some applicants are asked to submit examples of their written work. The Cambridge website lists the pre-interview assessments, which may include a reading comprehension, problem-solving test, or a thinking skills assessment; in addition to a paper on the subject itself. Applicants to Oxford must also take an admissions test for many courses, and written work may be a requirement. These tests are described by those in the know as 'the pathway to interview', which applicants are advised to prepare for as they would an A-level exam. Those who are shortlisted are invited to interview in early to mid-December, all of which are online. Applicants to Cambridge must also complete an online Supplementary Application Questionnaire (SAQ) by October 22 (6pm UK time) in most cases. Interviews can be online or in-person. Applicants receive either a conditional offer or a rejection in the new year. For more information about the application process and preparing for interviews, visit **www.undergraduate.study.cam.ac.uk** or **www.ox.ac.uk/admissions/undergraduate**.

# Oxford College Profiles

### Balliol

Oxford OX1 3BJ      01865 277 777      balliol.ox.ac.uk

Undergraduates: 418      Postgraduates: 445      undergraduate@balliol.ox.ac.uk

Famous as the alma mater of many prominent post-war politicians, from Harold Macmillan to Yvette Cooper, the college is named after John de Balliol. While maintaining its reputation since 1263 as the oldest academic site in the English-speaking world co-founded by a woman, Balliol also poses the triple "threat" (to study) of a student-run bar, popular café and excellent theatre – the Michael Pilch Studio. Historically a regular in the Norrington table's top ten (although it ranks 20th in the latest edition), academic excellence and social responsibility are college hallmarks. Students and tutors inhabit rooms in both the Garden Quad and the beautiful Front Quad, now equipped with a ramp to make the college accessible. Undergraduates are guaranteed accommodation for all the years of their course, while graduate students are lodged in beautiful Holywell Manor or the new accommodation at the Master's Field, where the College has its own sports facilities. The impressive medieval library hosts 70,000 books and periodicals. Friendly librarians also host popular quiz and ghost story evenings. Balliol runs access programmes for year 10 and year 12 students as well as taster days and other events for would-be applicants.

### Brasenose

Oxford OX1 4AJ      01865 277 822      bnc.ox.ac.uk

Undergraduates: 380      Postgraduates: 260      admissions@bnc.ox.ac.uk

Tucked beside the Radcliffe Camera, Brasenose is in the heart of historic Oxford. Renowned as a friendly, diverse, medium-sized college it admits 111 new undergraduates each year, across 18 science, medical science, social science and humanities subjects. Admissions selectors focus on applicants' academic potential and passion for the subject area. Across the three years from 2020 to 2022, 80.6% of UK students admitted to Brasenose were from state schools (the third-highest proportion among Oxford colleges). Students run a lively range of clubs, societies and social events, such as The Brasenose Arts Week, yoga sessions, dog walks and musical recitals. Welfare and academic support services for students are well-resourced. Dining (both formal and informal) is provided in the 16th century dining hall, with vegan, vegetarian and gluten-free options available at all meals. The Brazen Nose door knocker, after which the college is named, was placed on the wall in 1890 and hangs above the high table. Brasenose undergraduate students are offered accommodation for all years of study, and both rooms and food are subsidised. Graduate students can apply for accommodation across two sites: Hollybush Row and St Cross Annex. Membership of the university gym at the Iffley Road Sports Centre is free for all students. The Brasenose boat club is one of the oldest in the world.

### Christ Church

Oxford OX1 1DP      01865 286 583      chch.ox.ac.uk

Undergraduates: 455      Postgraduates: 230      admissions@chch.ox.ac.uk

Christ Church remains one of the most imposing sites in the university and boasts the largest quad in Oxford. Its impressive scale, beautiful meadow and religious foundations continue to attract students, academics and tourists in large swathes. Founded by Cardinal Wolsey in 1525, it is also the Cathedral of the Oxford diocese. The Very Reverend Professor Sarah Foot was installed as Dean of Christ Church in July 2023. She is the first woman to be appointed to the role in the college's 500-year history. Bowler-hatted porters, a listed 18th-century library, daily formal dining and wooden-panelled shared "sets" (double rooms) characterise the overall feel of student life here. Accommodation covers all four years and ranges from the Blue Boar 1960s concrete block (for first-years) to the beautiful rooms in Peck quad (the domain of second-years) and the impressive Meadows and Old Library rooms (mostly for third- and fourth-years). UK students from lower-income households (up to £50,000 per year) can have up to 50% subsidy on accommodation and dinners. Christ Church is the Oxford college with the highest proportion of UK students from Black, Asian, and Minority Ethnic groups – who represented more than a third of the intake across the three-year period from 2020 to 2022. Dining is in the infamous Harry Potter hall, which hosts two servings every evening, one informal and one formal. Students choose between two student bars: The Buttery, open daily, and The Undie, from Wednesday to Saturday. The college's newly refurbished art room is a base for practical work and regular exhibitions. The accent on extracurriculars at Christ Church includes an impressive choir, as well as music and drama societies. Christ Church is also active in rowing, and plans are afoot to create a new Centre for Entrepreneurship and Innovation, where all students will have the opportunity to polish their business building skills.

## Corpus Christi

Oxford OX1 4JF        01865 276 693        ccc.ox.ac.uk
Undergraduates: 277    Postgraduates: 100    admissions.office@ccc.ox.ac.uk

Small but mighty Corpus Christi offers a tight-knit community. Progressive principles distinguished the college's foundation in 1517 by Richard Fox, Bishop of Winchester – whose coat of arms shows a pelican in a selfless act of charity. Fox's focus on humanist learning had a strong influence on the college's impressive 16th-century library. The original bookstacks sit alongside the newly opened Spencer Building, which provides a modern library and workspace containing 70,000 volumes. Recent exhibitions have showcased Corpus's very own Magna Carta and King James Bible manuscripts. Academic expectations are high; medicine, English, classics and PPE (philosophy, politics and economics) are especially well-established. The college describes itself as an inspiring oasis for study and friendship. Its affable atmosphere is nurtured within beautiful buildings between Christ Church meadow and the High Street. The college provides one of Oxford's most generous bursary schemes, which bestows travel, book and vacation grants. Corpus's postgraduate community represents 25 countries. Quirky extracurriculars include the Cheese Society and an annual tortoise race. The large and modern Al Jaber Auditorium is used for music, drama, art exhibitions and film screenings. Corpus's drama club, The Owlets, is highly regarded, while its sports teams usually pair up with another college. 2024 marked the 50th anniversary of the tortoise fair, an annual summer gathering in Corpus' gardens featuring live music and the famous inter-collegiate human tortoise race.

## Exeter College

Oxford OX1 3DP        01865 279 668        exeter.ox.ac.uk
Undergraduates: 385    Postgraduates: 309    admissions@exeter.ox.ac.uk

The fourth-oldest Oxford college, Exeter has been situated in the heart of town on Turl Street since 1315 – one year after it was founded. It boasts spectacular views from the Fellows' Garden, which overlooks Radcliffe Square. Following a major restoration, Exeter's Victorian library is open again, 24/7, boasting a lift and fully accessible toilet, extra reader spaces and flexible seating for individual and group study. Undergraduates are guaranteed three years of college accommodation and can take advantage of Exeter's new on-course support programme, designed to ease the transition from school to university. Located ten minutes away on Walton

Street, Exeter's modern Cohen Quad has won awards for its architecture. Its fusion of glass, stone and cherrywood characterise the quad's 90 en-suite bedrooms, café, study and social hub, breakout rooms and auditorium. Exeter's students take pride in the college's warm and accepting character and a wide range of festivals celebrated in the Jacobean dining hall encourages everyone to experience their own and other traditions. The college was the first in Oxford to appoint a sustainability coordinator to help reduce carbon emissions, cut waste and enhance biodiversity. Among its alumni Exeter counts many prominent 20th-century writers, including Martin Amis, Philip Pullman and JRR Tolkien. Arts-based extracurriculars are particularly strong, with an annual Arts Festival – shared with neighbours Lincoln and Jesus – as well as regular live music nights and summer garden plays.

### Harris Manchester

Oxford OX1 3TD    01865 271 009    hmc.ox.ac.uk
Undergraduates: 100    Postgraduates: 170    admissions@hmc.ox.ac.uk

Harris Manchester is unique as Oxford's only college exclusively for mature students (aged over 21). It was originally founded in Manchester in 1786 to provide education for non-Anglican students. Following spells in both York and London it settled in Oxford in 1889, moving to its current central site in 1892 where it enjoys beautiful buildings and grounds just off Holywell Street. In 1996 Harris Manchester received its Royal Charter as a full College of the University of Oxford. The college is known for its close-knit, friendly atmosphere. Helping to create social bonds, all members of the MCR (middle common room, for graduate students) are also members of the JCR (junior common room, the term for the undergraduate student union at most Oxbridge colleges) – which has a student-run bar. Close to the Bodleian, Harris Manchester's own library is excellent and boasts the best student-to-book ratio of any college. All accommodation is on the main site and students can generally live in for at least the first and final years of their course. Meals are included in the fees, meaning self-catering is not an option for students living in college, but Harris Manchester has a reputation for excellent food. Students dress in their academic gowns for formal dinners on Monday and Wednesday evenings. Due to its small size the college offers a more limited range of degree courses. Many sports teams join other colleges and students have free membership of the Iffley Road gym.

### Hertford College

Oxford OX1 3BW    01865 279 400    hertford.ox.ac.uk
Undergraduates: 415    Postgraduates: 298    undergraduate.admissions@hertford.ox.ac.uk

A skyway linking Hertford's Old and New Quads on opposite sides of New College Lane is one of Oxford's most recognisable landmarks: Hertford Bridge, also known as the Bridge of Sighs. The college is one of the most centrally-located, nestled in a corner of Radcliffe Square next door to the Bodleian library. A pioneer of access, Hertford celebrated 50 years of admitting women in 2024 and its established outreach programme for state school students has been operating since the 1960s. The college continues to accept among the highest intakes of state school students at the university and in the three years from 2020 to 2022 78.5% of UK undergraduates came from the state sector. Hertford has a generous bursary scheme for undergraduates as well as scholarships for graduate students. College-owned accommodation is available across all years, and subsidised meals (including the popular weekend brunch) can be enjoyed in the historic dining Hall. There are plenty of extracurricular activities on offer as well, including a wide range of sports, a music society and chapel choir, subject societies, and a thriving JCR and MCR. Welfare, health and wellbeing support is available 24 hours a day, as are study and academic skills sessions.

## Jesus

Oxford OX1 3DW     01865 279 700     jesus.ox.ac.uk

Undergraduates: 384     Postgraduates: 334     admissions.officer@jesus.ox.ac.uk

Founded in 1571 by Queen Elizabeth I at the request of a Welsh lawyer and clergyman, Jesus is the only Elizabethan college at Oxford. The college is situated on a small site off Turl Street in the historic heart of the city, meaning students are just a few minutes' walk from the university libraries, science campus and humanities buildings. Known for being a friendly college, Jesus also provides a programme of financial support and outreach. Jesus' Cheng Yu Tung Building opened in 2022 and combines new postgraduate facilities with open-plan teaching and research spaces, the Cheng Kar Shun Digital Hub and a café, gym, exhibition space and multifaith room. College academics are engaged in interdisciplinary research in fields from climate change, astrophysics and medical research, to medieval history, classics and law. Off site, Jesus has squash courts and extensive playing fields with hockey, cricket, football and rugby pitches, grass tennis courts, netball courts, a boathouse and a sports pavilion. The lively JCR is housed in modern accommodation and runs a diverse programme of student events throughout the year, including the annual Turl Street Arts Festival. Jesus holds a shared ball with Somerville every three years.

## Keble

Oxford OX1 3PG     01865 272 708     keble.ox.ac.uk

Undergraduates: 465     Postgraduates: 550     admissions@keble.ox.ac.uk

One of Oxford's largest and most distinctive colleges, Keble's Victorian Gothic polychromatic brick facade looks onto University Parks. Its "holy zebra" stripy brickwork was intended to mark the college from its predecessors and attract attention and funding. Keble's dining hall stands out of the crowd too: it is the longest in Oxford – its epic proportions reflecting Keble's 1870s foundational premise that students should eat together regularly. The dining hall is hung with an exhibition of Keble portraits by photographer Fran Monks, showcasing individuals who represent resilience and tenacity from different genders, disabilities, ethnicities and socioeconomic backgrounds. Café Keble and the Red Brick Oven, the college pizza bar, are both open throughout term. Student productions run from the O'Reilly Theatre every fortnight, making Keble one of the best places for drama. Each year there's a lively Arts Week run by students as well as the acclaimed Early Music Festival. Undergraduate accommodation is provided for three years; some students choose to live out in their second or third year. Its vibrant community spirit provides Keble students with a covetable social life. The graduate community is based a short distance from the main site at the HB Allen Centre with 250 new rooms. Keble's sporting facilities are excellent, with gyms on both sites, a sports ground for football, cricket, netball and tennis 15 minutes away, as well as shared squash courts and a boat house.

## Lady Margaret Hall

Oxford OX2 6QA     01865 274 310     lmh.ox.ac.uk

Undergraduates: 417     Postgraduates: 300     admissions@lmh.ox.ac.uk

Lady Margaret Hall (LMH) began in October 1879, when nine women entered the college and became the first females to receive an Oxford education. Co-educational since 1978, LMH continues to widen access: it was the first college to establish a foundation year for students from underrepresented groups and paved the way for the Astrophoria Foundation Year, the university-wide scheme. Its situation just north of the city centre allows LMH an enviable expanse of green space compared with more central colleges. Beautiful gardens back onto the Cherwell River and the grounds include a punt house, tennis and pickleball courts and a hockey/football pitch. The college has a strong reputation in PPE with Nobel Peace Prize laureate Malala Yousafzai among its graduates. The college's art scene is supported by its library's extensive collections in the arts and humanities. The library is spread across three floors and contains 75,000 books. Music has become a strong focus at the college: there is a concert series, music recording studio, several student-run ensembles and visits by guest artists. Accommodation is guaranteed for first, second and third-year students, and includes recently built rooms in Pipe Partridge, a graceful neoclassical building with 64 en-suite bedrooms which also houses the Simpkins Lee Theatre. LMH is among the pioneers of supporting student wellbeing at Oxford and was one of the first colleges to appoint a head of wellbeing, along with a dedicated study skills support team.

## Lincoln

| | | |
|---|---|---|
| Oxford OX1 3DR | 01865 279 836 | lincoln.ox.ac.uk |
| Undergraduates: 328 | Postgraduates: 340 | admissions@lincoln.ox.ac.uk |

Ivy-covered medieval buildings distinguish the setting at Lincoln, which is counting down to its 600th anniversary in 2027. The college is located centrally on Turl Street, next to Exeter and Jesus. A strong performer in the Norrington table (in second place in the most recent edition), Lincoln prides itself on academic as well as extracurricular activities, and is known for being an unpretentious and friendly smaller college. Lincoln's supportive environment includes a welfare team, college nurse, and a college counsellor, while its environmental efforts were recognised with a second gold sustainability award in 2024. The college launched the West Midlands access programme, Pathfinders, in 2022 – which may in time shift the dial on Lincoln's intake of students from state school, which at 61.5% across the three years from 2020 to 2022 was among the lowest of the Oxford colleges. Deep Hall, the college bar, is popular with students and serves lighter food. There are generous subsidies for food and accommodation, with a large number of bursaries and hardship awards. The college offers scholarships for graduates and also rewards undergraduates who perform well in examinations. City-centre accommodation is provided for all undergraduates; graduate students are housed in Bear Lane or Little Clarendon Street nearby. Drama and music are popular: the Oakeshott Room in the refurbished Garden Building is a well-used venue for screenings and performances, especially during the Turl Street Arts Festival.

## Magdalen

| | | |
|---|---|---|
| Oxford OX1 4AU | 01865 276 063 | magd.ox.ac.uk |
| Undergraduates: 415 | Graduates: 190 | admissions@magd.ox.ac.uk |

Perhaps the most beautiful Oxford college, Magdalen has its own deer park and riverside walkway – grounds so inspiring that C. S. Lewis, who taught at the college, is said to have dreamt up Narnia while strolling around them. The choir sings from its bell tower to mark May Morning. Magdalen is the majority owner of the Oxford Science Park, which is known for its medical and life science technology firms. Tutors are renowned for their world-leading research and encourage applicants with a strong interest in their chosen subject and excellent academic ability. Magdalen has a history of placing within the top five of the Norrington Table (although it is 12th in the most recent edition). Around a quarter of students receive financial support – from travel grants to funding for creative projects. College diversity and inclusivity initiatives include packages for care-experienced students and support ranging from counselling and mentoring to financial help. One of its big draws is access to beautiful in-college rooms, which all cost the same for undergraduates. For graduate students, Magdalen has begun a major expansion of scholarships. Strength in drama is on show at the Magdalen Players' production in the gardens each summer, and the Florio Society (poetry) and Atkin Society (Law) are among the extensive extracurricular options. The college has punts – popular with students and tourists alike – and the Magdalen boat club is the oldest sporting club at the college.

## Mansfield

Oxford OX1 3TF          01865 270972          mansfield.ox.ac.uk
Undergraduates: 265     Postgraduates: 235     registrar@mansfield.ox.ac.uk

Opened in Oxford in 1886, Mansfield's original purpose was to educate nonconformist ministers. It draws on its history to cultivate intellectual autonomy and freedom, valuing diversity and difference. "Tell me what it is you plan to do with your one wild and precious life?" Mansfield principal Helen Mountfield asks freshers when they arrive, quoting poet Mary Oliver. Most of them come from state schools: 93.2% in the three years from 2020 to 2022 – the highest state-sector intake of all Oxford colleges. "The 93% isn't a quota," says Mountfield. "We take people wherever they come from, we look at them on merit, and we try to find the people we think will most make best use of a place here and benefit from it most." A short walk from the science area and university libraries but in a quiet position near to University Parks, the college is fairly central and occupies attractive Victorian buildings. There are extensive facilities considering its size, including the popular Crypt café and chapel dining hall, plus a well-stocked main library and three specialist reading rooms (for law, PPE and theology) open 24 hours a day. All undergraduates are housed in college accommodation, either on the main site (where all first-year undergraduates live) or in college-owned and -run accommodation in Oxford. The Hands Building is home to the law faculty's Bonavero Institute of Human Rights, providing a lecture space, and additional accommodation. The heart of students' social lives, the college atmosphere is relaxed and close-knit, with friendships forged within entertainment, sports, music and drama facilities and events.

## Merton

Oxford OX1 4JD          01865 286 316          merton.ox.ac.uk
Undergraduates: 322     Postgraduates: 223     undergraduate.admissions@merton.ox.ac.uk

Merton is top of the most recent Norrington table, based on 45 of 77 students scoring a first in their finals. It is rarely outside the top three of the ranking. Its academic reputation has earned Merton the "where fun goes to die" moniker – a nickname refuted by the college's fortnightly bops, white-tie Merton Winter Ball and annual Merton Society Garden Party. Merton is also one of Oxford's most ancient and prestigious colleges, founded in 1264 by Walter de Merton, Lord Chancellor of England. It houses Europe's oldest academic library in continuous use and offers a wide range of subjects. The curricular breadth goes some way to explaining the extent of its achievements. Luminous alumni include T.S. Eliot, physicist Sir Antony Leggett, Naruhito, Emperor of Japan, chemist Frederick Soddy, J.R.R. Tolkien, former Prime Minister Liz Truss, Dame Philippa Whipple, and mathematician Professor Sir Andrew Wiles. The college is located close to the city centre, with beautiful gardens and easy access to meadows leading down to the river. Some of the cheapest accommodation across Oxford colleges is guaranteed for all years of undergraduate degrees, alongside generous bursaries and grants. Merton's extracurriculars include sport, music, poetry, drama, and subject societies. Facilities span two libraries, music practice rooms, a multi-faith prayer room, bar and games room, as well as an on-site gym, and a boathouse. The chapel choir is renowned, with its Girl Choristers drawn from the local Oxfordshire community.

## New College

Oxford OX1 3BN          01865 279 272          new.ox.ac.uk
Undergraduates: 432     Postgraduates: 405     admissions@new.ox.ac.uk

Founder William of Wykeham was the first to build a college as an integrated complex in 1379 and New College became a model for the Oxford college layout. Its ancient foundation makes New College one of the oldest at Oxford. Within the large and architecturally striking college lies a relaxed and diverse community. New College boasts an enchanting common room and memorable walled gardens. The grounds make a perfect setting for the white-tie Commemoration Ball, held every three years. The college's charms have made on-screen appearances in *Mamma Mia 2: Here We Go Again*, *His Dark Materials* and *Harry Potter and the Goblet of Fire*. An impressive academic record is just as prominent and New College is often in the top ten of the Norrington table, (although it ranks 14th in the latest edition). A commitment to outreach work is evidenced by the college's Step-Up programme, which has been in operation since 2017. In recent years the college, along with two others, has also taken on responsibility for outreach provision in Wales. Music, drama and sport are prominent and are all aided by excellent facilities. The Clore Music Studios, which opened in 2019, provide state-of-the-art practice facilities while the chapel and antechapel host regular classical concerts and performances by the world-famous New College Choir. The college houses the vast majority of undergraduates in college accommodation, which has been enhanced by the recently opened Gradel Quadrangles two minutes away from the main college site.

## Oriel

Oxford OX1 4EW    01865 276 555    oriel.ox.ac.uk
Undergraduates: 335    Postgraduates: 227    admissions@oriel.ox.ac.uk

Known for its immaculate Jacobean front quad and striking portico, Oriel enjoys a central location on the south side of High Street, directly across from the University Church of St Mary. The fifth-oldest college at Oxford, its history spans almost seven centuries. In just the past century it has produced two Nobel Laureates, at least ten Olympic medallists and numerous luminaries in the arts and culture. Nicknamed "Toriel" due to its Conservative reputation, the college's controversial statue of Cecil Rhodes (an alumnus and benefactor) now includes a plaque describing him as "committed British colonialist" who exploited the "peoples of southern Africa". A strong sporting tradition is supported by facilities which include a sports ground, multiple gyms, squash courts and a boathouse. Oriel is described as having a "strong crew spirit" due to its strength on the river. Academics are equally to the fore and the college usually appears at the upper end of the Norrington Table, most recently topping it in 2016, though it sits just below its midpoint in the latest edition. Accommodation is guaranteed for the duration of study, graded from A* to D, with varying rents. All years live, eat and socialise together and the college's small size helps create a friendly atmosphere. The recently renovated Hall, with its English Gothic hammerbeam roof, is a popular feature. Meals are served six days per week, including two sittings for dinner with formal or informal options. Graduate housing is off the popular Cowley Road under a mile away and includes several recently renovated flats. A play is performed in the quads each summer.

## Pembroke

Oxford OX1 1DW    01865 276 412    pmb.ox.ac.uk
Undergraduates: 396    Postgraduates: 247    admissions@pmb.ox.ac.uk

Blending traditional and modern architecture, Pembroke is known for its relaxed atmosphere. Tucked away off St Aldates, the college sits opposite Christ Church in a quieter part of the city centre. The main site contains four quads: Old, Chapel, North and The Rokos, including five recently developed buildings. Promoting a supportive and down-to-earth approach to college life, its community is nevertheless lively and ambitiously intellectual. There are talks and panels with high-profile figures, as well as opportunities for Pembroke's own academics and students to share their research. Pembroke offers a range of joint honours undergraduate courses – from PPL (psychology, philosophy and linguistics) to European and Middle Eastern languages. History is both a strong subject and a strong presence around college: founded by King James I in 1624, Pembroke celebrated its 400th anniversary in 2024 and its grounds feature tributes to the Pembroke fallen as well as plaques to honour alumni such as James Smithson and J.R.R. Tolkien. The McGowin Library is open 24/7 and its special collections include works by alumnus Samuel Johnson. Pembroke's outreach work under the "OxNet" programme targets pupils living in the North West, North East and London. The college has also recently partnered with Rochdale Development Agency to provide a programme of academic engagement for the most able pupils across Rochdale, Heywood and Middleton. Rowing is strong and there is a variety of other extracurricular activities too. Almost all undergraduates and many graduates live on site and share meals together in the Dining Hall. The Sir Geoffrey Arthur Building, an off-site accommodation annexe situated on the banks of the River Thames, has recently expanded to provide more accommodation and facilities for both students and new academics.

## Queen's

Oxford OX1 4AW          01865 279 161          queens.ox.ac.uk
Undergraduates: 377    Postgraduates: 209    admissions@queens.ox.ac.uk

Located just off the High Street, Queen's imposing neo-classical buildings and bell tower create a grand entrance to the college's large, supportive and stimulating community. A multi-million-pound extension to the library delved underground to create an award-winning space that houses an accessible research centre with materials ranging from medieval manuscripts to digital resources. The library at Queen's now comprises three distinct reading rooms from different eras in history. The college's next masterplan is on sustainability: a review of existing buildings and their activity has recommended innovative solutions for reducing energy use and carbon emissions. Academically, Queen's is strong in a range of subjects and offers a diverse array of degrees. The college's Translation Exchange outreach centre specialises in languages and international culture and works with schools to boost language-learning among pupils. Queen's also partners with the Access Project to help deliver tutoring and mentoring support for disadvantaged students to get to top universities. An annual budget (of £108,450 in 2024) funds grants and loans awarded by a student finance committee. Facilities are splendid, with accommodation offered throughout undergraduate courses – some in annexes around central Oxford and a third on the main site, mostly en-suite. The college is fully catered, providing three subsidised meals a day. The lecture theatre is used for concerts and screenings. Sport, drama and music are all important parts of college life, particularly the Trinity term garden play and the mixed-voice chapel choir – recognised by Classic FM as 'one of the world's most renowned choirs'. Queen's has a popular beer cellar and extensive JCR facilities; afternoon tea is a daily highlight.

## St Anne's

Oxford OX2 6HS          01865 274 840          st-annes.ox.ac.uk
Undergraduates: 464    Postgraduates: 514    admissions@st-annes.ox.ac.uk

Like its motto, Consulto et audacter (purposely and boldly), St Anne's is bold and modern. It gained full college status in 1952 but has been widening access since 1879, when it was founded as the Society of Oxford Home-Students – allowing women to study in affordable halls without having to pay for college membership. Today, the college aims to be the home of choice for the brightest and most ambitious students of every background. Each year it funds 40 "Study Abroad" visiting students and it is also the only college to offer paid internships for its students – based in the UK, India, Serbia and Japan. Rooms in its purpose-built complex are decided by ballot and accommodation is guaranteed over three-year courses.

Renovations are currently underway on the college's Bevington Road buildings to update the accommodation and the new library and academic centre on Woodstock Road is a point of pride. The college is particularly strong for music: a student-led society encompasses various ensembles and hosts a termly showcase for all abilities. The college Arts Week includes drama, talks, film and dance classes. St Anne's is conveniently positioned for the University science area and is immediately opposite the Schwarzman Centre for the Humanities, currently under construction, the base for faculties of English, History, Linguistics, Languages, Music, Philosophy and Theology from 2025. Many students cycle to the university sports ground, although there is an on-site gym and nearby sports field.

## St Catherine's

Oxford OX1 3UJ      01865 271 700      stcatz.ox.ac.uk

Undergraduates: 513      Postgraduates: 500      admissions@stcatz.ox.ac.uk

Established in 1962, "Catz" is the youngest of any Oxford college and has the most undergraduates. Occupying a spacious site, it offers a vast 36 undergraduate subjects. Arne Jacobsen's modernist design for the college strikes a chord with those seeking to avoid the uniformity of some others. Positioned right by the English, law and social science faculties, Catz is characterised by a laid-back atmosphere but achieves excellent results – and ranks sixth in the latest Norrington table. Extensive facilities include the modern, spacious library housing more than 60,000 books. There is also a theatre, an on-site boathouse, squash courts, a water garden, an amphitheatre, a free gym and car park – a rare feature among Oxford colleges. A progressive JCR compounds the less traditional feel and with the largest bar in Oxford, Catz has a sociable reputation, hosting "bops" (big organised parties) throughout the year. Increased welfare support has seen the appointment of a college counsellor and a fund for transgender students. Large student numbers and generous sporting funds bring strength in extracurriculars – particularly in men's rugby, women's football and drama. Catz students also take active roles in writing, directing and acting. The annual Cameron Mackintosh Chair of Contemporary Theatre has seen visiting professorships held by Arthur Miller and Sir Tom Stoppard. Rooms are small, but warmer than in older colleges – and are available on site for first-, second- and third-years.

## St Edmund Hall

Oxford OX1 4AR      01865 279 009      seh.ox.ac.uk

Undergraduates: 379      Postgraduates: 339      Visiting students: 27      admissions@seh.ox.ac.uk

Known fondly as "Teddy Hall", St Edmund Hall is among the oldest Oxford colleges, dating back at least to 1317, and likely to the 1190s when St Edmund of Abingdon taught on the site. The college is located just off the High Street on the quieter Queen's Lane and its library is housed in the church of St Peter-in-the-East, with its (medieval) crypt one of Teddy Hall's many hidden gems. With an emphasis on securing further learning opportunities for its students, the college hosts programmes such as the Centre for the Creative Brain, Access Hall Areas, and the Geddes Lecture. Many of its academics are actively pursuing world-leading research, showcased on the college blog, that provides opportunities for students to understand cutting-edge ideas, concepts and phenomena. There is a literary slant too: Teddy Hall hosts a writer in residence, journalism prizes, weekly student-run writers' workshops and publishes multiple annual publications. The college community is known for being lively, social, creative and vigorously sporty. Food is excellent with Formal Halls and celebratory dinners marking diversity events and religious festivals throughout the year. Undergraduate accommodation is offered for two years, with first years housed in medieval college quads a stone's throw from the Bodleian; off-site rooms are at Norham Gardens, close to the University Parks, and East Oxford. The Norham St Edmund development currently under construction at Norham Gardens will provide fully accessible accommodation suites – built to Passivhaus standards and zero-carbon principles – within a new quadrangle and biodiverse gardens, as well as indoor communal spaces.

## St Hilda's

Oxford OX4 1DY          01865 286 620          st-hildas.ox.ac.uk
Undergraduates: 400     Postgraduates: 195     admissions@st-hildas.ox.ac.uk

Hilda's location just beyond Magdalen Bridge and towards Cowley creates a campus feel, and the college has excellent facilities. These include an exceptionally well-stocked library, one of the busiest JCR-run student bars and the modern Anniversary Building with 52 student bedrooms. The library emerged from a major refit in November 2023, making it more accessible and adding rooms for a law library and reading. The college boasts beautiful gardens instead of the more typical Oxford quads and hosts the impressive Jacqueline du Pré Music Building and recording studio. Founded in 1893 as an all-female college, Hilda's started admitting men in 2006 and now has an equal gender split. The college prides itself on inclusivity: a "class liberation officer" represents those who self-identify as working-class and St Hilda's has its own multifaith room. An extensive range of scholarships, bursaries, and grants supports students. Sport is particularly strong, with excellent hockey, football, and cross-country competing successfully in inter-collegiate "Cuppers" tournaments. The Hilda's College Ball is Oxford's most affordable while the riverside setting is ideal for punting season, during which students can use St Hilda's own punts. Round tables in the dining hall encourage a friendly atmosphere. Second-year students are accustomed to living out, though the 2022 purchase of two central Oxford properties means St Hilda's can now house undergraduates for the duration of their studies.

## St Hugh's

Oxford OX2 6LE          01865 274 910          st-hughs.ox.ac.uk
Undergraduates: 431     Postgraduates: 558     admissions@st-hughs.ox.ac.uk

Fourteen acres of green space and red-brick Edwardian buildings combine with more recent facilities to create a campus at St Hugh's. From its beautiful, spacious site in north Oxford, the college is modern and progressive in its outlook and enjoys a thriving culture of teaching, research and intellectual engagement across the arts, humanities, sciences and social sciences. Students can cycle into the city centre or arrive there on foot in 15–20 minutes. A welcoming atmosphere prevails and St Hugh's offers strong welfare support. There are scholarships and prizes for undergraduates, graduates and prospective applicants, and financial support for travel, academic projects and hardship is available. Accommodation is guaranteed to all undergraduates for the duration of their first degree and rents are lower than average; several rooms are specially adapted for the use of students with disabilities; graduate accommodation is also available. The (subsidised) food is consistently excellent, with regular formal dinners a particular highlight, and there is a popular café on site. The Howard Piper Library, an elegant 1930s art deco building, is one of the largest of Oxford's college libraries, housing over 85,000 books, and is open 24/7. In the Dickson Poon University of Oxford China Centre on the St Hugh's site students also have access to the KB Chen Library to consult the holdings of the Bodleian without leaving college. St Hugh's has music rooms and a gym and shares sports facilities, including a boathouse, with other colleges.

## St John's

Oxford OX1 3JP  01865 277 317  sjc.ox.ac.uk
Undergraduates: 443  Postgraduates: 291  admissions1555@sjc.ox.ac.uk

St John's enjoys a prime spot – a few minutes' walk from the Bodleian and the High Street. The college buildings combine traditional limestone quadrangles (the Front and Canterbury Quads) with modern accommodation blocks (Kendrew Quad and the Beehive Building) and the spacious new Library & Study Centre. Founded by London merchant tailor, Sir Thomas White, in 1555, the college traditionally produced Anglican clergymen. Its early history prioritised medicine and law, though it has expanded into the arts and humanities over the past half-century. St John's has a reputation for both academic and sporting success and it ranks eighth in the most recent Norrington Table. There are College teams for rowing, football (men's and women's), rugby, netball, badminton, squash, tennis, cricket, darts, croquet and ultimate frisbee and there are two squash courts, two free gyms, a boathouse and a large sports ground. Being one of the wealthiest Oxford colleges enables cheaper rent and food for students and access to generous academic prizes and book grants. Other than sports, extracurriculars include a chapel choir, drama society and orchestra and all can make use of the state-of-the-art auditorium. Music practice rooms are equipped with keys, drums and piano. The St John's Inspire Programme is divided into pre- and post-GCSE support for non-selective state-school applicants and runs an Inspire Year 13 twilight session for university preparation.

## St Peter's

Oxford OX1 2DL  01865 278900  spc.ox.ac.uk
Undergraduates: 351  Graduates: 228  admissions@spc.ox.ac.uk

St Peter's is known for its friendliness, informality, excellent relations between students and tutors and strong commitment to diversity and inclusion and student support. It was founded as St Peter's Hall in 1929 to offer an Oxford education to students with limited financial means and was granted college status in 1961. The college admits about 100 new undergraduates and about 90-100 new postgraduates each year. Located in the heart of Oxford, the college is close to University departments and libraries, and with easy access to both bus and railway stations. All freshers live in college in single study bedrooms and up to half of its second-year students can live in college rooms, as can any third or fourth-years who wish to. Student housing is either on the main college site or in annexes five minutes' walk away. The dining hall caters for a variety of different diets and budgets, favouring fresh ingredients and original recipes. The student-run St Peter's College bar and flourishing programme of community activities and opportunities add to the warmth of college life. Both the beautiful college library and the dedicated law library are open 24 hours a day. Its intake of UK students from state schools (58.8% across three years from 2020 to 2022) is among the lowest of the Oxford colleges. But St Peter's employs a full-time access and outreach coordinator working with schools, teachers, parents and carers in the college's dedicated link regions in Enfield, Waltham Forest, Merseyside and the Isle of Man.

## Somerville

Oxford OX2 6HD  01865 270 619  some.ox.ac.uk
Undergraduates: 446  Postgraduates: 341  academic.office@some.ox.ac.uk

Named after Mary Somerville, the pioneering scientist and writer, Somerville was founded in 1879 as one of the first two Oxford colleges for women and was also the university's first non-denominational college. It has accepted men equally for more than 20 years. Located just off St Giles it borders many of the university's faculty buildings – including mathematics, philosophy, engineering and physics. It is also close to Oxford's new humanities building, due to open in

2025. Somerville continues to expand on its promise to include the excluded through one of the strongest portfolios of scholarships and early career support at Oxford. In 2024–25, Somerville launched the RISE Campaign – aimed at galvanising its community around four pillars: resilience, inclusivity, sustainability and excellence. The centrepiece of RISE is the Ratan Tata Building, due to start construction in 2025 to Passivhaus standards, which will support interdisciplinary working. Eminent Somervillians include Nobel prize winner Dorothy Hodgkin, novelist AS Byatt, and Margaret Thatcher. The college has an impressive 100,000-volume library and funds one of the best Arts Week programmes in Oxford. Food is great value and there are student kitchens in all buildings. College rooms on the central site are provided to all undergraduates and some first-year postgraduates. Extracurriculars include an excellent chapel choir, a baking society and a boat club. Despite having tended to fall towards the bottom of the Norrington table, it made an impressive rise into the top ten in the latest edition. Somerville remains one of the most international colleges and has particularly strong links to India through the Oxford India Centre for Sustainable Development, which it hosts.

### Trinity

| Oxford OX1 3BH | 01865 279 900 | trinity.ox.ac.uk |
| Undergraduates: 319 | Postgraduates: 145 | admissions@trinity.ox.ac.uk |

Minutes from the Radcliffe Camera and High Street, Trinity is in the heart of the city – though its long drive, friendly porters and renowned lawns make it a peaceful haven. The new Levine Building has modernised the college and its facilities. It contains the de Jager Auditorium, five new teaching rooms, 46 student bedrooms, an informal study space and a popular café. Trinity hosts an annual programme of public lectures and performances that attracts high-profile musicians and speakers. Access and outreach have gained momentum and many students now volunteer for the paid student ambassador programme supporting the college's outreach work in Oxfordshire, Milton Keynes and the North East of England. Trinity offers financial support through grants, travel bursaries and other funds available to students. Extra-curriculars are popular, particularly the boat club and the chapel choir. The Trinity Players stages a garden play every summer and Trinity Arts Week is well-established. First- and second-years live in college, with "sets" (double rooms) popular with second-years. Third- and fourth-years mostly live out, either in "Stav" (on Staverton Road), on Woodstock Road or in privately rented Cowley properties. The college food is renowned – especially Monday's steak-and-brie night and weekend brunches. Formal hall is held three times a week, though new student kitchens provide a social space for informal dining.

### University College

| Oxford OX1 4BH | 01865 276 677 | univ.ox.ac.uk |
| Undergraduates: 427 | Postgraduates: 280 | admissions@univ.ox.ac.uk |

The precise founding history of "Univ" is a subject of debate. According to the generally accepted legend, it was founded by King Alfred in 872 – although, more likely, its origins lie with William of Durham in the 13th century. Despite its ancient roots Univ is one of the most forward-thinking colleges. Its Opportunity Programme, launched in 2016, paved the way for a university-wide scheme called Opportunity Oxford. Baroness Valerie Amos LG, the Labour life peer and former United Nations official, became Oxford's first black head of house in 2019, and the second black woman to lead an Oxbridge college. A generous bursary scheme for students includes travel grants for study trips abroad. The college is centrally located on the High Street and provides in-college accommodation to first- and third-years – either in flats, sets or single rooms – with second-years housed in a comfortable annexe near Summertown.

Both men's and women's rowing continue to excel. College members have access to a chalet in the foothills of Mont Blanc. Two 24-hour libraries and proximity to the Bodleian make Univ ideal for book lovers. The chapel choir is excellent, and students put on an annual garden play.

## Wadham

Oxford OX1 3PN     01865 277 545     wadham.ox.ac.uk
Undergraduates: 471     Postgraduates: 217     admissions@wadham.ox.ac.uk

Wadham occupies an imposing and attractive site opposite Trinity on Parks Road and offers one of the largest selections of course combinations, including languages, of any college. Known for its leftist politics and activism, Wadham prides itself on a liberal and laid-back atmosphere. Wadham's impressive "Back Quad" buildings opened in October 2022. Part of Wadham's Access to Excellence access programme, they were the first to be built specifically for outreach work. Overseen by Wadham's warden Robert Hannigan, two more building complexes – the William Doo Undergraduate Centre and the Doctor Lee Shau Kee Building – consolidate the college's commitment to widening participation and supporting students at every step of their educational journey. The college reached 37,782 pupils across 991 access events in a recent seven-year period. Weekday dinners are served in the 17th-century hall, though there are no gowned formal sittings. Undergraduates are guaranteed on-site rooms in their first and final years; other years are offered modern off-site accommodation. Average college rents are increasing by nearly 10% by 2025–26, but there will also be more generous accommodation assistance bursaries. The JCR and MCR have combined to form a students' union at Wadham and the college's social calendar includes Queerfest, an annual highlight, and Wadstock – an open-air music festival in Trinity (summer) term. The Holywell Music Room is the oldest purpose-built European music room.

## Worcester

Oxford OX1 2HB     01865 278 391     worc.ox.ac.uk
Undergraduates: 449     Postgraduates: 200     admissions@worc.ox.ac.uk

Before the dissolution of the monasteries, 15 abbeys had lodgings in Gloucester college, which was re-founded as Worcester College after the benefaction of Sir Thomas Cookes (a Worcestershire baronet) in 1714. Today, as one of Oxford's most popular colleges Worcester takes pride in an inclusive ethos and diverse intake of students, along with maintaining beautiful grounds and a strong academic reputation. Undergraduates live in college for three years and Worcester is the only college to have sports fields on site – thanks to the fact it was on the edge of the city in the 18th century. The famous Hall and Chapel, with interiors by James Wyatt and William Burges, remain in daily use and the older buildings continue to house students and the JCR. Worcester's extensive gardens are a good spot for croquet – or ultimate Frisbee – and the college's head gardener has a popular Instagram account. The award-winning Sultan Nazrin Shah Centre – containing lecture theatres, rehearsal spaces and a dance studio – looks over Worcester's lake. Arts and humanities lovers enjoy the Arts Week, regular concert programme, instrumental tuition scheme and summer Shakespeare performances by the Buskins dramatic society. Including the law library, there are three libraries: the modern reading rooms with 24/7 access contain 65,000 volumes; the impressive Old Library houses important European manuscripts, special collections, prints, architectural drawings and early printed books. The college hosts a popular Commemoration Ball every three years. Good food is served at formal hall three nights per week, where students stand at the entrance and exit of tutors, accompanied by grace – often in Latin but also in other languages and from other social and faith traditions.

# Cambridge College Profiles

### Christ's

Cambridge CB2 3BU    01223 334 900    christs.cam.ac.uk
Undergraduates: 446    Postgraduates: 290    admissions@christs.cam.ac.uk

Christ's has a reputation for high academic standards achieved by hard-working students across both the arts and sciences, and aims to balance its student community equally between the two. Often found in the top spot of the Tompkins table, it settled for second place in the 2024 edition of the list. Students at Christ's enjoy tranquil grounds a stone's throw from the city centre, including the Darwin Garden, named after its famous alumnus, and an outdoor swimming pool. Most undergraduates live in college, although a few students are nearby in terraced houses on King Street and Jesus Lane. On the main site just over 50% of rooms are en-suite. This includes small single bedrooms in the Modernist 'Typewriter' building (New Court) and large double bedrooms in Second Court. More traditional rooms and sets (a study room and bedroom) are in First Court. Yusuf Hamied Court opened in 2023 providing postgraduate accommodation, meeting rooms and a performance space. Christ's offers a range of postgraduate studentships alongside top-up bursaries for some undergraduate groups (including students from Scotland and Northern Ireland), grants to support extracurricular activity and financial assistance with summer research projects. There is plenty to keep student life vibrant, from the Yusuf Hamied Theatre, which hosts student productions as well as Christ's Cinema, an art society, and the oldest music society in Cambridge. Students can also borrow art for their rooms through the Picture Loan Scheme.

### Churchill

Cambridge CB3 0DS    01223 336000    chu.cam.ac.uk
Undergraduates: circa 485    Postgraduates: circa 340    admissions@chu.cam.ac.uk

Students at Churchill enjoy the largest single site of all the Cambridge colleges – encompassing 42-acres of sports fields and 1,000 trees – while being just a short cycle from the city centre. The location neighbours the West Cambridge site, where many of the university's major science departments are based – particularly useful for the 70% of Churchill students who study STEM subjects. However, as a large college with over 800 students, arts, humanities and social science students are numerous too. Churchill is famous for its distinctive post-War Brutalist architecture – bay windows overlook the lawns in nearly every part of the college – and its campus holds a comfortable library, an archive centre, gym, theatre, music centre with recording studio, squash and tennis courts, art studio, workshops and grass pitches. Undergraduates are guaranteed on-site accommodation for the entirety of their degrees. Over 40% of student accommodation is en-suite. Churchill is proudly one of Cambridge's least traditional colleges: students are welcome to walk on the grass, they are not required to wear academic gowns to formal dinners, and the college has a strong commitment to widening participation. The college has achieved an effectively even gender split in the last few years, and is a strong academic performer with a relaxed and friendly atmosphere.

### Clare

Cambridge CB2 1TL    01223 333200    clare.cam.ac.uk
Undergraduates: 501    Postgraduates: 299    admissions@clare.cam.ac.uk

Dating from 1326, Clare is Cambridge's second-oldest college and offers delightful garden views leading out onto the Backs and the River Cam. Much of Clare has been a construction site in recent years, as the college has been transforming Old Court. The college now boasts a River Room Café with riverside terrace, a great spot for students to socialise. Many of the more formal spaces have been refurbished and made fully accessible for the first time. Clare has a world-famous choir and the college often hosts music recitals, as well as intimate gigs in the popular and atmospheric underground Clare Cellars bar. Rooms in Old Court offer a traditional experience, while Memorial Court, across the river, is close to the university library and the humanities and science departments. All freshers live in Memorial, Thirkill or Lerner Courts. Students in their second year often live at Castle Court, closer to the boathouse on the slopes of Castle Hill around a 13-minute walk from the main site. The college has its own punts, an enthusiastic boat club and access to good sports facilities. Sir David Attenborough is among Clare's famed alumni.

## Corpus Christi

Cambridge CB2 1RH    01223 338 000    corpus.cam.ac.uk
Undergraduates: 315    Postgraduates:210    admissions@corpus.cam.ac.uk

Many know Corpus Christi for its famous clock, the Chronophage, displayed on the outside of the Taylor Library in Kwee Court. A small and bustling college with a welcoming feel in the heart of Cambridge, Corpus Christi is home to the Parker Library, which houses a collection of medieval manuscripts. It also stores the college's ancient drinking horn – given upon its 1352 founding and made from the horn of an aurochs, an extinct cattle species. All undergraduates are guaranteed accommodation with a "ballot" for selecting rooms after first year. Some students are housed in ancient rooms, others are accommodated away from, but close to, the main site, in the Beldam, Bene't Street and Botolph Court buildings; a new residence, Mogford Lodge, has now opened. The renovations to the medieval Dining Hall were shortlisted for a RIBA award while the Old Court is said to be the oldest continually inhabited court in either Cambridge or Oxford. At the main site there is also a cosy underground bar for socialising. The college has its own gym, tennis and squash courts and playing fields. Corpus joins with King's and Christ's Colleges to form collaborative "CCK" sports teams. At Leckhampton, the postgraduate campus just over a mile away, the gardens are renowned as among the most beautiful in Cambridge and swathed with wildflowers in summer. The small but much-used theatre, Corpus Playroom, is where students university-wide stage plays and comedy nights. In 2024 the college accepted its fifth cohort of Bridging Course students from underrepresented groups, who attend a three-week residential course before they matriculate, and will continue to offer approximately ten places each year. Corpus also participates in the STEM SMART widening participation programme and created the Pelican Programme to support arts and humanities applicants.

## Downing

Cambridge CB2 1DQ    01223 334 800    dow.cam.ac.uk
Undergraduates: 474    Postgraduates: 456    admissions@dow.cam.ac.uk

Built in a neoclassical style in the 19th century, Downing's appearance differs from other colleges. Grand buildings open onto the Paddock lawn – a popular spot for relaxing in the post-exam period. The college was originally founded for the study of law and natural sciences, and while it is still popular with scientists, lawyers and geographers – thanks to its fall-out-of-bed-and-into lectures proximity to their faculties – it is now home to an eclectic body of students of all subjects. Through the Downing 360 campaign, the college aims to raise £40 million by 2027 to increase the number of fellows, remove accessibility barriers and fund renovations. On the sports front, the college is known as a fearsome opponent, while for arts and culture there is the 160-seat Howard Theatre – a vibrant drama society that hosts a festival of student writing each year. Downing also has its own student-run annual literary magazine, The Leaves, and hosts exhibitions of modern and contemporary art. Students either live on-site or in a house bordering the college. Downing has some plush accommodation with double beds, while more than half of the rooms are en-suite and laundry services are free. A refurbished Bene't Place building opened in 2024, with two self-contained flats for fellows, kitchens, offices, supervision rooms, shared-study spaces and a multi-faith space. A lively social scene centres on the comfy Butterfield Café and Bar, which hosts pub quizzes and live music in the evenings and makes a casual study space during the day. Downing opened a wellbeing centre in 2022.

## Emmanuel

| Cambridge CB2 3AP | 01223 334 200 | emma.cam.ac.uk |
| Undergraduates: 516 | Postgraduates: 227 | admissions@emma.cam.ac.uk |

Often known among the university community as 'Emma', the college was founded by Puritans in 1584, when Sir Walter Mildmay envisioned Emmanual as 'an Acorn, which when it becomes an Oak, God alone knows what will be the fruit thereof'. Today the college aims to equip every member with the knowledge and skills they need to flourish in life – including through extra-curricular interests, volunteering and career development. Students love Emmanuel for its open, collaborative and supportive environment, central location, and the weekly load of laundry included in their rent. The beautiful grounds connect its historic buildings to nature and green spaces, and the majority of undergraduates are accommodated on the main site for the first three years of their degree. Accessible, practical facilities – both newly built and refurbished – provide education centres, social spaces and private study areas for the entire college community. The elegant Christopher Wren chapel hosts concerts organised by the music society, while the large paddock lawn and open-air swimming pool are popular in summer.

## Fitzwilliam

| Cambridge CB3 0DG | 01223 332 000 | fitz.cam.ac.uk |
| Undergraduates: 512 | Postgraduates: 284 | admissions@fitz.cam.ac.uk |

"Fitz" was founded in the mid-1800s to offer an affordable way to access a Cambridge education. Access to higher education is in the college's DNA and Fitz remains committed to this founding purpose, as witnessed by the number of undergraduates from the maintained sector (85% of 141 students in 2024–25). The college moved to its Castle Hill site in 1963. Fitz's buildings are eclectic and award-winning – from a Regency house, once home to Charles Darwin's widow, to modern icons such as the boat-shaped Chapel and the magnificent Lantern Roof on the Central Building. Fitz boasts a spacious and bright library, open 24/7, designed for modern study needs. All Fitzwilliam students are accommodated for the duration of their courses, never more than a five-minute walk from the main college site. All students have access to well-equipped kitchens, complete with hobs and ovens and shared living spaces, but they always have the option to eat in the spacious and modern hall or catch up with friends in the Café and Bar. The college gardens are extensive and sit at the heart of the main site, offering a beautiful view from many of the student bedrooms and plenty of open space to relax, read and socialise. At Fitz, everyone walks on the grass. The college has a strong reputation for music, drama and sport – particularly football. Excellent facilities include music practice rooms, a large auditorium, a gym and squash courts on site, and large playing fields just five minutes from the main site.

## Girton College

| Cambridge CB3 0JG | 01223 338 999 | www.girton.cam.ac.uk |
| Undergraduates: 540 | Postgraduates: 373 | admissions@girton.cam.ac.uk |

Boasting many exceptional women as alumnae, Girton's pioneering history began with its foundation in 1869 as the UK's first residential college offering higher education to women. It is now co-educational and home to a dynamic community of scholars – led since 2022 by Dr Elisabeth Kendall, the 20th Mistress (Head of House) of Girton College. An oasis of calm and green space, its Victorian red-brick architecture is set in over 50 acres of natural woodland and orchards giving students space to think and breathe, while just a short distance out of the buzz of central Cambridge. Top-notch facilities include three gyms, football, rugby and cricket pitches, netball, tennis and squash courts, as well as an indoor heated swimming pool. A café-bar serves as a social hub and another cellar bar hosts JCR events. As a low-carbon college, Girton has won awards for energy efficiency and has an eco-friendly green roof. Student rooms range from the atmospheric Victorian to the modern en-suite in Ash Court. Off-site accommodation is in college-owned houses or at Swirles Court, in the new Eddington area. Just over a third of undergraduate rooms are en-suite. One accommodation corridor in the main building is reserved for women and nonbinary students. Girton has its own museum and an artsy extracurricular scene – including the famous People's Portraits exhibition. The College participates in the Foundation Year programme for students from disadvantaged backgrounds.

## Gonville & Caius

Cambridge CB2 1TA    01223 332 413    cai.cam.ac.uk
Undergraduates: 620    Postgraduates: 256    admissions@cai.cam.ac.uk

One of the oldest colleges at Cambridge, Caius (pronounced "keys") was founded as Gonville Hall in 1348. Its undergraduate population is among the largest and Caius's main site, Old Courts, features three peaceful courtyards in the heart of town and a fine view of Senate House. There is also a beautiful 19th-century library and a chapel that claims to be the oldest purpose-built chapel in Cambridge, with walls dating back to 1390. Unlike other colleges, Caius serves a three-course meal, six nights a week, in hall. There is a cafeteria sitting at 6pm, and for the second students are required to wear their formal blue gowns (often with jeans or sports kit underneath) to file into hall. A unique dining policy obliges undergraduates to pay for 31 dinners a term in advance, with the aim of encouraging a sense of community. Forty college clubs and societies provide plenty to get involved with. All freshers live on West Road by the Sidgwick Site (where most humanities and social science subjects are taught). This includes the Stephen Hawking Building, which offers 75 modern, en-suite rooms, while the Brutalist Harvey Court has its own JCR and some of the rooms boast balconies. Many second-years live in rooms overlooking shops in the city centre or in houses near the vibrant Mill Road. More traditional rooms are in the Old Courts, and these often host third-years. Caius has a boathouse and gym. In the past, the college had some of the lowest state school intakes (just 57% in 2020) but its programme of outreach initiatives, assisted by a dedicated TikTok channel run by the admissions and outreach team, appears to have helped it turn a corner: that figure rose to 75% in 2024.

## Homerton

Cambridge CB2 8PH    01223 747 111    homerton.cam.ac.uk
Undergraduates: 632    Postgraduates & PGCE: 843    admissions@homerton.cam.ac.uk

Homerton is one the biggest Cambridge colleges. It is also the youngest; gaining official college status in 2010 – although it was initially founded in London more than 250 years ago as a "dissenting academy". Set in 25 acres of grounds close to the main railway station, there is plenty to keep students busy, and Homerton can give the impression of a self-contained campus. A 15-minute cycle ride brings students into town. The benefit of space means accommodation is mainly en-suite and of a high standard and the college has its own orchard and extensive grounds. Recent upgrades to facilities include the £8 million dining hall and buttery, which opened in May 2022. There is an on-site gym and the college shares a sports ground and boat house with St Mary's school. An auditorium and 18 en-suite bedrooms in North Wing are further recent additions. Homerton has many engineering students and its proximity to the Cambridge Biomedical Campus at Addenbrookes is convenient for medical students, although Homerton students can study any of the undergraduate subjects offered by the university. In line with its history as a teacher training college – and its location next to the Faculty of Education – students of education Tripos are another significant contingent. The master, Lord Simon Woolley, became the first black man to head an Oxbridge college when he took the helm at Homerton in October 2021. The college is among those to offer places within the landmark Foundation Year programme, launched in 2022, and welcomes five foundation students per year.

## Hughes Hall

Cambridge CB1 2EW    01223 334 898    hughes.cam.ac.uk
Number of current students: Undergraduates: 179; Postgraduates: 883
ugadmissions@hughes.cam.ac.uk

Known for being close-knit, multicultural and informal, Hughes Hall provides a ready-made community of mature students from more than 80 countries. Student ages range from 21 to over 70 and around half are women, 80% are postgraduates, more than half are international, and 20% are part-time. The college was founded in 1885 "to change Cambridge". The college enjoys views over the university cricket ground and sits alongside Mill Road, a hub for cafés, restaurants and independent shops. Hughes Hall has a strong record on the sports pitch and the river, with its rowers historically performing well in the intercollegiate Bumps competition and featuring in Boat Race crews. Accommodation (nearly 400 rooms, 70% on the main college site) ranges from traditional to modern, all with kitchens and many with en-suite facilities. There are roof terraces, couples' flats, city houses, accessible rooms, and a student-run bar. PGCE students and students taking courses longer than one year are prioritised for accommodation and all undergraduate students are offered college accommodation throughout their course, including for the summer vacation if they wish. Hughes Hall launched its Pathways programme in 2023, designed to scaffold students' learning with academic support, a sense of community, personal wellbeing and transferable skills for the future. In 2022 former diplomat Sir Laurie Bristow became president.

## Jesus

Cambridge CB5 8BL    01223 339 339    jesus.cam.ac.uk
Undergraduates: 529    Postgraduates: 395    undergraduate-admissions@jesus.cam.ac.uk

Close to the city centre and with acres of picturesque grounds Jesus occupies a covetable location. Facilities range from the ancient 12th-century chapel, believed to be the oldest university building in Cambridge and predating the college by 350 years, to the modern West Court complex – with student common rooms, a games room, and the Roost café that doubles as a popular bar in the evenings. Jesus' red-brick buildings date back to its foundation in the 1500s. The grounds are punctuated by a permanent modern sculpture exhibition and the college's own collection contains work by Sir Antony Gormley and John Bellany, among others. Students are permitted to roam on most – but not all – of the lawns in summertime. The West Court Gallery often hosts impressive exhibitions, including the annual student-run John Hughes Arts Festival. Jesus also has on-site pitches for football, rugby and cricket, as well as squash and tennis courts and a recently renovated gym. Students can showcase their musical abilities at the

Blues and Chill evenings or at the college's song-writing competition with the Centre for Music Performance. All undergraduates are accommodated for every year of their degree, not just the first three – a feature especially welcome for medical students. Other facilities include a multi-faith space, a kosher staircase and free washing machines and dryers. The college hall, known as "caff", has recently been refitted, along with the kitchens, which are now heated sustainably by ground source heat pumps. Jesus's master, former media executive Sonita Alleyne, became the first black woman to lead an Oxbridge college when she took on the role in 2019. The May Ball is glamorous and popular. In recent years, Jesus has regularly recruited around 75% or more of its UK students from state schools – among the highest proportions of all Cambridge colleges.

## King's

Cambridge CB2 1ST        01223 331 100        kings.cam.ac.uk
Undergraduates: 451      Postgraduates: 398    undergraduate.admissions@kings.cam.ac.uk

King's iconic chapel is a landmark synonymous with Cambridge. The college itself is renowned for being one of the least traditional and most progressive, offering an inclusive and diverse environment to applicants from all backgrounds. Located in the historic city centre on King's Parade, the mid-sized college is in a plum spot for most faculties and departments, as well as shops and cafés. Its picture-postcard setting is a draw for tourists too, and its famous carol service is broadcast by the BBC on Christmas Eve. There are plenty of extracurricular opportunities, from music to rowing to political debate. Students can use the art studio, grow their own food in the student allotments, or hire one of the College's punts to explore the city from the River Cam. The college prides itself on offering a supportive community that combines academic commitment and a lively social and artistic scene. In the summer, students can sit in the beautiful Fellows' Garden or walk by the wildflower meadow behind the chapel – with a view of The Backs that often includes a herd of cows. A successful current fundraising campaign is providing for stronger financial and pastoral supports to those who need them, and to house all undergraduate and graduate students in college accommodation for the first time. Rooms range from traditional to more modern and often en-suite in updated or new buildings. While most of the undergraduate rooms are on the main college site, in 2022 King's opened new accommodation a short walk away for graduate students and their families, built with a very low carbon footprint. King's has a reputation for good food from sustainable sources, and student formals always have vegetarian starters. After dinner, students can relax with friends in the well-stocked and recently refurbished College Bar. For those who prefer to cook for themselves, there are plenty of well-equipped student kitchens and dining areas around the college.

## Lucy Cavendish

Cambridge CB3 0BU       01223 332 190        lucy.cam.ac.uk
Undergraduates: 467     Postgraduates: 611    admissions@lucy.cam.ac.uk

Lucy Cavendish College is the fastest growing and most diverse college in Cambridge. "Lucy" (as it is known to its members) welcomes students of all genders aged 18 and over and boasts a truly international community, with students from 85 countries. A champion of widening access to Cambridge, Lucy Cavendish became the first college to admit over 90% of its UK undergraduates from state schools in 2022, while over 60% were from under-represented or disadvantaged backgrounds. Furthermore, 10% were eligible for free school meals, and around one in four were the first in their family to attend university. Entry standards remained intact: incoming students following STEM subjects achieved three A*s at A-level, on average; while arts, humanities and social sciences students arrived with only marginally fewer UCAS tariff points. The college's free online Academic Attainment Programme has proved an effective Cambridge outreach initiative.

Lucy Cavendish housing is either in college or in nearby houses, close to those fellow "hill" colleges St Edmunds and Fitzwilliam. There is also an attractive apartment complex on Histon Road. Students can stay in women-only sets if preferred for religious or cultural reasons. There are also some flats for couples. In 2022, the college opened a new accommodation facility, providing 72 en-suite bedrooms and a ground floor café, in a building that meets top sustainability standards. 100% of the college's electricity is supplied by renewables. The college's Fiction Prize is in its 15th year in 2025. A wide range of sporting opportunities for students include participating in both university-level teams and the college's own extensive selection of sports clubs. The college also offers a wealth of resources for students with entrepreneurial ambitions – such as seed funding prizes, enterprise initiatives, and one-to-one mentoring with industry professionals.

## Magdalene

Cambridge CB3 0AG    01223 332 100        magd.cam.ac.uk
Undergraduates: 350    Postgraduates: 274    admissions@magd.cam.ac.uk

Renowned for its ancient and beautiful grounds, Magdalene boasts the longest river frontage of any college. Its historic courts are situated alongside the Cam and its chapel was built in the 1470s. Tradition means the college still hosts one of the university's few white-tie summer balls every other year, while its modern outlook makes Magdalene a firmly 21st-century seat of learning. Its airy library, unveiled in 2021, features study spaces for 90 as well as an archive centre and art gallery, and won the RIBA Stirling Prize in 2022. The college's most famous alumnus, Samuel Pepys, is immortalised in the Pepys Building, which houses a collection of 3,000 of the diarist's books and manuscripts. In 2021, almost 50 books and pamphlets belonging to Mary Astell, sometimes considered the "first English feminist", were also found in the library. The MDS theatre society is very active and students can hold theatre productions at Cripps Auditorium, a space with 142 seats. The sports pitches are shared with St John's (both colleges have a sporty reputation) and Magdalene also has its own Eton fives court on site. The JCR has two punts that are free for students to use from March 1st until the last Saturday in October. Students live either in the main courts, in the village on the other side of Magdalene Street or in college-owned houses a few minutes' walk away. All undergraduates are guaranteed accommodation for all three or four years of their course. The college has expanded its student Health and Wellbeing Service and in 2022 appointed a head of wellbeing, who is also a counsellor.

## Murray Edwards

Cambridge CB3 0DF    01223 762100        murrayedwards.cam.ac.uk
Undergraduates: 349    Postgraduates: 279    admissions@murrayedwards.cam.ac.uk

One of only two women-only colleges at Cambridge (Newnham is the other), Murray Edwards occupies an iconic Modernist campus on Castle Hill, close to the other four Cambridge 'Hill Colleges'. A supportive atmosphere prevails at this informal, relaxed college, and students at "Medwards" (as it is often known) are served its famous weekend brunch in hall, under a domed roof that has inspired the "Dome is home" refrain. The college also houses the largest collection of women's art in Europe, including work by Barbara Hepworth, Paula Rego, Tracey Emin and Lubaina Himid, and hosts regular exhibitions. There's plenty of ambition along with the easy-going atmosphere: women's achievements are encouraged in all spheres. A Women in STEM Festival attracted the Vice-Chancellors of both Cambridge and Oxford as speakers and a new Enterprising Women programme, in partnership with Astra Zeneca, will support female entrepreneurship for students and recent graduates across the university. The college's pioneering Gateway programme ensures a strong focus on academic skills and career preparation. A wide range of scholarships and awards helps to support students' travel or internships. Currently, 71% of home undergraduates are from state schools and the college participates in the university's Foundation Year scheme. There's a strong eye on the environment, with students encouraged to join and organise green events. The laid-back feel extends to the gardens, where students can pick herbs and vegetables, as well as walk and picnic on the grass. All freshers are housed together in modern accommodation – almost all rooms are en-suite and benefit from famously large dining kitchens with freezers. A three-storey Art Café/Bar adorned with artworks overlooks spectacular Fountain Court and there is a comprehensive wellbeing service. Sport is strong: there's an on-site gym and tennis and squash courts, and the Boat Club is on a roll. In 2021, Dorothy Byrne, former Channel 4 Head of News, became College President.

## Newnham

Cambridge CB3 9DF    01223 335 700    newn.cam.ac.uk
Undergraduates: 430    Postgraduates: 300    admissions@newn.cam.ac.uk

Located across the road from the Sidgwick Site, Newnham's beautiful 18-acre grounds feature gardens, sports pitches and tennis courts. Students can relax on the lawns and get their hands dirty with the thriving gardening club. Founded in 1871 so that female students could attend lectures, long before they could become members of the university, Newnham celebrated its 150th anniversary in 2021. One of only two female-only colleges remaining at Cambridge, Newnham has a growing number of postgraduate students. It counts alumnae who include Mary Beard (a fellow), Sylvia Plath, Diane Abbott and Emma Thompson. Newnham participates in the Foundation Year programme for students from disadvantaged backgrounds and offers grants, travel, rent and other bursaries. In 2022 the college appointed a wellbeing adviser to support student health, and its sports clubs include a strong rowing club, badminton, football and netball. With 100,000 volumes including 6,000 rare books, Newnham boasts one of the best-stocked college libraries at the university, and there is also a well-appointed art room open to students. Newnham is partly powered by renewable electricity sources and upgrades to the estate include a new porters' lodge, gym (free to use) and café, as well as 90 en-suite rooms. The college also boasts some of the plushest student kitchens in Cambridge, while rooms for conferences and supervisions are in the Dorothy Garrod building, named after Cambridge's first female professor.

## Pembroke

Cambridge CB2 1RF    01223 338 100    pem.cam.ac.uk
Undergraduates: 534    Postgraduates: 282    admissions@pem.cam.ac.uk

Pembroke has remained in its original location (on what is now Trumpington Street) for centuries, having been founded by Marie St Pol on Christmas Eve of 1347. Within its walls, Cambridge's third-oldest college has tranquil gardens, a wild orchard and Christopher Wren's first chapel. Renovations to the Mill Lane site across the road are enlarging the college's footprint by a third and creating 110 bedrooms. The ambitious development is making way for more on-campus living and enhancing educational and social spaces, but there are no plans to expand student numbers. Phase 1 of Mill Lane opened in June 2023. Resources including the Ray and Dagmar Dolby court accommodation (named after the late Dolby sound inventor, who left £35m to his former Cambridge college, and his philanthropist widow) and leisure spaces are due to open in 2025. The extra rooms will boost current provision: most first-years live in the modern Foundress Court and in New Court, and should be prepared to share bathrooms as en-suites are uncommon. Currently, many second-years tend to move away to Selwyn Gardens behind the Sidgwick Site, or to Lensfield Road near the station. Many desirable third-year rooms are in terraced houses on Fitzwilliam Street. Pembroke's food is popular – particularly brunch – and formal dinner is traditionally served every night. Pembroke students make the most of an arty extracurricular scene, including the Pembroke Players, one of the largest college drama societies. Other clubs include the Music Society, the Stokes Scientific Society and Pembroke Politics. There are plenty of sports teams, an on-site gym and sports grounds 10 minutes away by bicycle. Around two-thirds of 2021 undergraduate entrants were state-school-educated. Alumni include Ted Hughes, and the actors Naomie Harris and Tom Hiddleston.

### Peterhouse

| | | |
|---|---|---|
| Cambridge CB2 1RD | 01223 331 403 | pet.cam.ac.uk |
| Undergraduates: 291 | Postgraduates: 188 | admissions@pet.cam.ac.uk |

Peterhouse is well located for both the science and the arts faculties. Cambridge's oldest college and one of its smallest, it retains some traditional idiosyncrasies, such as hosting a white-tie ball every other year and formal hall dinners that glow atmospherically by candlelight each night. Peterhouse is also one of the wealthier colleges and as such can offer travel grants, academic awards and high-standard accommodation. Students are housed either on site or not more than five minutes away for all years of their degree. Most freshers live in St Peter's Terrace – grand Georgian houses on Trumpington Street – or in the William Stone building, an eight-floor high-rise dating from the 1970s. Though it shares sports grounds with Pembroke, Peterhouse has its own squash court and a modern gym. It also has one of Cambridge's wilder outdoor spaces, known as the Deer Park – where no deer live but plenty of students roam in summer. Two libraries, the Perne and the Ward, provide plenty of quiet learning space. Peterhouse's beautiful 17th-century chapel boasts a recently rebuilt organ and has a strong tradition of worship and music, which is supported by a lively mixed choir mainly drawn from college members. Rooms in Fitzwilliam Street were renovated in summer 2021, its old brewhouse has been converted into a music facility, and Peterhouse has plans to landscape its outdoor spaces around Cosin Court to create courtyard gardens with a focus on health and wellbeing.

### Queens'

| | | |
|---|---|---|
| Cambridge CB3 9ET | 01223 335 511 | queens.cam.ac.uk |
| Undergraduates: 536 | Postgraduates: 532 | admissions@queens.cam.ac.uk |

Queens' buildings sit on both banks of the River Cam, connected by the striking, wooden Mathematical Bridge. Walking through the college campus provides a quick course in architectural history via buildings that hail from every era since its 1448 foundation. With one of the largest college populations, Queens' has a lively outgoing atmosphere, felt especially in the new courts. The active Bats dramatic society puts drama centre stage. Sport is also strong – Queens' tends to field several Blues team players and its own clubs cover everything from chess to water polo, with strong men's and women's football teams. Its biennial May Ball is a popular fixture that welcomes big-name bands. An annual Arts Festival features student work with a range of events and it has a non-auditioned choir as part of its music society, MagSoc. Most first-year students are housed in the modern Cripps Building, while second- and third-years are allocated accommodation through a ballot system. Students have the option of sharing a set of rooms or having their own bedsit.

### Robinson

| | | |
|---|---|---|
| Cambridge CB3 9AN | 01223 339 143 | robinson.cam.ac.uk |
| Undergraduates: 402 | Postgraduates: 285 | apply@robinson.cam.ac.uk |

Robinson's 1970s architecture is distinct from the Cambridge stereotype, while its gardens are typically beautiful. Students may walk on the lawns and Robinson is known for its welcoming, inclusive atmosphere and buzzing social life. Robinson is a short walk or cycle from the city centre and only metres from the University Library. Most humanities and science departments are within easy reach, and for students studying at more remote sites, the college is on the route of the university's subsidised U bus. Accommodation is comfortable and modern, around half of it en-suite, and freshers live in the central college block overlooking the gardens. In later years, students tend to opt for houses in the college gardens bordering the campus. Student societies abound: aspiring dramatists can organise productions with the Brickhouse Theatre Company, and those interested in sport can join one or more of the successful teams (the Robinson College rugby team were the 2023/2024 Shield Winners, and the ladies netball team made it through to the Cuppers final). The college has a reputation for excellent food, with the Garden Restaurant and Red Brick Café-Bar serving a range of options daily. In 2024, 64% of new UK entrants were from state schools. There is a focus on offering a high level of support to all Robinson undergraduates and the college opened a dedicated wellbeing centre in October 2022.

## Selwyn

Cambridge CB3 9DQ    01223 767 839    sel.cam.ac.uk
Undergraduates: 444    Postgraduates: 307    admissions@sel.cam.ac.uk

Arts and humanities students can roll out of bed five minutes before lectures begin if they live in Selwyn – whose gardens are so close to the Sidgwick Site that the faculties of economics and divinity overlook them. West Cambridge is also a quick cycle away for STEM students. Sitting near Newnham and the University Library the college is a short walk from the city centre on the other side of the River Cam, and enjoys an impressive range of freshly renovated facilities after extensive fundraising. The Ann's Court development features a 140-seat auditorium and the Bartlam library opened in 2021. The sleek, recently renovated café-bar buzzes in the evenings and makes a popular study space during the day. Selwyn consistently has one of the highest intakes of home students from state schools – 81.1% in 2023 – and has rocketed up the Tompkins table to sit fifth in the 2024 edition (up from 14th in 2022). In further evidence of its academic achievements, the college also topped the whole university for its percentage of good honours degrees (firsts and 2.1s) and had the lowest number of thirds/fails. All students are accommodated for every year of their undergraduate degree. First-years are guaranteed en-suites and tend to live together in Cripps Court. Selwyn has a strong musical tradition, and the chapel choir has recorded numerous albums and toured the world. The college launched a bridging programme for selected freshers in September 2024, aimed at building study skills before they start their courses, which is continuing for 2025 entry. Selwyn shares sports and tennis grounds around a mile away. It also shares its boathouse with King's and Churchill. At the end of first term, the college hosts a popular winter event called the Selwyn Snow Ball.

## Sidney Sussex

Cambridge CB2 3HU    01223 338 800    sid.cam.ac.uk
Undergraduates: 400    Postgraduates: 241    admissions@sid.cam.ac.uk

Founded in 1596, Sidney is the youngest of the "old" Cambridge colleges, and among the smaller ones by population. It is located in the heart of Cambridge, minutes from the river, moments from the ADC student theatre and close to Jesus, Christ's, Trinity and St John's. Accommodation, including all first year's, is largely on the main site but also extends into the surrounding streets. The dining hall is cosy and one of the best value Formal Halls in Cambridge, making it consistently popular with students. Sidney is a musical college with an atmospheric chapel where all are welcome at the candlelit Vespers. The very active choir tours regularly and releases critically acclaimed recordings. Sidney also offers organ scholarships. Sidney participates in the Foundation Year programme and runs a preparation week for freshers, with a focus on wellbeing and easing the transition to college life. The college's travel fund provides grants to students planning new experiences over the long vacation, and a mentoring programme. Sidney's new EQUIP programme offers further support to students to help them thrive within the Cambridge system. The student-run Sid Bar is known for its "bop" dance nights and is a popular meeting place for students from across the university. It is also the venue for free wellbeing activities, including yoga and guided meditation. Sidney's extensive grounds provide a relaxing place to wander, study and enjoy May Week garden parties. The Sidney May Ball, held every two years, is another a popular choice. Sports teams are more enthusiastic than competitive and membership of the college gym is subsidised. Sidney is the college of broadcaster Carol Vorderman and former Foreign Secretary David Owen, as well as four Nobel prize winners. The head of an early student, Oliver Cromwell, is said to be buried within the college grounds.

### St Catharine's

Cambridge CB2 1RL    01223 388 300    caths.cam.ac.uk
Undergraduates: 467    Postgraduates: 372    undergraduate.admissions@caths.cam.ac.uk

Students at "Catz" invariably mention two main reasons for choosing this mid-size college: its prime location in the heart of Cambridge city centre and the sense of community – commonly described as friendly, supportive and close-knit. Catz celebrated its 550th anniversary in 2023 but is looking to the future with an investment of over £30 million to modernise its student accommodation and facilities. A new dining hall, gym, music room, multifaith prayer room and garden room were opened in 2022 by alumnus Sir Ian McKellen (whose signed photograph adorns the wall of one accommodation block). Previous additions include the McGrath Centre, which includes an auditorium for events, film nights and performances, a junior common room and a bar. Students are guaranteed accommodation for their three- or four-year courses at Catz: undergraduates live on the main site in their first and third years, while second-years usually live in flats located a few minutes away at the St Chad's site, where there are also two new houses for fourth-years. Catz is one of only a handful of colleges to field a team in all sports leagues organised by the University of Cambridge. 2024 was a stellar year, with Catz students being crowned football, hockey, badminton and skiing champions. Students have access to large sports pitches (including astroturf for hockey), indoor and outdoor courts for racquet sports, and a boathouse for rowing. After announcing a commitment to net zero carbon emissions by 2040, Catz has installed six air source heat pumps and submitted plans for almost 200 roof-mounted solar panels. Catz students enjoy the distinction of a cheese course at formal hall and the college holds a May Ball every other year. Students can attend one at Corpus during the "off" years. In 2024, over 74% of UK students came from the maintained sector.

### St Edmund's

Cambridge, CB3 0BN    01223 336 250    st-edmunds.cam.ac.uk
Undergraduates: 200+    Postgraduates: 600+    admissions@st-edmunds.cam.ac.uk

A college for internationally minded students, aged 21 and over, Eddie's has a friendly, warm and egalitarian atmosphere which creates a home from home feeling for its vibrant community of global thinkers, with over 800 students and 250 senior academics and professional members representing over 80 nationalities. The college's leafy 10-acre site is just a 10-minute walk from the city centre and the river Cam. Its location means students are immersed in the historic and cultural offerings of city life but can still relax and unwind back at its tranquil campus setting. A broad range of accommodation types ranges from the modern and contemporary facilities of Mount Pleasant Halls to the more historic, traditional rooms in the Norfolk Building, dating back to 1896. Eddie's offers a number of scholarships to students from diverse and non-traditional backgrounds. Students from all faiths and none are welcomed, while St Edmund's is unique among the University of Cambridge colleges for having a Catholic chapel and Dean. It takes a relaxed approach to traditions: there is no fellows' high table in hall, and students, fellows and college staff dine together. The college aims to be particularly supportive of student parents through its St Teddy's Club, featuring family lunches and gatherings. The notion of 'community' lies at the heart of Eddies' ethos. As well as its informal and friendly atmosphere, it offers several programmes to help foster meaningful connections, such as a Bridging Programme for new mature undergraduates, to help them adapt to Cambridge's academic environment, and a Civic Engagement Programme where staff and students work together with the wider community. Opportunities to get involved in student life range from volunteering in the Eddies' student-run bar, to taking part in open mic nights or rowing in the Boat Club.

## St John's

Cambridge CB2 1TP     01223 338 703     joh.cam.ac.uk
Undergraduates: 626     Postgraduates: 356     admissions@joh.cam.ac.uk

With the River Cam snaking under the Bridge of Sighs, past grand ivy-covered buildings, St John's enjoys a fairytale setting. Inside, the college hosts a vibrant community with myriad cultural and sporting activities. A large and wealthy college, St John's offers generous financial support to its students and the state school intake increased to 68.3% in 2023. All undergraduates are guaranteed accommodation, which helps build the strong sense of community St John's is famed for. Crossing the ancient courts from room to dining hall, laundry, gym or bar is rarely achieved by students without running into someone they know. There are more than 40 student-run societies and sports teams provide ample amusement outside lectures, labs or the well-stocked college library. "Maggie", as the boat club is affectionately known, is the oldest in Cambridge and a force to be reckoned with on the river. In 2022, the world-renowned college choir began admitting women and girls. The award-winning Buttery, Café and Bar are popular spaces to eat and socialise, with stylish interiors blending the historic and contemporary. Food is well-subsidised and caters for all diets, with Saturday brunch a highlight. St John's May Ball is known as among the most fabulous and was voted one of the best parties in the world by Time magazine.

## Trinity

Cambridge CB2 1TQ     01223 338 422     trin.cam.ac.uk
Undergraduates: 739     Postgraduates: 336     admissions@trin.cam.ac.uk

Arguably Cambridge's most famous college, Trinity was founded by Henry VIII in 1546. It has vast grounds on the Cam and the largest undergraduate population at the university. The college retains some of its quirkier traditions, including the Great Court Run (made famous by Chariots of Fire), where students try to run around the court faster than the clock can strike 12 twice – itself a Trinity tradition. The former college of Sir Isaac Newton and led today by Dame Sally Davies, the former chief medical officer, Trinity is known for its popularity with STEM students. But humanities undergraduates are well represented too, and follow a long line of Trinity literary luminaries, historians and philosophers from Byron, Tennyson and AA Milne to Wittgenstein and Bertrand Russell. The college takes on a studious atmosphere in exam time and is consistently high-performing: Trinity topped the Tompkins table of 2024, up from second place in the previous edition in 2022. As the richest of the Cambridge colleges Trinity offers quality accommodation and bursaries as well as pastoral support. Trinity runs the You'll

Fit In webinar and residential course for Year 12 students from backgrounds under-represented in top universities. Even so, in 2023 it had one of the lowest intakes from state schools of any of the colleges (52.7%). There are 750 rooms across the college available for undergraduates, a third of them en-suite. The gym, located across the River Cam, is surrounded by sports pitches and there are courts for badminton, tennis and squash. The college punts are popular on summer afternoons and the renowned Trinity College Choir has toured extensively. Students socialise at the two-floor JCR which includes a popular café-bar, while Trinity's candlelit formals are held in its stunning hall.

## Trinity Hall

Cambridge CB2 1TJ    01223 332 535      www.trinhall.cam.ac.uk
Undergraduates 404    Postgraduates 228    admissions@trinhall.cam.ac.uk

Founded in 1350 Trinity Hall (nicknamed "Tit Hall") is compact, with plenty of charm and not to be mistaken for its larger neighbour Trinity. Home to Cambridge's smallest college chapel, year groups are also relatively small, which creates an intimate atmosphere. The college's riverside setting makes for enviable views of the River Cam from the Jerwood library. A short walk across Garrett Hostel Bridge offers access to the Sidgwick Site and the university library. Market Square is also just a few minutes away. All first-years are housed on the central site, where the cafeteria, coffee shop, bar, library, chapel and main music room are also located. The Thompson's Lane off-site accommodation is also centrally located. There are en-suite rooms in WYNG Gardens, while there are also more affordable single rooms in Bishop Bateman Court. Many students live at the Wychfield site, further afield, also the base for sports facilities which include squash and tennis courts, plus grounds for football, hockey, rugby, cricket and netball. Alumni include the scientists Stephen Hawking and Nobel Prize-winner David J. Thouless, actor Rachel Weisz and Olympic medal-winning cyclist Emma Pooley. Music is an important part of college life, and students have access to resources such as the recently opened WongAvery Music Gallery, with rehearsal spaces. Former BBC World Service editor Mary Hockaday took up the role of master of Trinity Hall in October 2022.

## Wolfson

Cambridge CB3 9BB    01223 335 918      www.wolfson.cam.ac.uk
Undergraduates 180    Postgraduates 550 (full-time) 300 (part-time)
ugadministrator@wolfson.cam.ac.uk

Wolfson is a highly international college with students from over 90 different countries. Approximately 50 new mature undergraduates (aged 21+) are admitted per year, and these students benefit from the college's expertise in supporting students with non-traditional routes to higher education. Founded in 1965, Wolfson is known for its egalitarian ethos and lack of hierarchy. There is no "high table" in the College dining hall, which means that academics, students, and staff all sit and eat together and learn from each other. This diverse learning environment is boosted by dedicated academic skills provision from the College library. The "WolfWorks" programme and Wolfson Writing Centre host regular skills workshops, and students are able to gain presentation experience in the college's annual student-led research conference. Undergraduates are guaranteed accommodation on the College site for the first three years of their course, which creates a strong community and campus feel. Students enjoy the beautiful college gardens and close proximity to key university locations including the Sidgwick Site, the University Library, and West Cambridge.

# **12** University Profiles

Students are increasingly keen to have their voices heard, going by the record participation attracted by the 2024 National Student Survey (NSS): it achieved a remarkable 72.3% response rate, the highest in 20 years. Collecting opinions from almost 346,000 final year students on a range of topics, including teaching quality, assessments, and mental wellbeing services the NSS is one of the largest surveys of its kind globally. The outcomes mostly match or exceed those from the 2023 survey, despite responding students having experienced significant pandemic disruptions prior to and during their studies. Results included 85.3% of students studying in England responding positively to questions relating to "teaching on my course" (up from 84.7% in 2023), 74% responding positively to questions around "student voice" (up from 71.9% year-on-year) and 79% giving positive responses to a query about how well their university's wellbeing services were communicated (an increase from 75.9%).

This chapter looks at the NSS and much more. It provides profiles of all 131 universities that feature in *The Times* and *Sunday Times* league table. It also has profiles of the Open University, which supplies the country's most part-time degrees; Birkbeck, University of London, which specialises in evening courses; and the University of the Highlands and Islands. Because of their special course or geographical circumstances, none of these appear in our main ranking.

Specialist colleges, such as the Royal College of Music (**rcm.ac.uk**) or institutions that only offer postgraduate degrees, such as Cranfield University (**cranfield.ac.uk**), are omitted. This is not a reflection on their quality, it is simply due to their particular roles. A number of additional institutions with degree-awarding powers are listed at the end of the book with their contact details.

Dating back to 1836, the University of London (**london.ac.uk**) is Britain's biggest conventional higher education institution by far, with a total of 250,000 students studying 3,700 courses. A federal university, it consists of 17 self-governing colleges, and most of its students are based in the capital. Further afield it also offers degrees at the Institute in Paris, and its global prestige attracts more than 40,000 students in 190 countries to take University of London degrees via distance learning. Its School of Advanced Study comprises eight specialist institutes for research and postgraduate education (details at **sas.ac.uk**).

The following University of London colleges have their own entries in this chapter: Birkbeck, Brunel, City, Goldsmiths, King's College London, London School of Economics and Political Science, Queen Mary, Royal Holloway, SOAS, St George's and University College London. Contact details for its other constituent colleges are given on page 442.

## Guide to the profiles

Our extensive survey of UK universities provides detailed, up-to-date information for their profiles. The latest campus developments, results from the National Student Survey, trends in application and social data, financial help available to undergraduates, research reputation and findings from the government's Teaching Excellence Framework inform their content. You can also find contact details for admission enquiries along with postal addresses and open day information.

We also include data under the heading "The Diversity Index" in Chapter 6. This is taken from our latest table on social inclusion that gives details of student recruitment and the socioeconomic and ethnic mix of each institution. The methodology for its data can be found on pages 94–100.

In addition, each profile provides information under the following headings:

» **The Times and Sunday Times** rankings: For the overall ranking, the figure in bold refers to the university's position in the 2026 *Guide* and the figure in brackets to the previous year. All the information listed below the heading is taken from the main league table. (See Chapter 1 for explanations and the sources of the data).
» **Undergraduates:** The number of full-time undergraduates is given. The figures are for 2020-21 and are the most recent from the Higher Education Statistics Agency (HESA).
» **Applications per place:** The number of applications per place for 2021, from UCAS.
» **Accommodation:** The information was obtained from university accommodation services, and their help is gratefully acknowledged.

## Tuition fees

Details of international tuition fees for 2024-25 are given wherever possible. At the time of going to press, a number of universities had not published these for 2024-25. In these cases, the fees for 2023-24 are given. Please check university websites to see if they have updated figures. As discussed earlier in this book, **tuition fees for UK students are rising to £9,535 from September 2025.**

It is of the utmost importance that you check university websites for the latest information. Every university website gives details of the financial and other support available to students, from scholarships and bursaries to study support and hardship funds. Some of the support will be delivered automatically but most will not, and it is up to applicants to explore the details on university websites, including methods of applying and deadlines, to get the greatest benefit.

In addition, in England the Office for Students (**officeforstudents.org.uk**) publishes "Access Agreements" for every English university on its website. Each agreement outlines the university's plans for fees, financial support and measures being taken to widen access to that university and to encourage students to complete their courses.

# University of Aberdeen

The UK's fifth-oldest university (and in our top 20 for the fourth consecutive year), Aberdeen's learning experience began at the 15th-century King's College building with 36 staff and students who studied the arts, divinity and law. Today, the curriculum covers 12 teaching schools offering almost 400 degrees, and undergraduates have the opportunity to switch and mix subjects as their interests broaden. The approach appeals to go down well with stuents: Aberdeen has risen to rank 7th for the wider student experience, according to our latest National Student Survey analysis, and 17th for teaching quality.

The university's research efforts in theology and religious studies gained some of the university's best results in the latest Research Excellence Framework (REF 2021), with Earth systems and environmental sciences, and public health also strong performers. However, Aberdeen has slipped to joint 63rd in our research quality ranking, 20 places down since 2014.

Aberdeen has discontinued some courses in genetics and its single-honours modern languages degree finished in 2023, though students may still take modern languages as part of a joint-honours programme. Environmental chemistry is new for 2025. Longstanding links with Aberdeen's offshore oil and gas industries open opportunities for engineering students. Boosted by its industry links, Aberdeen has leapt 19 places in the Graduate Outcomes survey, now occupying 28th place with 82.2% of leavers in highly skilled jobs or further study within 15 months.

Further afield, Aberdeen runs a partner campus in Qatar, a pre-medical course in Sri Lanka and an international exchange programme with Curtin University in Perth, Western Australia.

The Old Aberdeen campus houses the imposing King's buildings, supplemented by modern facilities such as the Sir Duncan Rice Library and the £35 million science teaching hub. Life sciences and medical students share Europe's largest health campus with NHS Grampian and the Aberdeen Sports Village features Olympic-standard sports and exercise facilities. The university also has a boathouse, climbing bothy and the oldest shinty club in the world, established in 1861. Activities in the great outdoors abound: the region has 150 miles of coastline and access to the Cairngorms national park.

All first-years are guaranteed a room if they apply by the deadline. Accommodation starts at £99 a week and no rooms cost more than £168 a week, with a small number catered. The Hillhead Student Village includes an outdoor gym and a community garden with plants from the university's Cruickshank Botanic Garden. Students have access to a free counselling service, therapy pets and free mindfulness sessions.

The university operates a contextual offers scheme and Aberdeen may also accept CCC at Clearing if offer holders do not achieve BBB. The university attracted around 16,500 applications in 2023, a decrease of 10% compared with the year before. Aberdeen is fourth among Scottish universities for the proportion of black and ethnic minority students it recruits (13.8%) but its achievement gap is tenth in Scotland overall.

Different bursaries and scholarships, both means-tested and merit-based awards, are offered according to whether applicants are from Scotland, the rest of the UK or abroad.

---

**King's College Aberdeen AB24 3FX**
study@abdn.ac.uk
abdn.ac.uk
ausa.org.uk

**Overall ranking 15**
(last year 19)

**Accommodation**
University provided places 2,184
Catered £103–£178 per week

**Student numbers**
Undergraduates 9,370
Applications per place 6.0:1
Overall offer rate 77.2%

**Fees**
UK fees £0–£1,820
RUK fees £9,250
International fees £20,800–£24,800
Medicine £50,100

abdn.ac.uk/study/undergraduate-open-day/
abdn.ac.uk/study/undergraduate/finance

# Abertay University

Abertay is an old hand at early adoption. The university launched its computer games degree in 1997 and, from 2006, was the first to offer degrees in ethical hacking. David Jones, the creator of the hit Grand Theft Auto, studied at Abertay and Sony chose the School of Design and Informatics to host one of the largest teaching laboratories in Europe for its PlayStation consoles. It is now behind the growing virtual production industry in Dundee, which will be valuable for students on the VFX programme.

It has also added competitive games and digital arts labs to reinforce its position at the forefront of video games education. All games students become members of UKIE (UK Interactive Entertainment) and benefit from industry mentorship and support.

Abertay makes an asset of its small size and now sits in 10th place in the wider student satisfaction measure. A combination of in-person and online teaching, including the ethical use of AI, has driven a six-place improvement to 11th in the teaching quality rankings. Among a relatively small submission across eight subject areas to the most recent Research Excellence Framework (REF 2021), the strongest performances were in art and design, engineering, food science and psychology.

Eight new degrees from 2024 include computer science and cybersecurity, and psychology with health sciences. Four are sports-based, including sport development and coaching, and strength and conditioning Offers vary by course from ABB to CDD at A-level or ABBB to BBC in Scottish Highers. Applications increased by 11% in 2024, of which 6–8% were through Clearing. Most courses have a work placement built in, with industry partners including Dare Academy, V&A Dundee and Santander, and there are mandatory interdisciplinary courses for all undergraduates. Abertay also introduced Scotland's first accelerated degree programme. But in our graduate outcomes analysis, Abertay has fallen 29 places to rank 98th.

Jute, jam and journalism were the industries that brought Dundee to life. In the past decade this heritage has been celebrated in regeneration projects in Scotland's fourth-largest city. At the city centre campus, the Annie Lamont Building, opened in 2022, provides a base for the cyberQuarter research and development centre, which boasts a liquid chromatography mass spectrometer, used to analyse molecules in the fields of food, health, sport and forensic sciences.

The campus also includes an exercise studio and gym, a gallery space for student projects and a monthly speaker series on creative and cultural topics. The free counselling and mental health service offers self-help resources, one-to-one therapy and seminars. About 600 study rooms are available from £129 per week. Priority goes to new entrants from outside the Dundee area postcode, students with disabilities and to those who have left care.

Abertay has a proud record for social inclusion and comes second in Scotland overall. It was the first university in Scotland to bring in a contextual admissions policy and offers varied routes to joining a degree programme, including part-time access and evening classes for those without formal qualifications who have been away from study for at least three years. About half of Abertay's students qualify for a scholarship or bursary, which can include an award of up to £12,000 for international undergraduates as well as several subject-specific scholarships.

---

**Kydd Building Bell Street Dundee DD1 1HG**
sro@abertay.ac.uk
abertay.ac.uk
abertaysa.com

**Overall ranking 74**
(last year 84)

**Accommodation**
University provided places 600
Catered £129–£202 per week

**Student numbers**
Undergraduates 3,864
Applications per place 4.5:1
Overall offer rate 86.2%

**Fees**
UK fees £0–£1,820
RUK fees £9,250
International fees £15,000–£15,500

abertay.ac.uk/visit/open-days
abertay.ac.uk/study-apply/money-fees-and-funding/tuition-fees

# University of Aberystwyth

Pack a Dry Robe as well as your books. The campus at this seaside university, affectionately known as "Aber", is quite a trek from most other parts of the country but when they get there, students find a sense of safety on the small-town campus where King Charles learnt Welsh in 1969. The university is bilingual and many courses can be studied wholly or partially in Welsh. Last year Aberystwyth was The Times and Sunday Times Welsh University of the Year and it retains second place in the wider student experience rankings. For teaching quality it ranks 7th, down from 3rd place last year.

Overall, three quarters of the university's research was rated as world-leading or internationally excellent in the Research Excellence Framework (REF 2021). Agriculture produced some of the best results, alongside food science, geology, sports science, and Celtic studies. Twelve degree options have been removed from a slimmed-down curriculum but the School of Veterinary Science has welcomed its fourth cohort of students on a programme run in collaboration with the Royal Veterinary College. Foundation degrees in veterinary nursing and in animal health began in 2024, while new courses in engineering and psychology with counselling are also being introduced.

The entry tariff for most degrees ranges from 96 UCAS points to 144, or or up to 16 points lower for enhanced contextual offers. More than 2,000 undergraduates were accepted in 2024, about a quarter of those were based in Wales and around 10% came through Clearing.

The university has jumped just one place year-on-year to finish 90th in our analysis of the Graduate Outcomes survey, assessing how many recent leavers find highly skilled work or return to study within 15 months. Each academic department has links with employers in the relevant sector. More than 40 undergraduate programmes across the faculties include an integrated year in industry or professional practice. The university also offers opportunities to study abroad.

The campus at Penglais is a 32-hectare site perched between Cardigan Bay and the Cambrian Mountains. The three-floor Hugh Owen library has been refurbished and the National Library of Wales is also on site. The university is investing in improving its flexible learning environments, research facilities, collaborative spaces and accessibility. The Aberystwyth Innovation and Enterprise Campus, providing world-leading facilities in food, biorefining and agric-tech, is at the university's Gogerddan site.

A self-powered gym opened in January 2024 and sports facilities also include an air dome, 48 acres of pitches, a pool and stabling for students' horses, as well as the local beaches, rivers and mountains of course. First years are guaranteed one of more than 3,000 accommodation places and students can choose mixed or gender-specific flats in revamped energy-efficient buildings. Welfare support includes a mandatory online module on sexual consent, a drug and alcohol service and daily drop-in sessions for mental health support.

Comfortably in our top 50 for social inclusion, Aberystwyth's efforts to broaden its intake include the Access All Aber residential visit for year 12 students from Wales who meet the criteria. About 30% of new undergraduates receive financial aid and there are bursaries available for care leavers, young carers and estranged students worth £1,500 per year of study. Entrance scholarships and merit awards of up to £3,000 come with an unconditional offer, based on exams.

---

**Penglais Campus Aberystwyth SY23 3FL**
ug-admissions@aber.ac.uk
aber.ac.uk
abersu.co.uk

**Overall ranking 48**
(last year 39)

**Accommodation**
University provided places 3,172
Catered £197 per week
Self-catered £110–£185 per week

**Student numbers**
Undergraduates 5,325
Applications per place 4.6:1
Overall offer rate 93.5%

**Fees**
UK fees £9,250
International fees £16,520–£18,830

aber.ac.uk/en/study-with-us/open-days/
aber.ac.uk/en/undergrad/before-you-apply/fees-finance/
tuition-fees/

# Anglia Ruskin University

A large institution with more than 30,000 undergraduates, Anglia Ruskin University (ARU) has a history of innovation. Its origins are in the Cambridge School of Art and it has long been the main provider of health and social care graduates in the east of England – producing qualified social workers, nurses and operating department practitioners and opening Essex's first medical school in 2018. The university's landmark merger with Writtle University College near Chelmsford in February 2024 has brought new courses across agriculture, botany and animal science and care. Other new degrees on the horizon include primary education with qualified teacher status, biomedical engineering, supply chain management and computer games design.

The Research Excellence Framework (REF 2021) credited nine subject areas with a world-leading impact, and ARU's music therapy research for patients with dementia received a Queen's Anniversary prize in 2022. In the Teaching Excellence Framework (TEF), ARU stepped up from silver to gold in 2023. Student experience was also rated gold in the report, but the university ranks outside the top 100 in both measures of our National Student Survey analysis. A major factor in ARU's overall low position in our main league table is its relatively low continuation rate of only 88%.

A contextual offer scheme operates in most subjects, including medicine. Unusually, Anglia Ruskin does not require maths A-level for some of its engineering programmes, as part of its efforts to diversify the intake. Many courses offer an optional year in industry and there is an on-site recruitment agency that fixes students up with paid temporary work and internships that fit around their studies.

ARU Writtle is the university's new 370-acre campus in the Essex countryside. The Peterborough campus boasts new teaching spaces for microbiology and engineering and an augmented reality facility. In Cambridge, ARU's city-centre campus has the red-brick arts school and hands-on facilities such as simulated hospital wards, crime scene rooms and a law clinic. In Chelmsford, the university's riverside base hosts the £20 million medical school. ARU also has two London bases, in the City and Docklands, mainly for business and law students.

Each campus houses a different mix of sports and social facilities. Cambridge is a student city geared up for undergraduates, while Chelmsford is not without history as one of the first Roman settlements. ARU Writtle guarantees a space in halls to first-years who confirm it as their firm choice by the end of May. At the other sites accommodation is more limited.

More than two thirds of students are aged over 21 when they enrol and widening access is part of the university's mission. Financial help includes the ARU Bursary and help with travel and laptop purchase for those who qualify, as well as a range of merit-based and sport scholarships. The university has co-produced a podcast series with students focusing on mental health, and offers both professional support and trained peer wellbeing mentors. In October ARU holds Shag (Sexual Health Awareness and Guidance) week to encourage students to think carefully about consent.

---

**Bishop Hall Lane Chelmsford CM1 1SQ**
answers@aru.ac.uk
aru.ac.uk
angliastudent.com

**Overall ranking 130**
(last year 115)

**Accommodation**
University provided places 1,119
Catered £134–£187 per week
Self-catered £120–£217 per week

**Student numbers**
Undergraduates 23,226
Applications per place 4.1:1
Overall offer rate 70.3%

**Fees**
UK fees £9,250
International fees £15,900–£18,600

aru.ac.uk/study/open-day
aru.ac.uk/study/tuition-fees

# Arts University Bournemouth

Design credentials are front and centre at Arts University Bournemouth (AUB), which has produced the world's first Instagram university prospectus. A university since 2012, AUB has diversified into a broad spectrum of creative fields within four schools: Arts and Communications; Design and Architecture; Arts Management; and Bournemouth Film School. From 2025 an online degree in creative writing will be available and the university is also launching its first apprenticeship, in model making. AUB has climbed 14 places in our research quality rankings following its best outcomes yet in the latest Research Excellence Framework (REF 2021). It was rated silver overall by the Teaching Excellence Framework in 2023 (down from gold in the previous assessment, in 2017). In our latest National Student Survey analysis AUB fell 38 places to 86th for students' evaluation of teaching quality, and to 102nd for their feelings about the wider experience.

Degree offers start at BBB at A-level or BTec diploma equivalent, and the highest requirements are AAB at A-level, or merit from a UAL extended diploma. Foundation diplomas and contextual offers, for those who qualify, offer other routes to entry. Around 8% of students gained places via Clearing in 2023. All courses other than architecture now have an optional one-year placement opportunity, and in a new initiative, a professional industry patron is dedicated to every undergraduate programme. Nevertheless, institutions with an art and design focus tend to occupy the lower ranks of our graduate prospects table; at 128th, AUB is fourth from bottom.

Located on the Jurassic Coast between Bournemouth and Poole, AUB's buildings are painted in pops of bright colour, with all teaching based on a single site. The university has restored the art deco Palace Court Theatre in the town centre and new fine art studios utilising north-facing light are under construction. Each department has specialist studio space, but students are encouraged to work together across disciplines to help them to pick up the collaborative skills they will need for an arts career.

AUB offers 1,131 study bedrooms and, although a spot is not guaranteed, there is sufficient space available for all first-years who want to live in. The university DJ provides the music to a range of social activities and events on campus, and the university's gallery hosts evolving exhibitions and panel discussions. Students share Bournemouth University's extensive gym, classes and courts at a subsidised rate. More than 200 AUB staff have been trained in mental health first aid and the university has teamed up with the NHS, Bournemouth University and local charities to offer a range of intervention and support services.

AUB has risen to =73rd in our social inclusion index. Those who complete the All Access AUB outreach programme qualify for a reduced conditional offer and about a fifth of entrants receive some form of means-tested financial assistance. There is pre-enrolment support available to help with travel costs, as well as £1,000 rent-reduction bursaries.

**Wallisdown Poole BH12 5HH**
admissions@aub.ac.uk
aub.ac.uk
aubsu.co.uk

**Overall ranking =78**
(last year 80)

**Accommodation**
University provided places 1,131
Self-catered £174–£244 per week

Edinburgh
Belfast
Cardiff London
**POOLE**

**Student numbers**
Undergraduates 3,524
Applications per place 4.5:1
Overall offer rate 67.3%

**Fees**
UK fees £9,250
International fees £18,950–£19,950

aub.ac.uk/open-days
aub.ac.uk/fees

# University of the Arts, London

Six distinct colleges dotted among the capital's cultural attractions comprise the University of the Arts London (UAL): Camberwell College of Arts, Central St Martins College of Art and Design, Chelsea College of Arts, London College of Communication, Wimbledon College of Arts and London College of Fashion (LCF), now based in the Queen Elizabeth Olympic Park. A new site in west London has freed up space within the colleges, allowing UAL to accommodate 3,000 more students and respond to demand from young creatives from the UK and beyond.

Innovation across the creative fields is long established at UAL, which has produced many nominees for the Turner prize, including the 2023 winner, Jesse Darling, and the university's former chancellor, Sir Grayson Perry. He has been replaced in the role by BBC news anchor Clive Myrie.

On a global scale, UAL is second for art and design in the QS World University Rankings 2024 for the sixth year running, and its large research submission has propelled it to 47th in our research quality index. However, UAL slipped from silver to bronze overall in the latest national Teaching Excellence Framework (TEF 2023). The student experience was also graded bronze, and the latest National Student Survey backs this up. UAL fails once again to breach the top 100 for teaching quality and the broader experience.

Most courses have some online elements, with AI approved as part of the learning and development process. Entry tariffs range from 80 UCAS points to 136 and in 2023 the university had more than 33,000 applicants, with 5,000 successful, just 3% via Clearing.

Students are based at the six colleges across London. Only first-year international students on a full-time course are guaranteed accommodation, while under-18s and disabled students are prioritised. High London rents require students to dig deep: the cheapest twin room is £166 a week, while at the other end of the scale are 14 premium studios at Wigram House, at £481.50 a week.

Halls Active provides UAL students with 200 low-cost hours of fitness, wellbeing and mindfulness activities in addition to the sports offered by the students' union. In-person and online counselling sessions are available and students can request appointments with professionals from black, Asian and minority ethnic backgrounds.

Outreach efforts extend to Saturday clubs for year 10 students and UAL operates an integrated contextual admissions process, helping UAL to maintain its spot in our top 50 for social inclusion. A bursary of £1,300 per year of study is awarded to all UK students who get a full maintenance grant, along with a separate hardship fund and a range of course-specific scholarships.

A relative lack of jobs in the creative industries won't come as a shock but it puts UAL towards the bottom of our analysis of the Graduate Outcomes survey, where it has fallen nine places to 124th. UAL is working hard to shift the dial on employment rates for creative graduates through an in-house recruitment service and links with global brands such as Microsoft, Levi's and Unilever.

---

**272 High Holborn London WC1V 7EY**
admissions@arts.ac.uk
arts.ac.uk
arts-su.com

**Overall ranking =40**
(last year 42)

**Accommodation**
University provided places 3,770
Self-catered £166–£482 per week

**Student numbers**
Undergraduates 17,240
Applications per place 6.5:1
Overall offer rate 44.8%

**Fees**
UK fees £9,250
International fees £25,780–£28,570

arts.ac.uk/open-days
arts.ac.uk/study-at-ual/fees-and-funding/tuition-fees

## Aston University

A work placement is a compulsory element of most Aston degrees, contributing to the university's impressive record on social mobility. Aston has ranked second in the country for three successive years in the English Social Mobility Index according to analysis by the Higher Education Policy Institute. Aston is also one of the best-performing pre-1992 institutions in our own social inclusion index, in =66th place. Its strong focus on graduate employability is backed up by its pioneering use of degree apprenticeships and partnerships with firms including Asos and GlaxoSmithKline, all of which keeps Aston in the top 25 in our analysis of the Graduate Outcomes survey.

Aston has grown from a College of Advanced Technology into a multi-faculty institution with schools across the applied sciences, social sciences and humanities. It boasts numerous specialised research centres and is delving into the potential of AI. Aston doubled the number of staff taking part in its submission to the latest Research Excellence Framework (REF 2021) compared with the previous national assessment in 2014, and places in the top half of our research quality ranking.

The university achieved the best possible results in the Teaching Excellence Framework (TEF) 2023, with gold in all three categories thanks to "outstanding teaching [and] feedback and assessment practices". Our analysis of the National Student Survey (NSS) lifts Aston 23 places to rank 74th for teaching quality, and up 34 places to sit within the top 20 at 16th for wider student experience.

Degrees in nursing studies (mental health), history, and international development management welcomed their first students in September 2024, while six courses have been withdrawn. Aston's medical school requires the highest entry grades – A*AA – and for other courses, the lowest requirement is CCC. Those who qualify for a contextual offer can expect a grade reduction of one or two grades. Applications to study at Aston have soared across the past decade to more than 23,000 in 2023, of whom 3,700 were accepted.

The 60-acre campus is a stone's throw from the centre of the buzzing student city of Birmingham. First-years who meet Aston's criteria are guaranteed student accommodation. Almost half of Aston's students are based at the highly rated business school and since February 2024 the campus has hosted Design Factory Birmingham – part of a global network of similar hubs in 25 countries. Sports facilities are divided across two locations and include a swimming pool with sauna and steam room, women-only gym, indoor courts and pitches for football, cricket and hockey. Qualified counsellors are provided as well as a multi-faith chaplaincy, disability services and residential support.

The university has the most ethnically diverse intake in England and Wales and is in the top 25 for students who are the first in their immediate family to go to university. Financial support includes merit-based and competitive scholarships, alongside grants of £1,250 to help students from households with an income of £42,875 or below to pay living expenses during an unpaid placement year or a placement year abroad.

**Birmingham B4 7ET**
ugadmissions@aston.ac.uk
aston.ac.uk
astonsu.com

**Overall ranking 35**
(last year 38)

**Accommodation**
University provided places 1,046
Self-catered £150–£164 per week

**Student numbers**
Undergraduates 11,534
Applications per place 6.3:1
Overall offer rate 66.5%

**Fees**
UK fees £9,250
International fees £18,250–£21,100
Medicine £45,550

aston.ac.uk/open-days/
aston.ac.uk/study/

# Bangor University

Few universities have such a breathtaking view, with the mountains of Eryri (Snowdonia) on one side and the Menai Strait on the other. The university in north Wales, funded by quarrymen and farmers in 1884, now has a broad curriculum spanning arts, humanities, business, engineering, environmental and human sciences. Bangor's newest development is the North Wales Medical School, launched in September 2024 and including clinical placements in mountain medicine and rural healthcare. Other new courses this year centre on media, business and communications, with more to come in 2025.

Bangor is one of the leading universities for Welsh-medium courses and came in the top 40 in our research quality index. Some of the best results were in earth systems and environmental science, and Bangor is in the top 20 in the 2023-24 People and Planet league table. The university's School of Ocean Sciences has its own research vessel, while other departments benefit from botanic gardens, a research farm and animal care facilities. Welsh universities did not take part in the latest Teaching Excellence Framework (TEF 2023), but in the previous assessment, Bangor was rated gold. The university has historically enjoyed high rates of student satisfaction, but our latest National Student Survey analysis shows a steep decline to 100th for the wider experience and 95th for teaching quality.

New entrants average 125 UCAS tariff points, putting Bangor in the lower half of UK universities. It has broadened the eligibility criteria for contextual admissions, and UCAS figures show that in the 2023 admissions cycle there were nearly 8,800 applications to study at Bangor, with almost 2,200 accepted. Students can choose to take a year's work placement at the end of their second year as part of almost all undergraduate degrees. The Bangor Employability Award accredits activities that are valued by employers and there are close links with the NHS, Santander Bank, BBC Cymru and Welsh Rugby Union. Despite these efforts, Bangor has dropped 23 places to =94th for graduate outcomes.

The university buildings are located in a compact coastal hub within walking distance of the city centre, creating a lively, campus-like atmosphere. Radiography students are based at the Wrexham campus. All first-years who apply before the advertised deadline are guaranteed accommodation at one of two student villages. Self-catered rooms start at about £88 a week and gym membership is included. There are more than 150 free clubs and societies for sports and other activities making use of the facilities in the centre at Ffriddoedd. Students are supported by halls' mentors, academic tutors and a range of wellbeing services. In our social inclusion index Bangor has maintained its overall rank of =35th, helped by its relatively high proportion of white working-class boys.

The university offers about 40 merit-based and sports scholarships each year. Students from the UK – but excluding Wales – may qualify for a £500 or £1,000 Bangor bursary and there are also bursaries for student carers, those who have been in care and students estranged from their families.

---

**College Road Bangor LL57 2DG**
applicantservices@bangor.ac.uk
bangor.ac.uk
undebbangor.com

**Overall ranking 64**
(last year 44)

**Accommodation**
University provided places 2,611
Self-catered £88–£230 per week

**Student numbers**
Undergraduates 6,659
Applications per place 4.1:1
Overall offer rate 82.9%

**Fees**
UK fees £9,000
International fees £17,000–£20,000

bangor.ac.uk/openday
bangor.ac.uk/studentfinance/new-undergraduates

# University of Bath

A fixture of our top ten for a decade, the University of Bath holds its own without being a member of the Russell Group. Its leafy self-contained campus is on the outskirts of the Unesco world heritage city. The university, established in 1966, offers courses across the sciences and humanities and is famed for its sporting prowess and high employment prospects.

Bath earned gold across all three categories in the Teaching Excellence Framework (TEF 2023), with course content and academic support singled out for praise. Students echo this; in our analysis of the National Student Survey it comes 6th for the wider student experience and 36th for teaching quality. The new Institute for Advanced Propulsion Systems caps almost half a century of automotive research. In the latest Research Excellence Framework (REF 2021), 92% of Bath's submissions were rated world-leading or internationally excellent, placing Bath in the top 30 of our index.

In 2023 Bath received more than 34,000 applications for 4,750 places, including 3.5% granted via Clearing. Computer science and engineering degrees command entry requirements of A*A*A, while social work and applied social studies require BBB. Contextual offers are applied automatically for about 30% of offer holders and completing one of the university's access schemes guarantees an offer. An integrated master's degree in pharmacy was introduced in 2024, in conjunction with the University of Plymouth.

Claverton Down, the main campus, boasts a range of modern teaching and research facilities. By the time students arrive in September 2025 the John Wood accommodation will have been redeveloped, and there are enough rooms available for first-years who apply by the deadline. An employability hub was added in 2023, helping maintain Bath's exemplary record for graduate outcomes. Two thirds of undergraduates spend a year gaining real-world work experience at one of more than 3,000 companies, while the university's careers service arranges up to 400 employer visits each year.

Bath boasts extraordinary sports resources. Its Sports Training Village is a national training centre for several Olympic and Paralympic sports and students have free use of most of its facilities, which include the UK's only bobsleigh and skeleton push-start track. Other extracurricular opportunities include art, dance, music and theatre. Help for students' mental health and welfare is available around the clock, from support groups and courses to specialist one-to-one counselling.

Social inclusion is a work in progress at Bath, which ranks 108th overall, losing ground by two places since our previous edition. Students from ethnic minorities make up about 20% of the Bath intake and just 2.3% are over 21. About 30% of Bath's new entrants gained scholarships and bursaries in 2024, with support focussing on those from households with an income below £30,000 and including a compulsory enrichment programme. A small number of talent-based arts and sports scholarships are available too. Based on academic merit, international students may qualify for fee discounts in the first year of study.

---

**Claverton Down Bath BA2 7AY**
admissions@bath.ac.uk
bath.ac.uk
thesubath.com

**Overall ranking 8**
(last year 8)

**Accommodation**
University provided places 4,262
Catered £209–£248 per week
Self-catered £139–£251 per week

**Student numbers**
Undergraduates 13,757
Applications per place 7.2:1
Overall offer rate 70.6%

**Fees**
UK fees £9,250
International fees £22,800–£28,800

bath.ac.uk/campaigns/undergraduate-open-days/
bath.ac.uk/topics/tuition-fees

# Bath Spa University

Bath Spa is riding high for its diversity and research credentials. In our previous edition it took the title of University of the Year for Social Inclusion, and it reaped its best results yet in the most recent Research Excellence Framework (REF 2021), thanks to projects such as an app to improve the wellbeing of social workers, and applying emerging digital media technologies in the publishing and theatre sectors. This has brought it up to 89th position in our research quality ranking.

Based four miles outside the city, the university's Newton Park campus features a nature reserve, a lake and rolling fields. Environmental sustainability is a contemporary theme at the university, which is ranked in the top 20 greenest institutions in the country by People & Planet. Two other campuses at Locksbrook Road and Sion Hill house arts and design faculties, and studio and workshop space respectively, while Bath Spa's Hackney outpost in east London focuses on business and management, and health and social care.

Despite triple silver in the Teaching Excellence Framework (TEF 2023), our latest analysis of the National Student Survey (NSS) results was not so positive. Bath Spa tumbles 36 places to rank =66th for teaching quality and 38 places to rank 109th for the wider student experience.

From 2024 the expanding curriculum offers degrees in economics and law, and forensic science. Undergraduate programmes in pharmaceutical science and music (performance) will be added in 2025. Bath Spa is a medium tariff university with a standard offer of BBC, while some courses accept CCC. If an applicant falls short of their offer, the university will take a holistic view of their personal circumstances, and in most cases confirm their place. For 2023 entry the university received almost 14,400 applications and 5,240 enrolments, about 10% via Clearing.

First-years who apply by the deadline are guaranteed student accommodation. Sports facilities on and off campus include a gym, netball and tennis courts, and floodlit pitches. For art and culture lovers there is a 50-seat auditorium, two recording studios, a 186-seat theatre and an outdoor amphitheatre. Services from mental health practitioners, a chaplaincy, disability advisers and 20 accredited care dogs are integrated, and all students complete compulsory training on sexual consent online during welcome week.

Despite being the University of the Year for Social Inclusion in our previous edition, the university has dropped out of the top 20 to rank 28th. The Bath Spa bursary of £4,000 across three years aims to remove financial barriers to higher education, while scholarships of £500 are paid to all students who enter Bath Spa with AAB or equivalent grades. A laptop fund provides up to £500 to students in need.

To help boost graduate employability, the option to add a professional placement year is offered on most courses and graduate creatives, freelancers and start-up entrepreneurs are offered free desk space. Nevertheless, Bath Spa remains in the bottom 15 for graduate outcomes, having fallen three places year-on-year to 117th.

---

**Newton Park Newton St Loe Bath BA2 9BN**
admissions@bathspa.ac.uk
bathspa.ac.uk
bathspasu.co.uk

**Overall ranking 76**
(last year 74)

**Accommodation**
University provided places 1,891
Self-catered £81–£296 per week

**Student numbers**
Undergraduates 10,406
Applications per place 2.7:1
Overall offer rate 78.2%

**Fees**
UK fees £9,250
International fees £15,750–£17,585

bathspa.ac.uk/open-days/
bathspa.ac.uk/students/student-finance/

# University of Bedfordshire

Formed by the 2006 merger of the University of Luton and De Montfort University's Bedford campus, Bedfordshire is a modern university with a professional slant; one of the UK's leading providers of training for physical education teachers, it is the education partner of Luton Town football club and Bedford Blues rugby union club. The institution stretches across sites in Luton (its largest campus), Bedford, Milton Keynes and Aylesbury.

In the latest Research Excellence Framework (REF 2021) creative writing and English were among the top-scoring subjects, while 60% of the university's research overall was assessed as world-leading or internationally excellent, placing the university at =85th in our research index. It is one of seven universities to have received only a bronze overall in the Teaching Excellence Framework (TEF 2023), and its business and management courses were investigated by the Office for Students, England's higher education regulator, in 2024.

Our National Student Survey analysis ranks it 60th for teaching quality and 78th for the wider experience. The proportion of students achieving firsts and 2.1s is among the bottom five in our table, as is the student-staff ratio, which together with low continuation rates, explains its position at third from bottom in our main table. Demand for places and new student numbers have also dropped in the last two years. In better news, Bedfordshire's achievements on carbon management, ethical careers, energy sources, waste and recycling, and water reduction have earned it an impressive third place in the
2023–24 People & Planet league.

Bedfordshire aims to boost careers for graduates through professional accreditations, paid internships and live experience projects. It has risen three places since last year to 113th in our graduate outcomes ranking but is still in the bottom 20.

From 2025 four new degrees launch across media and social policy as well as a range of degree apprenticeships. Degree courses demand a UCAS tariff of 96 to 120 points. A widening participation university, Bedfordshire includes foundation years on many degrees and considers applicants' individual skills and background, though contextual data is not part of the admissions process. Every full-time home undergraduate received some form of financial help in 2024, from a minimum bursary of £1,000 to funds of up to £6,700 for care-leavers or estranged students, as well as a range of sport and merit-based scholarships. Bedfordshire recruits the highest proportion of students from non-selective state schools (99.7%), but has plunged 43 places to 81st in our social inclusion ranking overall.

Many students live at home and commute, but first-years are guaranteed a space in student accommodation, divided across the Luton and Bedford campuses. Proximity to London is a big draw, but the campuses offer plenty. Students have access to a range of sports facilities and can access free fitness activities. Cultural life on campus is supported by fashion and interior design studios, two theatres, a television studio and four dance studios. Bedfordshire has been a member of the University Mental Health Charter since 2021 and student information desks can be accessed in a variety of ways.

---

**University Square Luton LU1 3JU**
study@beds.ac.uk
beds.ac.uk
bedssu.co.uk

**Overall ranking 129**
(last year 130)

**Accommodation**
University provided places 1,085
Self-catered £118–£230 per week

**Student numbers**
Undergraduates 9,862
Applications per place 4.3:1
Overall offer rate 75.3%

**Fees**
UK fees £9,250
International fees £15,600

beds.ac.uk/open-days
beds.ac.uk/howtoapply/money

# Birkbeck, University of London

Birkbeck has been a disruptor in higher education since its foundation more than 200 years ago, based on a radical vision to provide higher education to working Londoners. Today it is in the vanguard of HyFlex technology that will allow (mostly postgraduate) students to take part in lessons remotely in synchronisation with those who are learning on campus in Bloomsbury.

It has long offered part-time study through evening classes on campus, accessible to students who combine work or childcare with their studies. In 2024 Birkbeck introduced undergraduate degrees with daytime teaching in law; business; management; psychology; health and social care and management; and biomedicine. Classes between 6pm and 9pm remain the norm.

Birkbeck withdrew from our league table in 2019 on the grounds that our measures place a heavily part-time university at a disadvantage. We continue to include it in our listings because of its unique place in British higher education.

A college of the University of London since 1920, the university was rated bronze in the latest Teaching Excellence Framework (TEF 2023), having held silver in the previous assessment six years earlier. The TEF panel nonetheless commended Birkbeck's "effective support for students to succeed in and progress beyond their studies". Its research profile, meanwhile, is in step with its peers.

Popular subjects for full- and part-timers are law; psychology; and business and management. New courses are being added in entrepreneurship and innovation; and environment, culture and communication.

The university has a strong record of recruiting undergraduates from disadvantaged communities, boosting social mobility and contributing to a diverse student body. It welcomes applications from people without standard qualifications.

Birkbeck is among the growing number of universities with an increasing financial deficit (£2.2 million in 2022–23), which has led to restructuring and voluntary redundancies to save on staff costs. Professor Sally Wheeler, the vice-chancellor, is optimistic about the university's future, saying: "Birkbeck is a place where we have new opportunities to exploit."

Collaborations with business provide students with pathways to industry through career workshops, mentoring and opportunities for entrepreneurship. Its digital career accelerator scheme supports those hoping to work in digital, data and technology roles.

The main campus in Bloomsbury, where its academic neighbours include University College London and SOAS, is close to Senate House – the art deco building housing the University of London's main library. Birkbeck's own library, science laboratories and student services are based at Malet Street.

Most Birkbeck students live at home but the housing team can help to find places in University of London intercollegiate halls. The George bar on campus is a budget-friendly option for socialising.

Wellbeing services provide practical, psychological and disability-related support. To help students finance their studies, the university offers budgeting workshops and guidance in navigating the student loans system.

University-funded awards include cash bursaries of up to £800 to help with study costs, awarded to students from low-income households. Those who qualify under a needs-based assessment may receive up to £4,000 a year through the Birkbeck Financial Support Scheme.

---

**Malet Street Bloomsbury London WC1E 7HX**
my.bbk.ac.uk
bbk.ac.uk
birkbeckunion.org

**Overall ranking N/A**

**Accommodation**
University provided places

**Student numbers**
Undergraduates N/A
Applications per place 4.5:1
Overall offer rate N/A

**Fees**
UK fees £9,250
International fees £18,060

bbk.ac.uk/prospective/open-days/
undergraduate-and-postgraduate-information

bbk.ac.uk/student-services/fee-payment/fees

# University of Birmingham

Offering a leafy 26-acre campus in Edgbaston, just outside the bustling city of Birmingham, the UK's first civic university has set its 21st-century sights on becoming a global top-50 university. A member of the research-intensive Russell Group, Birmingham has maintained its ranking in our main academic league table, and climbed to joint 80th in the QS World University Rankings 2025. The university achieved superb results in the national Research Excellence Framework (REF 2021) and ranks tenth in our research quality index. Some of its best outcomes were in physics, environmental sciences, computer science, philosophy, theology, social work and law.

Birmingham came out of the latest Teaching Excellence Framework (TEF 2023) rated silver overall and gold for student outcomes thanks to its "tailored approaches", but bronze for student experience. In our analysis of the latest National Student Survey, the university has climbed three places for teaching quality to 109th and holds steady at =79th for the wider undergraduate experience. The High Fliers Graduate Market 2024 report showed Birmingham to be the most targeted UK university by the largest number of top graduate employers, including Lloyds Banking Group, Jaguar Land Rover and Goldman Sachs. In our analysis of the latest Graduate Outcomes survey, Birmingham ranked 16th, a slight drop from =14th last year.

New degrees for 2024 focus on drama, creative writing and medical physics, while from 2025 there will also be courses in cultural and creative industries, liberal arts, arts and sciences, and natural sciences.

Birmingham attracted nearly 56,500 applications in 2023 for 7,000 places. Birmingham's entry requirements start at BBB and go up to A*A*A. Contextual offers are typically one grade lower than standard, while Pathways to Birmingham, a programme aimed at widening participation, sees offers reduced by two grades. Only 4% of the 2023 cohort gained places through Clearing. Birmingham's decade of development began in 2016 and many buildings are already in use, from energy-efficient student townhouses to specialist labs for engineering and molecular sciences. Students who need a screen break can turn to the 12-acre Green Heart outdoor space. Birmingham's rich cultural diversity is another of its big appeals, with galleries, museums, libraries and concert venues aplenty both on campus and in the city. For sports, besides on-campus facilities, students can use the exceptional venues created to host events at the 2022 Commonwealth Games: glass-backed squash courts, a 50m swimming pool, climbing wall and multipurpose arena.

Rooms in halls are guaranteed for first-years who meet the criteria and a self-selection process allows students to pick their own room and post a biography. To support students, there are wellbeing officers in every school and the university partners with the NHS and the Children's Society. Like other research-intensive universities, Birmingham tends to perform poorly for social inclusion, ranking 97th in our latest index. The £2,000 Chamberlain Award is part of an attempt to improve on that, and about one fifth of 2023's new students received one of Birmingham's scholarships or bursaries.

---

**Edgbaston Birmingham B15 2TT**
admissions.bham.ac.uk/newenquiry
birmingham.ac.uk
guildofstudents.com

**Overall ranking 22**
(last year 22)

**Accommodation**
University provided places 6,565
Catered £153–£258 per week
Self-catered £99–£223 per week

**Student numbers**
Undergraduates 24,406
Applications per place 8.0:1
Overall offer rate 65.4%

**Fees**
UK fees £9,250
International fees £22,080–£30,330
Medicine £48,660

birmingham.ac.uk/study/undergraduate/open-days
birmingham.ac.uk/study/undergraduate/fees-funding

# Birmingham City University

Professor David Mba – the first black vice-chancellor at Birmingham City University (BCU) – took up his role in October 2023, determined to improve opportunities for others and make an impact on a city that has earned a reputation as a leading student destination where the populations from five universities create a vibrant atmosphere. BCU's City Centre campus is in up-and-coming Eastside, where the £70 million STEAMhouse innovation centre mixes it up to encourage collaboration between the arts, science, technology, engineering and maths sectors in a Victorian former factory.

Sports and exercise degree courses make use of Alexander Stadium, one of the main venues for the 2022 Commonwealth Games, and links to the Royal Birmingham Conservatoire gives access to a 500-seat concert hall as well as rehearsal and teaching spaces for performing arts students. BCU's Centre for Equality, Diversity and Inclusion in the Arts holds public lectures and workshops, while BCU's environmental commitments include investing more than £9 million in carbon reduction measures at the City South Campus.

In the Teaching Excellence Framework (TEF 2023), BCU won silver overall, silver for student outcomes and gold for student experience. The TEF panel commended "the use of research in relevant disciplines, innovation, professional practice and extensive employer engagement". Results from the latest National Student Survey (NSS) do little to back this up, however; in our analysis BCU has dropped down to 82nd for teaching quality and risen marginally to 77th for overall experience. In the latest Research Excellence Framework (REF 2021) BCU more than doubled its submission, compared with 2014 and creative writing and English produced the best results.

New degrees for September 2025 include BSc (Hons) degrees in game design; game technical art; game programming; and game technology. Entry requirements range from 32 UCAS tariff points for music to 136 for architecture. Foundation degrees, HNDs and contextual offers provide alternative routes in to the university for those who qualify. BCU has about 50 professional accreditations for a wide range of its courses, and these are bolstered by the Graduate+ range of extracurricular, employment-related activities. More than 1,500 trainees are enrolled on BCU's 15 degree apprenticeships, but BCU has fallen nine places year-on-year to be ranked 101st in our analysis of the Graduate Outcomes survey.

Up to a quarter of first-years tend to live on campus, while the majority commute from home. Accommodation is guaranteed to full-time new undergraduates who meet the September deadline. Pre-entry appointments are available for any students who want to discuss what mental health support is available at BCU and the university's mental health and wellbeing team operates Monday to Friday, 51 weeks of the year.

Work to widen participation includes student mentoring and summer schools under the AimHigher scheme as well as BCU undergraduate literacy tutors, who practise reading and comprehension skills with children aged 4–11. The university has jumped 12 places to rank 40th overall in our social inclusion table. For ethnic diversity, BCU ranks =14th. Students from low-income households who enrol via the Accelerate partnership can qualify for a £1,000 scholarship in the first year. Applicants who arrive with 144 UCAS points or more can qualify for a High Achievers' Scholarship worth £1,000.

---

**University House 15 Bartholomew Row**
**Birmingham B5 5JU**
admissions@bcu.ac.uk
bcu.ac.uk
bcusu.com

**Overall ranking =107**
(last year 110)

**Accommodation**
University provided places 2,746
Self-catered £105–£206 per week

**Student numbers**
Undergraduates 20,966
Applications per place 5.3:1
Overall offer rate 73.9%

**Fees**
UK fees £9,250
International fees £16,085–£26,195

bcu.ac.uk/student-info/open-days
bcu.ac.uk/ student-info/finance-and-money-matters

# Birmingham Newman University

A name change in 2023 has rooted the university to its location in southwest Birmingham. As its academic focus diversifies, Birmingham Newman has branched out with new facilities, most recently expanding its School of Nursing and Allied Health to include space for new degrees in paramedic science, occupational therapy and physiotherapy. For now it is still one of the smallest universities in our guide, with just under 3,000 students, and this personal touch is reflected in superb rates of student satisfaction. Birmingham Newman takes fifth place in our analysis of student satisfaction measures.

The university was rated silver for all three scores in the government's Teaching Excellence Framework (TEF 2023). In the latest Research Excellence Framework (REF 2021) Birmingham Newman doubled the size of its academic submission compared with 2014. 94% of its work in English was assessed as world-leading or internationally excellent. However, it is near the bottom in our research quality index in =126th, and with only 87.2% of students projected to carry on from the first to second year of their degrees, it has fallen to 125 in our rankings.

Entry requirements begin at an accessible 48 UCAS tariff points and no course demands higher than 120 points. Contextual offers reduce this by eight points for eligible students. Applications are at record levels, with 13 per cent of undergraduates coming through Clearing. Every full-time degree has a work placement module, and the university has particularly strong links with educational institutions and healthcare trusts across the West Midlands. This is bearing fruit, and the university has risen from 120th to 79th in our graduate outcome rankings.

First-year students are guaranteed one of the 276 places in university-owned accommodation, much of which is brand new. The modern campus has had £20 million of investment in recent years, with the new halls of residence accompanied by immersive laboratory spaces. A mock law court, computer science laboratory and a careers and employability hub have also been added, and work is continuing to make the campus more environmentally sustainable. The local area is quiet and residential but student-friendly nightlife, shopping and culture are within easy reach in Birmingham's city centre. A well-equipped fitness suite and performance room as well as a 3G sports pitch, sports hall, gymnasium and squash courts are on campus.

The university offers the services of wellbeing and mental health advisers as well as a disability and inclusion team. Birmingham Newman is top among English universities in our social inclusion index thanks to recruiting the second-highest proportion of students who are the first in their family to go to university (69.3%), the fifth-highest proportion from non-selective state schools (98.3%) and the sixth-highest proportion with a disability (14.1%). Birmingham Newman also supports parents of first-generation applicants to understand the higher education processes. One Sanctuary Scholarship is awarded each year to forced migrant students, and the Newman University Support Fund provides up to £1,750 a year for those experiencing hardship, as well as supermarket and travel vouchers.

**Genners Lane Bartley Green**
**Birmingham B32 3NT**
admissions@newman.ac.uk
newman.ac.uk
newmansu.org

**Overall ranking =90**
(last year 125)

**Accommodation**
University provided places 276
Self-catered £105–£200 per week

**Student numbers**
Undergraduates 1,875
Applications per place 4.9:1
Overall offer rate 87.6%

**Fees**
UK fees £9,250
International fees N/A

newman.ac.uk/study/open-days/
newman.ac.uk/study/student-finance/undergraduate-finance-information/

# Bishop Grosseteste University

Named after Robert Grosseteste, a 13th-century bishop of Lincoln, BGU stands out for its high rates of student satisfaction, as reported in successive National Student Surveys (NSS). In fact, in our latest analysis BGU comes top in the UK for satisfaction with teaching quality and =7th for the wider student experience. Such unparalleled NSS outcomes reflect the personal touch that is the hallmark of a small university with fewer than 1,700 full-time undergraduates.

The institution, which was founded in 1862 as an Anglican teacher-training college for women, gained university status in 2012. While teaching degrees remain the focus, BGU offers a range of subjects to students of all faiths and none.

The university was awarded triple silver in the government's Teaching Excellence Framework in 2023, drawing praise for its "highly effective teaching, assessment and feedback practices". Theology produced BGU's best results in the latest Research Excellence Framework (REF 2021).

From September 2024 the curriculum gained degrees in mathematics, computing and data science; criminology; environmental psychology; music and special educational needs; and business and Tesol (teaching English to speakers of other languages). A foundation year joins the criminology course from 2025 and there is a portfolio of degree apprenticeships.

Applicants require between 96 and 112 points in the UCAS tariff. Contextual offers reduce the standard offer by 16 points. Applications and new student enrolments decreased at BGU in 2023 to their lowest numbers for the past decade but the university registered a 34% increase in applications for 2024 entry by the end of March. BGU is =54th in our analysis of graduate prospects, up from 73rd last year. The university's business centre provides support for start-ups and its social economy hub develops links with social enterprises, charities and community groups.

Based on a leafy site a few minutes' walk from Lincoln Cathedral, BGU has two halls of residence on campus. The supply of bed spaces is set to double, which should help the university get closer to meeting the demand for halls of residence. Accommodation is first come, first served, with priority given to those who live outside the local area. Other facilities of note include an extended library housing student advice and learning development teams, and specialist teaching space for archaeology boosted by more than £427,000 funding from the Arts and Humanities Research Council.

BGU is one of two universities in Lincoln, where the student vibe is livelier than the city's quaint, historic reputation might suggest. The Venue, at the heart of the campus, operates as a theatre by day and a cinema by night, and students can take time out in the Peace Gardens. BGU has a range of indoor and outdoor sports facilities, while cultural activities fall under the auspices of the chaplaincy, ranging from a weekly discussion group to theatre trips and a chapel choir. Mental health support comes from a student advice team and a 24/7 mental health app. BGU has jumped five places to ninth overall in our social inclusion index. Nearly a third of undergraduate students qualified for some form of financial support in 2024, with bursaries of up to £3,600 a year available.

---

**Longdales Road Lincoln LN1 3DY**
courseenquiries@bishopg.ac.uk
bgu.ac.uk
bgsu.co.uk

**Overall ranking 86**
(last year =89)

**Accommodation**
University provided places 548
Self-catered £123–£205 per week

**Student numbers**
Undergraduates 1,605
Applications per place 2.3:1
Overall offer rate 91.9%

**Fees**
UK fees £6,935 (Foundation) – £9,250
International fees £10,200 (Foundation) – £13,600

bgu.ac.uk/open-days
bgu.ac.uk/apply-now/fees-and-funding

# University of Bolton

Students at Bolton tend to be among the most satisfied with their time at university. Consistent good feedback in the National Student Survey (NSS) has kept the university in the top ranks of our analysis for teaching quality and undergraduate experience, a success echoed by in a gold for student experience in the Teaching Excellence Framework (TEF 2023) leading to an overall silver. Contentment is boosted by a Life Lounge on campus where a team of mental health professionals provide support to students. However, the TEF panel noted the university's above-average dropout rate, and our latest NSS analysis shows a step down to 38th for satisfaction with teaching quality and 62nd for the wider undergraduate experience.

At the end of 2024, the Office for Students approved a name change for Bolton to the University of Greater Manchester, reflecting its presences in Trafford, central Manchester and Wigan as well as its home town.

An expanding curriculum has gained more than 20 new degrees over the past two years, and another four launch in 2025. In the latest Research Excellence Framework (REF 2021), Bolton submitted a broader body of work than in 2014, with the best results coming in English and engineering. However, as results improved across the sector, Bolton fell 16 places to 129th in our research quality rankings. Research facilities include the Centre for Islamic Finance and the National Centre for Motorsport Engineering – through which the university helps to run a professional motor racing team

For three-year degrees offers range from 96 to 120 UCAS tariff points, while foundation degrees entry may be gained from 48 points. The university does not make contextual offers. Nearly four in ten new entrants in 2023 gained their places via Clearing. Thanks to integrated career skills training and an active careers service engaging with local, regional and national employers, Bolton has leapt 26 places to =71st for graduate prospects compared with our previous edition, according to the latest Graduate Outcomes survey. Fifteen months after completing their degrees, 74.8% of Bolton graduates were in high-skilled jobs or continuing their studies, up from 73% last year.

Bolton's Deane campus houses a £31 million health, leisure and research centre and the Greater Manchester Business School. The new £40 million Institute of Medical Science at the Bolton Royal Hospital site. will feature tech-enabled facilities to accommodate students on courses including physiotherapy, nursing and midwifery. Bolton has also established an outpost in Salford and, much further afield, a campus at Ras al-Khaimah in the United Arab Emirates. On-campus sporting opportunities are provided by indoor facilities as well as outdoor pursuits such as kayaking and paddleboarding at the university's Anderton Centre. Off-campus, a partnership with Bolton Arena means that students can use its facilities at Middlebrook.

The 383 rooms available in Bolton's Orlando Village are allocated on a first-come, first-served basis but the majority of students live locally and commute. Six in ten entrants are the first in their family to go to university, around two in ten are from deprived areas and seven in ten are aged over 21 when they enrol. Students who have served for at least three years in the armed forces qualify for an award of £500 a year for three years, while bursaries for students who have lived in care are worth up to £3,000.

---

**Deane Road Bolton BL3 5AB**
admissions-team@bolton.ac.uk
bolton.ac.uk
boltonsu.com

**Overall ranking 119**
(last year =106)

**Accommodation**
University provided places 383
Self-catered £139–£199 per week

**Student numbers**
Undergraduates 7,156
Applications per place 4.6:1
Overall offer rate 61.0%

**Fees**
UK fees £9,250
International fees £15,950

bolton.ac.uk/open-days
bolton.ac.uk/student-life/fees-and-funding

# Bournemouth University

Life's near a beach at Bournemouth University (BU); seven miles of sandy Jurassic Coast shoreline is on the doorstep, and the New Forest National Park is not far away either. A Fairtrade university and with EcoCampus Platinum status, the university ranks tenth in the People & Planet 2023–24 university league table. With 100 degree programmes across 20 subject areas, BU has become renowned for computer animation, TV and media production, music and sound production degrees, as well as its well-regarded tourism courses. New degree courses in esports, digital technologies, and education psychology began in September 2024.

Communication, cultural and media studies, and leisure and tourism performed well in the latest Research Excellence Framework (REF 2021). However, BU dropped 16 places to rank 80th in our research quality rating, against stronger gains at other universities. BU was awarded silver overall in the Teaching Excellence Framework (TEF 2023), with silver for student outcomes but only bronze for the student experience. In our latest analysis of the National Student Survey, BU has slipped five places to 114th for teaching quality and risen five places to 98th for overall experience.

With an average of 113 UCAS tariff points, Bournemouth is =108th for entry standards. After a record year for applications in 2022, the demand for places has cooled. Those who meet the AccessBU criteria may find their offer reduced by up to 16 UCAS tariff points. BU is 61st in our analysis of graduate outcomes, down fom 55th last year. Dedicated university staff help students to find the ideal work placement posting in a range of workplaces, and there are also good opportunities to study abroad.

First-years who select BU as their first choice by the deadline are guaranteed one of 3,800 study bedrooms. The university has invested more than £200 million in its facilities, adding gateway buildings on each of its campuses: Talbot (the main site) and Lansdowne (home to the faculty of health and where most accommodation is based), a short bus ride away. The Talbot campus boasts everything from industry-standard TV and motion-capture studios to sports halls and a spin suite. Support teams work with BU's faculties to offer pastoral and academic help, including an out-of-hours welfare duty officer and in February 2023, BU opened the Retreat drop-in centre to provide help in a crisis.

Placed 70th overall in our social inclusion table, BU is in the top 20 for its proportion of white working-class male students, one of the most underrepresented groups, and nearly half of new students in 2023 were the first in their family to go to university (46.5%, =45th). Bournemouth's black achievement gap, at minus 31.3% (90th) lets the university down. BU maintenance bursaries for students from low-income households (up to £16,000) provide £800 a year, and care leaver bursaries of up to £12,000 are also available. Scholarships are offered to reward academic excellence, musical or sporting talent, and there is a dedicated scholarship awarded to female students of cybersecurity.

---

**Fern Barrow Poole BH12 5BB**
futurestudents@bournemouth.ac.uk
bournemouth.ac.uk
subu.org.uk

**Overall ranking 82**
(last year 81)

**Accommodation**
University provided places 3,800
Self-catered £141–£254 per week

**Student numbers**
Undergraduates 12,574
Applications per place 4.8:1
Overall offer rate 80.2%

**Fees**
UK fees £9,250
International fees £17,800–£18,000

bournemouth.ac.uk/study/undergraduate/open-days

bournemouth.ac.uk/study/undergraduate/
undergraduate-fees-funding

# University of Bradford

In step with its goal to be an engine of social mobility, the University of Bradford has invested in a range of projects, from decarbonising the campus to supporting underrepresented groups to enrol, and working to decolonise the learning and teaching strategy. The UK's No 1 university for social mobility for the past three years in the Higher Education Policy Institute's annual ranking, Bradford is 15th in our social inclusion index, down from the top ten last year.

In the Teaching Excellence Framework (TEF 2023) Bradford was awarded triple silver but our latest National Student Survey analysis shows declining satisfaction with both teaching quality (down nine places to 125th) and the wider undergraduate experience (down 35 places to 118th). The university's Peace Studies and International Development department celebrated its 50th anniversary this year, and in 2022 the university launched the Bradford-Renduchintala Centre for Space AI. The Research Excellence Framework (REF 2021) highlighted strengths in archaeology, engineering, accounting and allied health subjects, but these gains were not enough to prevent a drop to 87th in our research quality index.

Courses at Bradford require between 64 and 136 UCAS tariff points, with new entrants averaging 126 points in 2022. About half of new undergraduates join via access, foundation courses or BTec qualifications and over a quarter of students in 2023 entered via Clearing. Bradford attracted a record number of new international students in 2023, with around one in five freshers (615 out of 2,950) from overseas. Contextual offers are available under the Bradford Progression Scheme. Bradford ranks 51st in our graduate prospects analysis, a notable achievement in a city ranked as the fifth most "income-deprived" local authority in England, with employment rates below the national average.

Accommodation is allocated on a first-come, first-served basis at the Green student village, although the majority of students live at home and commute in. Minutes from the centre of Bradford, the university's City campus is self-contained. To encourage biodiversity there are beehives, edible gardens and buildings made from hemp. Among Bradford's specialist developments are the Digital Health Enterprise Zone, the Lady Hale mock court and the Wolfson Centre for Applied Health Research, which opened at Bradford Royal Infirmary in 2019 in partnership with the University of Leeds and Bradford Teaching Hospitals NHS Foundation Trust.

Undergraduate life includes students' union events and celebration of religious festivals. The university supplements a peer support wellbeing scheme with its own counselling service. Sports facilities include a swimming pool, climbing wall and squash courts, and the city has new and refurbished facilities opening this year as part of its status as the UK's City of Culture 2025.

More than two thirds of entrants are the first in their family to go to university and nearly three quarters are from black and ethnic minority backgrounds. More than 3,000 cash bursaries are awarded to students with a household income below £30,000. A number of country-specific scholarships help attract international students from Pakistan, Ghana and sub-Saharan Africa, among other regions.

---

**Bradford BD7 1DP**
enquiries@bradford.ac.uk
bradford.ac.uk
bradfordunisu.co.uk

**Overall ranking 111**
(last year 108)

**Accommodation**
University provided places 1,002
Self-catered £72–£128 per week

**Student numbers**
Undergraduates 7,669
Applications per place 4.0:1
Overall offer rate 84.5%

**Fees**
UK fees £9,250
International fees £19,560–£23,290

bradford.ac.uk/study/open-days
bradford.ac.uk/money/fees

# University of Brighton

This south coast university with buckets of seaside charm on its doorstep has had an ambitious makeover and its growing research profile has helped continue its march up our main academic rankings (up 16 places to 71st). The closure of Brighton's Eastbourne campus has left it with three sites: Moulsecoomb – the biggest campus and the focus of recent development, Falmer – fresh from a revamp for provision within sport, education and health, and City – a stone's throw from the pier and the base for art and media courses. Brighton's status as one of the most successful post-1992 universities for research was cemented by its results in the Research Excellence Framework (REF 2021), which propelled it to 87th in our research quality index.

In step with Brighton's professional and vocational focus, it fields a diverse portfolio of degree apprenticeships including teaching; civil engineering; social work, and nursing. It runs the Brighton and Sussex Medical School in a longstanding partnership with the University of Sussex. The School of Education and School of Sport and Health Sciences merged in summer 2024 as part of an overhaul of the curriculum that will lead to 18 new degrees while nine courses within the humanities are withdrawn. In the government's Teaching Excellence Framework (TEF 2023), Brighton's overall silver award reflected strong student outcomes, but in our latest National Student Survey analysis Brighton remains at the lower end for teaching quality (120th) and the wider undergraduate experience (122nd).

With an average of 114 UCAS points, Brighton is 107th for its entry standards. Contextual offers were introduced in 2024 for students who meet the criteria for widening participation. Santander funds £1,050 grants for six-week internships at small and medium-size businesses and there are a range of other placement and workshop schemes aimed at boosting employability, but Brighton has dipped 23 places to 85th in our analysis of graduate prospects.

Brighton's 2,954 spaces are sufficient for all first-years who apply in time to be guaranteed a space across the three campuses. Brighton is a student-friendly city packed with diverse delights. Sea air, laid-back attitudes and a gritty coastal charisma have long attracted undergraduates to Brighton – not to mention the club scene. Sports facilities are available for use at the Falmer campus and the fitness facility at Moulsecoomb opened in 2022. #NeverOK is the university's pledge to tackle all forms of harassment, sexual misconduct, violence and abuse. Wellbeing workshops, the Togetherall 24/7 online mental health service and a network of student residential advisers constitute the wider support system.

Brighton has fallen for the first time in two years in our social inclusion index, dropping eight places year-on-year to =62nd. However, it's ranked 22nd overall for its proportion of disabled students and is in the top 30 for white working-class males, a particularly underrepresented group. About a quarter of new admissions in 2024 qualified for one of Brighton's bursaries, including the Brighton Boost, a package of £1,250 towards the cost of halls or up to £500 in travel costs for those living elsewhere. Students who qualify also get a leg-up finding work through the student employment agency. Merit-based scholarships are offered, too, including up to 15 for sport.

---

**Mithras House Lewes Road Brighton BN2 4AT**
enquiries@brighton.ac.uk
brighton.ac.uk
brightonsu.com

**Overall ranking 71**
(last year 87)

**Accommodation**
University provided places 2,954
Self-catered £96–£249 per week

**Student numbers**
Undergraduates 12,089
Applications per place 6.7:1
Overall offer rate 72.0%

**Fees**
UK fees £9,250
International fees £15,900–£16,900
Medicine £44,500

brighton.ac.uk/studying-here/visit-us/open-days/
brighton.ac.uk/studying-here/fees-and-finance

# University of Bristol

Bristol is more in demand and as ambitious as ever. A record 61,000 applicants chased just under 7,000 undergraduate places in 2023. It has risen five places to rank 11th in our new league table, while also moving up a place in the QS world rankings, where it sits 54th in the list's 2025 edition. Bristol's outstanding strength in research distinguishes the university: in the latest Research Excellence Framework (REF 2021), 94% of its submissions were rated world-leading or internationally excellent. Bristol is placed 6th in our research quality index, with notable entries in engineering; medicine; law; chemistry; geography and environmental science; dentistry; modern languages; natural sciences; social policy and social work.

The university is also making strides in its environmental and ethical performance, sitting 16th in the latest People & Planet league table (and third among its Russell Group peers). In the Teaching Excellence Framework (TEF 2023) Bristol achieved silver overall and silver for student experience, and has added breadth to the course offering this year with twelve new degrees added for 2025.

An earlier start to the academic year greeted Bristol students in September 2024, with welcome week kicking off on September 9. The move is part of a structural shift that will also include an earlier start to the summer break. And instead of exams taking place after the Christmas holidays, mid-year assessments will take place in December – allowing for a holiday season minus revision stress.

Most teaching takes place on Bristol's main campus in Clifton, where standout facilities include the £56 million Life Sciences Building and the Richmond Building, which houses two theatres and one of the city's largest gig venues.

The university precinct merges into the city, with neogothic edifices contrasting with newer buildings. Further afield, in Stoke Bishop, the university has a botanic garden with more than 4,500 plan species. The £500 million Temple Quarter Enterprise Campus is opening in 2026 and will expand the university footprint by seven acres.

Bristol demands grades of BBC to A*A*A for entry, but is also a pioneer of contextual offers, which accounted for about a quarter of offers in 2023. The latest High Fliers graduate market report rated Bristol the fifth most targeted university by large employers, and our analysis of the national Graduate Outcomes survey puts Bristol at =17th. More than 20 degrees incorporate a year in industry or professional placements, as well as opportunities abroad through links with more than 150 universities around the world.

Sports facilities are spread across five sites, while the students' union offers nearly 400 student-run societies, sports clubs and support networks. Bristol guarantees accommodation to first-years, as long as they apply by the end of June.

Bristol's 24-hour residential life service is an example of its "whole university" approach to mental health and wellbeing, which includes services offered by faculties. Personal and senior tutors provide support with academic and pastoral issues, and students can opt to provide the name of a trusted contact whom the university can call if it has concerns. The university continues to analyse the contributing factors behind a cluster of suicides in recent years, and its efforts have been recognised with the University Mental Health Charter Award. Bristol has made modest gains in our social inclusion index in recent years but remains outside the top 100. There is a generous bursary and scholarship scheme benefitting about a quarter of students through means-tested and merit-based awards.

---

Beacon House Queens Road Bristol BS8 1QU
choosebristol-ug@bristol.ac.uk
bristol.ac.uk
bristolsu.org.uk

**Overall ranking 11**
(last year 16)

**Accommodation**
University provided places 6,725
Catered £165–£280 per week
Self-catered £105–£235 per week

**Student numbers**
Undergraduates 22,460
Applications per place 8.8:1
Overall offer rate 58.0%

**Fees**
UK fees £9,250
International fees £23,900–£46,500
Medicine £42,800

bristol.ac.uk/study/undergraduate/visits/open-days/
bristol.ac.uk/study/undergraduate/fees-funding

# Brunel University London

Named after the engineer, this west London institution strives to be the UK's leading technical university, although the original focus on STEM, education and management has expanded to include the performing arts, humanities, health and sport sciences. Brunel's medical school began taking international students in 2022 and 2024 marks its first intake of 50 UK students. In the arts, Brunel has attracted some well-known figures to the teaching staff over the years, with the author Will Self a professor of modern thought. The comedians Jo Brand and Lee Mack are ambassadors for the university's Centre for Comedy Studies Research.

From October 2024 Brunel became the 17th member of the University of London federation, and has inched up in both global listings and our own rankings. In our latest National Student Survey analysis, the undergraduate experience rating saw a rise of 54 places to 61st. Satisfaction with teaching quality has improved modestly from 125th to 111th. However, in the government's Teaching Excellence Framework (TEF 2023) the university is one of only seven to be rated bronze overall, downgraded from silver in the previous assessment. Sport and exercise science produced good results for Brunel in the Research Excellence Framework (REF 2021), along with anthropology and allied health subjects. Overall, 72.7% of Brunel's submission was assessed as world-leading or internationally excellent, putting the university at 72nd in our research quality index.

Grade requirements span from CDD to AAB, with contextual offers usually at the lower end of this range. Brunel is a pioneer of sandwich degrees to boost graduate employability and its Professional Development Centre nurtures relationships with a variety of businesses locally and nationally. Graduate prospects are declining after a brief improvement last year, with our analysis placing Brunel =103rd, down 20 places from our last edition.

Accommodation on campus is guaranteed for all first-years who apply in time but a large proportion of Brunel students live at home and commute. With all facilities on site, students can get wherever they need to be within 10 minutes. Since 2014 the university has pumped more than £150 million into its Uxbridge campus, where striking new buildings and landscaping contrast with original 1960s architecture. The Quad North building at the heart of the campus has simulated hospital wards and clinical skills laboratories.

Brunel is a regional training centre for UK Athletics with superb facilities. There is also a World Rugby-approved artificial pitch and strength and conditioning gym, part of a partnership with Ealing Trailfinders Rugby. Team Brunel was the first to introduce a branded sports hijab to boost participation among its female Muslim students and the university has a women-only gym. Away from sport, there is an annual musical theatre production.

One of the more successful pre-1992 universities in our social inclusion index, Brunel draws the third-highest proportion of students from black and ethnic minority backgrounds in England and Wales. Means-tested bursaries include a specific allowance for care leavers and there is also a range of merit-based scholarships.

**London Kingston Lane Uxbridge UB8 3PH**
admissions@brunel.ac.uk
brunel.ac.uk
brunelstudents.com

**Overall ranking =107**
(last year =119)

**Accommodation**
University provided places 4,209
Self-catered £150–£347 per week

**Student numbers**
Undergraduates 11,547
Applications per place 6.1:1
Overall offer rate 70.7%

**Fees**
UK fees £9,250
International fees £19,430–£23,615
Medicine £49,395

brunel.ac.uk/study/open-days/undergraduate-open-days
brunel.ac.uk/study/undergraduate-fees-and-funding

# University of Buckingham

Two-year degrees are the norm at Buckingham, which introduced the model as Britain's first private university, founded in 1976. The progressive fast-track programmes mean students can pack their undergraduate studies into two 40-week academic years (compared with three years of 26–30 weeks at most other UK universities) starting in either September or January. The course offering delivered by six academic schools matches the range at other UK universities, despite its bijou size: Buckingham has only about 1,600 undergraduates on its leafy riverside campus. The expense of private tuition fees – £27,750 a year for UK students living on campus – is higher than mainstream institutions but offset by saving a year's living costs. Buckingham's medical school is a popular choice for its 4½-year MBChB.

The original riverside campus is on three sites – the main hub in Hunter Street, Chandos Road and Verney Park – in leafy Buckingham, tucked into a bend of the Great Ouse. All courses will soon be taught in Buckingham, after the decision to close the university's costly campus for medicine and health sciences students in Crewe, Cheshire by 2026, six years after it opened.

The highest riser in our previous edition's league table and shortlisted for University of the Year 2024, Buckingham has plunged 58 places to 114th in our main academic rankings, not least as a result of precipitous falls in student satisfaction. Our latest National Student Survey analysis places Buckingham 108th for teaching quality, down 48 places, and down 54 places to 128th for student experience. Buckingham does not take part in the national Research Excellence Framework, although students can expect to be taught by academics who are active in their field. Rated silver overall in the Teaching Excellence Framework (TEF 2023), Buckingham is known for its face-to-face, small class tutorials. The curriculum gained eight new options in September 2024 including liberal arts, computing (gaming pathway), history with politics, and digital marketing. Buckingham's Centre for Heterodox Social Science has dived into the culture wars with a low-cost online course studying progressive illiberalism — better known as "wokeism".

Some foundation programmes ask for DD, or 48 UCAS tariff points, while at the upper end you'll need ABB (128 points) to get into medicine. Buckingham attracted more than 1,400 applications in 2023, a new record, and almost half of the 440 freshers in 2023 came from outside the UK. A micro-internship scheme connects students with industry partners but Buckingham has dropped out of the top 20 of our graduate prospects rankings to =57th.

All first-years who apply by the deadline are guaranteed a room in halls of residence. The main campus has a bar and fitness facilities, and a refurbished refectory with social learning space. Student-led clubs and societies cover a range of interests, and every student has regular meetings with their personal tutor, who provides academic support as well as signposting students to other services as needed. The university's wellbeing department offers counselling, mentoring and wellbeing advice. Life is tranquil in rural Buckingham while the brighter lights of Milton Keynes are a 20-minute drive away. Students in Crewe are close to both Liverpool and Manchester.

Buckingham is in the top 20 for its proportion of black and ethnic minority students (60%), but the university has slumped to second from bottom in our social inclusion index for England and Wales. The High Achiever scholarship of £2,000 is given to those achieving AAB (or equivalent) at A-level. Means-tested bursaries offer support up to a maximum of £4,000.

---

**Hunter Street Buckingham MK18 1EG**
admissions@buckingham.ac.uk
buckingham.ac.uk
su.buckingham.ac.uk

**Overall ranking 114**
(last year =56)

**Accommodation**
University provided places 473
Self-catered £140–£235 per week

**Student numbers**
Undergraduates 1,522
Applications per place 3.2:1
Overall offer rate N/A

**Fees**
UK fees £9,250–£13,875
International fees £14,800–£19,733
Medicine £40,000–£45,000

buckingham.ac.uk/study/visit-us/open-days/
buckingham.ac.uk/admissions/fees

# Buckinghamshire New University

For students looking for advice on wellbeing, finance and careers, Buckinghamshire New University's (BNU) £20 million Dove development has everything in one place at the High Wycombe campus, along with an airy atrium space, a café and roof gardens. New degrees shocase the university's practical accent with engineering design, building and construction engineering, aerospace engineering and civil engineering joinding the curriculum. Hands-on teaching highlights include sessions at Pinewood Studios for film and television students and a partnership with Thames Valley Police to deliver policing programmes.

The university does well on rates of student satisfaction with teaching quality (10th in our analysis). For the undergraduate experience more widely, it remains comfortably in the upper half of UK universities (down 25 places to 46th). It achieved triple silver in the Teaching Excellence Framework (TEF 2023), and moved up five places in our research quality rankings to 118th based on its results in the latest Research Excellence Framework (REF 2021). Art and design; history of art; geology, and sports sciences produced some of the best results. However, at odds with the TEF's findings was a 2024 Office for Students report raising concerns about business and management courses at BNU, including that the university was not consistently providing a high-quality academic experience.

Entry requirements range from 40–64 UCAS tariff points to 120–144. BNU makes contextual offers to qualifying students and in 2023 received more than 12,600 applications for 3,700 places – including 18% via Clearing. Despite its proactive industry links, BNU remains in the bottom 30 of our graduate outcomes rankings at =105th.

The main campus at High Wycombe has benefited from £100 million of spending over the past decade. A variety of simulation facilities are being added in a £3.6 million investment to give health and social care students hands-on experience. The historic Brunel Engine Shed opposite High Wycombe station is being converted into a community space and public art gallery for students' work. Most of BNU's healthcare students are based in Uxbridge, northwest London, and a third site in Aylesbury hosts nursing, business, law and apprenticeship courses.

Most BNU students live at home, allowing the university to guarantee all first-years who want to live in halls one of its 881 student bedrooms. 45% of these are at the minimum rate of £86 a week. BNU funds free sports and recreational activities through the students' union's Big Deal programme. There are more than 30 sports clubs and links with professional clubs in the region, and BNU has one of only five swimming performance centres approved by Swim England. The Human Performance, Exercise and Wellbeing Centre has a three-lane running track with 3D motion-capture technology. BNU has expanded its mental health support services with mentors specialising in conditions such as ADHD and specific learning difficulties.

BNU performs well in our social inclusion table but this year has dropped six places to 21st. The university has the third-highest proportion of mature students at 85%. Nearly one in five new entrants qualify for one of BNU's wide range of scholarships or bursaries, including the £1,100-a-year bursary for gypsy, traveller, Roma, showman and boater communities – a rarity in higher education and offered with the guarantee of accommodation and support from a mentor.

---

**High Wycombe Campus Queen Alexandra Road**
**High Wycombe HP11 2JZ**
admissions@bnu.ac.uk
bnu.ac.uk
bucksstudentsunion.org

**Overall ranking 122**
(last year 127)

**Accommodation**
University provided places 881
Self-catered £86–£197 per week

**Student numbers**
Undergraduates 16,787
Applications per place 3.4:1
Overall offer rate 63.8%

**Fees**
UK fees £9,250
International fees £15,000

bucks.ac.uk/study/undergraduate/open-days
bucks.ac.uk/study/fees-and-funding

# University of Cambridge

Founded in 1209, the second-oldest university in the English-speaking world sits fifth in both the QS and Times Higher Education global rankings. In our table, Cambridge's eight-year reign at the top ended in 2021 and this year it has slipped out of our top three to rank fourth. The university's research pedigree was confirmed in the latest Research Excellence Framework (REF 2021), which rated 93% of Cambridge's work world-leading or internationally excellent. Although second in our research quality analysis overall, compared with institutions that share its broad academic range, Cambridge's outcomes are the strongest. The university leads in 19 of our subject tables, more than any other university, and places =4th in our graduate outcomes analysis.

Cambridge offers a more intimate setting than its rival, Oxford. The city centre is dominated by the low-rise medieval quads, grand Tudor entrances and yellow sandstone buildings, many of which are linked across the River Cam by much-photographed bridges. Entry standards are high, with offers of A*A*A or A*AA at A-level, but these grades are not a guarantee. Instead, admissions are in the hands of the 31 distinctive, historic colleges, and about 80% of applicants are interviewed. The "pool" system gives the most promising candidates a second chance if they miss out on their first choice of college, but Cambridge reconsiders fewer applicants than Oxford does. Cambridge does not enter Clearing and does not have a formal policy of making contextual offers. However, a fully-funded foundation year was launched in 2022, enabling disadvantaged students to progress to a range of undergraduate degrees in the arts, humanities and social sciences.

The majority of lectures are in person, with some also recorded. These are supplemented by small-group teaching delivered by the colleges. Cambridge students ended their boycott of the National Student Survey (NSS) this year and our analysis of the results shows high rates of satisfaction with teaching quality (=30th) but a poorer overall experience (=116th). Cambridge was awarded triple gold in the government's Teaching Excellence Framework (TEF 2023), and is top for continuation rates. In October 2024 the first students embarked on the new four-year Design Tripos degree, merging engineering with architecture and materials science.

Most students are guaranteed a space in college-owned, catered accommodation for three years, some for four. Facilities include 100 libraries, specialist museums, laboratories, surgical suites, concert halls and theatres. Terms are intense at only eight weeks, but undergraduates tend to throw themselves into the social side too. Events, societies and sports clubs at both university and college level offer everything from anime esports to rowing and opera, as well as numerous cheap watering holes.

Since 2022, Cambridge has boosted investment in counselling services. Each college also has a senior tutor, nurse and wellbeing adviser. The proportion of state sector admissions reached 72.6% in 2023, including grammar schools, and ethnic diversity has improved to rank 57th since the Stormzy scholarship was introduced in 2018. Generous financial support includes more than £10 million awarded through the means-tested Cambridge Bursary, which pays up to £3,500 a year. About one in three UK undergraduates receive the bursary, and colleges and academic departments may make additional awards.

*See Chapter 13: Applying to Oxbridge for college profiles and more information on the admissions process.*

---

**Student Services Centre New Museums Site**
**Cambridge CB2 3PT**
admissions@cam.ac.uk
undergraduate.study.cam.ac.uk
cambridgesu.co.uk

**Overall ranking 4**
(last year 3)

**Accommodation**
College websites provide accommodation details.

**Student numbers**
Undergraduates 13,114
Applications per place 6.2:1
Overall offer rate 24.4%

**Fees**
UK fees £9,250
International fees £25,734–£39,162
Medicine £67,194

undergraduate.study.cam.ac.uk/events/cambridge-open-days
undergraduate.study.cam.ac.uk/fees-and-finance

See chapter 11 for individual colleges.

# Canterbury Christ Church University

The cobbled streets of Canterbury offer a charming backdrop to student life in a cathedral city richer in real ales than raves. University status was conferred in 2005 on this former Church of England teacher training college. Canterbury Christ Church University (CCCU) has the blessing of the former Archbishop of Canterbury, Justin Welby – who is its chancellor. It remains a Church of England foundation but admits students of all faiths and none. And it's a broad church — with a burgeoning curriculum, rising numbers of degree apprenticeships and ambitions to support wider access into higher education.

CCCU was awarded a triple silver in the Teaching Excellence Framework (TEF 2023) and teacher training courses are rated "good" by Ofsted. In 2024, its chemical engineering degrees achieved international accreditation by the Institution of Chemical Engineers. CCCU is also known for its strong programmes in health and social care, nursing and policing. In the latest Research Excellence Framework (REF 2021), CCCU more than doubled the proportion of its work that was judged to be world-leading compared with 2014. The university sits (just) inside the top 100 in our research quality index. In our analysis of the National Student Survey, CCCU ranks 77th for teaching quality and 110th for undergraduate experience. One of the worst continuation rates in England and Wales continues to hold CCCU back.

Foundation years are offered for a number of degree courses, with a standard offer of DDE at A-level (64 UCAS tariff points). First-year entry to a degree course usually requires BBC (112 points), rising to ABB (128 points) for physiotherapy. Almost a quarter of students entered through Clearing in 2023. Employability is embedded in courses and the university teams up with industry and local businesses to keep courses up to date. However, CCCU has fallen one place to =68th in our graduate outcomes analysis.

All CCCU's accommodation is off campus, none of it catered. For first-years who want to live in, university-approved rooms are guaranteed as long as students apply by the end of July. On the main site, the new Verena Holmes building for Stem subjects also incorporates the Kent and Medway Medical School, while the Daphne Oram Creative Arts Building has facilities for motion capture and extended reality. Some courses in media, childhood studies, education and health are based at either the purpose-built campus at Broadstairs or the expanded Medway site at Chatham's historic dockyard, with further affiliated sites in Greenford, west London, Birmingham and Manchester.

The students' union has returned to the main Canterbury site to boost the sense of community. On-campus sports facilities are supplemented by links to various local sports clubs. Mental health services include counselling, drop-ins and workshops, and students can seek support at the chaplaincy. CCCU sits 24th in our social inclusion index, and 27% of undergraduates received some form of financial assistance in 2022–23. Support includes academic scholarships for students who achieve at least ABB at A-level or equivalent, as well as sports and music scholarships.

---

**North Holmes Road Canterbury CT1 1QU**
courses@canterbury.ac.uk
canterbury.ac.uk
ccsu.co.uk

**Overall ranking 109**
(last year 114)

**Accommodation**
University provided places 1,258
Self-catered £124–£200 per week

**Student numbers**
Undergraduates 19,697
Applications per place 0.7:1
Overall offer rate 84.4%

**Fees**
UK fees £9,250
International fees £15,500
Medicine £47,900

canterbury.ac.uk/news/opens-days-what-to-do-on-a-university-open-day
canterbury.ac.uk/study-here/fees-and-funding/ug-fees-funding-and-student-finance

# Cardiff University

Applications to study in the heart of the Welsh capital reached record numbers in 2023 when more than 46,000 students chose Cardiff. The academic clout of Wales's only Russell Group university is a draw, as is the lively culture of this walkable city. Professor Wendy Larner, a social scientist from New Zealand with a research focus on globalisation, governance and gender, is the university's first female vice chancellor. She has started the Big Conversation – a chance for staff and students to share their views on the university and shape its strategic direction.

Cardiff received glowing results in the Research Excellence Framework (REF 2021) with 90% of its submission rated world-leading or internationally excellent, most notably in philosophy; communication and media studies; education; and architecture. In common with many research-intensive institutions, however, Cardiff has tended to receive lukewarm responses in the National Student Survey. In our new analysis Cardiff has fallen by 23 places to 117th for teaching quality but risen two places to 83rd for undergraduate experience.

Pale stone buildings around Cathays Park are the elegant heart of the campus, where a £600 million upgrade includes the Centre for Student Life, bringing study space and a lecture theatre under the same roof as support services, and new facilities for computer sciences, mathematics and architecture. Healthcare sciences share a 53-acre campus at Heath Park with the University Hospital Wales, including a mock hospital ward and operating theatre and Wales's only dentistry school.

Offers range from BBC up to A*AA, with contextual offers – received by about 28% of UK entrants – either reducing this by one grade or lending extra points in the interview process. About 15% of Cardiff's new undergraduates in 2023 entered through Clearing. An online BA in modern Chinese is new for 2024 and an online modern languages course is on the way in 2025.

Sixty-five sports teams keep students on their toes and there are more than 200 student societies, not least for performance and artistic pursuits.

All first-years who apply by the deadline are guaranteed one of 6,030 rooms for between £119.21 and £168.84 per week, of which about 6% are catered. Self-help resources, neurodiverse group counselling, peer-to-peer support and one-to-one counselling are available to those who need them. With various outreach partnerships, Cardiff remains in the top 100 of our social inclusion index and is eighth out of the 21 Russell Group universities in England and Wales.

Financial support is offered to about 20% of students. As well as the main Cardiff University Bursary, there is targeted support for unpaid carers, care leavers, estranged students and armed forces veterans. A memorial fund for the Aberfan disaster pays up to £1,500 over three years to students with family links to Merthyr Tydfil, and merit-based scholarships are offered for engineering, music and Welsh.

Cardiff has improved in our analysis of the Graduate Outcomes survey to rank =13th, with students benefitting from strategic partnerships for internships, work placements, and entrepreneurship opportunities.

**Cardiff CF10 3AT**
enquiry@cardiff.ac.uk
cardiff.ac.uk
cardiffstudents.com

**Overall ranking 32**
(last year 25)

**Accommodation**
University provided places 6,030
Catered £147–£169 per week
Self-catered £119–£167 per week

**Student numbers**
Undergraduates 21,568
Applications per place 5.9:1
Overall offer rate 70.9%

**Fees**
UK fees £9,000
International fees £22,700–£28,200
Medicine £43,700

cardiff.ac.uk/study/undergraduate/open-days-visits
cardiff.ac.uk/study/undergraduate/tuition-fees

# Cardiff Metropolitan University

Rising student numbers are helping to drive 21st-century investment at Cardiff Metropolitan University with an expansion into low-carbon futures and environmental sustainability. At 6th in the People and Planet league of UK universities in 2023–24, Cardiff Met is aiming for net zero carbon emissions by 2030. The university also aspires to be the leading Welsh sporting university. Its Cyncoed campus is already the base for governing bodies including Welsh Athletics and Team Wales, which prepares for competition in the Commonwealth Games, and 40 athletes from Cardiff Met competed in Birmingham in 2022.

Cardiff Met has been transforming its curriculum, adding more than 40 degrees over the past five years. New courses for 2025 include BSc degrees in health and wellbeing, and psychology and criminology, and BA degrees in game art, and interior architecture. In the latest Research Excellence Framework (REF 2021) the university climbed to 78th, with 79% of submissions judged world-leading or internationally excellent. Feedback from the National Student Survey has improved markedly, and Cardiff Met has leapt to 52nd for teaching quality and 49th for undergraduate experience.

Both of Cardiff Met's campuses at Llandaff and Cyncoed are close to the city centre. The Cyncoed campus is the main site for student housing and sport, including the National Indoor Athletics Centre, an archers' arena, tennis and fitness centres and a swimming pool. A strength and conditioning facility and improved pitch-side facilities for rugby and hockey are on the way. At Llandaff, a new drone research studio has been added at the Cardiff School of Technologies. The School of Art and Design houses workshops for ceramics and fabric treatment to augmented reality technology and audio visual equipment.

Unusually, Cardiff Met has as many students enrolled via a network of 13 partner colleges around the world as it does at the main site. These links provide opportunities to study abroad in countries including Greece, Sri Lanka, Singapore and Oman.

Entry requirements range from 80 UCAS tariff points (CDD at A-level) to 128 (ABB). Contextual admissions apply to all courses and just over a fifth of new students enrolled via Clearing in 2023. Across all five of the university's academic schools there are links with industry partners, from John Lewis to local startups. In our graduate prospects analysis, Cardiff Met's charge up our table has been arrested, with a fall of 11 places to =75th.

First-years are guaranteed a room if they apply by the end of May, and more than a third of rooms are catered. The university hopes to reduce car journeys to campus and encourage students to use the Taff Trail. Cardiff Met takes pride in its sense of community and friendliness. The city itself is a thriving student hub. From students' union activities to Welsh Premier League sides in men's and women's football, there is plenty of opportunity for extracurricular activity.

For students struggling with their mental health, Cardiff Met offers psychoeducational workshops, one-to-one counselling and online help. During the summer, the university runs events to help new students get ready for the start of term. Two years ago Cardiff Met was in the top 30 in our social inclusion index but is now 56th. About a fifth of new students qualify for financial assistance, with awards including performance and elite sports scholarships, a grant for refugees and asylum seekers, and funds worth up to £3,000 for applicants studying in the Welsh language.

---

**Western Avenue Llandaff Cardiff CF5 2YB**
askadmissions@cardiffmet.ac.uk
cardiffmet.ac.uk
cardiffmetsu.co.uk

**Overall ranking =66**
(last year 78)

**Accommodation**
University provided places 2,098
Catered £208–£224 per week
Self-catered £140–£154 per week

**Student numbers**
Undergraduates 8,078
Applications per place 3.4:1
Overall offer rate 82.0%

**Fees**
UK fees £9,000
International fees £16,000

cardiffmet.ac.uk/study/opendays/
cardiffmet.ac.uk/study/finance/Pages/Undergraduate-Students.aspx

# University of Central Lancashire

Offering a lower cost of living than its northwest neighbours, Preston has a friendly reputation. It is the main site of the University of Central Lancashire (UCLan), which also has campuses in neighbouring Burnley, and Westlakes, in Cumbria. At the end of 2024, the Office for Students approved a name change for UCLan to the University of Lancashire, and the university expects to be operating under its new name by September 2025. A large, modern university of around 17,000 undergraduates, UCLan's broad curriculum includes one of the biggest portfolios of degree apprenticeships in the country across engineering, the built environment, professional services, and health and wellbeing.

Rated silver overall in the Teaching Excellence Framework (TEF 2023), UCLan won praise for its "highly effective support". Our analysis of the National Student Survey (NSS) puts UCLan in 51st place for teaching quality and 66th for the wider student experience, an impressive step up from last year. In the latest Research Excellence Framework (REF 2021), some of UCLan's best results were in physics; social work and social policy; and the allied health professions. The university gained four places in our research quality index to place =82nd.

Taking one giant leap on UCLan's space-research path, and based on links with UCLan, Nasa's base in Preston is the British outpost for the United Nations Office for Outer Space Affairs. University researchers are working with those from the UN's Platform for Space-based Information for Disaster Management and Emergency Response (UN-Spider) to bridge the technology gap to ensure that all countries can access observations from space to prevent and mitigate disasters.

The Preston campus is home to the £35 million Engineering Innovation Centre and a £60 million student centre. The first cohort of students enrolled in the vet school, which is the UK's 11th, in 2023. At the Burnley campus, in the heart of the Pennines, the university's courses promise small class sizes in the historic Weavers' Triangle area of the town. The Westlakes campus focuses on nursing and other health subjects.

Entry standards range from 96 to 144 UCAS tariff points. Foundation years are offered on most courses and nearly 30% of 2023's new students benefited from UCLan's contextual offers, which apply to all except some dental and pharmacy degrees. Work placements benefit from UCLan's links with the NHS, BBC and Lancashire Constabulary, among other organisations. In our graduate outcomes analysis, UCLan has risen to 77th, boosted by the university's new Spark service for apprenticeships.

Sports centres, a gallery and cinema are just some of the spaces where students can enjoy down time. The wellbeing service provides one-to-one counselling, course-specific workshops, and emergency accommodation if needed. There is help to combat rising living costs too, in the form of free food in UCLan refectories. There are 1,356 student rooms in Preston, 129 in Burnley and 131 at Westlakes, with accommodation guaranteed for first-years in Preston.

UCLan has fallen nine places in our social inclusion index to 26th. The vast majority of students are from non-selective state schools and the university's Return to Study taster courses target over-21s who may not have formal Level 3 qualifications. The UCLan Scholars' Programme is for Year 12 students from the northwest of England, and those who complete its workshops qualify for a contextualised offer and a bursary of £500 a year. Other awards include bursaries of up to £2,000, across three years, for those from low-income households.

---

**Preston PR1 2HE**
cenquiries@uclan.ac.uk
uclan.ac.uk
uclansu.co.uk

**Overall ranking 96**
(last year 111)

**Accommodation**
University provided places 1,616
Catered £135–£210 per week
Self-catered £85–£149 per week

**Student numbers**
Undergraduates 16,928
Applications per place 4.4:1
Overall offer rate 69.0%

**Fees**
UK fees £5,760 (Foundation)–£9,250
International fees £16,400–£37,000
Medicine £50,000

uclan.ac.uk/open-days
uclan.ac.uk/study/fees-and-finance

# University of Chester

Not too big, not too small, Chester is just the right size for most students. A restructuring of academic life has organised all courses into three new faculties to promote interdisciplinary teaching and research, and share skills for future employment. First established as a teacher-training college in 1839, Chester continues to offer a wide range of teaching courses, as well as popular degrees in nursing and midwifery, business and management, psychology, law, agriculture and sociology. A number of courses in criminology and creative arts are new additions.

The university gained a triple silver in the Teaching Excellence Framework (TEF 2023): overall as well as for the student experience. The TEF panel praised the work of the university for "effectively raising the profile of graduates among employers" and the university engages with more than 1,400 employers for work-based learning modules and placements. In our graduate outcomes analysis, Chester has improved by 20 places to 59th, with 76.3% of students in highly skilled work or further study within 15 months.

Its TEF rating is slightly at odds with Chester's recent dip in the National Student Survey, however. Only five years ago the university ranked in the top 30 for both of our student satisfaction metrics but in our latest analysis, Chester is 78th for teaching quality and 124th for the wider undergraduate experience.

Students are based at the 32-acre Exton Park campus is ten minutes' walk from the walled city centre. A second campus at Queen's Park houses the Chester Business School and medical, nursing and midwifery courses. There are also campuses across Birkenhead, Shrewsbury and Warrington.

Theology, health subjects and sports and exercise science produced some of Chester's best results in the latest Research Excellence Framework (REF 2021) with 51% of research assessed in the top tier, but against bigger gains at other universities, Chester slipped to 110th place in our rankings.

Applications have fallen 17% since last year. Typical entry requirements are 72 UCAS tariff points for a foundation year, and 112–120 UCAS points for standard undergraduate degrees. Contextual offers may be considered. First-years are guaranteed a room and nearly a fifth of hall spaces are catered, though plenty of Chester students live at home.

Most sports facilities are near Exton Park, and there are also opportunities to take evening classes in a foreign language, volunteer, run a society and join a team, band or theatre group. Students can self-refer into the student counselling service, access low-intensity cognitive behavioural therapy sessions or take part in wellbeing sessions such as a men's mental health group.

Ranking 17th in our social inclusion index (down from 13 last year), Chester succeeds in recruiting more white working-class male students than most universities. A fifth of entrants are drawn from deprived areas. Financial help starts with travel bursaries of up to £100 to attend taster events such as open days or interviews. There are bursaries of £1,500 for those who have been in care, are carers, or are estranged from their families – as well as for students from gypsy, Roma, traveller, showman and boater communities.

**Parkgate Road Chester CH1 4BJ**
admissions@chester.ac.uk
chester.ac.uk
chestersu.com

**Overall ranking 89**
(last year 100)

**Accommodation**
University provided places 1,380
Catered £195–£200 per week
Self-catered £111–£167 per week

**Student numbers**
Undergraduates 7,931
Applications per place 5.4:1
Overall offer rate 74.8%

**Fees**
UK fees £9,250
International fees £10,250 (Foundation) – £13,950

chester.ac.uk/study/visit-us/open-days/
chester.ac.uk/student-life/fees-and-finance/

# University of Chichester

With one campus in the cathedral city and another in Bognor Regis, the University of Chichester started out as a teacher training college in 1839. Teacher training remains an established strength at this small institution in West Sussex, known for its close-knit atmosphere and rated outstanding by Ofsted in May 2023, with inspectors reporting that trainees "value the nurturing family ethos". Chichester became a university in 2005 and is also known for its performing arts, social sciences and sports provision.

The focus is broadening, however. A School of Nursing and Allied Health opened in 2021, and a £35 million Tech Park in Bognor Regis houses a welding floor and fabricating laboratory for engineering degrees. Additions in September 2024 included degrees in computing and biomedical science, as well as degree apprenticeships in diagnostic radiography and speech and language therapy.

The Bishop Otter campus in historic Chichester includes a music block, the recently opened School of Nursing and Allied Health, and specialist sport facilities including an environmental climate chamber to simulate extreme heat, cold and altitude. Five minutes from the sea, the Bognor Regis campus has a new community diagnostic centre as well as the flagship Tech Park. An intercampus bus service links Bognor and Bishop Otter, which each have students' union bars, while the local towns have their own social scenes as well as seaside activities and countryside charm.

Sport; history; and English and creative writing produced the best results in the latest Research Excellence Framework (REF 2021) but against stronger performances elsewhere Chichester dropped to 114th in our research quality index. The overall gold in the Teaching Excellence Framework (TEF 2023) is up from silver in the previous assessment. Our latest National Student Survey analysis ranks the university 28th for satisfaction with teaching quality but feedback for the wider undergraduate experience has nosedived, prompting Chichester to fall to 107th in that metric.

Admissions standards range from CCC to ABB and 10% of applicants gained places through Clearing. This year the university has introduced a contextual admissions policy to applicants from disadvantaged backgrounds. Chichester is at =71st for graduate outcomes after rising 46 places in our previous edition. Chichester's apprenticeship programme draws on the expertise of businesses such as the energy supplier SSE and Rolls-Royce, and most of Chichester's degree programmes provide work placements.

There are 1,310 residential places and first-years are guaranteed a room if they make the university their first choice and get their housing application in on time.

Students can get help via "Ask Wellbeing" drop-ins. Up to four sessions of counselling are offered, along with support groups. Chichester also sets a £30,000 budget aside for subsidising assessments by an educational psychologist for neurodiversity or specific learning difficulties. Chichester has fallen 17 places in our social inclusion index to 59th but scores well for disabled recruitment. The university awards £300 per year of study to students from households with incomes under £25,000. A gifted athlete programme is worth up to £400 per year and comes with support including performance analysis, psychology, nutrition advice and physiotherapy – and sports kit.

**Bishop Otter Campus College Lane Chichester PO19 6PE**
admissions@chi.ac.uk
chi.ac.uk
ucsu.org

**Overall ranking 62**
(last year =53)

**Accommodation**
University provided places 1,310
Catered £177–£201 per week
Self-catered £118–£193 per week

**Student numbers**
Undergraduates 4,310
Applications per place 5.0:1
Overall offer rate 76.0%

**Fees**
UK fees £6,624 (Foundation) – £9,250
International fees £15,840–£17,220

chi.ac.uk/study/open-days-and-campus-tours/open-days/
chi.ac.uk/study/undergraduate/fees-finance

# City, University of London

The former City, University of London merged with the healthcare specialist St George's to form a new institution – City St George's – from summer 2024. For now, the two London universities will operate "dual running" until full integration is achieved, which is why we are continuing to list them separately here.

Current and prospective students are members of City St George's, University of London, which aims to become a significant supplier of the capital's health workforce.

Impressive results for City in the latest Research Excellence Framework (REF 2021) paved the way to 37th place in our research quality rating, up 14 places year-on-year. Overall, 86% of the university's submissions within 13 subject areas were rated as world-leading or internationally excellent – a marked improvement on its performance in REF 2014.

In a remarkable turnaround for student satisfaction, City leapt from =116th in our previous edition to 37th for the wider undergraduate experience, according to our analysis of the National Student Survey. Satisfaction with teaching quality rose 24 places but remained outside the top 100.

The university has invested more than £140 million in developing its sites since 2012. Much of it has gone on improvements to the main campus in Clerkenwell, where resources include a 240-seat lecture theatre, students' union facilities and a multifaith area. The City Law School's home at Northampton Square features a technology-led mock courtroom.

In the Teaching Excellence Framework (TEF 2023), City garnered silver overall, bronze for the student experience and gold for student outcomes. Academic life at City, the second-most ethnically diverse university in our analysis, is structured around six schools: policy and global affairs; communication and creativity; health and psychological sciences; science and technology; Bayes Business School; and the City Law School.

An augmented reality/virtual reality design learning centre is available for engineering, computer science and applied mathematics students. From 2025 mathematics with business joins the curriculum.

One of City's strongest performances is its graduate outcomes, for which it ranks 45th for the proportion of leavers in high-skilled jobs or on postgraduate courses 15 months after finishing their degrees. The MBA at Bayes (formerly Cass Business School) was ranked seventh in the UK by the Financial Times in 2024.

Students get discounted access to the CitySport gym in Islington, which has more than 120 stations, a sports hall and studios for dance and yoga.

There are 1,136 rooms in university-endorsed halls and first-years are guaranteed a spot as long as they accept an offer and get their housing application in before June 30.

City's health and wellbeing services offer support delivered by professionally trained counsellors, advisers and tutors. Students can access workshops, counselling and referrals to external services. They also have use of the Togetherall mental health self-help app.

On the financial front, the Bayes Undergraduate Scholarship for Black British students is awarded to ten Bayes scholars annually. The City Education Grant is a bursary of £1,500 a year for those from households with zero income, as assessed by Student Finance England.

---

**Northampton Square London EC1V 0HB**
ugenquiries@city.ac.uk
city.ac.uk
citystudents.co.uk

**Overall ranking 49**
(last year 66)

**Accommodation**
University provided places 1,136
Self-catered £195–£293 per week

**Student numbers**
Undergraduates 11,507
Applications per place 5.6:1
Overall offer rate 58.4%

**Fees**
UK fees £9,250
International fees £16,230–£27,860

city.ac.uk/prospective-students/open-events-and-fairs
city.ac.uk/prospective-students/finance

# Coventry University

Forward-thinking Coventry has introduced success coaches, who work with students one to one and in group coaching sessions to bolster self-confidence, time management and presentation skills. The Phoenix+ programme, another innovation, provides work experience and development as students progress through their courses at the university, a three-time winner of our Modern University of the Year award (2014–16) and shortlisted for University of the Year in 2021.

Having evolved from the Coventry College of Design, founded in 1843, now its focus is global and the institution has become one of the UK's biggest recruiters of students from other countries. The Coventry University Group has hubs in Brussels, Beijing, Dubai, Rwanda and Singapore and in 2023 there were more than 22,000 students studying overseas for Coventry degrees.

The university has expanded its research centres, increased staff and developed purpose-built facilities. This paid off in the results of the latest Research Excellence Framework (REF 2021), in which 70% of Coventry's submission was classed as world-leading or internationally excellent. The outcomes triggered a huge 35-place rise in our research quality index to 73rd, from =108th based on the results of the previous national assessment, REF 2014.

Coventry's most recent accolade was a gold rating overall in the Teaching Excellence Framework (TEF 2023). Awarding gold for student experience and silver for student outcomes, the TEF panel said the university's "physical and virtual learning resources" supported "outstanding teaching and learning". However, Coventry has slipped from its former top 20 position for student satisfaction to 34th for teaching quality and 31st for the wider undergraduate experience in our new National Student Survey analysis.

Coventry is renowned for its innovative ethos. Some courses have a common first year, for example, enabling students to mix and learn with those from related courses, and potentially switch degrees at the end of year one. There are no end-of-year exams: assessments may take the form of coursework, projects and presentations.

A new BSc in psychology with counselling is being introduced in 2024 alongside a range of higher education certificates. Entry requirements range from 128 UCAS tariff points – equivalent to ABB at A-level – (mainly for four-year integrated master's courses) to 96 points (CCC) for degree-level study. Contextual offers offer a reduction up to 24 points. In 2023, 17 % of new students entered through Clearing.

A mentorship programme links industry professionals with final-year students to develop their career goals. Overseas opportunities for UK students range from field trips to a semester or year abroad studying, working or both. In our analysis of the Graduate Outcomes survey, Coventry ranks =75th, down just one place since our previous edition, with 74.4 % of leavers finding highly skilled jobs or returning to study within 15 months.

First-years who make Coventry their firm choice are guaranteed a space in halls, but many students commute from home. Coventry has jumped 15 places this year to be ranked 37th in our social inclusion index overall. Its ethnic diversity is in the top quarter of universities in England and Wales (23rd). The university's flexible start times for its degrees are designed to fit around personal and work commitments.

Care leavers can apply for fully funded accommodation in halls for up to four years. Sports scholarships provide up to £3,000. A range of other scholarships offer support.

---

**Priory Street Coventry CV1 5FB**
ukadmissions@coventry.ac.uk
coventry.ac.uk
yoursu.org

**Overall ranking 54**
(last year 58)

**Accommodation**
University provided places 1,880
Self-catered £140–£188 per week

**Student numbers**
Undergraduates 24,160
Applications per place 5.1:1
Overall offer rate 88.5%

**Fees**
UK fees £9,250
International fees £16,800–£20,050

coventry.ac.uk/opendays
coventry.ac.uk/study-at-coventry/finance

## University for the Creative Arts

One of the seven specialist arts universities in our league table, UCA's course offering covers all things creative-industry related, from fine art to virtual and immersive reality, interior design to silversmithing. With campuses in Canterbury, Epsom and Farnham, UCA puts the creativity into the commuter belt. UCA's ten-year history as a university can be traced back to a number of small arts schools in Kent and Surrey, whose alumni include Tracey Emin and Dame Zandra Rhodes. Rhodes is UCA's chancellor emerita.

UCA's performance in the latest Research Excellence Framework (REF 2021) far outdid its results in the previous national assessment in 2014, triggering a 56-place rise up our research quality index to 56th. Overall, 78% of the work was rated world-leading or internationally excellent. The university is known for employing staff who are practitioners, and its staff-student ratio is in the top ten.

However, results from the latest National Student Survey (NSS 2024) send UCA plummeting 65 places to 98th based on feedback about teaching quality. Responses about the wider undergraduate experience put UCA in 125th place, falling 22 places year-on-year. In our main academic table, UCA has lost ground by 14 places and is now 73rd.

UCA achieved silver overall in the Teaching Excellence Framework (TEF 2023), down from gold in the previous assessment in 2017, along with silvers for the student experience and student outcomes. Degrees in body art (histories, cultures and practices) and fashion (millinery, accessories and shoe design) launch in 2025.

Standard requirements vary between 32 UCAS tariff points for entry on to integrated foundation year courses up to 128 points for architecture. In addition to grades, the university assesses portfolios and auditions.

Industry links proliferate, such as a partnership with the National Theatre and an acting course that is accredited by Spotlight and Equity UK. However, UCA has dropped one place to return to the bottom of our graduate prospects index, with 56.8% of former students in highly skilled work or postgraduate study within 15 months of finishing their degree.

The Canterbury School of Architecture promotes collaboration between student architects, designers and fine artists. The UCA Canterbury campus also hosts degree courses in fine art, interior design, graphic design, and illustration and animation.

There are 1,149 bed spaces spread across its three campuses – not quite sufficient for it to guarantee accommodation to all first-years, but students who apply before the deadline should expect to secure a place. UCA is in the top 20 for recruitment of mature students (56.6%, 15th). It has risen 16 places to 12th place overall for social inclusion. Help with travel and equipment is available for students.

Financial support includes up to three Sir Ray Tindle scholarships, which provide £1,500 per year for students on media courses. The Elaine Thomas bursary for care leavers is of the same value. The Grenfell Tower Scholarship offers a full fee waiver to survivors of the 2017 fire in London. One student per course is picked to win the UK Excellence Scholarship – worth £1,500 off the first year's tuition fees.

---

**Falkner Road Farnham GU9 7DS**
admissions@uca.ac.uk
uca.ac.uk
ucasu.com

**Overall ranking 87**
(last year 73)

**Accommodation**
University provided places 1,149
Self-catered £128–£191 per week

**Student numbers**
Undergraduates 5,965
Applications per place 5.1:1
Overall offer rate 97.0%

**Fees**
UK fees £9,250
International fees £16,950–£17,500

uca.ac.uk/study-at-uca/opendays
uca.ac.uk/study-at-uca/fees-finance/

# University of Cumbria

One of the youngest universities in our guide, Cumbria gained university status in 2007 and has big ambitions. By autumn 2025 it will have opened the Pears Cumbria School of Medicine in Carlisle – a partnership with Imperial College London and backed by £5 million in philanthropic support from Pears Foundation.

Students are based at seven campuses, stretching from the Lake District to Canary Wharf in east London. The main campus caters for courses in education, health, sport and business. The Ambleside campus on Lake Windermere in the Lake District National Park offers the UK's biggest programme of outdoor education courses plus conservation and forestry degrees. The newest campus, Canary Wharf, is for students taking health, education and business courses.

Cumbria was rated silver overall in the latest Teaching Excellence Framework (TEF 2023), up from bronze in the previous assessment in 2017, along with silver for student outcomes, but only bronze for student experience.

The university maintained its 124th place in our research rankings, based on the results of the latest Research Excellence Framework (REF 2021). Yet low proportions of firsts and 2.1s among Cumbria's graduates contribute to the university's ranking in our league table, as have faltering rates of student satisfaction expressed in the National Student Survey. In our analysis of the latest data, Cumbria has fallen 29 places to 128th based on feedback about teaching quality, and 15 places to 126th for responses about the wider undergraduate experience.

Cumbria uses contextual information and data and will give eligible applicants an offer at the lower end of its standard UCAS tariff range for their course, which ranges from 104 to 120 points. A quarter of 2023 entrants received a contextual offer and more than a fifth of new first-years gained their places through Clearing in the same year.

For graduate prospects, Cumbria is experiencing a renaissance with 74.8% of leavers in highly skilled work or further study 15 months after finishing their degree, according to the Graduate Outcomes survey. This lifts the university 31 places to rank =71st, returning to the middle reaches of our graduate prospects measure for the first time in three years. Cumbria's portfolio of 12 degree apprenticeships has about 2,000 trainees on courses that include paramedic science; midwifery; professional forestry; and project management.

About a fifth of students want to live in and accommodation is guaranteed to first-years.

Cumbria is 11th in our social inclusion index, leaping 13 places in a year and 36 over two years. The university's school outreach programme is targeted towards low-participation areas.

The Cumbria Bursary for students from low-income backgrounds provides £1,000 per year of full-time study, or £500 per year of part-time study. One Sanctuary Scholarship is awarded to a forced migrant student each year, waiving tuition fees for up to four years, providing campus accommodation year-round for free, and £3,000 per year of study.

**Fusehill Street Carlisle CA1 2HH**
enquirycentre@cumbria.ac.uk
cumbria.ac.uk
ucsu.me

**Overall ranking 128**
(last year 129)

**Accommodation**
University provided places 619
Self-catered £88–£141 per week

**Student numbers**
Undergraduates 4,985
Applications per place 4.0:1
Overall offer rate 76.4%

**Fees**
UK fees £9,250
International fees £13,575–£16,400

cumbria.ac.uk/events/open-days/
cumbria.ac.uk/study/student-finance/

# De Montfort University

Not too big, not too small – Leicester's size and relative affordability are a draw for the city's large student population. The university began in 1870 as the Leicester School of Art, founded to provide education and training for workers from the city's booming industries. The university has a target of net-zero carbon emissions by 2032 and finished in the top 10 of the People and Planet league table for 2023-24.

In the latest Research Excellence Framework (REF 2021) more than 60% of De Montfort's (DMU) research was judged as world-leading or internationally excellent. The university entered the largest number of academics yet and featured more research carried out by women and ethnic minority academics than it has before. However, against stronger performances by other universities, the results triggered a 29-place fall for DMU in our research quality rankings to 96th position. It has also dipped in the government's Teaching Excellence Framework (TEF 2023), from gold in 2017 to silver, underpinned by silver for student outcomes but only bronze for the student experience.

Feedback from undergraduates in the National Student Survey (NSS) gives De Montfort a boost to 105th place (up from 115th) for teaching quality and 81st (from 110th) for the wider student experience, our latest NSS analysis shows.

Entry standards are at the more accessible end of the scale, and with new entrants averaging 108 UCAS points, DMU is =121st for entry standards. Contextual offers have just been introduced.

True to its roots in local industry, De Montfort University offers guaranteed work experience – a placement year or accreditation by professional bodies – for all of its undergraduates. Our analysis of the Graduate Outcomes survey shows a downward trajectory in the past year, however, with 69.3% of leavers in highly skilled work or postgraduate study within 15 months (105th, down four places).

Unusually for a campus university, DMU is located in the city centre and is housed in buildings ranging from medieval to 21st-century architecture. Investment of £136 million has upgraded teaching and learning spaces including the Yard – a £5.5 million extension for the Faculty of Business and Law – which also has revamped facilities in the Great Hall of Leicester Castle Business School. A £6.5 million Digital Tech Learning Hub is on the way, combining creative teaching and learning facilities for cyber and computer science.

There are more than 1,030 spaces in halls of residence – sufficient for the university to guarantee a space to first-years who apply by the deadline.

More than half of DMU's students are from black, Asian and ethnic minority backgrounds, placing the university 25th in England and Wales on that measure and in our social inclusion index overall. Its efforts earned the university a silver award in the Race Equality Charter in 2023, the first for a British university.

A wide-ranging package of awards largely benefit those from low-income backgrounds, or who have left care or are estranged from their families. Most are worth £1,000 a year.

---

**The Gateway Leicester LE1 9BH**
enquiry@dmu.ac.uk
dmu.ac.uk
demontfortsu.com

**Overall ranking 113**
(last year =119)

**Accommodation**
University provided places 1,030
Self-catered £95–£159 per week

**Student numbers**
Undergraduates 19,414
Applications per place 2.5:1
Overall offer rate 86.7%

**Fees**
UK fees £6,165 (Foundation) – £9,250
International fees £15,750–£16,250

dmu.ac.uk/study/undergraduate-study/open-days
dmu.ac.uk/study/fees-funding

# University of Derby

A university since 1992, Derby traces its roots back to the Diocesan Training Institution for School Mistresses founded in 1851 and its hallmarks are industry engagement and a curriculum informed by research. It is rated gold in the government's Teaching Excellence Framework (TEF 2023) – with gold for the student experience and silver for student outcomes – and despite a seven-place drop for student satisfaction with teaching quality in our latest National Student Survey analysis it still ranks a respectable 23rd. The university has also fallen six places to 42nd for responses about the wider undergraduate experience.

In the latest Research Excellence Framework (REF 2021), education and geology produced some of the best results, helping to raise the university six places in our research quality index to =111th. Derby's scientists lead on sustainability research with their international work on restoring damaged coral reefs. There is also research strength in biomedical and clinical science; creative and cultural industries; data science; business; economic and social policy; public services and zero carbon.

There are more than 60 new degrees in 2024, including programmes incorporating sociology, international relations, entrepreneurship and media content creation, history and law. In 2024, a suite of applied programmes in AI was added to the curriculum, with a focus on its use in criminology, digital marketing, healthcare, human resources and psychology. Degree apprenticeships in occupational health, social work, and physiotherapy have been introduced.

The majority of 2024 applicants had predicted results of 120 UCAS tariff points, equivalent to BBB at A-level. The university's grade requirements range from 112–136 points,

reduced by two grades or 16 points by a contextual offer. Applications were down by about 8% in 2024 but enrolments went in the other direction, with more than 3,300 new starters.

Derby offers applied, hands-on learning in simulated "real world" environments, such as a crime scene house for forensic science students, a replica crown court, a Bloomberg financial markets laboratory and an NHS-standard hospital ward. The East Midlands institution has also been awarded £1.2 million by the Office for Students to develop its degree apprenticeship programme, building on existing tie-ins with industry partners. According to our analysis of the Graduate Outcomes survey, tracking the numbers in highly skilled work or postgraduate study within 15 months, Derby continues to improve slightly. In our 2023 guide it was 93rd, rising to 88th a year ago: now it is 83rd. Derby's halls were voted best university housing in the UK in the Global Student Living Awards for two years running (2022 and 2023). There are enough spaces to guarantee a spot to all first-years who apply by the end of July.

The Gogglebox star Baasit Siddiqui, an alumnus of the university and a former teacher, is helping to spearhead Derby's popular Get Ready for Uni programme, with skills-based workshops covering topics such as academic writing, cooking, and building self-confidence. Derby is sixth for recruitment of students from deprived areas (24.8%) and =18th overall in our social inclusion index, a rise of three places year-on-year The university's commitment to inclusivity has also gained it Athena Swan Bronze and the Advance HE Race Equality Charter.

University of Derby bursaries of up to £1,000 are awarded according to a sliding scale of household income. Almost a third of students receive financial support.

---

**Kedleston Road Derby DE22 1GB**
askadmissions@derby.ac.uk
derby.ac.uk
derbyunion.co.uk

**Overall ranking 77**
(last year 82)

**Accommodation**
University provided places 1,962
Self-catered £115–£183 per week

**Student numbers**
Undergraduates 11,195
Applications per place 4.6:1
Overall offer rate 72.9%

**Fees**
UK fees £9,250
International fees £14,045–£14,900

derby.ac.uk/open-days/undergraduate/
derby.ac.uk/study/fees-finance/

# University of Dundee

The youthful vibe of Scotland's sunniest city is reflected in a sense of purpose and regeneration in the University of Dundee's curriculum – with a broad range of options from creative art to accountancy, law and dentistry.

Founded in 1881, the university developed alongside the city's industrial rise. Today, the university is renowned as a centre of research in life sciences, a field of expertise that has earned it a global reputation, and helped propel Dundee to rank =39th in our research quality index.

The Scottish universities did not take part in the latest Teaching Excellence Framework 2023, but Dundee was rated gold in the previous assessment six years earlier. However, rates of student satisfaction have been patchy in recent years. In our latest analysis of the National Student Survey, Dundee ranks 63rd for satisfaction with teaching quality, climbing from =77th last year, but has sunk to 104th for the broader experience from =85th.

Degrees in Islamic accounting and finance were introduced for 2024, as well as international business with marketing in practice. A BSc in digital interaction design will be discontinued from 2025.

Dundee's entry standards are in the upper quarter of our academic league table: new students entered with an average of 179 UCAS tariff points in 2024. Course requirements for degree-level study range from AAA at A-level to CC, and in Scottish Highers it is AAAAB to CCC. In 2023, 14% of entrants received a contextual offer, which include a guaranteed interview, reduced grades and a place at the university's access summer school.

Wide-ranging services are available to help students get a head start in the jobs market. Dundee is a partner in the Tay Cities biomedical cluster project, which aims to create 280 biomedical jobs by 2033 and generate more than £190 million for the local economy by 2053. The university has risen seven places to the top 20 in our analysis of the Graduate Outcomes survey, with 83% of leavers in highly skilled work or postgraduate study within 15 months.

Dundee's self-contained city campus has benefited from about £200 million of redevelopment, adding the £50 million Discovery Centre to its modern facilities. The medical school has its own 20-acre site while nursing and midwifery students are 35 miles away in Kirkcaldy. All full-time first-years are guaranteed accommodation if they apply by the deadline.

The university's summer schools and outreach programmes engage with more than 2,000 potential entrants a year. Dundee is sixth in Scotland for recruitment from low participation areas and fourth for its proportion of disabled students. It is ninth out of the 15 Scottish institutions in our guide for social inclusion overall.

Dundee offers one of the most generous financial support packages among UK universities. The university offers an uncapped number of awards for Scottish students based on academic merit and/or financial need. The Rest of UK bursary is worth £3,000 per year of study and the global citizenship scholarship for international students pays £4,000 a year towards tuition fees.

---

**Nethergate Dundee DD1 4HN**
dundee.ac.uk/contact
dundee.ac.uk
dusa.co.uk

**Overall ranking 36**
(last year 33)

**Accommodation**
University provided places 1,924
Self-catered £151–£186 per week

**Student numbers**
Undergraduates 10,756
Applications per place 6.5:1
Overall offer rate 62.5%

**Fees**
UK fees £0–£1,820
RUK fees £9,250
International fees £21,900–£26,600
Medicine £52,105

dundee.ac.uk/open-days
dundee.ac.uk/

# Durham University

Up two places to rank 5th in our main academic table's tightly-packed top ten, Durham is shortlisted for University of the Year 2025. The university has a collegiate structure similar to Oxford and Cambridge, with 17 colleges in total. The first, University College, was established in 1832. First-years live in their colleges, most of them in prime spots near the university campus and which serve as important social hubs, but teaching at Durham takes place centrally. A research-intensive institution, it ranks 89th in the 2025 QS World University Rankings and is in the top 200 of Times Higher Education's 2024 global rankings. In our domestic research quality index, which is based on results of the latest Research Excellence Framework (REF 2021), Durham is 23rd, a drop of seven places compared with its performance in the previous national assessment, REF 2014. Some of the best results were in education and geography; archaeology; and forensic science. Classics and ancient history; theology; and sports science also did well.

Teaching is done in person with additional support found in the university's Academic Skills Centre. The latest Teaching Excellence Framework (TEF 2023) gave Durham gold in student outcomes, underpinning silver overall. The university remains in the top ten in our graduate prospects measure, rising another two places this year (sixth). Durham is among the ten universities targeted by the largest number of top graduate employers in 2023, according to High Fliers. Over the past 12 months the university has facilitated 995 employer events and advertised more than 10,000 graduate jobs and work experience opportunities across a range of sectors.

In our latest National Student Survey analysis, students' evaluations of their teaching prompted a 15-place rise to 56th for teaching quality, though for the wider experience the university dropped from =77th to 82nd in the student satisfaction rankings, but rose to 56th (from =71st) for teaching quality. New for 2025 entry is a four-year integrated masters in engineering (bioengineering). No courses are scheduled to close.

Competitive entry requirements start at ABB and rise to A*A*A. The university attracted more than 34,000 applications for 2023 entry, when just over 4,600 new students were accepted onto courses. For students who qualify for Durham's contextual offers, there is a two-grade reduction from the standard requirements, which just under a fifth (18%) of 2023's UK applicants received.

Durham's colleges offer accommodation for all first-years who apply by the deadline, with more than 7,600 places available. Durham was our Sports University of the Year for 2023 and sport continues to be a big part of student life. The collegiate structure leads to intense rivalry, and participation rates are high locally and nationally, in the British University and Colleges Sport (BUCS) league.

Durham has jumped two places from the bottom (113th) in our latest social inclusion index and remains one of three universities with less than half its intake from non-selective state schools. Progress can be seen in increased numbers of students from areas of low participation in higher education (7.5%, 81st). The university reports a 70% rise in black British undergraduates between 2018 and 2023, albeit only 1.7%.

The Durham Grant Scheme is the main source of bursary provision for UK students. Grants have been increased to a maximum of £2,500 a year for students from households with incomes below £30,000. Those with household incomes between £30,001 and £47,200 qualify for grants ranging from £2,495 to £780 per year.

---

**The Palatine Centre Stockton Road Durham DH1 3LE**
durham.ac.uk/study/askus
durham.ac.uk
durhamsu.com

**Overall ranking 5**
(last year 7)

**Accommodation**
University provided places 6,012
Catered £273–£289 per week
Self-catered £175–£191 per week

**Student numbers**
Undergraduates 17,360
Applications per place 7.3:1
Overall offer rate 62.0%

**Fees**
UK fees £9,250
International fees £23,500 – £32,500

durham.ac.uk/visit-us/open-days/
durham.ac.uk/study/undergraduate/fees-and-funding

# University of East Anglia

The University of East Anglia (UEA) has a strong tradition of research, including from the renowned Climatic Research Unit on campus and the world-leading Tyndall Centre for Climate Change Research. The £75 million Quadram Institute has a remit to improve health and prevent disease through innovations in microbiology, gut health and food. Another standout strength is UEA's creative writing course, whose alumni include Ian McEwan, Tracy Chevalier and Sir Kazuo Ishiguro, and the university hosts an annual literary festival.

In the latest Research Excellence Framework (REF 2021) 91% of the university's submission was classified as world-leading or internationally excellent, pushing it up 15 places to enter the top 20 of our research quality index (17th). A triple silver rating in the Teaching Excellence Framework (TEF 2023) highlighted the university's "outstanding" physical and virtual learning resources "which are tailored and used effectively to support outstanding teaching and learning".

More than ten degrees are closing, among them politics and economics, marine sciences, and global development with anthropology. Placement years, study abroad and foundation years are being added to a range of courses.

Standard offers range from BBB to AAA. A nuanced approach to contextual offer-making includes the university's Medicine With a Gateway Year programme. Other degrees may offer one or two grades lower than the standard rate to those who qualify, which was about 10% of entrants in 2023. Nearly one in five (19%) entrants gained their place through Clearing.

At =35th in our analysis of the Graduate Outcomes survey, which tracks how many students have moved on to highly skilled jobs or postgraduate courses within 15 months of finishing their degree, UEA has fallen two places since our previous edition and 11 places since 2022.

The campus covers nearly 360 acres and includes fens and meadows that are home to otters, deer, hares and rare orchids – as well as the more commonly spotted students, who can enjoy nature trails and a "silent space" in the Dutch garden. A significant project to improve teaching and learning facilities at Lasdun Wall is under way, following the completion in 2021 of Productivity East, a £7.4 million interdisciplinary hub for engineering, technology and management, and the opening of the £30 million New Science Building in 2020.

UEA has 3,488 spaces in its halls and endorses another 170 spaces in privately operated accommodation. Prices start at a budget-friendly £90.30 a week for students sharing a twin room. First-years who apply by the deadline are guaranteed accommodation. It has fallen ten places in our social inclusion index, to 79th. However, it is in the top 20 for its work to close the black achievement gap (18th).

Bursaries of £800 to £2,500 a year can be received as fee waivers, accommodation discounts or cash, and are automatically considered using household income information from Student Finance England. Merit-based scholarships are available in music, sport, social sciences, medicine, the arts and the sciences.

**Norwich Research Park Norwich NR4 7TJ**
admissions@uea.ac.uk
uea.ac.uk
ueasu.org

**Overall ranking 33**
(last year 26)

**Accommodation**
University provided places 3,488
Self-catered £90–£298 per week

**Student numbers**
Undergraduates 13,167
Applications per place 4.5:1
Overall offer rate 76.7%

**Fees**
UK fees £9,250
International fees £20,600–£26,100
Medicine £42,300

uea.ac.uk/visit/uni-open-days
uea.ac.uk/study/fees-and-funding#tuition

# University of East London

The role of the University of East London (UEL) in the regeneration of the east of the capital continues with the development of a new Stratford Medical Campus where students will be able to live, study and socialise while they gain the skills for a career within the NHS. UEL is up 77 places this year on teaching quality, taking the national title. Its "careers first" approach is designed to equip students to stand out in the fourth industrial revolution.

In the latest Research Excellence Framework (REF 2021), the best results came in computer science; allied health, and social work and social policy. Performance in a broad range of research subjects improved markedly since the previous assessment in 2014, but against sector-wide gains UEL fell from 76th to 105th in our research rankings.

A silver rating overall in the Teaching Excellence Framework (TEF 2023) was a step up from bronze six years earlier, when the university was held back by low graduate employment rates. The latest TEF panel awarded the student experience bronze and student outcomes, silver. The university has seen some slight improvement, jumping five places in the last year to be ranked 120th overall, with 63.6% of graduates in highly skilled work or postgraduate study within 15 months.

However, the TEF findings appear at odds with the university's completion rate of 87.5% – which places it 115th in the UK, and its proportion of graduates in high-skilled jobs 15 months after their degrees. Results of the latest National Student Survey show vast improvement: satisfaction with teaching quality has risen to 12th place – up from =89th last year – and satisfaction with the wider experience is 30th, up from =92nd.

UCAS tariff for undergraduate entry ranges from 64 points (for foundation years) to 120 points. While UEL does not make contextual offers it does apply a holistic approach to admissions and accepts a wide range of professional qualifications. The university will also make assessments based on significant and relevant work experience, as well as portfolios, interviews and auditions.

UEL has two halls of residence on campus, in distinctive waterside buildings. First-years who want to live in are guaranteed a room if they meet the eligibility criteria and apply by the deadline.

In our social inclusion index UEL ranks 51st. Most undergraduates are from ethnic minority populations (63.1%) and 51.7% are the first in their family to go to university (=33rd). A significant proportion of undergraduates (38.3%) are at least 21 on entry and the university offers the option of starting courses in January as well as September.

The largest award is the merit-based vice-chancellor's scholarship of £27,750, available to recipients as cash or a fee waiver over three years. Dean scholarships, also merit-based, are worth £13,500, while the prestigious UEL sports scholarship is worth up to £6,000 per year. The university also offers engagement, progression and hardship bursaries of up to £3,000 per academic year for students from low-income households.

---

**Docklands Campus University Way London E16 2RD**
study@uel.ac.uk
uel.ac.uk
eastlondonsu.com

**Overall ranking126**
(last year 131)

**Accommodation**
University provided places 1,160
Self-catered £165–£220 per week

**Student numbers**
Undergraduates 10,718
Applications per place 4.4:1
Overall offer rate 66.7%

**Fees**
UK fees £9,250
International fees £14,580–£14,820

uel.ac.uk/study/undergraduate/undergraduate-open-days
uel.ac.uk/study/fees-funding

# Edge Hill University

Edge Hill has forged a path as one of the UK's leading modern universities and was crowned our Modern University of the Year in 2021. Purpose-built facilities include a £13 million Tech Hub with biotechnology laboratories for research into disease prevention, DNA sequencing, cloning and genetic treatments. Based on a 160-acre campus near Ormskirk in the northwest of England, the university is investing £35 million in a new students' union with spaces for everything from societies to socialising, all with the latest tech built in.

Results of the latest Research Excellence Framework (REF 2021) showed that 62% of the work submitted was assessed as world-leading or internationally excellent. Hospitality; leisure; recreation and tourism; and information systems and management produced the best results. But against stronger performances elsewhere Edge Hill fell 20 places in our research quality index, compared with its position based on the previous REF exercise in 2014.

In the government's Teaching Excellence Framework (TEF 2023) the university was rated silver overall. The new rating was underpinned by gold for Edge Hill's student experience and silver for student outcomes. Since then, however, rates of student satisfaction expressed have plummeted: in our latest National Student Survey analysis Edge Hill has fallen to 119th for undergraduates' feedback on teaching quality (down 35 places) and it has lost 40 places to rank =104th the wider experience.

Undergraduate degrees demand from 104–112 UCAS tariff points, up to AAA for medicine. Less than 10% of students come through Clearing. Edge Hill does not have a formal contextual admission policy, but the university's commitment to widening access underpins a flexible approach to offers that takes applicants' personal circumstances into account.

Our analysis of the Graduate Outcomes survey, based on the proportion in highly skilled work or postgraduate courses within 15 months, shows an eight-place rise to =54th, just above the middle ground for UK institutions.

The 1930s-designed Main Building has been refurbished providing en suite accommodation on campus and bringing the number of rooms available to 2,592 rooms. First-years who apply by the housing deadline are guaranteed one.

Edge Hill has a longstanding commitment to widening access to higher education and is currently ranked 43rd overall. Schemes to broaden participation include the pre-entry Fastrack access programme, which has operated for more than 20 years and offers a seven-week preparation for some degrees for those returning to university or wanting to boost skills.

Excellence scholarships of up to £2,000 are paid over the duration of a degree and reward success outside a student's course. Edge Hill also awards £2,000 university scholarships to students who contribute to equality and diversity. The student opportunity fund – worth up to £2,000 – accepts applications for career-enhancing opportunities.

Non-means-tested academic achievement awards of £1,000 are given to the highest-performing student in each subject area based on end-of-year results and sports scholarships are of the same value. There are £1,000-a-year bursaries for care leavers and eligible disabled students.

---

**St Helens Road Ormskirk L39 4QP**
admissions@edgehill.ac.uk
edgehill.ac.uk
edgehillsu.org.uk

**Overall ranking =84**
(last year 69)

**Accommodation**
University provided places 2,592
Self-catered £85–£150 per week

**Student numbers**
Undergraduates 10,109
Applications per place 4.5:1
Overall offer rate 69.6

**Fees**
UK fees £9,250
International fees £16,500
Medicine £16,500

edgehill.ac.uk/study/visit-us/open-days/
edgehill.ac.uk/study/fees-and-funding/

# University of Edinburgh

Established in 1583, Edinburgh has a charismatic estate that reflects its long history, from university buildings in the historic Old Town to the Nucleus Building – the recently opened student and staff hub on the 115-acre King's Building campus a couple of miles out of the city.

One of the UK's big hitters for research, Edinburgh is 11th in our research quality index. 96% of its submission to the latest Research Excellence Framework (REF 2021) was assessed as world-leading or internationally excellent. Some of the best results were in psychology; biological sciences; English; politics; pharmacology and pharmacy; anatomy; and computing. On a global scale, Edinburgh is in the top 30 in the QS World Rankings.

Undergraduates benefit from research-led teaching and provision is broad, extending across 60 subjects and almost 400 degree programmes. Fieldwork, industry placements and opportunities to study abroad are embedded in its courses.

Rates of student satisfaction at Edinburgh remain persistently low however, a fate shared by many research-intensive universities. In our new National Student Survey analysis, Edinburgh is third from bottom for teaching quality (down six places) and although it does better for the wider student experience, a ten-place decline brings it to 122nd place this year.

The first students of a new degree in global law began courses in September 2024 and from 2025 a degree in biological sciences begins. There are no courses scheduled to close.

High academic standards are the norm, with courses demanding from BBB up to A*A*A*. Edinburgh was an early convert to contextual admissions, which undercut the standard retirements for eligible students. In 2022 about one in five new entrants received a contextual offer. Edinburgh attracted more than 71,000 applications in 2023 (around 40% from international students), a 9% decline compared with a record number the year before.

Careers are promising for those armed with an Edinburgh degree. High Fliers' research graduate market report puts Edinburgh in the top 15 universities targeted by the largest number of leading employers for 2022–23. However, the university fell out of the top 20 to 31st in our last edition and according to our latest analysis the proportion of graduates in high-skilled jobs or postgraduate study 15 months after leaving has fallen a further two places (33rd).

The university is set across five main campuses spread across the city, from the historic Old Town and the £8 million Health and Wellbeing Centre, which offers a sanctuary of calm, to the Usher Institute within the College of Medicine and Veterinary Medicine.

There are 6,581 residential places reserved for undergraduates, nearly a third of them with breakfast and evening meals included. All first-years who come from outside Edinburgh's city limits are guaranteed a room.

The Access Edinburgh Scholarship for UK students is worth up to £5,000 and based on individual circumstances and household income. In 2023–24 nearly one in five Scottish students qualified for one plus 15% of those from the rest of the UK.

---

**Old College South Bridge Edinburgh EH8 9YL**
futurestudents@ed.ac.uk
ed.ac.uk
eusa.ed.ac.uk

**Overall ranking =17**
(last year 13)

**Accommodation**
University provided places 6,581
Catered £187–£327 per week
Self-catered £87–£324 per week

**Student numbers**
Undergraduates 25,208
Applications per place 10.3:1
Overall offer rate 37.4%

**Fees**
UK fees £0–£1,820
RUK fees £9,250
International fees £26,500–£37,500
Medicine £37,500–£51,000

ed.ac.uk/studying/undergraduate/open-days-events-visits/open-day
registryservices.ed.ac.uk/student-funding

# Edinburgh Napier University

There is a serious work ethic at Edinburgh Napier University thanks to an emphasis on industry-focused courses with embedded placements, which translates to a top 50 rank for graduate outcomes. In keeping with its career-driven ethos, the university offers eight graduate apprenticeships (known as degree apprenticeships in England and Wales), including in cybersecurity; civil engineering; and software development.

Edinburgh Napier already has a strong record in the annual National Student Survey (NSS), and its latest results yet again put it in front of the other Edinburgh universities. In our analysis of 2024's NSS the university is 53rd for satisfaction with teaching quality and =48th for the broad undergraduate experience.

The university boosted its research reputation in the latest Research Excellence Framework (REF 2021); its results showed one of the biggest improvements compared with the previous national assessment, in 2014. The proportion of work achieving world-leading or internationally excellent rose from 53% in 2014 to 68% in 2021 – rising 21 places to 74th in our research quality index.

Degrees in intercultural business communication and marketing management or tourism management welcomed their first students in September 2024.

Scottish Highers entry requirements range from BBC up to AABB. The university publishes two offer levels for courses: standard and minimum. To be eligible for the minimum requirement, which is two to three grades lower than standard, applicants need to meet one of a range of contextual admissions criteria. About 15% of students were admitted through Clearing.

Analysis of the latest Graduate Outcomes survey shows that Edinburgh Napier is 41st in our graduate prospects table, with 80% of graduates in highly skilled jobs or further study within 15 months, a strong performance despite a two-place fall in rank from a year ago.

Merchiston, one of the university's three campuses, hosts creative arts subjects. Overlooking Edinburgh, the Craiglockhart campus hosts the Business School, featuring a curved lecture theatre known as the Egg. Sighthill, 20 minutes away by tram, is the base for the schools of nursing, midwifery and social care, complete with mock hospital wards and a high-dependency unit.

Student accommodation is at three halls of residence: Bainfield; Slateford Road, for nursing students and postgraduates; and Orwell Terrace, which is predominantly for the over-20s. The university can guarantee a space to all first-years from outside Edinburgh who apply by the deadline.

While undergraduates from Scotland are eligible for the national scheme for financial help, students from the rest of the UK and Ireland qualify for the university's attractive financial packages – paying tuition fees for only three years of their four-year degree course, and cash awards of up to £3,000. The level of support depends on students' financial circumstances and achievement. There are also merit bursaries of £1,000 per year of study for those who achieve at least BBB at A-level or equivalent qualifications.

**Sighthill Court Edinburgh EH11 4BN**
ugadmissions@napier.ac.uk
napier.ac.uk
napierstudents.com

**Overall ranking 59**
(last year 60)

**Accommodation**
University provided places 1,240
Self-catered £117–£197 per week

**Student numbers**
Undergraduates 10,334
Applications per place 5.5:1
Overall offer rate 65.3%

**Fees**
UK fees £0–£1,820
RUK fees £9,250 (£27,750 max, 4yrs)
International fees £16,680–£19,340

napier.ac.uk/study-with-us/undergraduate/meet-us/open-days
napier.ac.uk/ study-with-us/undergraduate/fees-and-finance

# University of Essex

The social sciences are Essex's longstanding academic strength. The university ranks 73rd for sociology in the 2024 QS World University Rankings and sits in the 51st to 100th band for politics. Politics and sociology were also to the fore for Essex in the most recent Research Excellence Framework (REF 2021), along with economics and modern languages. Across all subject areas, 83% of Essex's research was rated world-leading or internationally excellent. While an improvement on its performance in the previous REF in 2014, even bigger gains elsewhere meant that Essex dropped 16 places to 41st in our research quality index

Essex celebrated its 60th anniversary in 2024, the year after it was rated triple silver in the government's Teaching Excellence Framework (TEF 2023) – overall and for the underpinning aspects of student experience and student outcomes.

The university's position in our academic ranking has fluctuated, going from the top 25 in 2017 – when Essex was shortlisted for our University of the Year award – to =56th, down from 54th in a year. The National Student Survey (NSS) keeps Essex leapfrogging up the ranks: from =92nd to 50th for teaching quality and 53rd to 25th for the wider student experience.

Eighteen undergraduate courses have been suspended, among them global politics; journalism and modern languages; sociology and politics; and accounting with economics. However, the curriculum has gained four new degrees: business and analytics; stage management; biotechnology; and a tourism degree. A new degree apprenticeship in biomedical science launches in 2025.

The majority of undergraduate courses require between BBC and BBB (112 to 120 UCAS tariff points). Essex introduced a contextual admissions policy for the 2024 admissions cycle; it undercuts standard offers by up to two A-level grades, or equivalent, to UK applicants who meet eligibility criteria.

The Knowledge Gateway on the Colchester campus is home to more than 90 businesses, many of which offer internships or employment. Essex has fallen outside the top half of our graduate prospects table, ranking =91st, based on the proportion of leavers in high-skilled work or further study 15 months on from their degrees, a drop of 14 places. The School of Life Sciences has extended its marine biology and aquatic sciences laboratory. Its new £3.5 million Smart Technology Experimental Plant Suite (STEPS) provides a research facility where the internationally acclaimed Plant Productivity Group are continuing to study how to improve crop photosynthesis.

The interiors of the six accommodation tower blocks on the main campus have been revamped in a multimillion-pound makeover. The university guarantees accommodation to first-years who make Essex their firm choice and meet application deadlines.

More diverse than most pre-1992 universities, Essex is =29th in our social inclusion index, rising slightly from =33rd last year.

Many awards are automatically applied and their number is uncapped. Their value ranges from between £250 to more than £10,000. Students from households with incomes up to £35,000 are eligible for the £3,000 Essex Futures bursary. Merit-based academic awards include a law scholarship.

---

**Wivenhoe Park Colchester CO4 3SQ**
admit@essex.ac.uk
essex.ac.uk
www.essexstudent.com

**Overall ranking =46**
(last year =56)

**Accommodation**
University provided places 6,084
Self-catered £106–£258 per week

**Student numbers**
Undergraduates 12,097
Applications per place 5.8:1
Overall offer rate 68.7%

**Fees**
UK fees £9,250
International fees £20,475–£30,275

essex.ac.uk/visit-us/open-days
essex.ac.uk/student/money

# University of Exeter

The coastal Russell Group university is putting its academic weight behind addressing the challenges of our time: climate change, healthcare provision and social justice. Exeter offers more than 400 courses in 40 subjects but wants to build a global reputation of expertise in sustainability.

Nearly half of Exeter's extensive submission in the latest Research Excellence Framework (REF 2021) was assessed as world-leading (particularly in sports science; theology; and area studies) and the university reconfirmed 18th place in our research quality index.

Its undergraduate provision was rated gold in the latest Teaching Excellence Framework (TEF 2023), as it was in the previous exercise six years before. Exeter also gained golds for student experience and student outcomes, attracting praise for courses that inspire its students "to actively engage in and commit to their learning, and stretch them to develop knowledge and skills to their fullest potential".

Exeter is accustomed to reaping positive feedback in successive National Student Surveys (NSS), where it tends to outdo many research-led peers. Our new NSS analysis shows a dip in form, however, with Exeter in =80th position for teaching quality (down 14 places) and 40th for the wider experience – a 16-place drop.

Offers for undergraduate degrees start at BBB and rise to A*AA. Exeter's contextual admissions policy undercuts the standard requirements by two or three grades — the upper credit is a more generous reduction than at most other universities. Almost a quarter (23%) of new entrants in 2023 received a contextual offer. Applications were up yet again in 2024, reflecting Exeter's all-round popularity. Even so, more than 10% gained a place through Clearing.

Exeter's TEF gold for its student outcomes reflects a strong record in the national Graduate Outcomes survey, which tracks how many students find highly skilled work or embark on further study within 15 months of finishing their degree course. Our analysis put Exeter in the top 20 for graduate prospects only two years ago, but it has since slipped to rank 31st overall.

Career and employment preparation modules are embedded across the curriculum for all first-years. More than 4,600 students opt for formal work placements as part of their course and Exeter's career-management platform advertised more than 14,000 opportunities, including graduate roles, internships, placements and part-time work.

The completion of the East Park student residences added 1,182 bedrooms to the Streatham site, taking the total to 6,469 and helping Exeter to guarantee a room for all first-years who meet the deadline.

The university ranks in the bottom ten (8th) in our latest social inclusion data. Just over half (57.5%) of its intake is from non-selective state schools.

A generous bursary and scholarship scheme includes the Access to Exeter bursary, worth up to £2,000 per year of study for students from households of under £30,000 incomes. Almost one in five entrants in 2024 received the bursary or hardship funding. Among other awards are sports performance bursaries of up to £3,000. Other merit-based awards include the global excellence scholarship for high-achieving international students.

**Northcote House The Queen's Drive Exeter EX4 4QJ**
exeter.ac.uk/enquiry
exeter.ac.uk
exeterguild.org; thesu.org.uk

**Overall ranking 13**
(last year 11)

**Accommodation**
University provided places 7,409
Catered £214–£239 per week
Self-catered £124–£199 per week

**Student numbers**
Undergraduates 22,774
Applications per place 5.0:1
Overall offer rate 82.0%

**Fees**
UK fees £9,250
International fees £23,700–£29,700
Medicine £45,700

exeter.ac.uk/undergraduate/visit/
exeter.ac.uk/undergraduate/fees

# Falmouth University

Falmouth attracted record numbers of applications – more than 8,000 – and new student enrolments totalled 2,600, with just 6% to be found in Clearing. Courses range from film, fashion design, theatre and performance, and music to business and entrepreneurship, marketing, photography, journalism, game development, and architecture – as well as a comprehensive offering in its founding specialisms of art and design.

Falmouth was awarded £7.2 million in government funding to develop its Centre for Blended Realities, where the mission is to blend cutting-edge computer science with innovation in the arts. Its innovations should further the burgeoning research profile of this small, specialist, south-coast institution.

Falmouth, which gained university status in 2012, achieved remarkable results in the Research Excellence Framework (REF 2021). 63% of its art and design submissions were rated world-leading or internationally excellent. The outcomes spurred a huge 52-place rise for Falmouth in our research quality rating.

Awarded triple silver in the Teaching Excellence Framework (TEF 2023), the panel noted that physical and virtual learning resources "are used effectively to support very high quality teaching and learning", and commended Falmouth's "use of research in relevant disciplines, innovation, scholarship, professional practice and employer engagement". Satisfaction with teaching quality (62nd) and the wider undergraduate experience (93rd) are on the slide, however, according to our analysis of the National Student Survey.

Applicants need 80 UCAS tariff points to qualify for an offer for an International Foundation Year (IFY) and a minimum of 104 points for an undergraduate degree. Falmouth holds interviews or auditions for most of its courses and will make contextual offers.

Students across all academic departments have opportunities to work on real projects in collaboration with industry partners. Exploring entrepreneurship is encouraged too, via a range of initiatives that include Falmouth's own incubator, Launchpad. However, in common with fellow arts specialists, Falmouth struggles in our graduate prospects analysis, based on the proportion of leavers in high-skilled work or further study within 15 months. At =129th, Falmouth lies second from bottom in our table.

A place in halls of residence is guaranteed to all first-years who apply by the deadline. Students can opt to have meals included at the Glasney Student Village accommodation. 8% of rooms are catered.

Just inside the top 90 of our social inclusion index (89th), Falmouth's outreach activities target schools and colleges in areas across the UK where progression rates to university are low. Initiatives include one-to-one peer support sessions with students to help applicants prepare for interviews.

About two thirds of 2023's new entrants qualified for financial assistance in the form of means-tested bursaries, international scholarships or hardship awards. The Falmouth bursary of £250 to £500 per year of study is awarded to students from households with incomes under £25,000. To help with the cost of course-related materials students may be eligible for a bursary of £100 to £400.

**Woodlane Falmouth TR11 4RH**
futurestudies@falmouth.ac.uk
falmouth.ac.uk
thesu.org.uk

**Overall ranking 73**
(last year 51)

**Accommodation**
University provided places 1,640
Catered £193–£239 per week
Self-catered £139–£261 per week

**Student numbers**
Undergraduates 5,336
Applications per place 3.1:1
Overall offer rate 64.6%

**Fees**
UK fees £9,250–£11,100
International fees £6,935–£19,950

www.falmouth.ac.uk/experience/open-days
www.falmouth.ac.uk/study/tuition-fees

# University of Glasgow

This ambitious and ancient institution founded in 1451 has a tradition of firsts. Glasgow was the first university in Britain to have a school of engineering and the first in Scotland to have a computer. Now it is extending its campus in the city's fashionable West End to develop modern facilities fit for the future. The £1 billion, decade-long investment which began in 2017 includes the James McCune Smith Learning Hub, a facility for 2,500 students that is named after an alumnus – the civil rights activist and first African-American to be awarded a medical degree anywhere in the world in 1837.

One of only two Russell Group universities north of the border, our Scottish University of the Year 2024 is linked with eight Nobel laureates. The results of the latest Research Excellence Framework (REF 2021) add contemporary sheen to the university's illustrious research profile. The results put Glasgow in 12th place nationally in our research quality index. The university has also secured another top 100 spot (78th) in the QS World University Rankings 2025.

Teaching quality takes a dive according to our latest National Student Survey analysis, tumbling from =92nd last year to 116th. The wider student experience also takes a hit, falling from =67th to 112th.

Offers range from CCC up to AAA at A-level and in Scottish Highers it is BBBB up to AAAAAA (which can be met with 4 A grades at SQA Higher and 2 B grades at Advanced Higher or six A grades in six Highers). Only 4% of undergraduates gained a place through Clearing.

Glasgow is 27th in our analysis based on the proportion of graduates in highly skilled work or postgraduate study after 15 months, rising slightly from 32nd last year.

Glasgow is not "a campus university" in the traditional sense and has three campuses around the city. As well as the McCune Hub, the redevelopment of Gilmorehill has produced the £50 million Clarice Pears Building, which opened in 2022 and has created a single multidisciplinary centre for the university's School of Health and Wellbeing. The university has increased spaces in halls of residence to more than 5,500. First-years who apply by July 14 are guaranteed a room.

Glasgow is showing progress in diversifying the intake, and 16.7% of new students come from the most deprived postcodes. Even so, Glasgow is among the lower reaches of our Scottish social inclusion ranking at 13th. Its black achievement gap, although still negative at minus 9.8%, is the leading result in Scotland.

While four-year courses are the norm in Scotland, students from the rest of the UK will find their fourth-year tuition fees (or the fees for a placement year) waived on the majority of degree courses. Access bursaries of £1,000 to £3,000 per year of study are available for students from England, Wales and Northern Ireland from low-income households.

---

**University Avenue Glasgow G12 8QQ**
ruk-undergraduate-enquiries@glasgow.ac.uk;
scot-undergraduate-enquiries@glasgow.ac.uk
glasgow.ac.uk
guu.co.uk; qmunion.org.uk

**Overall ranking 16**
(last year 12)

**Accommodation**
University provided places 5,538
Catered £204–£225 per week
Self-catered £121–£273 per week

**Student numbers**
Undergraduates 20,862
Applications per place 6.2:1
Overall offer rate 63.6%

**Fees**
UK fees £0–£1,820
RUK fees £9,250
International fees £25,290–£30,240
Medicine £56,520

gla.ac.uk/explore/visit/undergraduate/opendays/
gla.ac.uk/undergraduate/fees

# Glasgow Caledonian University

Its mission is to be the "university for the common good" and Glasgow Caledonian University (GCU) has added a 21st-century focus to make its graduates career-ready. More than half of its undergraduate programmes are accredited by professional bodies and most include a work placement, and it is Scotland's leading provider of graduate apprenticeships (equivalent to degree apprenticeships in England), including civil engineering, cybersecurity and accountancy. GCU is also one of the largest providers of graduates to NHS Scotland and has been responsible for training most of Scotland's non-medical eyecare professionals for more than 50 years.

The results of the latest National Student Survey (NSS) keep the university on an even keel, up four places for both measures: satisfaction with teaching quality (65th) and the wider student experience (53rd). Courses are organised within three schools: computing, engineering and built environment; business and society; and health and life sciences. Helping to fuel its league table ascent is an improved research profile. Nursing and allied health subjects produced some of the best work in the Research Excellence Framework (REF 2021), contributing to a rise of 11 places in our research quality index (66th).

GCU's School of Computing, Engineering and Built Environment is one of Britain's leading teaching centres for building and surveying. The Glasgow School for Business and Society offers highly specialised degrees such as entrepreneurial studies and risk management.

BScs in ophthalmic dispensing management, and biosciences degrees paired with food bioscience and microbiology are in the pipeline for 2025. The university's degree in food science will be withdrawn at the same time.

Offers for undergraduate degrees range from 147 UCAS tariff points (AAA at A-level) to 96 (CCC), and in Scottish Highers it is BBCC up to AABBB. Minimum entry requirements apply for those eligible for contextual offers, which were made to about a fifth of new entrants in 2023. Clearing accounted for 16% of admissions in 2023.

In our analysis of the latest Graduate Outcomes survey, GCU slips back into the top 40 (34th) based on the proportion of graduates in high-skilled jobs or further study 15 months on. GCU's British School of Fashion has teamed up with companies including Marks & Spencer, which has a design studio for postgraduate study in London and funds scholarships.

Early application is advised: there are only 655 residential places, and only 70% of applicants were housed in halls in 2024. Off campus, private rentals are stretched in Glasgow due to a shortage of properties. The historic West End's red-brick flats are popular – if you act fast.

GCU sets a high bar for social inclusion, ranking fourth among Scotland's 15 universities. With 22.1% of its intake from deprived areas, it is second among its Scottish peers. Awards are funded from a £2 million pot per year and include a £6,000 cash-back bursary for RUK (Rest of the UK) students, paid over three years followed by a fourth-year fee waiver.

---

**Cowcaddens Road Glasgow G4 0BA**
studentenquiries@gcu.ac.uk
gcu.ac.uk
gcustudents.co.uk

**Overall ranking 44**
(last year 50)

**Accommodation**
University provided places 655
Self-catered £125–£148 per week

**Student numbers**
Undergraduates 13,038
Applications per place 3.8:1
Overall offer rate 67.2%

**Fees**
UK fees £0–£1,820
RUK fees £9,250
International fees £15,200

gcu.ac.uk/study/opendays
gcu.ac.uk/study/tuitionfees

# University of Gloucestershire

The University of Gloucestershire's Countryside and Community Research Institute on its Oxstalls campus is the largest rural research centre in the UK and produced some of the university's best results in the latest Research Excellence Framework (REF 2021). Art and design also performed well and Gloucestershire doubled the number of subject areas assessed, compared with the previous REF in 2014. Overall, 47% of the university's submission was rated as world-leading or internationally excellent. Even so, the university slid three places to joint 111th in our research rankings due to improved performances across the sector.

Gloucestershire earned triple silver in the Teaching Excellence Framework (TEF 2023). Assessors commended its "supportive learning environment and access to a range of very high quality academic support" as well as its effective use of "physical and virtual learning resources to support very high quality teaching and learning". Students were found to engage in their learning, supported by effective practices that "stretch students to develop their knowledge and skills".

Rates of student satisfaction, which tumbled in our previous National Student Survey analysis – falling 50 places to 103rd for teaching quality and down 44 places to 106th for satisfaction with the wider undergraduate experience – have been mixed this year. Gloucester has gained ground for teaching quality, where it ranks =90th, but lost ground for wider experience, falling to 115th.

The university's portfolio of degree and master's-level apprenticeships encompasses 20 subject areas; about 1,100 students were enrolled at the last count. Three of these programmes are recent additions designed to fill skills gaps: healthcare science practitioner (ophthalmic imaging); healthcare science practitioner (vascular science); and facilities manager.

For undergraduate degrees, offers range from 96 to 128 UCAS tariff points. For courses with an integrated foundation year Gloucestershire accepts 48 UCAS points for entry. The university does not have a contextual offer scheme; rather, it tailors offers to applicants based on interview performance or the strength of their application. For mature students professional experience is taken into account and lower than standard offers may be made. Clearing accounted for almost a fifth (17%) of admissions.

A team named Your Future Plan operates at all of the university's campuses, offering careers and employability services such as a mentoring programme, placement opportunities and keynote speakers. Its services are available post-graduation too. A proportion of 76.4% of graduates in high-skilled jobs or further study 15 months on from their degrees, a rise of 3.7% compared to last year, has risen Gloucestershire to =57th in our table.

Gloucester guarantees accommodation to all first-years in halls on or near campus.

In 61st place in our social inclusion index – down 22 places year-on-year – Gloucestershire is eighth in England and Wales for its proportion of white working-class boys, the most underrepresented group at university.

Awards include a £1,000 cash payment in the first year only, to students progressing from partner schools. More than 20 sports scholarships are awarded each year.

---

**The Park Campus The Park Cheltenham GL50 2RH**
admissions@glos.ac.uk
glos.ac.uk
yourstudentsunion.com

**Overall ranking =90**
(last year =112)

**Accommodation**
University provided places 1,778
Self-catered £132–£240 per week

**Student numbers**
Undergraduates 5,952
Applications per place 4.0:1
Overall offer rate 81.9%

**Fees**
UK fees £9,250
International fees £16,600

glos.ac.uk/visit-us/open-days/undergraduate-open-days/
glos.ac.uk/finance/fees-and-loans

# Goldsmiths, University of London

Britain's creative royalty – and real royalty – have studied at Goldsmiths: the designer Mary Quant; artist Damien Hirst; Oscar-winning director Sir Steve McQueen; three members of the pop band Blur; and Princess Beatrice. Mr Loverman author Bernardine Evaristo earned her PhD in creative writing here.

The university's progressive outlook is a draw and its courses have clout. Goldsmiths ranks 21st in the world for art and design in the QS World University Rankings by Subject 2024, and 48th for the performing arts.

It found itself in the news for less favourable reasons when a £16 million budget deficit was reported in 2023 and strike action was threatened in a row over staff redundancies to save money. The strikes were called off, along with a marking and assessment boycott, after an agreement in time for the start of the 2024-25 academic year.

The sense of uncertainty and unrest was reflected in the latest Teaching Excellence Framework (TEF 2023), when Goldsmiths was rated bronze. Despite an appeal, the TEF results (student experience requires improvement; student outcomes bronze) stand. Goldsmiths is the only university in our guide to be told by the Office for Students that its provision requires improvement.

However, the TEF panel tempered its assessment by commenting that "research in relevant disciplines, scholarship and professional practice" contributed "to a very high quality academic experience".

Founded in 1891 by the Worshipful Company of Goldsmiths, the original institution focused on classes in the arts and sciences at the site in New Cross, southeast London, that the university occupies today. Its reach now includes social sciences and humanities, management, law and computing.

In the latest Research Excellence Framework (REF 2021), 79% of work submitted by Goldsmiths was rated world-leading or internationally excellent. Anthropology; art, design and visual cultures; media, communications and cultural studies; and sociology produced some of the best results. It is comfortably in the top half of universities in our analysis of research quality (49th) although it slipped 13 places compared with its performance in the previous REF 2014.

Despite modest improvements in rates of student satisfaction, the university remains rooted in the lower reaches of our new National Student Survey analysis: Goldsmiths is 124th for satisfaction with teaching quality and 127th for satisfaction with the wider undergraduate experience.

The university has some of the capital's best facilities for the creative arts, including dedicated space for design students, research laboratories and music studios with industry-standard equipment.

About 15% of entrants received one of Goldsmiths' range of scholarships and bursaries in 2024. Awards include fee waivers for students from the borough of Lewisham and scholarships worth £3,000 a year of study for mature students.

Help for students includes specialist counsellors, financial advice and wellbeing support officers. A holistic approach means academic and personal tutors are also points of contact for those in difficulty.

Most study bedrooms are near campus and none further away than a 30-minute commute. First-years are prioritised and international students who apply by the deadline are guaranteed a space.

---

**New Cross London SE14 6NW**
course-info@gold.ac.uk
gold.ac.uk
goldsmithssu.org

**Overall ranking 80**
(last year 96)

**Accommodation**
University provided places 1,395
Self-catered £176–£389 per week

**Student numbers**
Undergraduates 5,519
Applications per place 5.2:1
Overall offer rate 69.8%

**Fees**
UK fees £9,250
International fees £19,640–£27,500

gold.ac.uk/open-days/
gold.ac.uk/ug/fees-funding/

# University of Greenwich

Greenwich counts two recent Nobel laureate associations: Abiy Ahmed, who became Africa's youngest leader aged 42, when he became prime minister of Ethiopia, and went on to win the Nobel peace prize in 2019; and the late Sir Charles Kao, who won the prize for physics in 2009 for his work in fibre optics.

Greenwich is based at three campuses: Avery Hill in southeast London, Greenwich Campus in central London and Medway in Kent. It was rated gold overall in the government's Teaching Excellence Framework (TEF 2023) – a step up from its silver in the previous assessment six years before – with gold for student experience and silver for student outcomes. The TEF panel rated the course content and delivery outstanding, noting that "student engagement is embedded, leading to continuous improvement".

Last year Greenwich was on the verge of entering the top 40 in the National Student Survey, getting =41st for teaching quality and =42nd for the wider student experience. Now it sits in the middle of the table, at 67th and 60th respectively.

A student-to-staff ratio of 20.9:1 puts Greenwich 122nd, and a relatively low rate of firsts and 2.1s (70.8%) contribute to the university's confinement to a position outside the top 100 of our main academic ranking.

The university gained government accreditation as an Academic Centre of Excellence in Cyber Security Research, and received £9 million in funding for computer modelling to tackle emerging environmental and societal challenges. Greenwich's improved performance in the latest Research Excellence Framework (REF 2021) spurred an impressive 19-place rise up our research rankings compared with the previous assessment in 2014.

The course offering broadened by more than 30 degrees in 2023, including wine production, and horticulture and animal-related courses. New for 2024 are degrees in computing for emerging technologies and data science.

Standard offers range from 104 and 128 UCAS tariff points. Contextual offers (16 points lower) are available for those from a low-participation postcode or who have spent time in care.

Barclays, Alcatel Submarine Networks and RSK are among companies represented on advisory boards that help guide the curriculum. Professional placements are built into some courses. But graduate prospects remain one of Greenwich's weaker suits, and it ranks 100th in our rankings for this measure – based on the proportion of graduates in high-skilled jobs or further study 15 months after leaving.

First-years are guaranteed a room in halls of residence if they apply before the June 30 deadline.

Greenwich is ranked 20th in our social inclusion table, buoyed by counting 58.4% of undergraduates from ethnic minorities (20th) and 57.1% the first in their family to go to university (=13th). A broad programme of outreach activities helps widen access.

Extensive support includes means-tested financial help for those from low-income households, such as commuter bursaries worth 50% of a student's monthly travel costs (up to £1,000 a year); accommodation bursaries of up to £700; and the one-off £700 Greenwich Bursary.

---

**Old Royal Naval College Park Row**
**Greenwich SE10 9LS**
courseinfo@gre.ac.uk
gre.ac.uk
greenwichsu.co.uk

**Overall ranking 102**
(last year 105)

**Accommodation**
University provided places 2,399
Self-catered £134–£354 per week

**Student numbers**
Undergraduates 15,621
Applications per place 4.0:1
Overall offer rate 77.7%

**Fees**
UK fees £6,165 (Foundation) – £9,250
International fees £17,000–£21,000

gre.ac.uk/events/opendays
gre.ac.uk/finance

## Harper Adams University

Founded in 1901, Harper Adams, which describes itself as "the university for food production and technology, animal health and wellbeing" gained full university status in 2012. It was our top-ranked modern university for six years in a row (2017–2022) and was named our inaugural Specialist University of the Year 2024, rising to 36th place in our main league table.

60% of the work submitted by Harper Adams to the latest Research Excellence Framework (REF 2021) was rated world-leading or internationally excellent – improving on the results from REF 2014, but not enough to stay in our top 100 for research. It now ranks 116th in our research quality table.

Harper Adams was one of only two institutions to be rated gold two years running in the government's Teaching Excellence Framework, in 2017–18. In the latest assessment (TEF 2023), Harper Adams achieved gold overall, with silver for the student experience and gold for student outcomes. Results in the latest National Student Survey are mixed: Harper Adams is 16th for satisfaction with teaching quality (up from =37th last year) but has plunged from =21st to 95th for satisfaction with the wider student experience.

Harper Adams is branching out into courses in robotics, automation, and mechatronic engineering; applied data science; and digital business management at its new site in Telford's Station Quarter. From 2024 the university is offering degrees in crop production; farm business management; livestock production science; applied animal science; and wildlife, conservation and ecology.

Applications and enrolments remain remarkably stable at Harper Adams. The highest demand of 136 UCAS tariff points is for the university's integrated master's degrees in engineering, while at the lowest end, foundation courses require 72 UCAS tariff points.

All students have a work placement in their penultimate year of study – which means that about a quarter of students are on a sandwich year at any one time. More than 200 businesses come to the campus each year at careers and recruitment fairs. However, Harper Adams has dropped 19 places year-on-year to rank 78th, according to our analysis of the proportion of leavers in highly skilled jobs or postgraduate study within 15 months.

The university has planted its first vineyard on the main campus in Newport, Shropshire, as a platform for viticulture teaching and to test varieties suited to a changing British climate. Harper Adams runs a working farm with 435 cows (with dairy and beef units), 200 sheep, 230 sows, and chickens and turkeys.

Accommodation is guaranteed on campus to those from abroad, or who are disabled or have left care. The university is almost always able to accommodate all first-years.

Harper Adams is the least ethnically diverse university in our guide which places it 94th in our social inclusion index overall. However, it is placed third for recruitment of disabled students

Scholarships funded by philanthropic and industry donations totalling over £564,000 were awarded post-admission to more than 136 students (both undergraduate and postgraduate) in 2022–23.

**Edgmond Newport TF10 8NB**
admissions@harper-adams.ac.uk
harper-adams.ac.uk
harpersu.com

**Overall ranking 53**
(last year 36)

**Accommodation**
University provided places 774
Catered £123–£190 per week
Self-catered £81–£143 per week

**Student numbers**
Undergraduates 2,447
Applications per place 4.6:1
Overall offer rate 86.4%

**Fees**
UK fees 9,250
International fees £16,500

harper-adams.ac.uk/study/991/open-days/
harper-adams.ac.uk/apply/finance

# Hartpury University

Perhaps it is down to the success of Clarkson's Farm, but applications to Hartpury University have risen for the past six years, totalling more than 3,600 for 2023 entry – about 10% via Clearing. Founded as an agricultural institute, it became a university in 2018 and offers a curriculum encompassing animal, equine, sport and veterinary nursing degrees.

This is the Cotswolds institution's fourth appearance in our academic league table. It earned triple gold in the Teaching Excellence Framework (TEF 2023), an accolade only 15% of higher education institutions received.

As part of a ten-year vision to turn its commercial Home Farm into an agri-tech pioneer, the university's Agri-Tech Centre for smart farming technology focuses on increasing productivity and profitability within livestock. Partnerships with more than 3,000 employers allow students to benefit from field trips, careers events and work placements.

Commercial businesses on-site near Gloucester include equine and canine therapy centres while Home Farm, which supplies Müller, offers opportunities across the food chain. At the Hartpury Sports Business Hub, launched in 2022, students and staff work on live briefs and real-world research consultancy.

Despite such efforts, Hartpury is six places from the bottom of our graduate prospects table (127th), based on the proportion of students who find high skilled jobs or return to study within 15 months of finishing their degree.

It sits in 57th place of our social inclusion index, shifting two places since ranking 55th last year. Its outreach activities focus on attracting care leavers, mature students, those from low participation areas, students with vocational and non-traditional entry qualifications, disabled students and students from black and minority ethnic backgrounds.

Up to 20% of entrants qualify for some form of financial assistance, with bursaries of £1,000 a year for those from households with incomes up to £42,000. Sports scholarships are not means-tested.

Investment is ongoing: the £12.75 million University Learning Hub, the base for the library and careers services, includes group work pods, study zones and open-plan social areas. Students will have access to a £5.8 million Veterinary Nursing Centre in 2024–25.

The curriculum has gained degrees in business management, biological sciences, equine dental science and environmental science.

Facilities at the university include the Sports Academy, which houses biomechanics and human performance laboratories, an anti-gravity treadmill and an altitude chamber. There are physiotherapy rooms, a gym and a sports hall.

A new academy is planned for the Five Acres site in the Forest of Dean and the university is a training centre for the British Rowing World Class and Pentathlon GB Pathway programmes.

There are 389 student bedrooms on site and a further 190 off campus. Hartpury says it will guarantee to find accommodation for first-year undergraduates as long as they hold it as a firm UCAS choice and apply by August 31.

Wellbeing officers and support workers offer daily drop-ins and one-to-one appointments. Counselling is available and there are sexual violence liaison officers. In 2022 Hartpury received a University Mental Health Charter award from Student Minds.

**Gloucestershire GL19 3BE**
admissions@hartpury.ac.uk
hartpury.ac.uk
hartpurysu.co.uk

**Overall ranking 116**
(last year =112)

**Accommodation**
University provided places 579
Self-catered £136–£183 per week

**Student numbers**
Undergraduates 2,039
Applications per place 4.2:1
Overall offer rate N/A

**Fees**
UK fees £9,250
International fees £16,500

hartpury.ac.uk/university/open-days/
hartpury.ac.uk/university/facilities/life-at-hartpury/finance

# Heriot-Watt University

The UK's first purpose-built National Robotarium is hosted by this former institute for mechanics at its Edinburgh campus. Students from Heriot-Watt and the University of Edinburgh are exploring how robotics and autonomous systems can address real-life issues.

Research at the centre, which opened in 2022, complements laboratories applying robotics to the study of ocean systems and assisted living.

The university, which takes its name from George Heriot and James Watt, two giants of commerce and industry, also has campuses in Orkney, the Scottish Borders, Dubai and Malaysia. Students have an opportunity to move between the five sites for a semester, a year or longer.

Physics did well in the latest Research Excellence Framework (REF 2021), with 97% of the subject's submission rated world-leading or internationally excellent. Joint submissions with the University of Edinburgh in mathematical sciences; architecture, built environment and planning; and engineering excelled. Heriot-Watt sits comfortably in the upper half of UK universities in our research quality index.

The Scottish universities did not take part in the government's latest Teaching Excellence Framework (TEF 2023) but Heriot-Watt earned silver in the previous TEF in 2017.

Our analysis of the National Student Survey keeps the university outside the top 100 for teaching quality despite a slight improvement from last year. It did better for the wider student experience, with a shift of 26 places up to 90th.

Many degree programmes include industry placements or projects and carry professional accreditation, which is reflected in buoyant rates of graduate employment. Heriot-Watt is 23rd in our analysis of the latest Graduate Outcomes survey, fourth in Scotland, based on the proportion of leavers in highly skilled jobs or postgraduate study 15 months after leaving.

There are new degrees in interior architecture and design; brewing and distilling; and games development and production. Options for graduate apprenticeships (known as degree apprenticeships elsewhere) are broader than at most Scottish universities and include design and manufacturing; IT software development; and civil engineering.

Riccarton, to the west of Edinburgh, is the university's academic headquarters, where a £6 million library refurbishment increased capacity to more than 1,000 study spaces. The Borders campus at Galashiels hosts courses in textiles, fashion and design, while the postgraduate Orkney centre specialises in renewable energy.

Undergraduate provision in Dubai focuses on management, engineering, built environment and fashion. The Putrajaya campus in Malaysia has courses in psychology, engineering and finance.

Music is a feature of student life at Heriot-Watt, with opportunities to join various choirs, bands and groups. With almost 2,000 university-owned rooms, accommodation is guaranteed to all first-years from out of town who apply by the housing deadline.

Daily drop-ins help students to contact a supportive counsellor. Workshops, group work and one-to-one sessions are among the services provided by qualified staff. Personal tutors may also refer students for wellbeing support.

Students from Scotland who meet eligibility criteria qualify for subject-specific and access bursaries. Those from England, Wales and Northern Ireland receive a £1,500 Travel Home Bursary in their first year of study.

**Edinburgh EH14 4AS**
studywithus@hw.ac.uk
hw.ac.uk
hwunion.com

**Overall ranking 51**
(last year 64)

**Accommodation**
University provided places 1,986
Self-catered £159–£230 per week

**Student numbers**
Undergraduates 7,216
Applications per place 5.8:1
Overall offer rate 73.1

**Fees**
UK fees £0–£1,820
RUK fees £9,250
International fees £18,704–£24,048

hw.ac.uk/uk/visit/edinburgh-campus-open-day.htm
hw.ac.uk/study/fees-funding.htm

# University of Hertfordshire

Shoot for the stars. The University of Hertfordshire's Bayfordbury Observatory houses one of the largest telescopes available to undergraduate or postgraduate students in the UK.

The Automotive Centre is the base for engineering teaching and has put graduates on the road to careers in Formula One, while the new Spectra building for the School of Physics, Engineering and Computer Science promises to inspire a generation of Stem students.

The university's two main campuses are in Hatfield, 25 minutes by train from London. It was founded as Hatfield Technical College in 1952 on the former de Havilland aerodrome site.

Hertfordshire rose 26 places to 60th in our research quality index, according to our analysis of the latest Research Excellence Framework (REF 2021), with some of the best results in allied health subjects, computer science and psychology. Overall, 78% of its submission was rated world-leading or internationally excellent.

In the government's Teaching Excellence Framework (TEF 2023), the university achieved silver overall – down from gold in 2018. The TEF panel said staff created "opportunities for students to engage in research and with industry, resulting in an outstanding academic experience".

Our analysis of the National Student Survey shows improvement, with Hertfordshire in 42nd place for satisfaction with teaching quality (up from 59th last year) and 32nd for satisfaction with the wider student experience (from 66th).

BSc honours courses in professional policing and business management joined the curriculum in September 2024. Degree apprenticeship programmes include computer science, engineering and health and social work.

Professional accreditations or approvals are often built into courses, and students leave with CV extras such as Microsoft qualifications or City & Guilds awards. Most courses offer work placements. Hertfordshire has risen eight places to 86th in our analysis of the Graduate Outcomes survey, based on the numbers who find highly skilled jobs or return to study within 15 months.

Hertfordshire is one of the UK's more socially inclusive universities, up nine places to 27th on this measure. Links with primary and secondary schools across the county encourage wider participation and the institution runs outreach events such as GCSE booster workshops and summer schools. It also attracts students from more than 140 countries.

Modern facilities are a hallmark: the School of Physics, Engineering and Computer Science has robotics laboratories, cybersecurity facilities, a flight simulator and a supersonic wind tunnel. The Enterprise Hub is a business incubator for start-ups and graduate entrepreneurs.

The £15 million Hertfordshire Sports Village on the de Havilland campus caters for all abilities, and social events feature live arts and music.

All first-years who meet the deadline for applications are guaranteed a study bedroom on campus. Counselling, mental health and disability support are available and students who are struggling can reach out to the wellbeing team as needed. There is a chaplaincy with volunteers from a range of faiths.

Undergraduate bursaries are offered and students who have left care, are displaced from their country or are adult carers are eligible for further support.

**Hatfield AL10 9AB**
ask@herts.ac.uk
herts.ac.uk
hertssu.com

**Overall ranking 83**
(last year 95)

**Accommodation**
University provided places 4,700
Self-catered £125–£263 per week

**Student numbers**
Undergraduates 14,036
Applications per place 5.5:1
Overall offer rate 63.0%

**Fees**
UK fees £6,165 (Foundation) – £9,250
International fees £15,500–£22,500

herts.ac.uk/study/open-days-and-events/undergraduate-events/undergraduate-open-days
herts.ac.uk/study/fees-and-funding

# University of the Highlands and Islands

Undergraduates at the University of the Highlands and Islands (UHI) can expect jaw-dropping scenery and a unique student experience. Its 12 colleges and research institutions, and more than 70 local learning centres, spread out across hundreds of miles.

They stretch from Sabhal Mòr Ostaig, on the Isle of Skye – the only centre of higher and further education in the world to provide its programmes entirely through Gaelic – to Shetland in the far northeast of Scotland and Campbeltown in the southwest.

Given its unparalleled locations, UHI has been using blended learning for more than 20 years to deliver teaching and learning, mixing online delivery with fieldwork and self-study. It is rooted in its communities, with a mission to provide locally-available higher education intended to boost the region's development by offering both further and higher education courses.

UHI has the most students who are the first in their family to go to a Scottish university (49.5%) and ranks third overall in our social inclusion index for Scotland.

Applications to the university have doubled in the past decade. Over half the students are aged over 21 at the start of their courses and more than 3,000 undergraduates study part-time, often juggling studies with work and childcare.

Course portfolios reflect needs near each campus. UHI works with diverse organisations including the Cairngorms National Park Authority and SSE, the energy company. Specsavers collaborated in the development of its optometry degree.

The latest Research Excellence Framework (REF 2021) found that nearly three-quarters of UHI research submitted was world-leading or internationally excellent, highlighting Earth systems and environmental science.

UHI's disparate sites, with a large number of part-time staff and further education students, make comparisons with other universities a challenge. It exited our overall rankings in 2017.

Among newly launched undergraduate degrees are theatre industry practice, sustainable architectural studies and Gaelic. There are graduate apprenticeships in civil engineering, construction and built environment, business and management, and early learning and childcare.

Colleges vary from outposts in Perth, Elgin and Inverness, where there are a dozen specialist research facilities, to much smaller research bases on the Isle of Lewis. A £9.5 million Life Sciences Innovation Centre opened in 2023 on the UHI Inverness campus, with funding to increase collaboration between academic researchers and industry.

UHI Perth is home to the Academy of Sport and Wellbeing, and there are sports halls at Inverness and Moray, as well as outdoor and watersports facilities at Fort William. At the Moray School of Art, students have access to an art exhibition space.

Most students live locally but the university offers more than 600 rooms at eight of its locations, just under half of them at UHI Inverness. Private rental and host family options are also used by students.

A "green button" online counselling service provides support via webcam, instant messaging, telephone or email.

UHI has 30 scholarships, bursaries and discretionary funds aimed at diverse groups, including students of engineering, aquaculture, songwriting and production students, and nursing.

---

**UHI House Perth Road Inverness IV2 3JH**
info@uhi.ac.uk
uhi.ac.uk
hisa.uhi.ac.uk

**Overall ranking N/A**

**Accommodation**
University provided places 639
Catered £157 per week
Self-catered £108–£188 per week

**Student numbers**
Undergraduates 5,256
Applications per place 1.6:1
Overall offer rate 60.7%

**Fees**
UK fees £0–£1,820
RUK fees £9,250
International fees £14,988–£15,996

uhi.ac.uk/en/studying-at-uhi/open-days/
uhi.ac.uk/en/studying-at-uhi/how-much-will-it-cost

# University of Huddersfield

The origins of the University of Huddersfield, one of the post-1992 institutions, lie in the Young Men's Mental Improvement Society, founded in 1841 with about 400 students. Today the West Yorkshire university has more than 23,000 students and is pouring £250 million of investment into creating a National Health Innovation Campus to tackle regional health inequalities.

The first of six buildings opened in 2024, named in honour of Daphne Steele, who became Britain's first black nursing matron in 1964. It has clinical teaching and research facilities to train nurses, midwives and other medical staff, plus psychology laboratories and specialist sports provision.

A focus on teaching quality is paying off: Huddersfield's lecturers have won 22 National Teaching Fellowships since 2008, the highest number in the country. The university maintained its gold record in the government's Teaching Excellence Framework (TEF 2023) by notching up gold overall and gold for both student experience and student outcomes.

Huddersfield was among the 40% of UK universities facing budget deficits in 2023–24 due to static tuition fees, inflation and a sector-wide decline in international student enrolments. In our analysis of the latest National Student Survey, satisfaction with teaching quality tumbled 17 places to 69th and satisfaction with the wider experience fell ten places, also to 69th.

Its best performances in the Research Excellence Framework (REF 2021) were in music and creative writing, but results were not strong enough to prevent an 18-place fall to 79th in our research quality index, compared with its position after REF 2014.

The university recently introduced degrees in civil engineering and musical theatre, and an integrated master's in optometry. It is growing its portfolio of degree apprenticeships to include training for academic professionals, diagnostic radiographers and digital learning designers.

Collaboration with more than 500 employers helps to keep the curriculum in line with industry needs. Huddersfield is ranked 70th for graduate prospects overall, based on the proportion of graduates in highly skilled jobs or further study 15 months after leaving.

The Queensgate campus, two minutes from the town centre, has purpose-built facilities by the Huddersfield Narrow Canal. A decade of development has produced the £31 million Joseph Priestley Building for science subjects and the £30 million Barbara Hepworth Building, whose digital and physical workshop facilities are designed for experimentation by art and design students.

Societies cover a wide range of interests and help to build community spirit among undergraduates. If Huddersfield's lively social life begins to pall, the brighter lights of Leeds and Manchester are nearby.

Students can find willing listeners among the university's team of wellbeing and mental health advisers and counsellors. HudLets, a student accommodation office run by the students' union, works with independent halls of residence and private landlords but the university does not own any accommodation. Most undergraduates live at home.

About three in ten new undergraduates qualify for financial aid. A first-year scholarship of £1,000 is available to students from low-income households who arrive with more than 120 UCAS tariff points.

---

**Queensgate Huddersfield HD1 3DH**
study@hud.ac.uk
hud.ac.uk
huddersfieldsu.co.uk

**Overall ranking =78**
(last year 76)

**Accommodation**
University provided places 1,367
Self-catered £88–£222 per week

**Student numbers**
Undergraduates 11,151
Applications per place 5.1:1
Overall offer rate 71.4%

**Fees**
UK fees £9,250
International fees £16,500–£19,800

hud.ac.uk/open-days/undergraduate/
hud.ac.uk/undergraduate/fees-and-finance

# University of Hull

Progressive thinking abounds in the ivy-clad redbrick buildings of Hull, one of Britain's oldest universities. It is investing in the campus on the outskirts of the city to become carbon-neutral by its centenary in 2027.

It also invests in its undergraduates with financial help extended to one in four students. The Chancellor's Scholarship was introduced in 2024, providing a full fee waiver to ten undergraduates in any subject each year.

Six bursaries of £2,400 a year are given to medical students from low-income households and there are merit-based awards for students who excel in maths and sport. A £10,000 scholarship paid over three years goes to an economics undergraduate from a low-income background.

Based in a region with comparatively low participation in higher education, the university performs well in our social inclusion index, where it ranks 10th overall. Hull's status as an official partner of Team GB, which extends to 2028, has been a game-changer for students on and off the sports field, providing them with opportunities to volunteer, gain work experience and take part in study initiatives and motivational talks.

The university was rated gold overall in the government's Teaching Excellence Framework (TEF 2023) underpinned by gold for the student experience and silver for student outcomes. Having previously rated silver, it was lauded for its "course content and delivery that inspires students to actively engage in and commit to their learning".

In the Research Excellence Framework (REF 2021), 82% of Hull's submissions were assessed as world-leading or internationally excellent, lifting it two places in our research quality index to 52nd. Since then, Hull has joined the Turing University Network, which unites researchers to work on global challenges in data science and AI, and it is leading the £2 million COAST-R project working to protect precarious coastal communities.

Satisfaction rates have shot up in our analysis of the National Student Survey, reflecting Hull's consolidation of support services into a single location on campus and enhanced pastoral and academic support. The university ranks 25th in the UK for satisfaction with teaching quality (up from 50th in our previous edition) and 34th for the wider undergraduate experience (up 25 places).

Everything is within a ten-minute walk on Hull's self-contained campus, where developments include a data science, AI and modelling (DAIM) facility. Virtual clinical environments enhance provision for healthcare students. For sports scientists, there is a new strength and conditioning suite alongside the laboratories.

The university's art collection in the Brynmor Jones Library specialises in art in Britain from 1890 to 1940, and Middleton Hall is a 400-seat cultural venue. Asylum is Hull's on-campus nightclub.

First-years are guaranteed a room if they apply by October 1. Shared live-and-learn spaces are being introduced in the Courtyard halls of residence on campus.

Any student who may be struggling to cope can turn to the mental health and wellbeing team for an appointment – or time with a therapy dog. There are self-help tools online and support around the clock via a student assistance programme.

**Cottingham Road Hull HU6 7RX**
study@hull.ac.uk
hull.ac.uk
hulluniunion.com

**Overall ranking 60**
(last year 67)

**Accommodation**
University provided places 2,229
Self-catered £150–£280 per week

**Student numbers**
Undergraduates 9,971
Applications per place 3.3:1
Overall offer rate 75.9

**Fees**
UK fees £9,250
International fees £16,500–£19,500
Medicine £43,950

hull.ac.uk/choose-hull/study-at-hull/visit-us/open-days
hull.ac.uk/choose-hull/study-at-hull/money

# Imperial College London

On your (exam) marks, get set, go! Applications to study at Imperial College London have doubled in a decade and getting into the UK's only specialist higher education institution for science, engineering, technology, medicine and business is tougher than ever.

At least nine people apply for each place and it's not hard to understand why. Imperial is our University of the Year for Graduate Employment.

The research heavyweight launched a new strategy in 2024, guided by the principle of "science for humanity". It plans to set up Imperial Futures: four cross-cutting "schools of convergence science" allowing academics from different disciplines to work with each other on global challenges. They will consider human and artificial intelligence; health, medtech and robotics; climate, energy and sustainability; and space, security and telecommunications.

From its west London stronghold, Imperial hopes to develop a British Silicon Valley. The Imperial WestTech Corridor will span the South Kensington campus, the Paddington Life Sciences innovation cluster centred around the St Mary's Hospital campus, the White City campus where partnerships with research businesses are based and Silwood Park, the university's rural site near Ascot.

Imperial is first in our research quality rating, having beaten Cambridge to the top spot in our analysis of the latest Research Excellence Framework (REF 2021), with 55% of its work assessed as world-leading. Its global clout was underlined by a rise to second place in the QS World University Rankings 2025, behind Massachusetts Institute of Technology.

The involvement of so many leading researchers in undergraduate teaching is a big draw as students have a chance of taking part in their projects. The university was rated gold overall in the government's Teaching Excellence Framework (TEF 2023).

In the National Student Survey, satisfaction rates have been less consistent, however. It is rated 33rd for its students' evaluation of the wider experience, falling from 12th in our previous edition.

Imperial tops our table for graduate prospects, based on the percentage of graduates who move on to highly skilled jobs or further study within 15 months (95.9%). Industry-facing activities and careers fairs keep the talent pipeline moving.

There are eight campuses across the capital and one in Ascot. Undergraduates in most subjects are based in South Kensington. There are more than 350 student-run clubs and societies to choose from and if anyone struggles to find the right fit, they can get help to set up their own.

All first-years who apply by the deadline are guaranteed a space in halls, from £136 (for a bed in a twin room) to £346 a week. After that, students must brace themselves for London's competitive rental market.

Personal tutors are the first point of contact for academic issues. Health and wellbeing services on campus include confidential counselling, meditation and mindfulness, and Imperial has a multifaith centre for worship.

Four in ten new UK students received the Imperial Bursary in 2022–23, worth between £1,000 and £5,000 per year of study on a sliding scale for undergraduates with annual household incomes up to £70,000.

---

**Exhibition Road South Kensington London SW7 2AZ**
engineering.admissions@imperial.ac.uk;
medicine.ug.admissions@imperial.ac.uk;
ns.admissions@imperial.ac.uk;
bs.recruitment@imperial.ac.uk
imperial.ac.uk
imperialcollegeunion.org

**Overall ranking 6**
(last year 5)

**Accommodation**
University provided places 2,977
Self-catered £177–£346 per week

**Student numbers**
Undergraduates 11,739
Applications per place 9.8:1
Overall offer rate 33.1%

**Fees**
UK fees £9,250
International fees £37,900–£41,650
Medicine £53,700

imperial.ac.uk/study/visit/undergraduate/open-days/
imperial.ac.uk/study/ug/fees-and-funding

## Keele University

Set in a leafy 600 acres near Stoke-on-Trent, the university's campus, known as the "Keele bubble", is home to a lively students' union and offers a self-contained sense of security and community.

Founded in 1949, Keele championed the then radical principles of interdisciplinary and multidisciplinary scholarship, including dual honours. It has embraced degree apprenticeships and continues to fly the flag for a broad-based higher education.

Through its Global Challenge Pathways, introduced in 2022, elective study options can be taken alongside a core degree and undergraduates engage with debates in issues such as social justice, sustainability, digital futures and global health.

Keele is comfortably in the upper half of our research quality index, based on outcomes of the latest Research Excellence Framework (REF 2021), in which 80% of the work it submitted was rated world-leading or internationally excellent. Some of the best results were in allied health; dentistry; agriculture; communication and media studies; archaeology; and general engineering.

The university was rated gold overall in the Teaching Excellence Framework (TEF 2023), repeating its success in the previous assessment six years earlier, bolstered by gold for the student experience and silver for student outcomes.

Rates of student satisfaction tumbled during the Covid pandemic but results of the National Student Survey analysis indicate that Keele – formerly our University of the Year for Student Experience – is getting back on track. It ranks 93rd for teaching quality (up from =104th in the previous edition) and 70th for the wider experience (a 20-place improvement).

Keele outperforms many pre-1992 universities in our social inclusion index, where it places well inside the upper half of UK universities at 53rd. It is 20th for recruitment of students from deprived areas.

Undergraduates may be eligible for up to £1,500 to support their academic and non-academic student experience, such as payments for a laptop or gym membership. There are also academic awards and externally sponsored scholarships.

The country's largest campus offers all the amenities of a small town – shops, a bank, a health centre and a pharmacy, along with bars and restaurants and even a hotel. The university's low-carbon energy generation park became fully operational in 2021.

Keele's latest business facility, Innovation Centre 7, focuses on digital technologies and brings small to medium-sized enterprises together with academics and students. A new mixed-use facility, Keele in Town, in nearby Newcastle-under-Lyme is due to open during the 2024–25 academic year. Next on the horizon is an Institute of Technology located in Stafford.

An active students' union and more than 200 clubs and societies contribute to the social scene. Sports facilities include tennis courts, a bouldering wall and a gym.

First-years who apply by the end of June deadline are guaranteed a place in halls of residence on campus.

Opportunities to discuss the benefits that good nutrition, exercise and connecting with others have on anxiety and mood are part of Keele's "whole community" approach to supporting students' mental health. Help is available through the Student Inclusion and Accessibility department.

**Keele ST5 5BG**
enquiries@keele.ac.uk
keele.ac.uk
keelesu.com

**Overall ranking =57**
(last year 68)

**Accommodation**
University provided places 2,505
Self-catered £109–£207 per week

**Student numbers**
Undergraduates 8,369
Applications per place 5.6:1
Overall offer rate 66.7%

**Fees**
UK fees £9,250
International fees £19,500–£28,000
Medicine £45,100

keele.ac.uk/study/opendays/undergraduateopendays/
keele.ac.uk/study/undergraduate/tuitionfeesandfunding

# University of Kent

Darwin, Turing, Woolf and Keynes are among the British scholars after whom the University of Kent's six colleges are named. Each has its own academic and residential facilities, and they fast become the epicentre of students' social life, especially in the first year.

Further attractions are to be found off campus in the student-friendly cathedral city of Canterbury and there is a second site at Medway, reached by a free shuttle bus.

One of the 1960s generation of universities, Kent enjoys a stable history in our academic league table, where it has been placed no lower than the mid-fifties since our first edition in 1998.

In the Teaching Excellence Framework (TEF 2023) Kent was rated silver overall (down from gold in the previous assessment, six years earlier), achieving silver for both the underpinning factors of student experience and student outcomes.

A strong performance in the latest Research Excellence Framework (REF 2021) nudged the university up a place, to =32nd, in our research quality index, holding its own against improving results sector-wide. The best performers were in architecture; classics; history; law; philosophy; social work and social policy; theology; and music and drama.

Rates of student satisfaction are improving, having tumbled during the pandemic. Our analysis of the latest National Student Survey puts Kent in 82nd place for students' evaluation of their teaching quality (up from =107th in our previous edition) and =72nd for the wider experience (a 25-place gain).

In common with many universities, Kent is responding to financial challenges – it was a big recruiter of students from the EU – and adapting its course portfolio "to better match future student demand". It is closing more than 50 undergraduate programmes across Canterbury and Medway from 2025, among them health and social care, music and art history, but retaining modern languages. There are new psychology-based degrees and economics-related courses.

At the Canterbury campus, set in 300 acres, recent developments include upgraded facilities for the natural sciences division and high-spec teaching laboratories for computing. Students on courses within the school of architecture and planning have been afforded more studio space in the Marlowe Building.

The Kent and Medway Medical School, a collaboration with Canterbury Christ Church University, offers about 100 places a year. The Medway site houses the School of Pharmacy and the Centre for Music and Audio Technology.

Kent is one of the best-provided universities for accommodation, which includes more than 600 catered rooms, and extends a housing guarantee to all first-years who apply by the end of June deadline.

There are plenty of student-centric venues among Canterbury's cobbled streets and the seaside charms of Whitstable and Margate are easily reached by public transport.

Student services range from counselling and mental health advice to wellbeing and addiction support. There is specific help for disabled and neurodivergent students.

The Kent Financial Support Package is open to those from households with incomes up to £30,000 and who meet other widening participation criteria. Merit-based scholarships are offered in several subjects.

---

**Canterbury CT2 7NZ**
AdmissionsKV@kent.ac.uk
kent.ac.uk
www.kentunion.co.uk

**Overall ranking =40**
(last year 52)

**Accommodation**
University provided places 6,090
Catered £160–£296 per week
Self-catered £129–£258 per week

**Student numbers**
Undergraduates 13,300
Applications per place 4.2:1
Overall offer rate 89.2%

**Fees**
UK fees £9,250
International fees £18,600–£22,700
Medicine £47,900

kent.ac.uk/courses/visit/open-day-dates
kent.ac.uk/courses/fees-and-funding

# King's College London

King's College London (KCL) is digging deep to invest in scientific education by excavating the Quad at its Strand campus to redevelop 3,000 sq m of subterranean real estate into laboratories and workspaces. Building on its history of scientific breakthroughs – which includes discovering the structure of DNA, developing the theory of electromagnetism and conducting the world's first human-to-human blood transfusion – KCL is investing £45.5 million to power the future of its explorations.

The university has launched two interdisciplinary research institutes, Net Zero Centre and the Centre for Physical Science of Life, and been busy recruiting 64 academic staff.

KCL graduates do well in the jobs market – it is placed =13th in our analysis of the latest graduate outcomes survey. Students are in the thick of all that London has to offer by virtue of its prime central locations, most of them close to the banks of the Thames near London Bridge and Waterloo.

The university ranks eighth in our research quality index after 55.1% of the work submitted to the latest Research Excellence Framework (REF 2021) was judged to be world-leading. Its best results were in allied health subjects; business and management; classics; clinical medicine; sport and exercise sciences; chemistry; modern languages; engineering; and theology.

KCL is rated silver overall and for the student experience by the government's Teaching Excellence Framework (TEF 2023). Assessors gave it gold, their highest grading, for student outcomes, reflecting its "tailored approaches that are highly effective in ensuring students succeed in and progress beyond their studies".

In global league tables that do not include student satisfaction in their metrics, KCL fares well. It is placed =40th by QS and =38th by Times Higher Education in their latest world rankings. The Florence Nightingale Faculty of Nursing, Midwifery & Palliative Care is rated No 1 in the UK and second in the world for nursing in the 2024 QS rankings.

In common with other London-based and research-led institutions, it sits in the bottom ten for how students rate teaching quality, although it fares better with feedback about the wider experience (=116th) in our new National Student Survey (NSS) analysis. Both are improvements on last year's student satisfaction ratings, contributing to a three-place rise in our main academic ranking for the university, lifting it inside the top 25.

The Strand site and the Waterloo campus house most of the non-medical departments. Nursing and midwifery are based at Waterloo, while medicine and dentistry are mainly at Guy's Hospital and the St Thomas' Hospital campus.

Halls of residence are spread out across the capital, with accommodation guaranteed to all first-years who apply by the deadline.

KCL provides support for students' welfare in areas such as race, sexuality and gender, and its Institute of Psychiatry, Psychology & Neuroscience offers individual and group counselling.

About a third of entrants in 2024 received some form of financial assistance. The King's Living Bursary is open to UK students from households with incomes up to £42,875.

**Strand London WC2R 2LS**
newstudents@kcl.ac.uk
kcl.ac.uk
kclsu.org

**Overall ranking =24**
(last year 27)

**Accommodation**
University provided places 5,590
Catered £284–£385 per week
Self-catered £155–£519 per week

**Student numbers**
Undergraduates 22,033
Applications per place 10.2:1
Overall offer rate 38.5%

**Fees**
UK fees £9,250
International fees £10,944–£54,313
Medicine £48,600

kcl.ac.uk/study/undergraduate/events/open-days
kcl.ac.uk/study/undergraduate/fees-and-funding

# Kingston University

A best-of-both-worlds suburban riverside location, with a 30-minute commute to central London, is one of the attractions of Kingston University, as is its new education model. Future Skills embeds training to boost employability within every undergraduate programme and prepares its graduates to stand out in an increasingly AI-influenced careers landscape.

The strategy gives students skills that employers value, such as problem solving, adaptability and digital competency.

Kingston's creative courses are among its most successful, achieving some of the university's best results in the Research Excellence Framework (REF 2021) and contributing to a 20-place rise in our research quality index, where it ranks 71st.

It also performed well in the Teaching Excellence Framework (TEF 2023), winning triple gold ratings (up from bronze), overall and for both underpinning factors of student experience and student outcomes. The Future Skills framework was credited by assessors as successfully contributing to "clear articulation of the range of educational gains students are intended to achieve, and why these are highly relevant to them and their future ambitions".

Kingston students are among the upper half nationally (61st) for rates of satisfaction with teaching quality. In our analysis of the results of the latest National Student Survey, it does better still for students' evaluation of their broad experience (55th).

The student population is one of the ten most ethnically diverse (65.1%) and more than half of its recruits are the first in their family to go to university (51.4%, 36th). An inclusive curriculum framework has been designed to make all students feel that they belong.

Courses introduced recently include marketing; criminal justice; psychology and counselling; interaction design; and historic building conservation.

Students are based at four campuses in southwest London. Penrhyn Road and Knights Park are near the town centre, Kingston Hill is a couple of miles away and a short bus ride links to Roehampton Vale.

The £50 million Town House at Penrhyn Road, which won the 2021 Royal Institute of British Architects Stirling prize, is a focal point offering an auditorium and informal learning spaces as well as a studio theatre, dance studios and a library.

The Kingston School of Art is based at Knights Park and Roehampton Vale features its own Learjet and flight simulator for aerospace students.

Tolworth Court outdoor sports facilities are three miles from the main campus and the Visconti Studio is the university's standout music facility, featuring an octagonal live room stocked with instruments and rare recording equipment.

Full-time students in their first year get priority for places but there is no accommodation guarantee. Just under 2,300 spaces are available in halls.

Students can access appointments with the disability and mental health service. There is a counselling team and an online social group aims to help tackle feelings of isolation.

Financial support includes the £2,000 Kingston Bursary, awarded to 500 entrants from low-income households in their first year. For those who have left care or are estranged from their families, bursaries of £1,500 per year of study are available.

---

**Holmwood House Grove Crescent Kingston upon Thames KT1 2EE**
admissionsops@kingston.ac.uk
kingston.ac.uk
kingstonstudents.net

**Overall ranking 97**
(last year 98)

**Accommodation**
University provided places 2,300
Self-catered £126–£226 per week

**Student numbers**
Undergraduates 11,993
Applications per place 5.0:1
Overall offer rate 73.5%

**Fees**
UK fees £6,300 (Foundation Early Years) – £9,250
International fees £16,800–£21,500

kingston.ac.uk/open-days/undergraduate/
kingston.ac.uk/fees-funding-and-payments

# Lancaster University

Control, alt, develop: Lancaster's InfoLab building on its 560-acre campus, visible from the M6 motorway, has been upgraded as part of a semi-immersive decision theatre and "data cyber quarter" laboratory. The facility is one of the largest of its type in the UK, supporting undergraduate degrees in computer science, cybersecurity and data science as well as postgraduate courses and research.

The university has recruited more than 30 academics to focus on digital threats and support cybersecurity initiatives in the northwest of England. It is part of a £220 million investment since 2013 to provide purpose-built facilities that help to maintain its position in the elite top 20 of our academic league table.

A research-led university founded in 1964, Lancaster reaped strong results in the latest Research Excellence Framework (REF 2021), with 91% of its work assessed as internationally excellent or world-leading. Lancaster outdoes seven Russell Group institutions in our research quality index, ranking 19th, with linguistics and mathematics producing some of the best results.

It is regularly among the top 150 universities in the world according to QS (=141st for 2025) and has rates of student satisfaction to match the research pedigree. Lancaster is 14th for satisfaction with the wider student experience and 30th for their evaluation of teaching quality, according to our analysis of the National Student Survey.

Awarded gold overall in the Teaching Excellence Framework (TEF 2023), the university was found to offer "a supportive learning environment in which students have access to a readily available range of outstanding quality academic support tailored to their needs".

There are new degrees in international management, data science, cybersecurity, and English literature and politics, as well as a suite of global religions courses. The option of a placement year or a year abroad is embedded in a wide range of courses including architecture, mathematics with economics, and English literature and politics.

Up five places and ranked 29th overall for proportion of graduates in highly skilled work or further study after 15 months, Lancaster's engagement with industry is sector-leading.

Impressive facilities include the Margaret Fell lecture theatre, the biggest on campus with capacity for 400 people, while Lancaster's architecture studio provides specialist facilities for up to 48 students. Among the newest additions is a second engineering building that features an electron microscope suite.

All students belong to one of nine colleges, where they sleep, study and socialise. There are more than 160 societies and good sporting facilities. Students can stretch their legs in the woods or commune with the campus ducks.

Through the university's mental health service, support is available from counsellors, social workers, mental health nurses, cognitive behavioural therapists and occupational therapists.

Undergraduates seeking accommodation can select two preference combinations of college/room/letting period before the university allocates places. First-years who meet the deadline are guaranteed a place.

A high proportion (44%) of UK undergraduates received support from Lancaster's wide-ranging financial package in 2024. This includes a £1,000 annual bursary for UK students with a household income of less than £30,000.

---

**Bailrigg Lancaster LA1 4YW**
ugadmissions@lancaster.ac.uk
lancaster.ac.uk
lancastersu.co.uk

**Overall ranking 12**
(last year 14)

**Accommodation**
University provided places 6,700
Catered £214–£238 per week
Self-catered £125–£236 per week

**Student numbers**
Undergraduates 12,855
Applications per place 5.3:1
Overall offer rate 84.6%

**Fees**
UK fees £9,250
International fees £23,750–£28,675
Medicine £45,315

lancaster.ac.uk/study/open-days/undergraduate-open-days/
lancaster.ac.uk/study/fees-and-funding/

# University of Leeds

More than 69,000 hopefuls applied for a place at this redbrick favourite last year, attracted by the lively nightlife as well as the research-led pedigree. The University of Leeds' future-facing academic ambition is to create graduates who make positive impacts as global citizens.

As such all students engage with the Leeds Curriculum, which aims to broaden their intellectual horizons and requires everyone to produce a final-year research project.

The university is focusing on research into pressing global challenges at its new Futures Institutes, the first of which – the Priestley Centre for Climate Futures – opened for the 2024 academic year. Next up are centres for health, society and education.

90% of a submission by Leeds academics across 28 subject areas was rated world-leading or internationally excellent in the latest Research Excellence Framework (REF 2021), up from 80% in the previous national assessment in 2014.

This led to a seven-place rise in our research quality index, into the top 20. Leeds is a consistent presence in the QS World University rankings, where it is =82nd in the 2025 edition, down from 75th the year before.

Rates of student satisfaction have varied. Leeds remains outside the top 100 for teaching quality (127th), although it re-entered it for the wider experience (=92nd) in our new analysis of the National Student Survey.

Awarding Leeds a silver rating overall in the Teaching Excellence Framework (TEF 2023) – down from gold in the previous TEF, six years before – assessors gave it a bronze for its student experience. Even so, the panel commended "outstanding rates of continuation and completion".

Developments at Leeds students' union should help to boost rates of student satisfaction. The Essentials hub gives students a route to wellbeing and financial literacy support services, and the Crossroads entertainment lounge has esports and gaming equipment.

Leeds supports students to complete work placements but is down 12 places for its proportion of graduates in highly skilled work or further study after 15 months, ranking =35th overall. Recent initiatives include students taking up placements at UK fintech companies through the Centre for Finance, Innovation and Technology.

A ten-minute walk from the city centre, the university campus continues to evolve. Helix, a digital innovation and learning space, includes immersive technology and prototyping equipment.

Sport is well provided for and there are more than 300 student-led clubs and societies. There are plenty of green spaces in an urban setting that is easy to navigate.

The university converted a gym into a holistic wellbeing studio and boosted staff numbers within its counselling and wellbeing service. Students who register for support are offered initial counselling, mental health or wellbeing appointments.

Awards include the Leeds Bursary, worth £1,000, £1,500 or £2,000 a year to students from households with incomes up to £36,000. There are also subject-specific scholarships based on academic merit.

Leeds guarantees a room to first-years who meet the housing deadlines and academic offer. Much of the accommodation is further from the city centre than the main campus.

---

**Woodhouse Lane Leeds LS2 9JT**
study@leeds.ac.uk
leeds.ac.uk
luu.org.uk

**Overall ranking 29**
(last year 24)

**Accommodation**
University provided places 8,483
Catered £187–£244 per week
Self-catered £107–£215 per week

**Student numbers**
Undergraduates 26,683
Applications per place 8.9:1
Overall offer rate 56.9%

**Fees**
UK fees £9,250
International fees £22,250–£27,750
Medicine £39,750

leeds.ac.uk/undergraduate-open-days
leeds.ac.uk /undergraduate-fees/doc/fees-undergraduate-fees

# Leeds Arts University

Arts and culture continue to thrive at the north of England's only specialist arts institution. Student life is based on the Blenheim Walk campus, a ten-minute walk from Leeds city centre, which has studios for film, music and photography, as well as a 230-seat auditorium and a specialist arts library.

The university, which has its own gallery and a graduate show, was founded in 1846 as the Leeds College of Art. Although relatively small, with about 2,000 undergraduates, it is expanding its course offering in line with growing student numbers and has been building a research culture.

Leeds Arts showcased its work for the first time in the Research Excellence Framework (REF 2021). It entered at the foot of our research rankings (131st) but work within the history of art, design and architecture departments was recognised as world-leading.

It was rated triple silver in the Teaching Excellence Framework (TEF 2023), with the panel noting "very high rates of successful progression rates" of Leeds Arts students. The university has a commendable record on student retention, with a continuation rate of 96.6%.

Students here are usually pretty content: only four years ago the university was in the top 20 for their evaluation of teaching quality, as expressed in the National Student Survey. It is in the upper half of UK universities for both teaching quality and the broad undergraduate experience in our analysis of the NSS.

Students can build their portfolios through live briefs and opportunities to show work at trade fairs, studios and galleries. Graduates can apply for funded studio and project spaces in Leeds.

Job prospects soon after graduation are always a challenge for art and design specialisms. According to our analysis tracking those in highly skilled work or postgraduate study after 15 months, Leeds Arts is fourth from bottom among UK universities.

New degrees in music production; games art; games design; and acting for screen began in 2024.

An extension to the Blenheim Walk building includes a 24-hour student hub, informal work areas and a roof garden. There is an arts and cultural slant to student societies, among them life drawing and open-mike nights. Leeds is home to five universities and renowned for its vibrant nightlife.

Leeds Arts follows a holistic approach to supporting students, who can access meetings with welfare advisers, mental health advisers or counsellors. Compassion-focused art psychotherapy is offered. Students are encouraged to develop an ethical understanding of consent via Consent Collective.

Halls are owned and managed privately, and students deal directly with the provider. There are enough places to house all first-years, although the university makes a guarantee only to international students who apply by the deadline.

Skin's Chancellor Scholarship of £3,000 a year for three years is named in honour of the university's first chancellor, the singer with Skunk Anansie. It is awarded to two UK students and one international student each year. The Creative Practice Support Bursary provides up to £1,100, paid in three instalments over three years to those from low-income households.

**Blenheim Walk Leeds LS2 9AQ**
admissions@leeds-art.ac.uk
leeds-art.ac.uk
leedsartsunion.org.uk

**Overall ranking 92**
(last year =89)

**Accommodation**
University provided places 592
Self-catered £123–£187 per week

**Student numbers**
Undergraduates 2,185
Applications per place 7.3:1
Overall offer rate 54.2%

**Fees**
UK fees £9,250
International fees £17,500–£18,600

leeds-art.ac.uk/apply/open-days/undergraduate-open-days
leeds-art.ac.uk/apply/undergraduate-fees-and-finance

# Leeds Beckett University

If the city's famous nightlife and relative affordability have not already sold it to prospective students, Leeds Beckett University can field a fine sporting pedigree. On the honours board are the triathlete Alex Yee, who struck gold at the Paris Olympics (sport and exercise science 2021), Sam Quek, field hockey player turned TV presenter (sport and exercise science 2010), Lucy Bronze, the England footballer (sports studies 2013), and the Paralympian cyclist Dame Sarah Storey (sport and exercise science 2000).

The Carnegie School of Sport at Leeds Beckett University (formerly Leeds Metropolitan) has excellent facilities and students who dream of joining the list are nurtured by the Leeds Talent Hub.

The university has nine academic faculties operating across two campuses, Headingley and City. It has edged into the top 100 in our research quality index, moving up three places to 98th with 53% of work submitted to the latest Research Excellence Framework (REF 2021) rated world-leading or internationally excellent. The best results were in sports sciences, followed by allied health and building subjects.

Leeds Beckett was rated bronze overall in the Teaching Excellence Framework (TEF 2023), down from silver in the previous assessment. For the student experience, the TEF panel awarded Leeds Beckett silver, reflecting improved rates of student satisfaction in the National Student Survey (it was 38th for satisfaction with the overall student experience and 48th for satisfaction with teaching quality in 2024). TEF gave the university bronze for student outcomes.

A relatively low continuation rate (90.4%, =90th) keeps Leeds Beckett in the lower reaches of our main academic table. In July 2024 the university regulator, the Office for Students (OfS), issued an improvement notice after 69% of its full-time computing students completed their course (below the required threshold of 75%).

Leeds Beckett said: "The university has implemented an action plan in respect of the subject area concerned and monitoring shows that we continue to make good progress."

The Carnegie School of Education opened newly refurbished facilities in Caedmon Hall at Headingley for the start of the 2024–25 academic year. The £80 million School of Arts building on the City campus has more than 2,500 students on 40 courses. Resources for research and hands-on learning have been boosted at the School of Health, which has a biomedical research laboratory.

Courses introduced recently include acting; fashion design; software engineering; business management with sustainable development; and applied sport studies in tennis.

Leeds Beckett guarantees accommodation to all first-years who make the university their first choice and apply by the deadline, although more than half of undergraduates live at home and commute.

Bursaries are extended to students from low-income and other disadvantaged backgrounds, covering work placements and professional development.

A multidisciplinary team offers counselling and mental health support for students, who can self-refer online. An initial consultation may lead to short-term counselling or referral to external services.

Ranked =66th in our social inclusion index overall, Leeds Beckett is in the top 20 for its proportion of white working-class male students (7.5%).

---

**City Campus Leeds LS1 3HE**
admissionenquiries@leedsbeckett.ac.uk
leedsbeckett.ac.uk
leedsbeckettsu.co.uk

**Overall ranking 88**
(last year 101)

**Accommodation**
University provided places 2,845
Self-catered £150–£239 per week

**Student numbers**
Undergraduates 15,985
Applications per place 5.2:1
Overall offer rate 77.6%

**Fees**
UK fees £9,250
International fees £8,000–£16,000

leedsbeckett.ac.uk/undergraduate/open-days/
leedsbeckett.ac.uk/undergraduate/financing-your-studies/

# Leeds Trinity University

With seven education institutions and a student population of about 70,000, Leeds is well geared for the changing nature of undergraduate life. After more than 50 years at one campus, Leeds Trinity University opened a second site in 2024 with a trading room, computer science labs and a law court.

The city-centre campus at Trevelyan Square supplements the Horsforth base six miles northwest of Leeds, which hosts a new Health and Life Sciences building.

Leeds Trinity was the first university in Yorkshire to receive the Race Equality Charter bronze award in recognition of its work to improve representation, progression and success of black, Asian and minority ethnic students.

Theology produced its best results in the latest Research Excellence Framework (REF 2021), while sport and exercise sciences, and leisure and tourism also fared well. Leeds Trinity takes 122nd place in our research quality rankings.

Rated triple silver in the government's Teaching Excellence Framework (TEF 2023), it drew praise for its "content and delivery that effectively encourage students to engage in their learning and stretch them to develop their knowledge and skills".

Since the TEF assessment, however, rates of student satisfaction have nosedived, with our analysis of the National Student Survey 2024 ranking Leeds Trinity 85th for teaching quality and 108th for the wider experience – down 61 places and 90 places respectively and at odds with its selling point of offering a personalised approach to study thanks to its relatively small size.

The university is subject to an investigation by the Office for Students (OfS), England's higher education regulator, into its franchised course provision. In 2024 the OfS said in a statement that "potential concerns" had been identified at the institution that "require further scrutiny", in relation to whether courses delivered by Leeds Trinity's subcontracted partners are high quality. At the time of writing, no outcome had been published.

Most of the university's degrees include professional work placements, while volunteering is also credited. It jumped eight places to be ranked =87th based on the proportion of students in highly skilled work or postgraduate study 15 months on from finishing a degree course.

Recent launches include computer science with artificial intelligence; computer science with games development; computer science with cybersecurity; broadcast and digital journalism; building surveying; and digital media production.

The Media Centre is its main hub of cultural and creative life on campus. Sporting facilities at Horsforth include a spin studio and two floors of gym equipment, an athletics track and courts for netball and tennis.

A mental health and wellbeing service provides assessments and therapeutic treatment as necessary. The myLTU app signposts support services and allows students to book appointments.

Halls of residence at Horsforth have space for students who apply by the UCAS deadline date, although there is no accommodation guarantee.

Students entering with AAB or the equivalent qualify for £1,000 academic achievement awards in their first year. The Leeds Trinity Bursary of £500 is awarded to those from low-income backgrounds in the second year of their undergraduate degree.

**Brownberrie Lane Horsforth Leeds LS18 5HD**
admissions@leedstrinity.ac.uk
leedstrinity.ac.uk
ltsu.co.uk

**Overall ranking 112**
(last year 92)

**Accommodation**
University provided places 700
Self-catered £100–£156 per week

**Student numbers**
Undergraduates 9,309
Applications per place 3.2:1
Overall offer rate 78.5%

**Fees**
UK fees £5,760 (Foundation) – £9,250
International fees £12,000–£14,500

leedstrinity.ac.uk/undergraduate/open-days
leedstrinity.ac.uk/study/fees-and-finance

# University of Leicester

With the motto *Ut vitam habeant* – "So that they may have life" – the institution that gave rise to the University of Leicester was founded in 1921 as a memorial to those who died in the First World War. It began awarding its own degrees in 1957 with the granting of a Royal Charter and pioneered DNA forensic science in the 1980s.

Today medicine and dentistry students represent about a tenth of Leicester's undergraduates and the university has opened the Stoneygate Centre for Empathic Healthcare, whose approach to medical education puts empathy at its heart.

In the latest Research Excellence Framework (REF 2021), 89% of the university's work was assessed as world-leading or internationally excellent. Some of the best results were in clinical medicine; archaeology; sports science; and history, contributing to a rise of 11 places in our research quality index.

Leicester sits at =26th, ahead of two of the 24 members of the research-led Russell Group, which Leicester's vice-chancellor, Nishan Canagarajah, would like the university to join. "Everyone looking at Leicester says, 'This should be a Russell Group university'," he said.

The university is committed to space research and Space Park Leicester is forecast to contribute £750 million to Britain's space sector over the next decade, creating 2,500 jobs in the East Midlands.

In our analysis of the National Student Survey, Leicester ranks 11th for student satisfaction with the wider undergraduate experience (up 51 places year-on-year) and 54th for their feelings about teaching quality (up 40). The university achieved a gold rating in the latest Teaching Excellence Framework (TEF 2023).

From September 2025 Leicester launches degrees in biomedical engineering, with both three- and four-year options, plus journalism and marketing.

The university seeks to include work experience opportunities for students in all its degree courses through partnerships with employers. Its endeavours to boost employability produced a three-place rise in our analysis, to =35th, based on the proportion in highly skilled jobs or postgraduate study within 15 months.

Nearly two-thirds (64.4%) of students are from black and ethnic minority backgrounds, putting the university in 11th place, and Leicester ranks 65th for social inclusion overall in England and Wales.

The Freeths legal scholarship is worth £4,000 a year for students from low-participation areas. From 2025 Leicester is offering a merit scholarship for international students, worth £3,000 or £5,000 a year depending on grades.

Modernisation is under way at the compact campus, a mile south of the city centre. The Georgian architecture of the Fielding Johnson Building, where the Law School is based, contrasts with modern academic blocks.

Leicester says all students who apply before September 1 will get a space in halls. Prices range from £77 a week to £263 a week.

There are more than 200 clubs and societies, and the university has a botanic garden as well as sports centres. Students are supported by a wellbeing team and anyone in crisis or managing a long-term condition can turn to counsellors, mental health advisers and workshops.

---

**University Road Leicester LE1 7RH**
admissions@le.ac.uk
le.ac.uk
leicesterunion.com

**Overall ranking =27**
(last year =34)

**Accommodation**
University provided places 4,057
Self-catered £77–£263 per week

**Student numbers**
Undergraduates 11,091
Applications per place 5.5:1
Overall offer rate 69.5%

**Fees**
UK fees £9,250
International fees £18,950–£25,900
Medicine £29,000–£47,000

le.ac.uk/open-days
le.ac.uk/study/undergraduates/fees-funding

# University of Lincoln

The University of Lincoln debuted at the very bottom of the league table in 1998 and now harbours ambitions of being a top-40 university. It has invested £400 million in facilities over the past two decades to keep up with its burgeoning footfall and academic focus.

A school of engineering opened in 2009 and it gained a medical school nine years later. Our 2021 Modern University of the Year is relaunching its on-campus home for contemporary and performing arts as Lincoln Arts Centre and the Barbican Creative Hub, a base for creative businesses in the region, is due to open in 2025.

The university joined an elite group when it was awarded triple gold in the government's Teaching Excellence Framework (TEF 2023). Physical and virtual learning resources were found to be "outstanding".

More than three-quarters (79%) of Lincoln's research was judged to be internationally excellent or world-leading in the latest Research Excellence Framework (REF 2021). History; social policy, allied health professions; and computer science performed well. Against stronger gains elsewhere, the university lost ground in our research rating, going from 58th (based on REF 2014) to 67th.

In 2024 the university was awarded the Queen's Anniversary Prize to recognise its work supporting the agri-food sector.

Lincoln's course portfolio continues to grow, with degrees in diagnostic radiography; chemistry for net zero; general engineering; and forensic toxicology.

The TEF assessors praised the university for deploying and tailoring "approaches that are highly effective in ensuring its students succeed in and progress beyond their studies". However, its performance in the latest Graduate Outcomes survey declined from =79th to 89th, based on the proportion of graduates in highly skilled jobs or postgraduate study 15 months on.

Efforts to widen participation include pre-course transition events and foundation years in more than 40 subjects for students whose qualifications fall short of the standard entry requirements. Lincoln rises eight places to =29th overall in our social inclusion index and its share of white working-class male students is in the top ten.

Home to a cathedral and a castle, Lincoln is a compact city popular with students (and tourists) who appreciate its sense of safety. The university has turned a former industrial site into a waterfront campus hosting resources such as the Great Central Warehouse Library. The Lincoln Science and Innovation Park is a joint venture with the Lincolnshire Co-op.

A sports centre on campus includes outdoor pitches and boxing classes, while the Lincoln Arts Centre has a 450-seat theatre and studio spaces.

Cygnet Wharf halls are reserved for first-year students, with residential wardens on hand around the clock.

Students can access a wellbeing hub via drop-ins, online or over the phone. The WOW (Wellbeing Orientation Welcome) summer school is a two-night experience for students with autism, Asperger's or other conditions that may make the transition to university more challenging.

Most new full-time undergraduate students received financial support in 2024. The University of Lincoln scholarship is awarded automatically to full-time UK undergraduates with household incomes of less than £45,875.

---

**Brayford Pool Lincoln LN6 7TS**
admissions@lincoln.ac.uk
lincoln.ac.uk
lincolnsu.com

**Overall ranking 56**
(last year 55)

**Accommodation**
University provided places 3,891
Self-catered £99–£199 per week

**Student numbers**
Undergraduates 11,819
Applications per place 4.2:1
Overall offer rate 85.4%

**Fees**
UK fees £9,250
International fees £15,900–£17,200
Medicine £36,400

lincoln.ac.uk/studywithus/opendaysandvisits/
undergraduateopendays/
lincoln.ac.uk/studywithus/undergraduatestudy/feesandfunding/

# University of Liverpool

An elite education in the thick of a legendary cultural hub: a rich student experience awaits at the University of Liverpool, a founding member of the research-intensive Russell Group.

The city, one of Britain's friendliest, has nightlife, culture and sport for all tastes. Students on many courses also have an opportunity to study abroad if they fancy a change.

University Square, the gateway to Liverpool's campus, has been redeveloped to be more open and inclusive. A colourful installation – part of the nationwide Neurodiversity Umbrella Project co-ordinated by the ADHD Foundation – underlines the point outside the Foundation Building, the headquarters for student services and careers advice.

Impressive results in the latest Research Excellence Framework (REF 2021) triggered a 16-place rise in our research quality index for Liverpool to 24th, with 91% of its work rated world-leading or internationally excellent, led by veterinary science; chemistry; psychology; and modern languages.

The university was upgraded to gold overall in the government's Teaching Excellence Framework (TEF 2023), and rated gold for student outcomes and silver for the student experience. Assessors praised the university's research and industry connections, which "are used to contribute to an outstanding academic experience for students".

For students on most courses, the university's global reach offers opportunities to study at one of more than 100 partner institutions, from America to South Korea.

Liverpool has produced a decisive return to form in rates of student satisfaction, measured through the annual National Student Survey (NSS). In our new NSS analysis the university ranks 27th for the broad undergraduate experience – a remarkable turnaround from =100th in our previous edition. It has risen 31 places to rank 73rd for students' evaluation of teaching quality.

Despite a two-place fall, from 28th last year, in our analysis of the latest Graduate Outcomes survey (based on leavers in highly skilled jobs or further study 15 months on), Liverpool remains in the top 30. Links with employers such as AstraZeneca, Unilever and Airbus help Liverpool students to get a taste of potential careers, via hackathons, guest lectures and work experience. Businesses in the region also offer internships and placements.

The main campus is about five minutes on foot from the city centre. Liverpool's Digital Innovation Facility (DIF), which opened in 2022, brings together computer science, robotics and engineering research. Students holding an offer or an interview for clinical courses can apply for accommodation from January, without making Liverpool their firm or insurance choice, and are guaranteed accommodation (like all first-years) if they apply by the end of July.

Wellbeing advisers provide ongoing help including clinics addressing low mood or anxiety. Therapeutic services for mental health include counselling and art therapy. A 24-hour confidential phoneline is available for those trying to cope with stress, debt, relationships or study pressures.

About a third of UK undergraduates with household income up to £35,000 receive bursaries from £750 to £2,000 as cash or fee waivers. Other financial aid is available for care leavers, mature or estranged students, and young adult carers.

---

**Liverpool L69 7ZX**
ug-recruitment@liverpool.ac.uk
liverpool.ac.uk
liverpoolguild.org

**Overall ranking 23**
(last year =29)

**Accommodation**
University provided places 4,959
Catered £242 per week
Self-catered £105–£248 per week

**Student numbers**
Undergraduates 21,619
Applications per place 6.7:1
Overall offer rate 72.1%

**Fees**
UK fees £7,500 (Foundation at Carmel College) – £9,250
International fees £22,400–£28,000
Medicine £42,700

liverpool.ac.uk/study/undergraduate/open-days-and-visits/register-for-open-day/
liverpool.ac.uk/study/fees-and-funding/

# Liverpool Hope University

One of the UK's smaller universities, Liverpool Hope maintains a close-knit vibe that allows students to explore the city's epic attractions at their leisure. Hope Park, the main teaching site, is in a suburb four miles south of the bright lights, while the Creative Campus is less than a mile from Lime Street station.

Supporting the university's broadening course offering, the i3 Building is opening at the Hope Park campus, featuring a simulation lab equipped with virtual reality hardware.

Liverpool Hope is Europe's only ecumenical university: students of all faiths and none are welcomed, and graduation ceremonies are held in alternating years at the city's Anglican and Catholic cathedrals.

It recruits the third highest proportion (11.4%) of white working-class male students, the most underrepresented group in higher education, and draws a fifth of its intake from deprived areas. The university ranks =38th overall in our social inclusion index of universities in England and Wales.

It lost ground in the latest Research Excellence Framework (REF 2021) compared with the previous assessment in 2014, dropping from =62nd to 106th. Theology and education produced some of the best results.

Awarding Liverpool Hope triple silver (overall and for the student experience and outcomes) in the Teaching Excellence Framework (TEF 2023), assessors praised "outstanding teaching, feedback and assessment practices".

The university maintains its top-20 rank for undergraduates' evaluation of teaching quality in our analysis of the latest National Student Survey (NSS). It is steady in the top 50 for the broad undergraduate experience.

Arts and wellbeing; contemporary craft; creative industries business management; digital creativity; music production; stage design and scenography; and sport and exercise nutrition have been added to the curriculum. More degrees launch in 2025, in acting; economics; game art and design; digital marketing; religion, theology and spirituality; religion, world views and spirituality; global philosophy and world views; psychology in business; and psychology in education.

The university aims to boost employability through links with Tate Liverpool and the Royal Court Theatre, local authorities and the NHS. However, graduate prospects remain weak and it dropped from 110th to 116th in our analysis of numbers in highly skilled jobs or further study 15 months after leaving.

Recent improvements at Hope Park added a moot courtroom for the School of Law and Criminology. Facilities at the Creative Campus include two theatres and an arts centre.

The students' union runs a buddy scheme and new students living in must attend a welcome talk about alcohol, drugs and sexual consent. Trained therapy dogs lift spirits and the counselling service provides a bridge to other agencies.

Accommodation is at Hope Park, Creative Campus and Aigburth Park. A space is guaranteed for entrants who apply through the main admissions cycle and the university does its best to offer rooms to those who apply through Clearing.

Financial aid is available for care leavers and merit-based performance scholarships reward talent in dance, drama, music and sport. The university awards ten Access to Hope scholarships of £3,000 a year.

---

**Hope Park Taggart Avenue Liverpool L16 9JD**
courses@hope.ac.uk
hope.ac.uk
hopesu.com

**Overall ranking =94**
(last year 88)

**Accommodation**
University provided places 1,140
Self-catered £95–£130 per week

**Student numbers**
Undergraduates 4,316
Applications per place 7.2:1
Overall offer rate 85.5%

**Fees**
UK fees £9,250
International fees £13,000

hope.ac.uk/opendays/
hope.ac.uk/undergraduate/feesandfunding/

# Liverpool John Moores University

Named after the late football-betting businessman of Littlewoods fame, whose philanthropic interests helped to fund its forerunner institutions, Liverpool John Moores University (LJMU) is one of the pioneers of degree apprenticeships.

As part of its 2030 Strategy, the university is boosting its earn-while-you-learn degree provision, launching programmes in 2024-25 such as youth work; transport planning; serious and complex criminal investigation; and construction management.

Among its areas of expertise is the Football Exchange (FEX) at the School of Sport and Exercise Sciences, which engages in research with clubs, governing bodies, commercial enterprises and community schemes.

LJMU achieved a gold rating for its student outcomes in the government's Teaching Excellence Framework (TEF 2023) assessment, underpinning a silver overall for the university and for the student experience.

Results of the latest National Student Survey show an enhanced appreciation for the broad experience by students, whose responses put the university =23rd in our analysis (up 11 places from our previous edition) and in the top 50 for teaching quality (=47th, a 21-place improvement).

LJMU submitted work from more than 600 academic staff in the latest Research Excellence Framework (REF 2021). Astrophysics; sport and exercise sciences; engineering; and English produced some of the best results, with 73.1% of the submission rated world-leading or internationally excellent. But against stronger gains at other universities, it lost nine places in our research quality index, falling to =76th.

The university is introducing five degrees in 2025: politics, philosophy and economics; criminology, international relations and politics; and computer science, offered with three pathways – artificial intelligence, data science or mathematics. Each degree has a foundation year option.

Life at LJMU centres on two campuses, City and Mount Pleasant, supporting about 27,000 students. Connecting them is the 3.5-acre Copperas Hill development, home to the Student Life Building and Sports Building. Specialist facilities include the six-storey, £27 million John Lennon Art and Design Building.

With 4,000 residential spaces in the city, LJMU guarantees accommodation to first-years. There are more than 100 university clubs and societies, and the city's social and cultural scene is hard to beat.

The Sport Building's facilities include an eight-court sports hall and a gym with 120 stations. There are more than 35 sports clubs and LJMU fields teams in the British Universities and Colleges (BUCS) league.

The university's policy on drugs and alcohol prioritises student safety and a team of wellbeing advisers is the first port of call for those experiencing mental health issues.

Support for students who have experience of care or are estranged from their families includes the John Lennon Imagine Award, an annual bursary of £1,000 supported by Yoko Ono's Spirit Foundation. In 2024 three in ten first-years received funding from a £2 million LJMU hardship fund.

Ranking 49th in our social inclusion index, LJMU is fifth in England and Wales for recruitment of white working-class male students, the most underrepresented group in higher education. It recruits more students from Northern Ireland than any university on the UK mainland.

---

**Student Life Building Copperas Hill**
**Liverpool L3 5AH**
courses@ljmu.ac.uk;
international@ljmu.ac.uk
ljmu.ac.uk
jmsu.co.uk

**Overall ranking =66**
(last year =70)

**Accommodation**
University provided places 4,000
Self-catered £85–£180 per week

**Student numbers**
Undergraduates 20,440
Applications per place 5.0:1
Overall offer rate 80.8%

**Fees**
UK fees £9,250
International fees £17,750–£18,250

ljmu.ac.uk/study/undergraduate-students/visit-us/
undergraduate-open-days

ljmu.ac.uk/discover/fees-and-funding/specific-fees-info/
undergraduate-finance

# London Metropolitan University

The institution known as London Met was created in 2002 by the first merger between two UK universities, London Guildhall University and the University of North London. It has never placed higher than 100th in our main academic table but the government's Teaching Excellence Framework (TEF 2023) recognised the glowing evaluations of its students with a gold rating for the student experience and a silver award overall.

Mature students account for three-quarters of undergraduates here. In the Research Excellence Framework (REF 2021) it placed 90th in our research quality index, with 60% of its research assessed as world-leading or internationally excellent. Maths produced the best result.

Completion rates are an issue, with only 79.1% of students projected to finish their degrees. The university was awarded bronze for the student outcomes aspect of the TEF assessment and the Office for Students (OfS) later issued London Met with an improvement notice, highlighting that it had failed to meet its standards on student outcomes.

Responding, Lynn Dobbs, the outgoing vice-chancellor, criticised the data used in the OfS benchmarks for being too old and not contextualised. London Met said that despite cost-of-living challenges, it was confident that continued investment in teaching and learning, and in student services would have a positive impact on future metrics.

The university is determined to grow talent to create local jobs. The first nursing students began in 2023, while undergraduates have started courses in construction project management, building surveying and real estate to fill skills gaps in the property and construction sectors. There are new degrees in architectural technology and physiotherapy.

Professionally focused degrees may help to continue the university's upward trajectory in our graduate prospects table (121st, up three places year-on-year after a five-place rise in our previous edition). However, it remains in the bottom ten, with 63.4% of graduates in highly skilled jobs or further study within 15 months.

Most aspects of London Met life centre on the Holloway Road campus in north London, where the angular graduate centre designed by Daniel Libeskind is a standout feature. It hosts the Science Centre's superlab, one of the largest teaching laboratories in Europe. The School of Art, Architecture and Design is four miles east in Aldgate, while Accelerator (a business start-up hub) is in Shoreditch, on the capital's tech doorstep. Over the next decade the university plans to spend £180 million on modernising and digitising its facilities.

Most students live at home and commute to their studies. The university does not own halls of residence but its website has information on private halls with affordable rooms.

London Met aims to ensure that more than 90% of students stick with their course, and offers emotional and practical solutions including counselling, help with disabilities and dyslexia, and a hardship fund. Gym membership is free.

Bursaries of £1,500 a year benefit students who have left care and the university offers grants to help those with children or adult dependents, disabled students and active or former members of the armed forces.

**166–220 Holloway Road London N7 8DB**
courseenquiries@londonmet.ac.uk
londonmet.ac.uk
londonmetsu.org.uk

**Overall ranking 127**
(last year 124)

**Accommodation**
University provided places N/A

**Student numbers**
Undergraduates 10,070
Applications per place 6.7:1
Overall offer rate 85.8%

**Fees**
UK fees £9,250
International fees £17,600–£19,250

londonmet.ac.uk/events/undergraduate-open-days
londonmet.ac.uk/applying/funding-your-studies/undergraduate-tuition-fees/

# London School of Economics and Political Science

Equidistant from parliament and the City in the heart of the capital, the London School of Economics and Political Science (LSE) is Britain's social sciences powerhouse. It stands at the top of The Sunday Times rankings of UK universities, ahead of St Andrews, Oxford and Cambridge.

Improving rates of student satisfaction were key to LSE taking first position, as was its record of helping graduates launch straight into professional careers. It rates second in our analysis of graduate prospects, with 92.5% of leavers in highly skilled jobs 15 months after finishing their degree.

The university's motivations impact life far beyond the Aldwych campus. Professor Larry Kramer, the president and vice-chancellor, believes it has an important role to play in helping to solve some of the most significant global challenges of our time.

"We are looking at democracy in retreat everywhere and governments not delivering what populations need," he says. "Fresh-water supplies are collapsing, new technology is creating big headaches as well as huge benefits, and climate change. All around the LSE there is work being done on these huge issues. My goal is to make sure we do more of this crucial work and that it gets out there."

The LSE was named top in Europe and second in the world for social sciences and management over nine consecutive years in the QS World University Rankings. In the most recent subject list, for 2024, it was sixth.

In the latest Research Excellence Framework (REF 2021), 93% of its submission was judged world-leading or internationally excellent, placing it third in the UK for research in our analysis. The best results were in economics; anthropology; social policy; health policy; and media and communications.

A sharper focus on mental health and wellbeing support has been part of the improvements made to boost the undergraduate experience. This increased the number of wellbeing and disability advisers, improved access to counsellors and extended 24/7 support through a partnership with the Spectrum.Life online service.

There have been healthy improvements in rates of student satisfaction, as recorded in successive National Student Surveys (NSS). Our analysis of the feedback ranked LSE 112th for the broad experience as recently as five years ago; now it occupies 40th position. Students' evaluation of teaching quality moved up seven places this year to =70th. The university was upgraded from overall bronze to silver in the government's latest Teaching Excellence Framework (TEF 2023).

Each department on campus has common rooms and study spaces. The LSE Library is one of the largest in the world devoted to the economic and social sciences. The Marshall Building, in Lincoln's Inn Fields, includes a sports centre and café alongside academic departments.

There are more than 4,100 university-owned or endorsed rooms, about 40% of them catered, with accommodation guaranteed to first-years who apply by the June deadline.

About a quarter of the intake claim some form of financial aid. Awards include means-tested bursaries of £500 to £4,000 a year. Means-tested scholarships are available in specific subjects.

---

**Houghton Street London WC2A 2AE**
lse.ac.uk/ask-LSE
lse.ac.uk
lsesu.com

**Overall ranking 1**
(last year 4)

**Accommodation**
University provided places 4,119
Catered £138–£401 per week
Self-catered £196–£469 per week

**Student numbers**
Undergraduates 5,556
Applications per place 14.5:1
Overall offer rate 20.6%

**Fees**
UK fees £9,250
International fees £26,184–£28,176

lse.ac.uk/study-at-lse/meet-visit-and-discover-LSE/experience-lse/undergraduate-open-day
lse.ac.uk/study-at-lse/Undergraduate/fees-and-funding

# London South Bank University

There is a professional, practical edge at London South Bank University (LSBU). From technology and baking science degrees to wide-ranging options in nursing and social care, it stands by a civic mission to provide "industrial skill, general knowledge, health and wellbeing" to the people and businesses of south London.

LSBU continues to recruit a quarter of each year's intake of students from the local area and is ranked 34th in our social inclusion index.

Founded in 1892, it is at the heart of the LSBU Group – a network south of the Thames that includes a further education college, a technical college, an academy school and a sixth form. It has one of the country's largest cohorts of degree apprentices.

LSBU maintained a silver rating overall in the government's Teaching Excellence Framework (TEF) 2023, underpinned by a silver for student outcomes and bronze for the student experience. The assessors highlighted its "very high continuation and completion rates". However, our data shows that across all areas the students' projected continuation rate of 88.2% is relatively poor, placing the university =110th for this metric.

Rates of student satisfaction have improved, according to our analysis of the National Student Survey, with LSBU ranking 70th for students' evaluation of teaching quality (up 27 places) and 89th for satisfaction with the wider experience (a 19-place gain).

The Research Excellence Framework (REF) 2021 rated 68% of research submitted by LSBU as world-leading or internationally excellent (up 14 percentage points compared with the 2014 REF), and it ranks 92nd in our research quality index.

Less positively, LSBU has been struggling financially, having written off £16.3 million in "bad debt" due to what it described as "weaker repayments" on debts, including tuition fees owed by international students. One of more than 50 UK universities to have announced plans to make redundancies, it reported a deficit of £16.4 million in 2022–23. It said academic job cuts were driven by a "changing student profile".

Most courses are accredited by professional bodies or developed in partnership with employers. Although rates of graduate employment plummeted to 107th in our previous edition, our analysis of the latest Graduate Outcomes survey, tracking the proportion in highly skilled work or further study after 15 months, showed a significant rise this year to =65th.

More than £65 million has been invested in the main Southwark campus and there is a business and healthcare campus in Croydon. New degrees are offered in photography; music production and sound design; and computer science.

In 2023–24 half of first-years lived in LSBU's halls, where allocation is based on distance from home but guaranteed only for international students. Access is free to sports facilities such as the Southwark gym and a wellbeing team provides support for mental health.

There are bursaries of up to £1,500 a year for care leavers, students estranged from their families and young carer students, while the Lawrence Burrows Education Trust helps those with a West Indian or Asian background.

---

**103 Borough Road London SE1 0AA**
lsbu.ac.uk/contact-us/enquiry-form
lsbu.ac.uk
southbanksu.com

**Overall ranking 100**
(last year 116)

**Accommodation**
University provided places 1,338
Self-catered £194–£268 per week

**Student numbers**
Undergraduates 10,516
Applications per place 5.1:1
Overall offer rate 55.8%

**Fees**
UK fees £9,250
International fees £14,900–£16,900

lsbu.ac.uk/study/study-at-lsbu/open-days
lsbu.ac.uk/study/undergraduate/fees-and-funding/

# Loughborough University

Loughborough attracts elite students with what it calls "the country's largest concentration of world-class facilities across a wide range of sports". Its medal count at the 2014 Paris Olympics included four golds and there were seven more at the Paralympics. At both competitions, the university would have made the top 20 in the medal table if it were a country.

Our Sports University of the Year 2025, Loughborough's teams topped the British Universities and Colleges Sport (BUCS) points table in 2023–24 for the 43rd consecutive time. Its campus hosts the governing bodies of British Swimming, England and Wales Cricket, England Netball, British Athletics, British Triathlon and British Weightlifting.

In 2024 it led the QS World University Rankings for sport for the eighth consecutive year. Research in sport and exercise sciences contributed some of its best results in the latest Research Excellence Framework (REF 2021). Although 91% of the submission was rated world-leading or internationally excellent, the university fell four places to 34th in our table against greater gains elsewhere.

The former Loughborough Technical Institute won triple gold in the government's latest Teaching Excellence Framework (TEF 2023) with the highest rating for student experience, student outcomes and overall. Loughborough's students also gave glowing feedback in the latest National Student Survey (NSS). The university is fourth for satisfaction with the wider undergraduate experience in our new NSS analysis, up one place year-on-year, and 32nd for satisfaction with teaching quality (up 26 places).

It occupies a 523-acre campus on the edge of the market town and is investing in digital laboratories with robotics and AI technologies to support teaching and research. Graphics and design disciplines are moving into renovated spaces, while the English department relocates to the School of Social Sciences and Humanities. A degree in energy engineering launches in 2025.

Loughborough has an east London campus at the Queen Elizabeth Olympic Park, where the focus is on postgraduate and executive courses, research and enterprise.

More than 2,000 undergraduates take work placements in a typical year and those hoping to start their own business can apply for a post under the Year in Enterprise programme. The university ranks 12th in our analysis of the latest Graduate Outcomes survey, with 86.3% of graduates in highly skilled work or postgraduate study 15 months after finishing their degree.

In addition to its many sporting facilities, Loughborough offers the extracurricular LU Arts programme, which hosts live performances, workshops and exhibitions. It has more than 6,000 rooms across 17 halls of residence, with 42% of places catered, and guarantees accommodation to all first-years who apply by the July deadline.

The Personal Best skills development programme helps first-years find their feet. For those struggling with mental health problems, a duty assessment team responds in a crisis and there is one-to-one or group mental health therapy.

Generous bursary schemes provide between £1,000 and £17,100 over three years for eligible students from low-income households, areas of low participation in higher education and those who have left care.

**Epinal Way Loughborough LE11 3TU**
admissions@lboro.ac.uk
lboro.ac.uk
lsu.co.uk

**Overall ranking 10**
(last year 10)

**Accommodation**
University provided places 6,124
Catered £159–£237 per week
Self-catered £117–£221 per week

**Student numbers**
Undergraduates 14,665
Applications per place 7.3:1
Overall offer rate 69.0%

**Fees**
UK fees £9,250
International fees £23,300–£28,600

lboro.ac.uk/study/undergraduate/visit-us/open-days/
lboro.ac.uk/study/undergraduate/fees-funding/

# University of Manchester

One of Britain's biggest universities located in one of the country's largest and most diverse cities, Manchester offers close to 500 undergraduate programmes and is the UK's most applied-to university. It registered almost 93,500 applications for entry in 2023.

England's first civic university, founded in 1824, is a member of the Russell Group of research-led universities. It received a £17.4 million increase in funding by Research England for 2022-23 – in third place behind Oxford and Imperial College London.

In the latest Research Excellence Framework (REF 2021), 93 % of the university's research was assessed as world-leading or internationally excellent, the top two categories. The results put it seventh in our research quality index.

Manchester retained a silver rating overall in the Teaching Excellence Framework (TEF 2023), underpinned by silver for the student experience and gold for student outcomes. Assessors praised "tailored approaches that are highly effective in ensuring students succeed in and progress beyond their studies".

The university has, however, dropped outside the top 25 of our league table due to persistently low rates of student satisfaction. This is not an uncommon issue among urban universities or those that are research-led, but Manchester remains in the bottom ten for satisfaction with teaching quality (126th) and the bottom 15 for the wider experience (120th) in our latest National Student Survey analysis.

Improvements to the large campus in the city centre may help. Six "cosy campus" spaces provide welcoming areas for students to relax, while podcasting studios, VR experience pods and flexible teaching spaces are available in the zero-emissions Flexible Learning Innovation Space at Booth Street East.

The university is a strong performer in global rankings in which student satisfaction is not a factor, achieving =34th in the QS World University Rankings 2025.

The £400 million Manchester Engineering Campus was completed in 2021 and the redevelopment of the Paterson building, after a fire, created double the space for a collaboration with Cancer Research UK and the Christie NHS Foundation Trust for cancer research. Off campus, the Jodrell Bank radio observatory is a Unesco world heritage site. The university has international centres in Dubai, Hong Kong, Shanghai and Singapore.

Academic options introduced for 2024 entry were an integrated master's degree in optometry; graduate-entry medicine; digital media, culture and society; education, leadership and culture; creative and cultural industries; and global development with international study.

The university owns and operates almost 8,500 rooms. All full-time first-years who apply by August 31 in their year of entry are guaranteed a space. Applications received after A-level results are handled in date order.

Students can access one-to-one mental health appointments with specialists, psychoeducational workshops and therapy groups. Financial aid includes the Manchester Bursary, worth £1,000 for a household income of up to £35,000 and £2,000 for a household income of up to £25,000. There is further support for students who have left care or are estranged from their families. Scholarships are available for black British students and in specific subjects.

---

**Oxford Road ManchesterM13 9PL**
study@manchester.ac.uk
manchester.ac.uk
manchesterstudentsunion.com

**Overall ranking =27**
(last year 23)

**Accommodation**
University provided places 8,466
Catered £160–£220 per week
Self-catered £113–£200 per week

**Student numbers**
Undergraduates 30,733
Applications per place 9.7:1
Overall offer rate 53.3%

**Fees**
UK fees £9,250
International fees £22,000–£30,000
Medicine £38,000–£58,000

manchester.ac.uk/study/undergraduate/open-days-visits/open-days/
manchester.ac.uk/study/undergraduate/fees-and-funding

# Manchester Metropolitan University

Newly planted trees and wildflowers are boosting biodiversity in All Saints Park, a focal point of Manchester Metropolitan University's (MMU) campus. Pedestrians and cyclists have priority over vehicles in the surrounding areas, which has helped MMU to take second place in the People & Planet University League, a ranking based on environmental and ethical performance.

MMU has also been voted the UK's top degree apprenticeship provider for five years running in the RateMyApprenticeship awards. The university works with more than 600 employers, including AstraZeneca, IBM, BAE Systems and McDonald's, as well as smaller businesses.

In the latest Research Excellence Framework (REF 2021), 30% of its work was considered world-leading, helping it to stand 51st in our research quality index. Some of the strongest results were in art and design; English; and sport, leisure and tourism.

The Manchester School of Architecture, run in collaboration with the University of Manchester, holds joint fifth place for architecture and the built environment in the 2024 QS World University subject rankings. Meanwhile, the multidisciplinary Manchester Fashion Institute provides undergraduate and postgraduate training in design, business, promotion, fashion buying and technology. MMU was awarded a gold rating overall in the Teaching Excellence Framework (TEF 2023), underpinned by gold for the student experience and silver for student outcomes. Assessors praised the "highly effective enhancement of employment prospects through real-world projects, simulations and placements".

In our analysis of the National Student Survey, MMU ranks 33rd in the UK for teaching quality (up eight places) and 26th for the wider student experience (up 18), helping to propel it into the top 50 of our academic league table.

The All Saints campus near the city centre is home to the School of Digital Arts (SODA), where students study film, animation, UX design, photography, games design and artificial intelligence. The Manchester Metropolitan Institute of Sport opened in 2022 and renovation of the library is under way.

All Saints also hosts the £75 million business school and engineering buildings. The faculties of education and health are in the Brooks Building, about a ten-minute walk from campus, while the home of science and engineering has been transformed in a £115 million development.

Manchester is packed with culture, sport, music and nightlife options – more than enough to keep students entertained. Access to MMU's counselling, mental health and wellbeing service is free of charge. The university runs wellbeing skills workshops throughout the year, covering topics such as mindfulness and managing anxiety.

The university had 3,165 spaces in halls for 2023-24. Allocation is on a first-come, first-served basis. An accommodation guarantee applies to full-time first-years who make MMU their firm choice and pay the rental deposit before the end of July.

There is a £750-a-year support package for UK undergraduates and foundation-year students from households with an income of £25,000 or less. There are also £1,500 bursaries for first-generation students who complete a pre-entry programme. In 2023 more than 500 students received a scholarship, bursary or prize funded by one of the institution's donors.

---

**Ormond Building Lower Ormond Street Manchester M15 6BX**
mmu.ac.uk/contact/course-enquiry/
mmu.ac.uk
theunionmmu.org

**Overall ranking =46**
(last year 59)

**Accommodation**
University provided places 3,165
Self-catered £137–£220 per week

**Student numbers**
Undergraduates 27,076
Applications per place 5.7:1
Overall offer rate 74.8%

**Fees**
UK fees £9,250
International fees £18,500–£30,000

mmu.ac.uk/study/open-days/undergraduate
mmu.ac.uk/study/undergraduate/funding-your-studies/
tuition-fees

# Middlesex University

Most of the Middlesex intake call Hendon, the university's base in northwest London, their campus, but its locations in Dubai and Mauritius cater for up to 4,500 students and 1,000 students respectively. Practice-based learning is the theme worldwide and the university's flexible course system offers a January start on some programmes.

Under its 2031 learning framework, Middlesex has pledged to teach students in cluster groups to boost engagement. Timetables are organised to help them to manage their studies alongside work, caring and other responsibilities.

The university's earn-while-you-learn route is flourishing: its portfolio of apprenticeship programmes attracts nearly 1,500 enrolments, with students training for careers in fields such as teaching, social work and policing.

Middlesex submitted work in a dozen subject areas to the latest Research Excellence Framework (REF 2021), in which business and management was its strongest area. Although it recorded an improvement in the REF 2021 compared with the previous exercise in 2014, rival institutions did better. The university slipped more than 20 places down our research quality ranking to =88th.

With only 86.1% of students projected to carry on from the first to second year of their degrees, it ranks among the bottom ten for continuation rates. Overall Middlesex picks up four places in our academic league table (117th).

It was awarded silver overall in the Teaching Excellence Framework (TEF 2023), underpinned by bronze for the student experience and silver for student outcomes. In our analysis of the National Student Survey 2024, Middlesex is 37th for students' evaluation of teaching quality (up from 91st) and 28th for student experience (a 55-place gain).

Five degree apprenticeships launched in September 2024, including digital marketer and data scientist, and there is a new degree in professional arts practice.

Community-based outreach initiatives help to widen participation at Middlesex, which is among the most successful universities in our social inclusion index. Only the University of Bedfordshire has a higher intake of students from non-selective state schools than Middlesex (98.7%) in our latest social inclusion data. About two-thirds of students are from black, Asian or ethnic minority backgrounds.

MDX Excellence Scholarships are worth £6,000 over three years to academic high-achievers. Students who need to apply for financial help from the Living Costs Fund can do so more than once. Merit awards of up to £2,000 and faculty prizes may be given to talented students and sports scholarships are available.

Investment in the main campus has consolidated library services and added academic buildings at the business school. For visual arts and design students there are music, radio and television studios, plus fashion and textiles workshops.

Sports facilities include a bouldering wall and fitness pod. The students' union hosts balls, swap and repair shops, and comedy nights.

Full-time first-years get priority in halls, but there is no guarantee. Once rooms are filled the university will help students to find private accommodation.

One-to-one short-term counselling is allied to mental healthcare support and coordination with external services. A disability and dyslexia team works across departments.

---

**The Burroughs Hendon London NW4 4BT**
enquiries@mdx.ac.uk
mdx.ac.uk
mdxsu.com

**Overall ranking 117**
(last year 121)

**Accommodation**
University provided places 1,133
Self-catered £175–£220 per week

**Student numbers**
Undergraduates 12,339
Applications per place 5.4:1
Overall offer rate 67.3%

**Fees**
UK fees £9,250
International fees £16,600

mdx.ac.uk/study/open-days/open-day/
mdx.ac.uk/study/fees-and-funding

# Newcastle University

Tracing its roots to 1834, Newcastle University was a founding member of the research-intensive Russell Group. It has more than 200 undergraduate degrees and sites in London, Singapore and Malaysia. But it is the city-centre campus and culture of Newcastle, and the nearby Northumberland coast, that make the university such a popular student destination.

Applications for 2023 entry were up by 7%, at just under 36,000 – the highest in six years. With more than 180 societies, students have plenty of opportunities to get involved. You don't have to be a party animal to thrive here, although those looking for a big night out are unlikely to be disappointed.

Efforts to develop sustainably have been part of its upgrades and Newcastle is ranked in the top third of UK universities in the People & Planet University League, based on environmental and ethical performance.

Newcastle has gained seven places in our main academic ranking, lifting it into the top 30. Powering its overall performance were improved rates of student satisfaction. Our analysis of the National Student Survey (NSS) shows a 45-place rise for the student experience, to 71st place. Students' evaluations of teaching quality were more positive too, resulting in a ten-place improvement to 112nd.

A silver rating overall in the government's Teaching Excellence Framework (TEF 2023), down from gold in 2017, was bolstered by silver for student outcomes. The student experience was rated bronze.

In the latest Research Excellence Framework (REF 2021) Newcastle had 42% of its work assessed as world-leading, led by English language and literature, to rank =26th in our research quality index.

On campus, resources at the Stephenson Building for engineering include Maker Space (a "student-centred zone for interdisciplinary collaboration, creativity and entrepreneurship") and facilities for research in digital manufacturing. The £4.6 million Farrell Centre transformed a department store into a project that is part research hub, part civic space.

Facilities off campus include commercial farms and a biological field station, while an ambitious Health Innovation Neighbourhood has planning consent at the former site of Newcastle General Hospital.

Halls are either within walking distance of campus or close to public transport links. Newcastle guarantees accommodation to first-years who make it their firm choice and apply by the end of June.

A counselling team offers appointments face to face, online or over the phone. Students can access a 24/7 emotional distress helpline and an online referral form to report hate incidents, discrimination, harassment or misconduct.

The university's efforts to increase the proportion of students from deprived areas has shown signs of success: one in ten students fit this cohort (the 70th best proportion). Like most Russell Group universities, Newcastle is outside the top 100 in our social inclusion index.

Bursaries of £1,000 or £2,000 a year are paid on a sliding scale to students from households with income up to £35,000, and there are one-off payments of £500 for income up to £40,000. There is a wide range of academic and subject-specific scholarships.

---

**Newcastle upon Tyne NE1 7RU**
apps.ncl.ac.uk/contact-us/general-enquiry
ncl.ac.uk
nusu.co.uk

**Overall ranking =30**
(last year 37)

**Accommodation**
University provided places 5,180
Catered £148 per week
Self-catered £98–£200 per week

**Student numbers**
Undergraduates 20,722
Applications per place 5.7:1
Overall offer rate 79.2%

**Fees**
UK fees £9,250
International fees £22,900–£28,700
Medicine £42,200

ncl.ac.uk/study/meet/undergraduate-open-day/
ncl.ac.uk/undergraduate/fees-funding/

# University of Northampton

Efforts to help combat the rising cost of living for applicants and students at the University of Northampton include the provision of free breakfast cereal to all on-campus students – a kindness extended to those who attend its open days. Eligible UK students get a free laptop when they enrol and have a compulsory study trip as part of their course, with travel and accommodation paid for by the university.

One of the UK's youngest universities, gaining full status in 2005, it was rated triple silver in the Teaching Excellence Framework (TEF 2023) despite its relatively low continuation rate, with only 88.5% of new students still studying one year later and less than two-thirds of students achieving a 2.1 or a first in their degree.

The TEF assessment took into account the impact of the delayed move of some of its courses to the Waterside campus in 2019-20 and a cyberattack it experienced in 2021.

Since then, however, Northampton has been subject to an investigation by the Office for Students, England's higher education regulator, which identified seven areas of concern relating to its computing courses. It also concluded that Northampton's semester teaching model – in which modules are taught and assessed within a 13-week term rather than over 26 weeks – gave students "little time to reflect on one topic before starting the next" and had a "negative impact on student outcomes".

In response, a spokesman for Northampton said: "This report does not represent the considerable investment and comprehensive improvements that have been made in the years between this stale data being gathered and the report being published."

Rates of student satisfaction with the undergraduate experience and teaching quality are inside the top 100 in our analysis of the 2024 National Student Survey. Although the university increased the size of its submission to the latest Research Excellence Framework (REF 2021), it fell into the bottom ten in our research quality rating, against bigger gains at other universities. Northampton has gained three places (125th) in our academic league table but remains in the bottom ten.

The Waterside campus, a few minutes' walk from the town centre, is located along the River Nene on a former brownfield site. At its centre is a four-storey Learning Hub where large lecture theatres were replaced by classrooms for up to 40 people and smaller lecture spaces.

The students' union occupies a prominent spot and the Sports Dome is used for teaching as well as recreation. Cycleways link the campus to the town.

All new full-time students are guaranteed a room in halls, either on or close to the campus or at Scholars Green Student Village about four miles away. Students can access counselling, mental health advice and drop-in support.

About seven in ten new entrants qualify for financial assistance from the university. Awards include fully-funded accommodation for students who have left care or who are estranged from their families, and £1,500 scholarships to undergraduates from the Northamptonshire area.

---

**University Drive Northampton NN1 5PH**
study@northampton.ac.uk
northampton.ac.uk
northamptonunion.com

**Overall ranking 125**
(last year 128)

**Accommodation**
University provided places 2,250
Self-catered £88–£195 per week

**Student numbers**
Undergraduates 9,497
Applications per place 4.4:1
Overall offer rate 80.9%

**Fees**
UK fees £9,250
International fees £15,200–£17,700

northampton.ac.uk/about-us/contact-us/open-days/
northampton.ac.uk/study/fees-and-funding

# Northumbria University

A leading light among the UK's modern universities, Northumbria continues to drive social mobility and provide a higher education bedrock to the northeast's talent pipeline. Based at two campuses in Newcastle-upon-Tyne, students can access nearly 200 undergraduate programmes. The city's affordability, friendliness and legendary nightlife are key to its appeal.

The Sunday Times Modern University of the Year 2025 rose six places in our new academic table, boosted by increasing student satisfaction. Our analysis of the latest National Student Survey put Northumbria =68th for students' evaluation of teaching quality and =55th for the wider experience (up 14 places and 30 places respectively).

It also moved up six places in our research quality index to 58th, based on our analysis of the latest Research Excellence Framework (REF 2021). Sport and exercise science, English language and literature, and geography and environmental studies did best.

Among recent advances in its research capacity, Northumbria has become one of 12 UK Centres for Doctoral Training in Artificial Intelligence and is developing the £50 million North East Space Skills and Technology centre on the City campus.

Launching in September 2025 are a degree apprenticeship in social work and a degree in digital design. Also new are degrees in film; product design; media and communication; furniture and product design; business and entrepreneurship.

Awarding Northumbria a silver rating overall in the Teaching Excellence Framework (TEF 2023), the judging panel reserved gold for the student outcomes aspect of the assessment, along with another silver for the student experience.

Located in the region with the lowest take-up of higher education in the UK, Northumbria draws 18% of its intake of students from areas of low participation (27th). It ranks =62nd in our social inclusion index, with its overall position held back by recruiting among the least ethnically diverse intakes (10.7%, 102nd).

In the heart of Newcastle, the City campus has had a £200 million upgrade over the past decade. The Coach Lane campus, three miles away, houses the Faculty of Health and Life Sciences. Further afield, the university has a base in London and offers courses in Amsterdam in partnership with the Amsterdam University of Applied Sciences.

The Sport Central development at the City site has a pool, sports science laboratories and a 3,000-seat arena. The cultural centre of the northeast, Newcastle is home to Baltic Centre for Contemporary Art and the university has its own Gallery North. Beyond the clubs and pubs, Blue Flag Tynemouth beach is a Metro journey from the city.

A counselling and mental health team offers face-to-face, online or phone appointments and a 24/7 helpline. There is a programme addressing bullying, discrimination, harassment, religious hate incidents and sexual misconduct.

Accommodation is guaranteed for all undergraduates who apply by June 30. Northumbria has more than 3,100 places in halls.

British students may qualify for one of 35 Northumbria Undergraduate UK scholarships, worth £4,000 in the first year. There are subject-specific awards and bursaries of £2,000 for care leavers, carers and estranged undergraduates.

---

**Sutherland Building Newcastle upon Tyne NE1 8ST**
bc.applicantservice@northumbria.ac.uk
northumbria.ac.uk
mynsu.co.uk

**Overall ranking 43**
(last year 49)

**Accommodation**
University provided places 3,123
Self-catered £117–£206 per week

**Student numbers**
Undergraduates 19,896
Applications per place 3.8:1
Overall offer rate 86.0%

**Fees**
UK fees £9,250
International fees £18,250–£20,750

northumbria.ac.uk/study-at-northumbria/visit-northumbria/university-open-days/
northumbria.ac.uk/study-at-northumbria/fees-funding

# Norwich University of the Arts

Home to a busy cultural scene, Norwich University of the Arts (Norwich Arts) traces its origins back to 1845 but is looking to the future with new courses and facilities. It fosters industry collaborations to ensure that its courses are professionally relevant and students are supported in securing internships and placements.

Founded as the Norwich School of Design, it has been a university only since 2012 and has fewer than 3,000 students. Based in the city centre, the Norwich Arts campus includes the Duke Street Riverside building, which has 100 rooms for first-year students above a lecture theatre and state-of-the-art teaching facilities. Bank Plain, a former bank, is being developed into a new home for student services and social spaces.

Norwich Arts made an impact in the Research Excellence Framework (REF 2021), in which 71% of its work in art and design was assessed as world-leading or internationally excellent. The much-improved results, compared with REF 2014, helped the university to jump from 86th place to 62nd in our research quality rating.

It was awarded triple gold in the latest Teaching Excellence Framework (TEF 2023), with assessors praising its "use of research in relevant disciplines, innovation, scholarship, professional practice and/or employer engagement".

Rates of student satisfaction have been changeable in recent years. Although our analysis of the latest National Student Survey shows a 32-place gain for students' evaluation of the broad experience, it brings Norwich Arts to only a ranking of 76th for this metric. Their feelings about teaching quality are stronger, putting the university at 57th despite a 12-place decline on this measure.

Norwich Arts leads a regional outreach network in partnership with Cambridge, East Anglia, Anglia Ruskin and Suffolk universities. It succeeds in recruiting 16.9% of undergraduates from deprived postcodes (=33rd), and only eight universities have a higher proportion of disabled students. Overall, it ranks 72nd in our social inclusion index for England and Wales.

The first students of degrees in creative computing; and creative technology and robotics began courses in September 2024. Courses are also starting in business management; electronic music and sound production; esports; marketing; and psychology.

New halls of residence have taken the university's supply of rooms to about 950 and it guarantees accommodation to first-years who want to live in. Student support advisers and external counselling services are available.

Financial support includes a contribution towards the cost of materials, equipment and other expenses where a student's household income is lower than £25,000. The university offers £1,000 a year to undergraduates who are in care or estranged from their parents.

Norwich packs plenty of student-friendly entertainment into its compact centre and is one of the UK's safest and greenest cities. The university's rich artistic life is enhanced by its East Gallery, a public art space showcasing exhibitions by internationally recognised artists, curators and design practitioners.

Students can access museums and art galleries free of charge and have access to the University of East Anglia's Sportspark, which includes an Olympic-sized swimming pool.

---

**Francis House 3–7 Redwell Street Norwich NR2 4SN**
admissions@norwichuni.ac.uk
norwichuni.ac.uk
nuasu.co.uk

**Overall ranking 81**
(last year 75)

**Accommodation**
University provided places 948
Self-catered £114–£206 per week

**Student numbers**
Undergraduates 2,632
Applications per place 3.4:1
Overall offer rate 82.5%

**Fees**
UK fees £9,250
International fees £18,000

norwichuni.ac.uk/events/undergraduate-open-days/
norwichuni.ac.uk/study-at-norwich/fees-funding//

# University of Nottingham

Demand remains high at the University of Nottingham, which occupies a beautiful campus in a buzzy city. Its broad choice of courses and subjects within a research-led environment enhance its appeal. Nottingham was also the Sunday Times Sport University of the Year 2024.

Engineering degrees have the biggest take-up, followed by business and management, and medicine and dentistry. Social life is vibrant, with about 400 student-led societies.

In the latest Research Excellence Framework (REF 2021) the university's submission within pharmacy and health sciences, and economics did especially well. It stands 22nd in our research quality index.

Significantly improved rates of student satisfaction drove a two-place rise in our main academic ranking. Analysis of the latest National Student Survey shows growing contentment with the wider undergraduate experience compared with a year earlier (up 22 places to 73rd) and teaching quality (up 17 to 90th).

Nottingham was rated silver overall in the Teaching Excellence Framework (TEF 2023), achieving silver for the student experience and gold for student outcomes. The TEF panel praised it for tailoring "approaches that are highly effective in ensuring its students succeed in and progress beyond their studies".

Courses introduced recently are an integrated master's in physics with a year in computer science; health promotion and public health; film and screen studies; art history and visual culture; and cultural and creative industries.

More than a third of Nottingham's students come from selective schools (104th) and less than a third are the first in their family to go to university (106th). It ranks 99th in our social inclusion index, up one place from our previous edition. More than a third of students are from ethnic minority backgrounds (48th).

Nottingham has long been a favourite recruiting ground for large employers such as Walt Disney and Unilever. In our graduate outcomes analysis, it secured a top-20 result, based on 83.3% being in highly skilled jobs or further study within 15 months.

The 330-acre University Park is one of Britain's loveliest settings for higher education, with lakes and parkland as the backdrop to modern facilities and historic buildings. Its layout is the blueprint for Nottingham's campuses in China and Malaysia.

Recent developments include a virtual reality classroom for students of product design and manufacture in the Engineering Science and Learning Centre. The £40 million Power Electronics and Machines Centre hosts low-carbon aerospace projects. The Castle Meadow campus will provide a new base for the business school.

The university has more than 8,500 rooms, including catered and self-catering accommodation, and first-years who apply by the July deadline are guaranteed a space.

Nottingham invests more than £1 million annually in services to support students with their mental health and wellbeing. There are wellbeing staff in academic departments and it has a report-and-support process for harassment and abuse.

About 30% of UK undergraduates qualify for bursaries worth £1,000 a year, where annual household income is less than £35,000, or another £1,000 award under other criteria. Most merit-based scholarships are means-tested.

---

**University Park Nottingham NG7 2RD**
nottingham.ac.uk/studywithus/enquiry.aspx
nottingham.ac.uk
su.nottingham.ac.uk

**Overall ranking =30**
(last year 32)

**Accommodation**
University provided places 8,527
Catered £224–£318 per week
Self-catered £125–£249 per week

**Student numbers**
Undergraduates 28,443
Applications per place 7.4:1
Overall offer rate 71.1%

**Fees**
UK fees £9,250
International fees £12,500–£35,750
Medicine £30,200–£52,500

nottingham.ac.uk/open-days/
nottingham.ac.uk/studentservices/services/tuition-fees.aspx

# Nottingham Trent University

One of the UK's leading modern universities, Nottingham Trent University (NTU) is also one of the largest – with more than 40,000 students based at four sites in and around the city, plus one in Mansfield and another in London. With courses from equine sports science to aerospace engineering, it records high rates of student satisfaction.

Ambitious investment in facilities includes the £45 million Design and Digital Arts Building, while away from the lecture rooms NTU is the top-ranked modern university in the British Universities and Colleges Sport (BUCS) table.

The university is powering ahead with more than 20 new BSc courses including fashion photography and wildlife conservation, many offered with a foundation year. There are also new degrees in business management and sustainability; and psychology (cognition and neuroscience).

The Sunday Times Modern University of the Year 2025 runner-up ranks 21st for satisfaction with teaching quality and 20th for satisfaction with the wider undergraduate experience in our analysis of the National Student Survey.

Results in the latest Research Excellence Framework (REF 2021) led to an impressive 26-place rise in our research quality index compared with the results of the previous national assessment in 2014. Law; engineering; allied health; dentistry; nursing; and pharmacy were the top performers, each with at least 98% of their submissions rated world-leading or internationally excellent.

In the Teaching Excellence Framework (TEF 2023), NTU achieved gold ratings overall and for the student experience, with silver for student outcomes. The panel described its "teaching, feedback and assessment practices to support student learning, progression and attainment" as outstanding.

More than a third of new students received some form of financial assistance from the university in 2023–24. Support includes a £750 a year bursary for students from households with incomes under £27,500, hardship fund payments and bursaries for care leavers and students who are estranged from their families. Some merit-based scholarships are offered.

The main City campus is the academic base for about half of NTU's students, while the Clifton campus houses the arts and humanities, and science and technology, including the new Health and Allied Professions Centre and the Medical Technologies Innovation Facility. Business, education, and sport and exercise science are studied at NTU Mansfield, and the east London operation in Whitechapel has a centre for digital arts, production and performance.

Students have access to superb sporting facilities, including an equestrian centre and the multipurpose Lee Westwood Sports Centre. Extracurricular cultural life falls under the NTU Arts umbrella, which runs an entertainment programme with bands, book clubs, crafting and excursions.

Students can book a room as soon as they have a firm offer of a place and first-years are guaranteed accommodation in Nottingham in university-owned, UPP or private halls.

NTU's student health and wellbeing services operate a "single front door" approach so students can seek help in person or by phone. Counselling sessions are available and support advisers offer tailored care for those of diverse backgrounds, such as care leavers and transgender students.

---

**50 Shakespeare Street Nottingham NG1 4FQ**
enquiries@ntu.ac.uk
ntu.ac.uk
trentstudents.org

**Overall ranking 42**
(last year 43)

**Accommodation**
University provided places 4,943
Self-catered £100–£241 per week

**Student numbers**
Undergraduates 31,608
Applications per place 4.3:1
Overall offer rate 90.1%

**Fees**
UK fees £9,250
International fees £17,150–£17,900

ntu.ac.uk/study-and-courses/open-days
ntu.ac.uk/study-and-courses/undergraduate/fees-and-funding

# The Open University

The Open University (OU) was widening participation in higher education before the term had been invented and remains the model for distance learning around the world. Founded in 1969 to promote educational opportunity for all, it employs thousands of part-time tutors to guide students through their degrees.

The OU offers a full range of undergraduate degree courses with no formal entry requirements and cheaper tuition fees (£7,272 a year), thereby opening doors to higher education that traditional campus-based institutions cannot. All students are classified as part-timers, regardless of whether they study at full-time intensity or not, which allows them to complete their studies without any of their benefits being affected.

There is no campus but about 1,200 full-time academics and 250 postgraduates are based at headquarters in Milton Keynes. Investment has boosted laboratory space by nearly 50% since 2016.

The OU attracts the biggest student numbers in the UK, with more than 100,000 undergraduates and 7,000 postgraduate enrolments.

Our rankings have never included the OU as it would be at a disadvantage in comparison with traditional universities where the focus is on teaching undergraduates on campus. Where comparisons are possible, it tends to perform well. In the latest Research Excellence Framework (REF 2021), 76% of its research was rated world-leading or internationally excellent.

Entering the government's Teaching Excellence Framework (TEF) for the first time in 2023, the OU celebrated gold overall, with silver for the student experience and gold for student outcomes. The panel commended "outstanding rates of progression for the provider's students and courses, particularly considering its specific context".

The university's "supported open learning" system allows students to work where they choose: at home, in the workplace or at a library or study centre. Tutorials, day schools or online forums and social networks provide contact with fellow students and work is monitored by continual assessment, examination or assignment.

All students have access to the OU Wellbeing app, which has tools to build healthy habits into daily life, the TalkCampus peer-to-peer support platform, and Shout – a 24/7 text-messaging service for anyone struggling who needs immediate support.

The OU has expanded into Higher Technical Qualifications (HTQs) and is broadening the provision of continued professional development (CPD) courses, in line with demand for upskilling and retraining employees from the government and employers. Enrolments for degree apprenticeships have also increased.

New degree courses are offered in international relations; counselling; marketing and business management; biomedical sciences; and design.

Widening participation is a core OU mission. The lack of entry requirements removes barriers, while its Access module helps those in need of an educational refresher to get up to speed.

Scholarships and bursaries provide financial backing, with an emphasis on fee reductions rather than cash awards. In 2024–25, 3,800 Access module students were expected to gain a free place.

Refugees arriving in Britain can study free of charge through the Open Futures Sanctuary Scholarship if they have been displaced from their homeland for political, economic, ethnic, environmental or human rights reasons.

---

**Walton Hall Milton Keynes MK7 6AA**
general-enquiries@open.ac.uk
open.ac.uk
oustudents.com

**Overall ranking N/A**

**Accommodation**
Not applicable

**Student numbers**
Undergraduates 140,215
Applications per place N/A
Overall offer rate N/A

**Fees**
UK fees £7,272
International fees £7,472

open.ac.uk/courses/what-is-distance-learning/events
open.ac.uk/courses/fees-and-funding

# University of Oxford

It may be steeped in nine centuries of educational history, but Oxford also looks to the future. The institution is rarely far from the headlines – hosting controversial Oxford Union debaters; advancing health programmes to fight diseases such as malaria; developing the AstraZeneca vaccine. For undergraduates, the opportunity to soak up a rich intellectual experience from academics at the cutting edge of their field is worth the effort of the competitive admissions process.

Although it has slipped to third place in our academic league table, the dark blues were ahead of the light blues for the fourth year running as Cambridge ranks fourth. Oxford remains unsurpassed for its ratio of students to staff (10.3:1), and its tutorial system (weekly groups of two or three students discussing ideas with their tutor) is a core feature.

The university is made up of colleges spread across the city. Applicants should weigh up the colleges' respective academic strengths, reputations and social blends to give themselves the best chance of winning a place and finding an environment where they can thrive.

Although Oxford is part of the UCAS system, the deadline for applications is much earlier than at most other universities (unless you are applying for medicine, veterinary medicine or dentistry). You can apply to either Oxford or Cambridge in any one year, but not both. Selection is in the hands of individual colleges.

Oxford is fourth in our research quality index with stellar results in the latest Research Excellence Framework (REF 2021), which rated 91% of its submission world-leading or internationally excellent. In global rankings, which take account of the research profile but not student reviews, Oxford has been ranked first in the world by Times Higher Education (THE) every year from 2017 to 2024, and it is third in the QS World University Rankings 2025. In THE's subject rankings, Oxford has held the crown for clinical, pre-clinical and health subjects for 13 years.

The university achieved triple gold in the Teaching Excellence Framework (TEF 2023) and learning resources were assessed as outstanding.

It has lifted its boycott of the National Student Survey and our latest NSS analysis puts Oxford in 19th place for student satisfaction with teaching quality – and first among its Russell Group peers. For satisfaction with the wider undergraduate experience, however, the results are less encouraging (124th).

Students live in college accommodation and rents vary. Oxford's eight-week terms are intensive but most rise to the challenge. A counselling service includes one-to-one sessions, therapeutic groups and workshops. Under a peer support scheme, students are trained to listen to others.

The number of applicants accepted from state and independent schools remains a hot topic. Oxford is 11th out of 115 universities in England and Wales for social inclusion overall.

It spends more than £9.5 million a year on financial support for students from lower-income households and about one in four students receive funding. Colleges often have their own funds, such as travel or books grants and academic prizes.

*See Chapter 13: Applying to Oxbridge for college profiles and more information on the admissions process.*

---

**University Offices Wellington Square**
**Oxford OX1 2JD**
ox.ac.uk/undergraduate/ask
ox.ac.uk
oxfordsu.org

**Overall ranking 3**
(last year 2)

**Accommodation**
College websites provide
accommodation details.
See Chapter 11 for individual colleges.

**Student numbers**
Undergraduates 12,268
Applications per place 7.4:1
Overall offer rate 19.7%

**Fees**
UK fees £9,250
International fees £33,050–£48,620
Medicine £43,670–£57,690

ox.ac.uk/admissions/undergraduate/open-days-and-visits
ox.ac.uk/admissions/undergraduate/fees-and-funding/
course-fees

# Oxford Brookes University

Oxford Brookes is known for its focus on preparing students for the workplace, helping them to secure placements, internships and employment opportunities. And it pays off – their solid early-career destinations keep the university comfortably in the upper half of our graduate prospects index over successive years.

An 11-place leap to 50th place in our main academic table reflects the 13:1 student-to-staff ratio at Oxford Brookes, outdone by only ten other UK universities, and rising rates of student satisfaction.

It ranks =67th for undergraduates' evaluations of teaching quality (up from 102nd) and 58th for their feelings on the broad experience (a 30-place improvement) in our latest National Student Survey analysis.

The university's engineering students continue to claim pole position at Formula Student UK, in which teams from around the world design, build, test and race a small-scale racing car. They won three competitions at the Silverstone event in 2024.

It was awarded a silver rating in the government's Teaching Excellence Framework (TEF 2023), underpinned by silver for student outcomes but only bronze for the student experience, reflective of previously faltering NSS outcomes. The assessors commended "a wide range of approaches to effectively support students to succeed in and progress beyond their studies".

More than 400 researchers in 15 subject areas were entered for the latest Research Excellence Framework (REF 2021), a 40% increase on the previous national assessment in 2014, and the proportion of work judged to be world-leading or internationally excellent grew from 60% to 70%. However, Oxford Brookes dropped 19 places in our research quality index to =76th.

In our analysis of the latest Graduate Outcomes survey, 77.8% of graduates were employed in high-skilled jobs or engaged in further study 15 months after their degrees, placing the university =52nd for graduate prospects for the second consecutive year.

A decade-long £220 million investment programme at Oxford Brookes is approaching its final stages. Buildings housing Stem subjects and the creative industries are due to open during the 2024-25 academic year at the main Headington campus. Nursing courses are based in Swindon.

New courses include fine art and history of art; business English with translation; and biodiversity and wildlife conservation.

There are more than 100 societies and about 40 sports clubs for students to choose from. The renowned Oxford Brookes University Boat Club has a boathouse complex on the Thames in Wallingford.

All students who make the university their firm choice or have it as their insurance choice are guaranteed accommodation. In recent years all those who entered through Clearing have been given a place, but it is not guaranteed.

A mental health and wellbeing support service provides advice for students. "Crafternoon tea" is a weekly drop-in for craft and conversation at the multifaith chaplaincy.

About a quarter of undergraduates received financial support from the university in 2022-23. Students from low-income homes are eligible for bursaries of £500 to £3,000 and there is extra support for those who have left care, are estranged from families or are young carers.

---

**Headington Campus Oxford OX3 0BP**
admissions@brookes.ac.uk
brookes.ac.uk
brookesunion.org.uk

**Overall ranking 50**
(last year 61)

**Accommodation**
University provided places 4,361
Self-catered £129–£210 per week

**Student numbers**
Undergraduates 11,716
Applications per place 2.0:1
Overall offer rate 82.7%

**Fees**
UK fees £9,250
International fees £15,200–£17,200

brookes.ac.uk/open-days/
brookes.ac.uk/study/fees

# University of Plymouth

Plymouth's coastal location provides the perfect learning and research environment for the university's renowned marine-related courses. Students have their pick of seaside pursuits away from their books and are handily placed to explore Dartmoor.

The university has been busy transforming its city campus to provide skills-boosting training for students, opening £100 million of facilities in the 2023–24 academic year, including a design and engineering building, a moot court and a cold-case unit for policing and criminology students. An updated Bloomberg suite is among resources awaiting Plymouth Business School in 2025.

Plymouth has won three Queen's Anniversary Awards for its research on microplastics and marine litter, and for widening access. Verified as a carbon neutral university in 2023, the university is pushing towards net zero and its environmental and ethical performance put it 20th in the 2023–24 People & Planet University League table.

It earned triple gold in the government's Teaching Excellence Framework (TEF 2023), overall and for the student experience and student outcomes. Assessors commended its "wide and readily available range of outstanding quality academic support ensuring a supportive learning environment for students".

Although more than three-quarters of its submission to the latest Research Excellence Framework (REF 2021) was rated world-leading or internationally excellent, its performance was outclassed by rival institutions and it fell nine places in our research quality index, to 65th in the UK.

Plymouth ranks in the top half of UK universities for student satisfaction with teaching quality but dropped to =97th for their evaluation of the wider undergraduate experience, based on our analysis of the National Student Survey.

It collaborates with employers who provide mentoring, mock interviews and work placements for students. The Cube incubator aims to inspire student and graduate entrepreneurs, nursing their business ideas through to execution and beyond. Plymouth is 43rd in our analysis of the Graduate Outcomes survey, with 79.7% of its graduates in high-skilled jobs or further study within 15 months.

One of a small minority of modern universities with both a medical and a dental school, Plymouth also has schools of nursing in Exeter and Truro. It plans to expand the curriculum with degrees in social work; osteopathy; technical game design; primary education; and education for sustainability. A campus in Penang, Malaysia, opened in 2022.

On the social front, the summer ball is an annual highlight. Arts and performance venues bring culture to campus, which also has a sports hall, fitness centre, dance studio and squash courts. The Mount Batten Watersports and Activities Centre is a ten-minute ferry ride away.

A place in university halls (or an accredited private alternative) is guaranteed to those who make Plymouth their first choice and apply by the deadline. More than 20 bursaries and scholarships are available, with extra help for students who have left care, are carers or are estranged from their families.

A weekly drop-in session is run by Plymouth's mental health, counselling and pastoral and spiritual support team. Students can refer themselves for mental health assessments, counselling and workshops.

**Drake Circus Plymouth PL4 8AA**
admissions@plymouth.ac.uk
plymouth.ac.uk
upsu.com

**Overall ranking 70**
(last year =70)

**Accommodation**
University provided places 1,897
Self-catered £129–£231 per week

**Student numbers**
Undergraduates 13,995
Applications per place 5.1:1
Overall offer rate 71.8%

**Fees**
UK fees £9,250
International fees £17,100–£25,000
Medicine £39,500

plymouth.ac.uk/study/open-days
plymouth.ac.uk/study/fees

# Plymouth Marjon University

The name of this small university comes from its founding London institutions – St Mark's College and St John's College – whose aim was to educate young orphans from the workhouses and help them to escape poverty by training them as teachers. Marjon moved to Plymouth in 1973, occupying an attractive campus from which eagle-eyed students can spy the sea as well as Dartmoor National Park.

Widening participation is ingrained and Marjon, which gained university status in 2007, ranks third in our social inclusion index. Based in an area with a low take-up of higher education, it recruits the highest proportion (13%) of white working-class male students. The proportion of disabled students is the fourth highest at 16.6%.

About 10% of entrants receive some form of hardship funding. There are grants of £2,000 a year for care leavers and students who are estranged from their families.

The university retains Church of England control but welcomes students of all faiths and none. It is diversifying its academic focus and developing facilities in step, while recording high rates of student satisfaction. Marjon comes third in the UK for students' evaluation of teaching quality in our analysis of the National Student Survey. It is in the top 20 for the wider undergraduate experience.

Health-related courses are the focus as the university plans its growth. There is a new nursing degree and it is launching degree apprenticeships in physiotherapy, speech and language therapy, and public health.

Marjon was awarded a gold rating overall in the Teaching Excellence Framework (TEF 2023), underpinned by gold for the student experience and silver for student outcomes. It is held back in our main academic table by its continuation rate (for which it ranks =120th), with only 86.5% of students projected to carry on from the first to the second year of their studies. This is often a side-effect of diverse student populations.

Teacher training remains a strength and in 2023 Ofsted rated its early-years provision outstanding, while training for primary and secondary age was considered good. Marjon benefited in our rankings from its decision to enter the Research Excellence Framework (REF 2021), after opting out in 2014, although it sits towards the bottom of our research quality index at 119th.

The university's vocationally focused courses have close links with employers. It is 64th in our analysis of the Graduate Outcomes survey, with 75.7% of its graduates in highly skilled jobs or further study 15 months after leaving university.

The institution's manageable size creates a close community. The Barjon bar and coffee shop is renowned for its reasonable prices and regular events. Plymouth, with plenty to offer, is a bus ride away. First-years holding a firm offer take priority in the allocation of the 454 self-catered rooms.

A health and wellbeing programme within the Sport & Health Centre encourages physical activity. Students can self-refer to an in-house counselling service, while university chaplains work with the students' union and the wellbeing and support team to create a broad safety net.

---

**Derriford Road Plymouth PL6 8BH**
admissions@marjon.ac.uk
marjon.ac.uk
marjon.ac.uk/msu/

**Overall ranking 75**
(last year 83)

**Accommodation**
University provided places 454
Self-catered £115–£173 per week

**Student numbers**
Undergraduates 2,121
Applications per place 3.7:1
Overall offer rate 77.2%

**Fees**
UK fees £9,250
International fees £14,500

marjon.ac.uk/courses/open-days/
marjon.ac.uk/courses/fees-and-funding

# University of Portsmouth

The UK's only "island city", separated from the mainland by the Portsea creek, is a draw for students who like the idea of studying by the seaside. The University of Portsmouth is among a minority to reach the top half of our main academic table (55th) while achieving a similar ranking in our social inclusion index (52nd).

Through a partnership with King's College London (KCL), the first medical students enrolled at Portsmouth in 2024 – a long-held ambition for the university. The four-year course, with graduate entry for the first cohort of 54 students, will result in a medical degree awarded by KCL.

The scheme is an expansion of a longstanding partnership with KCL in which the London institution's dental students work with Portsmouth's to enhance their collective clinical experience.

The university has a London campus in Waltham Forest, where it launched its first undergraduate courses in 2024. It hopes to have 5,000 students in the capital by 2029.

Portsmouth earned gold overall in the Teaching Excellence Framework (TEF 2023), underpinned by gold for the student experience and silver for student outcomes. The TEF panel said it showed outstanding tailored approaches "that are highly effective in ensuring its students succeed in and progress beyond their studies".

A focus on research paid off in the Research Excellence Framework (REF 2021), which moved the university into the top half of our research quality index (61st). Physics led the way with 100% of its REF submission rated world-leading or internationally excellent.

Our analysis of the National Student Survey showed Portsmouth improving to =28th for teaching quality and =23rd for the broad experience, which helped to raise it ten places in our main academic league table.

Like much of the higher education sector, the university has been hit by financial troubles. In 2024 it announced redundancies as part of an "academic reset" and faculties may be merged further down the line.

Halls of residence are near the Southsea seafront, known for its quirky shops and lively social scene. Facilities at the £57 million Ravelin Sports Centre include a ski simulator, squash courts and a fitness centre. The smaller Langstone campus, on the outskirts of Portsmouth, is dedicated to outdoor sport. The university has more than 35 competitive sports clubs as well as a volunteering programme that offers opportunities such as youth and adult coaching and refereeing.

Support for students begins before they start their studies through the Get Connected event in September. Beyond enrolment, they can self-refer online to advisers and counsellors through the wellbeing service.

New students who apply by the June deadline and make Portsmouth their firm choice are guaranteed accommodation. Places in halls are allocated in the order they are received, so early applications pay off.

Financial support includes a £750-a-year bursary for students with a household income of less than £25,000 and there are several sporting scholarships.

New courses on offer include global dispute resolution; fashion communication; psychological sciences; geoinformatics; geomatics; survey engineering; and mathematics with machine learning.

University House Winston Churchill Avenue
Portsmouth PO1 2UP
admissions@port.ac.uk
port.ac.uk
upsu.net

**Overall ranking 55**
(last year 65)

**Accommodation**
University provided places 3,444
Catered £155–£200 per week
Self-catered £114–£149 per week

**Student numbers**
Undergraduates 17,020
Applications per place 4.8:1
Overall offer rate 80.4%

**Fees**
UK fees £9,250
International fees £16,200–£19,200

port.ac.uk/study/open-days/undergraduate-open-days
port.ac.uk/study/undergraduate/undergraduate-fees-and-student-finance

# Queen Margaret University, Edinburgh

A discovery trail meanders by a pond and hedgerows, through a meadow and woodland at Queen Margaret University (QMU). The Outdoor Learning Hub, opened in 2024, is especially useful for trainee teachers but all students are welcome to connect with the natural world here.

QMU's ambitions are big but the university has fewer than 5,000 full-time students at its campus in the seaside town of Musselburgh, ten minutes by train from the centre of Edinburgh.

Its primary education degree is a relatively new introduction to the institution, which was founded in 1875 as a cookery school. Food and hospitality teaching remains a strength and an entrepreneurial culture prevails.

The Innovation Hub, a joint project with East Lothian council, is due to open in 2025, offering space for small and medium-size enterprises, with laboratories for research and knowledge exchange. Thrive, a collaboration with Scotland's Rural College, helps to equip students with skills for the food and drink industries.

New degrees have begun in digital marketing and public relations; and cultural and creative industries.

QMU recorded one of the biggest declines in our main academic table year-on-year, tumbling 42 places to rank =105th. Despite its popular peer-assisted learning scheme and free hot meals on campus in a cost-of-living rescue package, feedback from the latest National Student Survey turned chilly. In our NSS analysis, the university crashed to 101st place for satisfaction with teaching quality (down 64 places year-on-year) and =120th for the wider student experience (down 72).

In our research rankings, QMU slipped to 97th on the basis of the latest Research Excellence Framework (REF 2021) compared with the previous exercise in 2014. Some world-leading or internationally excellent work was identified, with the best results in communications, cultural and media studies; speech and language science; and nursing and allied health professions.

Thanks to the university's strong international links, students are able to work towards QMU qualifications at partner institutions in Nepal, Uzbekistan and Sri Lanka.

The landscaped grounds and modern buildings of QMU's purpose-built campus, on the southeastern side of Edinburgh, are within easy reach of the city centre. With 800 spaces, the university does not guarantee accommodation but it prioritises disabled and care-experienced students as well as those from outside the EH postcode.

Library upgrades are among the recent improvements. As a specialist institution for the creative industries, the university has performance and rehearsal space used for a busy calendar of student productions.

QMU promises a "student-centred approach" with a culture of personalised support. Among its initiatives to boost contentment on campus, there is a part-time team of "student champions" who work with their peers and university staff. Students struggling with their mental health can self-refer to the counselling and wellbeing service.

While Scotland has its own funding system, undergraduates from the rest of the UK may qualify for bursaries. There is also support for student carers, those who served in the armed forces and students who are estranged from their families.

**Edinburgh University Drive Musselburgh Edinburgh EH21 6UU**
admissions@qmu.ac.uk
qmu.ac.uk
qmusu.org.uk

**Overall ranking =105**
(last year 63)

**Accommodation**
University provided places 800
Self-catered £133–£160 per week

**Student numbers**
Undergraduates 3,432
Applications per place 6.6:1
Overall offer rate 55.3%

**Fees**
UK fees £0–£1,820
RUK fees 9,250
International fees £9,250–£17,325

qmu.ac.uk/open-days-and-meeting-us/
undergraduate-open-days/
qmu.ac.uk/study-here/fees-and-funding

# Queen Mary, University of London

Stereotypes have no place at this institution, a member of the elite Russell Group with East End roots. Queen Mary, University of London (QMUL) manages to achieve success in both our academic league (ranked 39th) and our social inclusion table (41st) – a rare combination.

Based in Tower Hamlets, the university continues its founding mission to improve lives through education. Undergraduates are mainly taught and housed in Mile End, on the biggest self-contained campus in the capital, and Whitechapel.

There are also campuses at West Smithfield, Charterhouse Square, Lincoln's Inn Fields and Ilford (for medicine and dentistry), and overseas operations in Malta, France, China and Singapore.

QMUL confirmed its standing in the Research Excellence Framework (REF 2021) with 92% of its submission assessed as world-leading or internationally excellent. The drama and film departments produced some of the best results, along with politics and international studies, engineering, economics and history.

The university achieved silver overall in the latest Teaching Excellence Framework (TEF 2023), including silver for student outcomes. A bronze rating for student experience is in keeping with its general record in the National Student Survey (NSS). In our analysis of NSS 2024, QMUL was 85th for satisfaction with the wider undergraduate experience (up from 107th) but lost ground on satisfaction with teaching quality (down four places to 121st).

Even so, the TEF panel found evidence of "a supportive learning environment, where students have access to a readily available range of very high quality academic support".

Initiatives to widen participation in higher education are well established and evolving. Among them is the Access to Queen Mary scheme, an 18-month programme helping to prepare students for higher education. Our figures show the university has the fifth-highest intake of students from black and minority ethnic backgrounds (75.5%) and the narrowest black awarding gap for degrees in England and Wales (1.9%). A 2021 report by the Institute for Fiscal Studies ranked QMUL as the UK's top university for social mobility.

There are about 300 societies and sports clubs. Music is well supported and QMUL is involved as a partner institution with the Season of Bangla drama festival and the UK Asian Film Festival.

Accommodation is guaranteed either on or near campus to first-years who have a firm offer and apply by June 30.

Since the pandemic, QMUL has poured investment into wellbeing services, providing support for international and independent students, and taking a proactive approach by running mindfulness workshops and a knitting group. Advice on housing, money, immigration concerns and emotional wellbeing is available and students can seek counselling and other talking therapies. QMUL has introduced mandatory training on sexual consent.

More than two-thirds of current UK undergraduates receive the Queen Mary Bursary of £1,000 or £1,700 depending on incomes under £35,000. Merit-based and subject-specific academic awards are offered, some of which are means-tested.

Management for social change is a new degree and from 2025 the university will offer applied AI; international business; and a distance-learning degree in pharmacology and drug discovery.

---

**327 Mile End Road London E1 4NS**
admissions@qmul.ac.uk
qmul.ac.uk
qmsu.org

**Overall ranking 39**
(last year 46)

**Accommodation**
University provided places 3,370
Self-catered £168–£213 per week

**Student numbers**
Undergraduates 17,414
Applications per place 8.6:1
Overall offer rate 61.4%

**Fees**
UK fees £9,250
International fees £23,350–£28,350
Medicine £48,700

qmul.ac.uk/undergraduate/openday
qmul.ac.uk/undergraduate/feesandfunding

# Queen's University, Belfast

The university where the Irish poet and playwright Seamus Heaney studied has a creative writing building named in his honour. A permanent exhibition and spaces for students to work can be found at the Seamus Heaney Centre in Belfast.

Queen's has invested heavily in its historic campus. Initiatives include the MediaLab facility and the £50 million McClay Library, which has computing and media services, IT training rooms and a language centre. A centre for the Global Institute of Educational Excellence is due to open in 2025.

Demand for places is high and the number of international students has more than doubled over the past decade, although Northern Irish students remain the biggest cohort.

The university ranks tenth in the UK for graduate prospects, based on results from the latest Graduate Outcomes survey, showing that 87.1% of its undergraduates had found high-skilled jobs or were engaged in postgraduate study 15 months after finishing their degrees.

Civic responsibility and economic prosperity are among the pillars of the university's strategy. It plays a leading role in the Belfast Region City Deal, a 15-year programme to boost growth, and has been awarded more than £170 million from the UK government and Northern Ireland Executive to develop three innovation centres in areas including advanced manufacturing, clinical research and secure, connected digital technologies.

The university's charter guarantees student representation, equal rights for women and nondenominational teaching. Hillary Clinton, the former US secretary of state, is its 11th – and first female – chancellor.

A five-place ascent of our academic league table was driven in part by much improved rates of student satisfaction. Results of the National Student Survey put it 45th for undergraduates' evaluation of the student experience (up from =74th) and 75th for their feelings about the teaching quality (up 19 places).

In the latest Research Excellence Framework (REF 2021) submissions from Queen's in agriculture, food and veterinary science; health and biomedical sciences; law; and engineering produced the best results. Overall, the university is 35th in our research quality rating.

There are close to 200 student clubs and societies, so plenty of opportunities for undergraduates to find like-minded people. The campus is a 15-minute walk from Belfast city centre and its nightlife, but the social scene is mainly based around the students' union, which forms part of the £42 million One Elmwood student centre. The arts are well supported on campus, where there is an arthouse cinema, a gallery and a studio theatre.

Rental costs are more attractive here than at many other locations in the UK. First-years are guaranteed accommodation as long as they meet the deadline at the end of June.

Students are offered free counselling sessions through local services and support is available from the university's team of disability and wellbeing advisers.

About three in ten undergraduates receive some form of financial support. Queen's has been stepping up its outreach efforts to attract disadvantaged students and redoubling its research links with universities in the Republic of Ireland.

---

**Belfast University Road Belfast BT7 1NN**
admissions@qub.ac.uk
qub.ac.uk
q-su.org

**Overall ranking 26**
(last year 31)

**Accommodation**
University provided places 4,168
Self-catered £85–£215 per week

**Student numbers**
Undergraduates 16,785
Applications per place 6.1:1
Overall offer rate 70.7%

**Fees**
UK fees £4,750 (Northern Ireland)
RUK fees 9,250
International fees £20,800–£25,300
Medicine £36,900

qub.ac.uk/Study/Undergraduate/open-days/
qub.ac.uk/Study/Undergraduate/Fees-and-scholarships

# University of Reading

Reading is one of the leading universities for the study of climate change, holding a Queen's Anniversary Prize for its research and teaching in the area. It was named our Sustainable University of the Year 2025 for the headway it made towards its ambition of being one of the world's greenest universities, and ranked top in the UK for its environmental and ethical performance by People and Planet 2023–24.

It has reduced its carbon emissions by more than 60% since 2009, with funding secured for the next phase of decarbonising the Whiteknights campus heating infrastructure. Students enrolled on its renowned agricultural degrees have access to 2,000 acres of farmland nearby.

Undergraduates who apply before the deadline and choose Reading as their firm choice are guaranteed accommodation. Almost all residential places are on the Whiteknights site or within easy walking distance.

Archaeology, art and design, and earth systems and environmental sciences contributed some of the university's best results in the latest Research Excellence Framework (REF 2021). Overall, Reading fell ten places in our research quality index since the last REF in 2014, to =39th, because gains were greater at other institutions. Reading was ranked at 172 in the QS World University Rankings 2025, up from 229 two years earlier.

The university has achieved silver ratings in the government's Teaching Excellence Framework (TEF 2023). Assessors commended its "use of research in relevant disciplines, scholarship, professional practice and employer engagement".

In our analysis of the National Student Survey, undergraduates' evaluations ranked the university 15th for broad experience (up from =31st) and 46th for teaching quality (a 23-place gain). The shift to a two-semester year from 2024, rather than three terms, was made with a view to boosting the student experience.

Study abroad is encouraged and students can sign up for summer school or a longer stint at its branch campus in Malaysia or a partner institution in Nanjing, in eastern China. Some courses allow students to study single-term modules overseas.

Courses introduced at Reading in the past two years include a four-year law programme, accountancy, biomedical engineering with professional experience and international development with a study year abroad.

An internship scheme provides paid professional work experience of four to 12 weeks, and Reading moved into the top 40 in our analysis of the Graduate Outcomes survey, based on 80.4% of its graduates being employed in highly skilled work or further study 15 months after finishing a degree.

More than 150 sports teams, clubs and societies are available, and the Reading Experience and Development (RED) awards promote one-off and long-term volunteering. The university runs "life tools" programmes to help students to build resilience and offers budgeting advice and a student support fund.

The Reading Bursary is worth up to £1,100 and offered to students from low-income households. For international students there are 100 Vice Chancellor Global Scholarships handed out every year, each of which is worth £4,000, as well as subject-specific financial help.

**Whiteknights PO Box 217 Reading RG6 6AH**
reading.ac.uk/question
reading.ac.uk
readingsu.co.uk

**Overall ranking =24**
(last year =34)

**Accommodation**
University provided places 4,982
Catered £163–£252 per week
Self-catered £151–£330 per week

**Student numbers**
Undergraduates 11,895
Applications per place 5.0:1
Overall offer rate 88.0%

**Fees**
UK fees £9,250
International fees £25,250–£29,950

reading.ac.uk/ready-to-study/visiting-and-open-days/opendays
reading.ac.uk/ready-to-study/study/fees-and-funding

# Robert Gordon University

Aberdeen's Robert Gordon University (RGU) is putting its considerable energies into new technology as the city faces radical challenges to its offshore industries. It has the world's first decommissioning simulator and the National Subsea Centre, opened in 2023, works in the North Sea and worldwide to develop smart digital and engineering solutions to enable a faster, more sustainable transition to a net-zero energy landscape.

In addition to engineering expertise, areas of study include computing, art and design, business and law, creative industries, health professions, and architecture and the built environment. Courses introduced r ecently offer psychology, criminology and games design.

RGU's best results in the latest Research Excellence Framework (REF 2021) were in computer science and engineering – not enough, though, to prevent a nine-place fall in the research quality rating. Its standing was buoyed by positive feedback from satisfied students in the National Student Survey (NSS): our analysis puts RGU 14th in the UK for teaching quality and =36th for the broad experience.

The university's career focus has led to a distinguished record in graduate recruitment. More than four in five (81.6%) graduates were working in highly skilled jobs or enrolled in postgraduate study 15 months after earning their degree. RGU has risen nine places in our graduate prospects index to rank 32nd and work experience is embedded across the curriculum.

At the Garthdee campus on the banks of the River Dee, where teaching is based, the landmark green-glass library tower symbolises the university's ambitions after £120 million of investment. To balance all the hard academic work, students have access to gyms, a swimming pool and exercise classes free of charge.

Aberdeen may seem a long way to travel for students from other parts of the UK, but rail and air links are excellent and it regularly features in lists of cities that offer a good quality of life. Mentors and a counselling and wellbeing service are on hand, with free appointments and training for students to act as peer support volunteers.

All students are entitled to free RGU Sport membership, with three gyms, badminton courts, bouldering and climbing facilities, and a sports hall available. There are more than 40 societies to explore and a wide variety of outdoor activities can be enjoyed on land and sea.

All first-years can be accommodated, although the university stops short of a guarantee and rooms offered may not be in the first choice of location. Standing 10th out of the 15 universities in our Scottish social inclusion index, RGU draws the lowest proportion of students from deprived areas (6.2%) but attracts the fourth-highest proportion of students aged over 21 (39.8%).

A small number of access scholarships are offered to students who meet widening participation criteria. There are scholarships available for entrants who move to RGU from elsewhere in the UK and for the larger numbers who travel from abroad to help to cover tuition, which is free to Scots.

---

**Garthdee House Garthdee Road Aberdeen AB10 7AQ**
admissions@rgu.ac.uk
rgu.ac.uk
rguunion.co.uk

**Overall ranking 61**
(last year 62)

**Accommodation**
University provided places 903
Self-catered £106–£172 per week

**Student numbers**
Undergraduates 8,221
Applications per place 4.4:1
Overall offer rate 70.1%

**Fees**
UK fees £0–£1,820
RUK fees 5,890–£6,930
International fees £16,490–£17,840

rgu.ac.uk/study/visit-us/open-days
rgu.ac.uk/study/courses

# University of Roehampton

Roehampton's 54-acre campus in southwest London blends historic buildings and woodland walks with modern facilities. The pioneering spirit of Digby Stuart, Froebel, Southlands and Whitelands (its founding colleges, some of the first to train women as teachers) lives on in its future-facing ambitions, with the introduction of degrees in sustainable engineering and technology, civil engineering, architectural technology and construction management.

Its academic pedigree is in evidence in Roehampton's impressive performance in the Research Excellence Framework (REF 2021), in which more than three-quarters of the research across 11 subject areas was rated as world-leading or internationally excellent. The arts and humanities fared well, with dance, drama and education producing some of the best results, as well as allied health.

Roehampton earned triple silver in the Teaching Excellence Framework (TEF 2023). The assessors noted that "exceptional support for staff professional development and excellent academic practice [was] embedded" across the institution. This finding came despite a controversial restructuring project that involved it dropping some arts and humanities degrees, and required more than 100 academics to reapply for their jobs.

Education courses remain a significant focus for the university, which has partnerships with more than 700 schools. Training for primary teachers was rated outstanding by Ofsted in 2023. Secondary-age teaching, a smaller area for the university, was rated good.

Roehampton was an early adopter of esports courses and attracts students by offering dedicated scholarships and what it bills as "the largest gaming arena of any UK university".

Next it plans to launch more programmes that can be studied online. The university balances this innovation with impressive research: it sits in our top 50 in this measure, which makes it the highest-placed non-specialist modern university for research.

A church minister degree apprenticeship launched in September 2024, to be followed by courses in civil engineering and physiotherapy.

The £1,000 Roehampton Bursary is awarded automatically in the first year to students who receive the full maintenance loan and the university offers merit-based scholarships for those who show promise in music and sport.

Roehampton slipped outside the top 100 of our league table, from 99th to 118th, largely because of lower rates of graduate employment. But the results of the National Student Survey (NSS) put it comfortably in the upper half of the table nationally.

Students are all members of one of the four colleges, which form a social hub and host formal dinners and balls in winter and summer. With more than 1,600 rooms on campus, first-years who apply by the deadline are guaranteed accommodation. More than 50 student clubs and societies include a vegan society, LGBTQ+ society and the long-running drama group the Roehampton Players, whose ranks have produced performers in the West End.

Sports facilities include four dance studios and a resurfaced multi-use games area. Gym Roehampton, on campus, is run by Nuffield Health. The university has a team of dedicated student wellbeing officers, as well as counsellors and specialist mental health advisers available every day of the week.

**Grove House Roehampton Lane**
**London SW15 5PJ**
ug.information@roehampton.ac.uk
roehampton.ac.uk
roehamptonstudent.com

**Overall ranking 118**
(last year 99)

**Accommodation**
University provided places 1,676
Self-catered £139–£220 per week

**Student numbers**
Undergraduates 7,619
Applications per place 5.0:1
Overall offer rate 84.4%

**Fees**
UK fees £9,250
International fees £15,488–£18,900

roehampton.ac.uk/study/open-days/
roehampton.ac.uk/study/fees-and-funding/home-undergraduate/

# Royal Agricultural University

Students who are happy to muck in and roll up their sleeves should feel at home at the Royal Agricultural University (RAU) on the outskirts of Cirencester. Renowned for its land-based learning, it offers hands-on experience at Coates Manor Farm, which grows wheat, barley and oilseed rape, the dairy complex Kemble Farms and Leaze Farm, with its 300-cow calving herd.

A partnership with the neighbouring Bathurst Estate gives students access to 15,000 acres of farmland, forestry, environmentally managed land, real estate and heritage properties, along with rural enterprises for teaching, research and knowledge exchange.

Entrepreneurial activity is encouraged and students can spend a sandwich year in industry as part of their degree. The RAU is one of only six universities to be made a centre of excellence by the Institute of Enterprise and Entrepreneurs. However, with only 68.7% of graduates in high-skilled jobs or further study 15 months after their degrees, it sits in the bottom 25 in our analysis of graduate prospects.

Rated triple silver in the government's Teaching Excellence Framework (TEF 2023), the RAU was praised for "excellent academic practice" across the university. Feedback from undergraduates in the latest National Student Survey was less favourable. It fell to the bottom of our table for satisfaction with teaching quality and the wider undergraduate experience (both 131st). In our main academic league table, the RAU continues to be held back by a student-to-staff ratio exceeding 21:1.

Half of the work submitted in the Research Excellence Framework (REF 2021) was considered world-leading or internationally excellent. The RAU leads a global group of agricultural universities researching sustainable business models to reduce food poverty, decrease the carbon footprint of agriculture and protect the livelihoods of farmers.

The university is offering new degrees in environment and sustainability, with foundation degrees added in equine management, residential estate agency, and business and enterprise.

About 11.5% of new entrants in 2023 qualified for financial help. Eligible students from low-income households can receive a bursary of between £1,000 and £3,500. With only 55.6% of the intake drawn from non-selective state schools, efforts to broaden its appeal include two Next Generation scholarships, which pay £6,000 a year to eligible students from a minority ethnic community. The Kaleb Cooper Agriculture Bursary, backed by Jeremy Clarkson's TV sidekick in Clarkson's Farm, aims to support students from a non-agricultural background.

A hub on the RAU campus houses student facilities, with room for lacrosse, hockey, rugby, tennis, croquet and netball to be played on site. To support welfare there are daily drop-ins with a mental health professional, the Talk Campus platform and free counselling referrals.

Accommodation is allocated on a first come, first served basis and students are advised to apply early. Fossehill Farm provides livery stabling for those who want to take their horse to university.

The RAU has a tradition of royal patrons and King Charles joined the list in 2024. Every British monarch since Queen Victoria has visited the university.

**Stroud Road Cirencester GL7 6JS**
admissions@rau.ac.uk
rau.ac.uk
rausu.co.uk

**Overall ranking 131**
(last year 104)

**Accommodation**
University provided places 290
Catered £203–£260 per week
Self-catered £193–£199 per week

**Student numbers**
Undergraduates 972
Applications per place 3.7:1
Overall offer rate N/A

**Fees**
UK fees £9,250
International fees £15,300

rau.ac.uk/courses/open-days-and-events
rau.ac.uk/student-life/finance-scholarships-and-bursaries

# Royal Holloway, University of London

Royal Holloway has always been a pioneer. It was formed from two of the few colleges where women could access higher education and its Founder's Building is a showstopper of Victorian architecture, described by contemporaries as a "source of amazement". Today it is a centre of excellence in cybersecurity research.

The campus in Egham, Surrey, also offers recording spaces; the Handa Noh Theatre is being fitted out with the latest in video production facilities; and the Emily Wilding Davison Building is to get a 24-seat gaming laboratory.

There was record demand for places at Royal Holloway in 2023, with more than 21,300 applications and 3,800 undergraduates accepted on to courses.

In the latest Research Excellence Framework (REF 2021), 88% of the university's work was assessed as world-leading or internationally excellent, led by success in music, communication and media studies, and geography. It sits in =26th place in our research quality rating.

Awarding Royal Holloway triple silver in the Teaching Excellence Framework (TEF 2023), assessors praised "the use of research in relevant disciplines, innovation, scholarship, professional practice and employer engagement to contribute to an outstanding academic experience".

Rates of student satisfaction are inside the top 50 (48th) for the broad experience but only 91st for students' evaluation of teaching quality, based on our analysis of the National Student Survey.

The CVstac employability framework, which aims to support students by identifying and building the key skills around social intelligence, innovation and self-management required by employers, is embedded into teaching. Responses to the latest national Graduate Outcomes survey put the university in 46th place (up six on the previous year) for the proportion of graduates in professional-level jobs or further study 15 months after finishing their degrees.

Royal Holloway has highly specialised facilities, including its own observatory and a recently opened £2 million drone hangar, part of the Omnidrome Research & Innovation Centre. The relatively sedate social scenes offered by Egham and nearby Windsor are sufficient for some students, while others prefer to explore central London, about 40 minutes away by train.

There are 2,812 study bedrooms for undergraduates. Entrants are guaranteed a place as long as they make Royal Holloway their firm choice and meet the application deadline. More than a fifth of rooms are catered.

A wellbeing department provides broad support encompassing mental health, disability and neurodiversity. There is access to counselling as well as help with financial wellbeing, and the services of chaplaincy and faith support teams.

About three in ten UK undergraduates qualified for one of Royal Holloway's bursaries in 2024. These help people from low-income households, care leavers and mature students from low-income households, with values from £500 to £3,000 a year. Scholarships are awarded competitively to recognise academic, sporting and musical achievements.

With more than 80 teams and good facilities, Royal Holloway enjoys a stronger sporting tradition than at some other University of London colleges. There is a fitness studio and sports hall on campus and the university has the use of a boathouse on the Thames.

---

**Egham Hill Egham TW20 0EX**
royalholloway.ac.uk/applicationquery
royalholloway.ac.uk
su.rhul.ac.uk

**Overall ranking 34**
(last year =29)

**Accommodation**
University provided places 3,096
Catered £143–£196 per week
Self-catered £125–£196 per week

**Student numbers**
Undergraduates 9,459
Applications per place 5.5:1
Overall offer rate 87.1%

**Fees**
UK fees £9,250
International fees £19,600–£26,500

royalholloway.ac.uk/student-life/visit-royal-holloway/open-days/
royalholloway.ac.uk/studying-here/fees-and-funding/

# University of St Andrews

St Andrews was the first university to break the Oxbridge duopoly at the top of our academic league table and remains ahead of its ancient rivals and top of the Scottish institutions. In our analysis of the National Student Survey, it ranks top for the broad experience and second for teaching quality.

The seaside university is renowned for its marine research, pioneering medical investigations at the Sir James Mackenzie Institute for Early Diagnosis and its work at the Handa Centre for the Study of Terrorism and Political Violence.

It is also famous as the meeting place of two alumni in particular: the Prince and Princess of Wales. Asked why he chose St Andrews, Prince William said at the time: "I love the hills and mountains and I thought St Andrews had a real community feel to it." He studied art history before switching to geography and is said to have locked eyes with the art history undergraduate Catherine Middleton in a dorm hallway in 2001.

St Andrews' academic activities are arranged into four faculties: arts, divinity, medicine and science, and it offers a four-year course structure. It provides scholarships and bursaries amounting to more than £2.8 million annually, with awards worth up to £4,400 a year.

More than 88% of the work submitted to the latest Research Assessment Framework (REF 2021) was assessed as world-leading or internationally excellent, earning the university 25th place in our research quality index. Some of its best results were in physics, earth sciences and modern languages. St Andrews takes the top spot for the proportion of its students who graduate with top honours (94.8%).

The university dominates the small town of St Andrews, northeast of Edinburgh. All first-years who apply by the June deadline are guaranteed a place at one of the halls of residence that encircle University Park.

St Andrews has the most ethnically diverse student population of the Scottish universities (17.4% of its students are from black or ethnic minority backgrounds), yet it is at the bottom of our social inclusion ranking for Scotland. It admits the smallest proportion of students from non-selective schools (56.2%) and the fewest students who are the first in their family to go to university (18.7%).

Pubs, societies, balls and sport are mainstays of the social scene. A £14 million redevelopment and extension supercharged the sports centre, and students can take part in football, rugby, shinty and lacrosse. For a cultural flourish, there is the Byre Theatre and two university museums. Musical students are well provided for, with ensembles ranging from the elite St Salvator's Chapel Choir, Byre Opera and St Andrews Symphony Orchestra to groups requiring no auditions.

The university runs services for counselling and coaching, as well as psychoeducational groups, cognitive behavioural therapy, mental health coordination and out-of-hours care. Its Equality, Diversity and Inclusion Project Fund provides grants of up to £2,500 to support student and staff projects whose aim is to enhance equality and inclusivity.

---

**College Gate North Street St Andrews KY16 9AJ**
admissions@st-andrews.ac.uk
st-andrews.ac.uk
yourunion.net

**Overall ranking 2**
(last year 1)

**Accommodation**
University provided places 3,793
Catered £199–£297 per week
Self-catered £164–£264 per week

ST ANDREWS
Edinburgh
Belfast
London
Cardiff

**Student numbers**
Undergraduates 8,719
Applications per place 10.6:1
Overall offer rate 26.6%

**Fees**
UK fees £0–£1,820
RUK fees 9,250
International fees £30,160–£36,840
Medicine £36,990

st-andrews.ac.uk/study/meet-us/in-st-andrews/ug/
st-andrews.ac.uk/students/money/fees/feestable

# St George's, University of London

St George's merged with City, University of London in August 2024, nearly 300 years after its establishment as only the second institution in England to provide formal training for doctors. The new City St George's University will play a key role as what its president, Professor Sir Anthony Finkelstein, calls a "health powerhouse".

St George's courses in medicine, pharmacology, biomedical science, allied and global health will complement current City courses in nursing, midwifery, speech and language therapy, optometry, counselling and psychology.

Until integration is complete the universities will operate a "dual running" policy, so we continue to list them separately here. Current and prospective students will automatically become members of City St George's.

Based in Tooting, southwest London, St George's trains doctors, paramedics, physician associates, biomedical scientists, radiotherapists, radiographers, physiotherapists and occupational therapists. It pioneered the fast-track, four-year MBBS (Bachelor of Medicine and Bachelor of Surgery) graduate-entry programme and the course is a popular route into the medical profession across the country.

St George's was upgraded to silver overall in the government's Teaching Excellence Framework (TEF 2023), up from bronze in the previous assessment. Although it achieved silver for student outcomes, it was rated bronze for student experience.

Successive poor showings in the National Student Survey (NSS) have taken a toll on the university's position in our academic table in recent years. It clawed back ten places to occupy 69th place in our 2025 edition, having been in the top 50 as recently as 2020. In our latest NSS analysis, St George's recovered ten places to reach 119th for satisfaction with teaching quality, slipping one place to 129th for satisfaction with the wider undergraduate experience.

In the latest Research Excellence Framework (REF 2021), more than a third (36%) of the submission was given the top rating of world-leading, lifting the university ten places to =42nd in our research quality index.

The university does a good job of retaining its students, standing =32nd in our academic league table for course continuation rates. Most of its courses are linked with employers who deliver healthcare and St George's graduates are in demand. The latest Graduate Outcomes survey showed 91.6% of its students were in highly skilled work or postgraduate study within 15 months of finishing. This puts it second only to Imperial College London for graduate prospects in our analysis.

The university occupies the Hunter Wing of St George's University Hospital, where there are study areas and computer rooms. The nature of the clinical programmes at St George's means that mental health and wellbeing support for students is included within the curriculum.

More than three in ten entrants qualify for financial help. The St George's Opportunity Fund Grant provides up to £1,700 for first-years from low-income households, then £1,000 for each year of study.

The students' union offers 120 clubs, societies and community projects. Prospective students who accept St George's as their firm offer and apply by July 1 are guaranteed one of Horton Halls' 486 self-catering rooms, a 15-minute walk away.

---

**Cranmer Terrace Tooting London SW17 0RE**
study@sgul.ac.uk
sgul.ac.uk
sgsu.org.uk

**Overall ranking 69**
(last year 79)

**Accommodation**
University provided places 486
Self-catered £202–£224 per week

**Student numbers**
Undergraduates 3,159
Applications per place 7.1:1
Overall offer rate 41.1%

**Fees**
UK fees £9,250
International fees £19,150–£21,250
Medicine £42,550

sgul.ac.uk/study/visit-us
sgul.ac.uk/about/governance/policies/tuition-fee

# St Mary's University, Twickenham

One of four Catholic universities in the UK, St Mary's admits students of all faiths or none at its 35-acre campus near the River Thames. The landmark Strawberry Hill House, built by Horace Walpole, has been in the university's hands since 1923 and houses a fine art collection.

Sport and exercise science are among Twickenham's strengths: the St Mary's Endurance and Performance Centre offers elite training and 14 of its athletes competed at the Paris 2024 Olympics. At the Teddington Lock sports campus, the facilities are used for fixtures organised by British Universities and Colleges Sport as well as lectures.

St Mary's was founded in 1850 to train teachers and the university's School of Education maintains its reputation, holding Ofsted's top rating since 2011. Student satisfaction is high: the university ranks ninth for feedback on teaching quality and 16th for the wider experience, based on our analysis of the National Student Survey.

The university moved to a three-faculty structure from 2023, focusing on business and law; education, theology and the arts; and sport, technology and health sciences. St Mary's was awarded silver overall in the Teaching Excellence Framework (TEF 2023), with gold for the student experience and silver for student outcomes.

It made great strides in the latest Research Excellence Framework (REF 2021), rising 23 places to 88th. Sport and theology were the leading subject areas. The continuation rate at St Mary's is a sticking point, however. Only 89% of students are projected to carry on into the second year of their studies (ranked 103rd).

The latest data shows that 79.8% of St Mary's graduates are in high-skilled jobs or postgraduate study 15 months after finishing their degrees, taking the university into the top 50 (up nine places to 42nd). Some degrees come with a professional accreditation from bodies such as the Chartered Management Institute and the Chartered Society of Physiotherapy.

First-years who apply before the June deadline are guaranteed a room. Almost all of St Mary's stock of more than 600 rooms in halls are catered and all are on campus. The Student Heart development was completed in time for the 2024–25 academic year, offering social and study spaces, a roof terrace and an upgraded bar.

Featuring in the upper half of our social inclusion index overall (54th), St Mary's draws most of its students (95.6%, 32nd) from non-selective state schools and more than a third (37.8%) are from ethnic minority backgrounds (43rd).

Students have access to help from mental health advisers as well as counselling and the 24/7 Togetherall online support platform. St Mary's is one of the few universities to make sexual consent training mandatory.

Sport scholarships are worth up to £2,000 and include free gym membership and nutrition support. An acting scholarship waives the fees for all three years of study. Students who have been in care or are estranged from their families are eligible for a £3,000 annual bursary. PGCE students and those from low-income households may qualify for bursaries.

**Waldegrave Road Twickenham TW1 4SX**
apply@stmarys.ac.uk
stmarys.ac.uk
stmaryssu.co.uk

**Overall ranking 52**
(last year 45)

**Accommodation**
University provided places 662
Catered £193–£297 per week
Self-catered £272–£324 per week

**Student numbers**
Undergraduates 3,457
Applications per place 4.8:1
Overall offer rate 88.5%

**Fees**
UK fees £9,250–£11,100
International fees £16,320–£16,980

stmarys.ac.uk/open-events/undergraduate
stmarys.ac.uk/student-services/funding

# University of Salford

Regeneration and integration are at the heart of the University of Salford. In the revitalised Salford Quays, a former technical college has brought new life to the Old Fire Station opposite its Peel Park campus. The once-derelict building has its own micro-brewery and in-house bakery.

This industry-focused institution prioritises building work experience placements and live briefs from working experts into degree courses to boost employability. Salford shot 27 places up our graduate prospects index to rank =54th, based on more than three-quarters of graduates being in high-skilled jobs or postgraduate study 15 months after finishing their degree.

A 19-place rise in our main academic table took Salford to 72nd, buoyed by improved rates of student satisfaction. It shifted up a level in the latest Teaching Excellence Framework (TEF 2023), where it earned silver overall.

The university also performed strongly in the Research Excellence Framework (REF 2021), in which 78% of its submissions were rated world-leading or internationally excellent.

New resources include the £16 million Energy House 2.0, made up of a pair of detached houses inside a chamber. Scientists can simulate wind, rain and snow, and a range of temperatures to establish the most effective ways to reduce carbon and control running costs in modern homes.

The North of England Robotics Innovation Centre serves small to medium-sized enterprises and the Greater Manchester Institute of Technology is due to open in late 2025. A degree in sports journalism launches the same year.

There are three campuses including one at the MediaCity site at Salford Quays. First-years are not guaranteed accommodation but 1,300 rooms are ringfenced for new undergraduates. About 75% of students are able to live-in.

Students can access leisure facilities including a swimming pool with sauna and spa, fitness suites and a multi-use sports hall. They are within striking distance of Manchester, which is ideal for top sport, culture, shopping and nightlife. Greater Manchester is a huge student hub and home to about 100,000 students.

Students can self-refer to the counselling and wellbeing service, which offers an initial triage appointment followed by in-depth wellbeing sessions, workshops and therapeutic groups. Salford's security team, students' union and accommodation provider share training and best practice on suicide prevention. There is also Rafiki, a student-led peer support listening service, and a 24/7 student care line staffed by counsellors.

Breaking into the top 50, Salford is up 20 places in our social inclusion index, ranking at 45th. Its proportion of students from non-selective state schools (96.8%) is in the top 25 and the proportion of students from deprived areas represents 16% of the intake, putting Salford in the top quarter of UK universities. Outreach work aims to raise aspirations among young people from low-participation neighbourhoods around Salford and Greater Manchester.

Financial support includes the Salford Inspire Fund of £150 a year for learning resources, plus an extra £350 for students from low-income backgrounds. Bursaries of £550 support estranged students, care leavers and student carers.

**Maxwell Building The Crescent Salford**
**Greater Manchester M5 4WT**
enquiries@salford.ac.uk
salford.ac.uk
salfordstudents.com

**Overall ranking 72**
(last year 91)

**Accommodation**
University provided places 2,161
Self-catered £118–£186 per week

**Student numbers**
Undergraduates 17,895
Applications per place 4.5:1
Overall offer rate 73.6

**Fees**
UK fees £9,250
International fees £13,750–£18,300

salford.ac.uk/undergraduate/open-days
salford.ac.uk/undergraduate/fees-and-funding

# University of Sheffield

Runner-up for the accolade of The Sunday Times University of the Year 2025, Sheffield takes a proactive approach to student wellbeing, encouraging participation in sport and physical activity and nurturing communities through more than 350 clubs and societies.

Annual participation grants of up to £150 are available for eligible students from low-income households, those with a disability or who have children, or forced migrants. Support is also available from personal tutors and faith and belief advisers.

Sheffield has one of the biggest university sports leagues and facilities near the main precinct include an upgraded gym, six floodlit synthetic turf pitches and a swimming pool. Outdoor pitches for rugby, football and cricket are a bus ride away. Scholarships for elite student athletes contribute to the university's strong sports record.

Its accommodation guarantee goes the extra mile, giving a place in halls to all first-years who apply by the end of August – even those who enter through Clearing. Rents are among the most affordable around.

The number of bursaries it awards is not capped and students from households with an income of £40,000 or less are eligible for awards of £250 up to £1,000 a year. Students who live in deprived areas, or within a Sheffield city region that has low progression to university, qualify for an extra £250 a year. There is support for care leavers, student carers and those who are estranged from their family, as well as merit-based scholarships.

The institution attracted record applications in 2023 (43,665) and is enjoying rising rates of student satisfaction, partly thanks to an award-winning students' union. At 14th, Sheffield is up four places year-on-year in our top 20.

The university, which joined the research-intensive Russell Group in 1994, excelled in the latest Research Excellence Framework (REF 2021), in which 92% of its work was rated world-leading or internationally excellent. In our research rankings it is 15th. Sheffield is just outside the global top 100 in the QS World University Rankings 2025 (105th).

Top-notch feedback in the National Student Survey is rare among Russell Group universities but Sheffield bucks the trend, in our analysis, ranking ninth for satisfaction with the student experience (up from 28th in our previous edition) and =26th for teaching quality (up 21 places). Recent campus improvements, including investment in health and wellbeing, may explain why contentment has grown.

In the Teaching Excellence Framework (TEF 2023), Sheffield gained silver overall, with silver for the student experience and student outcomes. Assessors identified as outstanding "a supportive learning environment".

Upgrades at Sheffield include extra architecture studio spaces in the Arts Tower building, simulators for dentistry students and learning spaces for computer science within the Diamond, the flagship building at the Faculty of Engineering. History, philosophy, archaeology and the Digital Humanities Institute were brought under one roof to support collaborative working.

According to the Graduate Outcomes survey, 82.9% of leavers were in highly skilled jobs or postgraduate study 15 months after receiving their degrees.

---

**Western Bank Sheffield S10 2TN**
study@sheffield.ac.uk
sheffield.ac.uk
su.sheffield.ac.uk

**Overall ranking 14**
(last year 18)

**Accommodation**
Catered £166 per week
Self-catered £96–£253 per week

**Student numbers**
Undergraduates 19,543
Applications per place 7.5:1
Overall offer rate 75.3%

**Fees**
UK fees £9,250
International fees £22,680–£29,110
Medicine £43,150

sheffield.ac.uk/undergraduate/visit/open-days
sheffield.ac.uk/undergraduate/fees-funding

# Sheffield Hallam University

Sheffield Hallam's mission is to transform students' lives and give everyone the chance to reach their full potential. It has opened doors to higher education to many who might not otherwise have considered it, offering support at the application stage and during the transition to student life.

The university ranks 13th overall in our social inclusion index and more than half of its intake is made up of students who are the first in their family to go to university (29th). It has the second-highest proportion of white working-class males (an underrepresented group) in England and Wales.

Although Hallam is based in a lively city, the proximity of the Peak District is a boon for cyclists and hikers. Most teaching facilities are at the City campus, housing buildings for Sheffield Business School, law, social sciences and architecture. Redevelopment here will feature Hallam Green, a leafy haven, as part of a 20-year, £220 million investment. The Collegiate campus is ten minutes by bus from the city centre and home to the energy-efficient £27 million Heart of the Campus building. All first-years are guaranteed a room in halls of residence.

Hallam's research reputation is growing (69th) and it is in the top half for graduate prospects (64th). In the latest Research Excellence Framework (REF 2021), 72% of its bigger and broader submission was rated world-leading or internationally excellent. Some of the best results were in sport; art and design; and the built environment and planning.

It earned gold overall in the Teaching Excellence Framework (TEF 2023), with silver for the student experience and gold for student outcomes. However, faltering rates of student satisfaction hold Hallam back in our main academic league table. Our latest National Student Survey analysis showed a slight year-on-year decline in satisfaction with teaching quality (=107th) but an improvement in the wider undergraduate experience, up eight places to =112nd.

New entrants are allocated three advisers – specialising in the academic side, employability and student support. Hallam is in the top half of UK universities (=64th) for its continuation rate, based on 92% of students projected to carry on from the first to the second year of their studies.

Students can seek support and counselling in groups or individually, or through faith and chaplaincy sessions. There is also a 24/7 online support platform.

Degrees introduced recently include children and childhood; climate, sustainability and environmental management; biomedicine and health science; general engineering; business management with finance; AI and robotics; and mechatronics and robotics engineering.

Foundation years have been added to about 20 courses within the College of Health, Wellbeing and Life Sciences.

The university invested more than £5 million in financial support to students in 2022–23 and awarded the Student Success Scholarship (between £600 and £2,100) to 17% of new entrants. Placement bursaries of the same value range are available to help students stay afloat during a year in industry. The performance athletes support programme is worth up to £3,000.

**Howard Street Sheffield S1 1WB**
shu.ac.uk/study-here/ask-a-question
shu.ac.uk
hallamstudentsunion.com

**Overall ranking =84**
(last year =85)

**Accommodation**
University provided places 4,500
Self-catered £91–£190 per week

**Student numbers**
Undergraduates 20,419
Applications per place 4.2:1
Overall offer rate 74.5%

**Fees**
UK fees £9,250
International fees £16,665

shu.ac.uk/visit-us
shu.ac.uk/study-here/fees-and-funding

# SOAS University of London

The former School of Oriental and African Studies has shifted focus from its roots in Britain's imperialist projects, training administrators to run the empire's colonies, to contemporary debates that challenge its founding function.

The London university pioneered moves to decolonise the curriculum, committed itself to challenging Eurocentrism and developed a toolkit for increasing inclusivity in teaching and redressing disadvantage through racism and colonialism.

With students from ethnic minority backgrounds making up 77.3% of its admissions, SOAS has the fourth most ethnically diverse student body in the UK.

A small university with fewer than 6,000 students, its anthropologists have been awarded nearly £8 million from Research England to help understand and address inequalities in access to mental health care in London and beyond.

SOAS has degree combinations across law, politics, economics, finance, business, management, the arts, humanities and languages, with a focus on Asia, Africa and the Middle East. More than 40% of undergraduate programmes offer the opportunity to spend a year studying in another country.

Its development studies course ranks =3rd in the 2024 QS World University Rankings and it climbed ten places to 36th in our research quality index, thanks to a strong performance in the latest Research Excellence Framework (REF 2021). 87% of the research it submitted was ranked world-leading or internationally excellent, with notable success in law, anthropology and music.

Last year SOAS entered our top 30 and was shortlisted for our Specialist University of the Year title. A double-digit fall in 2025 was due to less buoyant rates of graduate employment and struggling rates of student satisfaction.

It ranks in the bottom five for students' evaluations of both teaching quality and the wider experience in our analysis of the annual National Student Survey. In the Teaching Excellence Framework (TEF 2023) it received only a bronze rating for student experience, although it maintained a silver award overall.

The university nurtures relationships with public sector organisations, charities, NGOs, law firms, consultancies and the cultural and creative industries. It fell 20 places to =65th in the latest national Graduate Outcomes survey.

Based in the University of London district of Bloomsbury, SOAS is known for its outstanding library, with more than 1.5 million volumes, periodicals and audio-visual materials in 400 languages.

IT facilities are being upgraded at the campus, which has a student-run radio station and a refurbished students' union common room. First-years who apply during the main cycle are guaranteed accommodation, with prices starting at £155 a week.

SOAS offers a student counselling service in one-to-one, group or workshop settings. A multifaith chaplaincy and a mentoring service also provide support. New students are required to take part in consent and active bystander training sessions.

Almost half of undergraduates received financial help from the university in 2024. Awards based on financial need include the SOAS bursary (£4,500 paid over the duration of a degree) and the University of London Scholars Programme. The International Academic Excellence Scholarship provides a £2,500 tuition-fee discount to overseas students.

**10 Thornhaugh Street Russell Square London WC1H 0XG**
study@soas.ac.uk
soas.ac.uk
soasunion.org

**Overall ranking 65**
(last year 28)

**Accommodation**
University provided places 1,385
Catered £205–£359 per week
Self-catered £155–£364 per week

**Student numbers**
Undergraduates 3,365
Applications per place 3.6:1
Overall offer rate 91.2%

**Fees**
UK fees £9,250
International fees £21,990

soas.ac.uk/visit/soas-open-days
soas.ac.uk/study/student-fees-and-funding

# Solent University

Hands-on, real-world teaching is to the fore at Solent University in Southampton, which has invested in immersive learning settings for its diverse courses. They include a ship and port simulation centre at Warsash Maritime School, the Human Health Lab replicating a medical ward and virtual production stage equipment for courses across CGI, computer gaming and the digital arts.

Among its specialisms, the university provides tuition for Merchant Navy senior officers, yacht certification and maritime safety management. Other courses are arranged under departments of sport and health; film and media; science and engineering; social sciences and nursing; business and law; and art and music.

New courses on offer include LLB law with business; LLB law with criminology; quantity surveying; and a degree apprenticeship in construction quantity surveying.

Solent's approach was endorsed by a gold rating overall in the government's Teaching Excellence Framework (TEF 2023), underpinned by golds for the student experience and student outcome – making it one of the few universities to achieve the TEF "triple gold".

In the Research Excellence Framework (REF 2021), 34% of the work submitted for assessment by Solent achieved the top ratings of world-leading or internationally excellent. Although modest, the scores prompted an improvement for Solent in our research quality index, where it moved off the foot of the ranking.

Solent does well on student satisfaction, especially in relation to students' evaluation of their teaching quality, which puts it at =26th (up 11 places) in our analysis of the National Student Survey. Students gave more positive feedback on the broad experience too, prompting a 16-place improvement to =51st.

Solent's main East Park Terrace campus is close to the city centre, with the £33 million Spark building at its heart with space for 1,500 students. Recent developments added an attractive new quad with outdoor space and a replica law court. The maritime simulation facility is at East Park Terrace, with the St Mary's dedicated maritime training centre nearby. The Warsash campus is about ten miles away, overlooking Southampton Water.

First-year full-time students who apply by the end of June are guaranteed a room. The sports complex on the main campus offers facilities for performance athletes as well as general use.

There are no waiting lists for counselling and mental health appointments, which are provided by Solent's therapy and mental health service, and students get a same-day response. Options include single-session therapy, blocks of counselling and cognitive behavioural therapy.

Joint 41st in our social inclusion index overall, Solent excels in its recruitment of underrepresented white working-class males. Almost a fifth of students are drawn from deprived areas and Solent's low dropout rate among these students is in the top 20.

Bursaries, of up to £1,500 and paid in instalments, target students who have left care, are local to the university, estranged from their families or who are carers. Sports scholarships are worth up to £5,000 and there is a £1,000 scholarship for black, Asian or ethnic minority students.

---

**East Park Terrace Southampton SO14 0YN**
admissions@solent.ac.uk
solent.ac.uk
solentsu.co.uk

**Overall ranking 98**
(last year 109)

**Accommodation**
University provided places 1,021
Self-catered £121–£159 per week

**Student numbers**
Undergraduates 8,128
Applications per place 4.8:1
Overall offer rate 92.4%

**Fees**
UK fees £9,250
International fees £16,125

solent.ac.uk/open-days
solent.ac.uk/finance

# University of South Wales

The University of South Wales (USW) is guided by a vision "to change lives and our world for the better" and focuses on equipping students with the skills and experience to give them every chance in their careers. Rooted in the regional economy, with campuses in Pontypridd, Cardiff and Newport, it offers more than 500 courses.

Pontypridd is the biggest site, with a £6 million Learning Resources Centre and new facilities for chiropractic students. It has acute care simulation suites for nursing and midwifery students and hosts USW's law programmes.

The Cardiff campus houses creative courses in the Atrium building, covering advertising, television, film set design and fashion. It also has dance spaces and photographic studios. Courses at the £35 million Newport base include cybersecurity, education and psychology.

USW was established in 2013 through the merger of the University of Glamorgan and the University of Wales, Newport. It has moved nine places up our league table over the past two years edging it further inside the top 100, ranking at =94th.

An improved performance in the Research Excellence Framework (REF 2021), compared with 2014, triggered a nine-place rise to 95th in our research quality index. Students are increasingly content with the teaching quality, according to their feedback in the National Student Survey, which puts USW =41st (up 13 places). However, their evaluation of the broader student experience is less upbeat, with a ranking of =97th (down five places).

Continuation rates are a sticking point. The latest figures show about one in ten students is projected to drop out between the first and second year of their degree: USW ranks 92nd on this measure. This can be a side-effect of a diverse intake, and with around four in ten USW students aged over 21 when they enrol, the university has the 22nd highest proportion of mature students in England and Wales.

Employability is built into its courses. In our analysis of the latest Graduate Outcomes survey, 71.1% of USW students were in highly skilled jobs or further study 15 months after finishing their degree (97th), up from two-thirds two years ago.

On the social side, Cardiff has a well-earned reputation as a student city that's hard to beat, while coastal and countryside adventures are within easy reach. There are halls of residence at all the campuses. USW has been able to accommodate all first-year, full-time students who have requested to live in halls, but demand changes annually.

A wellbeing service encompasses specialist mental health support and counselling. There are also wellbeing groups, craft workshops and book clubs.

Ranking 31st overall for social inclusion, USW recruits the eighth-highest proportion of students from deprived areas in England and Wales, and 96% are drawn from non-selective state secondary schools.

Financial packages include the USW Gwent Bursary of £1,000 for students open to contextual offer holders resident at a NP postcode at the time of applying. The university offers scholarships to reward attainment in sport and in Welsh-medium study.

---

**1 Lantwit Road Treforest Pontypridd CF37 1DL**
equiries@southwales.ac.uk
southwales.ac.uk
uswsu.com

**Overall ranking =94**
(last year 97)

**Accommodation**
University provided places 1,412
Self-catered £112–£186 per week

**Student numbers**
Undergraduates 13,281
Applications per place 4.2:1
Overall offer rate 89.4%

**Fees**
UK fees £9,250
International fees £14,950–£15,260

southwales.ac.uk/open-days/
southwales.ac.uk/money

# University of Southampton

Southampton's ten-year investment in its estate includes a supercharged sports offering with £40 million-worth of extra facilities. At the main Highfield campus, an extension to the Jubilee Sports Centre includes a martial arts space and a cycling studio.

The university has six sites within easy reach of each other in the city, plus another in Winchester and a Malaysian operation in Iskandar Puteri. Highfield is getting a new flagship teaching and learning building, scheduled to open in 2027, with an academic workspace for the faculty of medicine.

A founding member of the research-intensive Russell Group, Southampton was placed =80th in the QS World University Ranking 2025. Its spot in the elite top 20 of our league table is bolstered by its performance in the Research Excellence Framework (REF 2021), in which engineering, allied health subjects and computer science produced some of its best results. Overall, about 90% of its work was rated world-leading or internationally excellent and Southampton sits at 14th in our research quality index.

Assessors from the Teaching Excellence Framework (TEF 2023) gave the university triple silver – overall and for the student experience and student outcomes. However, rates of student satisfaction have declined. In our analysis of the National Student Survey, undergraduates' reviews of teaching quality put Southampton at =97th (down 35 places) and their evaluation of the wider experience ranked it =74th (down 40).

Courses introduced recently include accounting, accountability and taxation; creative computing; sustainable luxury (formerly textile design); and an integrated master's in medical technology, innovation and design.

Opportunities for volunteering and entrepreneurship add to the student experience, while the city's just-big-enough appeal makes it a magnet for school leavers dipping their toes into independent living. The university guarantees accommodation in a single room for all firm and insurance applicants who apply by the July 1 deadline.

A "Welcome to Southampton" module supports the academic transition to higher education and consent training is mandatory for all students. Mental health and wellbeing help is accessed through the Student Hub.

Nearly a quarter of UK undergraduates here tend to receive a bursary of £1,000 or £2,000 per academic year, based on household incomes of £30,000 or less. Merit-based scholarships are also available.

It sits 106th overall in our social inclusion ranking and is in the top half of universities for the proportion of students who are from ethnic minority backgrounds, who represent a third of the intake. About seven in ten students went to non-selective state schools and 31.9% of the intake were the first in their family to go to university. To widen participation in higher education among schools in areas with low progress rates, it runs programmes that support young people from primary school to sixth-form.

The university made a 12-place leap up our graduate prospects index to rank 15th, based on 84.3% of graduates being in high-skilled jobs or postgraduate study 15 months on from finishing their degrees. Most of Southampton's courses offer a year in employment and undergraduates are encouraged to study abroad.

---

**University Road Highfield Southampton SO17 1BJ**
enquiry@southampton.ac.uk
southampton.ac.uk
susu.org

**Overall ranking 19**
(last year 17)

**Accommodation**
University provided places 6,426
Catered £191–£227 per week
Self-catered £135–£214 per week

**Student numbers**
Undergraduates 15,086
Applications per place 8.6:1
Overall offer rate 71.7%

**Fees**
UK fees £9,250
International fees £22,300–£28,900
Medicine £28,900–£56,600

southampton.ac.uk/open-days/undergraduate
southampton.ac.uk/study/fees-funding

# Staffordshire University

At this Potteries institution with an eye for innovation, one of the latest developments is a competitive esports facility at the main Stoke-on-Trent campus. Computer games have been on Staffordshire's curriculum for more than 20 years and it was the first UK university to introduce an esports degree. From a £2.7 million investment, the esports arena features player desks and audience seating, networked with a broadcast studio.

The university has a reputation for practice-based learning across the academic disciplines, coining its approach "simmersive" to reflect the immersive experiences in simulated facilities on campus. At the forefront of widening participation in higher education, Staffordshire moves seven places up our social inclusion index, to rank fourth in England and Wales. It recruits more than a quarter of its intake from deprived areas and has a strong retention rate.

A university since 1992, Staffordshire is based at campuses in Stoke-on-Trent, Stafford and London. It was rated triple silver in the government's Teaching Excellence Framework (TEF 2023), overall and for the student experience and student outcomes. The most popular subjects were computing, creative arts and design, and nursing and midwifery.

Staffordshire fell outside the top 100 in our latest rankings, in part because of faltering rates of student satisfaction. In our analysis of the National Student Survey, it dropped to =114th for undergraduates' evaluation of teaching quality (down 63 places).

In the Research Excellence Framework (REF 2021), 68% of Staffordshire's submission was rated world-leading or internationally excellent. It ranks 30th in our research quality index, up from =85th the previous year. New degrees on offer include artificial intelligence; cloud computing; software development; and cybersecurity.

The Stoke-on-Trent site hosts the Catalyst building, the base for apprenticeship and skills training. The Centre for Health Innovation in Stafford has one of the world's largest immersive and interactive suites. With technology that alters real-world settings, the space can change from a patient's home or hospital to an airport or store.

Further south, the university doubled the size of its Here East London campus near Queen Elizabeth Olympic Park with a £3.5 million extension. Courses in London cover gaming, computer science and cybersecurity.

Students who make Staffordshire their firm choice and apply for accommodation before the end of August are guaranteed a room. Once there, they can access wellbeing support face-to-face or remotely. Out-of-hours provision and crisis support are on hand too, as is the online Togetherall platform.

Staffordshire's efforts to promote social mobility have achieved considerable success. As well as the high proportion of students who come from deprived areas, six in ten are from families where the parents did not go to university.

About 1,200 new entrants access financial help in their first year, more than in previous years due to £750 "cost of living" scholarships for students from households with lower incomes and bursaries for adult nursing students. The Denise Coates Foundation, founded by the Stoke-based co-chief executive of the gambling firm Bet365, funds bursaries for Staffordshire students.

---

**College Road Stoke-on-Trent ST4 2DE**
enquiries@staffs.ac.uk
staffs.ac.uk
staffsunion.com

**Overall ranking 101**
(last year =93)

**Accommodation**
University provided places 1,186
Self-catered £95–£158 per week

**Student numbers**
Undergraduates 9,757
Applications per place 2.6:1
Overall offer rate 83.5%

**Fees**
UK fees £9,250–£11,100
International fees £16,750–£19,000

staffs.ac.uk/visit/undergraduate-open-day
staffs.ac.uk/student-life/fees-and-finance

# University of Stirling

At the gateway to the Scottish Highlands, Stirling's 330-acre campus beneath the Ochil Hills is one of the most beautiful in the world. From the pool in the £20 million sports centre, swimmers can see the natural green space outside. Campus Central's atrium is the focal point of student life, with plenty of study areas.

Glasgow and Edinburgh are within easy reach but students wanting to broaden their horizons further can opt to spend a semester or a year studying at one of Stirling's 70 partner universities across four continents.

Stirling was the first UK university to pioneer an academic year of two 15-week semesters instead of three terms. Its research prioritises global challenges, aiming to change lives and create a more sustainable world.

The institution's research record remained consistent in the latest Research Excellence Framework (REF 2021), in which almost 80% of the submission was rated world-leading or internationally excellent. Some of the best results were in agriculture; veterinary and food science; geography and environmental science; and social work and social policy.

Stirling ranks 50th in our research quality index and the Institute of Aquaculture stands out for its pioneering work in the food production sector.

Deteriorating results year-on-year in our analysis of the National Student Survey contributed to the university 's ten-place fall in our main academic table. Students recorded declining satisfaction with teaching quality (down 55 places to =103rd) and the wider undergraduate experience (down 42 to =92nd).

Students can find a mentor within a global network connecting them with staff and alumni. The university's Innovation Park hosts start-ups and established businesses, and collaborative research projects. Academic faculties work alongside the careers service to offer internships, placements and volunteering experiences to students. But with just over two-thirds of leavers in high-skilled jobs or further study 15 months after finishing their degree, Stirling lost ground by nine places for graduate prospects (67th).

Students have a wide choice of sports clubs to join and there are artificial pitches for hockey, football, rugby, Gaelic football, lacrosse and American football, and an all-weather athletics track. More than 70 societies welcome members and cater for most interests. The Macrobert Arts Centre presents a programme of films, dance, drama, comedy and music.

Accommodation is getting a makeover and first-year undergraduates who live more than 20 miles from campus are guaranteed a room in halls, as long as they confirm their place and meet the housing application deadline. The wellbeing, mental health and counselling service offers support including one-on-one therapy.

Students from the rest of the UK (who do not qualify for Scotland's funding system) are eligible for an Undergraduate Merit Scholarship of £1,000 a year for three years if they achieve at least AAB at A-level or equivalent. To sweeten the deal, Stirling waives tuition fees in the fourth year of study for those from England, Northern Ireland, Ireland and Wales. The Reid Family Scholarship of £8,500–£21,525 helps Scottish students who meet the criteria for widening participation.

---

**Stirling FK9 4LA**
admissions@stir.ac.uk
stir.ac.uk
stirlingstudentsunion.com

**Overall ranking 63**
(last year =53)

**Accommodation**
University provided places 2,892
Self-catered £97–£215 per week

STIRLING
Edinburgh
Belfast
London
Cardiff

**Student numbers**
Undergraduates 8,840
Applications per place 6.5:1
Overall offer rate 75.6%

**Fees**
UK fees £0–£1,820
RUK fees 9,250
International fees £17,200–£21,300

stir.ac.uk/study/visit-us/undergraduate-open-days/
stir.ac.uk/study/fees-funding

# University of Strathclyde

A decade-long £1 billion investment in Strathclyde's campus has transformed provision for learning and teaching, sport and student support, while enhancing academic resources across areas including physics, biomedical engineering and manufacturing.

The Glasgow university attracts the fourth-highest entry standards in the UK and has the biggest engineering faculty in Scotland, with more than 40 degree courses. Rates of graduate employment place it in the top 20 nationally.

Feedback from undergraduates in the National Student Survey 2024 reflected positive experiences for most, with Strathclyde ranking =38th for teaching quality and 30th for the broad student experience in our analysis.

The university performed strongly in the latest Research Excellence Framework (REF 2021), with almost 90% of its research rated world-leading or internationally excellent. The submission by its School of Government and Public Policy achieved the best results. However, against rising standards elsewhere Strathclyde dropped nine places to rank 30th in our research quality index.

Strathclyde is home to one of Europe's largest university research groups for electrical power, engineering and energy. It is part of Scotland's graduate apprenticeship network as well as delivering degree apprenticeships validated in England. Subject areas include cybersecurity and civil engineering.

Links with employers such as Rolls-Royce, GlaxoSmithKline and the Fraunhofer Centre for Applied Photonics provide opportunities for student internships and graduate roles. An SME internship programme has proved a fruitful path to graduate jobs. Strathclyde ranks =20th in the UK for graduate prospects, based on 83%

being in high-skilled jobs or postgraduate study 15 months after the end of their degree.

Glasgow is one of Britain's leading student cities, brimming with culture and nightlife, and with more than 90 parks and gardens. Away from their studies, Strathclyde students can choose from about 200 societies and nearly 50 sports clubs.

The £31 million sports centre has a six-lane, 25m swimming pool, two sports halls, squash courts, a café and specialist health facilities. A room in halls at the university includes sports centre membership. Priority goes to first-years who apply by the deadline.

Students who reach out for mental health and wellbeing support are offered a triage appointment and services are delivered in person and online. A daily Zoom drop-in facilitated by counsellors is available to all, for direct support, advice or just a friendly ear. Sexual consent and bystander training has been provided by the students' union for a number of years.

With 13.4% of students from ethnic minority backgrounds, Strathclyde is more ethnically diverse than all but four other Scottish universities. Nine out of ten students were state-educated and the university ranks seventh in our Scottish social inclusion index.

There are scholarships and bursaries to support students from the rest of the UK and abroad, who do not benefit from Scottish students' funding arrangements. The Strathclyde Access Bursary provides up to £3,000 to students from England, Wales, Northern Ireland and the Republic of Ireland. An accommodation bursary adds £1,000 to those from the rest of the UK.

---

**16 Richmond Street Glasgow G1 1XQ**
study-here@strath.ac.uk
strath.ac.uk
strathunion.com/

**Overall ranking 20**
(last year 20)

**Accommodation**
University provided places 2,021
Self-catered £110–£149 per week

**Student numbers**
Undergraduates14,542
Applications per place 6.6:1
Overall offer rate 49.5%

**Fees**
UK fees £0–£1,820
RUK fees £9,250 (£27,750 max)
International fees £18,050–£27,750

strath.ac.uk/studywithus/openday
strath.ac.uk/studywithus/feesfunding

# University of Suffolk

There is a personal feel to the University of Suffolk, thanks to its relatively small size and friendly waterfront setting in Ipswich, ten minutes from the town centre. It has retained its character despite expanding facilities to meet the demand of a growing number of applications, with additions such as an on-campus gym, outdoor sports pitches and a careers zone.

Suffolk's exemplary record in our social inclusion index, where it ranks 7th in England and Wales, is boosted by its successful recruitment of mature students; more than nine in ten undergraduates are older than 21 when they enrol.

The institution was established as University Campus Suffolk in 2007 and gained independence nine years later to award its own degrees as the University of Suffolk. Since then it has branched out in Great Yarmouth, where a former department store is being transformed into a library and the University Learning Centre, which will offer degrees and diploma courses from Suffolk, East Coast College and the University of East Anglia.

Suffolk made its first submission to the Research Excellence Framework (REF) in 2021, in social work and social policy – 68% of which was rated world-leading or internationally excellent. It earned an overall silver rating in the Teaching Excellence Framework (TEF 2023), underpinned by silver ratings for student experience and student outcomes.

Evaluations in the National Student Survey raised Suffolk's rank in our analysis up 16 places (to =63rd) for teaching quality and up 27 (to 96th) for the student experience.

The university maintains close relationships with businesses. Measuring graduate prospects, however, it slumped to 93rd place, based on 72% of graduates being employed in high-skilled jobs or further study 15 months after their degrees.

Suffolk's continuation rate is its lowest-performing metric in our main academic league table, with 79.7% of students projected to continue from the first to second years of their studies.

Suffolk's healthcare provision expanded with the introduction of a degree in dental hygiene and dental therapy. The Legal Advice Centre gives law students the chance to get practical experience and offers free advice to the local community on family and business law.

Sports facilities include an all-weather floodlit pitch, two grass pitches and upgraded changing rooms, and the Move gym in the Athena Hall student accommodation building. Suffolk usually has enough rooms to go around, although there is no formal accommodation guarantee.

Students can apply for means-tested annual bursaries of £500 and a digital technology fund, worth £300 to go towards IT equipment, supports blended learning.

Support for mental health includes one-to-ones for issues such as managing anxiety and help for students who have suffered trauma or a suicidal crisis. Counselling and computerised cognitive behavioural therapy are available, as well as specialist mentoring and workshops.

A third of Suffolk's students are from ethnic minority backgrounds, which ranks it in the upper half of universities for its ethnic diversity. The university draws 23% of its intake from deprived areas, which is the tenth highest proportion.

**Waterfront Building 19 Neptune Quay**
**Ipswich IP4 1QJ**
admissions@uos.ac.uk
uos.ac.uk
uosunion.org

**Overall ranking 124**
(last year =106)

**Accommodation**
University provided places 752
Self-catered £105–£205 per week

**Student numbers**
Undergraduates 13,464
Applications per place 1.9:1
Overall offer rate 55.8%

**Fees**
UK fees £9,250
International fees £15,090–£18,380

uos.ac.uk/life-at-suffolk/visit-us/open-days
uos.ac.uk/life-at-suffolk/funding-your-studies/undergraduate-study

# University of Sunderland

A £250 million, ten-year overhaul is taking shape at Sunderland's three locations – in the city centre, at St Peter's on the banks of the River Wear and in London at Canary Wharf. Murray Health, the city campus home for Sunderland's School of Medicine and School of Psychology, opened in 2024, the same year that the first cohort of medical doctors graduated from the School of Medicine.

New esports, business and management facilities are open, complementing environmental improvements to the Sunderland campuses. Work has started at St Peter's on three large simulation labs for esports, law and market research.

The Canary Wharf campus offers business, healthcare, tourism and hospitality courses at undergraduate level. Sunderland also has a Hong Kong operation, which delivers business and tourism courses.

This ambitious institution is at the vanguard of opening the doors to higher education. Its intake includes the second-highest proportion of students from deprived areas (27.9%) and fourth-highest proportion of those whose parents did not go to university (61.7%). Sunderland is placed eighth overall in our social inclusion index of England and Wales.

A triple silver rating in the government's Teaching Excellence Framework (TEF 2023), overall and for the student experience and student outcomes, commended the university for its engagement with students. Rates of student satisfaction are comfortably in the upper half nationally. The university is =38th for students' evaluation of teaching quality and =61st for their feedback on the broad experience.

In the Research Excellence Framework (REF 2021), more than 70% of the work it submitted was rated either world-leading or internationally excellent. Some of the best results were in art and design.

But Sunderland has lost ground on both National Student Survey-based measures, which contributed to it falling 12 places and ranking outside the top 100 of our main academic ranking.

The university is working to improve its continuation rate. With 86.3% of students projected to carry on from their first to second year of their studies, it stands in the bottom ten on this measure.

An accommodation guarantee applies to first-years who meet the appropriate deadlines, and the Panns Bank and Scotia Quay halls were recently revamped. Many students live at home and commute to university. The CitySpace Fitness facility on the City campus includes a swimming pool and a seven-metre climbing wall. Students can learn to ski at a dry slope nearby.

Mental health and welfare options include the Shine a Light project, which helps ethnic minority students who may not want to access support services. Counselling is provided onsite or online, in a range of languages. The university's bursaries, ranging from £500 to £3,000, last for three years. Priority goes to students with low household incomes and those from groups not well-represented in higher education. Care leavers qualify for £2,500 per year of study, while School of Medicine bursaries include free accommodation.

The university offers 21 degree apprenticeships, with more than 900 trainees. Subjects include teaching, journalism, nursing and social work.

---

**Edinburgh Building Chester Road Sunderland SR1 3SD**
student.helpline@sunderland.ac.uk
sunderland.ac.uk
sunderlandsu.co.uk

**Overall ranking =105**
(last year =93)

**Accommodation**
University provided places 1,130
Self-catered £81–£138 per week

**Student numbers**
Undergraduates 11,899
Applications per place 3.2:1
Overall offer rate 62.4%

**Fees**
UK fees £8,750 (Foundation) – £9,250
International fees £16,000

sunderland.ac.uk/open-days/
sunderland.ac.uk/help/parents/fees-funding

# University of Surrey

Undergraduates here return such positive feedback in each year's National Student Survey (NSS) that it consistently ranks in the upper tiers of our table of student satisfaction. Surrey was placed =3rd for the broad experience and 15th for teaching quality in our latest NSS analysis.

The university is not resting on its laurels. Campus and academic advances include the opening of MySurrey Dots hubs, which provide spaces for study, clubs, socialising and events, and welcoming its first medical students in September 2024, to build on its reputation for delivering high-quality nursing and allied healthcare courses.

Surrey's two campuses, Stag Hill and Manor Park, are about a mile apart and a ten-minute walk from the centre of Guildford. The university is in the top 30 of our research quality index and garnered very good results in the latest Research Excellence Framework (REF 2021), in which 41% of its work from more than 660 academics was assessed as world-leading. Economics produced some of the best results.

Hospitality and tourism courses at Surrey are a magnet for students worldwide, and it was judged to be top in Britain and 15th in the world for hospitality and leisure management in the QS World University Rankings 2024.

It was also rated triple silver in the Teaching Excellence Framework (TEF 2023), with assessors commending its "physical and virtual learning resources that are tailored and used effectively to support outstanding teaching and learning". Surrey is not immune to the financial pressures facing UK higher education, though. In 2024 the vice-chancellor, Professor Max Lu, announced restructuring plans, including voluntary staff redundancies, to help reduce a £10 million deficit.

The university's focus on producing work-ready graduates is paying off: 83.7% of its graduates were in high-skilled jobs or further study 15 months on from finishing their degrees, the Graduate Outcomes survey shows. This put Surrey =17th for graduate prospects, up nine places.

New courses are planned in business economics and data analytics; games design; criminology and psychology; and international airline and airport management.

Under the Team Surrey banner there are more than 45 sports clubs for all abilities. The £36 million Sports Park has a 120-station gym, an interactive squash wall and an Olympic-sized swimming pool. Productions are staged at the university's four theatres and there is an annual Morag Morris Poetry Lecture.

First-years who make Surrey their firm choice and apply by the deadline are guaranteed a place in halls of residence. On-campus accommodation can also be offered to students who come through Clearing.

The Centre for Wellbeing offers virtual, phone and in-person appointments, and students have access to a consultation with a counsellor or a one-to-one meeting with the mental health practitioner team.

About 10% of the UK undergraduate intake of 2024 received the main bursary, worth £2,500 a year, for students from households with incomes of less than £20,000 and in areas of little participation in higher education. Support is available for those who have left care or are estranged from their family.

**Guildford GU2 7XH**
admissions@surrey.ac.uk
surrey.ac.uk
ussu.co.uk

**Overall ranking 21**
(last year 21)

**Accommodation**
University provided places 5,870
Self-catered £77–£205 per week

**Student numbers**
Undergraduates 11,140
Applications per place 7.1:1
Overall offer rate 65.3%

**Fees**
UK fees £9,250
International fees £15,000–£26,300

surrey.ac.uk/open-days
surrey.ac.uk/fees-and-funding

# University of Sussex

Development studies is the university's standout strength on a global scale: in 2024, for the eighth consecutive year, Sussex was ranked top in the QS World University Rankings for the subject. At its 12 research Centres of Excellence, set up in 2023, academics are also addressing societal challenges such as genome-damaging diseases, quantum computing and AI.

Sussex has a good record on course continuation rates, with 96.1% of students projected to carry on from the first to second years, ranking =24th. Strong results in the Research Excellence Framework (REF 2021) led to a position of =32nd in our research table.

Some of its strongest work was recorded in communication, cultural and media studies; sociology; art and design, and education. Overall, 89% of the submission was rated world-leading or internationally excellent.

The university was rated silver overall in the Teaching Excellence Framework (TEF 2023), with silver for student outcomes and bronze for student experience. Our analysis of rising student satisfaction in the National Student Survey (NSS) jars with the TEF finding: Sussex was up 45 places according to feedback on teaching quality (65th) and 67 places for satisfaction with the wider undergraduate experience (=25th).

The parkland campus at Falmer is about four miles from the centre of Brighton. Sussex has about 5,000 residential spaces, almost all on campus and enough to guarantee a room to all first-years who apply by the deadline. By 2026, the first few hundred of 2,000 new study bedrooms is due to open on the West Slope, along with a health and wellbeing centre.

In 2024 about 30% of entrants qualified for some form of financial assistance, which included the Sussex Bursary of £1,000 in the first year to students from low-income households and £500 in subsequent years. There is extra support for students leaving care. Academic scholarships are available for those studying music, engineering, business, sport or the environment.

Sussex received its Royal Charter in 1961 and from the outset took an interdisciplinary approach to teaching and learning. Undergraduates can study for a single or joint honours degree, or choose a major/minor course, spending 75% of their time on their core subject and 25% on another.

The first quantum technology students began in 2024, while the university has established degree apprenticeships in advanced manufacturing engineering; business analytics and digital technology; and data science and AI.

Undergraduates are encouraged to take work placements, study abroad or learn a language, and can make use of mentoring and internship schemes. Sussex fell 23 places year-on-year to rank =87th in our analysis of the Graduate Outcomes survey. Fifteen months after finishing their degree, 73% of graduates were in high-skilled jobs or postgraduate study – a performance that limited the university's rise in our main academic league table.

Sussex has rules to protect lawful freedom of speech and expression for staff, students and visiting speakers. It has a pro-vice-chancellor for culture, equality and inclusion, and became a University of Sanctuary in 2020, offering two scholarships a year for forced migrants.

**Sussex House Falmer Brighton BN1 9RH**
ug.enquiries@sussex.ac.uk
sussex.ac.uk
sussexstudent.com

**Overall ranking 38**
(last year 48)

**Accommodation**
University provided places 5,055
Self-catered £125–£209 per week

**Student numbers**
Undergraduates 14,228
Applications per place 5.2:1
Overall offer rate 93.0%

**Fees**
UK fees £9,250
International fees £21,500–£25,000
Medicine £44,500

sussex.ac.uk/study/visit-us/undergraduate/open-days/

# Swansea University

A charming coastal location is just one of the attractions of our Welsh University of the Year 2025. Research facilities are being developed and Swansea is proud of creating an inspiring environment for centres of excellence across Stem subjects and the humanities.

Academic life falls within three faculties: medicine, health and life science; humanities and social sciences; and science and engineering. The university hosts the Morgan Advanced Studies Institute, which opened in 2021 to promote transformative interdisciplinary research.

Situated along the M4 corridor, Swansea has similar numbers of applications and enrolments from both sides of the Severn Bridge. It offers many of its degrees as four-year courses, with a year spent in industry or abroad.

The university was founded in 1920 to serve the needs of local industry – an ethos still evident in its 500 partnerships across 53 countries with the likes of Rolls-Royce, Fujitsu and NHS Wales. More than 40 companies run operations across its two campuses, Bay and Singleton Park.

In the latest Research Excellence Framework (REF 2021), 86% of the university's work was rated world-leading or internationally excellent, with some of the best results produced by medicine and life science subjects; mathematics; and geography.

Swansea has been climbing the QS World University Rankings too, with a leap of 118 places in 2024. In the latest listings, it broke into the top 300.

Rates of student satisfaction are improving. In our analysis of the latest National Student Survey the university ranked =76th for positive feedback on teaching quality (up eight places year-on-year) and =64th (up 15 places) on the wider undergraduate experience.

Its efforts on sustainability earned Swansea eighth place in the latest People & Planet University League (2023–24), which ranks institutions on their environmental and ethical performance.

More than four in five graduates (81%) were in high-skilled jobs or further study 15 months on from receiving their degrees, ranking Swansea =35th for graduate prospects. The Swansea Employability Academy helps students to secure paid internships and co-ordinates programmes for career development.

The 65-acre Bay campus doubled the size of the university. It has accommodation for 2,000 and hosts the £33 million Computational Foundry, as well as the School of Management. A 20-minute bus trip takes students to the Singleton Park campus, which has facilities for social sciences; health and social care; medicine; geography; and physics.

The university has more than 3,700 residential spaces, enough to guarantee accommodation to all first-years who apply by the deadline. Swansea's social scene includes the popular pubs and bars of Wind Street (learning to pronounce it correctly – "Wine Street" – is lesson No 1). There are more than 150 societies and the Sports Park has an indoor athletics and hockey centre.

Welfare services include the SafeZone app, which gives students immediate access to the security team. Residence Life co-ordinators and faculty-based student experience officers are also on hand.

Swansea scholarships reward academic, musical and sporting merit. Students studying in the Welsh language can also qualify for funding.

---

**Singleton Park Swansea SA2 8PP**
admissions@swansea.ac.uk
swansea.ac.uk
swansea-union.co.uk

**Overall ranking 37**
(last year 41)

**Accommodation**
University provided places 4,340
Catered £174–£198 per week
Self-catered £142–£258 per week

**Student numbers**
Undergraduates 15,862
Applications per place 3.7:1
Overall offer rate 79.2%

**Fees**
UK fees £9,250
International fees £16,550–£25,750
Medicine £43,850

swansea.ac.uk/open-days/
swansea.ac.uk/undergraduate/fees-and-funding

# Teesside University

Teesside is powering ahead with an ambitious overhaul of its facilities. The BIOS building opened in 2023, with £36.9 million of resources ranging from simulated operating theatres to cutting-edge laboratory spaces, and is being followed by Digital Life, a centre for AI and robotics.

Based in Middlesbrough, it plays an outstanding role in widening participation and was a 2025 runner-up in the Sunday Times University of the Year for Social Inclusion category. Three in ten of its undergraduate intake come from areas of socioeconomic deprivation – no university recruits a higher proportion.

The majority of Teesside students (57.3%, ranking =11th) are the first in their family to go to university and its recruitment from non-selective state schools (98.6%) is the third-highest.

There are subject-specific scholarships encompassing arts and media, business, science, computing, engineering, nursing and health, worth from £2,000 to £27,000. Sports performance scholarships reward elite student athletes.

The university reached 44th place (up from 60th) in our graduate prospects index, based on 79.2% being engaged in high-skilled jobs or further study 15 months after their degree.

It swept the board with gold in the government's Teaching Excellence Framework (TEF 2023), one of an elite group to gain the top rating overall and for both underpinning factors: student experience and student outcomes. The panel praised "highly effective and tailored approaches to supporting students to achieve educational gains, particularly in relation to employability".

But its undergraduates provided much cooler feedback in the most recent National Student Survey (NSS). Teesside was 59th for teaching quality (down 36 places) and =90th for the wider experience (a 52-place drop) in our new analysis.

Almost two-thirds of Teesside's submission to the Research Excellence Framework (REF 2021) was rated world-leading or internationally excellent, and it sits in 94th place in our research quality index.

The main campus in Middlesbrough includes dedicated bases for the International Business School and the School of Social Sciences, Humanities and Law. A smaller site in Darlington has bioinformatics and imaging laboratories for use by the School of Health and Life Sciences.

At the London campus at Here East, Teesside students choose from courses in animation, gaming, visual effects, business and computer science. Students can study flexibly through a blend of face-to-face and online learning.

Sports clubs and societies are mainstays of Teesside's social scene. The Olympia complex in Middlesbrough incorporates a sports hall with capacity for 500 spectators, a climbing wall and gym. The Saltersgill Pavilion, two miles away, has four rugby union pitches, and the university is a stakeholder in the River Tees Watersports Centre.

Rooms are allocated on a first-come, first-served basis and in 2023–24 about 90% who wanted to live in got a place in halls. Middlesbrough also offers affordable private rents.

Personalised support is the goal for Teesside's mental health service, which has one-to-one counselling and runs workshops to promote a healthy lifestyle. The sleep and lifestyle management clinic provides advice for students learning to make the best use of their time.

---

**Teesside University Middlesbrough TS1 3BX**
enquiries@tees.ac.uk
tees.ac.uk
tees-su.org.uk

**Overall ranking 104**
(last year 102)

**Accommodation**
University provided places 912
Self-catered £85–£165 per week

**Student numbers**
Undergraduates 9,629
Applications per place 3.4:1
Overall offer rate 76.5%

**Fees**
UK fees £6,150 (Foundation) – £9,250
International fees £17,000

tees.ac.uk/opendays/
tees.ac.uk/fees

# Ulster University

With 34,000 students in Belfast, Coleraine and Derry-Londonderry, Ulster sits comfortably in the top half of our graduate prospects index. It is a pioneer of blended learning and its online recordings (provided for every module for more than 20 years) are popular with students.

In our National Student Survey (NSS) analysis, the university ranks =20th (up from =24th) for satisfaction with teaching quality and 22nd (a one-place gain) for the wider experience. It is 45th in our research quality index; 87% of its submission to the 2021 Research Excellence Framework (REF) was rated world-leading or internationally excellent, with the strongest results in allied health subjects.

The university's £363.9 million Belfast campus in the cathedral district was one of the biggest academic capital builds in Europe. At Coleraine, an inshore marine research vessel provides opportunities to monitor coastal waters. There is also a £6.5 million media centre here, reflecting Northern Ireland's emergence as a leading film and television centre.

At Derry-Londonderry, Ulster is expanding its medical school's presence on campus and at Altnagelvin Hospital, in conjunction with Derry's City Deal. The medical school is run in partnership with St George's, University of London.

Ulster has branch campuses in London and Birmingham, offering courses in business, computing and engineering in partnership with QA Higher Education.

The university recently introduced courses in food and business innovation; accounting and finance; law with politics and international studies; liberal arts; animal healthcare and bioveterinary science; and veterinary nursing.

Degree programmes often feature a work-based learning component. More than three-quarters of graduates were in high-skilled work or further study 15 months after finishing their degrees, according to our analysis of the latest Graduate Outcomes survey. This maintains Ulster's position comfortably in the upper half of UK universities.

At the High-Performance Sports Centre at Jordanstown, the base for the Sports Institute Northern Ireland, cameras are installed at the sports hall and outdoor pitches for performance analysis and live-streaming matches. The Coleraine site is home to the Riverside Theatre. Ulster's student TV channel, Offshoot TV, launched in autumn 2024.

A place in one of more than 2,800 rooms in university accommodation is guaranteed for all first-year students who apply by the July 7 deadline.

Mind Your Mood, Ulster's student-led mental health and wellbeing campaign, runs training sessions to build resilience. Counselling is available through an external provider, complemented by a 24/7 online support hub.

Ulster has an extensive outreach scheme and an excellent record in widening participation at university-level education. Almost all the undergraduates are from state schools, but we do not include Northern Ireland universities in our social inclusion index because of regional differences in the education system.

Up to a third of admissions qualify for some form of bursary. Support targets those from households with incomes of less than £19,203 and includes access bursaries of £475 a year, which can be topped up to £1,000 to help with costs of one year's student accommodation. The An Droichead Scholarship is open to Irish-language students.

Cromore Road Coleraine BT52 1SA
study@ulster.ac.uk
ulster.ac.uk
uusu.org

**Overall ranking 45**
(last year 40)

**Accommodation**
University provided places 2,826
Self-catered £102–£227 per week

COLERAINE
Edinburgh
Belfast
London
Cardiff

**Student numbers**
Undergraduates 15,970
Applications per place 5.5:1
Overall offer rate 81.2%

**Fees**
UK fees £4,750
RUK fees £9,250
International fees £17,010
Medicine £38,550

ulster.ac.uk/study/undergraduate/open-days
ulster.ac.uk/student/fees-and-funding

# University College London

Our 2024 University of the Year has a pioneering past: it was the first British university to accept students regardless of religion or social background and the first to admit women on equal terms. Now University College London (UCL) is striding into the future at its second campus.

UCL East at Queen Elizabeth Olympic Park in Stratford offers cross-disciplinary and interdisciplinary degree programmes, allowing for project work and collaboration. Research labs and studios at the One Pool Street building provide a setting to explore ecology, robotics, urbanism, culture, disability and heritage.

The university is spearheading the art of "disagreeing well" at a time of polarised debate. Its events and online resources aim to draw staff, students and the wider community into discussing how those with very different views can exchange ideas and coexist harmoniously.

UCL is the biggest component of the University of London Federation with about 40,000 students at its Bloomsbury base in central London. They can benefit from co-curricular and extracurricular activities in sport, the arts and volunteering under the Student Life Strategy programme running until 2028.

The university is fifth in our research quality index, based on the latest Research Excellence Framework (REF 2021), in which 93% of its work was rated world-leading or internationally excellent. UCL's research pedigree has helped to secure a top-ten spot in the QS World University Rankings for the past 13 years running.

UCL gained silver overall in the Teaching Excellence Framework (TEF 2023), with silver for student experience and gold for student outcomes. Yet students have given it mixed reviews in successive National Student Surveys (NSS) - a common trend at research-led, big city universities. In our new NSS analysis, UCL ranks 115th for student satisfaction with teaching quality, down from 88th in our previous edition. It fares better for feedback on the wider undergraduate experience (59th, a fall of 22 places). The Student Life Strategy, a collaboration between UCL and the students' union, is aimed at improving the situation.

Degrees launching in 2025 include art and technology; communications; philosophy and computer science; and youth, society and sustainable futures. Demand for places continues to rise.

About three in ten of the university's UK undergraduates receive financial aid. Its main undergraduate bursary is awarded to those with household income below £42,875. Accommodation bursaries are offered in the first year to students from lower-income and widening participation backgrounds.

On the main campus, finance students use a virtual trading floor and the medical school is among Europe's largest. At UCL East, the One Pool Street building houses a lecture theatre that doubles as a cinema. The Marshgate building has workshops and the UCL Institute of Making.

First-years who apply in time have priority for more than 8,000 residential places. UCL guarantees university accommodation to students aged under 18, care leavers and those with additional needs for the duration of their studies.

UCL's mental health support includes counselling, psychiatric support and workshops. Those seeking to boost their wellbeing can also spend time with therapy dogs.

---

**Gower Street London WC1E 6BT**
ucl.ac.uk/prospective-students/
undergraduate/admissions-enquiries
ucl.ac.uk
studentsunionucl.org

**Overall ranking 7**
(last year 6)

**Accommodation**
University provided places 8,067
Catered £216–£374 per week
Self-catered £145–£443 per week

**Student numbers**
Undergraduates 23,022
Applications per place 10.2:1
Overall offer rate 27.0%

**Fees**
UK fees £9,250
International fees £25,900–£41,000
Medicine £50,300

ucl.ac.uk/prospective-students/open-days/
undergraduate-open-days
ucl.ac.uk/students/fees-and-funding/

# University of Wales Trinity St David

Students enjoy the community spirit and small class sizes at the University of Wales Trinity St David (UWTSD); it ranks third in Wales and eighth in the UK for student satisfaction with teaching quality, based on our analysis of the latest National Student Survey. A high achiever in our social inclusion index, sitting within the top 20, it draws 97.7% of its undergraduates from non-selective state schools and nearly 80% are mature students.

There are six campuses: four in Wales (Lampeter, Carmarthen, Swansea and Cardiff) plus Birmingham and London. Accommodation, split between Lampeter and Carmarthen, was recently upgraded. There is no guarantee but it is rare for a first-year student to miss out on a room here.

Founded in 1822, UWTSD is looking to the future with its £9.3 million Innovation Matrix, part of the waterfront Innovation Quarter in Swansea, designed for sharing research and knowledge with businesses and entrepreneurs. It registered an improved performance in the latest Research Excellence Framework (REF 2021), sitting just outside the top 100. Its best results were in art and design, education, Celtic languages and literature, theology and psychology.

The university's automotive engineering courses are based at Swansea, which is also the location of the flagship College of Art. Lampeter is the home of humanities, including archaeology and creative writing.

Carmarthen offers programmes in the creative and performing arts, plus a growing portfolio within the school of sport, health and outdoor education. Courses in Cardiff cover musical theatre, while in Birmingham and Oval, south London, there are business-focused and health and social care degrees.

A seven-place rise in our main table was down to impressive feedback recorded in the NSS, but UWTSD is held back by only 70.6% of students achieving firsts and 2.1s, and it has the 11th highest student-to-staff ratio (20.3:1). Its continuation rate is another sticking point, with a relatively high proportion of students dropping out of their studies before the second year. However, this is often a result of a diverse intake, and four in five UWTSD students are aged over 21 when they enrol.

Although there are opportunities to gain professional qualifications, work placements and internships with partner organisations, UWTSD was dragged into the bottom ten of our graduate prospects ranking with a three-place drop (to 126th), based on 59.6% of its graduates being in high-skilled jobs or further study 15 months after finishing their degrees.

Swansea, Cardiff, Birmingham and London are buzzy student hubs, while Carmarthen and Lampeter have their own charms, not least breathtaking scenery. A counselling unit and mental health advisers provide support for student wellbeing. Self-help resources can be accessed through the Togetherall online platform and the Feeling Good app.

Bursaries are available and broad provision, including awards for laptops and broadband grants, benefits nearly three in ten entrants. There is specific help to support inclusion and diversity, such as the transgender and non-binary student wellbeing bursary, parents and carers bursary, and ethnicity equality bursary.

**Carmarthen Campus College Road Carmarthen SA31 3EP**
admissions@uwtsd.ac.uk
uwtsd.ac.uk
uwtsdunion.co.uk

**Overall ranking 110**
(last year 117)

**Accommodation**
University provided places 462
Self-catered £94–£130 per week

**Student numbers**
Undergraduates 10,593
Applications per place 2.9:1
Overall offer rate 80.1%

**Fees**
UK fees £9,000
International fees £13,500

uwtsd.ac.uk/open-days
uwtsd.ac.uk/student-finance

# University of Warwick

This West Midlands powerhouse has been a fixture in our top ten since our first edition and was shortlisted for the accolade of University of the Year 2025. On a 750-acre site near Coventry, it is undertaking a ten-year campus masterplan with new and repurposed study centres on the way.

A £100 million investment in arts and humanities has resulted in world-class facilities in the Faculty of Arts Building and a new site in Venice, which is popular with art history students. The Marsh Observatory opened in 2023 to train the astronomers of tomorrow.

Students benefit from a research-intensive environment and undergraduates enjoy their studies. Our latest analysis of the National Student Survey shows high levels of satisfaction with teaching quality (=33rd) and the wider undergraduate experience (13th).

Top honours went to Warwick in the government's Teaching Excellence Framework (TEF 2023). It was one of 26 universities (out of 228) to achieve triple gold for its overall grade, student experience and student outcomes. The TEF panel noted that its biggest subject areas are business (Warwick Business School occupies part of the Shard in London, as well as a base on the main campus), economics, maths, engineering and politics.

The university stands =69th in the 2025 QS World University Rankings and achieved impressive results in the Research Excellence Framework (REF 2021): 92% of its work was rated world-leading or internationally excellent. Warwick has partnerships with universities in Europe, North America, South America, Australasia and east Asia to offer its intake opportunities to study abroad.

Courses introduced recently include English and classical civilisation; child and family; global politics, with an integrated year in Brussels; design and global sustainable development; and international management with a foundation year.

Warwick ranks just outside the top ten for graduate prospects with 86.4% of leavers in highly skilled jobs or further study 15 months after finishing their degree. It is also a regular among the ten most targeted universities by leading graduate employers, coming sixth in 2023–24, according to the High Fliers Research Graduate Market report.

In the top 100 of our social inclusion index overall (92nd), the university admits relatively low numbers from non-selective state schools (62%, 105th). The Warwick Bursary, paid to about 900 UK first-years in 2024, is awarded on a sliding scale from £1,000 to £2,000 a year to students with household incomes under £35,000.

The sprawling campus features ancient woodland and a sculpture trail, while for less contemplative moments the students' union is the centre of social life. There are more than 300 societies and a Sports and Wellness Hub.

The university has more than 7,000 rooms in halls and first-years who make it their firm choice, or hold an unconditional offer, are guaranteed accommodation if they apply by the end of August.

Before starting their course, students must complete the Warwick Values Programme, which covers behaviour relating to alcohol, drugs and sexual consent, and racial, LGBTQ+ and social tolerance. A wellbeing support team oversees disability services, student funding and mental health.

---

**Coventry CV4 7AL**
ugadmissions@warwick.ac.uk
warwick.ac.uk
warwicksu.com

**Overall ranking 9**
(last year 9)

**Accommodation**
University provided places 7,400
Self-catered £121–£245 per week

**Student numbers**
Undergraduates 17,858
Applications per place 8.1:1
Overall offer rate 62.7%

**Fees**
UK fees £6,750 (Foundation) – £9,250
International fees £24,800–£31,620
Medicine £28,930–£50,430

warwick.ac.uk/study/undergraduate/opendays/
warwick.ac.uk/services/finance/studentfinance/fees

# University of the West of England

Nearly 40,000 students feel at home at the University of the West of England (UWE Bristol), which offers a wide subject mix over three campuses. But growing popularity has not stopped it from charging towards its net-zero emissions target – it ranks 11th in the People & Planet league table based on environmental and ethical performance.

Diverse, cultural and with epic nightlife, the university's attractions are clear. At the main site, Frenchay, it is investing more than £300 million to upgrade facilities. The City campus is spread across four sites in the heart of Bristol, one at Bower Ashton and three of them contemporary art centres. In Fishponds, a 15-minute bus ride from the city centre, the Glenside health campus has beautiful grounds.

UWE Bristol holds a silver rating overall from the government's Teaching Excellence Framework (TEF 2023), underpinned by a gold award for the student experience and silver for student outcomes.

Results of the National Student Survey show the university has yet to return to its pre-pandemic heights of student satisfaction, when it ranked in the top ten for the broad experience and 11th for teaching quality; it now occupies a bottom-half position for both. In turn, it lost some ground in our main academic ranking, although it recently recorded a four-place gain.

More than three-quarters (76%) of the work it submitted for assessment in the Research Excellence Framework (REF 2021) was rated as world-leading or internationally excellent, with the best results in architecture, built environment and planning; allied health subjects; communication and media studies; engineering; and law.

UWE Bristol is 69th overall in our social inclusion index. Only 7% of its students come from grammar or independent schools and the university ranks in the top 30 for its recruitment of white working-class males (6.7% of the intake). Nearly one in five students (18.9%) are from ethnic minority backgrounds.

The students' union, sports facilities and a 24-hour library can be found on the Frenchay campus. At City, modern design studios are part of a £37 million investment to help prepare students for jobs in the creative industries. The Fabrication Centre and the Centre for Print Research are at Bower Ashton. The £5 million optometry and clinical skills centre on the Glenside campus contains learning space for trainee paramedics, occupational therapy students, nurses and students of optometry.

An accommodation guarantee at all three campuses applies only to students who meet the application deadline. UWE Bristol's wellbeing service includes access to counselling, a chaplain and an out-of-hours team. Courses such as peer-assisted learning workshops help students to build resilience.

About 27% of students received financial aid in 2024 through bursaries and scholarships or from the Student Support Fund. The £500 low-income bursary is paid every year of study, subject to annual assessment. There is extra support for students who are parents or carers, or who have left care or are estranged from their families. Subject-specific or individually funded scholarships are based on merit and widening participation criteria.

---

**Frenchay Campus Coldharbour Lane Bristol BS16 1QY**
admissions@uwe.ac.uk
uwe.ac.uk
thestudentsunion.co.uk

**Overall ranking 68**
(last year 72)

**Accommodation**
University provided places 5,779
Self-catered £110–£275 per week

**Student numbers**
Undergraduates 23,512
Applications per place 4.9:1
Overall offer rate 74.0%

**Fees**
UK fees £9,250
International fees £15,850–£16,500

uwe.ac.uk/courses/open-days
uwe.ac.uk/courses/fees

# University of West London

The University of West London (UWL) is a model of reinvention in the higher education sector, having transformed from the former Thames Valley University (which finished bottom of our league table in 2001) into today's top-60 institution.

Its success is secured by a knack for finding out what makes students tick, demonstrated by consistently elevated results in National Student Surveys. UWL ranked 13th for satisfaction with teaching quality and 12th for positive feedback about the wider undergraduate experience in our latest NSS analysis.

An inclusive approach to admissions starts a supportive journey through university for students here. Non-academic experience is given weight as well as exam results during the selection process, and widening participation is ingrained at UWL. It recruits the sixth-highest proportion of mature students in England and Wales, representing three-quarters of the intake in 2023.

High staffing levels are notable: UWL's student-to-staff ratio of 12.9:1 puts it in the top ten. Assessors from the government's Teaching Excellence Framework (TEF 2023) rated the university silver overall. It awarded UWL gold for the student experience but only bronze for student outcomes. Our analysis shows the university ranks =110th for its continuation rate (88.2%). However, the TEF report highlighted "educational gains that are relevant to students' ambitions, and consistent with the institution's goals as an engine for social mobility".

UWL has campuses in Ealing and Brentford, while the Berkshire Institute for Health in Reading provides a base for nursing and midwifery students. There are more than 800 spaces in halls. Students can access support for their mental wellbeing whether they are in crisis or have long-term needs.

The university invests more than £3 million a year to fund bursaries, scholarships and targeted support designed to promote access to education and encourage students to fulfil their potential. About half of full-time undergraduates qualify for financial assistance such as the UWL Aspire Bursary of £100 for books and £1,000-a-year undergraduate bursaries for those from low-income households.

As part of its commitment to research, UWL created the Centre for Inequality and Levelling Up and the Institute for Policing Studies. It ranks 93rd based on the results of the Research Excellence Framework (REF 2021) in which nearly 80% of its submission was rated world-leading or internationally excellent.

New courses include esports and livestreaming; sports management; data science; business analytics; social sciences; sports psychology; and sports and exercise science.

Specialist learning facilities at UWL are designed to prepare graduates for the world of work: they include a Boeing 737 flight simulator with commercial airline software and a flight management system. The university has a mock courtroom at Ealing and a hospital simulation centre at Brentford. The Who co-founder Pete Townshend gifted the university a collection of synthesizers to be housed in the Townshend Studio on the Ealing campus.

The university's £13.8 million leisure centre in Gunnersbury Park is one of London's largest outdoor sports facilities, while the Freddies social space presents bands from UWL's London College of Music.

St Mary's Road Ealing London W5 5RF
undergraduate.admissions@uwl.ac.uk
uwl.ac.uk
uwlsu.com

**Overall ranking =57**
(last year 47)

**Accommodation**
University provided places 826
Self-catered £234–£399 per week

**Student numbers**
Undergraduates 14,183
Applications per place 6.3:1
Overall offer rate 66.4%

**Fees**
UK fees £9,250
International fees £16,250

uwl.ac.uk/whats-on
uwl.ac.uk/study/undergraduate/funding-bursaries-and-scholarships/undergraduate-tuition-fees

# University of the West of Scotland

The University of the West of Scotland (UWS) offers career-focused degrees with an emphasis on real-world experience. A reputation for widening participation in higher education goes before it, and the university tops our Scottish social inclusion index.

UWS has four campuses in Scotland – Ayr, Dumfries, Lanarkshire and Paisley – and another in the Docklands area of London. It organises teaching through four schools, in business and creative industries; computing, engineering and physical sciences; education and social sciences; and health and life sciences.

A 20-place gain in our graduate prospects measure (82nd) suggests UWS's focus on employability is paying off. Our analysis of the latest Graduate Outcomes survey shows that about three-quarters of leavers are in high-skilled jobs or further study 15 months after finishing their degree.

At the pre-hospital simulation centre on the Lanarkshire campus, healthcare students learn to develop clinical skills in an immersive environment. Music students take part in the EuroGig project, which enables them to perform abroad, or develop their careers via UWS's record label, Damfino. A partnership between the university and OneRen, Renfrewshire's culture, leisure and sports charitable trust, is behind the redevelopment of Paisley Museum.

UWS's portfolio of financial support includes childcare funds to help eligible student parents meet costs that may otherwise stand in their way of attending university. Most courses leave Wednesday afternoons free to encourage students to take part in sport and social activities, and membership to gym and fitness facilities at the Scottish campuses is free. There are sport scholarships of £500 to £1,500. A counselling service is available and there is support for students who struggle to engage with their studies.

Sport and exercise sciences, leisure and tourism, and physics led the way for UWS in the Research Excellence Framework (REF 2021), with 71% of the submission assessed as world-leading or internationally excellent. The university's Institute of Clinical Exercise and Health Science is responsible for some of its leading research.

Up five places in our main academic table, the university is boosted by rates of student satisfaction with teaching quality. In our latest National Student Survey analysis, UWS rose 24 places to =47th, as a result of feedback on teaching, and up eight places (to =104th) for satisfaction with the wider undergraduate experience. It is held back, however, by its continuation rate (125th) and a student-to-staff ratio of 22.4:1 (=125th).

In Times Higher Education Impact Rankings for 2024, which measure progress in delivering the United Nations' Sustainable Development Goals, UWS ranks 16th in the world for its success at reducing inequalities.

New degree courses include collaborative health and social care; environmental science and sustainability; business with sustainability; project management; and events and tourism management.

Students have a wide range of cultural options. UWS Radio is a hybrid student and community station that broadcasts from Ayr, while the students' union venue is at the Paisley site. The Ayr and Paisley campuses have 696 beds between them, with allocation on a first-come, first-served basis.

**Paisley Campus Paisley PA1 2BE**
ask@uws.ac.uk
uws.ac.uk
uwsunion.org.uk

**Overall ranking 121**
(last year 126)

**Accommodation**
University provided places 696
Self-catered £98–£170 per week

**Student numbers**
Undergraduates 12,737
Applications per place 4.4:1
Overall offer rate 64.1%

**Fees**
UK fees £0–£1,820
RUK fees £9,250
International fees £15,500–£18,000

uws.ac.uk/study/open-days-info-sessions
uws.ac.uk/money-fees-funding

# University of Westminster

With campuses dotted around London's West End, Westminster appeals to students who thrive in the thick of things. The headquarters at 309 Regent Street, the university's original home, is now the School of Humanities and School of Social Sciences.

At the Marylebone campus, business and management courses are the most popular undergraduate programmes. An expanding curriculum includes degrees in games art, policing and fashion photography.

The leafier setting of Harrow, northwest London, provides the setting for the institution's high-profile School of Media, Arts and Design. Facilities here include studios for music, film and television.

Art and design produced the university's best results in the latest Research Excellence Framework (REF 2021), keeping pace with many leading institutions. Overall, Westminster sits in the upper half of UK universities in our research quality index (59th). It achieved triple silver in the Teaching Excellence Framework (TEF 2023).

A three-place rise in our main academic ranking was powered by improvement in our latest analysis of the National Student Survey. Westminster rose 42 places to rank 46th for satisfaction with the student experience in our analysis. For satisfaction with teaching quality, it moved up 11 places to =107th.

With 61.2% of students working in high-skilled jobs or furthering their studies 15 months after graduating, according to the latest data. The university is 123rd for graduate prospects; its Centre for Employability and Enterprise may bring a renewed focus when it opens in 2025.

There are new degrees in contemporary retail; sustainable business management; marketing and data analytics; law and criminal justice; international communications and international business; and a range of business management courses.

Westminster is a member of the Mental Health Charter programme, which brings together universities to share good practice on mental wellbeing. Students can take part in one-to-one sessions with wellbeing advisers, counsellors, mentors and mental health practitioners.

Students at the Harrow campus enjoy basketball, netball and volleyball in the sports hall. Membership of all university sports facilities and teams is free. At the Quintin Hogg Memorial Sports Ground in Chiswick, there are extensive grounds for football, rugby, hockey, lacrosse, cricket, tennis and netball.

Room allocation in halls is first-come, first-served, and there is no accommodation guarantee. About 65% of first-years are able to live in one of the university's 1,030 rooms. Westminster has a high proportion of commuter students who live at home.

There are about 300 means-tested Westminster Bursaries of £500 per year of study. Care leavers and students who are estranged from their families may qualify for extra bursary support. There are scholarships of £5,000 a year of study for high-achieving black and ethnic minority applicants from low-income households.

Westminster is in the top 50 in our social inclusion index (44th) and its student population reflects London's diversity. The university recruits the seventh-highest proportion of students from black and ethnic minority backgrounds (69.9%) and more than half the intake is made up of students who are the first in their family to go to university.

---

**309 Regent Street London W1B 2HW**
course-enquiries@westminster.ac.uk
westminster.ac.uk
uwsu.com

**Overall ranking 120**
(last year 123)

**Accommodation**
University provided places 1,030
Self-catered £186–£304 per week

**Student numbers**
Undergraduates 14,350
Applications per place 4.4:1
Overall offer rate 79.7%

**Fees**
UK fees £9,250
International fees £15,400

westminster.ac.uk/study/open-days-and-events
westminster.ac.uk/study/fees-and-funding

# University of Winchester

The university, on a wooded hillside overlooking the cathedral city of Winchester, began as a Church of England teacher training college in 1840. It gained its charter in 2005 and has expanded into a multi-faculty institution encompassing humanities and social sciences; education and the arts; business and digital technology; law, crime and justice; and health and wellbeing.

Winchester is a small university of about 8,000 students, but it's big on community spirit. The chancellor is the actor and comedian Hugh Dennis, star of the BBC's Outnumbered and Mock the Week.

Awarding Winchester triple silver – overall, and for student experience and student outcomes – in the government's Teaching Excellence Framework (TEF 2023), assessors were impressed by the "excellent academic practice" embedded across it.

In the latest Research Excellence Framework (REF 2021), it tripled its proportion of world-leading work compared with the previous assessment in 2014, but fell 24 places to 107th in our research quality index against bigger gains elsewhere. Theology was among the strongest subjects.

Lower rates of student satisfaction contributed to a fall of 18 places in our main academic league table (103rd). Winchester tumbled 20 places in our latest analysis of National Student Survey feedback on teaching quality (=82nd) and 44 for satisfaction with the wider undergraduate experience (=101st).

The university also fared much less strongly in the latest graduate employment figures (down 18 places to =108th). Staff walked out on strike in June 2024 to protest about threatened job cuts and increased workloads.

It gained 12 places in our social inclusion index for England and Wales (47th), boosted by a relatively high proportion of disabled students (11.1%, 12th). Most of the intake (92.5%) is drawn from non-selective state schools (61st).

The university has links with more than 30 primary and secondary schools in Hampshire, running initiatives to raise attainment in literacy and English language. Support packages are offered to disadvantaged groups including care-leavers. About 40% of entrants qualify for some form of financial support, including income-based bursaries of £200 a year.

The King Alfred and West Downs campuses have specialist facilities including psychology and sports labs, a performing arts studio and a recording suite. The West Downs Gallery on campus hosts exhibitions by students and alumni.

Students can get to know each other relatively quickly in this compact, peaceful city. Those with a flair for music can choose from several performance groups and there are more than 100 societies and sports teams.

Free fitness classes are a perk at the university gym on the King Alfred site. The nearby Winchester Sports Stadium has an athletics track and a floodlit all-weather pitch.

First-years who apply by the June deadline are "usually guaranteed" one of 1,949 residential spaces.

Freshers week has workshops on mental fitness and throughout the year there are sessions on how to manage stress and anxiety. Students have access to counselling, mental health mentors and therapeutic groups that include bereavement support. There is out-of-hours support from outreach workers, housing and security services.

**Sparkford Road Winchester SO22 4NR**
admissions@winchester.ac.uk
winchester.ac.uk
winchesterstudents.co.uk

**Overall ranking 103**
(last year =85)

**Accommodation**
University provided places 1,949
Catered £200 per week
Self-catered £144–£198 per week

**Student numbers**
Undergraduates 6,536
Applications per place 5.1:1
Overall offer rate 84.1%

**Fees**
UK fees £9,250
International fees £16,700–£21,800

winchester.ac.uk/News-and-Events/On-Campus-Events/Open-Days-/
winchester.ac.uk/student-life/Students-and-money/

# University of Wolverhampton

Work-ready skills are to the fore at Wolverhampton, a university forged from the 19th-century mechanics institutes that provided vocational and general education to working men. Its mission is still to transform lives and the university has been adapting its course portfolio to reflect industry needs and investing in facilities where students can cut their teeth.

There are three campuses (Wolverhampton, Walsall and Telford) plus a £120 million site in Springfield, which regenerated an old brewery into a specialist construction and built environment centre.

No university recruits a higher proportion of students whose parents did not go to university (70.7%) and few have a more ethnically diverse student population (24th). Wolverhampton also attracts more mature students back to learning than all but 16 other universities.

Research by the Higher Education Policy Institute put the university in the UK's top ten for social mobility, and tailored financial assistance is available for the diverse student population. There are £1,000 scholarships for women in engineering.

Rising to sixth for social inclusion, Wolverhampton has lost ground in our main academic league table, falling into the bottom ten. Poor continuation rates – often a by-product of a diverse intake – are among the sticking points. Only 86% of students are projected to carry on from the first to the second year of their degree.

Our latest National Student Survey analysis shows Wolverhampton remains =54th for student satisfaction with teaching quality. However, the wider undergraduate experience attracted less positive feedback (86th, down ten places year-on-year).

For Wolverhampton's vice-chancellor Professor Ebrahim Adia, raising participation in higher education is a personal priority. The first in his family to get a degree, he has called for the government to pay a social mobility premium to institutions that create opportunities in communities where few people go to university.

The most recent Teaching Excellence Framework (TEF 2023) rated Wolverhampton bronze (down from silver in the previous assessment), commenting that it "fosters a supportive learning environment". The TEF report noted that the largest numbers of full-time students were within nursing and midwifery (14.3%), business and management (12.7%) and health and social care (10.7%).

More than half of Wolverhampton's submission to the Research Excellence Framework (REF 2021) was judged as world-leading or internationally excellent (109th).

At City campus in Wolverhampton, the Screen School helps creative and digital students to develop their ideas. The university has invested in new facilities for healthcare, nursing and paramedic students based at Walsall and City. The Walsall campus is also the base for high-quality sports facilities including the Active Wellbeing, Rehabilitation and Performance Centre. In Telford, the Centre for Health and Social Care trains key workers.

The university's halls are among the UK's most pocket-friendly, with rooms starting at about £94 a week. Allocations are made on a first-come, first-served basis.

A mental health and wellbeing team offers group work and one-to-one sessions. There are staff and students working across academic departments to put student welfare first, from the disability and inclusion team to wellbeing champions.

---

**Wulfruna Street Wolverhampton WV1 1LY**
admissions@wlv.ac.uk
wlv.ac.uk
wolvesunion.org

**Overall ranking 123**
(last year 118)

**Accommodation**
University provided places 1,081
Self-catered £96–£114 per week

**Student numbers**
Undergraduates 11,615
Applications per place 4.5:1
Overall offer rate 76.5%

**Fees**
UK fees £9,250
International fees £14,950–£15,450

wlv.ac.uk/news-and-events/open-day/
wlv.ac.uk/apply/funding-costs-fees-and-support/

# University of Worcester

Worcester is increasingly on the front line of training students for careers that make a positive difference to society. Education courses are a key strength for the university, founded as a teacher training college in 1946, and healthcare provision is flourishing too.

The Three Counties Medical School serves Worcestershire, Gloucestershire and Herefordshire, with a remit to address health inequalities in the region. It shares facilities, including a simulated GP surgery, with students on the university's broad range of courses in the health professions.

The medical school's Elizabeth Garrett Anderson Building is on the Severn campus (one of four), which hosts sporting facilities including an indoor arena for wheelchair athletes. The university's subject mix extends across nine academic schools including arts and humanities, psychology and business.

A rise of four places in our league table took Worcester into the top 100. This was partly driven by a top-ten performance in our new sustainability metric, based on People & Planet's university league that assesses environmental and ethical performance.

In the latest Research Excellence Framework (REF 2021), a third of Worcester's submission was rated world-leading or internationally excellent, with some of its best results in art and design; history; and sport and exercise science. However, it fell out of the top 100 (121st) compared with its performance in the previous national assessment in 2014.

Triple silver – overall, for student experience and student outcomes – was awarded to Worcester in the Teaching Excellence Framework (TEF 2023). Rates of student satisfaction have yet to return to pre-pandemic form. In our analysis of the latest National Student Survey, Worcester ranked =90th for feedback on teaching quality (down nine places year-on-year) and =74th for satisfaction with the wider undergraduate experience (down ten). Further campus investment may help to shift the dial.

The St John's campus houses science facilities including the National Pollen and Aerobiology Research Unit. The digital arts centre and drama studio are also here, while the City site incorporates the former Worcester Royal Infirmary and the Hive library. The Lakeside campus is the base for outdoor learning and an activity centre.

The student population of more than 9,000 brings a youthful vibe to a historic setting against a backdrop of rolling countryside that is a big part of the university's appeal.

Accommodation is guaranteed for first-years who firmly accept an offer and apply by the June deadline. Rooms are allocated on a first-come, first-served basis.

Worcester's programme of student welfare initiatives includes prompt access to counsellors and other mental health practitioners. Free workshops are offered covering topics such as managing anxiety and perfectionism.

Academic Achievement scholarships worth £1,000 are awarded to eligible undergraduates in their second and third year of a degree course. Sports scholarships and bursaries are also available.

Work placements of up to 12 months are offered within degree courses and students benefit from links between the academic schools and related organisations. The focus on employability translates into a top-50 place for the university in our analysis of the latest Graduate Outcomes survey.

**Henwick Grove Worcester WR2 6AJ**
admissions@worc.ac.uk
worcester.ac.uk
worcsu.com

**Overall ranking 99**
(last year 103)

**Accommodation**
University provided places 1,010
Self-catered £131–£221 per week

**Student numbers**
Undergraduates 6,822
Applications per place 4.2:1
Overall offer rate 76.3%

**Fees**
UK fees £9,250
International fees £16,200
Medicine £46,500

worcester.ac.uk/study/open-days/
worcester.ac.uk/study/fees-and-finance/

# Wrexham University

The rebranded Wrexham University, or Prifysgol Wrecsam – formerly Wrexham Glyndŵr – garners glowing reviews from its students. It ranks fourth for satisfaction with teaching quality and 18th for satisfaction with the wider undergraduate experience in our analysis of the National Student Survey, up three and 11 places respectively.

Wrexham, a city since 2022 and the youngest in Wales, may be enjoying the Hollywood shimmer that emanates from Wrexham AFC through its ownership by the actors Ryan Reynolds and Rob McElhenney. But the university's claim to fame is being the most socially inclusive in England and Wales for the seventh consecutive year of our analysis.

It has risen seven places in our main academic league table (to 115th) since our previous edition. Behind the boost is an improved performance in the latest Graduate Outcomes survey, as well as higher rates of student satisfaction.

Social work and social policy courses contributed to Wrexham's best results in the latest Research Excellence Framework (REF 2021), with some world-leading research. However, the university fell to =125th in our research quality index in the face of improved performance across the sector compared with the previous national assessment in 2014.

Wrexham is held back from further ascent of our league table by a poor continuation rate, with 83.7% of students projected to carry on from the first to second year (127th). A student-to-staff ratio of 22.4:1 also weighs it down.

It has risen 54 places in our graduate prospects index, with 74.7% of leavers in high-skilled jobs or further study 15 months after finishing their degree, according to the Graduate Outcomes survey. Uefa qualifications are included in the university's football programme, and art and design graduates can rent a free studio space to start a business.

The latest addition to the main Plas Coch campus is a Health and Education Innovation Quarter, with a simulation centre to provide immersive learning. Wrexham's Advanced Composite Training and Development Centre (a partnership with Airbus, which has a plant nearby) carries out research into the efficiency of materials used in aircraft. The School of Creative Arts in the town centre has been upgraded and the National Football Development Centre at Colliers Park has facilities for degree programmes in sports science and coaching.

Among degrees introduced in 2024–25 are software engineering; quantity surveying; architectural design; and applied business. The university is committed to keeping the Welsh language alive and there are opportunities for bilingual study across a range of courses.

Demand for the 321 residential rooms is greater than supply, so not everyone who applies gets a place. Priority goes to full-time first-years, those who live the furthest from campus and students with social or physical needs.

All students can access counselling and mental health advice, and care leavers are given extra support. Financial aid includes a £1,000 cash award and a 25% reduction in university accommodation fees, awarded to students who are the first in their family to go to university.

---

**Mold Road Wrexham LL11 2AW**
enquiries@wrexham.ac.uk
wrexham.ac.uk
wrexhamglyndwrsu.org.uk

**Overall ranking 115**
(last year 122)

**Accommodation**
University provided places 321
Self-catered £125–£178 per week

**Student numbers**
Undergraduates 2,156
Applications per place 4.8:1
Overall offer rate 57.9%

**Fees**
UK fees £9,250
International fees £11,750

wrexham.ac.uk/visit/undergraduate-events
wrexham.ac.uk/fees-and-funding

# University of York

For school-leavers who want academic stretch without urban overwhelm, York is a strong contender. The research-intensive institution is based on 500 acres of parkland on the outskirts of the city known for its Roman roots, Viking history and must-see Minster.

The collegiate structure is a draw for undergraduates, who are housed and hang out in their college with others from different year groups and disciplines. The system reflects the university's founding aims to integrate academic, social and residential activities.

Ranked ninth in our research quality index, York's ambition to be a university for public good is evident in its research themes, which cover environmental, social and economic challenges. It has schools for research and teaching: business and society; arts and creative technologies; and physics, engineering and technology.

Rarely outside our top 20, York does well across most of our indicators for success. Its top-ten position for research follows superb results in the latest Research Excellence Framework (REF 2021), in which 93% of its work was rated world-leading or internationally excellent. Language and linguistics; education; philosophy; and sociology performed best.

York's strength in teaching is recognised with a gold rating overall in the Teaching Excellence Framework (TEF 2023), underpinned by gold for the student experience and silver for student outcomes.

The academic year is based on a semester structure. The year is divided into two blocks, each involving a week's induction, 11 weeks of teaching and four weeks of assessments.

Feedback in the National Student Survey hints at discontent with the teaching on campus, however. In our latest NSS analysis, York fell 42 places year-on-year to rank 94th for satisfaction with teaching quality. It remained in the upper half of UK universities for evaluations of the wider undergraduate experience (=64th, down 25 places).

York was one of the first British universities to host businesses alongside academic centres of expertise. The Science Park houses organisations ranging from start-ups to global enterprises across the creative, digital media, IT and bioscience sectors. Work on a £35 million student centre was paused in 2024 as the university gets to grips with increasing costs.

All students can take a placement year and host organisations have included Amazon and Warner Brothers. Our analysis of the latest Graduate Outcomes survey shows such initiatives are paying off: 82.7% of graduates are in highly skilled jobs or further study 15 months after leaving – a top-25 result.

With more than 5,000 cycle parking spaces on campus, students can get on their bikes and avoid the 30-minute walk to the city centre. First-years who apply by the end of July are guaranteed a room.

The university's mental health services include Talk Campus, which provides peer support in 26 languages online, and a 24/7 phoneline staffed by clinicians.

The York Bursary of £2,000 in the first year and £1,000–£1,100 in subsequent years is paid to students whose household incomes are under £35,000. Care leavers, estranged students and refugees are also eligible for support.

---

**Heslington York YO10 5DD**
ug-admissions@york.ac.uk
york.ac.uk
yusu.org

**Overall ranking =17**
(last year 15)

**Accommodation**
University provided places 4,937
Catered £148–£238 per week
Self-catered £99–£224 per week

**Student numbers**
Undergraduates 15,035
Applications per place 5.8:1
Overall offer rate 78.9%

**Fees**
UK fees £9,250
International fees £23,700–£28,800
Medicine £43,950

york.ac.uk/study/undergraduate/visits/open-days/
york.ac.uk/study/undergraduate/fees-funding

# York St John University

York St John (YSJ) opened with one student, 16-year-old Edward Preston Cordukes, who arrived in 1841 to begin his teacher training. Admissions look a little different these days at the city's oldest higher education institution, which became a university in 2006. It welcomed more than 2,500 new undergraduates in 2023 after a record 11,620 applications, according to the latest UCAS figures.

The growing footfall is in step with YSJ's increasing success at widening participation: it shot up 31 places year-on-year to rank 16th overall in our social inclusion index for England and Wales.

Our University of the Year for Social Inclusion 2025 remains a relatively small institution where a personal touch distinguishes the undergraduate experience. The 11-acre city campus has a delightful setting, with a blend of historic and modern buildings amid manicured lawns.

Lectures, seminars and workshops take place face to face. New courses are available in paramedic science, midwifery and radiography.

Underpinning a silver rating overall in the Teaching Excellence Framework (TEF 2023), YSJ earned gold for the student experience and silver for student outcomes. The assessment panel commended "teaching, feedback and assessment practices that are highly effective in supporting students' learning, progression and attainment".

The university's superb record on student satisfaction has cooled. In our latest National Student Survey (NSS) analysis, it ranked 22nd for students' evaluation of teaching quality (down nine places) and 42nd for their feedback on the wider undergraduate experience (down 17).

58% of YSJ's submission to the latest Research Excellence Framework (REF 2021) was judged world-leading or internationally excellent (115th). Overall, the university has fallen 16 places in our main academic rankings year-on-year, mostly because of a weaker performance on graduate prospects (107th, down 23 places), as well as its reduced NSS scores.

YSJ is among the many UK universities forced to find cost-saving measures recently and job cuts were announced in May 2024.

With views of York Minster, the campus is based on Lord Mayor's Walk near the city centre. First-years who apply by the deadline are guaranteed a place in halls, which cost between £125 and £190 a week.

The university has spent £100 million in recent years to improve facilities. In 2021 the Creative Centre opened as a base for drama, music, media production and computer science. The Foss building has two nursing teaching wards, community consultation rooms and skills laboratories. York Business School is based in the De Grey building. YSJ also operates a London campus, near Canary Wharf, for postgraduate courses.

The students' union has more than 50 clubs and societies. Quiz nights, karaoke, live sport and music are hosted at the campus venue.

Counsellors and advisers on mental health and welfare tailor their services to the needs of students, who can book an appointment to spend time with the YSJ therapy dog, Blue.

YSJ's package of support includes £800-a-year scholarships for students from ethnic minorities with a household income below £42,000. Another low-income scholarship is worth £250 a year.

**Lord Mayor's Walk York YO31 7EX**
admissions@yorksj.ac.uk
yorksj.ac.uk
ysjsu.com

**Overall ranking 93**
(last year 77)

**Accommodation**
University provided places 2,134
Self-catered £125–£190 per week

**Student numbers**
Undergraduates 5,538
Applications per place 4.6:1
Overall offer rate 84.7%

**Fees**
UK fees £9,250
International fees £11,500–£14,000

yorksj.ac.uk/study/undergraduate/meet-us/open-days/
yorksj.ac.uk/students/your-finances

# Selected Specialist and Private Institutions

This listing gives contact details for selected higher education institutions not listed elsewhere within the book. They range from small specialist colleges to private universities offering a wide range of courses. Some have degree-awarding powers of their own, while some are affiliated with other universities. Those marked * are members of GuildHE (www.guildhe.ac.uk). Fees are for a single year of study, correct for academic year 2024/5. We expect many of these to rise in line with the increased cap mentioned on p.

## 1 Specialist colleges of the University of London

**Courtauld Institute of Art**
Somerset House Strand
London WC2R 0RN
020 3947 7711
**www.courtauld.ac.uk**
Fees: £9,000 (Overseas £27,000)

**London Business School**
Regent's Park, London NW1 4SA
020 7000 7000
**www.london.edu**
Postgraduate only

**London School of Hygiene and Tropical Medicine**
Keppel Street, London WC1E 7HT
020 7636 8636

**www.lshtm.ac.uk**
Public and global health

**Royal Academy of Music**
Marylebone Road
London NW1 5HT
020 7873 7373
**www.ram.ac.uk**
Fees: £9,250 (Overseas £28,250)

**Royal Central School of Speech and Drama***
Eton Avenue
London NW3 3HY
020 7722 8183; **www.cssd.ac.uk**
Fees: £9,250 (Overseas £29,050)

**Royal Veterinary College**
Royal College Street
London NW1 0TU
020 7468 5000; **www.rvc.ac.uk**
Fees: £9,250 (Overseas £16,430-£47,960)

**University of London Institute in Paris**
9-11 rue de Constantine
75340 Paris Cedex 07, France
(+33) 1 44 11 73 83
**ulip.london.ac.uk**
Fees: £9,250 (Overseas £12,000)

## 2 Specialist colleges and private institutions

**Arden University***
Campuses in Coventry, London, Birmingham, Manchester & Berlin
0800 268 7737; **www.arden.ac.uk**
Fees vary – blended learning

**BPP University***
Aldine Place, 142-144 Uxbridge Road, London W12 8AW
03300 603 100
**www.bpp.com**
Fees vary by subject and course

**Bristol Old Vic Theatre School**
1-2 Downside Road, Clifton, Bristol BS8 2XF
0117 973 3535
**www.oldvic.ac.uk**
Fees: £9,250 (Overseas £22,050)

**Central School of Ballet***
21-22 Hatfields, Paris Garden, London SE1 8DJ
020 7837 6332
**www.centralschoolofballet.co.uk**

Fees: £9,250 (Overseas £23,151)

**Dyson Institute of Engineering and Technology***
Tetbury Hill, Malmesbury, Wiltshire SN16 0RP
01285 705 228
**dysoninstitute@dyson.com**
**www.dysoninstitute.com**
Paid degree courses – no fees

**Glasgow School of Art**
167 Renfrew Street
Glasgow G3 6RQ
0141 353 4500
**www.gsa.ac.uk**
Fees: Scotland £1,820 annual fee; RUK £9,250 (Overseas £23,500)

**Guildhall School of Music and Drama**
Silk Street, Barbican, London EC2Y 8DT
020 7628 2571
**www.gsmd.ac.uk**

Fees: £9,250 (Overseas £24,250-£25,720)

**The University of Law***
Campuses in Birmingham, Bristol, Guildford, Leeds, London, Manchester and Nottingham
0800 289 997; **www.law.ac.uk**
Fees: £9,250 – three-year course (Overseas £22,150). Higher annual fees for two-year courses

**Leeds Conservatoire***
3 Qaurry Hill, Leeds LS2 7PD
0113 222 3400; **www. leedsconservatoire.ac.uk**
Fees: £9,250 (Overseas £15,700–£20,700)

**Liverpool Institute for Performing Arts***
Mount Street, Liverpool L1 9HF
0151 330 3084; **www.lipa.ac.uk**
Fees: £9,250 (Overseas £19,500)

**London Academy of Music and Dramatic Art***
155 Talgarth Road, London W14

9DA; 020 8834 0500**www. lamda.ac.uk**
Fees: £9,000 (Overseas £24,155)

**London Contemporary Dance School**
17 Dukes Road, London WC1H 9PY
**www.theplace.org.uk**
Fees: £9,250 (Overseas £22,000)

**The London Institute of Banking and Finance***
4-9 Burgate Lane
Canterbury, Kent CT1 2XJ
(Student campus in London)
**www.onlinedegree.libf.ac.uk**
Fees: £9,250 (Overseas contact school)

**National Centre for Circus Arts***
Coronet Street, London N1 6HD
020 7613 4141; **www. nationalcircus.org..uk**
Fees: £9,250 (Overseas £18,000)

**Northeastern University London***
Devon House, 58 St Katharine's Way, London E1W 1LP
020 7637 4550
**www.nchlondon.ac.uk**
Fees: £9,250 (Overseas £21,000-£25,000)

**Pearson College**
6 Mitre Passage,
London SE10 0ER
**www.escapestudios.ac.uk**
Fees: £9,250 (Overseas £17,995)

**Arts University Plymouth***
Tavistock Place,
Plymouth PL4 8AT
01752 203434; **www.aup.ac.uk**
Fees: £9,250 (Overseas £16,500)

**Regent's University London**
Inner Circle, Regent's Park,
London NW1 4NS
020 7487 7700
**www.regents.ac.uk**
Fees: £20,500-£25,000

**Rose Bruford College***
Lamorbey Park, Burnt Oak Lane, Sidcup, Kent DA15 9DF
020 8308 2600

**www.bruford.ac.uk**
Fees: £9,250 (Overseas contact school)

**Royal Academy of the Dramatic Arts**
62-64 Gower Street, London WC1E 6ED
0121 331 5901; **www.rada.ac.uk**
Fees: £9,250 (Overseas £25,137)

**Royal Birmingham Conservatoire**
200 Jennens Road, Birmingham B4 7XR
0121 331 5901; **www.bcu.ac.uk/ conservatoire**
Fees: £9,250 (Overseas £27,500)

**Royal College of Music**
Prince Consort Road,
London SW7 2BS
020 7591 4300; **www.rcm.ac.uk**
Fees: £9,250 (Overseas £28,500)

**Royal Conservatoire of Scotland**
100 Renfrew Street,
Glasgow G2 3DB
0141 332 4101; **www.rcs.ac.uk**
Fees: Scotland, £1,820
RUK £9,250 (Overseas £27,698)

**Royal Northern College of Music**
124 Oxford Road,
Manchester M13 9RD
0161 907 5200
**www.rncm.ac.uk**
Fees: £9,250 (Overseas £27,900-£29,500)

**Royal Welsh College of Music and Drama**
Castle Grounds, Cathays Park, Cardiff CF10 3ER
029 2034 2854
**www.rwcmd.ac.uk**
Fees: £9,000 (Overseas £20,790-£30,000)

**St Mary's University College***
191 Falls Road, Belfast BT12 6FE
028 9032 7678
**www.stmarys-belfast.ac.uk**
Fees: £4,710; RUK £9,250 (Overseas contact college)

**Scotland's Rural College**
Campuses at Aberdeen, Ayr, Cupar, Dumfries, Oatridge, West Lothian and Edinburgh
0131 535 4000
**www.sruc.ac.uk**
Fees: Scotland, £1,820
RUK £7,500 (Overseas £16,000-£33,000)

**Stranmillis University College**
Stranmillis Road, Belfast BT9 5DY
028 9038 1271
**www.stran.ac.uk**
Fees: £4,710; RUK £9,250 (Overseas £18,800)

**Trinity Laban Conservatoire of Music and Dance**
King Charles Court
Old Royal Naval College, Greenwich, London SE10 9JF
020 8305 4444
**www.trinitylaban.ac.uk**
Fees: £9,250 (Overseas £21,860-£25,800)

**University Academy 92***
UA92 Campus,
Brian Statham Way,
Old Trafford,
Manchester M16 0PU
0161 507 1992
**www.ua92.ac.uk**
Fees: £9,250 (Overseas £16,101-£24,151 [two-year course])

**University College, Birmingham (UCB)***
Summer Row,
Birmingham B3 1JB
0121 604 1000
**www.ucb.ac.uk**
Fees: £9,250 (Overseas £14,000-£15,500)

**UCFB (University Campus of Football Business)***
Wembley Stadium
London HA9 0WS
14th Floor, 111 Piccadilly, Manchester M1 2HY
0333 060 9850
**www.ucfb.ac.uk**
Fees: £9,250 (Overseas £14,950)

# Index

# FIND CLARITY AMID THE CLAMOUR